John Britten

It's not the critic who counts. Not the man who points out where the strong man stumbled or where the doer of great deeds could have done them better. The credit belongs to the man who is actually in the arena. Whose face is marred by dust and sweat and blood. Who strives valiantly, who errs and comes up short again and again. And who, while daring greatly, spends himself in a worthy cause so that his place may not be among those cold and timid souls who know neither victory nor defeat.

—Theodore Roosevelt

John Britten

Tim Hanna

CRAIG
POTTON
PUBLISHING

DEDICATION

To Mary Rose Hanna

ACKNOWLEDGEMENTS

I wish to acknowledge particularly the late Howard Paterson, one of the trustees of the John Britten Cathedral Junction project, who more then anyone, was responsible for this work finally being published. I wish to thank Allan Wylie, who read and marked up my manuscript no fewer than three times, and whose criticisms and corrections were the making of it. I am also grateful to Dennis White, who read and corrected the work on behalf of the BEARS, and Tim Stewart, who read it on behalf of the Team. I'd also like to thank Chris James, Lindsay Williamson, Alan Cathcart, Susan Sayer, Steve Green and the countless others whose contributions made this work possible. I must make a special mention of the late Eddie Ridgen, the first to welcome me into the BEARS fraternity when I turned up at the annual BEARS picnic, held on his farm in Canterbury. Finally, my very special thanks to my partner Mandy for her optimism and her faith.

First published in 2003 by
Craig Potton Publishing, 98 Vickerman Street,
PO Box 555, Nelson, New Zealand. www.craigpotton.co.nz

ISBN 1-877333-08-5

Printed by Astra Print, Wellington, New Zealand

Contents

Preface

When I began researching this book I discovered that John Britten did not seem to have known anyone who kept a diary. This made researching his life and works somewhat complicated as his story was held in the collective memory of a community of people whose numbers seemed to expand in any direction I cared to explore. Many of those whose memories became part of this account often did not remember things the same way or even in the same chronological order as each other, a situation additionally complicated by the obvious variety of opinion about what it all meant and the occasional stubborn silence.

It was inevitably something of a trial. A trial in which I hope there is no judgement, only a sincere attempt to understand why, given the usual human frailties, things happened the way they did. The great majority of the quoted material in this book is from interviews that I conducted or personal correspondence. In a few cases I have used material whose source is unknown, and accordingly, I apologise to anyone who has not been acknowledged.

This is largely a story about one extraordinary individual, but it is also the story of a number of others, all of them talented and most of them equally individual. Together they were 'the Team', which built the Britten V-twins, possibly the fastest four-stroke motorcycles in the world for a time, machines that could wheelstand at 150 mph in top gear simply by opening the throttle and could hurtle all the way up to 185 mph and beyond. Machines that, furthermore, presented a vision of motorcycle design to the legions of fans they enthralled that was, at least in part, romantic—a romance featuring an individual standing against the status quo, a drama played out against the sound of thunder.

Let no one seek to diminish the difficulties of John Britten's undertaking or decry his achievements. John Britten was a dreamer and motorcycles have a habit of inspiring dreams in those who fall prey to their seductive guiles. He was set apart from his fellow dreamers, however, by the depth of his talent, the tenacity of his character and the strength of his spirit. Most dreamers are defeated simply finding the starting point, the moment when dreaming must give way to action. John Britten was different. He had the ability to think his dreams through and to quantify what would be for most the wildest flights of pure imagination, reducing them to ogical, achievable steps. He was by nature an adventurer, a man who knew that nothing was ever gained until it was attempted, and he acted boldly and with confidence. It was true that once he accepted a place in his family's business he had money to pursue his passions. However, it was equally true that having money was never a guarantee of success. And money is a relative measure. He had to be very, very clever. He had to achieve a number of critical goals, any one of which would have required a corporation to dedicate many times more than the amount he spent in total. There was no research and development department, no vast resource of top-flight specialist engineers and advanced computer modelling facilities. He therefore had to achieve his critical goals from a stand-up start because he could never afford anything like the money an established manufacturer would spend doing a fraction of what he attempted.

And so to all who contributed to the remarkable story of Britten Motorcycles, I say, as Lindsay, whom you will meet in this account, would say, 'Good on ya.'

And to the rest of you, happy trails.

—Tim Hanna, August 2003

Introduction

I met John Kenton Britten a few times. The first time was in 1993 when I walked into his office in an old commercial building called Kenton Chambers in downtown Christchurch to keep an appointment. I wanted to write about him for a magazine and after some protracted negotiations he had reluctantly agreed to an interview. The fact that he worked in an office rather than a shed at the bottom of his garden, as was then the popular conception, was the first surprise. The second was that the building shared an old family name with him. It was the first intimation of the standing John's family enjoyed in Christchurch, where four generations of Brittens had worked diligently to become a solid, established and successful presence in society. By this time John had been the subject of a television documentary and quite a number of stories in the international motorcycle press. Like most people, I had formed from these the impression that John Britten was a somewhat intense man with a shy but engaging manner who struggled mightily in the solitude of his simple workshop to create the most ferociously powerful and daringly innovative motorcycle in the world. Instead, I found him sitting behind a very smart desk, his own handiwork as it transpired, looking highly groomed in a beautifully cut, dark suit. If this was also not exactly what I expected, neither was his opening remark, which was 'I hate talking to journalists.'

I told him that was all right—I didn't really consider myself a journalist. And so we talked. He told me that he was a property developer who liked designing and building things in his spare time instead of watching television. Property developers, he said, were megalomaniacs. He pointed through the window at the city below and told me that he wanted to move streets and buildings around so that everything could work better, and he outlined an obviously enormous plan in broad, bold brushstrokes that meant little to me, a stranger in town, but made his eyes light up with excitement. We went to lunch and talked about ornithopters and architecture, evolution, yacht design and ... motorcycles. At some point the discussion turned to personal motivation and he said something that was probably as responsible for my writing this book as anything else. He said he had always believed that if he did the things he wanted to do the rewards would follow. Later that afternoon we dropped into the Britten workshop, a spacious and generously equipped building, located a five-minute walk away from the office, where I encountered a team of fellows beavering away in different sections of the place on various parts of Britten motorcycles. Night fell and still the work went on until John gathered them all up and we went out to party. I wrote my piece and shortly after that John phoned me to say that he had enjoyed reading it. 'I think you got me,' he said candidly.

I next encountered him up at the racetrack at Pukekohe where two Britten motorcycles were contesting a round of the 1994 New Zealand Formula One Championship. The first of the two races began for the Britten Team with pandemonium, as John made a last-minute decision to switch tyres. I can't remember now if he wanted wets, drys or intermediates but, typically, it was what everybody else did not have. The delay denied Loren Poole, one of the two Britten riders, his place on the grid and it looked like he might miss the start altogether. During the madness I wound up standing in the wrong place outside the tent—John, careering around the outside, ran straight into me and we both ended up on the ground. Amid the growing panic as the back tyre on Loren's Britten refused to bite on the metal starting rollers, which were misted with light rain, he laughed. And then he helped me up. Loren's bike finally fired and, as he was easing up to the back of the grid with the clutch out, the flag fell. He opened the taps blasting straight through the field on the back wheel to lead into the first corner, such was the power of an already unleashed V-1000. Of course, his tyres were cold and other bikes soon slipped past.

In the second race John and I watched from the embankment as Jason McEwen, the other Britten rider for that season, hammered his V-1000 around the track, rubbing shoulders with Robert Holden, one of New Zealand's true motorsport heroes, who was pounding his Ducati along on the very ragged limit. The two were in a race of their own, way out in front of the rest of the field. Every time they went through the awkward high-speed flat-camber corner that leads onto the pit straight, so close they might have been connected by a very short rope, John was on his feet punching his fists into the air, roaring warnings and encouragement. And as they droned off into the distance he broke into a kind of dance, actually more of a crazy, arrhythmic shuffle, which he accompanied with loud whooping and hollering.

While we were waiting for the bikes to come around again John calmed down, resumed his seat and told me he still derived enormous pleasure from just walking around his machines, considering them from different angles. Sometimes, he said, that alone almost seemed sufficient reward for his efforts, but then there would be another day at a racetrack when he would rediscover the incomparable thrill of watching a talented rider wring out the best his machine had to offer.

As we walked back through the pits, a band of Hell's Angels greeted him affectionately and he exchanged a few words with a couple he obviously knew. As we went our different ways someone said that they loved the bike and there was a quick murmur of agreement. And they said 'love', not 'like'. No one tried to shake his hand or pat him on the shoulder—it was enough that he acknowledged the compliment with an open grin and a word of thanks. It was a great day and I looked forward to the next one.

But there would never be a next one and I will never forget the strange sense of unreality that accompanied the news just a few months later that John Britten had only weeks to live. Just before the end I was back in Christchurch staying with one of his many, many friends. There was reason to celebrate in the Britten Team because they had just won their first International Championship, in the British, European and American Racing Class, or BEARS as it was known. This was the class John and his friends had started in 1983 in order to continue racing their non-Japanese motorcycles at their local racetrack without having to compete against Japanese motorcycles, which were by then too quick for the likes of Triumphs and Nortons. The idea had proven enormously popular locally and had been the catalyst for John to build a BEARS bike that could foot it in any company. The idea had then spread rapidly through much of the rest of the motorcycling world, finally spawning an international series in 1995. The World BEARS Championship had been contested for the first time that year and Britten motorcycles had cleaned up. The television news showed a still photograph of John and the rider who had taken the championship, Andrew Stroud. John was sitting up in bed, looking gaunt and wasted. Next to him, Andrew was holding the prize, a huge glass cup. A recording of John's weak and laboured words was played over the image. He congratulated his team and said how very thrilled he was to win, and by the time he had delivered his brief statement my host was in tears. It was just a plain rotten, bastard of a situation and many people had great difficulty accepting it.

There was another day at Pukekohe, six months after John's death, for classic race bikes and a Britten was there to do a demonstration. Andrew Stroud, who was John's favourite rider, tore off a quick lap, wheel-standing the big barking V-twin all over the track. He finished this circuit by standing the bike on its shark nose with a savage application of the front brake, before proceeding on the front wheel for an impressive distance. When he had reached the part of the track that faces the middle of the stands he subsided back onto two wheels. A great, rolling cloud of white smoke quickly enveloped the machine and the crowd caught only occasional glimpses of Andrew shuffling the bike about before both disappeared in the smoke completely. How long they remained hidden was hard to say, but the bike suddenly launched itself, very nearly vertically, out of the smoke with Andrew standing bolt upright on the pegs. All eyes followed him as he kissed the front down and tipped into the sweeper at the end of pit straight. We looked back as the smoke drifted gracefully away from the launch site and the Britten droned off into the middle distance—and we saw a big, black, rather neat B smeared on the light grey track surface. There was a cheer but it was somewhat ragged, as if all the hard men up in the stands had collectively caught something in their throats.

Two-and-a-half years later I was again in the South Island researching this book, riding around on my Norton for the better part of a year. Along the way I met many riders who had memories of John to share. He had a remarkable selection of friends in many different areas but none were more loyal to him than his mates in the motorcycle fraternity. I expected wariness on their part but instead found the company of this hardy southern band congenial and encouraging, and in time learned something of the spirit that had encouraged John Britten to reach so far beyond anything anyone ever expected of him.

Throughout the period when the Britten motorcycle was being developed and raced, and for some time before that and ever since, the chill of economic depression breathed coldly through New Zealand. This was most obvious in the country's provincial towns where struggling businesses were often surrounded by the empty buildings left by those that had already shut down. Old towns founded on sweat, ambition and forethought, all once busy and full of purpose, had fallen on hard times. People who owned property lost their savings as values slumped. Tourist dollars went only to a few very select places. Farming wasn't generally worth a damn. Manufacturing had been gutted by cheap, uncontrolled imports from Third World countries where child and slave labour were acceptable.

Many of New Zealand's major national assets, including such items as the telecommunications system, railways network, forestry (including the biggest planted forest in the world) and generous natural gas resource, had been traded away. No practical answer had by then been proffered, except to allow the country's slide into permanent penury to continue by selling what was left, including the land itself, to her new foreign masters.

Many BEARS racers were struggling to stay out of debt, or, in even more cases, to manage the debt they had. Certainly it was harder for many to indulge in pleasures like motorcycle racing. In spite of this I never encountered any of the resentment that one would normally expect from those who were struggling toward those who, like John, had always enjoyed the security of inherited wealth. I believe the reason for this lay in something John Britten once alluded to in a television interview. He said he was awed by the way people around the world really seemed to love his motorcycle and he thought they did so because they saw the machine as a victory for the individual. I'm sure he was right. In all the dealings I had with the BEARS fraternity, no matter how threadbare they may have been, they were always proud of John. And they claimed him as one of their own even though he was, by most of their standards, rich and privileged.

I was also privileged to meet many of John's personal friends who had not been involved in the motorcycle project, and to share with some of them the relaxed and generous hospitality they once shared with John. I survived one of Robin Judkins' legendary post-'Coast to Coast' parties, when a seemingly limitless supply of Speight's beer— the major sponsor of the marathon running, canoeing and cycling event he started—and methode champenoise fuelled a shindig to rival any I'd ever attended. And then there was the invitation to attend a barbecue hosted by Derek and Rebekah McCullough, proud owners of the only house their old friend John Britten ever personally helped to build using the revolutionary sandstone and expanding styrene foam composite system he'd invented and developed. I arrived early and had a good look around their home, which was perched high on a steep slope overlooking the ocean where a brisk, chill wind whipped trails of spume from the crests of the waves. There was a generous open kitchen and lounge-cum-party area curled around a big deck with large folding doors linking the outside and the indoors. The walls looked like big blocks of earth-toned stone, revealed as being half a foot thick at the window and door openings. We were out of the wind and the evening was mild, but as the sun set a long, low, wet, cloud rolled in from the sea and blanketed the hill. Temperatures on the deck plummeted. One had only to step back through the still open doors, however, to find the house pumping out the most cosseting warmth. It was a superb illustration of the structure's quite outstanding thermal qualities. Rebekah told me that she could not, and would not, ever live in another house, and that she would eventually die in it. Derek nodded in agreement. 'This is our terminal home,' he said.

During the final weeks of my stay in the South Island I lived in John's old seaside holiday home at Church Bay on the shores of Lyttelton Harbour. One very dark night when the wind was moaning through the pine trees Robin Judkins made his way out from town and we spent the evening talking about old times. His old times with John. About how they would convene late at night in some quiet pub when they felt the need to unburden themselves of the press of the dreams, plans and reflections that drove them both. He recalled how at these meetings they would unleash a flood of words and ideas on one another, each trying to say as much as possible before the other interjected. He also told me how in the final weeks he sent a picture postcard to John every day featuring a graphic he knew would interest his old friend. And then he told me that to understand John's story you had to know that everyone who knew him was in love with him. I took that with a heaped teaspoon of salt, but subsequently, even after I'd spent time with the bitter and the disillusioned—and there were a few—I began to wonder if it wasn't actually true. Later that night as I walked up the drive with Robin he told me how on another dark night walking there with John a tree branch had poked John in the eye. And just as he told me this, the same thing happened to me. I cursed and Robin laughed.

'That's just like him,' he said. 'He always demanded the last word, even if he had to stay up all night to get it.'

CHAPTER ONE

First Steps

In January 1989, a small group of motorcycle enthusiasts gathered at Ruapuna Raceway on the Canterbury Plains in the South Island of New Zealand. It was a practice day and a number of other riders were running off laps out on the track. Although it was high summer and the plains are known for the endless parade of hot, dusty days the season brings, it was a dull afternoon with low clouds. The group wheeled a dark grey motorcycle with white wheels and a white exhaust system down off a trailer hooked up to a Mercedes 280SL. The motorcycle looked like a tough piece of race kit, unlike any recognisable make, while the Benz looked as if it had seen slightly better days, as did the faded maroon 1936 Ford Coupe that was driven onto a set of rollers used to start the bike. After one of the crew had perched the motorcycle on the rollers another fired up the V8 Coupe. For some time nothing much happened and then suddenly the V-twin motorcycle barked into life. It was no symphony. The sound was harsh, raw and penetratingly loud.

Out on the track the machine circulated erratically as the engine spat and popped, while a plastic hose poking out the back of the bodywork dribbled a steady stream of oil from the crankcase. For the rest of the afternoon the group fiddled with its innards between hesitant laps, tweaking the fuel-injection system in a vain attempt to find smooth running and power. They fidgeted uncomfortably when other riders stalked over to complain about the oil the machine was leaving on the track. When the light finally faded the group loaded the bike back on the trailer and a somewhat forlorn little cavalcade headed back to Christchurch. Obviously they had a long way to go before the bike would even run reliably, let alone win a race. It was hardly an auspicious start, but great endeavours and abject failures often begin in the same humble fashion. For John Britten, the man responsible for the grey machine, it was just another set of obstacles to be overcome or, in other words, business as usual.

In time, the Britten motorcycle would go on to capture the imagination of a nation not given easily to bestowing such celebrity, as well as motorcycle enthusiasts around the world. John Britten would stun the motorcycle establishment with a series of racers that would carve out a reputation for being among the most ferocious 4-stroke motorcycles ever built. The fact that they were also breathtakingly, outrageously different added an element of genuine consternation for established motorcycle manufacturers. For them, design was of necessity a slowly evolving process with small advances following equally slow market acceptance. It would have been courting disaster to act without such restraint. To their chagrin, however, a growing multitude of fans, and a significant part of the international motorcycle press, would in time regard the Britten as a dynamic package of fresh thinking that made everything else look old hat. Every heartbreaking failure and every victory added fresh lustre to the evolving romantic saga of a brilliant privateer defeating the best with a motorcycle he made himself in his backyard shed. The reality that John Britten was by most standards a wealthy man, and that far from being a garden shed, the space he laboured long and hard in with a growing band of highly talented helpers was more exactly the workshop wing of his mansion (and then a succession of industrial buildings culminating in the substantial art-deco ex-railways building owned by one of the companies in his property development group), did not substantially alter his achievements, or the odds against success. To enthusiasts of motorcycles, design and the competitive spirit the unfolding story of the Britten motorcycle was an inspiration for reasons that transcended pure results, although there were plenty to celebrate.

In some ways John Britten came to represent all things to all people. For many New Zealanders his endeavours were a tonic against the unrelenting programme of dominant New Right market-force ideology that insisted New Zealand could only follow where more powerful markets led, to the point where local industry had been all but destroyed in a slavish rush to join the new global economy. The promise of trickle-down rewards for those not in a position to benefit from the feeding frenzy that accompanied the dismantling of what had been one of the most successful and benevolent social experiments in the world proved hollow. Instead, generational unemployment had become a harsh reality for many families, 'trickle down' resembling nothing so much as being pissed on by the new rich.

To critics of the New Right, John Britten's achievements were proof positive that New Zealanders did not have to follow meekly; that they could do anything they set their minds to do and could do it brilliantly. It was in that sense a reaffirmation of a splendid national value that stated that New Zealanders, forced to accept the responsibility of self-sufficiency by their very isolation, had developed the ingenuity and audacity to attempt and succeed where others faltered. It was a triumph for the little man that all could rejoice in. To defenders of the New Right, on the other hand (and the arguments between both sides very neatly divided the country down the middle), his successes proved that an open-market economy was effective because it favoured the individual and encouraged enterprise.

John Britten had little if anything to say on the subject, which of course made his success available to both sides of the argument. It did not matter what political, economic or social view New Zealanders had when they considered John Britten; he was simply 'the motorcycle guy'—a diffident, personable hero for difficult times. It is probably not an exaggeration to say that he was popularly revered.

John (who also answered to Johnny among his friends) Kenton Britten was born in Christchurch on 1 August 1950 ten minutes before midnight and half an hour before his twin sister Marguerite. As he weighed in at a hefty 8.5 pounds and his sister 7.2 pounds, their mother, Ruvae, must have felt relieved of a substantial burden. (Pronounced Roo-vay, John's mother's name is of Fijian origin.)

The twins' father, Bruce Britten, was a businessman who had inherited his father's successful bicycle manufacturing and retail business, Butler Cycles, which he shared with his brother David. The two brothers were at the head of a family that had originally hailed from a small, rural community in England, the beginning of the new line having arrived in Canterbury in the form of one George Britten in the 1880s.

When George Britten first stepped off the sailing ship that had battled its way around the world to bring him to Lyttelton Harbour, he found himself among a thriving society already proudly self-reliant, an achievement that was only partly explained by New Zealand's extreme geographic isolation.[1] The rapid success of this, the British Empire's most southern outpost, reflected various propitious circumstances peculiar to the settlement of southern New Zealand, all of which boded well for new arrivals such as George.

Unlike their northern New Zealand counterparts, the new settlers of the south were little troubled by the objections of local Maori. The native population of the South Island, already comparatively sparse, had been viciously cut back around the time of the early settlements through savage incursions by predacious northern Maori war parties armed with muskets. The survivors therefore offered little impediment to the new arrivals' ambitions, and when the First Fleet splashed its anchors into Lyttelton Harbour in 1850 land was virtually free for the taking.

The English immigrants who established Canterbury were drawn for the most part from rural stock rather than from the ranks of craftspeople living in England's cities. Although they were generally poor and unskilled they were not, as was the case in Australia, convicted felons and their warders. They were industrious and solid, and they made dependable neighbours. Because they were not specialists, and had not specialists to go to, they became jacks-of-all-trades. With the kind of absolute confidence that only absolute religious and cultural certainty can inspire, they set about the enormous task of transforming the mysterious, forest-shrouded land in which they found themselves into a northern English landscape. To quite an astonishing degree they succeeded. And they did so very quickly.

Ballast stones in Lyttelton Harbour told the story. In the earliest days of the Christchurch settlement, sailing ships from the mother country arrived full of supplies. These included all manner of foodstuffs, fabrics, tools and machinery and even prefabricated housing. After discharging their cargo they then loaded up with ballast rocks for the return voyage home.[2] Within twenty years, however, the ships were dumping ballast rocks, brought all the way from Plymouth, into Lyttelton Harbour and were taking cargo, mostly wool and grain, back to England. In just two decades the southern settlement had become largely self-sufficient and it was making money.

Until relatively recently, New Zealanders on the whole accepted an egalitarian ethic that generally denied the accumulation of great wealth for a few in favour of adequate means for the many. However, if there was an early exception to this it was on the plains and in the high country of the South Island, where farmer barons soon accumulated great wealth, primarily through the export of their wool to the hungry mills of north England. It was the kind of wealth that allowed them to buy the very best the world had to offer, including of course the very latest of mechanical innovations for modern farming and urban living. At that time, when the British Empire was at its most influential and the Industrial Revolution at the height of its momentum, such innovations were astonishingly numerous and ingenious. Enthusiasm for such machines almost became a popular mania and local entrepreneurs were soon involved in their manufacture, taking on the challenge not only of replicating the devices sent out from the industrial mills of Mother England, but also improving them and inventing new ones of their own.

Of all the new machines none made a greater impact on the general populace than the bicycle. At first it was strictly an indulgence for the wealthy, but very quickly ordinary citizens realised the unheralded mobility offered by the new machines. Christchurch, being situated on a flat plain, was the perfect place for cycling and by the 1880s it seemed that everyone was doing it. Soon a number of local manufacturers had sprung up, among them the company Butler Cycles Ltd, which would eventually play a significant part in the lives of George Britten's son, two of his grandsons and one of his great-grandsons.

As he surveyed his new home, however, it was unlikely that George entertained any thoughts of bicycles. His one ambition was to resume in better circumstances the farming life he had left behind in Ashley Guise, the tiny English country village where his family had lived for countless generations. He was lucky enough to meet and marry Catherine Pigeon, the daughter of a Banks Peninsula farmer, after whose family Pigeon Bay was named. Catherine was an accomplished landswoman and was known throughout the district as an outstanding side-saddle rider. The couple's farming prospered on the peninsula and, as was the fashion of the day, they had a large family, including a son called Arthur George.

By 1914 Arthur had made up his mind to leave the farm and he managed to buy the tiny bicycle manufacturer Butler Cycles Ltd. He hardly had time to open the doors under his new management, however, when war broke out in Europe and he joined the army, training as a gunner in the artillery. Along with most of the young men who made up his generation, he endured the miserable hell of the trenches in France, but returned home at war's end. While away he had learned that his father had abandoned his mother and, severely upset by the news, he undertook to look after her, a pledge that rested easily with Isabel, the woman he married shortly after his return. Her father had brought his wife and five children to New Zealand from Scotland, where he had been a printer, to find a better life for them. By all accounts it was a wise decision and after some initial privations the family thrived.

Isabel was sixteen years old when she arrived and she was already a devout woman who prayed every day for several hours on her knees for those she loved, a habit she was to hold all her life. She and Arthur were engaged shortly before he left for war and married soon after he returned. The marriage was a happy one. Arthur shared his wife's faith and understood her fervour, in time providing her with a small room where she could practise her devotions without interruption. The couple had three girls and four boys, but two of the boys died while still very young, one of meningitis and one from a fall, leaving Bruce, the elder brother, and David. Arthur died at the age of sixty-four, after suffering from a weak heart for many years, whereupon Bruce took over the business, which under Arthur's steady guidance had grown into a solidly successful if unspectacular enterprise.

Bruce proved to be a businessman of a more ambitious nature and he soon began to build up the company. In addition to pushbikes, he began to sell motorbikes and acquired agencies for ranges of lawnmowers, whitegoods and televisions. Brother David joined him in the business and they did very well. Bruce built a splendid home in Christchurch and then built an equally smart holiday home in Queenstown, the alpine resort town on the shores of Lake Wakatipu in Central Otago.

David Turner, a contemporary of John's and a person destined to become one of his close life-long friends, first encountered the Britten family at home in Queenstown.

> It was an impressive modern structure built of stone and timber. Even though I was

> only about nine I knew it was very stylish. I was surprised to find the children already in bed when Dad and I arrived, as it was only seven at night. The twins were in bunks and John had the top one. He leaned over and gave me this warm, open smile. There was a beautiful aura in that room that I remember to this day. The Britten family home in Christchurch was an equally graceful, modern structure in the fashionable suburb of Fendalton. It was set on generous sweeping lawns bordered by a stream that flowed with crystal-clear spring water like most such streams that run through the city. The home was an immaculate setting for an immaculate family. Ruvae was very involved in ikebana, the ancient Japanese art of flower arrangement, and the interior of the house generally reflected the fastidious simplicity that is the hallmark of Japanese art and design. Shoji Hamada, the famous Japanese potter, who was revered in his homeland as a living national treasure, actually stayed there on a visit to New Zealand.

Bruce's interests were somewhat less esoteric. He travelled to America on a number of occasions and was tremendously impressed by the 'can-do, up and at 'em' aspect of the American national character. He became a determined modernist.

Many visitors to the Britten household of John's childhood saw various items of domestic electric gadgetry and experienced such American basics as instant coffee for the first time. It was often the first place they saw the very latest sporting equipment. The Britten family was equipped with moulded-plastic ski boots, for example, years before they became available in New Zealand. A weed-free, white-stone-chip driveway approached the house across the perfectly manicured lawn. Fine new cars and shiny new bikes were always parked in the garage. The house was arranged in an L-shape around a large pool and the rooms inside were large and airy. The family played tennis in crisp, new whites and entertained with tasteful precision. Life was pleasantly rather than relentlessly social.

Among the many visitors, however, was one who remained disinterested in all such things. Bruce's mother, Isabel—'Gran' to his children—was as always far more interested in the promise of eternal life than anything as obviously transitory as instant coffee or flower arranging. Isabel's love for her grandchildren was, like her faith, absolute and overpowering and she visited often. John and his sisters adored her in return, completely entranced by the indomitable little Scottish lady who continued to drive her car well into her nineties, reminding everyone with gusto and bright, shining conviction that there was more to life than the material rewards of this Earth.

For their first few years John and his sister (because they were born on different days they were never referred to as twins) operated as a single unit. Ruvae recalls that the two conversed in their own language and at school learned as one person. In most respects they were quite opposite and therefore complemented each other well. They divided tasks evenly and played to their respective strengths, so, as it turned out, Marguerite did all the reading while John did the arithmetic.

Ruvae remembered John laughing constantly but said that even tickling Marguerite would not raise a giggle. Marguerite, she said, was shrewd and careful. She would lick all her lollies and put them back in the package while John would scoff all of his straight away. (Marguerite was not that shrewd because John would apparently eat her lollies next, anyway.) When both were young adults John kept his accounts on the floor of his car while Marguerite kept immaculate books. According to their mother, Marguerite was always placidly even-tempered while John, like his older sister, Dorenda, could be fiery. If you could have boiled them up, Ruvae said, you would have had a perfect individual.

It was partly to overcome the fact that they were operating as one individual that they were separated at age eleven, when John became a day-pupil at St Andrew's, an exclusive private school catering to the scions of the establishment in Christchurch.

David Turner also attended St Andrew's, a highly regimented school run by a board of old boys with an ex-Royal New Zealand Army brigadier as a headmaster. It was, he recalled, an establishment that typically prided itself on its sporting traditions and maintained rigid discipline with generous lashings of the cane.

> It was not uncommon for the headmaster to have an entire class lined up outside his door waiting to be given a couple of strokes across the bum for something or other. You would go in one door and out another. We were expected to wear our school uniforms at all times and we caught hell if we were seen wearing mufti by a master or a prefect during the weekend. When that happened you could only spend the rest of the weekend shuddering in anticipation of being called up at Monday morning assembly for a beating. But John seemed to avoid most of that and I don't recall him being caned much. Actually I don't remember him being in trouble of any kind, he just quietly got on with his own programme.

As was the case so often, John seemed able to enjoy the things he liked while disregarding the rest, and yet the odd, chance remark later indicated that the threat of failure, a threat that hung over him throughout his time at St Andrew's, and the summary brutality of its administration, was not always lightly born. When John was later celebrated as something of a national hero, a teacher at his old school approached him to see if he would speak there and was asked, 'Are they were still torturing kids?' Typically, however, he obliged.[3]

From an early age John showed an aptitude for mechanical matters, something he was more likely to have inherited from Ruvae than his father, who had little interest in such practicalities even though he owned a business manufacturing bicycles.

Friends who attended primary school with John remember how at the age of about eight he brought a Revell scale model V-8 engine to class, complete with all essential internal mechanisms. He had completed the assembly of the kit-set and used it as a prop for his comprehensive morning talk on the dynamics of the internal combustion engine, a dissertation that left his teacher and fellow pupils in a state of bemused silence. It was an uncharacteristic performance from a boy who normally kept his own counsel in class, but John spoke so assuredly on his chosen subject that many children who witnessed his performance remembered it for the rest of their lives.

John earned pocket money working for Bruce at the Butler Cycle workshops from the age of about eight, and he spent many happy hours there during the weekends. David Turner's father owned a printing business in a similar old wooden commercial building across the road in the heart of Christchurch, and in the upstairs loft where the presses sat, lead letters were everywhere wedged between the wooden floorboards. David recalled his first visit, at about the age of nine, to the bicycle workshop, where he found John spray-painting bicycle frames that were hanging in the loft. Instead of dull lead letters, there were necklaces of shiny ball-bearings glistening seductively in the floor-cracks as John methodically went about his task.

'There was always,' David recalled, 'a kind of careless magic surrounding John. It was something he seemed quite unaware of and that made it even more pointed.'

By the age of ten John was assembling bicycles and he had also built a go-kart. His original drawings for the go-kart still exist and it is reported by his neighbours at the time that he seemed to find increasing speed out of it, until finally his fellow go-karters could no longer keep up. At home his father was happy to encourage his son's enthusiasm for mechanical activities by supplying a properly set-up workshop, and from a very early age this was one of John's favourite places.

The happy atmosphere in the loft that David Turner shared with John when he visited was apparently a rarity at Butler Cycles, where Bruce Britten had a reputation as a hard taskmaster to those he employed, yet another attitude he apparently gleaned from his visits to America. Not long after David's visit, Bruce relocated Butler Cycles to new premises in the city that featured a gleaming showroom and set about ratcheting the business up another notch by establishing a comprehensive maintenance division. Soon Butler Cycles employed sixty staff.

One former employee recalled that each morning Bruce, like a general, would inspect all the salesmen who worked in the showroom while they stood stiffly at their appointed posts. It was understood that each would snap out a respectful 'Good morning, Mr Britten' while he appraised them in cold silence. Bruce also insisted that they stand all day at their stations (with the exception, of course, of their legally protected breaks), carefully isolated from one another and without chairs, while he observed them through the large window of his office. The former employee believed that Bruce had read somewhere that a healthy turnover of staff was desirable and that he therefore contrived to fire a regular stream of them. Few lasted longer than six months.

According to Ruvae, Bruce tired of the retail business about the time the children were leaving school and so he sold it for a handsome sum, embarking on a second successful career as a property developer. For nine years he was also a city councillor, his standing as a pillar of society and a leader in the business community now assured.

Bruce's experience as a councillor was somewhat marred, however, when the very council he served elected to rezone a precinct in which he had purchased considerable property in such a way that his plans for a residential development were thwarted. But it was a minor setback compared with the fate awaiting his brother David, who elected to remain in retail only to be wiped out by the onset of an economic downturn in the early 1970s.[4] Fortunately for Bruce, the situation was suited to those with cash in hand who could buy property cheap and develop it with freely available loan money. He continued to do very well.

And until it became apparent that his son's activities in the workshop were more of the nature of a vocation than a hobby, Bruce was a tolerant and even indulgent father. He was a hunting, fishing, outdoors type who included his children in such pursuits when he could. His own youth had included the kind of high jinks that were almost expected of wealthy young Cantabrians, including a spell in the airforce, where he learned to fly and incurred the wrath of his superiors by buzzing an aunt's tennis party with a Tiger Moth trainer.[5]

Bruce encouraged his children to exercise and always stayed in shape himself, finding time throughout his life to play tennis five days a week (in winter after first carefully applying fake tan to his legs). He also had a golf handicap in single figures and played a round at least once a week. He was always up for new experiences and took up scuba diving in late middle age. Often he would dive on his own while Ruvae stayed on the boat. Even in later life, when most men his age would have been happy to accept a comfortable chair with a warm pair of slippers and a good book, Bruce refused to slow down. To celebrate his sixty-second birthday he learned to fly a helicopter and then he bought one. (According to Ruvae, the Robinson helicopter he shouted himself was ostensibly purchased to allow them to get into the backcountry to go trout and salmon fishing, but as there was no room for luggage she ended up driving the car there anyway.) He and Ruvae walked all the major trails in the South Island (and that's a lot of walking by any standards) and Bruce bungy-jumped at the age of sixty-five. (The jump was free to pensioners, an added incentive according to Ruvae.) He also whitewater rafted (in a punishing class-5 river) and made a parachute jump. And throughout their lives Bruce and Ruvae travelled abroad a great deal, usually without the children.

The effect Bruce's somewhat dogmatic pragmatism had on his son was at the very least a complex matter. However, it was certainly true that John loved the time Bruce was prepared to share with him and he absorbed many of his father's values and interests. Although John could never bring himself to shoot anything, he did become a keen fisherman with both rod and spear, and he always loved nature. Bruce encouraged all his children to enjoy outdoor activities and all had lessons in a diverse range of sports. These included sailing P Class yachts (New Zealand's classic learner's sailing dinghy), horse riding (which John quickly became proficient at and bored with) and skiing behind the family jet-boat. Bruce was also a pioneer in the jet-boating scene, Canterbury being the home of this universally acclaimed invention.[6] It was an exciting and potentially hazardous pastime, given the wild and woolly reputation of many of the rivers the jet-boaters navigated, and to test his children's life jackets Bruce had the youngsters put them on before he threw them off the end of a wharf. They all floated.

Like his father, John excelled at tennis and played the usual games New Zealand boys played, principally cricket and rugby, but he never showed any real interest in team sports and avoided them as far as possible. Jet-boating, on the other hand, became a life-long passion. When John finally acquired his own jet-boat he drove it so hard he succeeded in sinking it at least three times.

Although John's childhood may be seen as a privileged one he certainly faced challenges that could well have proven overwhelming. His father was a driven individual who could at times be domineering and intolerant, a considerable burden for a young boy who tended to be more sensitive than outgoing. It was a situation that could easily have been exacerbated by a condition John suffered and that Ruvae fortunately recognised when he was still very young. Like most parents she began reading to him when he was little more than a baby, encouraging him to pick out words. By the time he was four years old she had noted a tendency for John to transpose common words like 'was' for 'saw', and she began to suspect that he might be dyslexic. As time went by it became increasingly obvious that this was indeed the case. Ruvae had been trained to teach reading using the phonics system and she employed this method to teach her son as best she could at home. Unfortunately, the phonics system was not then in vogue in primary schools, where it had been replaced by the Look and Say technique, a method of teaching that

Ruvae knew was hopelessly inappropriate for John. With his teachers largely unable to help, Ruvae continued to teach him, mostly from the Janet and John books of an earlier period. She did so throughout his time at primary school until he could just manage to read and write. However, he later easily satisfied examiners that he should have a reader and writer for his degree exams, without which he would certainly have failed.[7]

When he was eventually able to instruct other people to write most of his communications, the only letters he bothered with were personal, including letters to business colleagues he considered personal friends. He had by then clearly abandoned any inhibitions he might have once had about simply expressing himself as best he could. His spelling was still primarily phonetic, but if it was difficult to ignore the incidental yet undeniable humour of his writing it was at least easy to understand. After all, a 'wishboan' is clearly a 'wishbone'. As is the sense of the question 'Can the pivot point of the bottom wishboan be on asentric bushers for ajustment?'

A number of people close to John claimed to know the name of the only book he was said to have read but it was invariably a different book. His mother, for example, thought it was Dale Carnegie's classic *How to Win Friends and Influence People*. One friend remembered him telling her, however, that it was *Zen and the Art of Motorcycle Maintenance*, a book concerned with the ethics of work that had misled him with its title but delighted him nevertheless. Yet another friend said that the only book John ever read was a book on time management by an author now forgotten. Kit Ebbett, a close friend who met him toward the end of his school days, could remember John battling through two books and confirmed that *Zen and the Art of Motorcycle Maintenance* was indeed one of them.

'The other,' Kit said, 'was an account of the Canterbury aviation pioneer Richard Pearse, a slim volume given to him by a girlfriend. He got through that in about 1988 and never finished another.'

John could certainly read technical manuals if he had to but he found it a tiresome task when he had too much to do. He enjoyed words most when they were associated with something graphic and he especially loved cartoons. Among his favourites were Gary Larsen's The Far Side collections and the adventures of Fred Gassit, an Australian cartoon canine written and drawn by Simon O'Leary, a New Zealander living in Sydney.[8]

As it turned out, John's dyslexia may well have been a blessing, albeit in heavy disguise. As he was to tell many school children later in his life, both personally and in a widely distributed school reader he helped write, such afflictions are often the goads individuals need to discover greater depths and talents within.

John Bain, another old friend, went through school with John from primary school at Elmwood School, and then through St Andrew's. From the beginning the two shared a fascination for mechanical things, which burgeoned in both into an enduring love of classic and performance machinery of all types.[9] John Bain was aware from the start that John's interest in such things was bound up in a wider love for all manner of creative expression, including his own art. Bain remembered how, even in primary school, John's artwork stood out with the brightest colours and the clearest designs. He was also aware that the way his friend thought was distinctly different from how most people thought. When they later sat together in physics class at St Andrew's, John had the habit of often volunteering correct answers to problems posed by the teacher. When asked to explain how he arrived at them, however, he would confidently launch into an explanation that had no connection with the textbook, leaving his teacher trailing helplessly in his wake.

By then Bain had also become aware of a quality of character that set his friend John Britten apart. It was the quality of tenacity, and it became very apparent when John acquired his first real machine apart from the go-kart. And what a machine it was.

He discovered it at the age of thirteen, while on holiday at a school-fellow's family farm deep in the south near the small town of Gore. As one would expect, John roamed far afield on explorations when not performing the various chores that are the lot of boys visiting in the country. It was on one such ramble that he came across an old bit of junk poking out of an irrigation ditch. Exploratory digging revealed that the rusted metal was part of an ancient motorcycle. This fired his imagination and he instantly determined that he would somehow get it home to work on it. The farmer was duly inveigled to take his tractor out to the ditch and the old machine was exhumed with the assistance of some heavy chains. Careful examination of the rusted mess revealed it to be a 1920s V-twin 1000cc Indian motorcycle. John managed to persuade Bruce that the machine was worth saving, and with the farmer's help the hulk was then dumped into a railway freight carriage for shipment to Christchurch. On arrival, Bruce picked it up with a trailer and took it home. John then wasted no time in getting the thing pulled apart. An early setback occurred, when he dismantled the engine in the family living room while his parents were away. Apparently the old thing had remained oil-tight all those years, but when John proceeded a bolt too far it dumped its entire crankcase contents on the very expensive pure wool, shag-pile carpet. The resultant black spot proved resistant to the combined efforts of John and his sisters to remove it.[10] However, the motorcycle project survived the moment of fury that followed the presentation of the black spot to Bruce and Ruvae. As his mother said, 'he was usually such a sweet boy.'[11]

John's enthusiasm for old motorcycles, and soon old trucks, was difficult for many of his friends to understand as, like most schoolboys, they were drawn to the latest, the most expensive and the fastest. In this, to a degree, they reflected the attitudes of their parents. The conservative and determinedly materialistic Cantabrian establishment, of which Bruce was a good example, then largely regarded anything other than a certifiable vintage car as being merely yesterday's junk.[12]

However, no matter how obscure his enthusiasms might have seemed to most of his peers, John made good childhood friends because his enthusiasm was infectious. Fortunately, there were also a select few, like John Bain, who actually shared John's interests and they were soon drawn into a succession of John Britten projects, each more ambitious than the last. From the outset, John Bain was singularly impressed with the way his friend went about his never-ending stream of tasks with a single-minded determination that saw them rapidly through to completion. He remembered the Indian being completed so quickly that he and his fellow helpers were constantly amazed at the amount of progress that occurred between visits.

John Bain also remembered whipping off from school on his pushbike with a number of fellow truants to turn the first of two 1920s International trucks John was to own over on its back so that the bottom could be painted. The truck had been obtained after yet another expedition in search of interesting mechanical detritus in the rich and fertile Canterbury region. John had learned to keep his ears open and to follow his nose, and when he heard that an old vehicle that had been used to power a ski tow was no longer required he followed it up and acquired it. Because the International had enjoyed a reasonably easy life with regular maintenance, at least on the engine, it was in quite sound mechanical condition. The body, however, was more filigree than fact and the general consensus was that John had taken on an impossible task.

The International was so rusted that those who saw it both before and after believed John probably welded in more new metal than was left of the original. Nor was it simply a matter of replacing missing or hopelessly rusted steel. John's restoration included such detailed work as the re-manufacture of the tumblers in the speedometer. It did not seem long to John Bain, however, before the ancient vehicle emerged from the shed, transformed into a bright yellow open-cab beauty with gleaming black wooden wheels and a solid, new wooden deck. But he also recalled that it proved quite horrible to drive, with brakes and steering that really demanded the strength of a number of large, husky men rather than one slightly built schoolboy.

Richmond Paynter, a neighbour who was three years older than John, also witnessed the first foray in the International. He had been conscious of John tapping away in his shed, which Richmond's bedroom overlooked, for as long as he could remember but had never felt more than a fleeting curiosity about John's strange and largely solitary activities. He had also observed John and his father driving in with trailer-loads of rusting junk on a number of occasions, but again had largely dismissed such activities as mildly eccentric happenings of no real interest. When the bright yellow and black truck emerged from the shed like a butterfly from a chrysalis and puffed off down the road with the skinny fifteen-year-old at the wheel Richmond was therefore somewhat taken aback. Later he heard that an American serviceman from the nearby airbase had spotted John going the other way and screeched his brand-new Mustang around to give chase. It could hardly have been a challenging pursuit but the serviceman was, according to the story, so taken with the truck that he offered John a straight swap for the Mustang. Richmond was even more surprised to hear that John had turned the offer down.[13]

David Turner was one of those who happily abandoned school to assist John with his projects and he remembered that the Britten house was nearly always empty during the day. 'John was so casual,' he said, 'that it never occurred to us that we would ever be caught. He would raid the larder and cook up generous baked bean feasts for lunch. His favourite food, then and later, were thick slices of bread with peanut butter but he particularly loved anything with mountains of sugar on or in it. If he had tea or coffee he'd always ladle spoonfuls of the stuff in. He was a sugar junkie.'

Once lunch was out of the way the happy truants got down to work. They lifted truck bodies on and off chassis and spent hours sanding the rust off old body panels. David remembered that on the one occasion when Ruvae did walk in, and he was busy sanding something back to bright metal with a group of friends, John was not even present. He seemed, even then, according to David, to possess the happy knack of being different without causing offence, or at least of getting away with it. A school class photograph taken in 1965 shows rows of freshly scrubbed fourteen-year-old boys resplendent in their identical uniforms and identical short-back-and-sides haircuts—except one. Beaming confidently in the back row is a cherub-faced youth with a bona fide Beatles mop top. It is a youthful John Britten looking very much like a younger version of Paul McCartney.

Although John's almost charmed ability to stay out of trouble was difficult to explain, Ruvae could offer a simple explanation for what she observed as a generous and selfless dedication of all those willing helpers, and it was something that would remain true for the rest of his life.

'I think they were there,' she said, 'because being with John was the most interesting place to be.'

It was at this time that John enjoyed his first foray into the world of design and commerce, with the encouragement of John Hughson, his maternal grandfather. John Hughson, after whom John was named, was a surveyor and an accomplished 'do-it-yourselfer', in the tradition of the remote and rugged West Coast of the South Island where he still lived. He had been there since 1908 after arriving on a sailing ship as an assisted immigrant from Britain, having abandoned the marginally more remote Shetland Islands. Then in his late twenties he had settled in the harsh extremities of the Buller Gorge, perhaps attracted by a familiar climate. Here, the emerald waters of the Buller River surge out of the mountains to wind across the boulder plane they have carved out of the steep foothills. Hot, clear summers are balanced by icy winters, with snow reaching down toward the valley and violent blasts of bone-chilling wind drawn across the Southern Ocean from the refrigerated voids of the Antarctic. It was a harsh, majestic and lonely place to start a new life, but John Hughson remained there until he was forty-seven years old. At that point he met and married the daughter of another immigrant Shetlander and moved to Greymouth, then a bustling West Coast port thriving on a booming coal industry.

Coincidentally, until his marriage Hughson was a V-twin Indian motorcycle rider, and it is quite possible that he was the first ever to ride the fabulous West Coast Highway, which he had surveyed, after it was opened in the 1920s. His wife, Margaret, was described by those who knew her as a fine woman who was sadly afflicted with an overly sensitive nature and a tendency toward depression. Tragically, her condition grew more acute until, as she approached old age, she was quite out of her poor mind. Her husband refused to even consider committing her, and as Ruvae had flown the nest and John was frail with old age, it was left to his son Peter to shoulder the burden of her care, a circumstance that doubtlessly contributed to Peter's own subsequent breakdown.

By all accounts John Hughson was a stoic and immensely patient man whose most vituperative utterance was the word 'bother', and he had a quiet but determined way of finishing every job he ever started. He was also a fit man who continued to ride his pushbike well into his eighties and, according to Ruvae, there was nothing he could not do if he wanted to.

It is easy to see that young John Britten may well have learned the habit of steady work and single-minded persistence from his grandfather, along with various manual skills. Among the latter was the ability to use a wood lathe, which John then used to turn up oversize candlesticks from native demolition timber. Because there were no supplies of oversize candles to go with them, he also made an arrangement to collect all the butt-end candles from a large Christchurch restaurant, which he then melted into his own moulds. The candles and candlesticks were popular, and John did brisk trade both selling them and re-supplying candles. Another early project was the design and production of his own ski boots, a task that led to his first experiences with fibreglass. The ski boots were not his only foray into footwear. Not long after, John spent time at the local blind institute where he learned about making leatherwear from those who worked in the leather shop. Using his new-found knowledge he produced a pair of leather boots and various other items, including belts and eventually a range of chamois-leather fashion items. From an early age it was clear that John Britten possessed, like his grandfather,[14] the confident and independent nature of the true individual.

CHAPTER TWO

Taking Flight

In 1964 St Andrew's School was rocked by rumours that senior members of the school were using marijuana. Somehow reporters got hold of the story and the rumours became a scandal. David Turner remembered that when he and John read about 'Reefer Madness at St Andrew's!' they were immediately intrigued.

'We had never heard of it before then,' he said, 'and straight away we wanted to try it. It took a while to find someone who could sell us a matchbox of the stuff but we were already enthusiasts. Anything that caused such consternation had to be interesting.'

Ruvae was far too shrewd not to know what was going on.

'John kept it in an old lamp in his room,' she said. 'He didn't know I knew but I'd check it every now and then to see how much he was getting through.'

As the end of his time at school approached, John increasingly joined in the hectic social life typically the preserve of the children of the privileged. Absent parents automatically heralded another lavish party, when the sons and daughters of the wealthy met to drink the purloined contents of the family bar. Friends remember that, although he still carried about him a strong air of reserve, John seemed suddenly to discover an ease with women that quickly became the envy of his male friends. His adolescent growth spurt had left him well over six feet tall with a slim, elegant build that he would keep for the rest of his life. His finely chiselled facial features, expressive dark eyes and thick, brown hair complemented an open and engaging manner that many of his female contemporaries found quite irresistible.

At times he pursued his interest in a succession of lovely young women with extraordinary single-mindedness. John Bain remembered John would often turn up with photos to develop in his brother's darkroom, and that one shot he had taken of a collection of people on a beach included a lithe beauty he was smitten with.

'She was just a dot,' said John Bain, ' but John kept blowing it up and blowing it up until he had a reasonable portrait of her.'

To express his feelings for another young partner he decided to make her a watch. Using the workings of another watch, he set about creating his own art-nouveau, solid silver body and bracelet. He went to see Kobi Bosshand, perhaps then the most famous jeweller in the country. Kobi, who lived in Akaroa, a beautiful little town first settled by French pioneers on Banks Peninsula, listened to John's plans and then told him that he could not hope to bend the silver in the manner he proposed. John persisted anyway and succeeded, winning Bosshand's surprised admiration. Next, John decided that he wanted a concave rather than a convex glass face. Again he sought out a number of aged masters of the craft of glass-working for advice, all of whom assured him that it could not be done. Again he persisted in spite of the negative advice, slumping the glass over chipboard moulds until at last he succeeded. The finished watch was a triumph, and the quality of the work had such an impact on those who saw it that decades later they all had clear and corresponding memories of exactly what it looked like.

John's relationships with girls, according to Kit Ebbett, often commenced with more than average intensity but soon metamorphosed into a kind of fraternal friendship.

> He always went for the most beautiful women in his world but he fell only for those who were sensitive, intelligent and talented to a rare degree. He was lucky enough to love, and to be loved, by a number of quite remarkable women from a very early point in his life, but his first real love remained a part of his life forever. She was a minister's daughter from Timaru and her name was Charlotte Thodey.[15] She had been head girl at Craighead School for Girls and she was as sensitive and perceptive as she was physically lovely. She and John shared many adventures and remained in close contact even after she moved to Sydney, where she became a renowned still-life artist. I believe that John was always looking for the perfect relationship with the perfect woman and that would be a tough role for any to play. Maybe that's why a number of relationships that seemed perfect, and particularly this one, didn't last.

With each fifteenth birthday in New Zealand comes a most precious rite of passage: the opportunity to become a licensed motorist. Like practically all of his peers, John was impatient to get behind the wheel and once he did he lost no time in discovering the limits of adhesion between the car and the road both horizontally and vertically. John Bain recalled being a passenger on a number of the occasions John managed to persuade Bruce to let him take out the big Pontiac V8 that was then the family's transport. In addition to sliding the big car at every opportunity, John also liked to take to the air. There was a humped railway crossing nearby where he regularly made a point of getting all four wheels off the ground while his passenger sat rigidly gripping the armrest with eyes screwed tightly shut. Shortly after this, when the Jaguar XJ6 was released onto the market, John persuaded Bruce that he really ought to have one, and the fun and games continued in the more refined ambience of wood and leather.

Another milestone that loomed, this one ominously, in every New Zealand teenager's life was the School Certificate Examinations. Conducted nationally, the exams were the first stage in identifying those who would be equipped to go on to have some kind of tertiary education and those who would not. Failure guaranteed relegation to the bottom streams of schooling and a tedious year learning bookkeeping and other simple skills before being tossed out into the workforce. The 'best of four subjects' pass mark was set at 200 and John managed 199. His failure was a potential disaster and he spent some weeks in nervous anticipation awaiting the results of the recount that he immediately requested. When it finally came he was immensely relieved to find that he had picked up the desperately needed point and had therefore squeaked home by the narrowest of margins.

At some point in John's school career the headmaster of St Andrew's told him that he would never amount to anything in life. Why he said it, and the circumstances surrounding the occasion, are long forgotten but the remark had a profound and galvanising effect on John, so much so that it is tempting to see the comment as a canny and constructive reading of both John's personality and his potential. At first he was terribly upset by the low estimation of his prospects, but he eventually took the somewhat brutal opinion as a challenge. He passed his University Entrance examinations two years later and after leaving St Andrew's went on to complete an Engineering Certificate at the local polytech.

While still attending the polytech, John wangled a job with a local glassware manufacturing company called Crown Crystal and worked in the design department, studiously picking the brains of anyone he felt might know something about the art of working with glass while observing all in his usual eagle-eyed fashion. His first real task was to design a tequila bottle for the brand Pepe Lopez, which David Turner, by now known to his friends as DT, recalled was quite square—'very different to anything else at the time.' By the time John left Crown Crystal he had learned much about the art of forming glass, something he would use to good effect in due course. His next job was with Carbonic Ice, another local company that made fire safety equipment. However, he was not long there before he passed his polytech examinations (with the assistance of a 'reader and writer') and left the company to attend Wellington Polytechnic, where he completed his studies by cramming a two-year design course into one year.[16] Once he had completed his New Zealand Certificate in Production Engineering, and much to Bruce's delight, John landed a job back at the Christchurch Polytech as a tutor in technical drawing.

For a while, as he made sporadic headway along the path of a teaching career, it looked as if young John Britten was going to straighten up and fly right, at least to those who either did not know him well or were only seeing what they wanted to see. The truth was, however, that his heart was not in the job and Kit Ebbett particularly remembered how frustrating and tedious John found marking student papers.

> He always left it to the last possible moment before starting on this work. Usually it was early in the morning, at the wrong end of an all-night session, when only very loud and very heavy metal music could still his longing to be somewhere else doing something different. Of course, the music at that hour would wake the household, which set Bruce off, and there were times when I really expected the seminal explosion. It never came. Bruce and John had a complicated relationship but they were very fond of one another. Bruce would listen to John and he would sometimes act on the things John said, as he did with the purchase of the Jaguar. Bruce used to give him his old shoes and things, because he at least understood that John needed them. He also gave him a succession of small Japanese cars. John did just enough that pleased Bruce to keep him mostly on side while positively glowing in any approval Bruce decided to give him. Underneath it all there was love between them, even if it wasn't always obvious.

Throughout John's childhood and adolescence Bruce had seemed to understand his son's need for solitude and largely left him to his own devices in the workshop he had thoughtfully provided, along with many of the tools John needed. Of course, few home workshops could ever be expected to carry the inventory of tools that John needed for his ambitious projects, and according to Kit he was constantly on the scrounge for specialist equipment. Kit quickly learned that lending anything to his younger friend was not a good idea if you valued the thing in question.

> Although he generally achieved absolute perfection in his finished product, he also created carnage in the tool department. I, like many, lived in fear of John borrowing a tool, as it was a minor miracle if it ever worked again. He couldn't understand anyone developing an attachment for tools. To him they were just expendable foot soldiers in the battle for perfection.

However, if Bruce was happy to let John potter about in his spare time, and regularly wreck the tool inventory, he was far from tolerant of what he regarded as his son's indulgent eccentricities. Bruce was a bottom-line man and had little respect for the esoteric, and if the end goal was not about making money he found it difficult to understand. Kit was a regular witness to the conflict between father and son and remembered that John's growing fascination with old machinery often triggered it.

It was inevitable that Kit should witness such conflicts, as he was often involved in John's expeditions to recover the 'old junk' that was so often the subject of Bruce's ire. Furthermore, Kit shared John's fascinations and was often complicit in pursuing such acquisitions in the first place.

> When I first met John in late 1968, it was to help him recover a 1937 Triumph Gloria Saloon. It turned out to be a lovely old carriage quite deserving of its somewhat grand title, but of course Bruce just saw more rubbish cluttering up his beautiful home.[17] John was not quite eighteen years old at the time and he'd learned of the Gloria through a boyfriend of his sister Dorenda's called Jim Slater. I also knew Jim, who was driving the recovery vehicle on this occasion, and so I was duly introduced to John. Jim had quite an influence on both of us because he managed to interest us in a raft of things he was enthusiastic about. Classic cars and architecture were just two of his passions and both became enduring interests for both John and I.

After John and Kit became good friends, John began to spend a lot of time at Kit's family farm, located on the southern end of the Canterbury Plains at Geraldine, times that Kit recalled fondly.

> Whenever John turned up at my home in Geraldine he seemed to bring the sunshine with him. This was not just some fanciful impression but something my mother and I often noticed and talked about. He always turned it round and said that he loved to visit because it was always sunny, but the truth was that it arrived with him. John always got on really well with my mother. They seemed to have a natural rapport and understanding. They used to talk for hours and I remember Mum was always trying to feed him up before his next adventure. She was always concerned about his lack of decent clothing or footwear, and he really did look like a tramp in spite of Bruce's hand-me-downs. He often said he wanted nothing to do with either his family's money or the family business and for many years he didn't. And he seemed to thrive on it.

When Kit commenced his engineering studies at Canterbury University he stayed for about six months at the Britten home, getting to know his young friend better.

> Although John had lots of interests, his main objective at the time seemed to be to broaden his life experience and expand his reality. Of course, one obvious way to do

this was through drugs and he was always a keen starter. He would smoke anything if he thought it would get him high but I believe most of the stuff he had early on was pretty mild. I bowed out because it never did anything for me but I remember him telling me about an experience he had with one of his schoolmates, John Vincent. Vin, as he was called then, remained perhaps the best friend he ever made at school and he was with John when John finally got hold of some first-class hashish. John said that they were alone at home when they tried it and that they soon began throwing very expensive crystal vases and the like to one another. John said that they found they could throw them and catch them single-handed and that no matter how difficult the catch might have been in normal circumstances they seemed to have all the time in the world to make it. In any event nothing was dropped. This was just as well, as breaking anything around the Britten household could prove very expensive, as I later discovered.

John was convinced by the vase-throwing episode that he had somehow changed the nature of both time and of what he called his 'molecular vibration'. He always had a true free-wheeling intellect and we used to get immense pleasure exploring some of our favourite topics over a bottle of wine—or what ever was at hand. One of his favourite topics for discussion was always 'concepts of time'. (This interested him almost as much as theories on human flight, his other enduring passion.) He really believed he could slow down time, and I suppose he did manage it by working twice as fast as any normal person and thereby achieving more in a short lifetime than many would in two. I remember once toward the end of a couple of bottles when we finally firmed up on a concept that time was not a fast river, running past us as we stood on the bank, but a lake we could swim about in. Free-energy theories and anti-gravity propulsion were also always worth another drink.

When I first arrived John was working on the Indian motorcycle, making a great effort to make the machine look brand-new. He and a school friend, Bruce Garrick, who partnered him in the restoration, achieved this goal with remarkable success. Mechanically, however, little was attempted. I remember that John and Bruce Garrick wheeled it around to the latter's home, where his father helped to get the thing running with the assistance of a smaller donkey engine. It did not run well, however, and although it looked wonderful in bright red livery it was hardly ever ridden. Bruce Britten was annoyed by the machine and resented it hanging around. He was a great thrower-out of all things he considered were past their prime and became increasingly intolerant of John's half-completed projects, especially when they began to be visible from the road. Somehow John shrugged it all off and continued to do what he wanted, which showed some mettle as Bruce could be very intimidating.

I believe Bruce was one of those people who could make things happen by projection. He liked me being around partly because he considered I was a moderating and sensible influence on John. I had had to run the family farm from a very young age when my father, who was an airforce fighter pilot, was killed in a crash. I had to look after my mother and the rest of the family and make some pretty stark choices early on. Bruce knew this and approved of me, I think, because I had accepted my responsibilities. All the same I still always felt that he was waiting for me to say something inanely stupid and I invariably did. Afterward I'd be at a complete loss to understand my own behaviour.

He also seemed poised for me to perform some gauche act of physical clumsiness and again I often did. One time I arrived at the house and walked into the living room and exchanged greetings with Bruce and Ruvae, who were sitting there. He watched me quietly as I sat down and breezily threw my arm over the back of the chair. There was a loud, expensive crash as I knocked this heavy vase off a table behind me. I stuttered out an apology and he told me coldly how much the thing was worth and that he had bought the last one. I swore I'd find a replacement and I did after much searching. Eventually I found two, the very last surviving examples, as I thought, in the country—in a shop in Timaru. They were indeed very expensive but I felt it was my chance to make a graceful apology and so I bought both. When I gave them to him he told me that he had already found one and had purchased it. I remember wondering silently just how many of the bloody things were still lurking out there and then told him that I would, of course, pay for that one as well. He nodded to show that he was satisfied, as I guess I would have been if I'd been in his position. One broken vase had been replaced with three.

He could be a damned difficult person where John was concerned. An evening would start well enough, but eventually Bruce would bring the discussion around to what was John currently doing and what the chances were of it enjoying any commercial success. Bruce invariably concluded that the answer was 'no'. Then he would slowly wind up and start berating John as a failure. He continued to do it right up until immediately before he died. For Bruce, time was a strictly linear commodity to be traded as efficiently as possible for money or pleasure. He found it impossible to understand projects that were not structured with a definite time-frame—they offended him. I always felt that John's relentless pursuit of excellence was a desperate attempt to get his father's attention and approval. I am sure that this lay behind the insane hours that he worked, hours that must have eventually contributed to the breakdown of his health. Tragically, Bruce continued to deny him that recognition until it was very nearly too late for both of them, something that I know hurt John badly.

In spite of Bruce's exasperation, the fleet of old iron continued to grow. An Ariel Square Four motorcycle found a place in the garage along with a second International truck he decided to equip with a gypsy caravan on the back.[18] Other, bolder, acquisitions were attempted after John discovered the joys of the magazine *Road and Track*. This respected American journal had a decided pro-motorsport bias, dedicating considerable ink to sports cars and motor racing generally. It also carried a heavy contribution of advertising, much of it by individuals selling desirable machinery. This last inclusion was fascinating to both John and Kit, and as the latter had an income he bought the magazines so that they could both share the contents. On one such perusal, as Kit recalled, they came across an advertisement for the late Bruce McLaren's personal M1 coupe.[19]

> We saw the ad a number of times and it was clear they were having trouble selling it, so we figured we might be able to swing a good deal. We decided if we could somehow secure the car we could recoup a bit of money doing demo laps at racetracks and by having it on show in shop windows, as well as having a heap of fun. We realised that Bruce was really our only hope and after honing our economic arguments we plucked up the courage to put the acid on him. He told us that in just a few years the thing would only be worth a fraction of the US$16,000 being asked and he wasn't in the habit of throwing money away. He was really quite scathing.
>
> That's when John decided to try selling the International truck in the US to raise a deposit on the McLaren. Then the M1 disappeared and we gave up, although it did later turn up in New Zealand. I remember we were amazed that the Americans let it slip away, although it did finally end up back in the States. By the time we tried pulling the same stunt on Bruce over a couple of airforce surplus Harvard aircraft he was seriously beginning to question the wisdom of letting me stay. We had got as far as the base commander at Wigram Airbase in our quest to acquire the World War II trainers, which the airforce was selling, and I recall how he looked at us as if we were something he had just wiped off his shoe. John looked like a refugee from Woodstock and the commander made it clear that the idea of two scruffy civilians such as we buying military aircraft was a remote and fanciful notion. Sadly, but predictably, Bruce agreed.

In the meantime, the caravan project carried on, the idea being to create a mobile think-tank in which John could pursue a consuming fascination he had long held with the flight of birds. The caravan took a lot longer than he anticipated and when it was finally done he had projects more pressing than his bird studies. Typically, however, he finished the job and drove it to Queenstown, where he left it in the local motor museum. Apart from a honeymoon foray with his new 'bride' up the vast gravel river plains that breach the mountain fastness, it remained there on display for the rest of his life. However, this change of plans did not mean that he ceased to wonder at birds and in particular about the secrets of their flight-control systems. He never stopped dreaming about a machine that he could strap on to his body that would allow him to fly as they did.

In part, this almost obsessive desire stemmed from a visit he and David Turner made to a mysterious clairvoyant while they were still at school, who told John that she could see him flying, a projection he took very seriously.

'He was absolutely fascinated by this woman,' said David, 'and took her very literally, although looking back she might well have been talking about his motorcycles. It suited him, of course, to take it literally. He wanted to fly as birds do, free and as unencumbered as possible.'

When talking about flying John seemed to favour an ornithopter, a machine that flew by flapping its wings. The most popularly known representation of an ornithopter is probably the design drawn up by Leonardo da Vinci. (The design was animated hundreds of years later by Walt Disney for an often shown television programme on flight.) There are many challenges involved in designing an ornithopter, not the least of which are the complexities of a bird's wing movement. (One look at the number of gears and pulleys da Vinci incorporated in his design illustrates the point.) However, such mechanical problems are magnified hugely if the craft is to be powered by its pilot. For starters, the human body has a much lower power-to-weight ratio than birds. Secondly, our musculature is singularly unsuited to the task of flapping. Our arms and shoulders, for example, can support our body weight only for a matter of minutes whereas, the equivalent muscles on a bird can, in some cases, power it through the air right across an ocean.

Predictably, such considerations failed to discourage John and he never ceased musing on the subject. His reflections on the way feathers seem to act independently in a bird's wing led him eventually to claim to have figured out many of the answers. Nobody seems to know exactly how he intended to succeed where no one else had, but he certainly told a number of people that he believed he could. It is probable that he had in mind a soaring device that would allow the birdman to store energy (by, for example, winding up a spring) for the odd series of flaps when they were necessary. He enthusiastically explained everything to a small number of close friends, none of whom regrettably understood sufficiently what he was saying to give a coherent account of his theories later.

Although the clairvoyant stimulated John's desire to soar, the source of his passion for birds and the way they flew originated from his contact with Ruvae's younger brother, Peter Hughson. Peter had an eerily intimate relationship with the birds that shared his world, and young John Britten enjoyed nothing more than listening spellbound to his uncle's highly original theories on their evolution, physiology and behaviour. Peter's effect on John, however, went far deeper than fostering an interest in birds. John often credited his uncle with teaching him to think freely and creatively, to think with his eyes wide open and his imagination fully engaged. In many respects he was John's mentor.

Peter Hughson was a brilliant, talented, eccentric and, tragically, often troubled individual. For many years he lived as something of a hermit after suffering a severe nervous breakdown. At times his illness led him to self-imposed and extended periods of almost complete isolation. It had not always been so. As a young man he had enjoyed some success working in the Canterbury Museum creating dioramas for the natural history section, but when it became necessary for someone to look after his ageing mother and father, he had little choice but to abandon his promising career. As has already been noted, Peter's mother suffered greatly with mental illness in her later years and Peter's father found it increasingly beyond his abilities to cope. And so Peter moved back to the coast.

After his mother died in 1968, Peter and his father moved to the family's small seaside holiday cottage where Peter further developed a technique he had mastered for making the flowers with which he'd dressed the dioramas at the museum. In particular, he found a way to make plastic orchids that were so realistic that they were in colour, texture and delicacy a precise re-creation of the real thing. The key to his success lay in the fact that he had found a way of infusing the colour into the plastic rather than applying it to the exterior. So accurate were his blooms that it is said a woman returning from a visit to the UK had her Hughson orchid seized by New Zealand Customs as vegetable matter prohibited from importation. On another occasion one of Peter's blooms was entered in a flower show where it won a first prize. A ready market was found for these remarkable objects in the United States and London, where, in the latter case, they were sold at Harrods. Some substantial efforts were made to persuade Peter to reveal his secrets, including visits from delegations sent from his distant markets, but he steadfastly refused to divulge his technique. In the mid-1960s, at the height of what he later referred to as 'The Plastic Age', Peter was easily making £100 a week when his friends were lucky to be making £20. Such was his embarrassment of riches that he worked only before breakfast, and still the money rolled in. Today, his orchids are treasured possessions of those fortunate enough to still have one.

Peter Hughson also became an accomplished scuba diver and travelled regularly to Fiji. Here he had such a profound impact on the people of the island of Vatulele, where he made his base, that they granted him the signal honour of being made a 'talking' chief. In this capacity he was expected to, and did, solve disputes, and generally to proffer guidance as he saw fit.

On these expeditions he was accompanied by his good friend and neighbour Cliff Dalziel. Cliff, who shared Peter's enthusiasm for diving, sought to escape the drudgery of stringing power lines for the Department of Electricity in the often appalling weather of the wet West Coast by becoming a pounamu carver.[20] To help Cliff learn his new craft Peter also took it up. Cliff remembered Peter arriving one day at his small workshop with a fragment of pounamu he had picked up on the beach. Sitting at the bench, he took up Cliff's tools for the first time and quickly produced a perfect little figurine of a traditionally attired elderly Japanese gentleman. When Cliff remarked with some astonishment at Peter's unheralded prowess, the latter merely gave the traditional sculptor's response that the figurine had been there all along—all he had done was to release it.

Without bothering to go through the trials and tribulations most people experience learning a new skill, Peter was soon acknowledged as one of New Zealand's most accomplished jade carvers. Established artists marvelled at his mastery of the lustrous, deep forest-green rock and many stayed with him in order to learn from the man who had not needed a teacher. Other forays into gourd and bone carving met with the same overwhelming level of critical success. Peter's wonderfully precise control of the materials he worked with, and his ability to interpret Maori design in a powerfully harmonious way that was at once traditional and thoroughly contemporary, marked him apart from those who merely repeated what had been done before. For a time the West Coast Highway, surveyed decades earlier by his father, seemed to flow through Peter's house, as people from all sorts of backgrounds sought him out. He commissioned extensions to his small army-surplus hut, which he shared with his father, and transformed it into a graceful two-storey cottage with an exquisite Japanese water garden. Set into his kitchen floor was a trapdoor above a fissure, where at high tide the water surged and penguins nested. His garden proper was an oasis of palms and all manner of other rare foliage alive with birdsong.

Peter had enjoyed a deep love of, and empathy with, birds from early childhood and this led him to develop a number of highly original theories to explain their very origins, and indeed the dynamic nature of all Earth's evolving life forms.[21]

Few could really understand him, and for most it was all just crazy talk, but his adoring nephew John Britten found Peter's passionate theories the stuff of fascination and intrigue. As a child and through his teenage years he visited Peter on many occasions, sometimes with friends, sometimes alone.

In 1967 the dark forces that had invaded Peter's life took over. The strain of looking after his parents and the pressure to sell the secrets of his orchids had now severely eroded his ability to deal with the world. His mental breakdown was a miserable, desperate affair with sporadic flights across the slippery mountains in his VW Beetle to a cool reception in Christchurch. According to David Turner, neither Bruce nor Ruvae welcomed the intrusion of Peter's mania on their carefully ordered lives, and he was institutionalised for a number of months by order of the court.

David accompanied John on various journeys to see Peter after things finally settled down and Peter had resumed his life at his beloved West Coast home.

> John was very spontaneous and sometimes he would suddenly decide to whizz over the Alps to spend time with Peter. I remember Peter's home having walls lined with pages torn from exercise books depicting futuristic cities he'd drawn that also somehow looked ancient. Streams flowed through and past homes, and there were copses of woodland integrated into the layouts. We never knew what to expect. Peter could be warm and welcoming or he might be in the grip of the most terrible delusional mania. Once he told us that his water was being drugged and that there were ships over the horizon directing rays into his home to take the tension out of his clock springs so that he couldn't tell the time. He wore strange hats, possibly his mother's, while collecting the eggs from his many hens, and he was also teaching them to read and do arithmetic. There were hieroglyphics all over the back door and I was suitably amazed when he asked them two plus two and they pecked the ground four times. John adored him.

Peter's slow recovery was not made in easy circumstances. The water garden was drained and with the end of 'The Plastic Age' money became tighter. A long and acrimonious fight over a rates increase erupted with his local council, which seems to have acted with peculiar vindictiveness toward an old man still suffering the effects of a terrible nervous breakdown. Sadly, Peter ended up spending his savings tilting at the power of the council in long, expensive litigation, finally losing ownership of his home.

Peter's tormentors allowed that he could still live in the house but he was prohibited from maintaining it. And so he persisted in what he later wryly referred to as a state of compulsory disintegration, the house unpainted, with weatherboards rotting and the roof rusting out. Each evening the house was plunged into darkness with the setting of the sun after the power was disconnected following yet another quixotic tilt against an increase in electricity charges. He continued, however, to draw great comfort from his friends the birds, and further developed his almost eerie rapport with them. Distressed at the number of wekas (or bush hens as he called them) being run over on the highway, for example, he took it upon himself to teach them to cross safely. He would wait until one emerged from the bush and would then engage their attention before showing them how, with shouted instructions and appropriate actions, to 'look both ways and then run like hell!'[22]

Back on the home front John had now acquired a new girlfriend and another car. The latter was a 3-litre Austin Healey, the former a dark-haired beauty called Marguerite Martini. John and Marguerite often headed over to the West Coast in the powerful British sports car, where they sometimes stayed with his Uncle Peter. They spent the rest of the time there combing the back-blocks for deserted houses and sheds in search of anything from forsaken vehicles to ancient taps and locks.

When Marguerite, who was a dental nurse, was transferred to Reefton on the West Coast, John abandoned the polytech, to Bruce's disgust, and moved west for three months to live with her. He spent his time wandering about the largely abandoned goldfields, talking to the old codgers who still eked out a living reworking the tailings and generally soaking up the history of the place

During the 1970s John increasingly found himself drawn to the values of the counter-culture, the youth movement then sweeping the world. A corporate life, he decided, was definitely not for him and he often told his friends that he could never work with his father in the family business. He went further, telling friends that he wanted nothing to do with the family money. For a number of years, with only a very few exceptions occasioned by outbreaks of biting poverty, he managed without his family's resources. Kit recalled that whenever he saw John he looked so skinny and ill-dressed that he 'wanted to give him five bucks'.

> I think for a while he was almost sleeping under bridges. He looked like such a tramp. We never knew when he might emerge from the guestroom having arrived in the middle of the night, but it was always delightful to see him. My mother used to fuss around him whenever she saw him and would try to keep him as long as she could to feed him up.

It is probable that John's decision to 'go it alone' had more than a little to do with Bruce's continuing disapproval of his son's lifestyle. It was also likely, however, that John relished the challenge of not only getting by but also flourishing without a lot of money. It was an attitude that was to become increasingly dominant in his psyche, and he would in future continue to take pleasure from undertaking and completing projects with considerably fewer resources than most people would consider necessary. It was all part of the fun of the thing.

However, for the moment it was time for rock and roll, for psychedelic visions and for hilarious and absurd happenings. John grew shoulder-length hair and largely abandoned footwear. He became a hippie.

After his sojourn with Marguerite was over, he left her on the West Coast and rented an old ex-schoolhouse in the countryside on the shores of Lyttelton Harbour. Typically, he had soon made the place comfortable, which included installing French doors. A telephone booth enclosing a long-drop toilet appeared in the garden.

Kit remembered it well.

> It was all glass windows from top to bottom and it gave the user a tremendous view of the road and of the harbour beyond. Unfortunately, whenever a car went past the occupants had an equally picturesque view in. Using it always made me quite nervous.

Before long a small community grew up centred on the house, and John and a number of close friends settled into the beatific lifestyle of hippie lotus-eaters. Some, including John's old school friend John—now known as Bodhi—Vincent, became involved in yoga, and a general atmosphere of mysticism pervaded what had by then become a small commune. The yoga was taken very seriously. A teacher was found locally and plans were made to travel to India to further their studies of the esoteric and spiritual. This did not mean, however, that there was not time for adventures. One expedition that was remembered well by both those who participated in it, and those who merely observed the finale, was to a foreboding spot where a swift stream called Broken River disappeared into a huge hole, to reappear some distance down the hill. It was no Sunday stroll—previous expeditions had met with tragedy when the rapidly rising river had trapped and drowned trampers. John had somewhere located enough miners' helmets with lights on them to equip his expedition and these were, quite literally, the only equipment carried. He had a theory that wet clothes made one colder than no clothes, so the crew stripped naked and plunged into the blackness. Some time later, cold and shivering, the crocodile of perhaps twenty bobbing lights emerged into the brightness of the afternoon to find itself in the midst of a church holiday camp. Apparently, the effect on the camp was somewhat electric. Six months later he did it again and this time, with a lot more water flowing in the river, someone was very nearly killed.

Life in the commune could probably have drifted on in such pursuits for years, but John suddenly found himself in possession of an airline ticket for a trip around the world. Bruce had apparently grown concerned that John's relationship with Marguerite, whom he continued to spend time with as often as possible, had become too intense and he therefore funded John on the six-month trip. A secondary objective was to provide John's sister, Marguerite, who was already in England and was apparently very homesick, with some company. In spite of his affection for Marguerite Martini and his reluctance to accept largess from his family, the offer was too good to turn down and John was soon winging his way to America, where he continued his journey by hitchhiking from the west coast to the east. His departure effectively ended his romance with Marguerite, but his life was soon full of new experiences and fresh adventures. On one occasion he was picked up by a group of people going to a rock concert and, typically, he was soon part of the party. While waiting for a ferry to take them to the island where the concert was to be held,

John watched in fascination as the car next to them waddled into the water and motored off. Amphibious cars would remain yet another lifetime enthusiasm.

Having completed his whistle-stop tour of the US he carried on to Europe. In Spain, a local motorist who was later revealed to be a big-time crime boss rescued John when he found him passed out on the side of a dusty Spanish road suffering acute dehydration and sunstroke. The man, who John later referred to as 'The Mafioso Dude', nursed him back to health and they formed a warm friendship, with John staying for some time in his home. Digby Hargreaves, who had been an early boyfriend of John's twin, Marguerite, was working at a Spanish ski resort in the mountains behind the Costa del Sol at the time and he recalled John later turning up with an exotically beautiful girlfriend in an MGA of dubious provenance that boasted a number of bullet holes. They stayed with him for several weeks before heading off for Morocco. John's time in North Africa is something of a mystery, but Kit Ebbett recalled many later conversations that suggested the experience was a profound and cathartic watershed.

'I formed an impression,' Kit said, 'that on this journey his last vestiges of conventionalism gave way to his natural instinct for rampant adventuring; that he finally gave way completely to his need for risky experiences that were close to the edge.'

Some time later Digby and John crossed paths in London, when John once again needed a place to stay and Digby found a friend who could oblige. John applied for a job as an engineering draftsman with a company that was competing for work on a section of motorway. Although it was completely outside his training, he was given the job and duly prepared detailed plans of the motorway for costing. The company eventually failed with their tender but John's work was judged competent and satisfactory. At some stage in London he also joined up with his sister Marguerite and they attempted to find outlets for a range of chamois-leather clothing that John had organised to manufacture back in Christchurch.

As might be expected, John enjoyed immensely the excitement of parties, pubs, and rock concerts, and the driving rhythms of London reinforced his conviction that life was for living, at pace and in the now. And as this attitude settled about him like a comfortable and familiar cloak, a fellow commuter waiting with him in a tube station one day somehow fell from the platform immediately in front of John and was killed by an approaching train.

'Which,' John said later, 'only goes to show that you never know what is waiting around the corner.'

CHAPTER THREE

Taking Root

Once back home again in Christchurch, John cast around for a new place to live. The commune had quietly fallen apart in his absence and in any event living in London had left him with a renewed enthusiasm for urban living. He found exactly what he needed in the form of old brick horse stables in the heart of the comfortably middle-class suburb of Riccarton. He had been aware of the building for many years and had often biked over while still a schoolboy to soak up the ambience of the fine old structure, with its clinging collection of decaying, jerry-built add-ons. The building had most recently been used as a factory by the Radiant Transfer Company, which made, predictably, all manner of transfers before they too finally abandoned the place. Once, the stables had served a grand nineteenth-century mansion, Mona Vale, but they had been separated from their parent estate by a railway line.[23]

Kit Ebbett often accompanied John on these early visits.

> Our interest in old buildings was stimulated by our mutual friend Jim Slater, who was way ahead of his time in Christchurch with his appreciation of old cars, old buildings and so on. One day, soon after John had returned from his OE [overseas experience], I was biking back from university and I noticed a 'For Sale' sign had gone up on the old stables during the afternoon. I couldn't get around to John quick enough, but he was out. Eventually I found him with a group of friends, including the daughter of a well-known and highly successful architect. I enthusiastically passed on the news and later that evening we planned how we would buy the place together and develop it to live in. We flew into gear, but our inexperience delayed matters and by the time we were ready to make a move the architect had bought it with the intention of converting it into three apartments. We were gutted.

DT remembered John contacting him the day after it had been sold. 'He could be

... ..erly distraught when things went wrong, but I had seldom seen him so deeply unhappy. He was devastated.'

Life went on, of course, and John was soon involved in fresh projects and adventures, the bitter disappointment of losing out on the stables left quickly behind. However, the buildings continued to hold a powerful attraction for him, and when he was offered an opportunity by the architect who now owned them to move in while plans for its development into apartments were finalised, John jumped at it. He and his friends soon compounded the general air of dereliction by littering the site with an eclectic selection of vehicles and paraphernalia, but it was obvious to all who could see beyond the clutter that the stables were far from a ruin. The main structure was actually very sound, its rude good health disguised only by the few crudely built add-ons. In plan it looked like a flattened 'U'. The side facing the railway line had an additional floor, perhaps having once been the carriage house with feed storage in the large loft above. Between the arms of the U was a courtyard where the horses were once saddled and harnessed, with stables opening all around. Not only was the building sound, it was also an elegant reminder of a slower, more genteel age, as the architect-owner could also plainly see. John Britten was in, but it was strictly temporary and so his occupation was somewhat tentative. For some time he lived under a parachute hung from external walls, and the site became a favoured hangout for all manner of folk who would often gather for evenings of hilarious excess around blazing bonfires.

John also turned his mind to the tricky business of earning a living. For a brief time he flirted with conventional employment and found a job with a well-known local mechanical engineering firm that gave him the task of designing a shingle crusher. Kit remembered spending a weekend going around various county contractors' yards looking at shingle-handling machinery. 'He was the first to admit that he didn't know what one even looked like, but he poked his head into the internal workings of these massive machines nodding his head like a surgeon with a patient. I never saw the finished article but I understand that it incorporated many unique features and worked very well.'

The job, however, was short-lived and it was not long before John was once again casting about for something to keep body and soul together.

While in London he had noticed that Tiffany-type leadlight lampshades were all the rage and, correctly anticipating that the fashion would soon spread to New Zealand, he decided to make them himself.

He began making his lights and lampshades at a garage owned by David (Dave to his friends) Purdue. Bruce Britten had long kept his petrol account at the Purdue establishment, which was located across the road from Butler Cycles, but Dave only really met John when he first arrived in the yellow International to put half a gallon of petrol in it. The garage housed Dave's collection of classic Jaguars, which immediately caught John's eye. Dave quickly warmed to the young man who so obviously shared his love of shapely motorcars, and the friendship grew to the point where Dave and his wife, Betty, were proud to consider themselves part of John's growing network of supporters. Dave liked having John around and offered him a little space at the garage to make his lights. At the same time John used the garage's equipment to further his knowledge of welding, with a certain amount of guidance from Dave, and eventually completed most of the gypsy caravan in a spare workshop. This involved skills that Dave candidly admitted were beyond his own. His young protégé was now on his own. Often, when some apparent impasse had been reached, Dave would urge John simply to hire someone with the needed expertise but, although John would not hesitate to seek advice, he always did the work himself and always looked for a new way to do it.

Dave remembered John being extremely shy through his teen years, something that was made obvious when it came time to lift the heavy caravan body onto the International truck chassis. Between the two of them they had organised about thirty people to help, all of whom duly turned up at the appointed hour. Being responsible for such a throng seemed to freeze John into fumbling inactivity and Dave was forced to take over. Organising the lift, he said, was as easy as saying, 'Right, half of you go on this side, half of you go on that side, get equidistant and lift!'

According to Dave, however, by the time John returned from his jaunt overseas he seemed to have discovered a facility to organise and command people, even if it never came easily to him. He remained, said Dave, far more comfortable leading by example, inspiring those with whom he worked with his enthusiasm. He gradually attracted a small team to work with him on his lights and lampshades, and the business moved from Dave's establishment via a number of flats to the Artists' Quarter in town, a ramshackle collection of disused industrial buildings set up primarily by Jim Slater, John and Kit's old friend and mentor. For a long time it was the creative hub of Christchurch and the site of some memorable partying.[24]

John and his crew shared the space with two other glass workers, both of whom were well established. Administration of the business was a somewhat casual affair, with all receipts and invoices, as well as the company's cash assets, being kept on the floor of John's car. However, in spite of such practices the business was sufficiently successful to keep the crew afloat.[25]

The pace of work was, however, erratic, primarily because John was more interested in creating crafted pieces that required some thought and real skill rather than in developing a semi-production run of items. His usual pattern was to custom-make an elaborate light with quite a high price—$800 was mentioned for a 'Parrot' light[26]—after which he would live off the proceeds until the need for fresh funds drove him to fulfil his next commission.[27]

Eventually, John decided he needed a retail outlet and for a while he rented a small space in a new mall downtown—a lift well that had, for some reason, not been utilised. Friends recalled a solitary young woman minding the place and that it was short-lived. However, the tiny space was later remembered by the lady who leased it to John as a charming and almost magical little corner in the midst of the commercial bustle.

Back at the stables, the growing collection of old mechanical detritus had been joined by a collection of parts that had once been a Triumph motorcycle. As unassuming as they may have been, the bits and pieces were to bring a significant newcomer into John's life and trigger a passion for motorcycles that would end up defining it.

If there is a point where the saga of the Britten V-1000 could be said to begin it was probably the moment when Allan Wylie, visiting the stables for the first time, noticed the collection of parts and asked John what he intended doing with them.

Allan Wylie's first real encounter with the Britten family had been in the wilds of Papua New Guinea when he met up with John's sister Dorenda. He was in PNG because his newly acquired Triumph Saint had been stolen in Sydney shortly after he arrived there from New Zealand. He had intended travelling on to England, but the Saint represented the funds for the fare and with no insurance he needed a change of plan. When friends in PNG with whom he corresponded learned of his difficulties, they suggested that as he was a mechanic he could easily get a job driving and maintaining trucks in New Britain. New Britain was at least somewhere far away in a very different land, a land with a reputation for wildness and drama. It was definitely travelling on. He already knew Dorenda vaguely from Christchurch and knew her partner, who operated coastal traders around the New Guinea coast, rather better, and so they met. When he returned eventually to Christchurch in 1976, five action-packed years after leaving, he decided to look John up.

> I had viewed the famous caravan around at Dave Purdue's shop and was much impressed with it. From what I knew John seemed like an interesting character and when I learned that he had moved into the old stables I went to see him. He was a bit preoccupied at first but his ears pricked up when I told him that I had just bought a collection of Triumph parts of similar age to his. I had spotted what proved to be a complete 1946 Triumph Tiger. He'd bought a dilapidated one from a mechanic who worked for Dave Purdue and had set about restoring it in his usual industrious manner. I don't think he'd had it for long but he'd already dismantled it and stripped all the old paint off the parts.

> I told him I was going to build a sort of Thunderbird with my bits and he told me he was looking for someone to help him with his motor and gearbox. I knew quite a lot about pre-unit Triumphs. I'd raced a Triumph-powered TQ Midget when I was seventeen and I'd owned a Tiger 100 and an early Bonneville. John obviously had the skills to paint the bikes, and so joining forces to rebuild both seemed the natural thing to do.
>
> He showed no particular skill as a mechanic but I'm sure he could have developed some if he'd set his mind to it. He had no need to; there are plenty of good mechanics in New Zealand. John's gift was a much rarer one than mechanical aptitude. His was the gift for original thought, for unbounded vision. He never had time for details. He could and did get other people who were good at details, to take care of those for him. I was one of them.

Allan's bearded countenance and somewhat studious demeanour belied a genial temperament always marked by an easy smile and a ready laugh. He was, however, a careful engineer who possessed a profound dislike of lash-ups or compromise. For him, the rushed job was anathema, a sure way to waste more time finally than was ever saved.[28]

Because Allan was so meticulous he was, to a degree, a perfect foil to John, whose restless impatience drove his projects with a merciless ferocity that took a heavy toll on both people and projects. The compromises that were demanded by such differing approaches were tougher, however, on Allan, because the projects they worked on together were from the beginning John's and John was footing the bills.

> When John and I disagreed over how something should be done, it was usually me who advocated the tried and true. John was more inclined to favour the quick and dirty. His impatience often drove him to come up with new ideas for doing things faster. Most of them didn't work, but you had to think carefully before rubbishing them because a few did. In any case, what John wanted to happen, happened. He was always the project leader.

It was entirely characteristic that John would listen to suggestions if they were made quickly enough and consider them briefly, but his equally rapid judgements were the end of the matter—at least until something went wrong, forcing a re-think. Given the very different natures of the two men it might be expected that, at least on Allan's side, the relationship might have been quite stressful. However, Allan was always quick to acknowledge a debt to John that he said had changed his life. John, he said candidly, sharpened up his thinking and made him challenge his own ideas. In moments of gentle reflection Allan also chortled at the memories of hilarities shared with a complex individual who could demand far more than he had a right to. A man, however, who very obviously had become a close friend, the kind that can encourage and facilitate you to develop and give the very best that is within you—for reasons you don't always entirely understand.

From the moment John and Allan met it was inevitable that riding motorcycles, racing motorcycles and eventually building motorcycles for others to race would become a logical course for John's restless and creative life to follow. It was also significant that as he headed toward his place in motorcycle history he had a formidable travelling companion by his side. Allan Wylie was his first associate, the first in what would become a very select company. The first to join the quest.

Not long after both machines had been finished, the event that John had been dreading suddenly and brutally came to pass. The architect was ready to proceed with his plans to convert the stables into three apartments and he wanted John out. Accordingly, John packed up his sparse possessions, took down his parachute and, with a heavy heart, moved into a flat with Allan Wylie.

John's depression was short-lived and he was soon involved in another grand adventure. Captivated as he was by the love of birds, it was hardly surprising that the moment he heard that a 'birdman' competition was to be held at Diamond Harbour, a small holiday settlement across the water from Lyttelton, he decided to enter. Entrants were to hurl themselves off a pier into the tide, the winner being the individual who achieved the greatest horizontal distance before the inevitable splashdown. John set to and designed a glider of aluminium tube, gaffer tape and black polythene that was to be foot-launched as a monoplane; the configuration he believed would provide minimum drag for his running take-off. Once airborne, however, he planned to pull a lever that would deploy a second wing, which would emerge from the monoplane wing and thus create a biplane. This second configuration was to provide maximum lift for greater distance before splashdown. He created his wings by wrapping a plastic envelope around a tubular leading edge, with the trailing edge being formed by a wire under tension, also within the envelope. When in monoplane mode the second wing's leading edge and trailing edge were to nestle on top. This arrangement exploited a peculiar property of aerodynamics, whereby the envelope, either as part of the collective wing or as two single wings, formed a perfect aerofoil section for any angle of incidence. Or so the theory went.

John enlisted Allan's help with trial flights of the machine and he duly turned up at the chosen site with his Model A pick-up. *Charles*, as the Ford was known, was to be the take-off platform. The host for the flight test was Colin Dodge, a keen young hot-rodder whose family farm offered big, flat paddocks that John considered ideal for the attempted launch.

John and Colin had become friends, at least partly, because Colin was more than handy mechanically and had some considerable experience stuffing V8 engines into T Bucket Fords and all sorts of other unlikely vehicles, as was the fashion among young horsepower addicts then and now. He had started bolting things together while quite young, his workshop then being the shelter offered by a gnarled old macrocarpa tree on his father's farm. One of his first projects was to tear the body off an old 1938 Humber that he then shortened before bolting the seats back on. Many happy hours thereafter were spent tearing around on the expansive shingle banks of the Waimakariri River.

Colin was also a keen mountaineer who had already won acclaim as an ice climber, having been a member of the four-man team that made the first winter ascent of the formidable east face of Aoraki/Mt Cook. He was more than willing to impart his expertise to John, who was equally eager to learn, and the two had spent a little time climbing on Mt Rolleston. Like Allan, Colin was a calm and intentional man with a patient and forgiving nature that nevertheless admitted to a tendency not to suffer fools gladly. He would eventually become John's second companion on the motorcycle quest. [29]

It was a fine summer day as Allan and Colin handed the glider up to John, who was perched on *Charles*'s tray. It is probable that the glider was a somewhat simpler version of the one John intended making, as Allan did not recall any second wing mechanism being fitted and the craft's first attempt at flight was definitely made as a monoplane.

The trio roared around the paddock with John hanging onto the top windscreen support. Allan steadily increased speed with John yelling encouragement, shouting that he could feel his shiny black plastic machine lifting. In spite of their best efforts, however, the craft stubbornly refused to take to the air and so the friends retired to the farmhouse for afternoon smoko. John later claimed that while they were engaged in this agreeable diversion, an unexpected gust of wind caused the unsecured craft to take flight before dashing itself into the ground. Others say that the black polythene covering melted like Icarus' wings in the sun. Neither Allan nor Colin recalled the glider doing anything but resolutely sitting on the ground, but the episode might have happened on another occasion. Whatever the truth, some of the glider ended up as a hothouse for tomatoes out on the Dodge farm while the rest languished for years in various sheds. Certainly none of it ended up at the bottom of Diamond Harbour.[30]

John had not long abandoned his birdman aspirations when he heard the most remarkable news. The stables were up for grabs once more, as Kit recalled.

> The architect had purchased a huge old historic property in Governors Bay on Lyttelton Harbour and had decided to liquidate some of his assets, including the

> stables. He offered the property to us at a very reasonable price and John and I decided to race back in. I visited John a couple of days later to discuss the purchase and found that he had already constructed a scale model of what he planned for the building. It was, even at this early stage, very similar to its final form and I could see at a glance that it was a plan for a grand, single-family home. I withdrew my involvement on the basis that any joint venture would inevitably have resulted in the sale of the building if one of us wished to withdraw.

John persuaded his mother to lend him the money he needed to purchase the property and then moved into one of the attic rooms. He commenced his reconstruction straight away, although his efforts were always very sporadic as he was easily distracted by the promise of fun and adventure. He shifted in his kilns from the Artists' Quarter and the toxic fumes of molten lead were now added to the general chaos. His activities attracted a lot of friends, who came and stayed and were soon roped into some aspect of the development. In the early days the police, who were sure that John was just squatting on the property, often raided the premises. They would shake him awake and try to move him along, much to his annoyance, especially as it continued to happen.

For some time John maintained an account at the corner store up the road and the growing group of friends survived in large part on a diet of burgers and chips. (The shop was known popularly as the 'dairy with no door', as it never closed.) Fleur Mair, the kind-hearted lady who lived next door, regularly provided additional sustenance of a more nutritious kind and her son, Mike Brosnan, became one of the regulars at the stables. He was soon flat out making lights and lampshades for the $3 an hour that John paid, and he kept making them for years. Broz, as he was popularly called, was a strong, stocky individual given to bouts of deep and suspicious truculence that were balanced by a frank and guileless manner. Broz, one of his friends later said, always called it the way he saw it, even if he often insisted on doing so when cooler heads might have remained silent. Until 1978 he had lived with his father, Mike Brosnan senior, an enterprising South Canterbury farmer who was a pioneer in organic sheep farming when the rural community regarded such notions as little more than loony. Broz, however, was more interested in motorcycles and he acquired his first machine, a derelict BSA 500 Blue Star, when just ten years old. His sometime mercurial nature was offset by an innate sense of design and considerable mechanical ability, demonstrated early on by his success in getting the BSA running. He hammered the old machine all over the remote hill country farm, so that by the time he hit the city as a teenager he was already a proficient rider and mechanic.

Ruth McCracken and Roland Logan were two other individuals who became part of the crew at the stables and went on to form lifelong friendships with John. Roland and John became, in the words of the former, a kind of mutual admiration society. Roland, who was several years younger than John, was also dyslexic and he believed that this helped forge the strong bond that grew between them.

By most accounts John found in Roland a flamboyant and joyful love of design that matched his own, plus a kind of nihilistic determination to have a huge amount of fun. They shared an appetite for adventure and the same humour that delighted in the obscure and the bizarre.

Among the many adventures they shared were a number of climbing expeditions on the challenging mountains of the Southern Alps, including a weekend climb of Mt Aspiring. Kit recalled the event:

> John was shockingly badly equipped, and Mum and I were most concerned for him when he dropped by on his way to the mountain. Climbing Mt Aspiring is a huge challenge, something that experienced mountaineers take very seriously. John's boots were just ordinary boots and his clothes just seemed like the threadbare things he always wore. The weather had been bad and many really well-equipped and professional teams had failed to get to the top quite recently. There were deaths on the mountain on either side of John's expedition but they fluked this amazing window of brilliant weather and made it. Mum and I were sure it was just John working his usual magic.

The climbing team was led by Ed Cotter, an older man who had been part of the team that first conquered Mt Everest in 1953, who recalled:

> I'd obviously climbed a lot, and two of the others, Colin Dodge and a mate of his called Jonathan Davie, had also climbed a fair bit. The rest of the team, consisting of John, Roland and Marney Brosnan (Broz's sister, who John was taking out at the time), were relative novices. I chose the route up the north-west ridge, a decision that meant a long trek around the mountain, starting early on the second day after staying in the hut on French Ridge. When the going became steeper I roped up with Marney and Colin and we began to belay one another while the other three carried on individually. Eventually, John and Jonathan made it to the summit after what I'd rate as a long and strenuous climb. It was a hell of an achievement for a first-timer.
>
> We got back down OK and started home. Then, when John was driving through a gorge on a metal road that was being rebuilt prior to sealing, we hit a rock protruding out of the bank, tearing open both tyres on that side. We were all completely buggered but John just whipped the wheels off, stopped a car and headed off to the nearest place, which was a tiny town called Omarama. He was back within the hour

> with new tyres on the wheels.
>
> John was tremendous fun and I always enjoyed being around him. He was as hard a party man as I was and we always had a great laugh. However, when something needed to be done there was never any mucking about, he just got on and did it.

Encouraged by this success, Roland and John went on to attempt an ascent of Aoraki/Mt Cook, New Zealand's highest mountain. On that climb they came within 100 feet of the summit before storm clouds rolled in, forcing them back down—a remarkable achievement given their very limited experience. They also discovered a poignant reminder of the frailty of human existence when they came across a pack and some gear perched on a lonely ledge high in the clouds, left behind just three days before when a climber had fallen to his death. The two friends shouldered the forlorn possessions and struggled back down with them, something at least for the dead climber's family to cling to.

Not all their adventures were in such remote places. They were excited by an episode involving Bruce Britten, who had visited a demolition site where he was having an old house torn down only to find all his workmen thoroughly inebriated. The workers had broken through to a forgotten cellar full of whisky, a temptation that had proven immediately overwhelming. John and Roland somehow convinced each other that many such cellars must exist, and they became particularly interested in a commercial building they had access to through Bruce's office. The building had been constructed over the site of an earlier establishment and the pair spent many nights climbing underneath it. Finally, they did find themselves in a cellar full of booze. Unfortunately, however, it was simply the cellar beneath a neighbouring restaurant and they left discreetly and empty-handed.

In Ruth McCracken, on the other hand, John found the kind of deep friendship that endures without such shared escapades. Ruth was cheerful, kind and caring, and would regularly arrive at work with a freshly baked loaf or a cake, a welcome addition to John's basic diet of fried fast food and sweets.[31]

In spite of John's somewhat ad hoc approach to manufacturing, the leadlight and lampshade business was expanding and he diligently mastered new skills as he needed to. Typically, he did so first by finding those who had the knowledge he needed. In order to cast his own traditionally ornate bases for his Tiffany lights, for example, he found a man who knew about lost-wax casting, which led him to another man, a potter, who gave him a kiln that was surplus to requirements. After much experimentation he was able to combine his newly learned knowledge with his newly acquired kiln to produce the lamp bases he wanted, thereby adding yet another skill to his growing armoury of expertise. It was an intensely time-consuming process, however, and he finally decided to have a local commercial foundry sand-cast the bases from his own patterns. (The same establishment turned out the castings he needed to complete his caravan.)

In addition to expanding his range of lighting and lampshades, John also began to build furniture, some of which he sold locally and some of which he exported to Australia. He was always ready to make new things. One visitor found him taking plaster moulds off a pile of grass clippings. He had been lounging about, sitting on the pile of clippings in the sun, when it occurred to him that he could make very comfortable fibreglass chairs from the impression made by his backside. When he eventually did so, they apparently proved every bit as comfortable as he had anticipated and sold very well.

In the meantime, work continued on the transformation of The Stables, as they were now officially titled. The new design was quite definitely not a restoration, as John intended a massive re-configuration of all the spaces, something that concerned his friends Dave and Betty Purdue, who urged an approach that was more sympathetic to the building's original character. John was not to be moved, however, and although his plans resulted in the project being massively more complicated and difficult than a straightforward restoration, he launched into it with a quiet resolution that brooked no dissention. When the job was finally done, the Purdues were happy to admit that he had been right. The building became John's vision and it worked wonderfully well. However, it was a long time coming.

Part of the entirely new construction was a glass- and steel-roofed atrium where the courtyard had been, featuring a recycled marble floor. One of the two wings also featured a recycled floor, in this case a wooden parquet affair that had been transported in one piece from a department store that was being demolished. To do this, John hooked up a number of trailers to his car and, in the dead of night, the assemblage crabbed through the deserted streets from the centre of town to The Stables. A policeman who happened upon the transport was heard to sigh loudly, express disbelief and then announce that he had had enough and was going home. Extraordinary, too, was the Heath Robinson-type machinery featuring old bicycle wheels and water flowing through a hose from a nearby tap that John improvised to turn and drill the tall sandstone column supports for the thirty-foot-high atrium roof. Later, the same machinery was modified to cut the salvaged marble to create a diamond- and dot-patterned floor.

One morning, following a dream that obviously included water, John began to dig a swimming pool inside the building. The digging became a kind of party, with helping hands turning up from all quarters. Halfway down, however, they discovered that the building was perched over a swamp and the whole structure seemed in imminent danger of collapse. The digging had been halted in the middle of the night when the happy band of diggers encountered massive tree stumps, remnants of the ancient forest hacked down by settlers a century before. The stumps soon disappeared beneath a rising well-spring of oozing black mud and the sides of the crater began to crumble into the dark slime. Convinced his property was about to be literally consumed by a black hole, John tore off and found sludge pumps to drain the excavation and props to shore everything up. Shutters were acquired with equal urgency and concrete was hurriedly poured in a state of high excitement. Because John was certain that the new pool should never be drained, lest it float out of its hole again and endanger the building, he chose a salt-water system and from that moment on the pool was never emptied. The pool immediately became the focal point of some wild parties, with naked revellers happily splashing away into the wee hours, often while work continued around them.

Gradually, the old buildings became a home, a transformation that was underlined by the arrival of the first of a long line of animals, as DT recalled:

> I was teaching pottery to girls in prison, and I decided to take John along with me to give the girls something to talk about. The excitement was more than the prison authorities thought appropriate and it was made clear to me that I was not to bring him again. However, on the way in he noticed a kitten in the gutter immediately inside the walls. It was pissing down and this little bedraggled Persian was just lying in the water. It looked like a totally fucked unit but he insisted on retrieving it. It recovered after lots of care and attention, and he called it Lectricity. Then Tessa [a refugee dog from Kit's farm] turned up at the flat and gave the cat hell, staring at it night and day. But when they moved into The Stables they both seemed to settle down and it was a happy home.
>
> John fell in love with a honey-coloured strong-eyed pup [Tessa] that I was more than happy to be shot of, and she became his constant companion for many years, dying in about 1995 at the age of sixteen. She was always trying to outstare any cats, rabbits, ducks and so on that she came across and he absolutely adored her.

The fact that he was concerned with fundamentally altering the structure of The Stables did not in the least distract John from considering the smallest details. Doorhandles, taps and other fittings were especially designed and cast, while an elderly immigrant European John hired produced exquisite joinery on site. Slowly the building evolved into something that captivated all who visited. The atrium ultimately became an oasis of tall palms and cool water, the hub of one of the most strikingly innovative and elegant homes in Christchurch. Regrettably, an ingenious hydraulic system working on mains water pressure that John designed and installed to open shutters in the atrium roof to let out the heat never performed well, and consequently the space was always uncomfortably hot in the heat of a summer day. In the evenings and throughout winter, however, both the ambience and the temperature were, according to those who knew the home well, perfect.

Lindsay and Margaret Williamson, two of the closest friends John would later make through his motorcycle adventures, spent many happy evenings socialising at The Stables, but for Lindsay there was always a reckoning to be paid at the end of the evening. 'When you went home afterwards,' he said, 'you felt like you were living in a car crate.'

Life at The Stables became a blend of hard work and hard play in a setting that was a somewhat schizophrenic mixture of a graceful home and a factory.

'Throughout the conversion John and Roland worked long hours year in and year out,' recalled Allan Wylie. 'When they were not building they made lights and lampshades as a succession of other part-time workers came and went. The haphazard nature of the lighting business gave way to a more or less organised production line. There was a mortgage to pay and building supplies to buy.' As always, however, it would not do to devote every waking hour to work. One guest at a dinner party that John held in the loft above the workshop, recalled that the food was exquisite, the table setting sophisticated and elegant and the company uproarious. She also remembered John grabbing her, as she was about to step through a door at the end of the room that led to nothing more than a 15-foot plummet to the ground. DT had just returned from the yoga trip to India and was one of the forty people invited that evening. He recalled that John had organised waiters and that the evening was intended as a return for all the dinner parties that John had enjoyed.

On another occasion John contrived a 'drive-in' movie theatre in the yard and screened one of his favourite 'road' movies, *Steelyard Blues*. The evening was complete with roller-skating waitresses delivering to the cars 'Hungarian' hamburgers, which were prepared by DT at the 'Hungarian Burger Bar by the Well' (the well being located right next to the workshop).

DT described the evening as a night of drama both on and off the screen.

> The entertainment commenced when the couple up front in this big old brown Chevy had a screaming argument and decided to leave. This meant that all the other cars had to move while they continued to abuse and berate one another in the most violent fashion. He was heir to a considerable fortune, which he and his girlfriend were busy blowing on hard drugs. They both tended to get a little emotional but they fascinated John. Unfortunately, they weren't around for long. He was jailed after a drug deal went wrong and then hospitalised while she went on the street before finally hooking up with a jockey. When the heir got out of jail he couldn't wrest her away

> from the jockey and he promptly fatally OD'd. A couple of months later she did the same thing. There were a lot of drugs around in those days although we didn't have a lot to do with pills. It was proper stuff—dope, coke and speed. I was living in this big stone place on the Port Hills called the Sign of the Takahe and there was nearly always a party there on Friday nights and most people would be totally out of it. There was always something going on.

DT's parties in the imposing old Gothic stone mansion that roosted on the eastern face of the Port Hills, many of which he and John planned and executed together, were the place to be for some time and were the occasion of much comment. At one such evening the guests found that they had to push their way through a room full of 'falling autumn leaves'. The leaves had been painstakingly tied in strings with almost invisible nylon fishing thread and then suspended from the ceiling. The effect was, apparently, quite surreal.

'The Chocolate Party' was another well-remembered soirée. To set the scene all the furnishings in the rooms had been transformed with rich, molten brown velvet and satin surfaces, and David served a splendid smorgasbord of chocolate everything. Great bowls of fruit, each piece dipped in chocolate, complemented chocolate sculptures of roast meats and seafood. And centre stage was John, naked, apart from a thick coating of chocolate all over his spare frame.

Work and play rolled along for John in one seamless continuum, with little notice taken of the time. Night or day, it was all the same. Many of his friends now recall that he would often be so engrossed in whatever it was he was doing that he would have no idea whatever of the time and he would work deep into the night. Quite what it was in his make-up and background that drove him so hard is obviously a complicated matter. To a handful of his closest friends, however, he confessed his belief that he felt he was racing against time and that he did not have a great deal of it.

As can be seen by the chocolate incident, John had discovered within himself a strong attraction to theatricality and he soon found a fresh outlet to express it. It was curious that he could be paralysed with shyness, as he was on the day the caravan body was lifted onto his truck chassis, yet could also happily stand naked in front of a roomful of people. But as DT pointed out, such paradoxical behaviour was quite typical of him. His character was essentially a paradox: at one level open and without guile and at another complex and contradictory. With a number of close friends he became critically involved in the stage-managing of a series of alternative fashion shows that were quite daringly innovative—and not without incident. An old butchery in Christchurch was turned into a fashion emporium called Tripe, which became the locale for a number of wild events. It was while wiring the now redundant chiller as a changing room that John managed to give himself a tremendous electric shock that knocked him out stone cold, but he survived the experience unscathed. One of the first 'happenings' there, known forever since as the 'Rude Show', opened with the lights slowly coming up to reveal a solitary figure crouched mid-stage. It was John wrapped in a multi-hued and glittering cloak that enfolded him like a pair of wings. As the music slowly swelled, he emerged to reveal himself naked beneath his gorgeous finery before the somewhat startled but, by all reports, mesmerised audience, an audience that included his parents, who were perhaps the most mesmerised of all.

An even bigger production was staged at a large motel/reception complex where John constructed a towering multilevel stage of scaffolding. The ambitious use of this industrial material for such a purpose was at the time highly unusual. He also installed closed-circuit television to relay the show to participants awaiting their cues in the motel rooms they had also hired. John's contribution to the proceedings was to glide out onto the silver stage in a sea of dry-ice fog (something few present had ever seen) wearing a glittering silver suit and balanced on hugely high-heeled aluminium shoes he had cast for the occasion.[32] All the models were friends and all were amateurs but, by all accounts, they gave a polished performance that presented the locally designed and obviously alternative fashion in new and innovative ways. It is perhaps indicative of John's powers of persuasion that one turn featured a beautiful young bare-breasted woman wearing angel wings. The impact of these events should not be underestimated. A number of the individuals involved went on to play key roles in the Wearable Art Awards that are still staged with considerable national and international critical acclaim in the city of Nelson.

In spite of such consuming commitments as the transformation of The Stables and the staging of exotic fashion shows, John still found the time and means to indulge his love of sports cars. He had thoroughly enjoyed his Austin Healy and had, for a time, owned a second 'hotter' Healey that he drove everywhere at its limit, or occasionally over it. Paul Pannel, a school friend who shared John's enthusiasm for sports cars, remembered him spinning it through 360 degrees on a club run on Banks Peninsula, as usual with little damage.[33]

John's first foray onto a racetrack was probably at the wheel of a celebrated South Island racing car, Ron Silvester's 1938 Chevrolet Coupe. The Chev, equipped with a red-hot Corvette motor and cutaway bodywork, had enjoyed considerable success but was getting a little long in the tooth to foot it with the wave of 'proper' racing saloon cars that began to edge out the homemade specials in the early 1970s. Later on the car enjoyed a new lease of life in historic racing, but for the moment it was enjoying a gentle retirement. However, on this occasion it had been dusted down to raise funds for charity by offering a drive to any would-be racer with a spare $50. Kit Ebbett and John went out to Ruapuna where John paid his money and was duly strapped into the big coupe. Kit recalled the following events:

> He took off like a scalded cat and absolutely caned the thing around the track. He was sideways most of the time, barely under control, with the engine bellowing like a demented animal. Every one at the track stopped what they were doing to watch. I wasn't surprised that the marshals only allowed him a couple of laps before they waved him in. It was one of the most lurid displays of pure recklessness I have ever seen. Of course, John was incredibly pissed off because he thought he was beginning to get the hang of the car when they stopped him and he complained that he hadn't had his money's worth. Everyone else thought he had, however, and I remember being extremely relieved that he hadn't smashed the old Chev into a railing or something. It was the first time I saw how brutal he could be with machinery. He treated machines the same way he treated tools.

John's cars were by no means uniformly exotic. Bruce had given him a brand-new Toyota station-wagon at some point and that became the runabout for the business for many years. For a time he also enjoyed puttering about in a Fiat Topolino. He particularly enjoyed driving around sitting on the roof of the baby Italian automobile with his feet dangling through the sunroof to operate the steering wheel and the hand throttle. How he operated the brakes, clutch and gearbox remains something of a mystery, but he found a way.

When Betty and David Purdue bought a house John was quick to phone and arrange an inspection. They were puzzled, however, by his insistence that they measure and tell him the width of the front door. The reason for his strange enquiry was revealed when he arrived, sitting on the roof of the Topolino, and attempted to drive it into the house. To the relief of the proud, new home-owners the front steps proved more than the Fiat could deal with, given the available run-up, and he had to walk in like everybody else.

Although motorcycles would become the grand passion of John's life, he remained a genuine enthusiast for motorcars all his life. And like all true enthusiasts he knew that they existed first and foremost to provide endless fun.

CHAPTER FOUR

Two Wheels Better

Given John's almost addictive need for speed, it is perhaps surprising that it took him so long to discover his true passion for motorcycles, machines that more than any other involved the rider in the physical reality of raw speed, that element the French call *la belle vitesse*. Although John had already restored the Indian, it was, as we have seen, doubtful that he ever really rode it. As he was still two years away from being legally entitled to apply for a licence when he completed his restoration, and given that his father Bruce was a stickler for propriety in such things, it is doubly doubtful that he did much more than start the Indian up in the first years he owned it.

Marguerite Martini remembered travelling to Wellington on a motorcycle she thought might have been the Indian during which they fell off it.[34] As has been noted, however, the Indian was restored cosmetically rather than mechanically, and as it never really ran properly it is likely they were astride something else. John finally ended up giving the Indian to Bruce Garrick and he did not see it again for many years. John also had an Ariel Square Four motorcycle quite early on in the piece, and Allan Wylie remembered from his conversations with John later on the subject that he had obviously enjoyed it. However, no one seemed to recall ever seeing him ride it.

It is therefore likely that the first motorcycle John ever really rode was the old 500cc rigid rear-end Triumph Tiger 100, which Allan soon had in one piece and running well. Allan recalled that:

> We restored both bikes over the summer of 1976–77 and as soon as they were ready to ride we took off on a shakedown tour of the North Island. Both bikes had the same gearing and almost identical engines, and I remember how satisfying the engine notes of the two machines were as they drifted in and out of phase while we blatted along.

> From the outset, however, I was concerned at the way John was riding. He was pushing way too hard for a person with his very limited experience and several times I tried to persuade him to take it easier. We were on a twisty back road just north of Wellington when he very nearly killed himself. We had stopped to get fuel and I took the lead as we headed off. I thought I might be able to curtail his exuberance and that he might learn a little from following a more experienced rider. However, John was not happy to trail along in my wake and tore past on the white line as we entered a blind left-hand corner. Unfortunately, there was a car coming the other way and I actually saw John glance off it before disappearing around the corner. The shaken driver stopped immediately and naturally I did too. He asked if my mate was all right but there was no sign of John. I carried on with my heart in my mouth and found the bike parked around the corner neatly against the bank. There was still no sign of John. After casting about in some confusion I eventually found him lying in the grass on top of the bank groaning in some pain. Luckily, the damage proved to be only a badly bruised leg and a hole in the gearbox cover. We bogged the hole up with Plastibond at the nearest garage and were able to carry on.

It was but John's first crash in a whole series that followed over the years, and considering what might have happened he got off relatively unscathed. That, too, would prove typical. Generally, the god of wrecks and crack-ups smiled kindly upon him in spite of his habit of always pushing that little bit harder.

Although Christchurch is located on flat-as-a-board plains crosshatched with ruler-straight roads, it was still a great place to ride a motorcycle. Twisty roads of the kind richly enjoyed by many motorcyclists were conveniently available on the adjacent hills of Banks Peninsula. Venturing further afield, however, brought even richer rewards. For those with a need for more distant explorations, the North Island was just a few hours and a ferry trip away. But the best was to be found to the west. The Southern Alps, which stretch north and south beyond the western edge of the plains, could be breached at Arthur's Pass, by a road that then wound down to the coast, where it joined the magnificent West Coast Highway. The highway flowed alongside the coast to the north and south and could have been constructed especially for sporting motorcyclists. The coastal ranges rear abruptly over the narrow coastal flats, massive rocks and sheer cliff faces breaking through the dense cover of trees, ferns and palms. Like most South Island roads, the West Coast Highway was well engineered and, due to the relatively sparse population, only modestly used. (North Islanders travelling there for the first time invariably marvelled at the absence of potholes.) With a dramatic and largely unspoiled landscape, the region enjoyed a fantastic reputation with international motorcyclists lucky enough to have toured in one of the best locales in the world.

John toured quite extensively on the Tiger for several years and his journeys included many visits to his Uncle Peter on the West Coast, often in the company of a mate or a girlfriend. As always he travelled everywhere at breakneck speed, but the motorcycle bug had bitten him badly and although he would always love touring, he was ready to notch his involvement up to another level. After he and Allan attended a couple of race meetings, held by the Classic Racing Register at Levels, the racetrack in Timaru, they began to consider the possibilities of going racing. It required only a small push and it was not long in coming. The local motorcycle club was running a few training days at Ruapuna, and John and Allan were persuaded to attend by one of the organisers.

The gentleman in question was Lindsay Williamson, then co-owner of Christchurch Motorcycles, a highly successful motorcycle dealership located just up the street from the Artists' Quarter. As has been previously noted, the Artists' Quarter was, at the time, the hub of a great deal of creative endeavour and enthusiastic partying, and it was through the latter activity that Lindsay and John first met. In time, Lindsay's infectious and effervescent enthusiasm for racing motorcycles would prove a key factor in persuading John to become involved. When they first met, however, Lindsay had little time for him or any of his Artists' Quarter cronies.

> Me and my cobbers were motorcycle racers and we thought the blokes down the road at the arty-farty place were mostly just bullshit artists even though they had good piss-ups. My mates and I started racing motorcycles from about the age of fifteen and motorcycles were always the focus of our lives. In the early years I raced mostly Triumphs and Nortons, and in 1976 I set up a wrecking yard with a partner, Gary Boote. A year later we were granted a Triumph dealership and following that a Suzuki franchise. In the 1980s we were going gangbusters shifting bikes and we also managed to come to an arrangement with the New Zealand Harley-Davidson franchise-holder to sell them. That's when we really started booming.

Gary and Lindsay interrupted business long enough to spanner on a Yamaha TZ250 race team in Australia and Malaysia, but Lindsay's big racing effort was made on Triumph motorcycles. Lindsay teamed up with John (universally known as Joe) Hannah, and the pair campaigned an 8-valve Triumph Bonneville 750 in Twins (2- cylinder) racing, along with a 4-valve machine in 750 Production events. It was a somewhat rearguard action against the by now dominant Japanese machines, and Lindsay recalled that they were, at the time, 'two dead serious nobodies in flashy red and blue leathers looking like a pair of done-up twits'. The results show, however, that he was being overly modest. On more than a few occasions Lindsay and

Joe were able to give their Japanese-mounted opponents a real hurry-up, and they sneaked home the odd win and a number of very good results.

Lindsay soon discovered that John Britten was far from being a 'bullshit artist', and that he was, furthermore, a fellow Triumph rider. Having made the discovery, he encouraged John to take up motorcycle racing with a cheerful optimism that was more than enough to persuade John to 'have a go'.

And so it was that John and Allan Wylie turned up at Ruapuna on their Triumphs to learn all about motorcycle racing. Allan, who already had a hot motor, was first to get into the groove and was more than a little pleased to pass Joe Hannah, who was astride his Sprung Hub Triumph, a machine that he managed to flog along in a highly competitive manner.[35] Joe's reputation as a hard charger on the track was matched by his reputation off the track, where his ability to party was well respected. It was therefore perhaps inevitable that the three should become firm friends.

'Beating Joe first time out was a surprise,' recalled Allan, 'as he already had some form on the old bike. However, it was clear that I had beaten him with higher power, not riding skill. Later, when the racing got more serious, I built him an engine similar to mine. We had many close battles after that.'

After this introduction to motorcycle racing Allan Wylie and John began competing casually. At first John continued to ride his Triumph on the road, but Allan soon made the decision to turn his machine into a full-blown racer and he made and fitted a single seat and a central oil tank.

John gradually followed suit, stripping bits and pieces off his bike, and Allan recalled that he went quite well but soon blew up his engine.

> John had little sympathy for machinery and the old '46 engine was fragile. He had no patience for niceties like warming up his bike before thrashing it mercilessly.
>
> John first took to the track in about 1980 but I'm vague on the details. My Triumph had become a dedicated racer some time before and I was already enjoying quite a bit of racing. When BEARS first started I managed to win a few before the new, hot stuff arrived on the scene.
>
> I remember John racing his Triumph at a Country Gents meeting at Levels in 1981 or 1982, where it broke its crankshaft. I also remember it at Levels again at an early BEARS meeting in 1983. By this time John had modified it quite a bit. He'd made an aluminium oil tank and possibly some special exhaust pipes. The oil tank split, causing a spectacular crash, which did a lot of damage to, among other things, the original steel petrol tank.
>
> About the next thing I remember of it was the Three Fools racing episode. I think John was working on the engine himself at this time, although he might have had

> some help—I wasn't involved myself. I recall him showing me a couple of high-compression pistons someone had given him. They had no oil-control rings and looked as if they'd been cast in holes in the ground. There was some interference between these pistons and the cylinder head when he tried to assemble the engine, so he attacked the combustion chamber with a grinder, leaving scars which can still be seen today.

The Three Fools expedition occurred in 1983 when Allan, Joe and John decided to compete in a race meeting that was to be held in February at Pukekohe racetrack, located about forty minutes south of Auckland. Allan recalled that he and Joe were on target with their race preparation, but that John was busy dallying with a visiting girlfriend and did not begin his preparation until departure was imminent. At this point Paul Pannel introduced John to his father, a fortunate introduction because Pannel senior had a metal wheeling machine. After cursory instructions John took over the machine and, to the great surprise of Paul's father, worked straight through for thirty-six hours. His achievement at the end of this marathon was a beautiful alloy petrol tank and tailpiece.

John had also produced a set of rear-set foot pegs with his own gear selector and brake pedal, a racing-style seat, a chain-guard for the open primary, and fitted twin Amal carbs with a common SU float chamber. Allan also believed that Dave Silcock, a well-known car racer and tuner, had been roped in to do a mild porting job on the head. The Tiger was now transformed from an old street bike into a real racer, but when it was loaded onto a trailer behind John's Toyota Corolla station wagon it was completely untested. He had simply run out of time.

The crew set off in high spirits. They had decided to call themselves Three Fools Racing for the purposes of the expedition, and a friend, Ashley Smith, had actually gone to the trouble of printing t-shirts emblazoned with the slogan 'Any Old Iron' in recognition of the fact that they were all racing iron-headed Triumphs. They quickly discovered that the groaning Toyota Corolla was barely up to carting four men (another passenger went along for the ride) and the three motorcycles on a trailer. It was high summer, and by the time they were a couple of hours north the Toyota was fizzing at the bung. From that point on the heater was run full time to help cool the hopelessly overloaded engine. This in turn seriously overheated the Three Fools and their passenger. When they eventually made it to the Desert Road, in the middle of the North Island, John decided to take a break and test his bike, and it was duly wheeled off the trailer and fired up. Unfortunately, when he had created the gleaming alloy oil tank he had neglected to include a restrictor in the oil return pipe to encourage oil to flow to the top end of the motor. The result was a quick melt-down, an outcome Allan believed may have been encouraged by the carburettor set-up causing the engine to run lean. Uncertain of the causes or the exact nature of the problem, John loaded the now defunct bike back onto the trailer and the overheated company continued on its way.

On arrival in Auckland, the crew went directly to Universal Motorcycles, a dealership that carried a comprehensive inventory of British motorcycle spare parts, and removed the cylinder head.

'We found that one of the valves had seized in its guide,' said Allan, 'due to a lack of oil. So we replaced the valve and guide from Universal's stock and put it all back together again. We arrived at the track and John charged out into practice. Unfortunately, the bike overheated and stopped again, and this time the strip-down revealed a melted piston.'

The *New Zealand Classic Motorcycle Race Register Newsletter* subsequently reported what happened next under the headline 'Methinks the Engine is a Trifle Hot John!' The article went on to say:

> Not to be outdone, after various calls for replacement parts it was off to knock up a sympathetic engineering works to weld the offending article and return at dark where work was called to a halt due to insufficient light and fatigue! It was then up at dawn to fit—literally, you know, with files and scrapers—the recalcitrant item. A reassembly and modification of the carburettor system, organised practice behind the 250 class event and into battle albeit at a slightly reduced pace. The Register applauds your effort John which shows the true spirit of Classic racing and all it stands for.

For Allan it was a salutary lesson on how not to go motor racing. But when John's 500 failed for the final time, he gave John his own Triumph, so that he could experience at least one race on a healthy machine. He soon regretted it.

'He missed a gear change,' Allan recalled, 'causing a big over-rev which I heard from trackside. It was a horrible noise that made me cringe and it turned out later that he'd slightly bent both exhaust valves. There was no time to do anything about it so I raced it as it was, a little off song. I was lucky with the handicapping and still won two races.'

In spite of such setbacks, work on transforming the Tiger into a demon methanol-burning racing machine now began in earnest. Allan remembered that the old Amal carburettors were ditched in favour of a new pair of 28 mm Amal Concentrics after Pukekohe.

> About that time the switch was also made to alcohol fuel. By then the bike was performing pretty well but it lacked reliability. The old 1946 crankcases bit the dust and cylinder barrels kept breaking at the flange. New 500 barrels were not available, so

> John had a special set made up from spheroidal graphite iron. These were cast as solid tubes by a local foundry. Cooling fins were then machined in to a depth of about 20 mm, which was adequate, as methanol engines tend to run fairly cool. (The fins would have been hopeless on a petrol engine.) Although the barrels were heavy they did the trick.
>
> John had me rebuild the motor at the garage where I then worked and from then on I did all the engine work. An acceptable level of reliability was soon achieved even though the engine was really beginning to make some power.[36]
>
> John now raced the bike a lot and I remember one occasion at the fiftieth anniversary meeting at Cust in 1986 when he won the 500 race. It must have been a hard ride. The gravel-road circuit was quite bumpy after storm damage and John's bike had no rear suspension or sprung saddle.
>
> Sometime later, during a routine rebuild, John asked if I could get yet more power from the engine. I enlarged the inlet tracts throughout, bored the carbs to 30 mm and opened the ports to the maximum possible size before fitting still larger inlet valves. This was the ultimate form the engine reached and it made pretty good power. Finally, I managed to fit the five-speed guts out of a Bonneville gearbox into the pre-unit construction gearbox cases on the Tiger, something Joe Hannah had already done. It was a tricky operation but the gearbox worked really well.

With the Tiger now both fast and reliable, John began to earn a reputation as a determined competitor. He developed into a bum-off-the-seat kind of rider who, predictably, pushed himself and his machine to the limit. His intensely physical riding style had much to do with the fact that the Tiger had no rear suspension and that the power it eventually developed was far in excess of the frame's capabilities. The more usual approach of gracefully tipping the machine into a corner, and then sweeping through with just sufficient throttle to load up the drive train before winding on the power for the exit, was not really an option. Instead, John had to grab the unwieldy but powerful twin by the neck and wring it. Corners were taken in a series of steps as he wrestled it around, with the frame flexing in the middle like a giant hinge.

Although the Three Fools team, per se, ceased to exist after just the one expedition, there were many more road trips to racetracks around the country and all were characterised by a certain amount of carefree fun. On one such trip during which the bikes were towed behind a 1936 Pontiac, a bottle of nitrous oxide was being passed around the car to all except the driver. Nitrous oxide is normally used in hospitals to stimulate people who were experiencing cardiac arrest. Recreationally, however, it is used to promote a minute or two of climactic hilarity. One of the painful side effects of using the gas in this way is that the metal outlet on the bottle promotes painful cases of 'freezer burn' on the lips, but the crew came up with a solution and a plastic hose was soon passed around while the bottle stayed in the back.

Another rider with whom John was destined to share future motorcycle adventures was fellow BEARS founder Steve Radcliffe. Steve was then racing Ducatis, and occasionally an ex-police 800 BMW, and he often shared the track with John. He remembered in particular the way John took a very different race line to everybody else.

> He had to find his own way around because he had to keep the power on at all times or risk taking a spill. He quite often did the latter anyway. Even so he was still pretty effective and I think that was because he had a kind of raw talent that suited his wild and aggressive style. During this period he developed a habit of clipping his fellow competitors on the arm, or tapping them on the back, as he went past. This was enough to put the fear of God into you without the need of further dramatics, but it could be especially scary when John seemed out of control. Unfortunately, it was often difficult to know if he was or was not. Most of the time the back wheel was stepping out while the front went in the other direction and the thing wobbled and weaved like a demented animal.

Steve also remembered that John stacked the Tiger pretty hard on a number of occasions on the open road around Christchurch before it became a dedicated race bike. 'Once,' he said, 'John wiped out going over Dyers Pass and planted himself in a bank. I think he was often pretty lucky to get away with it. The Triumph's lack of cornering was perfectly matched by its lack of brakes. When all else failed John could call upon them, but they were unlikely to be home. He had made his own double-sided front brake from two period Triumph items but apparently they were never up to much.'

According to Allan, the cycle parts on the Tiger were now thoroughly worn out, which greatly added to its caprices under the influence of far more power than it was ever designed to handle.

'On one occasion,' he said, 'when I did not have a ride, John gave me the Tiger, but one quick outing was enough. I think it broke down before I could take it out again, which was just as well for me because I really did not enjoy riding it.'

In spite of the machine's somewhat spiteful nature, however, John did enjoy it. More than that, he relished it. Fellow riders recalled that he usually finished toward the top of the field against much more recent machinery—when he finished.

'He always took off like a man possessed,' said Allan. 'He'd be clear of the majority of the field soon after flag fall—up with the guys at the front. Sometimes

I would not see him again until it was all over, but there were quite a few occasions when I rode past John lying on the side of the track with the Tiger lying nearby. I beat him quite a few times that way.'

Those involved with motorcycles often find that they tend to take over. As always John continued to pursue many different interests through his late twenties, but motorcycles were never far from the foreground. With the Tiger dedicated to racing, he turned to other machines for everyday use. Fortuitously, he had a friend, Tony Friel, who had discovered a way to get motorcycles into New Zealand that avoided most of the duties that both discouraged such imports and maintained high prices for both new and used machines.

Motorcycles were not subject to the same level of import duty in Australia and were available there for perhaps half the price they commanded in New Zealand. Strangely, however, the duty on second-hand bikes imported into New Zealand from Australia could be calculated either on the basis of the ex-factory price or the Australian market value. By electing the latter option it was possible to reduce the duty significantly. It was an opportunity not to be missed.

Before long, John, Roland, Broz and an American John had befriended called Chris James had all acquired gleaming Ducatis. Chris, or CJ as his new friends quickly renamed him, was a bespectacled American with a spare frame and a distracted air that turned to intense and focused attention the moment his interest was aroused. He had arrived in New Zealand in 1973, a wandering hippie seeking a change from the years he had spent driving busloads of backpackers through war-torn Afghanistan. He had made his way into Christchurch from the outlying airport on foot by following the Avon River, the shallow ribbon of translucent water that glides through the city on its way to the sea from the plains. As he approached the city centre he chanced upon a small health-food shop and decided to buy a sandwich. It happened that the man in front of him in the queue was John Britten and the two immediately struck up a conversation. John was a friend of Kevin Brookfield, the owner of the shop, and the three soon settled down to a serious natter about life, the universe and everything. Eventually, John invited CJ to come next door to the Artists' Quarter to see the work he was doing with leadlight lamps and lights, and by the end of the day he had offered CJ a place to stay. It proved the beginning of a life-long friendship.

John took delivery of the first Ducati, an 860GTS that he soon sold. The next bike brought in was a red 900GTS that John and Tony sold to Broz, who had been assiduously squirrelling away his $3 an hour. As it transpired, Broz was lucky to receive his machine in one piece after John took it for a quick 'burn-up' prior to handing it over. Boz recalled the incident:

> He came down the street past The Stables on my 900 with the bike lurching horribly from one full lock to the other. It was so violent he actually dented the tank. It was bloody frightening to see my new bike bucking and weaving like that. On the one hand I was scared he'd fall off and wreck it, and on the other I wasn't sure if I wanted to ride it myself if it was going to behave like that. However, he hung on and in all the time I had it I never managed to provoke anything even remotely like it.

John and Tony also imported a black Darmah, which ended up in Roland's hands, and two red Darmahs for themselves. All this activity did not escape the notice of the Customs Department, which eventually swooped on The Stables with a full-scale raid. Roland remembered John laughing at two of the department agents who turned up and asking them if they thought they were Starsky and Hutch. The agents were not amused and demanded to know what John knew of the New Zealand drug industry, an enquiry that provoked further gales of laughter from their suspect.

Allan caught the Ducati bug but decided to go to Australia to buy his machine himself. However, when his 860GTS bike arrived in New Zealand, along with another one for John, he found himself being charged large amounts of duty that was calculated using the highly undesirable method. Considerably annoyed, he paid up, but John, who had also been caught out, took on the department. The result was a battle that involved some of the most convoluted story-changing Allan had ever witnessed. However, to his utter amazement John won and his duty was duly reduced.

Why John and his friends so favoured Ducatis is not hard to fathom. The handsome and powerful machines are overtly sporting and they have that cachet of good breeding that the Italians manage so well. For John and his friends, Ducati was quite simply the benchmark that other manufacturers failed to achieve.

Trips to distant places happened for no better reason than that there was a pub there that served beer. Or a party to go to. Or motorcycle racing to attend. One such expedition was the annual pilgrimage to the Hawkesbury Road Races near Blenheim, held every Labour Weekend (in late October). Usually the group would break the journey there and back by staying with friends at Kaikoura, and it was always a fun trip with great racing to watch at the Hawkesbury circuit, a lovely loop of meandering country road that included a number of bridges. However, the trip did not always pass without drama. On one occasion, at a place called Blue Duck Creek, Tony smacked straight into the cliff-face that runs the length of most of the Kaikoura coast, breaking his ribs and writing off the front end of the bike. The bike he was riding was actually Roland's, who complained bitterly about the damage, blaming the rider for being 'too zonked to keep it together'.

More often than not on such trips the bikes were a ticket to biker parties and, always ones for a party, John and his friends did not hesitate to attend. At one such gathering they arrived just in time to see a tall, wild-eyed man in black leathers being hauled off another who had somehow aroused his resentment. Jon White was the mercurial individual and his lack of patience with those he considered had wronged him was well known. Had anyone suggested at the time to John that Jon White would play a significant part in his motorcycle future, John would very probably have expressed amazement. He detested violent behaviour and, within certain bounds, always kept a tight reign on his own conduct. Nevertheless, Jon White was destined to add a chapter to John's story that was as valiant and bold as any other.

As the 1970s rolled into the '80s the crew from The Stables was able to racket around in an out-of-control fashion, generally living the life of Riley.

Typical of their adventures was the rock concert that CJ, ever the entrepreneur, staged on the West Coast at a celebrated beauty spot to the north of Greymouth called Punakaiki. He had a number of bands and odd-ball talents to entertain the crowd, including a man who played the spoons. Mike, John and Roland all turned up on their Ducatis and parked them in the dog pound Chris had thoughtfully provided. They then purchased all the alcohol Chris had available, to the disgust of the other patrons, and after storing the booze in the handy kennels they settled in for a marathon session. Being the West Coast it was not too long before solid rain had reduced everything to mud, but the fun continued with undampened enthusiasm, as CJ recalled.

> Someone had thoughtfully brought along a few sticks of gelignite to spice up the planned fireworks display and Roland managed to get his hands on one. Shouting that he was going to wake up the hippies, he lit a fuse and threw the blazing stick onto rocks on the bank of the nearby river where muddied festival patrons were bathing. At that moment Tony staggered out of the bushes and, after tripping over on the rocks, fell over on the fizzing gelignite, smothering the fuse. Undeterred, Roland retired to the campsite and threw a spare glass jar of petrol on the fire where it sat unbroken for most of the rest of the evening before John finally kicked it off. The music raged on and the party continued into the wee hours, when they finally finished the booze and everything else and fell over to sleep. When they all finally came to the next day to ride home, it was generally agreed that it had been a bloody good time.

On another occasion they trooped over to the West Coast to hold speed trials. In those days you could wait beside the West Coast Highway for hours without seeing a vehicle. They measured and marked out a series of lines on a straight section of road and then tore up and down timing, one another over various distances, including a flying mile for all-out top speed.

One of the best West Coast adventures of all, however, was the time John took the gypsy caravan to Queenstown and left it at the local car museum. By then Broz had acquired a TR6, which for some reason had brakes that often caught fire, and he accompanied John, who drove the truck. Roland also went along for the trip on his Ducati. They took the longest route possible, visiting people all along the way. Two nights were spent with John's uncle, Peter Hughson, and another night was spent on the shores of Lake Wanaka with Robin Judkins, who had by then just staged the first of the multi-sport events that would make him rich and famous. John and Robin had met a few years earlier when John turned up to look at a Model T that Robin owned. Robin recalled:

> He had admired my brother's Hupmobile, which we had used to tow the Model T home, but he thought the Ford was stuffed. I already knew that but I could start it and I wanted to show that it at least ran. I had somehow wired up the strange ignition with a dodgy system of my own, and after priming the carb I hit the switch and got the full force of the magneto through my body. This was really shocking in every sense. I think I was still quivering with smoke coming out my ears when he left. After that I saw him at parties from a distance but I only really talked to him again when he turned up in the International.

On the morning following their arrival, Robin introduced John to kayaking on the Motatapu. John set out with his usual reckless exuberance and soon capsized. According to Robin, it was more through good luck than good management that John was not drowned, but he insisted on getting back in and carrying on.[37] Although Robin and John would take some time getting to know each other properly, the day marked the beginning of another very special friendship. Soon the small, erratic convoy was heading south again. It was a beautiful summer and all was well with their world at least. The trip was a slow crawl for the International, from one pub to the next, where the rest of the party waited patiently with lagers in hand, along one of the most beautiful, and one of the emptiest, highways on the planet.

With John now racing both his Tiger and Ducati, his racing calendar was fairly full. In addition to club racing, he and Allan both enjoyed racing the Triumphs in historic class racing. The bikes were of a certain vintage and they were, apparently, technically original enough to qualify. The Classic Race Register held meetings at rural South Island circuits such as Cust and Levels, and John and Allan turned up regularly. They had also raced the Triumphs in the occasional, and far more exclusive, Country Gentlemen's races at Wigram Airfield.

The Country Gents, as they were popularly known, organised meetings at a number of South Island venues, including Levels and Wigram. The latter was the airforce base just outside Christchurch where the runway was converted to a racetrack by the usual addition of drums and hay bales. These meetings were intended for the benefit of classic enthusiasts, and the advanced state of tune of both John's bike and Allan's occasioned some concern. Of course, it probably didn't hurt that John had the social weight to ensure a warm welcome at any of these events, but he managed to test even these excellent connections. His exuberant, and sometimes lurid, style and his fiercely competitive nature (on bikes and in cars) did not always fit comfortably with the Gents, who took a fairly social approach to their racing. He was 'spoken to' by race officials a number of times over the years for his antics and was given to understand most firmly that he should tidy up his act. Apparently he did, at least enough so that nothing ever came of it, in spite of some quite spectacular episodes.[38]

The Canterbury Autocycle Club, with encouragement from Lindsay Williamson, also organised a few races for non-Japanese machinery at Ruapuna, and John and Broz become involved when they heard about a practice day. Although Lindsay had hardly noticed them up until then, he nevertheless suggested to the two that they consider going north to Manfeild to have a go in the 1981 Castrol Six-Hour. His suggestion may well have been somewhat tongue-in-cheek, and his enthusiasm for the idea may have been fuelled by more than a touch of mischief, but Lindsay had always been a firm believer in the value of giving something a go. The 'something' in question, however, was nothing less than the absolute pinnacle of New Zealand road racing, an event that attracted the cream of New Zealand talent. It was a tall order to expect that a couple of rookies could do anything but make fools of themselves, but when the time came in mid-November they loaded John's 900SS on a the back of an Isuzu pick-up, loaned by Lindsay for the event, along with Broz's wire-wheel 900SS as a spare, and went north to catch a ferry.

Manfeild is located a couple of hours north of Wellington, on the flat wind swept plains of Manawatu. The track is a real scratcher's circuit with long straights and tight corners, a layout that rewards hard, aggressive riding. The favoured mounts in the Castrol Six-Hour race for production motorcycles in 1981 were the Honda CBR1100s of hotshot riders such as Australians Michael Cole and Malcolm Campbell, and the Suzuki 1100 Katanas being campaigned by the likes of Robert Holden and Neil Chivas. But they were far from the only potential winners at the circuit, where a fast and highly competitive field had gathered to do battle.

Lindsay and Joe probably weren't two of the potential winners, but they were there with their Triumph Bonneville, ready to fly the flag for Britain. They were obviously involved in their own programme and didn't have time to pay much attention to John and Broz, and the two found themselves very much on their own. Generally, the arrival of a couple of hippies with the two Ducatis on a pick-up was greeted with some passing mild amusement but other than that they were largely ignored.

John and Broz soon realised that they were hopelessly outclassed. It was bad enough in the paddock. The other teams had well-equipped trailers and smoothly organised mobile workshops. They had spares. They had food on tap. But it was worse on the track, as Lindsay remembered.

> Both John and Broz found they were being treated like absolute bunnies. The other riders gave them no racing room and they were both stunned at the sheer pace of the field. This was the real stuff, not club racing or belting around on old pom-bombs. They both ended up falling off in practice and packed a big sad and went home. They didn't even wait to watch the race. It had been like taking chickens to the slaughter-house. A lot of people would have given up after an experience like that but John just got in deeper. He really loved racing and we soon accepted him as one of the boys. We called him 'Sack of Shit' Britten because of the way he hung off that old Triumph, but he didn't behave as if he thought he was anything special and we liked him. He was OK.

It was Broz who finally called a halt to proceedings at Manfeild after he had taken a particularly violent tumble that nearly dislocated his shoulder. But, as Broz recalled, it was not the end of their adventures for that particular trip.

> We were driving south toward Wellington alongside the Main Trunk Line. For quite a while we had a big goods train travelling beside us, and I had half an eye on it when I suddenly saw showers of sparks coming from under a carriage right next to us. I said something to John and he looked over at it, and then the whole thing slowly tipped over, dragging more carriages with it, and before we had a chance to react huge bogies were flying through the grass towards us. We slid to a halt and one of the bogies stopped on the road right in front of us. We sat there for a couple of minutes and then all these people arrived from nowhere and started poking around, so we got underway again. We had only gone a few miles when another train going the other way went past. John and I looked at it disappearing up the line toward the crash and John said, 'I wonder if he knows?' There was no phone around or anything and the Isuzu was pretty slow, so there was nothing we could do. I don't recall that there was ever any news of a second accident so I suppose the second train driver must have stopped.

It was not hard for Broz and John to justify their early departure from Manfeild. Clearly, discretion was not only the better part of valour, it was better than trashing their prized Ducatis, and their persons, to no useful effect. The yawning gap between the highly organised teams and their own effort, however, and the sheer ability of the faster riders, did not rest easily with John. He had failed and he had failed abjectly. It was a salutary lesson but it was a lesson he was determined to learn. According to Lindsay, 'From that day he never got motorcycle racing out of his system.' Far from being discouraged by his failure at Manfeild, John left fired with determination to take on the best and beat them fair and square.

Back in Christchurch, John continued racing both the Ducati and the Tiger as a clubman, joining in the fun and games, enjoying the friendly and relaxed rivalry and camaraderie, and generally refining his abilities as a motorcycle racer. As usual, he only really had one speed and that was flat out. Allan recalled that John still crashed fairly regularly, but he was improving and beginning to enjoy some good finishes. The South Island was spoiled for circuits. In addition to the races held at the recognised racetracks, there were annual events on urban street circuits in Dunedin and Invercargill, plus a number of splendid rural road circuits like the one at Hawkesbury.

Unfortunately, the competition on offer through the available events was less than satisfactory for either the Ducati or the Triumph. It was all very well to do well on the Triumph against the classic crowd, but it was less than satisfying when the competition proved less than taxing. Worse still when you had to slow down to avoid being kicked out.

On the other hand, racing the Ducati against fields of Japanese machinery in club racing was frustrating for the opposite reason. The Japanese bikes were just too fast. This harsh reality affected all those racing the contemporary (and, as it transpired, largely final) offerings from British manufacturers as well as all the other current Italian and American machinery.

Triumph Bonnevilles and Tridents, BSA Lightnings and Rocket 3s, Norton Commandos, bevel-drive Ducatis, Moto Guzzis, Laverdas, Benellis, BMWs and Harley-Davidsons were no match for Yamahas, Kawasakis, Hondas and Suzukis. They simply failed to make the podium and after a while that became boring.

This then was the background to what proved a somewhat fateful day when a group of racers turned up, again with Lindsay Williamson well to the fore, at an event organised by the Classic Racing Register.

The events that followed have achieved a kind of notoriety in motorcycle circles. The version most often repeated in the BEARS fraternity had the Classic Register types expressing dismay at the prospect of sharing the track with a bunch of real bikers who liked to go hard. It was a classic establishment versus outlaw story. And that, according to Allan, who was there at the time, was all it was—a good story. 'The newer bikes,' he said, 'were simply not eligible.'

However, it does seem true that somehow or other tempers flared and some unkind words were exchanged. It would appear that the last words belonged to George Begg, a man justly famous for his efforts in a string of race cars bearing his name. He was one of the Classic Register members present that day and he was reported to have told Lindsay and his mates to 'Fuck off and form your own club!' It proved to be useful advice, and when they did just that and made it a wonderful success George Begg was one of the first to congratulate them.

It is hard to know who first thought to follow through with the idea of forming a club, but somehow the decision was made and it quickly gathered momentum. Local enthusiasts Stu and Sue Whyte placed an ad in the *Christchurch Star* inviting those who were interested in racing motorbikes other than Japanese machines to meet at the Ocean View Hotel in Governors Bay.

The Ocean View was an old pub and a favourite stop-off on Banks Peninsula for sporting motorcyclists. About twenty keen competitors turned up, including John Britten, and the meeting got down to tin tacks. Also present at the meeting was Ray Shearman, an older gentleman who rode an even older Indian motorcycle. Ray was also a member of the Auto Cycle Union (ACU), the then governing body of motorcycle racing (now Motorcycling New Zealand, or MNZ), and he would play a vital role in steering the disparate collection of motorcyclists in the right direction to satisfy officialdom. It was the first of several meetings that eventually resulted in the group becoming affiliated with what was left of a 1950s milk-bar cowboy outfit called the Corsair Motorcycle Club, which had by then metamorphosed into a motocross club for off-roaders. On 29 March 1983 the first pre-race meeting was held in the Corsair clubrooms. One of the matters to resolve was just what to call the new group, and there was much lively discussion about it. Joe Hannah suggested that because the meetings always involved a generous quantity of lager the name Beers might be appropriate. Dennis White (brother of Jon) then made the short step from Beers to BEARS—British, European and American Racing, with the 'S' standing for supporters or society, though this was never officially decided. Shortly thereafter, Ashley Smith, the same artist who had created the 'Three Fools' t-shirts, created the now famous logo of a speed-crazed grizzly barrelling along on a British Twin, a machine clearly modelled on John's Tiger.

So it was that on 29 May 1983 the first BEARS meeting was held at Ruapuna, with twenty-five riders attending. From the beginning, the club was determined to attract new members and supporters with an inclusive and welcoming attitude. No doubt the cheering influence of a few jugs of amber fluid assisted in the formation of this noble and generous resolution, but the attitude persisted and membership of the club flourished.

By January 1984, when the club held its first Sound of Thunder meeting at Ruapuna, BEARS racing had become so popular that 2000 spectators turned up to watch. In the early days the overwhelming majority of the field was English, with the odd 860 and 900SS Ducati (these were generally agreed to be too long in the wheelbase to be much good on the tight Ruapuna circuit). However, as the racing grew in popularity so did the variety of competing machinery. In addition to the marques already mentioned, Aermacchis, BMWs, Cagivas, Gileras, KTMs, Maicos, Montesas, Moto Guzzis, Moto Morinis, Husqvarnas, Laverdas, Royal Enfields, Weslakes and a host of sometimes weird and often wonderful specials appeared out of the woodwork.

The track marshals at the first Sound of Thunder meeting were drawn from the ranks of wives and girlfriends, and by all accounts they managed the job wonderfully. Another large team of volunteers ensured a well-run meeting, while two wives who were nurses looked after the medical side of things. To cover costs, Lindsay's wife, Marg, and three of her friends walked around with buckets collecting donations. The meeting was conducted in a festive and convivial atmosphere and set the tone for the years to come. Traditions of openness and generosity established that day were maintained even as the organisation became bigger and more professional. Although the club soon gave up the buckets in favour of an entrance fee collected at the gate, access to the pits always remained free. The only decision that did eventually change, to the regret of most concerned, was that prize money should be paid evenly to all classes right down the field, so that sometimes even the last place-getter was paid. This change was probably inevitable, however, given the explosion of interest that followed when machines arrived from all over the country and from overseas.

By the time of the 1986 Sound of Thunder meeting about 10,000 spectators were watching full grids of trick machinery, some of it from Australia, compete for up to $20,000 of prize money. To put the attendance figures in perspective, it should be noted that the meetings were attracting bigger crowds than the New Zealand Grand Prix. By then the club was so well organised and funded that it was able to pay the Australians, who were invited over by Lindsay Williamson, to ship their bikes over.

Although it seemed to the organisers that the press was spoiling for an incident to brand the event with a big, bad biker label, the years delivered only one. This occurred when a non-patched gang prospect fired a pistol into the ground in the vicinity of the rival Highway 61's president before running off, eventually into the arms of the law. To their credit, the Highways elected not to retaliate and the episode essentially fizzled out. In spite of this laudable record, however, the Sound of Thunder meetings always enjoyed the patronage of a huge police contingent. As there was nothing for them to do they spent the weekends in a special room drinking coffee and enjoyed the racing like everybody else.

The parties thrown by BEARS were always lively occasions, but the club never lost sight of the fact that it was largely made up of family people. The annual BEARS lolly scramble at the Sound of Thunder was typical of the kinds of activities that appealed to small and big kids alike, with a helicopter slowly flying over the crowd while one of the many volunteers shovelled sweets out of the open door. Lindsay was forever arranging activities for kids such as tricycle racing, go-kart rides, and, for the slightly older, Vespa racing. Nor was it just at the track that families were encouraged to participate. The annual BEARS picnic in the country, for example, was well patronised by BEARS racers and their wives and kids. One of the main activities was racing a couple of old cars on a paddock around a course laid out with hay bales, to the amusement of all concerned.

Another popular series of BEARS activities, begun in 1984, was the annual speed trials at South Eyre Road, a dead-straight two-lane road that speared through the Canterbury countryside. Having obtained permission to close the road for the trials, the club then accurately surveyed set distances and organised sophisticated timing equipment to record such events as the flying quarter-mile.[39] Allan Wylie won the inaugural event with a speed of 122.94 mph on his Triumph 650, a pretty impressive result for the old twin. The event was a complete success, and each year it attracted an ever-increasing number of entries. For John and the Tiger, however, one of the early trials very nearly resulted in complete disaster. Allan recalled:

> Typically, John arrived late with his Triumph for the riders' briefing one year. At the briefing we had all been advised to stay on the right side of the centre-line to avoid a nasty bump on the left, right in the speed-trap area. Nobody thought to warn John and when his turn came he hit the bump at terminal velocity. With no rear suspension, the jolt unseated him and the resulting tank slapper was terrifying to watch according to witnesses. Somehow or other he held on and finished the run with an average that was still well over 100 mph.

The atmosphere of cooperation that existed between competitors particularly moved Jim Sykes, who was elected the first president of the club.

> We had the odd drama but nothing serious. On the whole, BEARS brought out the best in people. If a rider did not have the money to get home we would lend them the gas at least and a few bucks. People were always lending gear. Boots, back braces, clutch cables, grommets, tools, advice—you name it. If someone needed something

to get them out on the track everyone would do their best to see they got it.

BEARS patronage was to prove a real boon to Ruapuna Raceway, as the racers and their families did something about the shortcomings that other clubs and organisations had ignored for twenty years. Of course, with so many paying spectators at the Sound of Thunder, the BEARS coffers were bulging and they could actually afford to do things that other clubs could not. Located on a barren, rocky river plain with precious little shelter, Ruapuna had always been a hot, inhospitable, dusty place in summer and a miserable, cold, windswept place in winter. The BEARS joined in an ambitious tree-planting programme and built the first toilet block in the pit area. They also assisted with funding major track extensions and helped construct a proper playground for children. Ruapuna Racetrack was not the only recipient of BEARS largess. The Intensive Care Unit at Christchurch Public Hospital was able to purchase a VCR unit with BEARS funding, and cleaning equipment was procured for a local spinal unit. The Aids Fund and the Special Olympics Organisation were just two of the other groups to benefit from substantial BEARS contributions.

Two further BEARS clubs, one in the Central North Island and one in Auckland, were quickly affiliated and, in double-quick time, the movement spread to Australia.[40]

By 1984 John was riding sufficiently well for Lindsay Williamson to think about racing with him at Manfeild in the Castrol Six-Hour. However, it was not entirely a matter of John's developing riding skills that encouraged Lindsay to consider the idea. He candidly admitted that he was by then aware of John's powers of persuasion, and he shrewdly calculated that John might be able to find the sponsorship that had eluded him. Accordingly, they teamed up under the banner Christchurch Motorcycles Racing Team, named after Lindsay's popular motorcycle shop. The K1000 BMW had just been released onto the market and, by good fortune, one just happened to be available. It apparently gave the owner, who may have been doing a stretch in prison at the time, enormous pleasure to know that probably the very first example raced in the world was on hire purchase. It would also be the only non-Japanese machine in the race.

The bike needed to be run in and Jon White took on the task, very nearly writing off himself, his pillion passenger and the bike with a heavy crash at the notorious Zig Zag, the switchback road that ran down the mountains to the west from the top of Arthur's Pass. However, the damage was soon made good and all was set for the big day.

John had done a good job finding sponsorship. He discovered in the process a talent—already spotted by Lindsay—for enthusing hard-nosed businesspeople who might usually have been expected to regard a group of relative novices racing a motorcycle of dubious suitability in one of the toughest motor-sport events in the country with some scepticism. With the bike duly emblazoned with the Canon Copiers' logo, the team headed north.

In any case, 'novice' was hardly a word to describe the spannermen who'd volunteered to help John and Lindsay for the event. Looking after the mechanical side of things were Allan Wylie and Mike Sinclair. Mike, who was a friend of Lindsay's, was then working as a mechanic for the American Randy Mamola Grand Prix team, racing 500cc NSR Hondas, and he was at home in New Zealand for the off-season. Mike and John immediately hit it off, and yet another vital cog clicked into place in the complex human machinery that would produce the Britten motorcycle.[41]

The BMW was not given much credence by the rest of the field but on the day it performed admirably. The real race was between the Honda VR1000s and the Kawasaki 900GPZ Ninjas, with two-stroke Yamaha RZ500s adding some spice. Amid all the excitement, however, John and Lindsay circulated on the BMW with few fuel stops and little wear on the rubber, finally coming home in a very credible eighth place.[42] The result showed one thing very clearly. John had indeed matured as a rider in the few short years since the earlier debacle at Manfeild. He could take some satisfaction at having arrived at a critical point in his motor-racing career, and to have arrived there in a very short time. But he must also have been very aware, as he laughed and drank with his fellow riders in the clubrooms after the race, that he had probably left his run too late. Too late, at any rate, to beat the twenty-year-olds who surrounded him to the next level of the sport he had grown to love. If he was ever to win a mention in the big book of motorcycle racing it would not be as a rider.

CHAPTER FIVE

Racing Now

In 1984 John married Kirsteen Price, a former Miss Canterbury and successful international model. He had pursued her for several years, in part through a long-distance correspondence, proof at the very least of the seriousness of his intentions. (Fortunately, as she was often candidly to acknowledge, she was as challenged as he was by the complexities of spelling and grammar.) Finally, John had sold his black Ducati and, after borrowing some additional funding from Allan Wylie, had flown off to New York to lure Kirsteen home to matrimony. As Kit Ebbett recalled it, the marriage marked a number of fundamental changes in John's lifestyle.

> Kirsteen was probably the princess he was looking for to set off his home and provide him with children. She was successful to the point where everyone made a fuss of her when she came home and he was a centre-stage sort of guy. And so he decided she was it and that was that. He had to have her and after a long pursuit he got her. They had a lot of good times together and had some great kids. They also had the kinds of difficulties two headstrong individuals can have—but they survived together and his friends were content to give him the space he needed to become a very committed family man.

The Stables, so long an open home to those who had worked in and on the house, was suddenly a very private residence, and John, so long the life and soul of the party, was suddenly highly selective of his company. John's hippie days had more or less ended when he bought The Stables in 1977, but throughout his days as a sporting motorcyclist he'd continued to enjoy a certain level of nihilistic hell-raising. Suddenly, however, it seemed all that was behind him.

According to Kit Ebbett, the pressure on John to do what had always been unthinkable—to join Bruce at Brittco, the family business—was now enormous.

> In the past, John had always been attracted to intellectual, creative and essentially gentle women. Kirsteen, however, was everything that you would expect a successful, international model to be. She was demanding, assertive and absolutely confident of the essential rightness of her opinions. Bruce now had a powerful ally who believed as he did that money, and the ambition to make money, were paramount in life. John resisted them both for months but gradually they wore him down and finally he capitulated. I remember how uncomfortable and embarrassed he was the first time I saw him in a suit. I think he really believed he had let the side down somehow.

Allan also recalled being puzzled the first time he saw John wearing a suit. He was equally bemused when John made reference to having an office. He had never had one of those before either. So far as Allan knew, John had thus far spent remarkably little time in anyone's office. Not long after that, while John was visiting him at Auto Restorations, Allan noticed him wander off to a quiet corner where he seemed to start talking to himself. Cell phones were then thin on the ground and someone asked Allan what John was doing.

> I said he was talking on his yuppie phone, a common name for them then. My comment must have stung him, however, because he rang me at home some hours later from a bar, judging by the background noise. He said 'Don't you have portable appliances?' I thought he was joking and told him that I didn't, that everything plugged in around at my place. He then hung up, leaving me utterly taken aback. I certainly had not meant to say anything hurtful but I realised later that it probably had something to do with the changes that had recently taken place in his life. When I'd first met John he showed no interest in his father's business and rejected everything to do with it. He knew that Bruce saw him as a failure and would sometimes refer to Bruce's protégé, Russell Boddington, ironically as 'my brother', as if Russell was filling the role really meant for John. After John began to work at Brittco I think he must have been sensitive about what his old friends would think about his apparent about-face and I must have touched a nerve.

It was a trivial exchange but it served to illustrate the distance that had suddenly grown between the two friends.

In spite of his sudden lurch into respectability, however, John kept on racing the Tiger as often as he could and continued to do so with all his usual reckless verve.

His determination to continue to do so was brought home forcefully to Allan one evening as he worked on the bike around at The Stables in preparation for racing the next day at Levels.

> Kirsteen was upstairs in the next wing giving birth to the first of their three children, Sam. She was screaming her head off while I was putting the gearbox together, and every now and then John would appear to see how I was going. At one point there was a particularly dreadful shriek and he looked at me and said, 'Isn't mother nature cruel.' Later he came back down and told me he had a son and he wasn't going to race after all. He asked if I would like to use the bike. I did end up taking both bikes but his was unsorted and I was happy to leave it alone in the pits.

Only two weeks later, however, John was back racing at Levels. Kirsteen was sitting on the embankment with their new son, who was wrapped up against the howling wind. To her astonishment, John's bike went flying past without a rider. Frantically, she peered back up the track and to her relief spotted him trudging back toward her.

John stuck with the Tiger for years and only really gave up racing it because of the pressure of time. Of course, a large part of the pleasure he derived from racing it came from the opportunity it afforded him to mix with all his old motorcycle mates. As the pressure of business mounted, however, he found it hard to afford the time to attend some of the more distant races. Lindsay Williamson had an answer to that.

> I persuaded him to borrow his old man's helicopter and I flew him down to Levels for a meeting. Dennis White[43], who was racing his Rickman, had already taken the bikes down and we just landed in the infield and went racing. He felt a bit fronty about it and I could tell he was embarrassed. John really didn't want to ask for the thing and he was a bit surprised when we got it. He told me that we'd never get it again and, sure enough, the following Monday Bruce sold it.

The fact that Lindsay took John for a tour of some of his cobbers' high country farms after the races, and that both lost track of time and had to fly home in the dark, probably had more to do with Bruce's decision to curtail John's helicoptering activities than anything else. Apparently, the bikes had arrived home from Timaru with Dennis White many hours before Lindsay and John, which rather defeated the purpose of taking the helicopter in the first place. And it caused those awaiting their return some anxious hours.

Finding the time to get to meetings was not the only area where the pressure of work compromised John's racing. Allan had been concerned about the state of the Tiger for some time, but John now seemed too busy to put matters right.

'Years of neglect since the restoration had taken their toll on the cycle parts,' Allan recalled. 'I doubt if John ever checked things like fork-oil level or wheel bearing play and the increases in engine power had only made things worse.'

In spite of the increasingly awkward and twitchy handling, John pushed the bike as hard as ever and mostly managed to stay on to finish the race. Sometimes, however, things did go wrong. At one meeting at Levels, the oil tank fractured, probably because John had neglected to use rubber bushes to mount it, which caused the alloy to work harder as it was subjected to the direct effects of engine vibration. The cracked tank had dropped oil all over his back tyre and the track, and he suddenly found himself flying through the air with the bike turning somersaults beside him. As usual, however, he scraped himself together and was none the worse for wear.

Why he wanted to race something so ostensibly compromised for as long as he did is the kind of question that is often asked of enthusiasts. The simple truth is that those who race obscure, or seemingly inappropriate, machinery do so because the challenge pleases them. It certainly seemed to please John. Whatever his reasons, the Tiger provided a solid education for the world of motorcycle racing, and those who raced with him agree that on a good day both he and the Triumph were formidable competitors. As Steve Radcliffe put it, 'No one ever rode a Tiger 100 faster than he did.'

Unfortunately it was not enough. John was determined to have at least one last shot at the next level in motorcycle racing, even if it meant doing two things he had never done before—racing overseas and racing a Japanese machine. And so he turned to the one person who had always encouraged him to reach beyond his known abilities, to find out what was inside and to test it. As always, Lindsay was keen to give it a go, and they sat down and worked out a strategy to get them across the Tasman Sea to the Australian Six-Hour race for production motorcycles at Oran Park. If Manfeild had been a taste of the big time, this was a very big bite.

Once again John's job was to organise sponsorship, and Canon Copiers came to the party with a $10,000 deal that John clinched when he offered to redesign their showroom in Christchurch. The deal also included sponsorship to contest the Manfeild Six-Hour race that would run several weeks after the Australian event. Finally, John negotiated a bank loan on behalf of the team to cover the remaining expenses while Lindsay secured a sharp deal with the Suzuki agents to provide one of the new, deadly fast Suzuki GSX-R750s. Steve Radcliffe flew up to Wellington, collected the bike and then ran it in bringing it back. Testing was challenging and involved a complete rebuild of the rear mono-shock to cure handling problems. They were without the reassuring presence of Mike Sinclair and both riders found the Suzuki uncomfortably cramped. John was determined to get in as much track time as he could, and turned up with the Suzuki at a BEARS practice day at Ruapuna. The presence of a Japanese machine occasioned a chorus of protests from the

BEARS riders at the track. John's argument that the club had been founded on the premise that rules were a nuisance was firmly rejected. There was, the BEARS riders insisted, at least one immutable rule and that was that Japanese motorcycles were absolutely banned from participation in BEARS events. Things got a little heated, but when one BEARS rider threatened to throw rocks at the Suzuki if John took it out on the track he finally gave up and went home.

Although John and Lindsay were completely unknown in Australia their Canon sponsorship ensured that they had one of the biggest, most comprehensively equipped, trailer-homes at the track. This so impressed the locals that, to their embarrassment, both riders found themselves being interviewed by Australian television crews who seemed to rate their chances a lot higher than they did. They were, after all, just a couple of club riders competing against the likes of such international racing identities as Wayne Gardner, Robbie Phillis, Richard Scott, Paul Feeney and a host of others with almost equally formidable reputations.

The race itself was a miserable affair in streaming rain on tyres that were something of an unknown quantity.

Some hours into the race John aquaplaned off the end of the straight at 137 mph. Thankfully, the place where he went down had a huge run-off area and he skidded so far it actually took quite a long time to find him. As usual, however, the damage to both bike and rider was relatively minor and the team was able to hammer everything straight again so that John and Lindsay could finish, albeit well down the field.

Steve Radcliffe, who was riding for another team, recalled, 'John was absolutely rapt to finish. He always stayed positive throughout a bloody tough race when a lot of big names failed to get home.'

Steve also recalled, however, his concern at the hours John kept prior to the race. 'I was amazed that John was still partying up in the kitchenette of the trailer as the night dragged on toward dawn. We were all telling him to go to sleep but he just kept bouncing along, even though he had to line up the next day to race. And this wasn't any old race. This was six bloody hard hours.'

However, if John appeared to be his usual uncaring 'press on regardless' self, it did not mean that he was not giving serious thought to his future. Now with a young son toddling about, he readily agreed to his wife's demand that his future race activities be restricted to classic events. After the next Manfeild six-hour race, he would no longer compete as a serious racer. If he had ever dared to dream of winning real glory as a motorcycle racer, the dream was now over.

The final outing at Manfeild was to illustrate succinctly both John's strengths and failings as a rider. Preparation was thorough, with a substantial inventory of spares being made up by the team, including a spare fairing and levers machined out of blank aluminium. Steve Radcliffe, who would share the riding with John this time, remembered working the usual crippling hours at The Stables preparing the bike, and it became a standing joke that John would not announce knock-off time until at least five in the morning. Steve would struggle awake around 11am to find that John had been hard at work since nine. Nevertheless, it was a confident and well-equipped team that turned up to race with spares, according to Steve, for practically everything that could break.

Once again John partied up, and this time Steve remembered being really annoyed when, at four in the morning, John was still well alight with an early track call just three hours away.

> John could handle the hours better than anyone I ever knew, but I believe the late hours did slow down his reactions that time. I went out in the morning and set a time of one minute and eighteen seconds, which was eighth fastest, and more than good enough for qualifying. With six hours of racing it hardly mattered where we were on the grid, anyway. Then John took the bike out for a practice and he hadn't even done half a lap before he damn near wrote the thing off cart-wheeling it into the infield.

The bike was dragged back to the pits where a disgusted Allan Wylie vented his frustration by demanding why John 'couldn't do even one slow lap?' They had intended spending the time before the race practising pit work, particularly tyre changing. Instead they were faced with hours of repairs. The fairing and instruments were a write-off, the bars and sub-frame were bent and worse, the alloy wheels, which they had no spares for, were buckled. Allan was so thoroughly 'shat off' about it all that he went off and had a shower. Later, John told him that he was quite hurt by Allan's comments, but there was work to be done and John was soon attempting the impossible, straightening the wheels with a heavy bar and a sledgehammer. With the most delicate touch, or as delicate as such tools allowed, he and Broz, who had come along to help out, succeeded in getting the wheels back into an acceptable shape to the general amazement of all concerned, and the bike was back in one piece in time for the start.

The race went very well, although there was a moment of concern when, after his first one-hour session on the bike, John seemed close to collapse. Allan remembered that John was completely dehydrated and had to lie down by the pit wall. Allan 'poured copious quantities of drinks into him' and by his next stint he had pretty much recovered. When the flag finally dropped they were circling comfortably in the middle of the field. For Steve it was a great result.

> I'd never ridden a Jap bike before and so it was a big change. It was also a fitting race for John to bow out on. Looking back I would say that he reminded me of riders like Jason McEwen, a man who would later ride for Britten Motorcycles. Like John was, he is a ferociously fast charger who just gets on with it. John was not an elegant or polished rider but he had raw talent and courage. He became a pretty good racer who could hold his own among some very professional company.

It was probably the best result John could have hoped for, and it was a lot more than most would have achieved in the time he allotted himself. However, as Lindsay had noted, motorcycling was bubbling in John's blood and he now needed a fresh challenge. The Tiger was still sitting in the workshop, of course, but somehow, after all he had been through, this did not seem enough.

There was, however, another way that John could remain in close touch with the sport and the people who pursued it. He could become a constructor. He could build a special for BEARS racing using Ducati running gear. He liked Ducati engines. He could build something really tricky, something really different. And he could get one of the new young hotshots to ride it. Somebody who could win some races and win some attention.

There would be a certain amount of development riding, in addition to which he'd be at the track more often, where he might race the odd classic.

It sounded like fun.

CHAPTER SIX

Off Again

The subject of building a dream bike incorporating all the latest technology and thinking was something that invariably cropped up when sporting motorcyclists gathered. Generally it was recognised that such speculation was more in the nature of entertainment and, unsurprisingly, such talk had flown about at The Stables for some time. One person, however, who had taken part in these discussions had always been determined to take up the challenge. And that was Broz.

> I'd bought a Ducati 900 Darmah engine and gearbox some time before from Ned Knewstubb. Ned had opened the first Ducati franchise in New Zealand up in Auckland and I got to know him after he moved down to Christchurch. He was always very helpful and encouraging about the idea of building a special and gave me a really good deal. Then I took off to Europe for a year and got a job driving a truck in the UK that took me to just about every little town in the country. I saved my money and invested it in a lot of hot-up bits for the Darmah engine before heading home, where I started making lights again for John. By then he was thinking seriously about building a bike as well and my project got intermingled with his.

The fact that John's and Broz's ideas about a 'special' seemed compatible was hardly surprising. John had also discussed the possibility of building a competition machine with Mike Sinclair thoroughly, and this had confirmed his idea that a Ducati special was the only way to go. The only Grand Prix capacity that interested John was 500cc racing, but this seemed out of the question and Mike wasted no time in saying so. John agreed. There were too many players in the field with unlimited amounts of money. John also agreed that Superbike racing was also out of the question because of homologation requirements for a set minimum production run of identical machinery. Clearly there was no immediate prospect of building more than one or two bikes. However, there were a number of popular race series he could contest. Battle of the Twins racing (BotT) and Formula One TT racing both offered a place for prototype machinery with few restrictions. Of the two, BotT racing offered the greatest challenge as it was a recognised class in both Europe and the USA, with separate annual championships on both continents, although it was not an international series. Such racing was more or less a 'ride what you brung' contest for twin-cylinder, 4-strokes with a capacity limit of 1000cc (soon to be 1100cc in the USA), and had little else in the way of restrictions beyond a ban on turbochargers, superchargers and funny fuel. And then, of course, there was BEARS racing, which had by now spread all over New Zealand and was firmly established in Australia.

At first glance, John's belief that he could build such a machine might seem somewhat overconfident and even arrogant. But there were plenty of precedents and he did not have to look far to find role models who illustrated what could be done when boldness and ability were combined.

One such character who had long fascinated John was an early Canterbury farmer by the name of Richard Pearse. It is likely that Pearse flew his home-built bamboo-framed monoplane, powered by an engine entirely of his own contrivance, in early 1903, about eight months before the Wright brothers (with whom Pearse corresponded) made their first celebrated hop. As we know, a slim volume detailing Pearse's achievements was one of the only books that John ever read.[44]

Bill Hamilton, father of the jet boat, was another inspiration.[45] Hamilton had enjoyed considerable success building hydraulic machinery until after World War II, when he turned his attention to the fast-flowing rivers that run east from the mountains to the sea. Determined to explore them by coming and going, as opposed to simply washing downhill in their grip, he developed and eventually marketed to the world the first successful jet-boats. As already noted, both John and his father Bruce were to become great enthusiasts of jet-boat adventures and could be numbered among the sport's very early pioneers.

Another of John's boyhood heroes, whose example clearly demonstrated that there were no limits to success other than those we place on ourselves, was Bruce McLaren, the race-car driver who founded one of the most enduringly successful Formula One car construction companies in motor-racing history. Although he hailed from Auckland and was not therefore a member of the southern fraternity of engineer-adventurers, his influence on John was pivotal. Throughout his boyhood John collected newspaper clippings about McLaren, and on his first visit to England he made a point of visiting the company. Later, nothing pleased John more than to be compared with these three remarkable achievers, and their various influences on him should not be underestimated.

In the world of motorcycle racing there were also a number of inspiring examples of extraordinarily talented New Zealanders who had contributed to both motorcycle design and motorcycle history. John was familiar with their accomplishments and undoubtedly derived encouragement from the fact that each represented a triumph of ingenuity and focused application over the power of the establishment.

Kim Newcombe was one such individual, a motorcycle mechanic and motocross rider from Auckland with some quite incredible achievements to his name. He had built his own Grand Prix motorcycle using a 4-cylinder, water-cooled German outboard marine engine, and against all the odds had raced to second place in the 1973 World Grand Prix 500cc Championship.[46]

There were also tremendously gifted race engineers, such as Wellingtonian Dick Lawton. A particular whizz with 2-stroke engines, Lawton prepared the engines that sent Geoff Perry, son of the famous Kiwi motorcycle racer Len Perry, on the road to motorcycle stardom on Suzuki TR500s and TR750s. Lawton's engines were often referred to by those who knew his work well as 'Araldite Specials' because the tuner used the material extensively to reshape the ports, part of Lawton's recipe for extracting outstanding performance.[47]

The man who built the frame for the 1970 Suzuki 500[48] that first brought Geoff Perry to the attention of the Suzuki company was another source not only of inspiration for John but also of brilliant new engineering ideas. Steve Roberts was an engineer and craftsman who, perhaps more than any other motorcycle constructor in New Zealand, deserved the epithet 'Renaissance Man'. Working almost entirely alone he pioneered a number of the technologies that John Britten and others would later exploit, and his name was associated with some of the most prominent names in New Zealand motorcycle-racing history. Apart from the motorcycles he built for Geoff Perry, he constructed machines for racers such as Keith Turner, Dave Hiscock, Dale Wylie, Robert Holden and Norris Farrow.

Steve Roberts learned all about working with aluminium, titanium and fibreglass as an apprentice with the De Haviland Aircraft Company before accepting a position with a major London Jaguar agent repairing crashed cats. Following that he joined the craftsmen building DB4s and Lagondas at Aston Martin. When Aston Martin suddenly found itself short of buyers, and had covered the company cricket field with unsold cars, Roberts was among those retrenched. Concerned at the way British manufacturing in general was taking a nosedive, he and his wife decided to check out the other side of the world and they duly arrived in Wellington, with just a few shillings to spare. Steve soon found a job at Wellington Polytech, where he taught panel beating for the next fourteen years before purchasing a 6-hectare farmlet 240 km north on the wild west coast just outside Wanganui. South Pacific Suzuki, then still in the hands of the Coleman family and still in Wanganui, contracted him to produce hoods for Suzuki four-wheel-drives in his new workshop, but he soon settled down to the serious business of making racing motorcycle frames.[49]

Eventually, Steve produced a series of monocoque motocross machines, but the idea of making such a unit the primary structure of the bike recurred to him when he read about a new material called Kevlar, a material apparently lighter than fibreglass but strong enough to make effective bulletproof helmets. He arranged for a friend with a fibreglass shop to import some Kevlar and carbon-fibre, which he then made up into various forms and attacked with a sledgehammer. He found the materials to be strong but brittle until they were combined layer by layer, when the resulting forms exhibited outstanding strength and impact resistance while remaining extremely lightweight.

Rod and Bob Coleman came up with the funding and just six weeks later the world's first carbon-fibre monocoque race bike was ready to take to the track. Once again, Steve had incorporated his usual refinements (such as his special swing arm and external ducting to an airbox) in a handsome machine that tipped the scales at just 155 kg, about 10 kg less than its aluminium predecessor. The construction also had the virtue of allowing the machine to be separated into two halves by releasing a handful of bolts.[50]

However, the pioneering construction was not the only unique feature of the new Suzuki special. When Dave had first discussed the bike's layout with Steve, the rider had suggested that the rear suspension unit could be hung underneath the bike. The two then put their heads together to figure out a way to make it work, and the result was a rear suspension that operated entirely in tension.

Steve was so excited by the final form of the rear suspension that he travelled down to Wellington to register it at the patents office, only to find a description of the exact system awaiting his return in the latest car magazines he subscribed to. It seemed Ferrari, Brabham and Lotus had all beaten him to the punch with their new race cars and, in fact, the progressive, tension-suspension principle had been tried before, by Moto Guzzi way back in 1928. Nevertheless, it was a first for modern racing motorcycles.

Sadly, the future for the world's first 'plastic' bike, as Steve fondly called it, was a lot less brilliant than its conception and execution. Things began to go terribly wrong when Dave's older brother Neville, himself an outstanding motorcycle racer, was killed competing in South Africa while Dave was testing his new machine. Dave then abandoned racing activities in New Zealand to take his brother's place in South Africa. But it was by no means the end of the story.

Robert Holden, one of the other keen Steve Roberts clients, purchased and campaigned first the aluminium monocoque and then the 'plastic' machine, winning a New Zealand Formula One Championship on the latter in the 1982–83 season. At that point a seasoned racer by the name of Norris Farrow—the most fearless competitor Steve ever met—commissioned a second bike and went on to take third place in the 1985 Australian Grand Prix, in spite of a bad oil leak.[51]

Steve would go on to be involved in the development of a series of Ducati-powered racers for Robert Holden to ride, including the celebrated special 'Fast 'n' Fragile'. However, Steve's legacy to motorcycle design went further than the victories scored by machines he contributed to directly.

Back in 1972 a Roberts-framed Suzuki 250 TR had taken a New Zealand National Championship with a young rider named Mike Sinclair on board. Steve recalled talking to Mike shortly after Dave Hiscock got going on the first plastic bike.

> I remember particularly telling him that I wanted to make carbon-fibre wheels as well as composite frames. By then I had developed a few ideas for a bike that would carry on where the radical machine made by the French company ELF left off. ELF had produced a series of race bikes with Honda four engines featuring single-sided, hub-steering, swing-arm suspension up front and a single-sided swing-arm to the rear. I thought about putting both suspension units under the bike and I discussed it with a few people, until someone told me that the French had done it already because he'd seen an ELF with the set-up a few months previously. So there you go. No matter what you think of, someone has already been there![52]

If Steve Roberts was a technical inspiration to John Britten, there was another Kiwi motorcycle racer and constructor whose efforts are perhaps most often mentioned as being in some ways forerunners to John's. This was the celebrated motorcycle speed king Bert Munro. The validity of comparisons between John and Bert is arguable, but the inspiration of Bert's achievements on several generations of sporting motorcyclists is beyond contention. In many ways he was the most uniquely gifted enthusiast of them all.

The story began in 1920 when Bert, who hailed from Invercargill, 585 km south of Christchurch, purchased a brand-new Indian V-twin Scout and set about extracting ever more power and speed from it. The long-running saga of single-minded determination, ingenuity and sheer skill that unfolded is highlighted by the humbleness of Bert's circumstances. He got by on the proverbial smell of an oily rag, sleeping in the damp end of a small shed while his beloved motorcycles (he also tuned and raced a Velocette) lived in the dry end. The bikes shared this space with a very basic lathe and various inventories of metals that at times included old aeroplane propellers, bulldozer tracks and truck axles. From these, using only his extremely modest equipment, Bert hewed engine and cycle parts in his quest for speed records, eventually achieving an astonishing 200 mph.[53]

As always, John wasted no time getting down to business once he had made his decision. His first thought was to build a streamlined fairing incorporating his ideas on the subject to fit Broz's planned special. Dennis White remembered going to see John at The Stables at this time, to find him whittling away at a big chunk of polystyrene with a pocket knife. It was the beginning of the project. As he intended to build the fairing using the latest miracle compounds, carbon-fibre and Kevlar, and had no experience in composite construction, John did what he had always done: he found an expert and learned from him.

Nick Williams was then a local manufacturer of motorcycle race-fairings and windscreen-blades.

> I had a few Triumphs and like most of my friends I used to turn up at the various happenings. There was a big annual gathering at Blenheim and I remember meeting John there. It was pretty hard core and a lot of the blokes looked down on John as being a bit namby-pamby. They were the kinds of guys who turned up in their leathers, got hopelessly pissed and then spent their time running people down to one another. John seemed quite different, and as I got to know him I realised that he was one of those rare individuals who would rather do something than just talk about it. He and his mates weren't big on going to the pub for a piss-up. They were more likely to have a few joints and make something, and I found that pretty refreshing. I was more than willing to join in and once I had, I found that working with him was a breeze because he was, as a workmate, so non-competitive. He encouraged everyone who was willing to contribute to put their ideas on the table and then we would all examine them. If the idea was found to be no good he did not make you wrong for bringing it up. I found that very empowering.

Nick explained to John how to build 'female' moulds from the polystyrene 'buck' John had by now whittled, into which they would layer carbon-fibre, Kevlar and epoxy resin. Before this could happen, however, the rough mould had first to be given a mirror-smooth finish. As always, John took the work to a man he knew could do the first-rate job he required. Bob Brookland was a sign-writer and keen BEARS supporter who raced a BSA B50. He first met John with Roland in the days when the Britten Glass Works was operating out of the Artists' Quarter and he painted John's red Ducati SS jet-black not long after. They quite often raced at the same events and Bob recalled helping John push-start the Tiger on a road outside Teretonga, the fast, bumpy track on the outskirts of the city of Invercargill, in a numbing blizzard of hail and snow. 'It was bloody cold anyway, but having alcohol all over my hands from tickling the carburettors as we ran along made it even worse. I thought I was going to get frostbite.'

Over the years Bob had been increasingly drawn into John's projects, including the protracted makeover of The Stables. John was constantly requesting all manner of materials be painted by Bob, including sundry items such as a pile of old domestic heating radiators John had scrounged from somewhere. Some of the requests were quite beyond the resources Bob commanded, and he finally made a rule that he would not paint anything that could not be carried into his premises. He remembered objecting when John turned up soon after with the two enormous front doors for The Stables, but with a bit of judicious wiggling and shuffling John managed to squeeze them sideways into the premises. He did not hesitate to remind Bob of the new rule, and Bob duly obliged and painted them. From the beginning Bob was an enthusiastic and passionate supporter of John's bike-building efforts, and vowed that so long as John had prototype racing motorcycles to paint he would do it for nothing. It was an undertaking he would honour right up until the end.

He gladly accepted the task of finishing the polystyrene mould and set to with polyester filler, or bog to use its more popular name. Many, many hours went into the mould as he alternately filled and sanded it until the finish was as perfect as he could make it.

Once Bob had completed his painstaking work Nick and John quickly produced the bucks they needed, and work on the body proceeded at pace.

When finished it was a spectacular blend of space age and traditional aesthetic values. It looked as if it had been moulded out of soap, with worn indents for the rider to fold into. The prow was characterised by a beak stretching over the front wheel, while winglets sprouted from the fairing to streamline the handlebars and rider's arms. At the rear, the tailpiece narrowed like a toothpaste tube to a wedge with a vertical trailing edge. The body also featured a faired headlight, indicators and a stylised little Kiwi, made from solid 'bog' that sat proudly on the end of the beak. The Kiwi also resembled the letter B. It was the first appearance of a logo that would eventually, in slightly modified form, become familiar to motorcycle-racing fans all over the world. The name 'Britten' was also prominently displayed on the side of the fairing.

Although the forks were properly mounted for the unveiling that soon took place in front of invited guests at The Stables, most of the rest of the machine was mocked up. Greg Atkinson remembered going to the christening, where John gave him permission to sit on the new machine. It failed to impress him and he recalled it as being generally uncomfortable and particularly 'horrible around the handle bars'. Greg frankly admitted, however, that he was later stunned at the way it went, with

'Mike Brosnan racing it bloody hard'.

'It only had an old bomb motor,' he said, 'and there was nothing high tech about it, but it went surprisingly fast.'

By the time of the unveiling Broz had become thoroughly concerned that he was being pushed aside from his own project and a serious rift was beginning to develop between the two men.

> I was happy to accept John's help when he told me he wanted to build a fairing for the project, but he started to behave more and more as if it was his. Finally, I just couldn't take it any more and I took the bike away to work on it without him. He then presented me with a bill for $900 for the fairing, which was a lot of money in those days when you consider that he only paid me $3 an hour to work for him. Not only that, but I had put a lot of hours into the fairing myself.
>
> I paid him and then, as I considered that the bike was now totally mine, I took his name off the side. This really made him cross and he wrote me an angry letter about it. In the end he made such a bloody fuss about it I put his name back on again. After that we were mates again and we got on as good as ever for years and years.

John and Broz had intended naming the bike 'Aero D One', and as John insisted on retaining the title for the next machine he was already planning Mike called his machine 'Aero D Zero'. It was known by that name from then on.

When Broz eventually finished it in 1985, the road equipment had been deleted and it was set up as a race bike. Its frame was a triangulated tubular structure of his own design that uncannily anticipated later Ducati units.[54] John had designed the swing-arm and it was a pleasingly sculptural aluminium unit that tapered toward the pivot in the horizontal plane and toward the axle in the vertical plane.[55] Fractures apparently occurred in the unit early on in the bike's career but they soon stopped, the result perhaps of the swing-arm 'working through' its built-in stresses.[56] Brembo pumps and three drilled iron rotors, the latter made up by Broz, with a pair of lightweight magnesium Lockheed single-piston callipers up front and a Fontana calliper at the rear, supplied the stopping power. The rear brake was only ever good enough to pass muster with the scrutineers, but as Broz 'never used it anyway' it was of little matter.

Broz very deliberately retained the 900 Darmah engine that powered it in a mild state of tune to ensure reliability. Changes included Ducati HiCom race pistons (one size over) on standard rods and crank. Imola cams activated 2-mm oversize inlet and exhaust valves in a gas-flowed head.

From the beginning Broz intended the machine to be a reliable workhorse and he therefore elected not to go down the 'alcohol' route. He opted for a pair of

Lectron flat side carburettors, the front one modified to run as a down-draft unit, bored to 40.5 mm to deliver 100-octane petrol. The engine produced about 20 hp over the standard item, with about 80 bhp *in toto,* and would spin up to about 9000 rpm.

The completed machine cost Broz about $12,000 to build, somewhat more than he had budgeted on, but it proved even more reliable than he had hoped for. Its only real failings were rods and crankpins, which Broz had to replace every year, and the first gear in the stock Darmah gearbox. (A Ducati modified three-dog item cured the problem.) Finally, a Ducati lightweight dry-clutch conversion replaced the standard item, a modification that gave, according to Broz, absolutely magic performance and totally reliable service. All in all, Aero D Zero was a highly creditable effort and Broz campaigned it more or less continually for the next five years, achieving some quite outstanding results along the way.[57]

The next Aero would be an entirely John Britten production. It would also be a lot more ambitious.

Although John was happy with the general shape he had devised, he wanted to ditch the frame altogether and run with only the bodywork acting as a monocoque structure. He also wanted a lot more power. For a while he toyed with the idea, hotting up a Ducati motor by making a 4-valve head, but when that looked to be beyond his immediate means he considered adapting the heads off a local speedway motor being built by a Christchurch company called Denco Engineering. With this in mind, a Ducati engine was dropped into the company, but the idea was rejected as being overly complicated and went no further. However, during his visit he was impressed by his first good look at the Denco speedway V-twin engine and by his meeting with the irrepressible gentleman who made them. It was the first step down what would prove a long and winding road.

Denco Engineering specialised in work on high-performance engines but their activities went far beyond those of most speed and engineering shops. Bob Denson, the founder of the company, actually produced a range of his own engines for speedway competition. These ranged from single-cylinder engines to a V8, all of which were methanol-burning and most of which were air-cooled.

Bob Denson's involvement in motorsport extended back into the days of his early youth in Christchurch, when he first watched powerboats racing off the local beach at Brighton. By the time he reached his teenage years he had managed to scrounge and install a worn Ford Ten engine in an old dinghy he called *Rastus*. He would lurk about during race days and then lunge into the fray for a few laps, crouched over the hot engine, breathing exhaust fumes while he operated the throttle on the carburettor with one hand and steered with the other. He would tear off before the wrath of race officials could be brought to bear, and in this manner he became a participant, if not a competitor. It was not long, however, before his enthusiasm earned him a more recognised place in the company of his fellow racers, and so at an early age he was rubbing shoulders with some of the most gifted and, in many ways outrageous, race engineers of the early post World War II period.[58]

During those years the fastest race boats competing in New Zealand were monster hydroplanes equipped with these 1500-odd horsepower engines. Young Bob was already hooked on horsepower and once in this somewhat megalomaniacal company his enthusiasm was fuelled further. The pursuit of raw horsepower became his vocation. He also possessed the natural aptitude needed to excel in his chosen field, and after serving a toolmaking apprenticeship with a local company he was made toolroom foreman at the age of just twenty-one. He rose through the company and was finally made manager, with eighteen engineers and ninety other staff under his control. Bob then accepted a job as the development engineer and manager of a company making light engineering products before setting up his own company in 1974. His new shop specialised in race engineering, and such was his fast growing reputation for fine work that he was soon one of a handful of customers entrusted with piston blanks by the American manufacturers Arias and Ross.

Bob Denson had not neglected the hands-on side of speed addiction through the years and had raced a number of hugely powerful hydroplanes to great effect. At the age of thirty-eight, however, he left the water and took up speedway racing, where he soon made a name for himself. His car was powered by a methanol-burning, air-cooled, 4-cylinder engine featuring sixteen valves that he built himself. A string of top placings followed, including a win in the New Zealand Midget Grand Prix, a third in the New Zealand Championships and a win in the 1988 South Island Midget Car Championships. Other engine-building projects included four alloy water-cooled V-8 engines, a second 4-cylinder, seven V-twins, one vertical twin and about eighteen single-cylinder engines. The V-twins were 60-degree units, designed with the narrow V because this could be made to fit between the frame rails of the popular 3/4 (TQ) Midget speedway racers. He also built a pair of flat four-boxer engines and completely rebuilt a 1951 Ferrari Formula One V-12.

Bob's engine designs, and indeed the castings from which he machined the finished products, were the work of an engineer and former professional motorcycle racer called Colin Lyster, an expatriate Rhodesian who had fetched up in the South Island of New Zealand some thirty years before.[59]

Colin Lyster and John Britten were never destined to meet, a circumstance that can in hindsight be seen as regrettable. Had they met when John was first considering purchasing the Denco V-twin, for example, Lyster would have certainly advised him against it. He would have told John that a speedway engine was designed to produce buckets of low-down torque for a minute and a half before being put away in a paddock—neither of which boded well for a road-racing motorcycle. And he might have thereby saved John and his friends a huge amount of frustration, heartache and pain.

Colin Lyster came from a farming family that had owned properties in northern and southern Rhodesia and in Nyasaland. He had graduated as an engineer from Johannesburg University in neighbouring South Africa while racing motorcycles whenever he could. Unfortunately, his hobby was somewhat rudely interrupted by the Rhodesian Army conscripting him on a number of occasions and sending him off to the Congo to help suppress the Mau Mau insurrection. In 1960 Colin decided to go to Europe where he could race motorcycles in peace.

> Being in the reserve meant that I could be called up time after time and my father thought it best if I took off and did something else. I thought I was probably good enough to earn a living racing motorcycles after enjoying some success at home and so I went off to Europe. I knew that a good Norton Manx would always beat a good Matchless G50 or an AJS 7R, unless it had Mike Hailwood on board, so I mostly raced Norton 350s and 500s along with a works Benelli 250. The Grand Prix races were dominated by the factory teams who cleaned up the trophies, and as there was bugger-all start money I concentrated on the smaller events. As a friend used to say at the time, 'You can't eat trophies.'
>
> I went to the Isle of Man for the TT as a member of the Rhodesian Team but realised after ten laps that I was just wearing out a good motorcycle trying to learn 37 miles of corners. I was with Jim Redman and I remember saying to him, 'This is where you guys get killed.' I did go back again with the RAC, but I never raced there and I'm glad I didn't. However, I raced every other circuit in Europe, doing all my own maintenance and a stream of modifications to my machinery. Slowly I won a reputation as a design engineer who understood pattern making and casting, and who could take a project from a pencil idea to a finished product. In time I became one of the 'Freelance Boys', a select group who were hired by the industry to complete specific projects. Most manufacturers find that it is a lot more cost- and time-effective to go outside their organisations to achieve something completely new, and in the case of the British motorcycle industry this was especially true. And so I found a reasonable demand for my services.[60]
>
> In the UK I had met and married a New Zealand girl, then Gillian Francis, who was quite a famous ballerina, and when the American work was finished in 1972 we decided to move to Christchurch, her home town. Two years later we moved to Nelson and I set up my own foundry and workshops and got back to business.

Colin built up a G50 for a racer called Neville Landrebe, and when Landrebe was sadly killed on a Yamaha, the G50, now known as the Lyster Matchless, ended up in racer Dale Wylie's hands. Colin also built complete wooden models for the G50, the 7R and the Manx engine. Subsequently, a number of complete engines were built up from his castings and in 1973 he designed and cast a single-cylinder speedway engine.

Apart from the speedway motors Colin's projects included the construction of two Chevette cars for the World Rally Championships, building a 32-valve, twin-overhead cam, aluminium version of the Chevrolet 350 engine for an Australian hydroplane and a slant-four version of the same motor.[61] However, by this time Colin Lyster had formed a kind of partnership with a certain nuggety speed demon in Christchurch. The somewhat acerbic engineer and the equally blunt machinist made an incendiary combination, and there would be sparks aplenty, but they rubbed along and for some time a string of Colin Lyster's engines would be known only by the name Denco.

Also present at the Denco workshop the day John Britten first walked in, in 1988, was Bob's assistant, a solidly built and neatly bearded young man by the name of Rob Selby, a toolmaker who, like Bob, was also a self-taught engineer. He had been working for Denco since 1979 and was also an enthusiastic motocross rider who consistently finished among the top five in South Island Championship races. Rob had come across Bob Denson when racing three speedway seasons on a 2-valve Jawa. At the time Bob was campaigning one of his own engines with another rider on board, and because he fixed crashed race machinery and made his own interesting gear Rob found himself spending quite a bit of time in Bob's shop. Eventually this led to an offer of employment that Rob accepted with alacrity, and twelve happy years followed. Rob found Bob a mine of information and great fun to be around.

Rob brought to the shop the deliberate and fastidious approach that is typical of toolmakers, but was soon undergoing severe behavioural modification at the hands of the ever-bustling Bob, who urged him to get rid of unwanted metal the fastest way possible. With his blue marker in hand, Bob drilled, gauged, hacked and cut great lumps away until the work was roughed out and ready for final minimal machining. Walking past Rob's lathe, he would crank up the speed and feed, urging Rob on with contagious enthusiasm.

Looking back on the years he spent at Denco, Rob recalled Bob as a clever, flexible engineer who could be something of an iconoclast. Bob's response to those who returned with bent and broken bits of his manufacture was generally to demand if it had looked like that when it left the shop. When he received the answer he was looking for, namely that the part had not looked like that when it left, he would shrug and walk away. At the same time, Bob maintained a remarkably even and cheerful temperament. On one occasion Rob remembered him accidentally whipping the final lobe off a camshaft he had been painstakingly finishing. Pausing only to exclaim 'Uh oh!', he fired the offending item into the scrap with one hand while calmly reaching for the phone with the other to order a replacement.

Once he was working for Denco, Rob began to consider the possibilities of racing a Denco single in a Rickman-type motocross machine. At the time there was an annual beach-racing meeting at Nelson, and with help from Colin Lyster, with whom Rob stayed while in Nelson, a 530cc, single-cylinder Denco engine was hooked up to a Norton gearbox, a comparatively simple matter with the old-fashioned chain-driven, separate-case gearbox. After shoehorning the assembly into a Suzuki RM250 frame, Rob then sallied forth and cleaned up all the prize money. The results were an embarrassment for the dealers who used the event to promote their wares by showcasing state-of-the-art production machinery. They were doubly annoyed when Rob did exactly the same thing the following year. At that point Rob and Colin decided that the bike really deserved a 'proper' bolted-up gearbox, and the decision was made to fit a Yamaha 650 unit. Initially, Rob attempted the work, but after experiencing some difficulties Colin was roped in and the gearbox was sent back up to Nelson. At that point Colin, Bob and Rob were all rather excited by the prospects for the Lyster-Denco singles. The beach racer had been quite spectacularly promising and there seemed every reason to suppose that the engines might make a solid contribution to New Zealand motorsport history. Nor was Rob the only rider to find merit in the engines.

It was not uncommon for American speedway riders and drivers to travel to New Zealand to compete, and Bob Denson enjoyed nothing more than having them try out his engines in speedway machines. A number of world champions, including Bobby Swartz and Bruce Penhall, took him up on the offer and both said complimentary things. Bruce Penhall was asked his opinion after riding a Denco single at a speedway meeting in Christchurch. He told the delighted crowd that the 'thing damn near tore my arms off'. Ivan Mauger, the world champion New Zealander, was also sufficiently impressed to ask Bob to build a number of engines, a deal that unfortunately would have required more engines than the small Denco team could cope with.

Rob's success on the beach encouraged him to think about taking his bike to the track, and he made up various sprockets to alter the final gearing. He had raced a TZ350 on one occasion at Ruapuna—where his motocross background was starkly revealed by his habit of taking the hairpin with the tail out and his foot down—and had enjoyed the experience. It was therefore timely when he encountered the ever-encouraging Lindsay Williamson, who urged him to try the special in BEARS racing. Lindsay brushed aside Rob's queries regarding the admissibility of a machine with a Japanese frame, and he found himself racing at Levels, where he experienced some difficulty finding the race line. He very nearly lost the plot altogether through the esses and found himself continually falling off the track, although fortunately not off the bike. Struggling badly, he wound up behind Joe Hannah, racing his sprung-hub Triumph, and was happy to discover he could at least stay with him. After slipstreaming Joe for a few laps the race line was revealed and he suddenly felt confident enough to try to take the Triumph down the main straight.

At this point, however, Rob was startled by the antics of another Triumph rider who exhibited what seemed an absolutely outrageous riding style. This rider hung so far off his flexing, rigid, rear-end motorcycle that his backside was nearly scraping the track—a view Rob registered in the few moments it took for the Triumph to blast past him and disappear into the distance. But such antics were only of passing interest to Rob, for there was work to be done. Coming onto the straight, he screwed on the power early and in typical Denco fashion bolted past Joe, only to encounter a huge pool of oil on the track right in his path. (Later, Joe registered a protest that Rob had gone past under the yellow flag being flown to warn riders of the oil patch.) The bike had by now hit the Denco rev wall and was no longer accelerating with the same electric urgency, but it still went slithering and squirming down the track after splashing through the black puddle. As Rob regained control he saw the formerly flying Triumph and rider now supine beside the track.

Walking around the pits later, Rob made a point of eyeballing the slender rider in the worn black leathers who had almost caused him to come to grief by dropping a sumpful of oil on the track. It was his first sight of John Britten.[62] It was hardly an auspicious moment, not even a meeting, but Rob would finally spend more time working on the Britten motorcycle project than anyone else—including John.

Allan Wylie was also racing that day and he recalled having some trouble getting past the Denco, which he noted was very fast coming out of the turns. But as it did not seem to make the same power as the revs rose, he found he could dispatch it relatively easily on the faster parts of the circuit. 'I didn't know then,' he added somewhat ruefully, 'that that was just the way Dencos go.'

The next time Rob saw John was when the latter wandered into Denco engineering with his bevel-drive Ducati block and started asking questions about the possibilities of grafting on a couple of Denco 4-valve heads. Both Rob and Bob spent some time considering the proposition with John but reluctantly concluded that it might prove too difficult to undertake with any real confidence. There was something about John's ability to grasp quickly the sense of the advice he was getting, and the way he used his obviously keen mind to drive the discussion toward a conclusion, that drew Rob in.

As Bob bustled off to resume his work, Rob found himself talking to John at the door. They talked for about ten minutes and Rob began to appreciate John's determination to build something new and innovative. When John finally went off, Rob was left pondering about the possibilities arising from the meeting. And about the strange but compelling nature of John Britten.

During the following week Bob and Rob continued to discuss the Ducati during smoko but were forced to conclude that they could see no clever way to achieve John's request. They shuddered at the prospect of the complex of welds that would be needed and anticipated an ongoing nightmare in achieving a satisfactory engineering set-up. And so nothing further happened until John dropped by to pick up his parts and became, once again, engrossed in conversation with Rob.

When Rob suggested John consider buying a Denco V-twin he was instantly aware of a rapidly quickening interest. A locally built monster of a speedway motor in a road bike had a certain obvious allure for John. It had been done before with engines like the English Weslake and it fitted a certain Kiwi hot-rod tradition. It would also make his machine truly unique. Yes, the idea had merit, if the motor could be made to fit the bill.

Why Rob thought it could is puzzling. He had enjoyed some success on his own single-cylinder machine, it was true, but this had been only in very particular circumstances—namely, racing on a beach. At its best the engine was never more than a low-down slugger, and the V-twin was simply that times two. It is hard not to conclude that, in his enthusiasm, Rob must have somewhat oversold the capabilities of the V-twins while at the same time minimising some of the problems. In any event, John then went into a huddle with Bob to talk money and ended up commissioning two engines. It is hard to imagine that he really knew what he was buying into, but as Bob was fond of saying, 'Racing is a hard game.'

In fact, the history of the Denco V-twin to date had been a story of mixed success. The first Denco V-twin speedway engine had been built by Bob in 1976 when two Denco singles were combined on a single crankcase to produce a 62-degree, 750cc V-twin for a TQ Midget. Bob raced the Midget to good effect, achieving a number of podium finishes and a 1000cc version for speedway sidecars soon followed. As we know, the range of engines produced at Denco would include 4- and 6-cylinder engines, and ultimately V8s.

Bob's first V-twin for sidecar racing had been supplied in 1982 to 'Big' John Warward, a Christchurch speedway rider, who built an outfit for it and then sold it to a Rick Saunders in Nelson. In 1985 Baz Fox of the Muthus Motorcycle Club in Palmerston North heard that the outfit was for sale. The three-wheeler had gained a reputation as a brutal but effective unit and Baz was intrigued. At the time he was defending a number of titles on his Weslake-powered outfit and was looking for a back-up machine.

> I went down to Nelson and tried the thing at a local meeting. Rick suggested I use his swinger, a bloke called Chop. He turned out to be the wildest man I've ever raced with. He made me wear this big, leather belt and as we powered into the corners he'd launch himself forward by hauling on it, which damn near pulled me off the back. I had to hang on like crazy anyway because the thing was so bloody fast it was scary. It just wanted to wheel-stand every time you gave it a handful and run into the wall, which was why Chop was so eager to chuck himself over the front wheel. I ended up breaking the lap record and then went home to think about it. I remember asking myself if I really wanted the thing, it was that frightening.
>
> Anyway I bought it and ran it as a second bike through the 1985–86 season when we won all the Provincial titles, the North versus South Island title and the New Zealand Grand Prix. The only thing we missed was the New Zealand and the North Island Championships. I won 103 races in a row so I didn't want to run the Denco unless I was pretty certain of a win.
>
> Our biggest problem with the engine was the total lack of support we had from Denco. The main reason I bought the thing in the first place was because it took a month to get parts for the pom-bombs I was riding and I thought a local job would be better. But it was worse. And when we got the bits they were unbelievably expensive. I sold [my machine] to Geoff Angel in Rotorua and he had a really bad crash on it and ended up with the handlebars through his chest. That peeled him back badly and he only just survived. The crash finished his racing. The Denco finally wound up in Napier with a father and son outfit, who built a new frame for it and they have been doing really well on it. The damn thing won't lie down and die.

Apart from reliability problems, the reluctance of the engines to make power at higher revs was a common cause of concern among those who ran Denco engines in speedway. This was only partly explained by Colin's design objective to produce an engine with loads of low-down torque. While achieving this it was obviously desirable that the engine should continue to make power at higher revs. The fact that it did not was, to a degree, symptomatic of both a lack of development and compromised design. Those who did attempt to race engines produced by the Denco-Lyster collaboration found that the development needed for reliable racing became their responsibility, a situation that was far from satisfactory given the somewhat limited resources available to most speedway teams. This was exacerbated by difficulties in obtaining spare parts and most found it easier to go back to the tried and true from established manufacturers.

Some of the difficulties at least were appreciated at the time by Colin Lyster, who watched as one opportunity after another slipped away.

> Allan Palmer used our 2.1-litre 4-valve at a speedway meeting in Christchurch and won straight out of the box in a new car, but there were a lot of complaints about the 4-valve set-up from other drivers and finally race officials banned it. So we built a 2.3-litre, 2-valve version and that cleaned up as well. Sleepy Tripp, the American speedway champion, was so impressed he wanted Bob to go to the US with him and build them there.
>
> Bob was the finest machinist I have ever known, but he was not an engineer and that led to problems. If something broke he'd just remake it heavier and then the problem, whatever it was, would impact elsewhere and something else would break. And he'd make that heavier. And so it went. He would not come back to me for an engineer's analysis and solution. I'd send him replacement castings and add one or two spares. I'd tell him to make them up for the boys, for when they needed them, and to maintain a certain stock level of vital bits. But he never would and every time they needed a replacement they had to wait for him to get around to machining it up.[63]

The track record for the Lyster-Denco collaboration, then, was on the whole interesting and ambitious, but flawed. Undoubtedly there were some good ideas, but they were sometimes poorly executed, usually insufficiently developed and inevitably inadequately supported. Regrettably, the history of the collaboration had been, up until the time John Britten walked into the shop, largely a record of thwarted promise and underachievement. It was not about to change.

Bob later said that when John ordered the two engines, he (Bob) formed the impression that John eventually wanted to build a limited production run of twenty road bikes and that the two air-cooled 1000cc V-twin engines were but the beginning. John had arranged for a series of studio shots of the first Aero D One (now Aero D Zero) to be taken shortly after the unveiling at Matai Street, and he now used one of the images to make up a poster with a French legend describing the machine as a new road bike. Kirsteen was still modelling from time to time and John now accompanied her on various shoots around the world. They were about to depart for France, where she had her next assignment, and he had decided to hawk his poster around at the Cologne Motorcycle Show to see if he could scratch up any interest. How successful he was in this is not known, but in any event by the time he arrived home he had resolved that the place to kick off the project was on the racetrack. His determination to get on with it was in no small way influenced by news from Broz that his own Aero was now up and running. In a return letter to Broz, scrawled on the back of a photograph detailing the rear brake and foot-peg on a race bike prepared by Mike Sinclair, John wrote:

> Thanks for your letter, I can't believe it's going. Fantastic! I've just been to the motorcycle and pushbike show in Cologne. No kidding, you could put all the shops in Christchurch together and they wouldn't be as big as this show. I walked for three days in the rain and just managed to get around, only stopping to look at all the important stands. I'm looking forward to building one for myself and riding it. (Can't wait!). I collected all the information for the parts for a production model. Regards John.

Unfortunately, when John turned up at Denco Engineering to pick up his finished engines some six weeks later he was incensed to discover that they had not even been started.

His plans had always included competing in the 1987 Sound of Thunder, at this stage only six scant weeks away, and he now urgently reviewed the situation with Bob, who reluctantly agreed to work to the deadline. It was at this moment that the ticklish question of a suitable gearbox came up. Presumably John had expected the matter to be addressed while he was away, but again nothing had been done. It was not a good start.

In the absence of anything better, Rob volunteered the Yamaha 650 box that Colin had prepared for his beach racer. He explained to John that all the extraneous holes had been filled and all that would be needed was an adapter plate and perhaps some primary gears. He stressed it was an ad hoc solution suitable only to get the machine up and running so that further development could take place. (His reservations quickly proved well founded. Not least of the problems associated with the gearbox was the fact that it had imperial fastenings while those on the engine were metric.) In spite of such concerns, however, both Rob and Bob also expressed confidence that they could produce a hairy-chested thumper that would make people sit up and take notice. And so, under pressure from the beginning to make an almost impossible deadline, they started.

Although married, Rob had not yet become a father and he was able to put additional hours into the project in the evenings, hours that soon began to bite deeply into the night and that would never be paid for. Somehow it did not matter. The project was the thing. Not John's project but simply the project, an all-consuming entity that in some way belonged to them all. As the pressure grew with the rapidly approaching deadline, the many misgivings Rob had about the long-term effectiveness of some of the engineering solutions they cobbled together were simply subsumed in the urgency of the moment. The piper would just have to wait for payment.

Allan Wylie also became involved with the new project. Like many of John's old friends, Allan had seen little of him since his marriage and it was good to reconnect.

> John had been in Europe for a while, and when I ran into him and he told me about the bike he was building at Denco Engineering, I was naturally intrigued. One night I went around to see it and was pretty impressed by what I saw. However, it was obvious that John and Rob needed help in some areas, help that I could provide. From that point I was sucked in.
>
> I started turning up at Denco in the evenings and working late to get the bike ready for the Sound of Thunder, all unpaid of course. John had been doing the composite work at home and at some time the entire project moved to Auto Restorations where I was, and still am, foreman of the mechanical department. The wide range of equipment there was ideal for building prototypes, and I worked there with Rob and John throughout the rest of the Denco project, donating God knows how many hours of my time. After a while you just stopped counting.

Because the second Aero body was to be a complete monocoque, with a reinforced area at the front of the incorporated fuel tank to take the steering head, John decided to construct the twenty-six separate sections that would make up the complete body entirely of uni-directional carbon-fibre, Kevlar cloth and high-density closed-cell foam.

As he still knew next to nothing about composite structures, John followed his usual practice of contacting those who did. At the time, the Bank of New Zealand Challenge had just returned to New Zealand from Fremantle, in Western Australia, after campaigning the first fibreglass boat to challenge for the America's Cup.[64] Later, John would claim that the design team had cast their eye over his plans and pronounced them to be structurally sound, but the people who spent the most time scrutinising his intentions were the suppliers of the composite materials used in the 'Plastic Fantastics', as the boats were popularly known, a company called HiModulus. The company was then located in the small town of Warkworth, north of Auckland, and over the following years it accumulated a fat file marked 'John Britten'. Far from being enthusiastic about John's intentions for the materials they supplied him, however, the design engineers at HiModulus were more often either incredulous or horrified.

Richard Downes Honey, who was a founding member of the HiModulus company, remembered that his dealings with John were always conducted with a degree of trepidation.

> He was a metals engineer trying to work with materials that behaved in very different ways. He'd use the wrong fibres or the wrong resins and he was always fearlessly experimenting in a way that really made us shudder. He'd blithely say that he'd added a bit of this or a bit of that and we'd tell him that he couldn't possibly send someone racing off down the road relying on whatever it was. He'd send up drawings and we'd take one look at them and tell him where whatever it was he intended building would break first. Using these materials in yachts is difficult enough, but in a high-powered motorcycle it's an even more uncertain proposition. The potential consequences of failure are so much direr. We had another motorcycle constructor called Steve Roberts approach us some years before. I remember him calling up and saying he wanted some of that 'Kelva' stuff that was ten times stronger than steel.
>
> Both Steve and John ended up doing exceptionally well, but it looked pretty hit and miss from where we were standing.

In spite of such concerns, the finished body was strong and rigid with an all-up weight of 12 kg.

John had designed the machine to come apart in two pieces, with the front wheel, forks and steering head constituting the front half; the engine, swing-arm and rear wheel made up the second part. The swing-arm was pivoted on the back of the gearbox, mounting on a solid chunk of alloy. All the metal components, including the engine, had a solid, hewn quality to them. It was all hard, sharp edges with little attempt made to slim down the cases or round them off. It seems that the completed machine was never weighed but, in spite of the absence of a frame, it must still have been a fairly hefty affair.

As the motor was not suitable to be a stressed unit, it was attached at multiple points to the bodywork, with large metal 'cotton reels' bolted onto the top of each cylinder for the top mounts. The location of the engine was always a matter of concern, with mounting points proving less sturdy than was desirable. Unfortunately, there was not time to refine the installation, as this would have involved a fundamental redesign of the engine casings.

From the beginning, the deadline imposed by John on the production of the motorcycle resulted in engineering compromises that inevitably led to a myriad of long-term frustrations for the collection of individuals who formed the nucleus of what would simply become known as the Team.

By now Allan Wylie was beginning to harbour serious doubts about certain aspects of the engine. Mark 2 Amal smooth-bore carburettors flowed methanol into the system via a manifold that featured a decided S-bend, something he suspected might rob power. One of his first tasks was to redesign the sidedraft Amals so that they worked vertically as downdraft units. This modification involved turning the float bowls through 90 degrees and setting up bleeds to stop them siphoning. He was able to get them to work well enough in this configuration but they always proved difficult to set up and tune. In the long term, this problem was greatly exacerbated by the fact that the body had to come apart before the carburettors could be accessed. There were other difficulties associated with the monocoque body, one of the worst of which was a leaking fuel tank. As noted, this was integrated with the body, but compared with petrol methanol is a notoriously difficult fuel to contain due to its lower viscosity, and the tank leaked badly. (Most speedway machinery runs with a fuel bladder to avoid this problem.) John tried smearing and sloshing various compounds into the tank via the filler, to little effect. According to Allan, it was likely that the methanol was reacting unfavourably with the materials John was trying to seal it in with; certainly it seemed to eat resins and fibreglass. There was nothing for it but to build an aluminium tank and mount it beneath the bodywork.

Owing to the complex shape of the bodywork, the new tank was a strange-looking item of many facets that Allan nicknamed the Loch Ness Monster. He remembered Robin Willan, a friend who was roped in to help, hacking away at the underbelly of the integral tank with an air-chisel as the bike lay on its back. It looked, Allan said, like a man gutting an animal. Inevitably, and in spite of their best efforts, the arrangement cost valuable fuel capacity, a serious matter given the greatly increased volume of methanol used to achieve the same performance as petrol.

When it all finally came together at Auto Restorations the new machine sported White Power front suspension with upside-down 54-mm forks up front and a rear suspension consisting of a White Power monoshock, which was mounted under the engine. The final specifications included a steering-head angle of 25.5 degrees with adjustable trail.

The front brakes were twin 315-mm rotors with Lockheed four-piston callipers, while the rear was a 250-mm rotor with a two-piston calliper. The wheelbase was 1425 mm and the wheels were state-of-the-art Marvic alloy items, probably ex-Kenny Roberts by way of Mike Sinclair, survivors of the previous 500 GP race season.

Finally, exhausted and scratchy, the Team was able to stand back, stretch their aching muscles and take a bleary-eyed look at the machine they had created. With its white exhaust system and wild body it looked sharp and mean, if a little rough around the edges. It also proved a pig to start, and by chance it was Allan's turn to be pushed when late that night it first barked into life.

The Auto Restorations workshops were located near the railway lines that ran through Christchurch and at that time the vicinity was dominated by vast railway goods sheds that were all but deserted after five in the afternoon. It was not unusual for loud and exotic machinery—like the Straight 8 Grand Prix Alfa Romeo that Allan helped restore—to be tested up and down the street, so the motorcycle did not attract undue attention. He did a short run and then handed it over to John, who ran back up the road and fell off while turning around. The problem was that the wet clutch would not disengage and it was almost impossible to find neutral. In spite of the reversals of the evening, and to the amusement of Rob, to whom such things were simply part of the process, John produced champagne to toast their success. Like some latter-day Frankenstein, he shouted his delight into the night. 'It runs, it runs!'

In what was to become a familiar scenario, the Team worked with mounting desperation to ready the bike for the Sound of Thunder meeting, by this stage just two weeks away. As time leaked away it became increasingly obvious that it would not be ready. Every time the Team ran the bike fresh problems surfaced, and the little testing they managed to slot in was perfunctory at best, invariably throwing up more questions than it answered.

In spite of all the doubts, however, John would not be persuaded to delay his debut as a constructor, and as the BEARS gathered to do battle the newest V-twin in the world took its place in the pits. The spectacular-looking machine, with its huge rear tyre and wicked, muscular powerplant (revealed to all when the side fairings were removed, which proved to be quite often), caused a sensation.

The BEARS fraternity were wildly excited by the sudden appearance of a radical machine whose existence most had not even heard rumours about, and they immediately claimed it as their own. This was a BEARS bike, built by one of their own fellows. If John ever had concerns about the reception the often acerbic BEARS boys would give his creation, they were quickly assuaged. From now on anything he cared to create would be OK with them. They loved the machine and they loved John for making it.

The bike had been given a resplendent red and green paint job by Bob Brookland in time for its debut.

'John turned up with the body poking out of his Mercedes,' Bob remembered, 'and told me he had to have it the next day. He was the kind of bloke that is incredibly hard to say no to because he had such passion for every project he did. I just set to and got it done and it did look pretty good although, to be honest, the finish on the body itself was a bit rough!'

On race-day the brand-new machine was even more reluctant to start. Luckily, when the crew were thoroughly exhausted from pushing it up and down the pits, with the lifeless beast going 'doof, doof, doof', and were about ready to give up, Allan had an idea. He duct-taped a flipped-up race-stand to the rear axle of the bike so that his Model A truck, *Charles*, could push it. (This was the same Model

A that had been used years before in the unsuccessful attempt to launch the bird-man plane.) Charles soon showed the Denco who was boss, and the reluctant V-twin was forced to fire up. And so John took to the track and the cheering BEARS crowd had their first opportunity to look at his work in action.

Unfortunately, there was not a great deal to look at. The Denco V-twin now revealed itself shamelessly for what it was, a low-end slugger incapable of making power at higher revs. John circulated slowly toward the bottom of the field in a couple of races, frustrated and disappointed at the way his big day was turning out. Worse was to come, however, for it soon became evident that the engine was not only suffering a tuning problem that seriously sapped its power, but there was also something fundamentally wrong with its engineering.

It was Allan who noticed that the engine was blowing oil through the head joints, an obvious indicator of leaking compression, and a quick test confirmed that that was indeed the case. Eventually, the trouble was traced to crushing cylinders, something Denco engines had apparently suffered from for some time. Bob had tried to solve the problem, as he usually did, by adding more metal, in this case to the cylinders—something that gave rise to the somewhat unusual bore and stroke ratios of his engines. Allan soon realised, however, that the real solution lay in reducing the diameter of the through-bolts that sandwiched the cylinder between the head and the crankcase. This could be achieved by machining long waists into them, allowing the bolts to stretch when the engine heated instead of lagging behind, which had the inevitable consequence of either crushed cylinders or permanently stretched bolts. He remembered showing Rob the studs in a Kawasaki crankcase that happened to be lying around, and which were waisted in this manner, but Rob was reluctant to change. There was some animated discussion about it, with Allan insisting the studs should be turned down from 12 mm to include 8-mm waists. After some heated debate, they compromised with 9-mm waists and that particular problem was largely solved.

After the dismal showing there was much discussion among the BEARS fraternity about the recalcitrant Denco engine, and of the best way for John to coax some performance from it. Greg Atkinson and Lindsay Williamson suggested to John that he send the heads to the famous American tuner Jerry Branch in California. They had enjoyed dealing with the congenial American, who had assisted them in their search for further power from their Harley-Davidson race bike. John took their advice and duly dispatched the heads for Jerry to see what he could do. Branch's initial reaction was far from reassuring, as he cryptically suggested that they melt them down and start again. However, he was persuaded to flow-test them, after which he pointed out various fundamental design problems, describing the inlet manifolds in particular as horsepower-killers.

Jerry's low opinion of the engine was probably justified in terms of it being a road/race engine. However, as we have seen, it had never been designed as such and once again Colin Lyster could only fume as he heard reports of his work being dismissed by a man who really did not know what he was looking at. But it was also probably true that the same lack of development that had hampered the engine after its design had also hampered it before. Colin may have achieved his objective of prodigious low-down torque, but the engine's inability to make power through the revs could not have been desirable for any kind of race engine.

In the long report Jerry sent to John outlining his opinions, he revealed a quite astonishing generosity in sharing technical information that must have, in many instances, been hard won. Possibly he did so because he saw New Zealand as being so far way from his customers that it did not matter. More probably, however, he simply admired the spirit that drove John to attempt to build his own competitive machine. Whatever the motivation was, Jerry stated his opinions clearly and backed them up with a wealth of technical data.

After several pages of considerably less-than-favourable opinion, but with many suggestions for revision and improvement, Jerry ended on a more positive note. 'If you have any more pictures of details on the bike I would appreciate seeing them as I really admire the job you have done.'

Naturally, the dismal evaluation, and all the other trials and tribulations experienced, were by now taking a toll on the relationship between Bob Denson and John. At this point, however, Bob offered to share development costs, a decision that went some considerable way to alleviating the growing tension. Allan considered Jerry's report carefully and then summarised the findings on a sheet of graph paper under the heading 'Options to increase power'. He identified six such options, which he listed thus:

> 1. Fit bigger valves to the existing heads with stock spacing, retain the existing guides and reduce the valve stem diameter under the head.
> 2. As above but with inlet valves closer together. This would reduce shrouding by the cylinder. Would the valve springs foul inside the buckets with the existing bucket spacing?
> 3. Make a new rear head with forward-facing exhaust. This would improve the cooling of the rear cylinder and permit straighter inlet ports using side draft carbs. Would there be room for the rear carb and where would it draw its air from? Is there room for exhausts? The lower carb position would eliminate the need for a fuel pump.
> 4. Alter the bore-stroke ratio to unshroud the valves and increase the rev potential. This would require a new crank, pistons, liners and maybe rods. This arrangement could be used with existing or new heads. Engine height could be lowered slightly

giving more fuel capacity and a lower centre of gravity.
5. Make two new heads with forward-facing exhausts perhaps changing the valve angle as well as their size and spacing. Inlet ports could be raised if casting allows. Deeper fins could be added with a view to burning petrol.
6. Change the exhaust pipes to Jerry's specs.

By the end of August John had weighed up all the options and had come to his decision. He wrote to Jerry (on BEARS letterhead stationery as he was, at the time, the club's secretary and treasurer) and thanked him for his report, adding that, 'of course, it is not always pleasing to get such bad news!' He then told Jerry of his plans, explaining that designing and manufacturing completely new heads was out of the question owing to the lack of time to make patterns for castings, given that the next racing season stated in November. Basically, the changes followed Allan's suggestions numbered 3 and 4 in the above list, and involved casting new barrels with a 95-mm bore and a new crankshaft with a stroke of 70 mm, making a 1000cc motor (exactly the dimensions of a proposed new 1000cc Harley-Davidson race engine Jerry had referred to in his report). At the new bore, John wrote, the existing valve centres in the heads seemed satisfactory, with the inlets being increased to 35 mm in diameter. This, he explained, allowed just enough metal between the ports for the seats. The increase in valve size was still way short of the area Jerry anticipated for his new 750cc Harley-Davidson race engine, but it was at least moving in the right direction.

John went on to tell Jerry that he had decided against new conrods, as this would enable the Team to complete the changes quickly and get out on the track.

'We are making up another rear head,' he wrote, 'to face the other way and converting back to a side draft carb on it.' He explained that this move would give them the desired 11-inch (28-mm) intake length and allow the elimination of the troublesome S-bend.[65]

'We would still be using the same front head,' he wrote, 'but we would weld it up so that you can have the shape that you need. You could straighten out the 65 degrees between the port and the cylinder bore and create the little hemi-chamber around each valve as we would weld this area up too. The rear head will be a new casting so there will be enough material for you to remove.'

Jerry readily agreed to John's request and a newly cast rear cylinder head was sent in the raw, along with a welded-up front head. Dennis White was going to Los Angeles with his family on holiday, and he was able to take the heads with him and deliver them to Jerry. During the following two weeks Jerry reshaped the ports, allowing Dennis to take them back to New Zealand at the end of his holiday, and thereby saving a great deal of time.

Britten V1000 F003—The Waterbike.

Successive Britten motorcycles were popularly known simply as Number One, Number Two etc. However, proper numbers were assigned and stamped on the crankcases where each number was preceded by a letter: F for Factory or P for Production. (Production bikes were built for customers.) In order of manufacture, the ten second-generation V1000s were:

F001 Owned by Cardinal Network and the Britten estate (Actually a V1100.) – NZ
F002 Owned by Kevin Grant ('The Waterbike') – NZ
F003 Owned by Te Papa Tongarewa Museum of New Zealand – NZ
P001 Owned by Roberto Crepaldi (Café Racers and Superbikes) – Italy
P002 Owned by Jim Hunter – USA
P003 Owned by Dr Mark Stewart – USA
P004 Owned by Barber Dairies – USA
P005 Owned by Mike Canepa (Ten K Racing) – USA
P006 Owned by Gary Turner – Holland
P007 Owned by an American collector. At last report still in its crate.

(Photo: Fraser Harding courtesty of Gardyne design and Spicers Paper)

Top: John Britten with his Triumph Tiger 100 soon after he had made an aluminium fuel tank, oil tank and tail piece. Note the lack of rear suspension. (Photo: courtesy Mike Brosnan)

Right: On the BMW raced at the Manfeild Six-Hour, Lindsay Williamson, John, Dale Wylie, Mike Sinclair. (Photo: courtesy Lindsay Williamson)

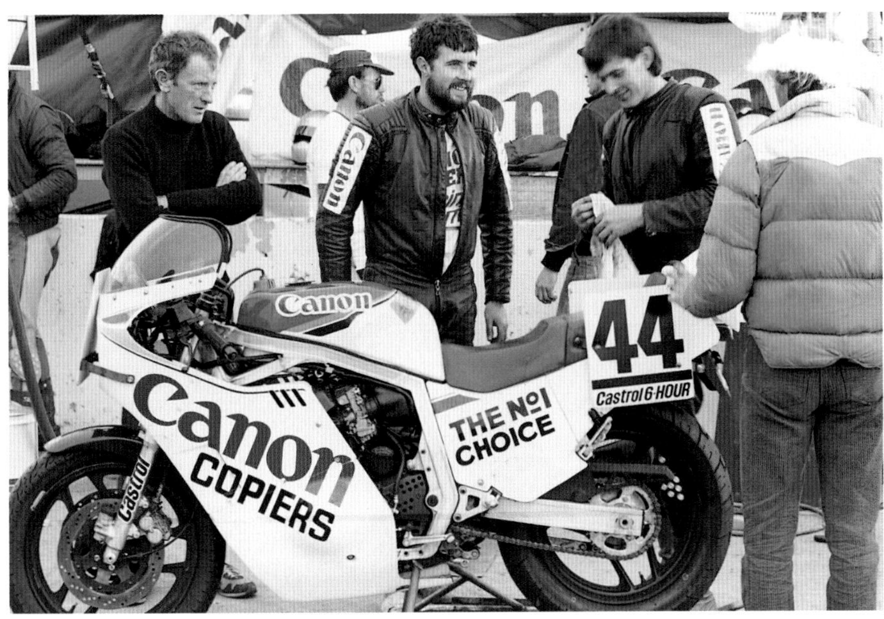

Top: John, Triumph, Sound of Thunder, Christchurch, 21 February 1988. (Photo: Steve Green). *Bottom:* Lindsay Williamson and John with the Suzuki GSX750 raced in Australia and at Manfeild, 1985. (Photo: courtesy Lindsay Williamson)

Top: Aero D Zero—largely mocked up for the camera. (Photo: courtesy Mike Brosnan) *Bottom:* As completed by Mike Brosnan with Ducati running gear. Sound of Thunder, Christchurch, 21 February 1988. (Photo: Steve Green)

Top: Britten Denco. (Photo: Alan Cathcart)
Middle: Britten Denco. (Photo: Alan Cathcart)
Bottom: Gary Goodfellow testing on the Britten Denco at Ruapuna. (Photo: Steve Green)

Top: Chris Haldane on the first Britten, practicing for the Sound of Thunder, 22 January 1989. Note white marks where fairing has grounded. (Photo: Steve Green) *Bottom:* Chris Haldane at Levels, Timaru, 1990. (Photo: Euan Cameron)

Top: Sound of Thunder, Christchurch, 1990. (Photo: Steve Green) *Bottom:* Assen, 1990. (Photo: Alan Cathcart)

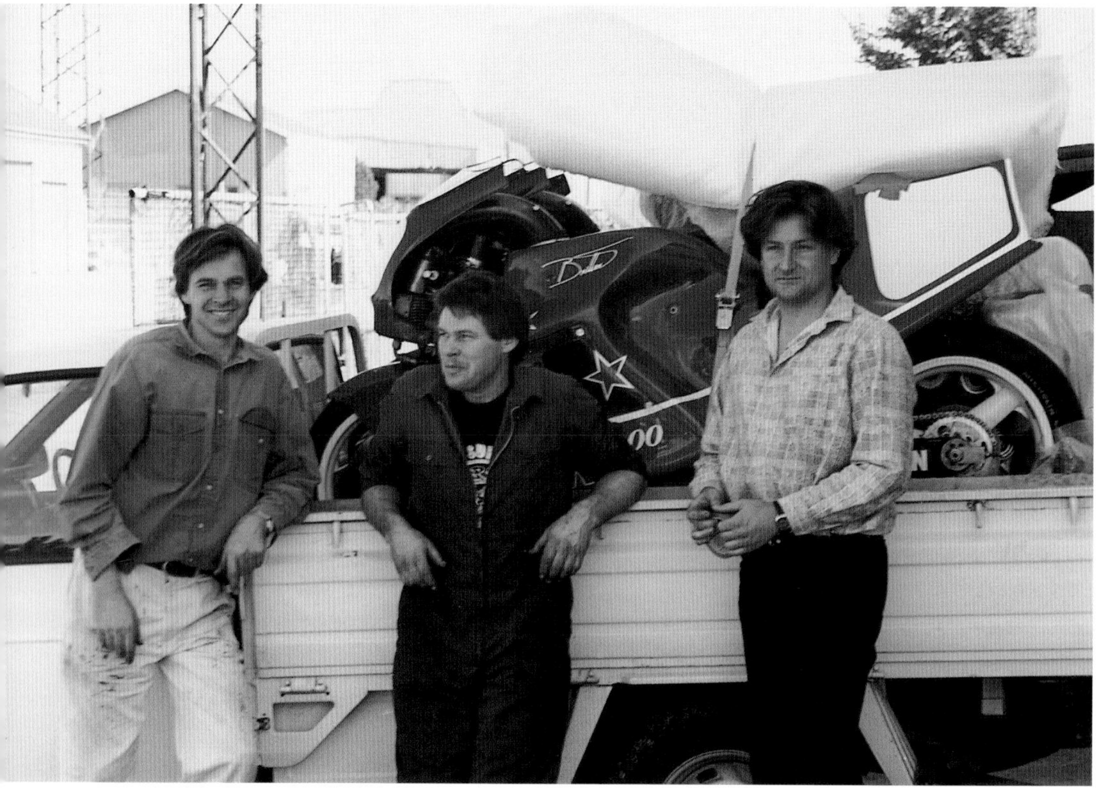

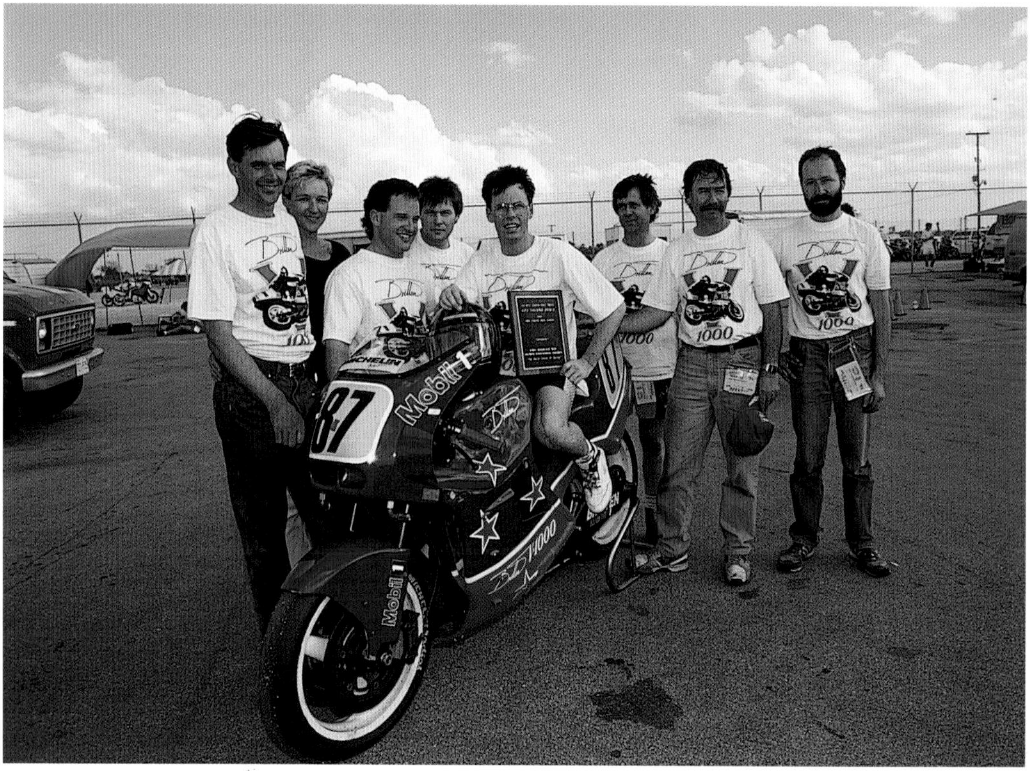
MICHELIN
87
Mobil
1000
Mobil

Left top: John Britten, Mike Brosnan and Murray Aitken ready to ship two Britten V1000s for the second atempt at Daytona. (Photo: courtesy Mike Brosnan) *Left bottom:* At Daytona, 1991. Left to right: John Britten, Dorenda Britten, Steve Crevier, Mike Brosnan, Paul Lewis (on bike), Colin Dodge, George Morrin and Mark Franklin. (Photo: Alan Cathcart) *Top:* Paul Lewis, second to Doug Polen at Daytona, Battle of the Twins, 1991. (Photo: Alan Cathcart)

Top: John and Mike Brosnan, testing at the Zolder circuit, Belgium, 1992 (Photo: Alan Cathcart)
Bottom: Allan Catchcart riding the Britten, Zolder test, 1992 (Photo: Alan Cathcart)

Top: Andrew Stroud, Sound of Thunder, 16 February 1992. A first Britten Motorcycles outing for 'The Maestro'. (Photo: Euan Cameron) *Bottom:* Chris Haldane, Sound of Thunder 16 February 1992. His last Britten ride for a decade. (Photo: Euan Cameron)

Top: Jason McEwen with Mike Brosnan and John, Manfeild Super Bikes 26 October 1992 (Photo: courtesy Mike Brosnan) *Bottom:* Manfeild Super Bikes, 26 October 1992. Jason McEwen gets the jump on Robert Holden, who is riding a very special eight-valve Ducati. (Photo: Euan Cameron)

Daytona, 1992. (Photo: Alan Cathcart)

Top: Jon White at the Britten workshop with the Streamliner.
(Photo: courtesy Jon White)

Right: August 1994. Jon White is shoehorned into the Streamliner on the salt, Salt Lake City, Utah.
(Photo: Dennis White)

Top: Streamliner frame at the Britten workshop with a dummy engine in place. (Photo: Steve Green)
Middle and bottom: Streamliner at South Eyre Road for the first land-speed record attempt, 27 November 1993. (Photo: Steve Green)

Top: John Britten wheeling the 'dustbin' out in pursuit of the land-speed record. South Eyre Road, Canterbury, 4 December 1993. (Photo: Steve Green) *Bottom:* Loren Poole launches the land-speed record run. South Eyre Road, Canterbury, 4 December 1993. (Photo: Steve Green)

Jerry had ported them as best he could, and flow figures were considerably improved, but it was now obvious to both John and Allan that they were a long way short of a clean sheet of paper possibilities.

Of course, all they had really done was to arrive at the point where Colin Lyster had been all along, and Colin's final thoughts on these developments revealed a growing sense of anger and frustration.

> When we raced the V-twin in speedway we didn't even machine the head castings. They were just bolted on as they came from the foundry and for what we wanted that was perfectly acceptable. To send those heads all the way to America to polish the ports was just fucking ridiculous. There were any number of people who could have done that right here. All my life I had developed my ideas on the basis of what I already knew. Here we had a situation where all these people were running around without a bloody clue in the world, throwing money at a problem that was only created in the first place because they had failed to think it through.

For John and the Team, however, it was a case of being in too deep to do anything except swim with the current. Happily, they were now working with one of the best independent designers in the world and he was clearly willing to encourage them with a free flow of invaluable information. However, now that they were beginning to understand the limits of what they already had they were also experiencing the frustrations of not being able to utilise fully what they now knew.

In spite of all the difficulties the bike slowly improved and started to become more reliable. When operated in its longer stroke form, the engine had run out of power well before it reached its rev limit, which was somewhere between 6000 and 8000 rpm.[66] However, the huge relative decrease in stroke cut piston speeds and resulted in an engine that would pull more revs and made more power higher up the range, even if its nature remained that of a slugger rather than a screamer.

Unfortunately, as is often the case, when you change one thing it impacts on another in a way that you cannot always anticipate. The modifications caused the old cylinder-crushing problem to resurface, because the bigger bore removed aluminium from around the sleeve. Over time, the cylinder would concertina and the flange on the sleeve would start to crack. To make matters worse, the cylinder shrinkage would eventually cause the piston to hit the head. Allan's lighter bolts still went a long way to solving the problem but it remained worrying to the team nonetheless. Naturally, the problems just added further allure, if any was needed, to the attraction of designing something from scratch that incorporated everything they were now learning.

Results were sufficiently encouraging, however, for John to take the bike to the

1987 BEARS Speed Trial on the straight rural road where the club had installed timing equipment. His chief opposition was none other than Broz on Aero D Zero. Although Broz's bike was not, in its individual parts, anything particularly ferocious, it was a reliable and competent machine that made the most of its superior aerodynamics, and Broz was able to give John a serious run for his money. The first encounter between the two was no easy victory for the Denco-powered special when severe fuel-starvation problems had to be overcome. John only made the winning flying-quarter-mile pass with a speed of 148.21 mph after Allan set up a tube into the tank that John could blow through with just sufficient force to pressurise it. This ensured adequate fuel flow, but he was lucky to keep the thing on the straight and narrow, as the effect of hyperventilating on alcohol was almost enough to knock him out altogether. He also found that the bike was faster in fourth gear than it was in top and that Broz's 'old banger Ducati'-powered Aero was only a whisker slower.

The fact that Broz's bike was as competitive as it was did have one positive aspect for John. As Phil Payne, the winner of the event the previous year, pointed out to him on the day, it meant at least that the fairing design John had come up with was 'spot on'. [67]

However, no matter how you looked at it Aero D One's narrow victory was disappointing, especially after all the work that had been done to get the motor to make greater power at higher revs. With nothing to lose John called Colin Lyster in Nelson to see if he had any ideas.

Colin recalled the phone call, possibly because it was one of the few chances he had to register his strong disapproval for the way the project had been managed.

> The engine had never been designed to do what John wanted and all I had been able to do was watch the lunacy. If they had worked with me in the first place we could have designed an engine with a clean sheet of paper that was suitable, but they didn't. John had called me previously, but it was a complete waste of time because everything they were trying to do was fundamentally flawed. The last time he called me he told me that the bike had managed 147 mph in fourth gear on South Eyre Road and only 146 mph in top. He asked me what I thought the problem was and I told him it was obviously running out of power. He asked me to go down and look at it but I really couldn't see the point. I told him he could bring it up to me but he didn't bother.

The episode marked the last time the two ever spoke, leaving Colin Lyster with brief memories of a man who he never met but later described as 'an arrogant little shit', and John Britten with a mission. One way or another John would produce a road-racing engine that was up to the job.

Shortly after the speed trials, Aero D One was taken to Ruapuna to be filmed for a local television programme featuring homegrown success stories. For reasons that were for some time a mystery, the bike ran a big-end bearing. Once repaired, John and Allan took the bike to Manfeild, where John intended to ride it in the opening rounds of the Brut 33 Series. However, he managed only a few laps in practice before it again ran a big-end bearing.

Allan puzzled over the successive bearing failures while they plied back to the South Island on the ferry. It occurred to him that the gearbox Rob had loaned to the project had been intended for a single-cylinder engine and that the oil pump, which was part of the gearbox, might not be up to the job of oiling twice the number of bearings. Although when asked about it neither Rob nor Bob would concede that the oil pump might have insufficient capacity, and that this might be the reason for the bearing failures, at John and Allan's insistence they replaced it with a higher volume unit. At the same time, the oil feed to the crank was changed to an axial rather than a radial flow by feeding oil in through the end of the shaft. The oil filter was moved from the oil tank (which was mounted in front of the motor) to the side of the crankcase, while the oil tank itself was replaced with a modified design. These changes seemed to obviate the problem as there were no further bearing failures.

All the improvements were finally beginning to pay off and the Team found they now possessed a machine that had more power than anyone involved in the project could readily trial. It was time to find a professional test rider, and after casting about John invited Gary Goodfellow to do the job.

Gary, or Goody as he was often called, hailed originally from Dunedin and had already established a formidable Superbike racing reputation in America and Canada. As a boy he had ridden a Kawasaki 90 road bike 18 km to school along loose dirt and gravel roads. The route ran parallel to the highway and he often raced the cars on it, 'falling off on average about four times a week'. He put knobbly tyres on the bike and did a little motocrossing on it before purchasing his first serious off-roader, a Bultaco Pursang. 'Many bikes and many races later' he took out the 1979 New Zealand 250 Motocross Championship on a Honda. He went on to become South Pacific Champion three years running and was twice runner-up in the Mr Motocross series in Australia. When he was barely out of his teens he competed internationally, with many commendable finishes in the European 125 Motocross Championship, before chucking it all in to sell Suzukis in Canada. He frankly admitted that he had found it too demanding to cope with the strains and stresses of living out of a suitcase and surviving at the budget-end of life, while at the same time struggling to maintain the high level of fitness his sport demanded. Finally, he decided that his heart really wasn't in it.

In his first year as a salesperson, Gary made CAN$60,000 in commissions and was able to set up his own shop in partnership with his former boss. He had found his niche and the business soon became the biggest motorcycle dealership in western Canada. But the racing bug had bitten and he was still suffering its effects. During the year before he bought his own shop he found time to do a little road racing, a new experience but one he found a whole lot easier than motocross.

> I was sitting watching a race at Westwood in 1982 and getting bored shitless because the racing was so slow. There was a great crowd of about 5000 at what was just a club meeting and they cheered like crazy every time anyone did anything remotely adventurous. I remember saying, 'I can go faster than that' to myself and then I decided I might as well do it. I borrowed a silver Suzuki Katana, or Can-a-tuna as we used to call them, off the floor at the shop and cleaned everybody up. The best thing about it was that nobody knew me from a bar of soap.

After buying out his old boss in a business called Vancouver Suzuki, Gary continued to road race, partly as a way of promoting the business but mostly because he found himself enjoying the experience. He was certainly good at it.

Riding a Suzuki GSX-R750 he would on occasion beat stars such as Wayne Rainey and Kevin Schwantz. He was particularly fast at Laguna Seca, a notoriously dangerous track where, in Rainey's words, the rider is 'shifting, sliding and bumping all the time'. To make a hazardous track even more demanding, a mistake under brakes turning into either Turn Eleven or the infamous 'Corkscrew' would drive the rider straight into a concrete wall. Gary had first-hand experience of this danger when in 1983 he broke both ankles doing just that.[68] Gary came back from his accident during the following season and once again set about mastering the demanding Laguna Seca circuit, displaying along the way an impressive combination of skill and courage.

Gary was enjoying himself so much on the track that when the chance came in 1985 to sell out the dealership, having already set up a second shop, he took the opportunity to become a professional racer. 'Business was getting tougher and road racing was getting easier. I put forty grand aside and decided to blow it on a year's racing. After that I'd figure out what I wanted to do next.'

He returned to New Zealand with a Production Suzuki GSX-R750 and a Superbike version of the same machine to compete in the 1985 Brut 33 Series. The series attracted a number of international riders to the tracks at Manfeild, Pukekohe and Ruapuna, and to the street circuits at Wanganui and Hamilton. During the series, Gary 'won a lot of races and had a lot of fun'. At the same time he made a lasting impression on his countrymen with his smooth but aggressive style, and in particular his ability to promote and control spectacular power-slides few riders in the world would have gotten away with. He also met John Britten.

> I met him track-side but I have no recollection of exactly where or when that was. I just know that we became friends and then slowly became very good friends. I saw a bit of him when I returned to New Zealand to do the same series the next year, and then after I came back to race in the International Superbikes rounds at Manfeild in 1987 we really hooked up. He was there with his race bike, which broke during practice. I didn't race either as my bike blew up in practice.
>
> He invited me to stay at his home in Christchurch, where I had a good look at the race bike, which was having a lot of work done on it. The place was a real mess and I saw this old motorcycle leaning up against a wall. It was absolutely coated in shit. I asked him what it was and he told me it was his own BEARS race bike. I couldn't believe he'd want to ride something like that and want to build the thing he was building. Later, I saw him ride the Triumph and although it was clearly unsafe he was pretty fast on it. When I became involved with the Denco project I stayed at his home and helped finish the new bike. By then we were fairly tight and there was never any question of being paid or anything. I did what I did from the beginning because I wanted to help. He was my mate.

After the first Brut 33 Series Gary had returned to Canada, where he won the 1985 Canadian Superbike Championship and claimed a hard-won fifth place in the US AMA Superbike series. It was a tough year that included a number of crashes, but it was a remarkable performance for a self-funded racer competing in his first year of professional road racing.

In recognition of his achievements in 1987, Gary was chosen to represent America as part of the country's eleven-man team at the annual Shell Oil's Trans-Atlantic Match races, a keenly contested two-day event held at Brands Hatch and Donington. He finished third overall behind winner Wayne Rainey and team captain Kevin Schwantz, with Texan Doug Polen in fourth place. It was the biggest drubbing ever inflicted on the British team, and it caused the racing world to take a close look at the outstanding outsider in third place.

Gary's results were sufficient to secure him a ride later in the year for Yoshimura Suzuki in the largest and most prestigious Japanese road race, the eight-hour Endurance race held at Honda's track in Suzuka. This race was enormously popular in Japan, with 300,000 fans turning up to watch 200 top road race teams from around the world vie with one another just to qualify. Gary and his team-mate Katsuro Takayoshi almost pulled off a huge upset victory, narrowly losing to Australian champion Kevin Magee.[69] Second place was good enough, however, to confirm Gary's reputation as an up-and-coming racer, in spite of the fact that he was by then a decade older than most of his competition. He was particularly noted for the ferocity of his starts, having 'hole-shotted' a number of fields featuring galaxies of stars, blasting through the lot of them at flag-fall to take the lead. But things don't always go to plan, and in a qualifying heat for the Rothmans Superbike Challenge at Westwood everything went spectacularly wrong. Gary stalled his Suzuki on the line and immediately raised his arm to signal the problem. Unfortunately, however, he was caught up in the explosive action of the start. A number of glancing blows swung him sideways and then he was knocked down. Some of the riders made it past him, but by the time the end of the field got to where he was lying the riders were doing about 60 or 70 mph and he was hit hard by several bikes. Another rider went down and was in turn run over several times. Immediately after the accident, Gary and the second rider were loaded into an ambulance and taken off to hospital, where their conditions were later described as stable. Fortunately, neither suffered any lasting damage although both were decidedly the worse for wear.

And so it was that when John Britten was looking for a rider Gary just happened to be in New Zealand enjoying a bit of 'R & R' after the crack-up. He had practised at Manfeild on his Suzuki Superbike for the New Zealand round of the International Superbike Series, but elected not to compete, deciding instead to concentrate on completing his recovery before risking life and limb again. Racing may have been temporarily abandoned, but Gary still felt up to the job of testing and he accepted John's offer to ride the new machine. He did not know it at the time but he was signing up for a long and often arduous campaign. From the beginning, however, he believed in John and had faith in his creations, and he soon became a staunch ally and a vital cog in the Team John was assembling to build and race motorcycles. In time, Gary and his French-Canadian wife, Paule, would shoulder a large part of the organisational burden, helping to arrange accommodation, transport, shipping, race practice sessions, riders, support crew and all the other tasks that need doing to campaign successfully internationally.

Work began immediately with an exhausting test programme at Ruapuna. By early 1988, the bike had completed a number of test sessions and the effort was beginning to come together. From the beginning, Gary was able to extract more speed from the machine. In only his third lap on it he was lapping the circuit four seconds faster than John ever had and he was going faster all the time. Both John and Allan expressed mounting alarm to Mike Sinclair, who had accompanied them, as Gary poured on the pace, regularly getting the bike seriously out of shape and leaving black lines on the track as he came out of the tighter corners.

Mike urged them to relax.

'He's a professional,' he told them. 'It's his job.'

The sessions, however, were not as rewarding as they might have been. As is often the case with extremely talented and aggressive riders, Gary's input into sorting the bike's handling set-up was regrettably limited. The trouble was that he had the skills to ride around problems, using his huge natural ability to compensate for the bike's shortcomings. But the test sessions were far from pointless, as with each one the bike became increasingly reliable. Better still, it was at last delivering real, tyre-shredding power.

Gary was now blazing unofficial lap times of dead on fifty seconds, which was the equal of the current lap record, and there was considerable speculation among the excited BEARS fraternity that he might just break the outright track record come the Sound of Thunder meeting. Certainly, both bike and rider seemed on exceptional form, with the machine now leaving even longer black lines behind it as it exited the fast sweeper onto the main straight. Debate about the prospects of a new record grew increasingly intense, as not all were convinced. At one point Eric Wood, a well-known local motorcycle shop-owner, vowed very publicly that he would eat a programme if Gary and the Aero achieved it.

The Dunedin Festival of Speed, a street race traditionally held a few weeks before the Sound of Thunder, was selected for Gary's debut on the big V-twin, and in the Formula One race, which kicked off the programme, Aero D One finally came good. Broz went along and spannered and for once the bike seemed determined to behave. Gary, on his home track, absolutely blitzed the field and took an easy win.

Phil Payne, who was also a good friend of Gary's, was at Dunedin as well, racing a Moto Guzzi Le Mans Mark 4, which was also set up to run on methanol. Like all the other competitors on that day in Dunedin, Phil found he simply 'could not live with Aero D One once it got the bit between its teeth'. During the first race he found Gary lapping him by going around the outside on the fast 100-mph corner before the straight. Phil was already quite wide, and so Aero D One was forced to take to the broken surface between the curb and the gutter. This did not unsettle Gary in the least and he poured on the power, pulling away with his rear tyre spitting a rooster tail of bitumen and gravel in Phil's face.

But Aero D One was not the sort of machine to behave meekly when given the slightest encouragement to do otherwise. The main event of the day was the Festival Cup, where the Aero was expected to dominate the field once again. Knowing that Aero D One was a handful to get off the line, due to its grabby clutch, Phil wound the Guzzi engine up and managed to pop his clutch at the perfect moment at the flag-fall. He hole-shotted everybody and kept his head down into the first corner. He could hear the Denco bellowing angrily behind him as Gary tried to push the bike through under-braking, but Phil held him off by forcing him wide. Although this in turn forced Phil to tip the Guzzi into the next corner very late, he managed to hang on to the race line through the bend. By now the weather had broken and heavy rain was falling on the already slick surface, a development that made the awkward off-camber street corners more dangerous than ever. The Guzzi slid badly at both ends as it crossed a railway line, but Payne could still hear the vicious growl of the Denco engine right behind him, so he kept the throttle open and rode through the tank-slapper that followed. (According to Allan Wylie, the engine noise resonated strangely inside the Aero's all-enveloping bodywork so that it sounded like an apple box with a motor inside it.) At the next corner Phil again managed to hold Gary at bay by leaving his turn in to the last moment. (By chance he had fallen at the same corner in practice, forcing Gary, who was behind him on that occasion as well, to follow him off the track.)

The Guzzi was quite a long bike and could not be flicked about like the Aero D One—which, after all, borrowed its dimensions from a Grand Prix machine—and Phil doubted he could keep it behind him for long. However, as he cranked the Guzzi into the left-hander that precedes the main straight, he became aware that the wailing clamour immediately behind him had disappeared. Next time around he found a dazed Gary standing by the hay bales staring at Aero D One lying on its side in the gutter. He had apparently gassed the bike up to take Payne coming out of the corner and the back wheel had suddenly lost traction. The bike then high-sided him, spitting him head first onto the track with sufficient force to break his helmet. Fortunately, other than being somewhat concussed and annoyed with himself he had escaped unscathed.

It was not the last time Aero D One would bite the hand that fed it methanol. Back at its home track testing resumed, with the next planned outing being the New Zealand Grand Prix at Ruapuna. Because of other commitments Gary was not available, and so John elected to do the test rides himself. On the Friday before the race weekend he was hurtling toward the end of the front straight at about 120 mph when the throttle jammed wide open. The front end slid out when he grabbed the front brake, and bike and rider went down together. John's leg became trapped between the track surface and the indentations Aero D One's all-enveloping bodywork provided for the rider's legs. By the time man and machine finally slid to a halt, John's little toe had almost been ground off along with a substantial section of the side of his left foot. Mike Sinclair, who was at Ruapuna for the test session that day, tore over in the Team's station-wagon to where John was lying and hurriedly wrapped up his mangled foot in a towel to stem the profuse bleeding. John then managed to climb into the car and Mike raced him off to hospital, where he was stuck in a bed for weeks, undergoing a painful series of skin grafts.

The throttle had stuck probably because the methanol fuel did not dissolve mineral oils as efficiently as petrol, resulting in a build-up of sticky residues on the carburettor slides. Because Aero D One ran two different ignitions, two kill buttons were fitted and these were situated so that both could be pushed down with the left thumb. Unfortunately, this was not easy to do and it required thinking about. Locking the front wheel while the rear continued to drive was a recipe for disaster but it was, under the circumstances, an easy mistake to make. It was also a very painful one, and John subsequently decided that his days as both a racer and a test pilot were over once and for all. From then on such activities would be left to the professionals.

But after throwing first Gary then John, Aero D One still had one more victim to claim. Allan and Mike worked late into the night to repair the damage for the meeting at Ruapuna, where international motorcycle racer and journalist Alan Cathcart was to ride the bike. The tall, balding young Englishman, known for some reason throughout the motorcycling world as Sir Al, had been offered a choice of rides, including Joe Hannah's hub, but he had decided on the spectacular-looking Aero D One. The go-between in these arrangements had been Lindsay Williamson, with whom Cathcart was staying. When Lindsay had visited John in hospital, John asked if he would also like a ride and so Lindsay rode it in several races on the Saturday. He managed to keep out of trouble while having a lot of fun on a machine he frankly described as a 'wild man's bike'. Alan Cathcart had a practice session on the Saturday, again without incident.

During practice racing on Saturday the rear shock reservoir had come adrift and had been slightly damaged by being dragged along the ground. Lindsay had strapped it back up and it seemed to function properly, but nevertheless he warned the English journalist to take it easy, which was good advice in any case—Aero D One was not a machine to be trifled with.

One of the most enduring problems with the engine, apart from the fact that it was always a brute to start, was that it was equally difficult to persuade it to run smoothly. It would often misfire, sometimes dropping one cylinder for a moment. The habit earned it the popular nickname 'the Br…Br…Britten'. It did just that as Alan Cathcart opened it up coming out of the sweeper leading onto the front straight at Ruapuna. He kept the throttle open, and while he still had the stuttering machine cranked hard over it abruptly chimed in on both cylinders. The sudden, vicious surge in power (of the kind that had nearly pulled American speedway champion Bruce Pinhole's arms off, only, presumably, twice as bad) combined possibly with a rear shock-absorber problem, threw Alan over the top of the bike and he flew onto the grass alongside the beginning of the main straight, breaking his wrist as he landed. By chance, Phil Payne was at the meeting and as he had just chucked away his Moto Guzzi Mille he joined the angry Englishman in the ambulance.

Although Alan Cathcart would later promote Britten Motorcycles, and BEARS racing, with carefully coordinated assistance from John, the relationship had clearly not yet evolved into the mutually advantageous arrangement it would become. His initial report on the machine that had so unceremoniously dumped him was scathing. He labelled the bike a lemon, but oddly, given the circumstances of his crash, he criticised the handling of Aero D One while describing the engine as a potential winner.

'Sadly,' he wrote, 'the chassis is completely and utterly inadequate to harness the performance of this engine. I think that if John Britten goes back to his first principles and maybe gets Ken McIntosh to design a chassis for him he'll have an extremely competitive motorcycle.'[70] John accepted the criticism with good grace but shrugged off the judgement, later explaining to a reporter:

> When you start off doing something like this the biggest problem is that people don't take you seriously. The attitude is that you're one of them so how can you be smarter. You have a credibility problem to overcome. You need to have the confidence in yourself to convince others around you that you are worthy of their assistance and support. Its hard work and you have to be prepared to accept the failures with the successes.[71]

The damage to the bike was again largely superficial and all was repaired in time for the Sound of Thunder meeting. On race day the bike drew big crowds, but few spectators had ever seen anything quite like it. The bike's already fearsome reputation, now enhanced by its violent rejection of Alan Cathcart, ensured that interest in it remained high, while its true potential was the subject of even more heightened gossip and embellishment. As it happened, however, Eric Wood's race programme was safe. With Gary back on board, Aero D One decided against breaking the track record and broke a gudgeon pin instead. And that was that.

This time the damage to the machine was never repaired and the episode effectively represented its retirement from competition.[72] Aero D One had raced for exactly one year, during which time it had won one race, rejected three riders and injured two. It had been a wild ride. John now felt he had gone as far as he could, or perhaps should, with the Denco. It was a brutal bastard of a thing and it always would be. However, if John had not exactly dined out on success with Aero D One he had at least tasted enough of the entrée to know that a fully sorted Denco-Wylie-Britten would in all probability have run away from the opposition in New Zealand. And if it could do that at home then why not take up the real challenge and take on the rest of the world? The rest of the world, however, or most of the regions that matter to motorcycle race teams, had outlawed methanol. As there was no way the Denco could ever run on petrol, because of the inevitable cooling problems associated with this much hotter fuel, a total redesign was inevitable. For this reason alone the lure of a project started on a completely fresh sheet of paper was irresistible. The next machine would be a Britten.

CHAPTER SEVEN

Enter the Britten

The precise moment John decided to start again from scratch with a motorcycle using his own engine in a radically different structure is, of course, impossible to know. It was certainly a gradual process that perhaps began when he and Allan Wylie first read Jerry Branch's comments on the Denco heads. Phil Payne recalled that while John was recovering in hospital after crashing Aero D One, he started talking about a water-cooled engine and a carbon-fibre structure quite different to Aero's all-enveloping monocoque. While they were still working with Aero D One, Mike Sinclair also had a number of conversations with John about building a completely original race motorcycle. Again he felt obliged to warn John against a Grand Prix 500cc machine, reminding him forcefully that he could never match the Japanese, whose resources were effectively limitless.[73]

Colin Dodge also talked to John about building a new engine during a visit to The Stables, when John showed him the Denco and complained about the trouble he was having. Colin examined the engine carefully and ventured the opinion that the number of parting lines in the engine, which he considered excessive, would fret badly. Colin suggested there and then that John would be better off starting from scratch with his own purpose-built engine, rather than persisting with the Denco.

Nick Williams, who had helped John with Aero's bodywork, remembered John angrily complaining about an engine or gearbox component that had later proved unsuitable, saying, 'I've had enough of this, I'm going to build my own motor.' By then he was obviously ready to commit himself to the project and only a few weeks later he showed Nick the completed patterns for a new set of heads that had been built up out of layers of custom wood.

Inevitably, the relationship between John and Bob Denson ended on a sour note, but Bob remained philosophical about the parting of the ways, which he said occurred without angry words.

> I'm probably a pig-headed old bastard and I had my set ideas. For example, I didn't like the idea of shortening the stroke because I reckon a big V-twin should have some legs on it. Once we'd ironed out the bugs it went pretty well and I think we all deserve some credit. After the motor broke its pin Rob machined up two pistons but John never picked them up. I think I chucked them away not long ago. We still did the odd bit of business. I remember when they later cracked a sleeve at Daytona on the first Britten engine John called up and said he wanted new ones and sent round a sample. Then he called back and said not to copy it and that Rob would fax through new dimensions. We did as he asked and then I called and said they were ready and to bring his chequebook. When he came round to pick them up he complained about the price. He said these were twice as much as the ones he'd been using. I just smiled and reminded him that those didn't work and that these would.

While he contemplated the vast challenge of building a competitive racing motorcycle from scratch, John was also becoming entangled in the most ambitious, and risky, property development of his career to date. It was a project that would expose him to a great deal of harsh and uncomfortable public criticism, much of it from the very avant-garde whose values he had once so proudly championed.

In many ways the project represented the final metamorphosis of the new corporate John from the old, unconventional, freewheeling John and it centred on the demolition of a rather splendid Victorian mansion. It suddenly seemed to many of John's old friends that he was strangely determined to make himself over in the exact image of his father. Certainly it was hard to reconcile the aesthetic, spiritual, nihilistic John they thought they knew with the John who was hell-bent on what seemed on the face of it to be a greedy, ruthless and thoroughly venal act of wanton vandalism. Of course, John ran no risk of offending the Christchurch establishment whose standards were, like most of the country's better-off, based firmly on black-ink evaluations. They would simply welcome John to a club he already belonged to as a birthright. The grand old Victorian 'pile' that would be at the centre of the growing furore was called Heatherlea and it was located just around a couple of corners from The Stables, where it overlooked the manicured lawns and graceful spreading trees of Hagley Park. According to Kit Ebbett, John had noticed that the place was for sale and had decided to buy it with his usual spontaneous enthusiasm.

> He really didn't know what he was going to do with it but it seemed too good to pass up. Of course, Bruce was horrified at the idea of putting up so much money without a comprehensive plan but I guess he felt John had to stretch his wings. Because of his misgivings, Bruce was unwilling to lend the money for the deal directly to John

> but he was amenable to guaranteeing John's loans and the property was duly purchased.

Bruce also insisted that Russell Boddington become John's partner in the deal, a move that tempered both John's lack of experience and his somewhat headstrong tendencies. Although it might have been expected that John would harbour some resentment against the man who had 'taken his place' with Bruce, this was not the case and relations between the two were always warm and cordial. Russell's assistance in the project was both welcome and, at that time, essential.

Kit remembered John being horribly disappointed when the hard sums were crunched and it seemed the old building had to go.

> He loved the building and had absolutely no thought of harming it in any way when he bought it, but then the banks got involved and he found himself stuck between a rock and a hard place. He salved his conscience by arranging for someone to remove it, but when they let him down he really began to panic. He offered it to me for $100,000 so long as I relocated it complete onto the farm, but I was having trouble at the time and I just couldn't do it. I was really torn by this, as the place was absolutely splendid. It easily contained more than $100,000 worth of in-built furniture, panelling, leadlighting and so on and it was in such good order.

John and Willy Trengrove, a close friend since childhood who was now an architect working for his father's firm, jetted off to Surfers Paradise to have a look at high-rise apartments before returning to oversee the demolition. Allan Wylie recalled reading a final press release from John bemoaning the fact that no one wanted to save the magnificent old house by removing it, an attitude that, in Allan's view, neatly overlooked the fact that John represented the only danger to it.

It was an attitude that also failed to placate many of the good citizens of heritage-sensitive Christchurch. Committees were formed and petitions drawn up to oppose the destruction. There were, at the time, no high-rise blocks on the park and it took all of John's skills, and one suspects Bruce's contacts within the Christchurch City Council, to win planning approval for the proposed tower. Allan recalled John's grim determination to proceed in spite of growing community opposition, including coteries of elderly women confronting him in the streets and hissing at him with anger. Only the wooden library and a fireplace survived from the old house, the former as a bar at the nearby Merivale Hotel and the latter in the Park Royal Hotel.

The new Heatherlea then went up, and as soon as possible Bruce and Ruvae moved in. If John was willing to show that he was part of the Brittco family then they certainly intended backing him all the way. Not that living in Heatherlea compromised in any way their high standards of accommodation. Panoramic views from their many large windows gave a 360-degree vista across the city to include the Port Hills to the east and the Canterbury Plains everywhere else, with city giving way to farmland in the middle distance and to the west the distant mountains stretching like a white line on a graph across the horizon.

The building did not lack design flair to complement the spectacular and, in the absence of other high-rises, unique views. Although the overall appearance of the structure was little different from other such vertical boxes, it did abound in quality detailing and the layout of the apartments was of the airy and spacious variety so beloved by interior designers. If the building was essentially conventional it was also well executed, and if everything sold as was hoped then it would also prove profitable. Unfortunately, this proved harder than anyone had expected, as Kit explained.

> John showed me around when it was nearly completed. While we were in the penthouse he told me that whoever bought that floor would make more money out of it than Brittco would make out of the entire project. He told me they had to let it go at a bargain basement price to achieve the percentage of sales needed to draw down investment capital. It was a tough outcome for a project that would always haunt John and he really regretted buying the place. He saw himself as the architect of its destruction and that was a bitter pill to swallow. But that's the development game.

Bruce and Ruvae had made their new home on the floor beneath the penthouse, which they then persuaded their old friend Sir Robertson Stewart to buy. Sir Robertson was chairman of PDL, a company that had enjoyed spectacular success manufacturing electrical fittings, and he was a central figure in established Christchurch society. Once Sir Robertson was on board, other society figures followed suit and then the rest, in Ruvae's words, followed the names. Unfortunately, given the severely reduced prices at which John was forced to sell, there were still insufficient sales to turn a profit and years later this was still the case.

One thing the project did clearly illustrate to John was the power of money and connections. Both had proven more than a match for groups such as the Historic Places Trust, which had managed to get the old home listed just a little too late to complicate John's demolition of it. His new-found clout was soon utilised again, this time to protect his own environment.

The occasion was an announcement by New Zealand Railways that it intended to build a station next to The Stables, a prospect John found intolerable. He worked the old boy network for all it was worth and secured a meeting with the Minister of Rail. When the minister failed to see things John's way, John threatened to record sound levels every time a train pulled in and out and to sue whenever there was a breach of the standards set for noise abatement. He had sufficient money and influence to win the day, power the opponents of the demolition of Heatherlea had lacked. This contrast that was not lost on Allan, who found both episodes somewhat distasteful.

> I lost a lot of respect for John over the wrecking of Heatherlea and for a while there I didn't have much to do with him. Even after he came back into my life it was a side of his that I really didn't want to know about.

With the unpopular Heatherlea project more or less under control, John was finally able to turn his attention once again to the much more agreeable matter of building his own, unique race bike. His first priority was to assemble the Team he needed to handle the new project. Given Colin Dodge's earlier advice, it was probably fitting that he should be the first to be asked. He was accustomed to John's casually framed requests for assistance but he was now approached with a very specific invitation: 'I am building my own BEARS bike and I want to compete in BotT racing in the States and in Europe. I'd be happy to have your help. Are you interested?' Colin was.

Looking back, Colin noted that willing helpers always surrounded John but that John chose very carefully the individuals with whom he wished to work on specific projects.

> John would keep you enthused and focused by making his hobby your hobby. It was not something you did for money and in some ways perhaps I was a bit of a sucker. He was always going on about not being able to afford anything, and maybe it was touch and go, but boy I ended up living harder than he ever had to. But he had a way of getting the best out of you and somehow that became the important thing. It became very personal. The goal was to achieve something that was better than anything you had ever done before.

Indeed, the magnitude of the commitment Colin had made was soon apparent. He found he worked usually till midnight, and often all night, in the large room next to the workshop at The Stables. For the first few weeks he and John talked through the general design parameters of the new engine. What was an ideal rod-to-stroke length ratio? Should the engine be square or over-square? John set up a drawing board and they began to cover sheets of A4 paper with sketches before moving onto bigger sheets and renderings in full size.

Mike Sinclair was overseas at the time, but he, too, became involved and he and John spoke often on the phone. And each time Colin turned up he found that John had progressed the full-size layout, determining aspects such as crank clearances. They talked a great deal about breathing and particularly the flow of air and fuel into the engine. Colin remembered John showing him the head of a Ducati, drawing his attention to the bends in the ports, something he was determined to avoid. The start point for the heads was the drawing that Jerry Branch had given John, and the American would continue to play an important role in the development of the engine, as John would often seek his advice. He quite clearly saw their relationship as one of mentor and pupil and later wrote to Jerry that his 'clear view of the laws of physics applied to port design, tempered by your vast experience, has been the key to the high performance of my engine'.

Colin also had quite a bit of literature on laminar flow and turbulence, and he read up on the subject and brought textbooks with him for John to look at. John, he recalled, would look at the pictures but seldom read anything. Of course, he already had some knowledge of laminar flow from his engineering studies and Colin recalled that he had a good idea of things like the size of the squish areas he wanted. They worked out the basic layout for the head by starting with the biggest valves that would fit and then went to the steepest valve angle they could manage for that valve size.

Discussions between the two were straightforward and positive. Colin recollected that John would listen carefully and cull elements from conversations that he felt were worth pursuing. If he felt a suggestion was not leading anywhere he would say so, but he was able to do it in such a way that Colin never felt put down. He worked, said Colin, in a way that was inclusive and non-competitive. Contributing greatly to the easy communication between the two was the habit they both shared of working through the night and of being able to function with very little sleep. John soon acknowledged that he had never before found a companion able to keep the hours that he could.

In the meantime, Allan Wylie had been fully occupied with his job at Auto Restorations and with restoring his old Christchurch villa.

> After the Denco project I'd had enough. I had projects of my own and I was happy to leave racing motorcycles behind me. When John asked me to be a consultant, however, I agreed. I thought that consulting, even if it was unpaid, wouldn't be too onerous. I'd also learned a lot from the Denco project, primarily how not to do it. The opportunity to contribute to a new design seemed an attractive challenge. I remember going with John to Rob's house one evening where we discussed the broad parameters of the new engine design such as bore and stroke dimensions, cylinder-

> included angle, type of head joint and so on. A couple of times I was called round to The Stables to look at full-size drawings and I remember discussing with John things like pump drives and water jacket design.

And so they drove forward, defining the project with greater and greater precision, realising as they went that the only way they would achieve their emerging objective was by creating much of the project afresh, from scratch. Colin remembered John making the comment at some point in the wee hours that they would have to be very careful not to buy in proprietary parts that would oblige them to make compromises. Colin readily agreed, even though he already had a good idea of the personal sacrifices such an approach might demand. They talked about ways of making the motor strong, because John had already determined that he wanted to hang nearly everything off it. Already he was thinking that the engine would be more than a structural member; it would be the structure. Colin felt the engine should be built like a car with wet liners for strength. They drew it up and tried to find the seemingly inevitable problems, but nothing fundamental emerged. It appeared that there would be no trouble casting it and it would certainly help to control the stresses where they would be most apparent (especially with the rest of the bike hanging off it), in the area where the barrels and the crankcase met.

In adopting this layout they could draw some confidence from the fact that a number of motorcycle manufacturers had already gone down this track. Some time prior to this, Phil Payne had given John a parts manual for the Honda VFR750, a V4 machine. One of the features of the Honda motor was that the non-removable wet-sleeve cylinders were housed within the top case, eliminating the need for a base flange or jointing face—the same layout John intended for his V-twin.

They determined that the sump would feature substantial webbing running right through the casting in preference to an oversized wall thickness. Strength would be achieved through engineering, not bulk. On the Aero the dry-sump oil tank had been located on the front of the engine behind the front wheel, while the rear suspension unit had been mounted horizontally under the motor. In the new engine the two were effectively swapped over, with the rear suspension now being carried in front of the engine and the oil supply in the wet sump under the engine.

Like the Denco, the new engine was to feature belt-driven twin overhead camshafts operating four valves on each cylinder. And like the Denco, although this had yet to be determined, it would end up being another narrow (60-degree) V configuration running without balance shafts. Vibration would be minimised by careful balancing and by using the lightest possible reciprocating components.

Unlike the Denco, however, it would be water-cooled. The motorcycle body was to be a variation of Aero D One, the primary differences being the deletion of the beak over the front wheel and further smoothing of the 'leg indentations', which would hopefully prevent the kind of accident that had befallen John. It would also be somewhat wider in order to house cooling radiators on either side of the engine.[74] Structurally, it was intended that the machine would be very different from its predecessor, with the engine acting as a fully stressed unit. The steering head was to be incorporated in a minimalist Kevlar and carbon-fibre twin-spar composite box that linked it to the top of the engine, while a Kevlar and carbon-fibre swing-arm would be mounted directly to the back of the crankcase. The front end would be cannibalised from the Aero—White Power USD (Upside Down) forks and twin-disc Lockheeed brakes with Marvic wheels. (Components for two complete front ends had by now been assembled.)

Having determined more or less what was wanted, the next job was to work out how to make it. Rob Selby remembered turning up at the first big brainstorming session after Mike Sinclair had returned to New Zealand. Also present at the meeting with John were Colin and Gary Goodfellow. The expanded Team now represented a formidable line-up of skills and talents.

In addition to his growing design and engineering skills, John had considerable experience in casting, both from his days working for Crown Crystal and Carbolic Ice and from his own light-making business, and he knew about such details as how to calculate margins for drawing out castings. He was also becoming pretty adept at working with the composite materials that would comprise much of the new machine. Rob had the knowledge of machining that was vital to the success of the project and Mike was a direct conduit to Grand Prix motorcycle-race engineering and development. Colin was the hands-on, nuts and bolts man, and Gary would ultimately ride the machine. For some reason, Allan Wylie was not present at the meeting, but as noted he had already accepted John's invitation to join the Team as a consultant. The meeting lasted long into the night.

Mike and John had drawn up the essential chassis and established the bike's dimensions using Wayne Rainey's 1985 Grand Prix Yamaha as a guide. This then became the determining factor for the overall shape of the engine. Having established the general layout and dimensions, it was then Rob Selby's job to connect the dots by drawing up the rest to John's specification. At this point John had also made a second, critical decision. There would be two bikes and a spare engine.

From this stage Allan Wylie began to assume a hands-on role in the project.

> [John] asked me if I would assemble the first two engines at work, as a paying job. I suppose he realised that this was the only way he could get me to do them. John had persuaded some government department to give him some money, about $20,000 from memory. I think it was some sort of development grant or export incentive. This he

> said would be used to pay the bill at Auto Restorations. I was a little uncomfortable with the idea of public money being used to finance a rich man's hobby, but since it would be paying my wages I was hardly in a position to complain. Of course, I was soon consumed by the project again, working forty hours a week for pay and probably a similar number in my evenings and weekends unpaid. In order to assemble engines that hadn't even been fully designed, let alone made, I found myself taking responsibility for the fabrication of all the ancillaries like the crankcase baffles, the oil pickup and relief valve, fuel delivery, ignition system and so on. I did so because John was such an inspiring guy to work with and I had total faith that this would be as fast as any twin in the world, including the then new 8-valve Ducatis.

To a degree, Allan was lucky to be able to involve both his personal and his professional life in the project. Rob Selby had no such choice, a circumstance that caused many unwanted complications and delays. He had recently left Denco to work for another engineering company, not as the result of any falling-out with his old boss and mentor, but because there was a chance he could purchase the business from his new employer. When this proved impossible he was already relocated and so he stayed put. Rob recalled that John actually seemed a little put out that he (Rob) had had the temerity to move without first consulting him. He wasted no time, however, in asking Rob to prepare all the drawings for the project and then to execute the machine work. Unfortunately, Rob's new employer frowned upon the kind of open-ended project John was pursuing, seeing such work as difficult to quantify and invoice. Because of this attitude, all the machining for the new engine had to be done at night or over the weekend. This was to prove frustrating for Rob, who had to go through the time-consuming process of setting up his lathe every night instead of being able to finish jobs in one hit. To compound his frustration, he could only watch as John whipped the parts away for Allan Wylie to assemble.

However, Rob's first task following that initial meeting would involve no cutting machines more sophisticated than a pair of scissors. Before he could even begin to turn the sketched vision that John and Mike had come up with into drawings, he had to determine the basic configuration of the engine. He began by cutting out a cardboard silhouette of the cylinders and crankcase, which he then rocked, rolled and generally manipulated until it fitted the proposed layout. A key consideration was that the engine (and more particularly the front exhaust headers) cleared the front suspension when it was fully bottomed out. Starting with a 90-degree cylinder layout on the cardboard mock-up, Rob narrowed the angle until it worked. And thus it came to pass that the new Britten would be, like the Denco, a 60-degree V. It was also crucial that the swing-arm pivot was in the right place in relation to the rear axle. The cardboard engine was rotated forward until the crank height was correct. The limiting factor here was that the crankcase split line was horizontal to the ground, meaning that the crank, gearbox and output shafts were all on one plane. When everything lined up it was then necessary to back the cardboard cylinders by 12 degrees, which then became the final configuration.

The heads were state-of-the-performance-fiend's-art, drawing heavily from current Formula One motor-racing practice. Basically, they were a 4-valve affair, with the intake and exhaust valves having an included angle of 30 degrees, and featuring a pent-roof combustion chamber, that incorporated a generous squish area and a centrally located spark plug.[75]

The heads were to be attached to the sub-frame, which in turn attached to the steering head, via lugs cast into the detachable camboxes.[76] Perhaps the most striking aspect of the head design was the way the inlet charge was introduced through ports that were as close to the bore axis as possible and as straight as an engineer's steel ruler. The inlet tract was 330 mm long and started with a 100-mm diameter that tapered down to the valve pockets. Feeding air into each port were trumpets big enough to swallow a man's fist. Because the rear cylinder's trumpet faced to the rear, the two trumpets would be fed by two separate external air inlets, one located in the seat hump and the other fed by a duct through the fuel tank. John and Colin talked about the location of the injectors on the inlet ports but were unable to come to any useful conclusions, so John contacted Jerry Branch, who again proved happy to help. After talking to him, a Bosch injector for each cylinder was located about halfway down the port, a deep installation by most standards.[77]

Unlike the inlets, the exhaust ports were gently curving, starting the turn that carried on into the exhaust headers. Each head had two camshafts, all four being driven by a single serpentine, high-torque drive belt with a semicircular tooth section.

When the engine was first drawn up by Rob he showed a separate belt driving each pair of cams, but John reduced this to a single belt.[78] The valves were in turn actuated by buckets and shims, the later being located beneath the buckets. The included valve angle was 30 degrees and an American company—Delwest—supplied the featherweight 30-gram titanium valves to John's specification.

John drew up the bottom of the crankcase, a deep wet-sump arrangement that accommodated the oil pump and the guts of the 5-speed Suzuki GS1100ET gearbox he intended using. It was envisaged that this would feature road gearing for first and second, and close-ratio gearing thereafter, but this never happened and stock road-ratio gears were used instead. The pivot point for the swing-arm was cast onto the rear of the crankcase, which was engineered to handle the considerable loadings this would involve.

With the engine designed, the next very obvious challenge was to work out a way to cast the heads and engine cases. John asked Colin if he would make the patterns, and Colin agreed, but neither had any idea how it might be done. Colin thought about it and then asked if the drawings could be sectionalised in plan view and elevation. For the next three weeks John took a break with his family in Australia while Rob spat out full-size drawings for Colin that represented 12-mm sections. Colin then glued the sections to 12-mm ply or custom wood and cut them out. Where the work was trickier, as in the heads, the sections were thinner—usually 5 mm. The next step was to glue the sections together with Araldite, after which Colin sanded them with a power file. The first patterns completed were for the top and bottom of the crankcase, and with dowelling for the bolt-holes it was finished with all the screw-in pieces, such as the oil-pump mounting lugs, in place. The work went smoothly and, much encouraged, Colin turned his attention to the heads. These were to prove a lot more difficult.

The biggest challenge was to make a solid rendition of the ports to suspend within the cores during casting. By then John had returned and he sourced the material used in making false teeth. (Typically, he consulted an expert—in this case a dentist—to get the information he needed about the material.) Colin remembered that it was quite expensive and that it was poured in as a liquid and then left to set. John extracted it slowly, trying not to break the rubbery material, and was duly rewarded with what Colin described as something looking like a 'small pile of those artificial bones for dogs'.

Even though extreme care had been taken with the cutting out of the patterns, a final problem with a hollow area had to be solved by pinning in extra material. Even so, the casting was reasonably successful, although Colin recalled that something did move and required additional work to remedy. The heads were then found to be quite porous, so were sent to an Australian company where they were impregnated under vacuum with Loctite sealer.

The choice of cams presented something of a conundrum. The first problem was that no one in the Team had the knowledge or experience to make particularly informed choices. Second, the choices available were limited to what was then available from the cam grinders. Initially, a Cosworth Formula One grind was tried but this proved to be just the beginning of a long quest for the perfect cam set-up that persisted to the end of the line. Essentially, every engine needs its own particular cams in order to meet most efficiently the performance requirements, but the expertise to achieve this was simply unavailable to the Team at the time. Designing a cam was a very different art to merely copying a hot cam, a task a number of grinders were well able to do.

When the first engine was built, the Team had no CAD (Computer Applied Design) programs to draw on, other than the distant facilities offered by Jerry. In the beginning, everything was done on an empirical, commonsense, seat-of-the-pants basis. Later, it would be possible to feed port-flow velocities, valve diameters, bore, stroke and compression ratios, inlet-exhaust configurations, camshaft overlap and duration, and so on into a computer and have it spit out horsepower readings for different revs. For now, however, it was necessary, as Rob put it, 'to suck it and see'.[79]

Rob now continued to churn out his sectionalised drawings, from which Colin made patterns for the top of the crankcase and cylinders. The cylinders were cast integrally with the upper half of the crankcase, which was, as noted, designed to split from the bottom half along the horizontal line running through the crank and gearbox shafts. The only other parting line in the motor was the one between the cylinder head and the upper crankcase, which was designed so that there was no need for a head gasket. John took on the job of heat-treating the castings in his wife's pottery kiln in the garage at The Stables. By now his activities had attracted the attention of a local filmmaker and photographer, Harry Ruffell, who asked John if he could film critical parts of the process to make a documentary film at a later date. John readily agreed. On one occasion he was happily explaining the process of heat treatment to the camera when he discovered that the washing-machine tub he was using to quench the casting had insufficient water in it. With every possibility that he had ruined the casting he frantically filled a bucket from the nearby swimming pool and topped up the tub. As it happened, no damage was done but, in spite of his insistence that fatigue actually helped him to focus by driving out extraneous thoughts, the workload was telling on everyone, including him.

The pistons chosen were Mahle-forged slipper types made of aluminium alloy, although when subsequently there were insufficient pistons to go around, some Denco items were used. The Mahle pistons were developed for Porsche to use in their pent-roof combustion-chamber race engines and featured very short cut-away skirts. The pistons used by the Team were actually supplied by the Australian company APEP (Australian Precision Engine Parts), which machined the Mahle casting to suit the Britten engine.[80] The pistons offered the high 13.5:1 compression ratio John wanted but came with their own inherent reliability problems. This was not a quality-control issue but a design complication arising from the fact that this particular piston was made to work in a Nikasil[81] bore. In such an application the Nikasil-coated alloy sleeve and piston material expanded at the same rate as they became hotter, allowing closer tolerances than were possible with the Britten engine, which had cast-iron wet liners pressed into the cylinders.[82] The combination of short skirts and loose tolerances when cold could result in the piston rocking within the bore, leading to cylinder-wall scoring and, potentially, to cold seizures, particularly of the front cylinder, a circumstance the Team would come to dread.

The next component to locate was a conrod. What was needed was a readily available off-the-shelf race item about 14 cm long. After casting about for some time, a titanium conrod of about the right length was found in America. The manufacturer, a well-respected company called JET, was prepared to custom-build rods to John's specification, but as the lead-time was unacceptably long John settled for an existing item. This was the rod JET made for a turbocharged DFX Cosworth race engine.

Unfortunately, the JET DFX rods were a fraction short, but there was a reasonably simple solution. The engine was simply shortened to accommodate them.[83]

While John was locating suitable rods, Rob went ahead and carved a new crankshaft. He started by roughing the shape out from a block of billet steel and then milling the final form and the oil galleries. It was then heat-treated and the bearing surfaces were double nitrided. Following heat treatment the first one was then reground, but this was found to be unnecessary and was not repeated on later units. When finished, the crankshaft weighed a substantial 12.5 kg and to handle it John elected to have it run in massive single-roller bearings set into the cases on each side. The reason for such a relatively heavy crank was not only longevity—and here again Jerry Branch's influence was probably significant. Both dirt-track and oval-circuit racing had developed in America with the same basic machinery, and a characteristic of that machinery was relatively heavy flywheels, a desirable property when engines were expected to run more or less at maximum revs most of the time.[84]

Allan Wylie continued to endure his share of challenging complications. Engine components were delivered to him, as soon as John could wrestle them from Rob, in various states of finish. During the day he worked on the bike for Auto Restorations, which then charged John for the time. They, in turn, paid Allan. After 4 pm, however, Allan worked for John, and he worked mostly for nothing other than the satisfaction of getting it done. The hours were tolerable only because he, like the rest of the Team, accepted that it was only through the power of their collective commitment that the project could be accomplished.

This is not to say that the obsessive (and grossly excessive) hours did not cause more than their fair share of stress. Allan recollected that for quite a bit of the time he was involved in the project he was not enjoying the experience. During weekends particularly he would dread the sound of the phone ringing or of John's Mercedes turning into his driveway. On one occasion, by way of thanks, John arrived and spent an hour or so helping Allan lay a brick path in his garden. Allan remembered John saying facetiously that he would have to take especial care to make sure the bricks were smooth so that Allan could scrape his knee when he rode the Guzzi around the corner of the house. Allan also remembered John's son Sam, now a toddler, earnestly moving piles of sand around as he lent a hand by undertaking various small constructions of his own. It was a welcome moment of weary levity before the real work of building a radical racing motorcycle rolled relentlessly on again.

Allan's job continued to be far more complicated than simply bolting things together. With the flow of components reaching him in varying degrees of completion, he spent a lot more time drilling, tapping, machining and lapping components than he did assembling them. In a number of cases he also designed, fabricated and modified them. Sometimes changes were necessary to make the work already done actually work properly. Sometimes he had to join a few dots that Rob had insufficient time to consider. On other occasions he rebelled against doing things that he considered inelegant.

It was intended, for example, that the cam bearings should be sealed with RTV (silicone rubber—a material used generously on the Denco motor to keep the oil inside). Allan, however, disliked the idea of cleaning the tenacious material from the jointing faces every time the top end was reassembled. Instead, he machined grooves in the bearing housings to take rubber O-rings.

Sometimes the design and manufacture of seemingly simple components could be frustratingly complicated. Allan's first version of the oil baffles in the sump cracked, for example, and it took two more rethinks before a more satisfactory arrangement was worked out.[85]

Colin was also kept frantically busy through this period laying up the body for the bike in the modified Aero D One moulds. These were laid up in the room next to the office at The Stables and were surrounded with heaters to cure the body panels. Colin recalled that there was 'all this crap around the place', and it was undeniably true that John seemed comfortable working in a complete mess. Of course, when working with inherently messy, sticky substances, like two-pot resins, any propensity to messiness is made that much worse and the workshop soon acquired an atmosphere that was almost pestilential. Greg Atkinson remembered being so appalled at the chaos that he wound up spending some considerable time trying to clean it all up. It was a losing battle.

'John just liked to get things done. How he did it and the mess he created doing it were not important to him.'

Nevertheless, work proceeded and the carbon-fibre bodywork was popped out of the moulds without any problems, following which jigs were made up for the sub-frame and swing-arm. At this point John took over the work and Colin took off to do a bit of building to revive his somewhat emaciated coffers. He was not away for long before John asked him to return, and his time on the project would increasingly be characterised by biting poverty.

Despite all the frustrations and on-the-spot improvisations, the project rolled along in an atmosphere of enthusiasm and excitement. Part of the reason for this was the fact that the structure John proposed for the new motorcycle was perhaps the lightest and simplest ever devised. All that was required to link wheels, engine and front suspension was a swing-arm and the top sub-frame referred to earlier. Such a layout had been tried successfully by the Daytona-winning Quantel-Cosworth, which had a swing-arm and sub-frame fabricated from dural sheet. John was confident he could achieve greater strength and rigidity and even less weight by constructing his missing links from Kevlar and carbon-fibre. To do this, he devised an ingeniously simple but effective technique that he dubbed the 'skin and bones' method.

The first jig completed was for the top sub-frame. Essentially, this located aluminium spools, which would become the steering head, bearing housing and the mounting points to attach the sub-frame to the lugs on the engine heads. In the case of the second jig for the swing-arm unit, the spools were used for the swing-arm bearing, the suspension-rod bearing and the wheel bearing.

John started the process by winding carbon-fibre in continuous strands (or rovings), four at a time around the spools in a repeating sequence. He took care to maintain an even tension on the strands, largely by feel. He also took care not to break or kink any strand as this would compromise the prestressed integrity of the final structure. The spools were deliberately made large for two reasons, the first being that the material would not go around right-angle bends, or even tight corners, without being made weaker. Carbon-fibre and Kevlar are best suited for gentle rounded forms, a factor that perfectly suited John's preference for organic shapes. The second reason for the large spools was that they offered a generous surface area for the material to bond with.

It was a long and laborious process, each winding taking one full 'John' day to do, a normal workday for John being anything between sixteen and twenty-four hours. The strands were wetted out with resin that had a retarding agent in it to delay hardening, the type being chosen a two-part epoxy. (This was later replaced by vinyl-ester, used for its superior wet-out properties.) John built an ingenious little device to apply the resin to the rovings, one that remained in use for years. This consisted of four rollers in a small, fabricated bath through which the roving was pulled as it unwound off its spool. Each roller ran over the next, with the rovings between ensuring that resin was squeezed into the material until it was saturated, after which point excess resin was automatically squeezed out.

When its required form was completed, the structure was a fully triangulated affair of great rigidity and it was this that comprised the bones of the finished item. The skins, or exterior casings, were made of a composite of Kevlar (which has good impact resistance) and carbon-fibre. Impregnated sheets of these two materials, pre-cut oversize, were laid into a mould in alternating layers. The extra material folded back on itself, making ten layers in all. The bones and the skin were made simultaneously and were introduced to one another while both were still wet. The complete structure was then filled with two-pack expanding foam and clamped in the mould with the finishing carbon-fibre sheet to the outside. (After the first sub-frame was made, John eliminated the foam as he felt there was a danger it might put pressure on the rovings.) Finally, it was cured at 50 degrees Celsius overnight in a home-made oven. The result was a unit with all of its component pieces 'fused' into a structural whole.

The completed swing-arm was then sanded with progressively lighter paper until it was satisfactorily smooth for Bob to paint with clear lacquer.[86] When finished, the deeply triangulated swing-arm weighed just 3 kg while the sub-frame weighed in at an equally impressive 4.25 kg.

Inevitably, there were some compromises when the overall layout of the bike was finalised. One of them was the location of the White Power spring-shock absorber for the rear suspension, which as noted was mounted forward of the front cylinder. It couldn't go beneath the rider's seat, where one might normally expect to find it, because the rear cylinder-injector trumpet protruded backwards and there simply wasn't room for it. (Later engines would turn the rear head around so that both trumpets were located in the engine V, feeding from a common air-box.) Rob, Mike and John actually drew the bike out on the garage floor, and after much drawing and erasing found it was the only place it could fit. In order to bolt the thing onto the exhaust port and clear the exhaust header, the unit was canted over a few degrees at the top. This meant that the bell crank, which turned the horizontal push-pull of the swing-arm-activated rod running beneath the engine into a vertical movement, did not pivot on the same plane—in turn meaning that it had to twist under load. The ultimate result was a series of failures of the crank, which was made from successively stronger materials (the final one being titanium) to get around the problem. The fact that the spring was sitting out front also meant that the radiator, or radiators as it transpired, had to go somewhere other than behind the front wheel. As noted, they ended up on either side of the front cylinder, which resulted in a wide body and some clearance difficulties with the finished machine when it was leaned over.

Because the rear shock was located in still air behind the wheel immediately next to the forward exhaust header, it also received a good roasting, which could not have helped its efficiency. On the other hand, the placement did help with the forward weight bias John was after, although Allan argued that this aim would have been better achieved by putting the shock somewhere else and shunting the engine forward a little.

With his new machine more or less falling into place, John began to give more thought as to where he might actually race it. He believed it was essential to break out of the small New Zealand scene into the international big time as soon as possible in order to attract powerful backing and make sales, two objectives that matched his overall aim of putting himself on the map as an international designer.

Battle of the Twins racing seemed an obvious first choice, as it encouraged mavericks who wanted to try something different. By 1989 it had grown from club outings featuring crowded grids of amateurs on tuned twenty-year-old machinery to some of the fiercest racing to be seen on some of the most technically interesting prototype machinery.

Of all the races on the calendar, however, the most established at the time was probably the America Pro Twins race, held every year at Daytona in Florida during the famous Cycle Week as a lead-up to the Daytona 200,[87] and it was at this race that John chose to debut his motorcycle on the international scene. In recent years the high banks of Daytona had become an annual showcase for big twins, with teams arriving to race from across the States in addition to Australia, Canada, England, France, Germany and Japan. It was time to add New Zealand to the list.

Cycle Week was an American phenomenon. Every year up to 120,000 bikers from all over the continent swarmed into Daytona and took the place over for a solid week of partying and racing. First staged in 1924, it had matured into the biggest single motorcycle-racing event in the US calendar, with championship events for road racers, motocrossers, flat-trackers and classic racers. Of course, not all the bikers were there for the racing. Most were simply along to socialise and a pronounced majority was astride Harley-Davidsons. It was a wild place to choose for a coming-out party.

From the time the first castings arrived in Allan's hands at Auto Restorations, the Team had just two months to build a motorcycle.

Allan began the final assembly for the 1989 Sound of Thunder with little if any time for screw-ups. Regrettably, however, the pace of work, the exhausting hours and the awkwardness of pursuing the project in three primary locations resulted in plenty of them. Allan recalled the activity of that time as a 'mad, desperate rush'.

> We worked late every night at Auto Restorations in a state of semi-chaos because many minor parts, and some major ones, hadn't even been designed. It was a case of design as you build and in many instances the first attempt was a waste of time because nobody could see the whole picture. The packaging of all the components is one of the most difficult design tasks on a racing bike, and until you've worked out where every component is to go the positions of none of them can be finalised. John was trying to do it backwards and everyone paid the price. I remember Mike Sinclair

> had done a lot of work at home on the throttle bodies to his usual impeccable standard. Unfortunately, much of his effort was wasted and the rear-throttle body in particular needed major reworking because it simply didn't fit in with other components. It was a case of two components trying to occupy the same space.

It soon became clear that even a best-outcome scenario for completing the bike would leave scant weeks to iron out the inevitable bugs before shipping it off to confront the best twins line-up in the world. The only way to deal with inevitable reversals was to work longer hours. Enormous pressure was placed on John's schedule by such circumstances as the condition of the cases for the second motor as they were delivered to Allan for assembly. Lugs had been welded on for the oil pump after the finish machining and this had distorted the cases. As a result, Allan found he had to do some of the finishing work afresh in order to get the oil pump to fit.

Throughout it all John carried on at a frenetic pace, completing his part of the project while balancing the whole deck of cards like a demented magician. Cajoling, encouraging, kidding and cracking jokes that he at any rate found unspeakably hilarious, or standing with his shoulders hunched forward, nervously smoothing his hair back, he kept everything moving forward by working hours that would kill another. His approach may have failed from time to time, but at least it had the virtue of simplicity: keep everybody focused on the immediate job at hand and solve problems as they arise.

For Allan the task was often to bridge the gap between hurried past conversations about various bits and pieces and their speedy realisation. Just before the first castings were done, for example, John rushed into the Auto Restorations workshop and asked Allan what the oil-pressure relief valve should look like, probably in order to determine how large a boss would be needed to take the valve. Allan drew a sketch and John raced off with it. Then, just weeks later, a casting arrived with a bore in it for the valve. And so Allan set to and made the valve. That was the system working at its best. Often, however, it seemed to Allan that John had everyone he knew with time on their hands making bits for the project, and this did not always produce quality work. After all, it was generally true that the best people did not have time on their hands but usually were busy. A good example of the kind of thing that happened as a result of the divergence of human input to the project were the oil-pump drive shafts that John brought in for Allan to fit. After a number of shafts had been rejected, Allan ended up making them himself.

The killing pace continued to accelerate as the project proceeded. Parts straggled in from external suppliers, to be seized by impatient hands and thrown into the mix. In addition to the gears, the clutch was also sourced from Suzuki, in this case a Suzuki GSX750 unit. Although designed to run wet, the clutch was operated successfully dry.[88] Also sourced from Suzuki was the trail-bike water-pump, which was driven off the opposite end of the oil-pump shaft by the primary drive.

At the very beginning of the project John went to some trouble to find carburettors for the new engine, but there was nothing available over 40 mm, which was clearly too small.[89]

The hardest thing to get into an engine is air but the secret to producing horsepower lies in ensuring that once there it is mixed in exactly the right proportion with the fuel. The difficulty facing the Team was that this proportion constantly changes throughout the rev range and through different throttle positions and engine loadings. The ideal mixture at full throttle at low revs is different to that required at full throttle at high revs. A carburettor is a passive instrument that is activated by induction vacuum and as such there is a certain built-in delay in its responses. The only way to obviate this was to abandon carburettors to history and embrace fuel injection.

When John eventually became convinced that he needed a fuel-injection system, Allan began asking around the traps. In response to his enquiries, when they were about half way through the assembly of the engine, Bob Richardson walked into Auto Restorations and offered his services. He was working with a company called Turbo Technology but he had also supplied a number of successful fuel-injection systems that he had designed and built for jet-boaters and rally drivers. These were marketed under the name Auto Logic, later renamed Link. Bob looked over the half-assembled engine and told John and Allan he was confident he could supply a system that would suit the Britten.

Encouraged by his assurance, John placed an order. With crucial input from Mike Sinclair, the Team proceeded to build the throttle bodies from aluminium. It was new territory for them and they had to learn as they went, but building the bodies proved surprisingly straightforward. The final assembly of the motor took place over Christmas at Allan's house in a last, frenetic effort. It was fortunate for the project that Allan had holidays to devote to it. A particularly vivid recollection for him was of the assembled engine casings resting on an old wooden stump he used as a chopping block in his garden. He was pressure-testing it for general watertightness by running a garden hose through it after 'bunging up all the holes'.

'If ever the work deserved the backyard tag, it was then.'

The Denco had been a brutal object of sharp corners and raw-machined alloy and steel, but the Britten engine was something quite different. Its form was smooth and organic. John had always preferred the look of the older round-case Ducati engines to the angular motors that replaced them, and his preference for moulded shapes was immediately obvious. Because it would be a fully stressed member of the motorcycle structure, the engine was not as svelte as it might otherwise have been (at 65 kg), but strength and solidity were communicated pleasingly in its architecture. If the classic English HRD Vincent motorcycle had survived this could well have been their engine for the new millennium. But there was no mistaking what it was—the word 'Britten' was cast onto the side of the cylinders.

In terms of a clean-sheet racing design the Britten V-twin was neither revolutionary nor innovative, but sitting there on that stump, even as an empty shell, it really was something else.

In the rush to get things done, however, little effort had been made to record exactly how it had all come together. This oversight took a long time to correct, and the absence of any records of the engine's specifications became acute when mechanics who had not been intimate with its construction were expected to maintain and even rebuild it. In an attempt to at least start down the track of proper records and eventually, he hoped, a workshop manual, Allan recorded the vital specifications of the engine in a blue exercise book. Until the advent of the second-generation Britten engine, the 'blue book' was really the only real record of what went on inside the Britten V-twin.[90]

Once again, the completion of the bike was hurried along to make the Sound of Thunder BEARS meeting at Ruapuna. Unfortunately, history repeated itself in quite a few ways. Once again, just like Aero D One, the machine was far from ready. Like Aero D One the bike had first been fired up at Auto Restorations, in this case just three days before it was to be raced. Like Aero D One Allan was the first to ride it. It ran but only just, and Allan recalled it 'farting and popping. It delivered about 8000 revs tops and I knew we had a long way to go. There was so much wrong with it. Many of the problems were clearly centred on the fuel-injection system and particularly on the computer. As soon as the ignition was turned on the injectors would start false triggering, indicating an interference problem in the system.'

Bob Richardson's fuel-injection system differed from most modern systems in that it was an analogue rather than a digital system and could only operate the fuel supply, so the ignition had to be managed conventionally and independently. On the plus side the system's controls were similar to those of a radio, and it was therefore straightforward to tune. The fuel mixture, for example, could be adjusted by simply turning a dial with a screwdriver. However, turbo-charged rally cars and jet-boat engines operate within a narrow range of conditions and, being single-point injection systems, are not terribly fussy. The Britten, unfortunately, was. A loss of performance due to the injection system was obviously bad enough, but it also represented a real danger for the rider. If a cylinder were to cut out under trailing throttle going around a corner, for example, the back wheel could easily lock up and throw the rider off. Another worrying scenario would be a repeat of the Cathcart episode, when a faltering cylinder suddenly exploded back into life as he powered out of a corner, high-siding him.

It slowly emerged that the analogue system was simply not smart enough or reliable enough for the application. The Britten engine ran at a wide range of throttle openings over a much wider spread of revs than either rally cars or jet-boats, and all its electrical components were very much more vulnerable to heat and vibration stress. Because the system was assembled from radio and stereo equipment, rather than military-specification electronics, it was simply not up to the unforgiving and tough environment of motorcycle racing. Later, John complained somewhat bitterly that electronic engineers were blinkered by a mindset that prevented them seeing the world beyond their own workbench.

'No matter how often you tell them that their product will not hack it,' he told a journalist, 'they refuse to consider you might know more about the way their stuff behaves in the real world than they do. In fact they are more likely to accuse you of breaking it.'

Problems with the fuel injection were compounded by an elementary error. The Team believed that they would be able to run the bike on a 'total loss system' electrically. In other words, they expected to be able to run a race on the power of a battery without having to generate charge. The battery they chose was a compact sealed unit marketed for burglar alarms and it certainly looked promising. It was used by a number of motorcycle racers at the time but they were only running ignition systems that drew a few amps. On the Britten, the fuel pump, a compact little unit that resembled a sausage, ran on eighteen amps. This meant that the battery could not supply juice for more than about four laps of a track the length of Ruapuna before it went completely flat. Nor was inadequate capacity the battery's only problem; it was also not designed to supply a heavy current draw.

When it became obvious that the bike needed a charging system, Allan frantically cast about for something suitable. Finally, he grafted on an alternator to supply charge to the EFI (Electronic Fuel Injection) system. The alternator itself was predictably taken from a GSX Suzuki, and after narrowing the rotor it was shoehorned inboard of the inlet-cam pulley on the rear cylinder. As there was no proper position for it, Allan used helicoils with 5-mm screws to attach the stator. He knew it would survive removal and refitting only a few times before the threads failed, but it was the best he could do.

Gary was back in Canada and John needed another test pilot for the new machine. Once again, Lindsay Williamson had the answer. Eighteen-year-old Chris Haldane, son of the well-known Auckland racer and motorcycle-shop owner Bob Haldane, was in Christchurch for a Formula One race at Ruapuna. At the time he was, in his own words, one of the youngest guys on the scene who was doing well.

He was using Lindsay's shed to work on his Yamaha FZR1000 when Lindsay told him about John's project. It was the first time Chris had heard of it; indeed, few people had any idea of what was going on around The Stables and in the workshops of Auto Restorations.

> I was very cautious about it. Basically, I had no idea what Lindsay was talking about when he first mentioned it and I more or less put it out of my mind. On race day at Ruapuna I think I managed to win one and had an oil leak put me out of the other while leading. John walked up and spoke to me in the pits after the racing and I was captured by something different in his nature. I don't know what it was but he immediately had my attention. He invited me to inspect the bike at Auto Restorations and when I did I realised that they were creating something special. It was all grey carbon-fibre and it looked like a pro job. It had AP Brakes, which were top notch, and the same tyres I'd been running on the Fizzer. He asked if I wanted to test it and I said that I would. They were working around the clock to get the thing finished and I think John expected to have it ready to run on a daily basis.

Chris then travelled back to Auckland to await John's call, which came some days later. He was wanted immediately. The Britten would be ready to test the following day.

'I shot down and then twiddled my thumbs for about a week just standing around,' recalled Chris, 'before the bike was finally wheeled onto the rollers. Then Allan jumped on and it fired up straight away. There was a bit of drama because the relief spring on the oil-pressure valve was too strong and it blew the O-ring out of the oil filter. But it fired up and ran. Very, very loudly.'

For John it was a moment of supreme triumph, glitches notwithstanding. It was certainly enough for John to justify opening a bottle of champagne, and there was much good-natured hooting and whooping into the wee hours. The next day, John, Allan, Chris and a small team of volunteers drove out to the track for the first test session. The bike was finished with a shining gel-coat over the raw carbon-fibre, but Allan was suffering intense sleep deprivation and to his weary eyes the finish appeared quite rough and the body did not look terribly professional. The wheels and exhaust were painted white, and the sides and bottom had been removed from the fairing. He recalled that much of the rest of the body was held together with zip ties and duct tape. A length of plastic hose made up a makeshift breather from the crankcase and it trailed out the back of the fairing blowing oil. For all that, however, it was a handsome brute and there was a sense of satisfaction in the air at having come thus far. Once again, Allan was astride the bike on the rollers when the engine caught and settled into the deep, resonating, slightly sonorous drone that from the first characterised a Britten at idle. Once again Allan was the first to ride the new bike, completing a few hesitant laps before handing over to Chris, who had a few reservations after his ride.

> My first impression of the thing was that it was quite cramped and I found it hard to get comfortable. I'm nearly six feet tall and Gary is quite short, so I didn't fit as well as he obviously had on Aero D One. I found the handlebar position really shocking after racing a production bike, but even though I never liked it I got used to it. The suspension worked beautifully and as the bike I'd been riding all year developed 140 hp I wasn't fazed by the power it made. The V-twin was probably significantly less powerful than my Superbike even when it was running smoothly, although it was hard to tell because it didn't run properly all that often. The fuel injection was a real problem and we struggled to even get the bike to run consistently.

At one point in the afternoon John raced off and returned with a new set of injectors that he had picked up, grumbling that he could have bought quite a good bike for the price of one of them. They made little appreciable difference. The day ended on a gloomy note and on race day at Ruapuna things were not much better, as Chris recalled.

> I managed a third or so in the main event, with Paul Pavletich on Dallas Rankine's "Fast 'n Fragile" Ducati special in front of me while Glenn Williams on the Anglo's 851 was in front of him. So it wasn't hopeless but it just wouldn't stay in tune. I also had this problem with clutch drag, which really interrupted the flow. However, the bike got a huge amount of attention.

Others present on that day remembered a wild kind of elation that greeted the bike's surprise appearance. The machine ran just well enough to give a hint of its considerable promise and the problems it was having could not dampen the huge sense of excitement it generated among the BEARS crowd. As they had with the Denco, they gave it their immediate and unqualified support.

The inescapable reality however, was that the bike would not run properly. And nothing the crew tried seemed to make any lasting difference. Allan, who knew full well how the day would go, went to the races but elected to keep clear of Team Britten. It was the third time in a row that John's bike had failed to deliver anything near its potential at the Sound of Thunder. It would not be the last.

The Team now had to face the fact that Daytona was just three weeks, and many thousands of kilometres, away and that they had enjoyed only a very average debut performance. Allan feared that the next stop for the Britten Motorcycle might be just that—a stop.

> Most people would give up after an experience like the Sound of Thunder and stop trying to race until they had sorted the problems, but not our Johnny. My own feelings when I realised that he was determined to go to Daytona anyway were of resigned despair. There was so much to fix on the bike. The fuel-injection system still did not work properly. But that was not the worst of it. The breather was still emitting oil and even if the other problems could have been overcome the thing would still have emptied its crankcase way before the end of the race. Fitting a reed valve was the solution to the oil emission problem but there was no time for anything like that to be done. John believed in miracles. He believed that if he just persisted things would come right. In that way he was quite unreasonably optimistic.

Chris continued to test the bike both at Ruapuna and more regularly on the straight at South Eyre Road.

> I can remember John standing beside me while we waited in the still morning air. He would shout, 'I can't see any cars coming—off you go!' Often the first run would be brilliant and then on the return, in top gear, it would seize. They kept increasing the bore clearances and doing a host of other things at the same time, so we never really established a baseline to work from. It was a problem I experienced with John right from the very start. He was in such a hurry. However, the bike handled brilliantly—it stopped beautifully and so on—except for this one big problem that became apparent when we took it to Ruapuna.
>
> This was the lack of ground clearance. The magnetos were located on the side of the engine and the fairing was really wide, with these ridges running down the side, probably to clear them. It would drag its arse on the ground when you leaned it in. The fairing was built really strong at the points in contact and it would unload the suspension as it scraped away in the most unnerving manner. You get to know your race lines, which vary a little from one bike to another, and it was strange to see these white lines inside the line I was following. It was residue of fairing from previous laps. The bike had to have constant repairs to the bodywork. I knew it would be possible otherwise to really lay the thing down, which made the shortcoming even more frustrating.
>
> The other bug, of course, was trying to get it to run right. I did hundreds of laps at Ruapuna with the computer box strapped to the tank altering the mixture at different revs under different loads, and we would achieve bursts of smooth running. It still wasn't shattering but I definitely got a sense of promise, enough to encourage me to hang in.

Gary Goodfellow had agreed to ride the bike at Daytona, and with only a couple of weeks to go before the race John sent him a fax to tell him of the Team's progress. Gary was in Japan testing the Yoshimura Suzuki Superbike and 600 Super Sport (along with Kevin Schwantz and Ron Haslam, both of whom he also expected to race against at Daytona). In his fax, John wrote:

> The bike looks good and runs well but still has to be tuned a bit. It handles great I think. It's light and the weight is low down and forward. It stops very quickly. The motor is smooth for a twin. Allan thinks that the fuel injection is no good but I rode the bike at Ruapuna for two hours last Sunday and it feels at least as good as carbs. As you ride it analyses the exhaust gases and a meter on the dash tells you if it is too lean or too rich—which helps tuning. You'll love the bike. It will get heaps of attention. You just have to WIN the race and PROMOTE the product. Two things that come naturally to you—ha! I've worked my arse off to make it exist. Now if it's any good we want people to learn and remember the make—BRITTEN! Thanks Gary for having the confidence in my work—maybe it will be good for both of us.

After the Sunday test session at Ruapuna John had joyfully reported to Allan that the injection set-up was perfect.

'It was wishful thinking,' said Allan. 'The set-up was better but it was far from satisfactory.'

In the meantime, doubtless buoyed by John's enthusiasm, Gary had also been busy chasing up some sponsorship money on John's behalf for the Daytona expedition with a Japanese garment manufacturer called Don Knit. The company already sponsored Gary's Superbike programme and Gary was soon able to inform John that they were interested in a deal.[91] He also expressed his enthusiasm for the coming contest.

'I am as excited about the bike running as you are,' he faxed to John. 'I have had reporters phoning me on what I am riding and I've been getting the interest up! Everybody will be interested for sure!'

He signed off the fax with a drawing of the top of the world balancing a big number one on it that had the word 'Britten' inscribed across its base. A chequered flag waved over the top.

In a follow-up fax Gary confirmed various arrangements and then mentioned some difficulties he had experienced in Japan.

'You wouldn't believe the problem I had with Yoshimura and Suzuki to get them to let me ride your bike,' he complained to John. 'In the end I told them they could get fucked so they agreed. I had this point written into my contract with both of them.'

Although John urged Gary to do well in order to promote the brand name 'Britten', one substantial expression of interest in the Britten engine had already been received. This had been initiated by Rod Coleman, who had recently sold his Wanganui-based motorcycle import, retail and maintenance business. Initially set up by Rod's father Percy, the business had for many years represented the Suzuki Motor Company in New Zealand. So successful had the Colemans been[92] that the Suzuki Motor Company had recently made them an offer for the business that could not be refused, and the company had duly changed hands.

Rod retained close links with the international motorcycle fraternity and counted among his friends one Hiro Miyazaki, a Japanese entrepreneur whose company, Brooklands Ltd, specialised in the manufacture of dress-up kits for Japanese motorcycles. Hiro had decided to expand his business and make complete 'European'-style motorcycles with non-Japanese mechanicals, and had therefore approached the Italian company Gilera to see if they would sell him engines. Unfortunately another Japanese company had already made an exclusive arrangement with the Italians, at which point Hiro heard about the Britten. Rod came to act as the go-between, but it was quickly obvious to all involved that even if John had been able to supply a reliable unit for 'domestic' consumption the price would have been prohibitively high.

The negotiations were therefore abandoned and it was clear John was far from ready to market anything beyond perhaps the experience that had been gleaned so painstakingly in the construction of the engine. The only people who might be interested in that as a proposition would be established manufacturers looking for a fast track into a performance engine they could manufacture themselves. Or maybe a company prepared to foot the bill for a showboat with their name on the tank. One thing was certain, the motorcycle would have to do a lot better than it had to date to attract such interest.

Nonetheless, John sent a letter to Rod Coleman with his estimate of the costs of producing a single Britten motorcycle. He put that figure, including all the imported cycle parts, at NZ$38,000, although he wrote that the sum could come down if he manufactured the machines in batches of ten. 'I have designed this motorcycle and motor to be the best in the world,' he added, 'and in a matter of months I will be able to prove that this motor produces more horsepower than any other twin in the world.'

It is interesting that John indicated a couple of months rather than a couple of weeks. Perhaps in his heart of hearts he knew that Daytona was not going to be the magnificent triumph he and Gary already seemed to be celebrating.

CHAPTER EIGHT

Stateside

Allan certainly was not celebrating as he worked frenetically to finish the second engine, and it became increasingly obvious that it would have to travel after the bike had been dispatched. John was keen to have the spare and therefore arranged for Allan to fly to Daytona, where he was to catch up with the rest of the Team.

> John did not intend to go to Daytona due to the pressure of work and he asked me to go. I was in two minds about making the trip because I knew the bike was not ready and it would take several miracles to even finish a race, let alone win. On the other hand a free trip to Daytona would be interesting and at least I'd learn something. And so I decided to accept and eventually I found myself flying off with an engine in my bag. When I eventually arrived at Daytona Airport I phoned the Speedway Inn where Goody and his crew should have been and was given a number to call. I called it and Goody answered, taking me aback somewhat with the news that he was at home in Canada, that he would be driving down and that it would take two to three days. With nothing better to do I hired a car and spent the time getting lost all over northern Florida, visiting Disney World and so on. I also went to Orlando Airport, where the race bike had been sent. I wasn't able to collect it but I did organise the customs clearance and verified that it had arrived intact. When Gary and crew finally arrived we collected the bike, took it to the track and set about getting it scrutineered.
>
> People's reactions to the bike were interesting and quite a few of the Americans thought that 'Britten' meant 'Britain'. I was constantly asked if it was the new Cosworth. Scrutineering, which is called Tech Inspection in the USA, posed a minor problem when the officials couldn't find a frame to wrap their tag around, and it was only after a lot of head scratching that it was attached to a fork leg. Passing the noise test, however, was a much bigger problem. We knew the bike would have to be below a specified decibel level at Daytona, but John refused to take it seriously. He

always thought such rules didn't apply to him; that they were for everybody else. Consequently, the bike had no silencer on it at all, just an open megaphone, and of course it was way too loud. My final desperate solution was to buy a can of baked beans, cut the top off, punch the bottom full of holes and wire it over the end of the megaphone. It probably cut power by about 80 percent and it was still a little too loud, but the officials took pity on us and passed it. Of course, the can then 'fell' off before the bike took to the track.

I'd been talking to John on the phone each night and he suddenly decided that he would come to Daytona after all. I think he arrived at about the time of the bike's first practice session. By then we were reasonably organised. Gary had driven down from Canada with a couple of his people, Red-Headed Colin and George Morrin. Red-Headed Colin was called that for obvious reasons and it came in handy I suppose when Colin Dodge arrived the next year. He made himself useful as a gofer and was good company. George, whose day job was as a postman, was a former Canadian Superbike champion. Since retiring he had established Morrin Racing—an outfit that managed various riders and was pretty active in the Canadian racing scene. He earned his keep at Daytona by hustling us a Cadillac from somewhere or other.

In order to qualify we had to do three timed laps, but in several attempts we could never get the bike to run long enough to do this. We were getting pretty desperate when Gary finally persuaded the officials to aggregate two lap times from one session with one lap from another and we were in.

The bike was showing tantalising flashes of its potential but constant glitches, mostly with the fuel system, kept spoiling the show. Eventually, it decided to run on only one cylinder and after much investigation I found a poorly soldered joint in one of the flywheel magnetos that seemed to be the cause of it. We'd run out of practice sessions and really needed to test the repair, so we borrowed a pick-up from a friendly guy at the track, loaded up the bike and starting rollers and drove out of town looking for a quiet country road. Having found a suitable spot, we fired the bike up and John hopped on. To the horror of us watchers, he roared off and disappeared around a bend at high speed on the wrong side of the road. He'd obviously forgotten which country he was in! Luckily, there was no oncoming traffic and the bike was sounding fine. So we loaded up and headed back to the track.

The atmosphere at the track was one of quiet excitement and mostly friendly competition. Allan was delighted one afternoon to find none other than Dr John Wittner, the man who had almost single-handedly dragged the famous old Italian motorcycle manufacturer Moto Guzzi back into motor sport, casting a critical eye over the Britten. To Allan's surprise he singled out the alternator for praise.

> I guess he liked it because of the crafty way I'd managed to squeeze it in. He couldn't have known how precariously it was mounted. Much later, when the next generation engine management system [EMS] was finally working properly, an alternator was mounted in its rightful place on the end of the crankshaft where the flywheel mags had been.

There was much to see from the other teams and in some areas Allan found the Britten somewhat poorer in comparison. In particular, he noted that the finish of the carbon-fibre on many of the other bikes showed that John's work left a lot to be desired. However, the bold Britten V-twin was also attracting its share of interest from other race teams, the public and the media and, in the absence of any requests from John for discretion, Allan had answered their questions as well as he could while working on the bike.

Once John arrived, he quite naturally took over the task of fielding such enquiries and began, in his usual fashion, talking up the machine to a degree that embarrassed Allan. A photograph taken at the time shows Allan crouching down while working on the machine, with a number of sceptical-looking visitors—most of whom were mechanics—watching on as John enthused about his bike to Steve Anderson, the editor of *Cycle Magazine.* Allan had talked with Steve on several occasions prior to John's arrival, and he was mortified to hear John quoting power and weight figures that were significantly enhanced over his own more modest estimates.

> I kind of hid behind the bike and tried to pretend it wasn't happening. These guys all knew that John was exaggerating and I could sense them losing respect for us. It was bloody embarrassing. The silly thing was that what we actually had was really impressive, although we could only prove it if we could persuade it to run reliably.

John's tendency to exaggerate was a curious but consistent aspect of his character, matched by an equal tendency to understate the problems he faced. But there was inevitably some kernel of truth in the exaggerations, a glitch on a dynamometer read-out that might promise hidden horsepower, or a best-scenario addition of component weights that might suggest a sum total just a few kilos shy of the reality. John wanted to make a splash for any number of reasons, ranging from enhancing the possibilities of future sales to establishing himself as a recognised international designer and he was, in addition to everything else, a powerful and persuasive salesperson. If, in the heat of the moment he stretched the truth a little, then that was, to him, just part of the game.

It is also probable that for John the difference between where he was at any particular moment and where he was going next was an out-of-focus landscape. What was sharply in focus, however, was the vision he carried in his head of the ultimate destination.

Of course, Allan was right, the truth was remarkable enough without what were, to him, embarrassing embellishments. But John's joyful passion for the project, and for its future, was a factor that contributed enormously to the growing awareness among the small community that shared his motorcycle dreams that the Britten was something special. At Daytona, John revelled in the opportunity to rub shoulders and swap stories with some of the motorcycle world's foremost independent, free-thinkers and, if he made himself look silly from time to time, he also made a number of powerful friends and allies.

As implied by the description 'independent, free-thinkers', such individuals who had gathered to race did not enjoy unqualified support from powerful manufacturers. They were on the whole enthusiastic and often ingenious amateurs. Although subsequent publicity, much of it generated by John himself, would claim that the Britten had taken on the might of the world's motorcycle manufacturers and given them a fright, this was hardly the case, then or later. His competition was not the best works teams in the world with all the vast resources of their respective factories behind them. His competition was largely keen-minded individuals like himself who wanted to achieve their individual visions outside the uniformity that strictly production-based racing imposes. That is not to say that the factories did not follow events with keen interest and levels of support that varied from the occasional hand to active assistance in development.[93]

The dominant force in Pro Twins racing at this time was the Fast by Ferracci version of the highly successful 8-valve 851 Ducati (bored and stroked to 888cc), with perhaps 118 bhp at about 9500 revs. Like Dr John and Moto Guzzi, the Ferracci team enjoyed a close relationship with the factory, but again it would be misleading to see them as a bona fide works effort. However, Ducatis were certainly there in numbers. Reigning US Champion Dale Quarterly was riding for Fast by Ferracci and was tipped as the favourite. Also astride an 8-valve Ducati, with American pistons giving a capacity of 907cc, was three-times US BotT Champion Jimmy 'Rubber Ball' Adamo.

The well-known American race bike engineer Don Tilley was there, too, with his enormously developed Harley-Davidson. Saddled with a twenty-year-old gearbox (the only five-speed the factory had made to that point), the Harley made about the same all-out power as the Fast by Ferracci Ducatis at an absolute maximum of 8000 revs. Not in evidence was any sign of the long-awaited 10-valve, double overhead camshaft, water-cooled Superbike that Harley, and particularly Jerry Branch, had been developing.

An immensely talented New Zealander by the name of Brook Henry was there with his Vee Two Engineering RV-1 (formerly known as the Webrook Ducati), ridden by Owen Coles. Brook, who based himself in Perth, Western Australia, had made a name sawing the right-hand sides off 900cc bevel-drive Ducati engines in order to convert them to belt drive. His team fronted with an immaculately prepared machine, which they had christened 'Alchemy', boasting a beautiful frame made by fellow New Zealander Ken McIntosh.[94]

Alan Cathcart, now somewhat mollified since his accident at Ruapuna on Aero D One, was there on another Australian Ducati, the ex-Kevin Magee/Bob Brown Pantah, which he was forced to ride when he experienced problems with his factory-supplied 8-valve. Two French riders on 888 Ducati Superbikes and a strong contingent of US riders, also on Ducatis, including five on 8-valve machines, completed the Ducati line-up, a formidable array.

The only Japanese-powered entry in the race was the Commonwealth Honda. Boasting an 857cc version of the Honda 750 V-twin dirt-track engine that could spin up to 10,000 revs, it made about 115 bhp. This year it was ridden again by the diminutive Australian rider Paul 'The Angry Ant' Lewis, the man who had looked all set to win the event on the same machine the year before until his engine broke.

Among the rest of the front-runners were two very special BMWs, one of them a Japanese entry. The German Handrich-Mayer BMW featured Krauser 4-valve heads and a Krauser space frame with maybe 105 bhp at 8200 revs. The Japanese BMW team had constructed their own frame and were running 2-valve heads with a claimed 95 bhp.

This then was the competition. It was tough because it was experienced. The riders were talented professionals. The machinery was reliable.

The 80-km race was becoming an increasingly popular part of Cycle Week, while a declining list of international entries characterised the main event, the Daytona 200, and associated 250cc races. This was due in large part to a lack of both start money and guaranteed prize money for overseas entries in the principal events. A further contributing factor in the decline of the 200—a race that had helped spawn international Superbike racing—was the insistence of the American Motorcycle Association (AMA) that only machines available for road use in the US could compete. This rule put the race at odds with the international Superbike fraternity by outlawing machines such as the Honda RC30 and the Bimota YB4. The Pro Twins Grand Prix, however, the race the Britten Team was there to contest, had attracted a record number of foreign entries and promised a thrilling spectacle for race fans.

Record numbers walked through the pit area before the race and the undoubted star of the entire show, according to Alan Cathcart, was the Britten. He later wrote that the machine drew 'a constant stream of admirers to its garage and was the unquestioned hit of the Daytona paddock. It's unlikely there will be much to match the Britten at Daytona for the conceivable future.' He added that 'while it was running it was undoubtedly the fastest bike on the track as Dale Quarterly found out when Goodfellow passed him on the banking!' Less encouragingly, Alan also noted the ongoing problems the Team were experiencing with the fuel-injection set-up.

Race fans were not disappointed with the race, which provided an epic struggle between Adamo, Lewis and Quarterly, and saw the last pip Lewis by a wheel length for the win after all three had tussled for the entire 80 km. Predictably, things did not go so well for the Britten Team, but it was not a day without honour. If anything can be described properly as a flash in the pan, the race was just that for the Team, but it was at least a bright flash. Alan Cathcart watched the whole thing from slightly astern and recorded the Britten's brief showing.

> When the flag fell Lewis charged into the lead, using the better acceleration of the lighter Honda to head off the Ducatis into the first turn. But before he got there he was overhauled by the incredible Britten, which lit up like a firework from the second row and out-dragged everything else to the turn. But then, tragically, Goodfellow slowed, banging his fist on the bodywork in frustration as the engine went dead. A fifty-cent connector in the fuel injection-wiring had broken—but not before John Britten's new creation, a device shorn of the eccentricities of his first effort, had made a considerable impression on US Pro Twins racing.

It was typical that John should blame a simple connector for the failure, and it was understandable that Alan Cathcart would repeat his explanation as fact. The truth was, however, that the Britten Team had no idea why the race bike stopped. Next time they tried it, according to Allan Wylie, it ran perfectly.

After the race was run there were the usual sessions when all the 'what if' recriminations and praises were aired. Third place-getter Jimmy 'Rubber Ball' Adamo was quite famous for his somewhat abrasive nature and his comments to Gary were less than encouraging.

'You're not gonna waste your time on that thing any more are you?' he asked.

Others were more congenial. Allan remembered standing at a urinal next to race-winner Dale Quarterly, who enquired cheerfully if 'you all are gonna bring your scooter back next year.' At that stage nothing had been decided about the future of the project and Allan could only respond that it was up to John.

The Team did remain to watch the main event, however, the Daytona 200, which Gary was to compete in on his Yoshimura Suzuki on the following Sunday. In the opening laps of the race he set a blistering pace and was comfortably settled in second place as the field began to string out. Then he encountered the one thing road racers dread as much as mechanical failure—oil on the track. He hit it at the worst possible moment, while braking hard for the high-speed chicane. Gary recalled:

> I was about to lap this Canadian lady rider, when she fell and oil wound up on the track. You speed up when you hit oil, and I was already doing about 140 mph so I came down hard.

The resulting spill was spectacular, with Gary and the bike cartwheeling and somersaulting down the track. Finally, he slammed into the wall of straw bales wrapped in plastic, a violent impact that added to the list of injuries he'd already sustained. An ambulance carted him off to hospital where he was found to have fractured his left arm, his right foot and most of his ribs. It was a nasty accident that effectively finished his season, although he still eventually came fourth in the final Superbike point standings.

With racing over, all that remained to be done was for John and Allan Wylie to deliver the bike back to Orlando Airport. But Allan remembered that even this simple journey did not pass without incident.

> On the trip from Orlando back to Daytona we were travelling in heavy traffic on the freeway at about 60 mph. John, in his usual impatient manner, was relentlessly tailgating the pick-up in front of us, making me nervous. My legs and feet were starting to feel very vulnerable in the forward-control van, and it seems I wasn't the only one made uncomfortable by John's driving, for the passenger in the pick-up suddenly spun around and made as if to aim an imaginary pistol at us. In Florida it pays to take such a warning seriously and John maintained a respectful distance from then on.

In the meantime, back in Halifax Hospital, Gary had been trussed up in plaster and was anticipating a long and exceedingly expensive stay.

> The Yanks didn't have the Canadian system of medical care and it was costing me thousands of dollars a day. Under the terms of my race contract with the AMA I wasn't allowed to discharge myself either, which really annoyed me. I knew I had to get out of there or kiss a fortune goodbye. Then we were told that there was going to be a space-shuttle launch and patients who were up to it would be allowed up on the roof to watch it. I got in touch with Red-Headed Colin and we cooked up a plan. Even though the Cape was a fair way away we got a great view of the launch from

> the roof, which was five floors high, and then while everyone was still watching the thing going up, Red-Headed Colin, who is a big fellow thankfully, picked me up and carried me down the fire escape. We drove straight out to the airport and caught the first plane out. The flight went to Denver and there were only first-class tickets available, so that's where and how we went. From there we picked up a flight back to Vancouver. I paid the bill as soon as I got home but the AMA were really pissed off about it and kept sending me threatening letters for quite some time.

While Gary was taking flight, John and Allan were also winging their way home. The expedition to Daytona had clearly shown that the bike had the potential to be a winner. It had also shown that over-confidence and under-preparedness were the primary reasons that it had not done better. It remained to be seen if the lesson would be learned.

CHAPTER NINE

Gremlins

John contacted Colin Dodge soon after his return and told him that he was uncertain if they should carry on with the bike. According to Colin, however, he was also far from discouraged, and if he was entertaining serious doubts about the project it did not take him long to get over them. 'I reckon we have the potential,' he told Colin with his next call, 'and I think we should do it.'

But it was a while before Colin returned to the exhausting grind, working for what was now known as Britten Motorcycles. (For some time to come John also used the name JK Britten Engineering.) In Colin's absence the Team had undertaken speed trials on their favourite country roads, where the bike had continued to behave erratically, and it was obvious that they were still a long way from where they wanted to be.

It was the beginning of an exhausting ongoing programme of dynamometer testing, as the Team struggled to find torque, revs, smoothness, responsiveness and reliability. The only dynamometer they could access was at Canterbury University, in the School of Engineering, which they had fortuitously been invited to use. Allan accompanied John out to the university with the race bike on a trailer to meet the faculty member who had issued the invitation, and they discussed an arrangement to use the equipment. However, the vice-chancellor soon got wind of the plan and immediately moved to put a stop to it. All of John's considerable powers of persuasion eventually managed to change the vice-chancellor's mind and the testing was allowed to go ahead, but even then permission was given with the greatest reluctance. It was soon apparent that the chancellor was not alone in his misgivings, as various heads of departments expressed rising concern that such noisy interlopers should be given access to the Engineering School's facilities. By then, however, the Team was in and the test programme was in full swing.

The young man who held the key to the 'dyno room', as it was called, was an engineering graduate then working on his doctorate called Murray Aitken. Murray was clearly interested in the motorcycle programme and started to hang around for the sessions after he'd let Colin and John in. According to Colin, this caused John some annoyance and he warned Colin to 'keep him away from the bike.' Later, however, after Murray had clearly demonstrated his ability to analyse complex problems, John modified his position and instructed Colin that he would let Murray 'do some big sums but he still was not to touch anything.' In time, this would change completely and Murray would become Moriaty (or Murrayati), an integral part of the Team.

In the meantime, the level of effort to get the bike to run right had ratcheted up several notches, as Colin recalled.

> The new pace was enough to make the previous months building the thing seem quite relaxed. We worked day and night, day after day. Sometimes some food would appear. Sometimes it did not. Sometimes John would stop for a coffee. Sometimes I had to make an excuse and head off to a shop somewhere just to get one. He was quite oblivious to such things, utterly consumed by the task at hand.

One of the first decisions to make concerned the troublesome fuel-injection system. The Team had to decide whether they should attempt to refine what they had, find a new injection system or switch to carburettors.

John had spoken to many top tuners at Daytona about the problems of fuel-injecting twin-cylinder racing bikes, and he had concluded from these discussions that no one other than Ducati had yet successfully managed it. Jerry had recommended an American MoTeC Systems unit, but that too seemed something of an unknown quantity and it was expensive. The American Hilborn Injection system, a mechanical device, had been discussed briefly, but it was Allan's opinion that excellent though it was in the applications that it suited, such as speedway and Indy Cars, it was a blunt instrument compared with electronic fuel injection. At that time another race team in New Zealand was struggling with similar problems. Dallas Rankine, owner of the Wellington company British Spares, had sponsored well-known local engine builder Dick Huurdeman and race-bike constructor Steve Roberts to develop an 8-valve Ducati with a Hilborn Injection system. Allan Wylie had witnessed first hand the 'grief and trouble' they had with the Hilborn set-up at the Sound of Thunder in 1989.

> We were having an equally miserable time with our EFI, so the score was nil all. We had starting rollers, which they didn't, and we offered to share ours, which meant that I got to witness their struggles up close. I think they eventually got their system running pretty well, but putting a Hilborn set-up on a bike that came with EFI seemed a backward step.

One thing that was now known was that the throttle position sensor (TPS) the Team had been using was not up to the task. The sensor was simply too frail for the environment in which it operated. A more robust sensor had therefore been procured and was ready to be tested. Naturally, it was hoped this would solve the problems. If it did not, and a reliable alternative EFI system could not be located, John was prepared to reconsider using carburettors.

'John had actually been given a pair of these huge flat slide carbs,' Colin recalled, 'by this guy Ray Plumb from the Commonwealth Honda Team at Daytona. Apparently he just walked up to John in the pits and handed them over. They sat on the shelf for ages and were nearly bolted up on a number of occasions as we struggled with fuel injection.'

In the midst of all the refining efforts devoted to the existing machine, John also made the decision to carry on and build the next two engines (three sets of castings had been made in the first batch), and to proceed with his planned second bike. It was by no means a universally popular decision within the Team. Allan felt that properly constructing and preparing just one machine was stretching their resources and endurance. But he also believed that if they gave it everything they had, one well-prepared machine could win at Daytona, the race that remained their first immediate objective. After all, they knew that if the engine could be persuaded to run consistently they were looking at somewhere around 120 bhp at perhaps 10,000 revs, in a machine that weighed no more than the lightest of the competition and handled at least as well. It was enough to win and to win handsomely. But John saw it differently. Rather than reducing the odds of failure by refining one machine, he was convinced that reducing the odds of unforeseen failure by doubling up on the entries was the way to go. He also wanted at least 145 bhp. It was his call. Allan remembered the final conversation on the matter when he put it to John that properly preparing one machine offered the best hope for victory at Daytona in 1990.

John listened carefully and then rejected the advice, saying, 'Yes, but are you ever really prepared?'

Another essential talent now entered the picture and became a part of the ever-evolving Britten Team. Hans Weekers had recently arrived as an immigrant from Holland, where he had worked with Mike Sinclair at Yamaha Motor Europe. Hans, a slim, tidy individual, had the kind of quiet control generally found in older men. A keen sporting motorcyclist, he had acquired his first machine, a Laverda 750, when he was just fifteen years old. It was the beginning of a life-long passion. After completing a Bachelor of Automotive Engineering, he joined the Yamaha testing and development facility in Holland, where he road-tested prototypes and worked on the dynamometer programme. The Kenny Roberts race team developed Yamaha's

Grand Prix bikes and production racers in the same facility, and it was through this association that Hans met Mike. Hans's test-riding activities took him all over Europe and Japan, while his work on the dynamometer programme in Holland led to some experience working on the shop's milling machine. This latter activity would stand him in good stead when he began drawing up items for manufacture by the Britten workshop because, unlike many designers, he was able to consider how the items in question could be machined from a standpoint of practical experience.

Hans first visited New Zealand to attend the wedding of his sister, who had already settled there, and decided he liked the uncrowded and unhurried nature of the country. Ironically, his first job in his adopted land, as a mechanic for a large Auckland motorcycle dealer, proved quickly detestable to him because the situation there was exactly the opposite of his first impressions.

> Everything was done in such an atmosphere of pressure. We could hardly finish each job properly and consequently the standard of work was very low. I had the greatest respect for the founder and owner of the business, but I could not say the same for those who managed the place.

It was with some relief that he found a job with a company that specialised in converting diesel engines to run on compressed natural gas, a job that entailed a methodical and creative approach to a constantly changing series of challenges.

With his new job came the time to consult on other projects, and it was at this point that John Britten phoned him. John had been given the contact by Mike Sinclair and already knew that Hans not only possessed the experience working on flow benches that Britten Motorcycles needed but had actually built his own bench. Meeting Hans was fortunate, as John had recently experienced a frustrating disappointment when he entrusted a pair of heads to an engineer in Auckland who specialised in tuning Ford BDA motors. The tuner had opened up the ports and had succeeded only in losing a lot of mid-range horsepower. After this dismal outcome John was eager to get back on track, and so asked Hans if he would take over the task of flowing the heads. Hans readily agreed and a deal was worked out.

It is interesting to note that both had a clear idea of the obligations and expectations of the other. Hans had no intention of working for nothing and he always charged for his effort. However, he was also happy to put in many additional hours on his home-made flow bench because it provided data that was of general value to him. John knew that Hans was a rare find and recognised that to keep his interest he would have to treat him as a professional. It was typical of John that he would willingly pay for something he needed and could not get elsewhere, but he had to be asked. Otherwise, he would accept the most inordinate effort without any thought of payment. It is also interesting to note that with this deal there was no subsequent confusion or argument.

In the meantime, Allan Wylie sometimes continued to assist John with dynamometer sessions on the engine, which continued to seize sporadically. One recurring problem, said Allan, was that John still failed to warm up the engines properly even though the problem of cold seizures was well known to them. This was apart from the possibility of a problem with cold oil draining away too slowly from under the cam buckets resulting, at least potentially, in hydraulic lock partially seizing the engine. Although the problem was difficult to quantify, the theory was simple enough. It was believed that once the engine was warmed up, and the oil was therefore less viscous, it could drain fast enough so as not to cause a problem. But when it was cold, the thick oil could form a hydraulic lock under the cam buckets. This would in turn stress the drive belt, which could flick over the cam sprocket teeth. Bent valves were just one part of the predictable carnage.

Allan particularly recalled one such episode when it seemed to him that John dragged him out to the dynamometer simply to watch him blow his own engine up by immediately sending the revs soaring toward the red zone. It was at this point that Allan decided he needed a break.

> With Colin back in the picture and with Murray and Hans involved, John was getting quite a bit of help and I felt it was a good time to leave. Frankly, the frustration and the disillusionment was all getting a bit much for me. I still believed in John's basic concepts, and in the bike's potential, but the way John was running the project convinced me that the potential was not going to be realised any time soon. The different ways we viewed the project, and the right way to carry it forward, caused some stress between us and I believe that damaged our friendship for some time. We didn't get really close again until John got sick.
>
> In the meantime, my house still needed fixing, my motorbike needed riding and I was no longer prepared to sacrifice so much in pursuit of somebody else's dream. Besides, I already had a real job that gave me all the technical challenges that I needed. John had such an amazing ability to draw you into his world and it had obviously worked on me several times. When I did leave the project there was no falling out; I just stopped turning up voluntarily and I heard from John less and less.
>
> I continued to visit from time to time, especially when John set up his workshop across the road from Auto Restorations in Carlyle Street, and I was always keen to talk to the people and see what they were doing. I did assist once with the assembly of the gearbox on engine number three, but for me it was time to move on.

Back on the engine front, Hans finished flowing the heads and reported to John that he could not materially improve them. They represented, he told John, a remarkable achievement. The Team had created a top end that would not respond to further development because it was as good as it could be without a total redesign. John, however, was in no mood to receive accolades. He remained determined to find more power in spite of the fact that the brief run at Daytona had clearly shown there was sufficient power to win and that what was desperately needed was reliability. So Hans now travelled south to join the search for more power, having left the bike shop in Auckland and with two weeks free before he took up a new position with the diesel-to-gas conversion outfit.

On the morning of his arrival at the university, Hans found himself staring at an old English water-brake dynamomter—a machine he knew was quite inadequate to accurately test a peaky, high-revving motorcycle engine.

Nor was that the only problem. Because of the nature of the dynamometer, the engine had to be tested separately with a power take-off on the end of the output shaft. Colin had set up the engine in a jig and so far as that went the arrangement was as good as it could be. The V-twin was fired up with an old twelve-volt starter motor but there was constant trouble with flat batteries and fried battery chargers, irksome complications that constantly eroded precious time.

And time was in short supply. To minimise disruption to the quiet academic atmosphere, the vice-chancellor had only reluctantly agreed to the use of the dynamometer outside normal university hours, but these hours were further restricted, when he complained that running the engine at night was disturbing the peace of the neighbours, many of whom were academics from the university. John refused to accept this and visited everyone who had complained, sometimes with flowers, laying on the charm as he desperately elicited from each of them an assurance that loud, mechanical noises late at night were not, after all, of the slightest concern.

The vice-chancellor remained resolutely unimpressed, however, and, in spite of John's efforts, he pronounced that the engine could not be run after six in the evening. This meant that the motor could only be fired up after 5 pm for one hour, so the sessions tended to be over just as the Team was beginning to get in the groove.

John then decided to circumvent the problem by operating before the university awoke. Hans was apprehensive, but John brushed his misgivings aside and they duly trooped in and started the engine up at 6 am. This resulted almost immediately in the vice-chancellor descending like the proverbial load of bricks and banishing them from the campus for ever. Hans recounted that he had never seen anyone grovel as much as John did then in order to win back their previous limited access.

> Boy, they made him plead and I really did not think he was going to win. However,

> it wasn't surprising that the university people had difficulties with what we were doing. When we ran that engine it would leap around on the jig like a mad thing and it was loud enough to hurt our ears, even with ear protectors on. We were all sure it was going to detonate like a hand grenade and we'd be pressed against the walls, trying to get as far away from the bloody thing as we could. But it never did. That engine did a lot of races afterwards; it was quite remarkable.

On a more positive note, Hans was pleased to find that he enjoyed working with both Colin and Murray. The latter was now increasingly involved in the project and Hans found a kindred spirit in his fellow engineer. Murray, he said, was careful with his measurements and sensibly conservative with his conclusions, maintaining a coolly dispassionate and analytical approach. Hans also recalled that no matter how much they swore and cursed over the occasional bout of inexplicable or capricious behaviour on the part of their erstwhile patron, they 'always loved John'.

> From the beginning I had a hell of a lot of fun with John. Some of those times were so crazy I could still not really talk about them without maybe getting into trouble. But they were bloody hilarious. However, the hours we worked really were mad. For some reason they did not seem to affect John, but I know Mike Sinclair always felt strongly that it was not a good way to work. He used to say that fatigue caused mistakes and mistakes caused accidents and accidents hurt people. But we carried on and we did so very much in such a short time. Mind you, it did not feel like a short time then. It felt interminable. John kept us going with this incredible energy he could always draw on. He would throw out this constant stream of ideas about all manner of things. Sometimes they made immediate, obvious sense. Often, however, you would hear them and think that cannot be. That's stupid. Then later, maybe a day or a week or a month later, you would remember it and it would not seem so far-fetched. And then you would start to think about it and suddenly it would not just seem possible. It would seem sensible, elegant and clever.

During early testing the Team was particularly concerned with operating temperatures, that the engine was developing hot spots and that these were causing some of the engine seizures. For a while, the two-ring Mahle pistons were suspected and full-skirted Ross pistons were tried, but that seemed to make no difference. Finding the cause proved elusive and frustrating. Colin remembered stripping an engine after one cold seizure and examining in minute detail the piston skirts, the piston crown and the cylinder bore without really gleaning any meaningful information.

The Team became extraordinarily fussy about warming up the engine, something that was easier to do when John was somewhere else, and changed the type of oil they were using. Much of the time they were running the engine as a single cylinder so that changes could be tried more quickly and cheaply. They lacked the time to test everything in sequence so they could really nail down the problems, but a combination of intuition and frantic work largely succeeded in producing a reliable engine—although seizures would always remain a cause of concern.

Throughout the test period drive belts also regularly snapped and many expensive American Delwest titanium valves were bent and written off. Hans was sceptical that hydraulic lock was the real cause of the problem, as the engine would run happily for long periods before the belt suddenly broke and the engine went bang. Like the cold seizures, the cause of the problem remained largely a mystery, but one way or another, by trying everything they could think of, they finally got on top of it.

One system that remained obdurately unreliable, however, was the EMS. In spite of all the modifications that had been made to the Auto Logic system it refused to work reliably and it was clearly time to try something new. But just what to try posed a major conundrum for John. He knew that none of the systems available had been developed for a big race bike and that spending a lot of money would give no guarantee of success. There was, for example, a Bosch system that on paper looked as if it might do the trick, but at NZ$40,000 per unit it was a lot to pay out for a system that might well prove to be as big a dud as the one they already had.

At that point John heard about a second local manufacturer who seemed worth talking to—David Steward, whose company Steward Electronics made an EMS system in Auckland. In a letter responding to John's initial inquiry, Steward wrote that his system was fully digital and that it managed both fuel and ignition advance, whereas the American MoTeC (and the Auto Logic system, come to that) managed only fuel. He informed John that his EMS computer fired the injectors sequentially and was synchronised to the intake cycle in a similar fashion to the pricey Bosch MPI.7 set-up. He suggested that, because the system could be set up to use any input as the main load-controlling variable, John use a throttle opening-sensor to control the system, which is what they were in fact already doing.

'The system,' Steward reported, 'sets the fuel quantity an advance amount at thirty-two positions of the main load-control variable at every 100 rpm step in the rev range.'

He further noted that the computer had tunable corrections for any input, including air temperature, engine temperature and altitude. Finally, he assured John that although the standard computer would require a slight enhancement to cope with the irregular timing of the 60-degree V-twin, 'this should not be a problem'. Nor could he see any problems with jointly fabricating a lighter case for the unit should one be desired. At just NZ$3375 all up John was definitely interested.

The very reasonable price did not discourage John from trying to persuade Steward to supply a system gratis in return for the international publicity and market interest John believed he could generate, but Steward firmly rejected the idea. John then requested that he be allowed to try the system on the dynamomter, but this was similarly rejected. Instead, Steward offered a hire arrangement for one month for about a third of the cost of the unit, to be credited against the cost of the unit in the event John purchased it. John went with this deal and thus began one of the most acrimonious relationships in the record of the development of the Britten motorcycles.

The first thing to do was to get the new system hooked up to an engine on the dynamometer to see what they had. Unfortunately, 'what they had' in the first instance was a terrible tangle of wires and an EMS that resolutely refused to manage the ignition.

By an act of good fortune, BEARS supporter Dennis White heard of the troubles with the new EMS and introduced John to Mark Franklin, the man who had set up the timing gear at South Eyre Road for the BEARS speed trials.

Mark was a softly spoken individual who generally only ventured an opinion after careful consideration, but he had a sly sense of humour that appealed to John and the two hit it off. In spite of Mark's perennially youthful looks he had worked for a quarter of a century for Air New Zealand's Instruments Section, which was based at Christchurch Airport, servicing their equipment. The facility also repaired and restored instruments for a variety of customers, including the Australian Airforce. Mark, who was a Norton Commando rider and a fervid BEARS supporter, told John somewhat redundantly that he knew a little about wiring and offered his assistance.

> I went around with him to the university where they had the engine set up on the dyno and saw this massive confusion of wires going all over the place. John needed a wiring loom for the thing and I was able to make him one that did everything it was supposed to do. I guess I just slowly got sucked in from that point on.

Unfortunately, a great deal more than a wiring loom would be needed before the system would work properly.

Although Colin Dodge suspected that the heart of the problem was the lightness of the components, the Team continued to struggle to eliminate spiking, which messed up the ignition maps, and other failures throughout the summer of 1989–90 without fundamentally changing the system.[95] A second major disappointment was the fact that, in spite of David Steward's assurances, the unit remained resolutely incapable of running the ignition system. At one point the bike was actually sent to Auckland for Steward Electronics to rectify the problems, but according to Colin they did 'only a half-arsed job on it' and tension continued to grow between Britten Motorcycles and Steward Electronics.

> The system would eat maps and the print-out would deliver nothing other than strings of zeros, but Steward's only response was to say that it couldn't happen. He accused me of causing the problem, demanding to know who the stupid bugger working on it was. We were trying to achieve our objectives and were not interested in defending anything that did not work. However, when Steward's stuff crapped out all he seemed to want to do was to accuse us of breaking it.

Despite the continuing unreliability of the EMS, and all the other complications such as the continuing seizures, the search for more power continued at a furious pace. However, the Team had completely worn out their welcome at the university and until they could come up with another dynamometer the only way to test an engine would be in the bike, on the road. Such testing was highly unsatisfactory while, as Colin recalled, important details were still being refined.

> In addition to trying to get the EMS to work we were playing with things like the shapes and lengths of the inlet trumpets in order to tap into more grunt, and configurations and lengths of exhaust systems. When the bike first went to Daytona it had a single exhaust system and we decided to try a dual-pipe set-up. We found this delivered more ultimate power but less torque through the range. John decided that more torque was more useful than all-out power and so we mostly ran the bike through the next season in New Zealand with the two-into-one exhaust on it.
>
> We also found, however, that a lot of the changes we tried with the exhaust system made no appreciable difference. We tried, for example, different pipe diameters with no measurable effect, and once we tried these really long, skinny pipes. John and I tore up South Eyre Road[96] at six in the morning only to find they, too, made no difference. John hated sharp bends, so the exhaust systems were always beautiful, flowing things but the engine did not seem that sensitive to variations within sensible limits.

Just as Hans had predicted, the engine delivered between 118 and 120 bhp when it was running right, and there it stuck. If John wanted more power he would have to take Hans's advice and more or less start again with new heads.

Progress on the second bike was rapid and it, too, was taken on a trailer out to South Eyre Road for testing, mostly like its twin in search of reliability from the fuel-injection system. At various times John, Chris Haldane and Robert Holden rode the machine, but the lion's share of testing fell to Colin.

Like most of the straight roads that grid the Canterbury Plains, South Eyre Road had a good smooth surface with gentle undulations, but it was only really just wide enough for two cars to pass one another comfortably. On most 'test' mornings John would make a run and then Colin would make several. He would roll the throttle on and off, then snap it open and shut, simulating racing conditions in order to fine-tune the electronic fuel map. Nearly all the flat-out runs fell to Colin, as John would tell him, with an apologetic grin, that his wife had forbidden him to do such things. Colin remembered that a friendly cow-cocky generally showed up, leaning on his gate and offering the use of his paddocks should they require them. Colin could not imagine what they might have wanted the paddocks for, but he did not fancy a high-speed entrance onto them through the tightly strung wire fence.

Colin had little experience of riding bikes, 'being more a four-wheel person', but he gamely hopped on what was even then one of the most powerful motorcycles ever devised and wailed off in search of its outer limits.

> We would get there at first light and spend half an hour before buggering off home. I really appreciated the way the vision would narrow as I leant over the tank and went for it. The computer print-out showed we were getting about 160 mph with me sitting squarely in the middle of the road. When I spotted a vehicle coming the other way I would slow down to about 120 mph and then speed up after it went past. On one occasion a black and white cop car flashed by in the opposite direction, but the officer was staring straight ahead as if I didn't exist. Sometimes between blats I'd look at the sheep on the other side of the fences and think about what would happen if one walked out on the road. But I was always keen. To me those runs were an awesome bonus.

John was distracted briefly from the problems of the motorcycle project when Rod Coleman introduced him to Robert (Rob) Ianucci, a New York lawyer with all the gritty characteristics usually associated with that background, and a completely dedicated motorcycle enthusiast. Rob and Rod had first met after Rob purchased an 'empty' AJS Porcupine for his collection of classic motorcycles. Rod had close associations with Porcupines, both as a former works rider for AJS and as a keen collector and restorer himself, and Rob had therefore contacted him in pursuit of 'innards' for his machine. After Rod subsequently accepted an invitation to visit and stay with Rob in New York, the two became friends. Rod, whose own collection of restored classic motorcycles eventually numbered nearly eighty, was astounded by Ianucci's private museum of works racers.[97]

Ianucci was in New Zealand as a guest of the Classic Motorcycle Racing Register when Rod telephoned John to introduce the two men to each other. Rob then came on the line and told John—who hadn't a clue who he was talking to but listened attentively all the same—that he was interested in representing Britten Motorcycles internationally. Their subsequent pleasant exchange of faxes seemed to open up all sorts of exciting possibilities. Ianucci was certainly well connected and his interest in Britten Motorcycles was at the very least flattering.

As the end of 1989 approached, John felt confident that they had solved enough of the problems to enter the first race bike in the coming New Zealand Formula One series. Chris Haldane, who had just returned from racing in Japan, agreed to ride the now red, white and green bike and Colin undertook the job of mechanic.

> John refused to learn anything about operating the laptop and he was never comfortable with basic spannering, so I suppose I was the only one who could do the job at that point. I did appreciate that John was a broad-brush-stroke design and engineering type. I knew he had more pressing things to do.

Although Colin had no previous experience of computer technology he was an able mechanic and with Mark Franklin's help he found he picked up the necessary computer skills quite readily. Basically, the computer was used to adjust the programming of the electronic fuel injection to deliver torque and horsepower settings throughout the rev range to suit particular tracks. Or so the theory went. In practice, it was more often a case of desperately trying to get the bike to run properly when it seemed the existing programme had somehow degenerated.

On 18 and 19 November the bike was on display at Manfeild during a World Superbike Round, a short respite before the Formula One Championship began.[98] Gary Goodfellow had come over from Canada to race in the Superbike event, where he managed a highly credible third place, and the meeting turned into a very enjoyable get-together for Gary and the Britten Team. John had decided to use the event to do a bit of fundraising for the forthcoming trip to Daytona and had hit upon the idea of a raffle. Entrants paid NZ$10 for the chance to win a ticket to travel with the Team to Daytona. Dennis White, who went along to support the Team and sell tickets, remembered that there was no shortage of takers.

> We sold all the tickets and John did pretty well out of it. The fellow who actually won was a guy called Lew Grant. He was a BEARS supporter at the time but not a club member. Later on he joined up and eventually became president, so he was a fitting winner.

After Manfeild it was time to head north to Pukekohe for the first round in the Formula One series. On race day it rained and the bike ran dangerously cool. Water also affected the electronics, and a minor place and a DNF (did not finish) were the best Chris could manage before he headed back to the South Island for the following rounds of the Championship. The rest of the season brought mixed results for Chris.

> I remember the race at Timaru best. I was doing really well in third place with the bike running absolutely superbly and we looked set for a pretty good finish. Then when the machine was grunting out of the hairpin it suddenly lost drive. I pulled off the track and sat there with the bike still in gear, idling beautifully, and thought I must have broken the chain. I was really quite surprised when I looked down and saw that it was still there, but there was nothing for it but to switch off. When we tore the bike down we found that the teeth were all stripped off the primary gear. To save a bit of weight John had had it ground down to just half the width we had been running and it failed. I never really understood why he would take a risk like that, but that was John.
>
> The final race was at Teretonga in Invercargill and that was one I'd rather forget. Once more I was up in the top four and once again I was going well for a high finish. This time it came to a very abrupt halt. I was in fourth gear and about halfway round the big 160-degree sweeper that follows the very long front straight. I was doing about 150 mph, cranked over as far as that fat bodywork would allow, when it suddenly went out of control and spat me straight over the high side onto the track. I picked myself up and limped over to the bike, which was lying on its side idling away in gear with the back wheel turning. The first thing I noticed was that the rear suspension rod running across the bottom of the sump was broken. John wasn't at the track but afterwards he was quite snaky with me and he insisted that the fracture was accident damage. Which meant, of course, that the crash was my fault. I never accepted that. The bike hadn't been leaving big skid marks coming out of that corner before, but this time there was a big one leading to the crash. We ended up coming fourth overall in the series, which I considered satisfactory given the successive failures we had suffered. I humped around for a few weeks feeling sore and I guess I was pretty annoyed with John's attitude as well.

The set-up for the rear suspension was one of the few things that Colin and John had been unable to agree about. Colin considered the off-centre bell crank poorly designed and engineered, and had anticipated that it would give trouble. Following Chris's accident, John went through the computer print-out and working back from the data decided that the mechanism had broken as a result of the crash rather than vice versa. In spite of the compelling case John made for his obviously preferred scenario, Colin remained unconvinced.[99]

Colin worked at a frenzied pace to finish the third engine, with the usual brutal regime of exhausting hours that allowed few comforts. On Christmas Day 1989 he took time off from the project only long enough to scoff down lunch with his family. As always the Sound of Thunder meeting at Ruapuna was only weeks before Daytona, and although John was reluctant to run a machine there he felt a powerful obligation to the BEARS fraternity to do so. The result of his decision to honour the obligation meant, of course, less time all round, along with more work over longer hours. For there were two Britten V-twins entered in the 1990 Battle of the Twins at Daytona—to increase the odds. Whether they would increase in the way John hoped or Allan feared remained to be seen. One thing that would not detract from the possibility of winning, however, was the choice of riders, with Gary on one and Robert Holden on the other.

In spite of his most recent experience with the bike, Chris Haldane accepted John's invitation to ride the number one Britten—now referred to as 001—at Ruapuna. In the first race, the bike, sporting a smart new blue and red colour scheme courtesy of Bob Brookland, thrilled the 10,000-strong crowd with a display of absolutely crushing superiority. In pouring rain Chris hammered the V-twin around the familiar track and pulled out an entire lap on the rest of the field. John, whose eyes were steadfastly focused on the impending race at Daytona, became concerned that Chris might be thrashing the machine to the point of risking damage, or worse that he might fall off, and started making frantic slow-down signals from the side of the track. Chris, whose eyes were steadfastly focused on the race in hand, ignored him.

> I was blowing everyone into the weeds and I wasn't slowing down for anyone. Everything jelled and no one could get near me. Jason McEwen tried to claw me back on the Anglo's Ducati 851 and went down big time on the kink after the dipper. After the race I was looking forward to going out and doing it again as the rain had stopped and the track was beginning to dry out. And then I had this really silly conflict with John about tyres. The track was now patchy but there was still plenty of water around. I'd been on wets in the first race and because I'd goosed the rear I wanted a new intermediate one. No doubt a drying track would use it up, along with what was left of the front, but that's motor-racing. But John disagreed. He said the Team was short of tyres for Daytona and insisted that I go out on slicks. It was a crazy decision. On the warm-up lap I nearly crashed and so I just pulled the pin and went back into the pits. I was really angry, and even when John apologised I couldn't help thinking that his actions could have gotten me hurt. Again! People were absolutely

> rapt in our showing in the first race and then we looked like complete idiots in the second.

If John felt like an idiot, and it would seem that he did judging by his apology to Chris, he did not dwell on it for very long. He had too much on his mind. Although the bike had gone brilliantly, he could not, infuriatingly, draw confidence from the performance. In spite of Colin's struggles with the EMS, the system continued to behave erratically. The worst of it was that although Colin had now wrestled it to the point where it could deliver a faultless performance, as it had just done at Ruapuna, it could also, abruptly and without warning or easily traceable cause, fail.

John had borrowed a second EMS from Steward Electronics, an EMS given reluctantly only because of such successive and largely mysterious failures, to use as an emergency backup and he now neglected to give it back. Of course, he needed it to run the second machine at Daytona. He made no secret of the fact that he was dependent on it, but he also made no secret of the fact that he considered that Steward Electronics had failed to deliver him the EMS they had contracted to deliver—a reliable unit that could manage a race bike. He therefore unilaterally suspended the relationship pending further results.

'When John refused to return the second EMS,' recalled Mark Franklin, 'it really got up David Steward's nose. He saw correctly that John was virtually getting two for the price of one. Of course, that was pretty irrelevant when they still did not do the job, but the action escalated the growing tension between him and John.'

Unfortunately, time had run out. Regardless of the rights and wrongs of the situation, two Britten motorcycles were due at Daytona and they would have to run with the EMS units as they were. Any recriminations or explanations would have to wait.

Britten Number Two, 002, was finally assembled on the day both machines had to be shipped out, more or less immediately after the Sound of Thunder. There was time to start the bike up but not to road test it before the nails were driven home in its crate and it was delivered out to the airport. But there was still work to be done on the third engine before Colin and John could leave, and Allan Wylie was roped in for a final time to help. He assembled the gearbox but found the parts poorly machined.

> Nothing fitted properly and I complained to John that for whatever reason this guy he'd roped in to do some work for him wasn't doing a good enough job. However, John defended the work and I was happy to escape without getting roped in again.

The gearbox was not the only thing to cause grief during the assembly of engine number three, and for a while it looked as if the Team would have to race without a spare. Typically, however, John refused to accept expert opinion that a critical casting was useless and unsalvageable. Colin recalled the eleventh-hour strategy.

> The bottom crankcase for the third motor had buggered up when it was cast and Rob couldn't machine it up. We had to get more material pigged up inside it and that warped it. John took it to a crowd in town who said it was stuffed and that nothing could be done with it. John ignored that and set to with a ball-peen hammer and belted it around until it was more or less the right shape. After that Rob was able to machine it so we could still build a third engine.
>
> Once it was assembled there was just time to briefly start it before we split it in half for the journey. The top end went in my backpack and the bottom went in a box and then we were off to Daytona.

After landing in Los Angeles, John and Colin uplifted their luggage and engine and took advantage of a spare day to visit Jerry Branch.

'Jerry liked the head,' said Colin. 'He had a quick peer at it and said it was a good-looking thing, but he immediately wanted to get in with a TIG and put another valve in it. I guess that is when John started thinking about doing the same thing.'

The following day they flew on to Orlando, and after arranging a van and a motel they uncrated the bikes in the car park and started work. As usual, Colin recalled, there were still pieces to be assembled while 002 had yet to be road tested.

> John was still trying to do too much. He never seemed to learn that you could push too far and lose the plot. We were still sticking bits and pieces of bodywork on the second bike along with ancillaries like the oil-catch bottle. We got it running again and puttered around in the motel car park but John was keen to find a backcountry road to have a serious blast on. It was probably just as well that we didn't find anything suitable as Americans frown on that sort of thing and our cause would not have been helped by John being thrown in the local pokey. So we waited until we got to Daytona.

When both bikes were more or less ready they loaded up the van and drove to Daytona, where Robert Holden and Gary Goodfellow were waiting. As he had done the preceding year, Gary was also riding a Superbike in the 200 and he was there with his usual team. Every one had a bit of a smile when Colin was finally introduced to Red-Headed Colin, and then John and Colin unpacked the bikes and started them up. To John's disgust, they encountered an immediate problem with the original EMS, which was running Robert's machine. To make matters worse, the computer printer they now had began to play up and they could scarcely read the information it was spitting out. This made it doubly difficult to identify the cause of the problem and, to the enormous frustration of the Team, a persistent misfire continued to plague Robert's bike throughout the week leading up to the race. John had carried the computer for both bikes with him as hand luggage on the flight from New Zealand and he wondered if the airport's X-ray machine might not have scrambled the program for Robert's bike.[100]

A further worry for the Team was the discovery of metal swarf through the engine that Colin had brought over as a spare—in spite of the thing having been started only briefly before their departure. Closer inspection revealed that the oil pump had not been functioning correctly, and as a certain amount of wear and tear was evident they gave it a thorough clean, assembled it and put it aside, crossing their fingers against it being needed.

Electronic problems now also began to dog Gary's bike, although as the management system worked more often than not it had obviously escaped being scrambled at the airport. As the bike was brand new, only a minimal amount of mapping of the fuel-injection and engine-management chip had been completed before departure from New Zealand, and Gary therefore had to complete the mapping by the seat of his pants with the dash-mounted tuner. Thankfully, he soon had the machine running reasonably well when it ran at all. On qualifying day, however, the EMS decided to run only one cylinder and it was as much as Gary could do to persuade it to do three-quarters of a lap at a time—which meant long, time-wasting retrievals whenever they sent him out to try the thing again. Colin eventually traced the problem to a blown transistor in the computer, but by then qualifying was over. For the second time Gary found himself pleading with reluctant race officials to let him start. This time he had to employ every arrow of persuasive power he had in his quiver—arrows sharpened, furthermore, by years of selling motorcycles—before they finally gave him permission to start, ignominiously from the back of the grid.

Infuriatingly, the electronic gremlins had not yet finished playing with him and during tyre scrub-in on race day another transistor in the computer blew. Once more Colin worked desperately to find the fault, measuring components to try to find the origin of the glitch. Finally, he traced it to incorrectly labelled Bosch injectors and he rewired the system to suit. His last-minute labours worked and Gary was able to take his place as the rearguard of the pack.

A final problem awaited him, however. His bike, 002 (Robert being on 001), was equipped with a new twin-pipe exhaust that had not been tested before. For the moment, John recognised that his machines would have to comply with noise restrictions and both Gary's twin-pipe system, and Robert's two-into-one system, incorporated effective mufflers. Through the season in New Zealand, with Chris riding, the single-exhaust system had, however, exhibited a severe resonance problem that had repeatedly fractured the rear air-box, and finally the Team were forced to bog it up with lots of goop to keep it together. It was immediately apparent, however, that the new twin system was even worse and the sound it made coming down the back straight caused Colin real concern.

In the lead-up to the race the two riders had been struggling to complete three- or four-lap practices, but despite their lack of success John still felt confident he had sufficient data from the outings they had managed to determine the amount of fuel that would be needed to complete the race. It was, he thought, less than a full tank, a handy weight-saving. When race day arrived, and Colin filled the tanks of the machines, John therefore instructed him to remove a certain amount from both bikes. Although Colin protested strongly against the plan, John insisted and he therefore began to take fuel out of Robert's bike. Attracted by the fuss, Gary wandered over and once John had left, he told Colin in no uncertain terms to leave his fuel alone.

'Bugger the weight,' he said, 'I'll take the gas.'

Despite all the problems, however, the two riders started well. Robert tore off after the race leaders from his twelfth-place grid position and worked his way up to fifth place on a machine that was running, in John's words, 'as sick as a dog'. But somehow or other it kept going and Robert stayed out there, finally working his way up to third. He would have crossed the line in that position, too, but on the last corner of the last lap he began to run out of fuel, with the spluttering bike dropping back to fifth before crossing the line. As Robert's bike was hauled into the pits John apologised to Colin over the fuel debacle.

'It was interesting,' said Colin, 'because in all the time I knew him it was the only time he ever apologised to me for anything.'

Gary had also gone surprisingly well for most of the race, his electronic gremlins now suddenly inactive. After the start, he had blasted his way through the field with a display of aggression and power that went some way to restoring both the morale, and the general standing, of the Britten Team. He had worked his way up from thirty-fourth to eighth place in just four laps, passing Ducatis, Moto Guzzis, Harleys and all as he hustled his way toward the front of the field. But as he proceeded through the minor placings, the rider immediately in front of him blew the race line on a corner and forced him onto the grass. He managed to stay upright but then had to let the whole field go past before he could rejoin the race. Undeterred he set about repeating his heroic charge.

Once more, he carved his way back through the field and once more the prospects of a high-place finish began to look increasingly hopeful. Then, as feared, the vibration from his twin-pipe exhaust fractured the rear air-box and the engine began to gulp superheated exhaust fumes. Gary used the handlebar mixture adjustment to lean the mixture out progressively, but was unable to improve on seventh place, immediately behind Alan Cathcart.

After the race, when the crew looked at the feed-out from the computer, they were amazed at the temperatures Gary's bike had sustained without either melting something or seizing, and the general consensus was that they had been exceptionally lucky to finish as well as they had with both machines.

One thing was clearly needed and that was more development time. Once again, the race had shown that when all went well they had the required pace to win—the bikes were timed at a highly impressive 175 mph on the straight—and the search for reliability would doubtless release at least a little more power. How best to pursue that development was, of course, a matter for consideration. When Gary suggested that both machines be left in his care, so that he could race them in Canada with Colin doing the spannering, John thought it over and agreed. So did Colin. It was his first trip abroad and he was eager to see as much as he could. And so while Gary flew home to Vancouver and John winged back to New Zealand, Colin spent the next week with George and Red-Headed Colin driving north in the van with two Britten motorcycles in the back.

CHAPTER TEN

Inheritance

The race bikes were not the only things that John left behind as he flew home to New Zealand. Also missing was 'one Britten motor V-1000 # 001 complete. Less only fuel-injection system, ignition system, exhaust. All pursuant to terms of agency contract between JK Britten Engineering and undersigned', the undersigned being, of course, Robert Ianucci.

The bike's clear promise at Daytona had impressed Ianucci and had encouraged him to consider seriously how he might market a limited run of engines. However, by the time Rob and John met at Daytona, two further players who were interested in the engines had entered the picture.

Following Gary's brief but spectacular display on the Britten at Daytona the previous year, Alan Cathcart had been busy singing the bike's praises and the journalist-racer and John were now firm friends. As early as late March 1989 he had sent a fax to John informing him that 'there is a strong opportunity for you to supply engines to a European company you will certainly have heard of—Bimota.'

Of course, John certainly had heard of Bimota, a boutique Italian manufacturer that had earned a deservedly illustrious reputation for its race bikes and road-registerable replicas. In particular, the company's Tesi, a Ducati-powered hot-rod with a revolutionary single-arm front suspension, had made an impact—both on the racetrack and on the streets—that was impressive out of all proportion to the small numbers produced. Cathcart went on in the fax to explain that he had previously been instrumental in initiating talks between the Italian concern and Norton to arrange a supply of the latter's rotary engines.

Bimota, who did not make their own power packs, was in trouble because the air-cooled Ducati Pantah engines they had been using had been discontinued. Unfortunately for them, the new generation of water-cooled Ducati motors were all needed for pumped-up Ducati production for at least the next two years. In the meantime, a fresh Aprilia V-twin engine that Bimota had signed up for was way behind schedule. To add to their woes, the Norton deal had then fallen through because, said Cathcart, the English company intended competing head to head with Bimota in the sports-bike market.

Cathcart reported that he had already contacted Bimota boss Giuseppe Morri with details of the Britten, writing, 'I don't know the Italian for "Shit off a shovel" but I think I conveyed its performance adequately.'

Sure enough, the technical manager of Bimota, Pierluigi Marconi, soon after sent John a fax asking for a full set of specifications for the Britten motor, promising that his company would 'of course warrant you the maximum reserve with the information.'

The third interested party was an American outfit by the name of The Classified Motorcycle Company. The company's CEO, Dan Wilson, had already corresponded with John, helping him source alternative supplies of cam belts as well as enquiring about the possibilities of being supplied Britten engines immediately before Daytona. Under pressure of time, and because of the possibilities offered by the proposed deal with Ianucci, John had fobbed him off, promising to get back to him after the race. By the time he did, however, further players had entered the arena.

It must have seemed to John that his bikes had the entire motorcycle world talking. And this after they had won only a couple of local races on the most remote racetracks in the world.

On the other side of the Pacific Ocean, and of continental North America, Gary Goodfellow and Colin Dodge had settled into their racing and development programme. The new base was, of course, Gary's latest successful motorcycle retail and repair business in Vancouver, and Colin soon found himself drawn into the relaxed Vancouver lifestyle. Compared with the dizzying whirl he had just escaped, his new circumstances were not far short of a perfect idyll and his short break easily became a long-term stay. With time to spare, he prepared the two bikes for the coming local season, refining a number of details that he had previously judged unsatisfactory, refinements he knew John would have opposed as being not worth the trouble. When racing commenced it was a relaxed, once-a-month affair at the Westwood track in Vancouver and, just once, in pouring rain, at Seattle. Colin spent hours testing both bikes on a dynamometer Gary organised, but the EMSs were still dogged by computer glitches and progress was negligible. Either they went, it seemed, or they didn't.

When they went, of course, the Brittens did so very well, and when, on a couple of satisfying occasions, they were able to display some of their potential they began to attract something of a local fan club. Canadian race crowds, it appeared, were ready to love the big V-twins just as much as the New Zealand crowds had.

According to Gary, by the time they finished the season the bikes had carved out an enduring niche in the hearts of the passionate Vancouver race fans who faithfully filled the stands at Westwood. A highlight of their Canadian season was a first-place finish in an Open Pro Superbike race, when Gary comprehensively defeated a field that included Yoshimura Suzukis and RC30 Hondas, all being campaigned with a degree of factory support. During the race he also posted an average lap of 96 mph, a new lap record. Here at last was the first international victory John had been waiting for and, indeed, the occasion could later be legitimately viewed as a turning point in Britten fortunes.

After the race, Gary added to the Britten's growing reputation by confidently informing the local press that, 'the machine could go faster still', a prediction he fulfilled during his next and final, appearance at the track, when he shattered his own lap record. The local paper, The *Province*, published a photograph of the man they also now called 'Goodie', riding around on his victory lap with a chequered flag grasped in his left hand under the bold heading 'Britten Lapping It Up in Westwood Adieu.' Gary at last had something to be excited about.

> We concentrated on the newer bike and developed it into an absolute weapon. There were problems, of course, with the EMS but otherwise it hung together pretty well. The time the back suspension collapsed was a rare exception. It was about halfway through the season and I was beginning to feel really confident with the bike. It was exceptionally fast and it handled beautifully, so I was chucking it about and sliding it all over the place and we were going faster and faster. This particular time I had it sideways, powering out of the esses, when it just kind of went 'donk'. The back wheel was rubbing on the inside of the bodywork and we just shuddered and shimmied to a halt.
>
> The only time I actually lost a race otherwise was to Steve Crevier, who was riding my Superbike. I wanted to run in the National Championships but they shut us out due to some homologation crap. By then we had 500 people turning up at the track on Wednesday night just to watch us practise, so the decision was really disappointing for the fans and me. Everyone wanted to see it run in the Nats and it was just a damn shame that it wasn't allowed.

Back in Christchurch, John was over the moon about the result in the Open Pro Superbike race and he scrawled out a fax to Gary, which read 'Congratulations and thanks! Thanks for having faith and riding so well. I wish I could be there.'

And in Christchurch, the *Press* reported the victory on 13 July with a story entitled 'First Win Sweet for Britten'. In the accompanying interview John was particularly pleased to draw attention to the presence at Westwood of various factory-backed machines. He went on to say of his own machines that, 'there's never been a bad mechanical failure. It's always been trivial things like a spark plug cap or loose wire on the computer.' He added that he had 'the product but not the backing. The factory-backed Ducati which won at Daytona had cost $300,000 to prepare for the race.'

If his comments seem to gloss over the odd major structural failures—like the one that had so unceremoniously dumped Chris—or the real status of the opposition, or many of the problems the bikes continued to experience that were far from trivial, his final comments reveal something more than a tendency merely to exaggerate. It was, perhaps, the first overt example of a habit that would in time cause some strong resentment and disappointment among those who had given generously of their time and talent to the project. For, in spite of his fax to Gary, he also did not hesitate to claim all credit for the victory for himself, attributing it to his 'single-mindedness'.

Throughout his life John Britten remained unapologetic for this attitude. If pressed, he would later say that propagating the myth that he worked in splendid isolation in a back shed had always been a very deliberate strategy. He would say that the myth was necessary to win the widespread sympathy and support that is traditionally the preserve of loners and outsiders. It was a debatable point of view at best. Even had he granted full recognition to the parts played by the rest of the Team, he would hardly have diminished the romantic lustre of the endeavour, or even the impression of underfunding and isolation he habitually cultivated. Nor would it have tarnished his own tenacious and often brilliant contribution, both as a designer and as the project leader. However, he often displayed an essentially generous spirit and on a number of occasions very publicly acknowledged what the press would increasingly refer to as his 'small band of dedicated helpers'. However, the small band remained largely nameless, faceless and sadly, in the case of those who found themselves unable to continue, often quickly forgotten.

It is also interesting to speculate what the true cost of his 'preparations for Daytona' might have been if had he been obliged to pay, or to pay in full, people like Allan, Colin, Rob Selby and Mike Sinclair, in addition to a number of others, for all the work they had done to realise the project. Had he done so, the sum attributed to the Ducati effort may not suddenly have seemed so exorbitant. It is also interesting to note how he continued to attribute the results of underpreparedness and a general lack of development to sheer bad luck.

All of these attitudes would impact on the story of Britten Motorcycles, sometimes in significant and unfortunate ways.

The splendid result at Westwood, however, was a clear victory and it was sufficient to encourage the Dutch Ducati club, organisers of a major BotT event coming up at Assen, to offer to pay to have the Britten compete. This was great news and a heartening indication that a significant degree of international recognition had now been achieved.

By now it was also obvious to John that his hobby had spun out of control and that he could only really indulge in it in the short term if he could use it to write off profits generated in property development. However, to do so he would obviously need to retain total control of the project, and this meant that he was not in a position to make good his various promises to present shares in the project to those who had contributed so much for so little. This was hardly critical while he was pouring money in with no returns, a situation that basically persisted throughout the history of the project, but he found himself confronted with a long-term conflict between what he had promised and what he could deliver. It was a conflict that he was never able to resolve. It was perhaps fortunate for him that those who had been promised a stake never really took him seriously and were mostly content to have merely played a part.

Of course, he was far from accepting that his motorcycle ambitions would never develop to stand on their own, and he thought deeply about the ways and means he might employ to secure their future. At about this time he told a local journalist that he had never calculated the total cost of his motorcycle project because he knew it would depress him. However, he now had a pretty shrewd idea of the money involved and he was also increasingly aware of the fact that the expertise he needed to move forward would not come free. This meant scaling up the project and either selling race replicas or building and marketing street bikes. Another possibility was to establish the company as a prototype design studio. Typically, he decided to do all three.

Meanwhile, the relationship between John and David Steward had reached, if it were possible, a new low point. With Colin complaining that the EMS was a spiteful and perverted unit, incapable of accepting further development or refinement, John was in no mood to accept David Steward's insistence that the causes of the ongoing problems lay entirely within Britten motorcycles. However, John felt that Steward deserved an explanation for his—John's—hardening attitude, and so he wrote to him toward the end of May telling him that, 'I must explain my actions because it is important to me that, even if we have strong disagreements, I'm still, in my own eyes, acting in a reasonable and honorable manner.'

In his letter John complained that he had experienced problems throughout the summer with stray figures getting into the maps. He rejected Steward's allegation that they had been entered in error by Colin, and pointed out that he had spent an enormous amount of time and effort trying to rectify the problem while missing opportunities to win races. He also pointed out that the system had only ever done half its job because it would not run the bike's ignition. He was, he informed Steward, therefore holding back payment on the second EMS until the bikes returned to New Zealand, when they could sort out the deal.

'In the meantime,' he wrote somewhat provocatively, 'you can consider that your EMS is being tested for you in the field. I have been patient over the summer, now it is your turn to be patient in waiting for the motorcycles to return.'

John's attitude enraged Steward, who sent an unsigned, scrawled fax in August 1990, which read in part, 'Until a cheque for the full amount..., NO more info/assistance/parts will be given! Can't you see that by breaking agreements with everyone that you come in contact with, you are slowing down or stopping development of your bike? Try thinking for a change.'

Clearly, if the EMS was ever to be sorted out it would have to be done by someone other than the company that made them. As it happened, the very person who could do just that had been waiting for an invitation to do so for some time. Instruments expert Mark Franklin was pretty sure he knew exactly what was wrong and how to fix it.

Back in Canada, Colin and Gary continued to work on the two bikes, but there was no real budget and Colin was again 'living poor'. He was glad of Gary's company, describing him as a hard businessman who respected those who stood up to him, and, because he was reliant on Gary, he was pleased to find him quite generous as well.

> He was also easy to get on with as a rider, although he was always a bit of a showman. Balancing that he was also fast and safe. I ended up staying with him at his home for about six months. It was just as well I had someone to look after me because John was hardly maintaining me. I would regularly run out of money altogether and I'd ring and tell him I had to come home. He would then usually send just enough to patch up body and soul, and would always dangle the carrot that if anything ever came of it all I would be part of it. And then he called and said that we were off to Europe, so at least I was going to see a little more of the world.

So Colin and Gary crated one bike for the trip home to New Zealand while Colin prepared the other as best he could for the Battle of the Twins race at Assen. The BotT race had been organised by the Dutch Ducati Club as part of the popular European BotT series, and it attracted very large crowds. It was therefore an excellent opportunity to show off a Britten motorcycle to the Europeans, always supposing that it could be persuaded to run properly.

There was, however, another important reason for going to Europe, and that was the Cologne Motorcycle Show. This was the same show that John had attended armed with his posters of Aero D One. It is held every two years and happened to be on the calendar just two weeks after Assen. John had arranged to meet representatives from Bimota there and he also hoped to meet a number of other interested parties who might want to discuss the possibilities of having him supply them with engines—in addition to perhaps selling a few race replicas.

Quite apart from the fact that the trip was heavily subsidised by his hosts, the decision to go was a natural outcome of John's growing preoccupation with just what exactly he was going to do with Britten Motorcycles. With this vexatious question in mind, he wrote to Gary to ask his opinion about the game plan they should follow at the Cologne show.

> Do we just promote the bike and then see what response we get or do we have some kind of marketing strategy? Can we sell 20 bikes direct from the factory as a limited collectible race bike with some sort of guarantee of spare parts for X years or is it essential to have dealerships to give the purchaser more confidence in the product? Or do we sell the motors only? Or, better still, the design? Or is the bike best used to promote other products?

Prior to the trip, John once again expended considerable effort persuading a New Zealand government body, in this case the Business Development Centre, to put up some money to cover expenses. In support of his efforts, he again wrote to Gary requesting him to write a letter portraying the trip to the Cologne Motorcycle Show as a marketing exercise. This he did, but the centre rejected the application because they did not fund marketing exercises. However, they were obviously impressed with John and his plans and bent over backwards to assist him, even going so far as to suggest that Gary write a new letter supporting the show as a market research exercise, an activity they did fund. Gary did so and some money was obtained. John then hit up the Dutch Ducati Club for money above the appearance money they were already prepared to pay, wryly adding that the top speed of his bike was over 180 mph and he would understand if they did not want a Ducati coming second in their race. Paul Vink, the organiser of the event, replied that Ducatis had come second once before and that it was still a good race, and furthermore the track was all corners so top speed did not matter. The club, he assured John, would do its best to secure funding, adding gracefully that it would be great to have an exotic machine like a Britten at their meeting. He climbed out on a thin limb to secure more money for John, even proposing that the club dip into its financial reserves.

'I was almost thrown out of the club for that,' he wrote to John later. 'Fucking money!'

After further negotiations, mostly between Gary and Paul, the club offered a generous arrangement of cash up front and a share of the gate. Paul pointed out that neither the Britten nor Gary Goodfellow were known in Holland and that some effort would have to be made to make them both familiar to the public in order to recover the club's hefty investment. They were extremely successful in doing so, and by the time the Britten arrived the race organisers had stirred up a great deal of excitement and curiosity.

John then decided to send his second bike, explaining to Paul Vink that the machine would travel at his expense and that having another on display would doubtless help the club in their efforts to promote the Britten.

He also contacted Rob Ianucci and asked him to return the engine he had, so it, too, could be displayed at the Cologne show. When Ianucci had borrowed the engine one of his express intentions had been to show it to Harley-Davidson, as both he and John hoped the company might be interested in either buying the technology or taking over the project as their race programme. This he had done after extracting promises from Harley-Davidson that they would not dismantle the engine. After a number of months, however, and without any kind of response from the American manufacturer, John had grown concerned at the length of time they had held his motor and he began to press for its return with growing urgency.

At the same time, he was confident that some of the work he had done marketing his product elsewhere looked likely to produce some returns. He therefore sent a copy of the contract he had signed with Ianucci to his own lawyer and asked what 'effect it might have on any orders or sales opportunities that might come my way at Cologne'. The contract was clearly tearing apart along the dotted line, but it would only be after threats of litigation had flown hither and thither that the engine would finally be returned. When it was sent back, John immediately had the motor torn down and complained that it was clear from the engineering clearances that the motor had been stripped and reassembled in the US. If this was the case, given the origin of the inlet tract design, the episode must rate as one of life's little ironies.

By 1990 the Dutch Ducati Club's annual race meeting at Assen had grown into a well-attended event, attracting a number of top entrants from within Europe. Already it was felt the club should be extending its challenge across the Atlantic and the governing race committee had given Alan Cathcart, who was an honorary member of the club, the job of drumming up interest in the event in the US—particularly among BotT and Classic competitors at Daytona. He had also been elected to recommend an outstanding competitor who the club might invite as a sponsored guest, and by a twist of fate it was this circumstance that opened the door to the Antipodean Britten.

Paul Vink, who continued to play a vital role in arranging the visit, had been involved in the Assen meeting from its inception, as he wrote later:

> The Dutch Ducati Club was founded in 1978 after a Ducati only circuit meeting at the track of Zolder in Belgium. By 1985 we attracted over 300 Ducati only entries and 2000 spectators.
>
> In 1987 the Zolder managing board decided that the Dutch Ducati Club race was now too big and made too much noise, so we had to change the venue. I was now part of the Dutch Ducati Club Race Committee and we began negotiating with the TT circuit at Assen. Our first meeting there was in 1987 and it could have been easily the last. We had a huge crash in the V-Twin-A class (a forerunner of the BotT) with one of the most beloved club members dying in hospital a few days later. We were put off racing for quite a while and during the winter there were strong discussions in the Dutch Ducati Club about going on or quitting altogether. When we finally decided to go on it was on the condition that we had to improve safety dramatically, meaning that we should run the event as a full-sized international event, with monitors and so on. The costs would thus double and that meant that we couldn't rely on the entry fees as our sole source of income. This meant we had to transform the club race into a professionally run international meeting which would attract 5000 spectators. In our view we had to add non-Ducati classes to the event and we decided on having Classic and the BotT races. The committee decided that I would be responsible for getting a representative grid and possibly Ducati factory-entries.
>
> Our first effort was an immediate success because we secured two new factory 851s, one to be ridden by Baldassare Monti, later a Suberbike ace, and the other by Walter Cussigh, an endurance racer. We also landed Steve Wynne's Ducati, which was to be ridden by Wayne Mitchell, and Roger Marshall who agreed to ride the famous Quantel Cosworth. The top of the German BotT riders Hartmut Müller also promised to come with his Norton F1 rotary along with Bernd Seeber on the VV-OAS II, a spectacular BMW with hub-centred steering. Finally, and most essentially, Alan Cathcart accepted our invitation to race the Bimota Tesi.
>
> We finally attracted some 7000 spectators and had over 60 entries in the BotT race. I was standing on the roof of the pit-building when the field was flagged away and I could hear the roar of the crowd above the thunder of the bikes—man that was truly emotional stuff.
>
> In the end the Battle of the Twins race was won by the Quantel Cosworth. The race drew a lot of attention in the motorcycle press and put our venue firmly on the map.
>
> BotT racing, and by now Sound of Singles racing as well, was making its mark all over the world. In 1990 we were inspired by Alan Cathcart, who had been made an honorary member of the Dutch Ducati Club, to add a Sound of Singles class and

to elaborate on our success with the BotT race by trying to get an even better entry list. Our targets were the Ducati works bikes, the Norton factory rotary F1, the Two Brothers Honda Team, The Dr John Moto Guzzi Team, the Fast by Ferracci Ducatis with James Adamo riding one of them and the Vee Two Engineering Ducati. Alan Cathcart was appointed to be our ambassador and he agreed to promote our event among the competitors at the BotT race at Daytona. The American teams were mostly unavailable due to colliding dates, but we aroused the interest of Dr John Wittner and the Moto Guzzi Team. This was good news but then Alan also produced this unknown quantity, the Britten, which he said had looked promising at Daytona. I knew of this creation through a little article in the German magazine *MO* and knew that it was high tech and that the Daytona bike was a new one. Alan succeeded in interesting John Britten to attend our meeting but after the first contacts via fax it appeared that we had to negotiate with Gary Goodfellow, who raced the bikes in Canada. Gary stated that only the costs of travel and expenses were to be met but estimated this at DFL10,000, about US$5000 at the time. This was a very tough demand, because getting the Dr John Guzzi with Dutch GP ace Kees Doorakkers was only the half of the amount. We spent two meetings discussing if it was worth the money but could not agree one way or the other. In the meantime, however, we obtained quite an amount of sponsorship to bring the Britten and the promise of some television coverage along with a lot of pre-race publicity in the Dutch motor-mags and the German magazine *MO*. With this in place we felt more confident to take the risk of bringing John and his machine over, even though we knew we would have to work hard to introduce the Britten to the public.

We were finally convinced that we should pay the money to get a racer nobody knew on a bike nobody would understand on a track they had never been to before because we were convinced that having John there in person would help to sell the bike to the public. Imagine our concern then when after everything was confirmed he told us he wasn't going to come after all. It spelled disaster. It was only the personal contact that I'd had with Alan, Gary and John that had given me the confidence to convince the other members of the committee that the Britten would be worth its money. After all I only had their word for it and now the man himself wasn't going to show. By then, however, it was too late for me to do anything about it.

Back in New Zealand, the Team were working frantically to complete the rebuild of the second machine, now virtually a new bike, and when the work came together with a few days to spare John decided he could go to Assen after all. The night before John left, he strolled into Phil Payne's shop with a bottle of Scotch. Phil was also off to Europe, to fulfil a dream by racing his Vee Two Alchemy at Monza, in Italy, and he was finally crating up his just finished machine after weeks of frantic effort. Later, he remembered John being pleased that someone else was also heading off halfway around the world with a bike that had yet to fire a shot.

> I hadn't slept for about three days and I felt completely wasted. The press came around after John and I had had a bit of a session and took photos of me looking unshaven and wild-eyed. John's whisky probably didn't help and he looked as crazed as I did—we looked like the worst pair of wicked heads in town. Even though, like John, I was completely stuffed I was quietly excited and really looking forward to being in Europe. BEARS had kicked in NZ$500 for my trip and I felt that John and I would both be representing the movement. It felt good to know we'd be in Europe together. As it worked out, however, I didn't run into him that time. My race at Monza went well and I managed a tenth place in the BotT race before I had to head home. So I didn't get to Assen. I left the bike with an Italian guy called Dino thinking I'd be right back to do some more racing. I didn't realise it would be two years before I returned.

In the meantime, Gary and Colin had arrived in Assen on the Wednesday before the race and met up with Paul Vink to clear the machine they had consigned from Canada through customs. To their intense consternation, they discovered that the paperwork was way out of order and the bike was effectively impounded, as Paul later explained.

> I was assuming that Gary would have arranged a Carnet de Passage for the bike since it was going to the big show in Germany to be exhibited at the White Power stand. However, Gary thought, and he was right I believe to think so, that I would clear the customs for him. As neither of us had done this customs wouldn't release the bike. It was then that Gary informed me that John after all was coming himself. He also confirmed that he would be bringing the other Britten although it was not apparently ready to race. We had a real problem on our hands but at least the news that John was coming was good. However, it was imperative to get the Canadian bike through customs and the only way to do it was by paying a bail of US$25,000. This really stumped me for a while. I didn't have the amount, the Ducati club didn't have it and Gary himself sure didn't have it. I decided to contact White Power because they would suffer too if the bike remained in custody. After phoning and faxing for two hours, WP agreed to deposit the amount and let a bank confirm the guarantee. So after three hours of sweating and desperation the bike was released.
>
> I had arranged a van for the Team and a bed and breakfast in Assen and they unpacked and then drove off to Zolder where Alan Cathcart was to test the bike. However, they were actually withdrawing the bike from Dutch jurisdiction because

> Zolder is in Belgium and we didn't have free borders back then. If they had been caught they could have been charged with smuggling and the bond money might have been at risk. Fortunately we didn't have a lot of control at the borders either and so I decided to take the risk and let them go without telling them about it. I thought they could always claim ignorance that way, but fortunately there was no bother.

When Gary had first heard the idea of having Alan Cathcart test a machine at Zolder he had expressed grave reservations about allowing the English writer to ride the machine, reminding John that, 'last time he crashed, blaming the bike'.

He did not hesitate to share his feelings with Alan.

'I gave him shit,' Gary recalled. 'I told him that the bike had real power, not like the crap he was used to. I warned him not to let it bite him and generally let him know that I had my eye on him.'

In spite of Gary's misgivings, the session went well and Alan Cathcart was duly impressed with the Britten, referring to it in subsequent articles as the fastest special and probably the fastest V-twin in the world. For John, the test had been a very deliberate strategy to generate a news story for the international motorcycle press that would, in Alan's words, 'let the world know you want to either sell the project to a recognised manufacturer or else put it into production yourself'. Having achieved the first part of that objective, and with the session having stayed nicely on two wheels, it was time to sally innocently back across the border into Holland.

In spite of having the acid placed on them for the US$25,000 bond, White Power treated John and Colin as honoured guests. Colin remembered that as well as being exceptionally hospitable they were also especially generous, giving John a new set of their latest suspension and the use of their workshops.

With everything under control for the moment, and with both bikes sitting snugly in the WP workshops, John offered to take Colin for a quick tour through Germany, Italy, Monaco and France in the van. Colin felt the trip was by way of a thank you for all he had done, and the pair had a relaxed time following their noses and stopping whenever, and wherever, the spirit took them. Once they were back at the well-equipped White Power workshop in South Holland, they made sure everything was as it should be with both bikes, confident that with a week up their sleeves they were looking good for the main event.

There was a huge surprise in store for John when some days before the race his father, Bruce, turned up and announced that he intended to stay for the big day. John was, according to Colin, tremendously excited to have his father with him and immediately decided that they would all share the room he and Colin had back at the delightful little hotel WP had organised for the team.

John's delight was short-lived, however, for Bruce soon revealed that the purpose of his visit was to pass on the news that he was leaving Ruvae and that he would in future reside in Australia, in the coastal resort town of Noosa in Queensland, where Brittco had various investments, including a supermarket. In addition to leaving home, Bruce also announced his complete retirement from business, and so a somewhat incredulous John suddenly found himself in control of the entire family firm.

The announcements, according to Colin, were a terrible shock for John, who had to absorb them while continuing with all the final preparations for the big race. Later, he would tell his friends that as a result of all the pain and confusion he felt over the news he made a solemn vow to himself that he would never abandon his own marriage.

However, in spite of the dramatic news, there was now finally a chance for John to show Bruce what Britten Motorcycles was all about. When the motorcycle project had first started, Allan Wylie remembered Bruce and Ruvae turning up at Auto Restorations to have a look at the goings-on, but it was clear, at least to Allan, that they did not at that time really understand or approve of their son's strange enthusiasm. 'They were really nice about it,' he remembered, 'but Bruce particularly was puzzled by it all. And you couldn't blame him. I was sometimes pretty puzzled myself.'

This time, however, Britten Motorcycles was no disparate collection of parts in a dimly lit workshop. It was a rising star in a bright firmament. The word was out that the Britten was an outsider worth watching, and the big crowd that was already beginning to gather to witness the enormously popular race was abuzz with talk of the quiet genius from the other side of the world and his fantastic creation.

Back at the shared accommodation, Colin was finding living with both Brittens somewhat trying. Bruce, he said, had little sympathy for the late hours he and John worked and was highly critical of the fact that they were still asleep in the morning, albeit at a still early hour, when he had already completed a good, brisk walk.

> He was a dogmatic bugger and although I met him as a stranger it didn't take him long to tell me all the things I was doing wrong. John kept the peace and explained to me that his father had virtually given up all his friends because they had allowed themselves to grow old. Sleeping after sunrise was to him a sign of the sloth he detested in his contemporaries and worked so hard to deny in himself. We co-existed but I couldn't say it was comfortable.

Saturday morning of the race weekend quickly arrived and with it a new set of problems for Paul Vink, who yet again had to pull several rabbits out of his hat to keep the Britten entry in the hunt.

> I got the chance of pushing the Britten into life together with Colin Dodge for the first of the three BotT training-sessions and it was as if there was suddenly thunder in Assen when amidst a large crowd the Britten exploded into life! I got a blast of pressure in my face from the exhausts when it fired up, which told me this was no ordinary engine. Then at scrutineering we sailed through with no problems—only admiring looks.
>
> However, our next stop was the sound-check and this time we met some very big frowns. The Britten was producing 113 Decibels (Db) where only 110 were allowed. That was a big problem because the jury wouldn't budge. So while John and the Team started thinking of ways to silence the beast we went into some lengthy discussions with the Technical Commission to persuade them to let the Britten take part. Finally it was decided that the Britten could train but that the bike would have to comply before it could take part in the race itself. Then the training got under way and after a couple of laps Gary went missing. It seemed that he went off the track in the southern loop because it had rained a little.

For Gary it was a decisive moment.

> The fact is that I just slid off the bike when I hit the damp track. The bike was fine but I cut the tendon of a finger on my right hand pretty badly and it looked awful. When it eventually healed it was set at a strange angle and it's stayed that way ever since. However, I had it shot full of painkillers and then I went to the race officials and showed them that I could still work the throttle but they wouldn't listen. So I was out and that was that. Something about the way that incident turned out persuaded me that it was time for a change. I remained committed to help John in any way I could but I never raced again. There and then I retired.

The 'something' that occasioned Gary's catharsis may have been the way John reacted to the accident. To Gary's dismay, his friend lashed out at him, accusing him of jeopardising all they had worked for in return for a moment of showboating. It was hardly fair, but John was now under tremendous pressure and there was no obvious answer to the problem.

But Paul Vink came up with a solution.

> The bike itself was OK but at eleven o'clock on Saturday morning it suddenly seemed that all our efforts had been wasted and we would have no Britten on the grid. For a while I had no clue as to what to do next. However, late in the afternoon I incidentally met Stefan Piwek, editor of *MO* who were the co-sponsor of the meeting. He

> told me another bad-news story about the German Superbike champ Hayri Winter. It seemed Hayri could not start on Sunday because of terminal mechanical troubles with his machine and would be without a ride. It occurred to us that the Britten had no rider and putting two and two together we dreamed up this unlikely combination. By now training was over and it meant that we had to convince Race Control that Hayri Winter was to replace Gary in the race without actually having ridden on the Britten. Again we received the most co-operation one could hope for. It was decided that on Sunday morning Hayri could feel his way round, riding in the Classic Demonstration provided he didn't get in the way or upset someone. Now there was one formality left—since Hayri hadn't trained, where should he be on the grid? After some discussion we all agreed that he should be on the same spot Gary would have been—seventh place.[101]

On the Sunday morning Hayri did a few laps and came back into pits very impressed with the performance of the bike, convinced that he could acquit himself and the Britten well in the race. The crowd, too, had become even more enthused with the Britten. Although it was too late to improve his grid position, Hayri, riding the machine for the first time, had nailed the second-fastest time in practice. However, there was scarcely time for the Team to exchange a few grins before disaster struck once more.

'The day was suffering from typical Dutch weather,' recalled Paul Vink, 'with clouds and sunshine constantly changing places and with always the threat of rain. Fifteen minutes before the start a heavy downpour soaked the track and again it seemed the Britten might fail to appear since there were no rain-tyres for it.'

Indeed there were not. And such was the ferocity of the downpour that sections of the track were left completely awash. The start was therefore delayed and when the rain stopped Paul, with the confidence of a local, reassured the Team that it was likely to hold off for at least another hour. With the prospect of a drying track, Hayri took his place on the grid and waited for race officials to declare conditions dry enough for racing. Meanwhile, back at the pits, there was absolute pandemonium as those who had the luxury of wet and intermediate tyres tried to figure out the right combination for the race.

The track was still slick with rain when the flag fell, and rain specialists like the German rider Oliver Schmidt went out hard to work up a lead before the track dried. Schmidt, who clearly relished the conditions and went straight out to the front, was chased hard by Robert Holden. The two riders thrilled the cheering crowd in the stands as they blasted down the start/finish straight in a huge vortex of spray, braking just as late it seemed as ever they did in the dry, while the Britten cruised around in the middle of the field. By lap two a dry line was beginning to show and

Hayri was able to up the pace, gobbling up the mid-field before attacking the front-runners. By mid-race the dry line was almost right around the track and those on wets were beginning to suffer heating problems as the cooling puddles evaporated. Back at the pits, the Team became increasingly excited as the Britten really began to get going. The exhaust had been stuffed full of polypads to pass the final noise test but the inevitable loss of horsepower was hardly apparent. Suddenly, the sun was shining brightly and the Britten was the bike to watch as Hayri scythed through the field up to third place.

'The crowd was going absolutely mental,' said Colin, 'roaring with approval when Hayri went by. By lap six we were in third place with four laps still to go. The bike was clearly so much faster than anything else and we knew Hayri had time to blast through to the front. We all thought we were going to win. Then the EMS decided to play up again and our race ended.'[102]

Back in the pits, Bruce was stunned. He had no idea that his son had attempted something so big, or that he was so obviously close to triumphant success. The sheer brilliance of the spectacle dazzled him, while the reaction of the 10,000-strong crowd to his son's creation, and to his son personally, utterly overwhelmed him.

For John, however, the race was another infuriating and bitterly disappointing failure, as Colin recalled:

> John always hoped that each time we played with the EMS we would somehow do something that would finally solve all the problems. I'd hear the engine start to go br…br…br…br and I'd just think there it goes again; I wonder what it is this time. However, John had a completely different reaction—he was so emotional about it. And at Assen he did exactly what he always did on these occasions. His head went down and his shoulders slumped and he cried out, 'I just can't believe it!'

If there was still a deficit between the disappointing race result and the positive public reaction to the bike, the compensation offered to John by the presence of his father more than made up for it. In the same way that all the other new fans at the track recognised the brilliant potential of the new Britten, and by extension the brilliance of its designer, Bruce suddenly appreciated his son for the individual he was. It was perhaps the greatest reward John could have asked for in return for his tireless efforts, and in spite of the confusion and pain his father's plans had caused him, he basked in a moment of powerful reconciliation, mutual enthusiasm and acceptance.

After the race, the English magazine *SuperBike* interviewed both John and Gary. John proudly told reporter Grant Lewis, who had raced an 851 at the meeting, that the Britten was the world's fastest 1000cc twin, the world's lightest 1000cc twin and the world's strongest 1000cc twin. Plus, he added, it boasted total mechanical reliability, a claim that neatly avoided any mention of electrical reliability.

Lewis, who was clearly impressed with all he had seen of the bike over the weekend, largely accepted John's contentions. In an article, entitled 'The Battle of Britten' and subtitled 'Enigmatic engineer, John Britten stands alone against the might of Ducati', Lewis later wrote that, 'the designer and builder is out there proving it on the race tracks. The bike is a direct one man challenge to the supremacy of the Ducati 851 in Battle of the Twins races around the world.'

John also used the interview to announce his intention to build a number of replicas for sale to anyone who wished to race in the Battle of the Twins and who could front up with US$50,000, about the price of a factory Ducati 888. Such customers, he explained, would be guaranteed a same-day-as-ordered parts-dispatched service.

Gary backed up John's enthusiastic appraisal of his own machine by telling the reporter that it was the best bike he had ever ridden.

> It handles better than anything I've ever raced. The power is perfect and it has a good top speed. The weight distribution is perfect too—it's all low down; it's very easy to ride. In the wet the bike will slide and when it grips there's no wobbling or weaving—it just resumes its course, steady as a rock. It has good power up to about 9,800 rpm but it begins at 4,000 rpm, and its driveable all the way.

John underlined the engine's tractability by telling Lewis that it made so much power because it was a longer stroke, a view he would soon review with dramatic consequences. He confidently told the reporter:

> Our stroke is 72 mm while the Ducati's is way too short at 64 mm. The bike will do 180 mph as it stands and rolls. The only thing slowing it down is the wide frontal area. We put tape over the radiators because they're too efficient. We don't need such big radiators because as a V-twin the engine has a very large surface area. Cooling isn't a problem. When I've fitted some slimmer ones the bike should hit 190 mph no problem. The bike hasn't drawn much serious attention yet and we hope Cologne will change that. We'd like to do something with it but if no one buys the design, we'll carry on and do it ourselves.

Hayri Winter was also answering questions from the motorcycle press, and being an established champion his comments carried considerable weight, as Colin noted.

> Thankfully the bike had done enough to satisfy him that all the sensational things

> that John had been saying about it were true, and he did not hesitate to share his regard for it with the press after the race. The fans already loved it, and having Hayri confirm their high opinions of both John and the bike was pretty terrific. I know it meant a lot to both John and his old man, so that was good. But that damned EMS was really pissing me off. I knew there were all sorts of things we needed to do to refine the bikes but until we could get them to run reliably there was no way to go forward.

Next stop for the two bikes was Cologne, for display on the White Power stand at the famous bike show. Here, the Brittens were a big hit and attracted an enormous amount of attention. Also, as Alan Cathcart had predicted, Pierluigi Marconi was at the show and he was indeed interested in Britten engines.

In the article Alan wrote for various motorcycle magazines following his test ride he also noted the Italian's interest in the engine, quoting him as saying:

> John Britten has designed and developed perhaps the only engine in the world today that gives the bike designer a completely free hand in chassis design by ensuring from the beginning that it is strong enough to be used instead of a normal chassis. He has given people like me the sort of four-stroke engine we would build ourselves if we had the opportunity. The fact that the specification also includes such important details as a narrow valve angle, correct bore to stroke ratio and excellent breathing with a direct inlet tract, as well as having been designed from the start to run on electronic fuel injection, makes this a very modern engine as well. I hope to be able to build a Tesi around it, if a self-starter can be incorporated successfully.

According to Alan, the Italian had indicated he would take an initial supply of thirty engines once details like the electric start had been finalised.

It is hard to know just how seriously John took any of the invitations to supply completed engines to established manufacturers. The prospect was so fraught with complications, not least of which was the cost and reliability of his engines, that it is hard to imagine that he ever seriously thought he could do it. However, he had already given some thought to the matter of attaching a starter motor to his engine, a challenge that presented some fundamental problems.

Primarily, they centred on the fact that large motorcycle engines, and especially large, high-compression, twin-cylinder engines, require commensurately big starter motors spun over by commensurably big batteries, neither of which is desirable in a carefully pared-down sports bike. The answer, John believed, was to go back to a bit of traditional technology, the decompression lever.[103]

Marconi was not the only designer interested in the Britten engine. Fritz Egli, the famous Swiss designer, was also keen to order a batch of six with which to equip his own BotT racers.[104] Such interest was much more to John's taste, offering as it did a fast track out of the myriad confusions that arose when he contemplated building a Britten engine for street use. Alan Cathcart reported John as saying that he'd 'rather hand the whole project over to Bimota, who have the means to put the bike or engine into production, rather than do it myself. I really only like building prototypes and developing them to the point that they achieve something. After that I tend to lose interest and want to get on with the next thing which right now is an aeroplane I've had an idea for...'

Was it possible that the attention John was receiving from such respected motorcycle engineers, engineers who furthermore needed real answers from him rather than vague assurances, was becoming somewhat daunting? Perhaps. However, the name Britten was rapidly becoming a kind of popular catchphrase. Maybe the thing to do was simply to carry on building and racing handmade motorcycles until something better occurred to him. By now, John had come too far to fail to arrive.

Looking back, Colin felt that Hayri Winter's positive comments, along with the interest generated by the Cologne show, did more to establish Britten Motorcycles' credibility than anything else up to that point. That credibility was soon working for them. John had read about a German dynamometer manufacturer called Dynotech and he was keen to obtain their support. Colin recalled that the company had obviously heard of Britten Motorcycles and when they visited seemed eager to help in any way they could.

> This guy from the company gave John plans and a computer program with a certain amount of hardware for an inertia-wheel dyno. This was exactly the thing we needed, as it constantly measured the energy going into the wheel, giving a torque reading for any given moment. This meant we would be able to get continuous readings, so we'd know accurately what the engine was doing across the whole rev range. It also measured deceleration, so we could also measure the amount of friction in the system.

Although the race result had been far from what John had hoped for, in every other way the European mission had been an enormously encouraging success. He had little time to take satisfaction from such success, however, before news from home brought him crashing down to the very depths of despair. With about three days to go before his scheduled flight out he learned that his father had died suddenly of a heart attack in Australia..

Colin found himself trying hopelessly to comfort John, who was utterly distraught and remained inconsolable. He did the best he could as John fell apart and then packed him off on the next flight to New Zealand, after which he quietly crated up the bikes and flew back to Canada. Shortly after arriving in Vancouver, he received a letter from John confirming that White Power had shipped the bikes back to New Zealand by sea and expressing his hope that it would not take them too long to arrive. He also confided that, 'Dad's death has got me down a great deal. I never knew how much of a step in life it is to have the closest in the bloodline leave you. In a way it is like a part of me dying. All the business matters just make me depressed. It is a sombre, sad job working through all his efforts.' He finished the letter by thanking Colin for his personal support in Assen.

John's life had now completed a U-turn following his days as a wandering, semi-itinerant hippy. He was now entirely responsible for the quite complex business of running and maintaining a considerable portfolio of properties. Bruce's death, however, heaped another level of responsibility onto his only son, because he had also left John, with just a few exceptions, the entire family fortune. Why he did this is difficult to know. Certainly, Ruvae could have expected at least half of her late husband's estate and had she contested the will she would undoubtedly have won at least that in court. To do so, however, was unthinkable, for it would mean opposing her only son. Obviously, Bruce believed when he made his will that John would ensure that all the family's needs were met, but it was still an unfortunate thing to do to the woman who had been married to him for nearly half a century. However, he clearly believed that John should have control of the family wealth in order to pursue his career as a developer and so that was that.

But the first effect of Bruce's decision was more immediate. John suddenly had the power and the means to carry on with Britten Motorcycles. Indeed, he had the means to do rather more than that. He could now drive his project onward and upward; he could shoot for the moon.

CHAPTER ELEVEN

Back to the Bowl

Having inherited a substantial fortune, John could now indulge almost any hobby that he cared to, leaving the family business to take care of itself under Russell Bodington's capable stewardship. However, it was not in his nature to sit back and collect rents, or to allow others to run the company on his behalf, and it was therefore not surprising that he should now choose to explore his new-found power. It was not enough merely to maintain the company. He was a developer now, both by profession and by nature, and he had to develop. The main consideration was the kind of the development he should undertake. Should he repeat the same tried and tested 'formula' development his father had so successfully pursued with prudent and conservative acquisitions of solid commercial properties? Or could he use his position to express his creative talents with something huge, daring, and startlingly innovative? Of course, it was no contest. He would do the latter.

And just to show that Britten Motorcycles was no passing fancy, he would also take that project to fresh heights, and he hoped competitive success, with a new generation of machine that would rewrite all the rules in one bold stroke. Perhaps there would be an established manufacturer, or a big corporate partner, who could manufacture his engine or a sports bike based on his designs. Perhaps not. But there would be a new Britten and it would be so beautiful, and so fast, and so plain bloody brilliant that it would not just turn heads, it would twist necks as it flew past.

Both bikes were now back in New Zealand but Colin Dodge remained in Canada, taking a well-earned holiday. Being a keen mountain man, he made for a ski field, where the team who looked after the sno-cats, graders, blowers and sundry equipment that kept the field running soon discovered his mechanical talents. He rewired something that had blown, and when the rest of the equipment was found to be in poor shape the works manager was sacked and Colin found himself with a job. Furthermore, it paid. His time with the Britten project was coming to a close and he knew it. In his heart he had already decided he had to move on, but the next rounds at Daytona and Assen were coming up soon and he once again agreed to wield a spanner. For two years he had eaten and slept Britten Motorcycles. He had laboured with single-minded dedication to build and develop the first bike. He had struggled mightily and patiently in Canada to try and sort out the problems with the EMS and a plethora of other teething troubles—and he had gone a long way toward doing so. He had lived on the tattered edge and he had asked only for enough to keep going. He had been, more than anybody else, John's loyal lieutenant. But he was tired and the constant presumption of his availability was beginning to annoy him. It was almost time to let it all go.

'I'd been repeatedly promised a stake in anything that came of the project,' he said, 'and John reiterated that promise when he got the Cardinal Network loan. He said we would repay that when we could and then set things up so I was finally rewarded. I didn't get too excited. I knew who would get paid first and it wasn't going to be me.'

The Cardinal Network money had been obtained following a cold call John made to a company that manufactured a product called LINC, an acronym standing for Logic Information Network Compiler. The parent company, Cardinal Network, later known as the Cardinal Group, was a high-tech software manufacturer in Christchurch that had carved out a solid international reputation for brilliant products and innovative management.

The founder of the company, Gil Simpson, was much impressed by John's enthusiasm and frankly admitted that John's ability to 'articulate the dream itself really got me in'.

> I don't involve the company in philanthropic works very much because frankly the corporate payback is very limited. But I knew this project was a winner. John wanted to totally change our perception of what a motorbike is and after that first meeting I believed that he could do it. I have often wished that I could build a computer program that does what he did. It is not about refinement. It is about being able to come at things from a different angle.
>
> When I look back on my entire business career it is clear to me that I only ever met one other like him. He was a Kiwi called Sir William Pickering and he headed the Jet Propulsion Laboratory in Pasadena. He was responsible for all the unmanned space probes until the early eighties. Mariner, Pioneer and all the rest—he was the space man! I met him when he accepted our invitation to open our building and we named the street after him.
>
> When John came to see me he wanted money to go back to Daytona and I gave him twenty-five or thirty [thousand dollars] and there was more later on. But I wanted to take it a lot further than just winning a few races. John involved himself in busi-

> ness as much as he needed to in order to get where he wanted to go. He regarded it as a place to get provisions. I wanted a future for what he was doing. He was making those first faltering steps and I would have helped to make it a business. We discussed it and I know he would have accepted that help. Sadly, though, there simply wasn't time.

Perhaps all the interest that his motorcycles were arousing internationally encouraged John to think about relocating his project to a dedicated home. More likely, however, was the fact that the motorcycle project was causing some domestic tension and it was clear that the workshop at The Stables could no longer provide a welcome haven for all those associated with it. The place he chose as a replacement was a stark, steel shed located in Addington, just a few minutes from the city centre in the light industrial ribbon development that followed the railway line through Christchurch. John paid little rent for it because of the imminent possibility that a new line might knock on the door at any time.

Although the move marked a final end to the days when sporting motorcyclists, and friends generally, could drop by to help out and enjoy a bit of a session into the wee hours at The Stables, it was a welcome change for friends such as Robin Judkins, who now felt comfortable wandering into the new place at any hour.

'It was somewhere for us to go without imposing on John's family,' he recalled, 'and in many ways things got back to the way they had been. Once again we started having fun.'

A circle of sorts had been completed some time prior to the move when Broz joined the Team. Unfortunately, Broz had then found himself with nothing to do. Although he had left a very good job with a company that serviced and maintained forklifts to join John at the latter's invitation, it was soon clear that with both bikes in Canada Broz was not yet needed.

'John messed me around for about a year,' he complained, 'and in all that time I earned no money at all. He was adamant that I needed to come on board when I did, but there was actually no need for me to have left my job so soon and all that happened was that I became poorer and poorer while he buggered around and I twiddled my thumbs.'

With the move to the new premises he finally had a job to get on with and he set about the task of establishing the workshop. He also moved in and set up residence, for which privilege he paid rent, bringing his considerable collection of tools with him. With his meticulous insistence on order, the Britten Motorcycle workshop started to resemble an organised enterprise. Broz's first task was to build and install a dynamometer, and he soon had 'the big wheel', as it was dubbed, in place, ready to measure horsepower accurately in any gear throughout the rev range as soon as the computer that Dynotech was programming for it in Germany arrived.

With fresh funds in the coffers, John decided once again to mount a two-pronged attack at Daytona. Although Canadian Steve Crevier and Australian Paul Lewis were organised to ride the two machines in the 1991 race, Gary Goodfellow generously decided to turn up with his crew to help out.

With two top riders and a full team to look after the bikes, the potential to pick up the elusive win looked good. John had even more reason to be confident—the EMS had finally received the kind of attention needed to make it reliable. After volunteering his services, Mark Franklin had waited for some time for John to take him up on his offer and had almost forgotten the matter when he received an invitation to morning tea around at The Stables. John was surprised and excited when Mark told him that he was confident he knew what the causes of the troubles were with the system and that he was sure he could fix them.

> The original computer connections were the first obvious problem. I told John that I thought the automotive stuff wasn't up to the job and suggested we make up our own system. He was keen, so I set about the task by changing the connections to aviation-style jobs and then designed a circuit board with a little case for it to live in. The computer was reprogramming itself whenever it was switched off, changing all the maps so that tuning refinements were continuously being lost. To stop that tendency I set up a new program with a non-volatile memory that kept the stored information intact. I redesigned the computer box with the computer in a shielded environment of its own and still ended up with something that was a lot more compact than the old system. I made up four systems and took them around to him. We put one on a bike and it fired up straight away. I remember being amused when John said, 'Oh, it goes!'
>
> I feel we only completely solved the problem with bike numbers nine and ten when we changed the system to an inductive pick-up. Generally, however, it did not take long to produce a system that was acceptably reliable.
>
> I actually spoke to David Steward a few times and he was most concerned that we were trying to rip off his software, which the system still used of course. I tried to point out that we were only trying to make it work but he was deeply suspicious.

The imbroglio between the two companies was finally eventually more or less to everybody's satisfaction when Britten Motorcycles began manufacturing the units to their own specification while paying Steward Electronics a royalty of NZ$1000 for each system. The emotional exchange had served only to sap energy that clearly would have been much better expended addressing the problems in the first place, problems that finally proved straightforward to solve. Successive failures of the engine-management systems had probably cost Britten Motorcycles several years of glory and that in its own way was a tragedy. But the gremlins had finally been driven out and the road ahead was clear. The EMS had been exorcised at last.

Before the Daytona race Colin flew down to Los Angeles, cleared the bikes through customs, rented a van and picked up Broz, who had flown in shortly after him. Broz was still steaming at the months of time he had wasted waiting for John to give him something to do, and more particularly some payment for doing it. Given his general mindset it was therefore unfortunate that when he finally got to do something he was teamed up with Colin, a man who had done more than enough himself for little or no reward to have to tolerate somebody else's grumpiness.

As it was the first time Broz had spent any time in California, Colin went to some trouble to show him around. They started with a trip to Magic Mountain, just north of LA, where Colin talked Broz into a ride on the infamous 'Free-fall'.

'He smiled when he saw the Mountain,' recalled Colin 'which was the first and only time I saw him do that. The 'Free-fall is a classic ride to subject someone like Broz to, someone who doesn't believe in showing emotion. He kept it together but his expression was still priceless.'

After driving all the way to Florida the two men still had time to spare, and so they decided to go to Disney World, an experience Colin had shared with John the year before. In spite of, or perhaps because of, the somewhat intense exposure Colin and Broz suddenly had to each other, they singularly failed to hit it off and even in Magic Land there was an edgy coolness between them.

In the meantime, the rest of the Team trickled in to Daytona. The substantial Canadian contingent, consisting of Gary, Red-Headed Colin, Gordy (Gary's general helper and gofer in the business back in Vancouver) and George, were first to arrive. John had offered George the title of Team Manager (even though John had no intention of allowing anyone to make important decisions other than himself) and George took the responsibility very seriously. By the time John jetted in, accompanied by his sister Dorenda and Mark Franklin (who was now beginning to wring some reliability out of the EMS), George had done much to ensure that the Team was ready to roll.

For Colin, however, things were going rapidly from bad to worse.

> Broz seemed to resent me being around. I'd start doing something and he would tell me I was doing it all wrong and take the job off me. He wouldn't let me do my work and I was beginning to get really pissed off because I knew how to do it. In all the time I spannered on Britten motorcycles nothing I did ever went wrong. John could see the problem, and he acknowledged it to me, but for some reason he could never bring himself to do anything about situations like that, no matter how negative they

> became. It was an odd failing but it resulted in a lot of wasted energy. I gave up trying to be nice and just walked away. The Canadians and Gary and I all got on really well so I spent my time with them. The trouble I was having with Broz, however, wasn't the only thing bugging me. It was as if my thoughts about pulling the pin were being reinforced by everything that was happening around me.
>
> The worst thing really was the fact that John was still trying to do too much at the last minute. For example, it seemed that the front end was light at high speeds on the banking, or something, and he had decided to pop-rivet these little winglets to the front of the fairing. It might have worked, I don't know, but he was practically sticking them on as the bikes were going down pit lane. You just don't do that sort of thing when you turn up to race. You do it beforehand or you don't do it at all. You cannot predict with certainty the effect of any change you make until you have tested it. It's a dangerous game and the business of running the race has to be your only priority.[105]

Also at Daytona at this time was Chris Haldane, who had accepted an invitation to compete in the AMA National Endurance Championship, which he was also eventually to win.[106] He was at The Bowl, as fans called the track—a reference to the curved embankments that made up part of it—to race his 170-bhp Suzuki GSX-R1100 in the two-hour race that was part of the Championship series. The race was one of the two main events that climaxed the week's activities, and Chris had time to socialise with his friends at the Britten pit just a few bays down from his own. Since the accident at Teretonga he had been unsure of his status with Britten Motorcycles, and indeed John had seemed surprised to see him when he puttered around on a small pit bike.

> I think John had more or less put me out of his mind, but when he saw me he kind of twigged that he'd overlooked something obvious. It was pretty silly not to have me riding. I knew the bike, I was on a roll and I was there. However, we hung out together and had a great night in town, after I won my race at the end of the week. I'd say we probably patched things up.

In fact, John had considered both Chris and Robert Holden as an alternative to Paul Lewis, the Australian rider he eventually signed up for the ride on the second bike, and he had asked Gary for his opinion. Although there were additional expenses involved in getting Lewis to Daytona from his UK, base Lewis's previous experience at Daytona won him the invitation for the ride, which he accepted.[107]

The two Superbike riders John had chosen were both talented, successful and utterly unalike. Paul 'The Angry Ant' Lewis was (as might be expected from his nickname) a small, slightly built chap with glasses. Naturally, he was not in the least bit angry, being politely affable and invariably well behaved. Three years earlier, after very nearly winning at Daytona on the Commonwealth Honda, he had gone on to win the Battle of the Twins series overall. Steve Crevier, the other rider, was also short, but he was stocky and unlike his team-mate he thoroughly enjoyed a little hell-raising. He had a reputation for showy riding and was particularly known for a habit of doing spectacular 'stoppies' in the pits, but he had several championships under his belt.[108]

Apart from the friction between Broz and Colin, the Team was a harmonious crew and, as was usually the case when spirits were up, no opportunities were lost to make one another look stupid. For some reason Crevier's bike had been given a minor amputation on the end of one fork leg to clear something or other, and because of this it did not protrude through the steering head as much as the other. Lewis noticed this and when he asked why it was so he was told that it was a special trick to tune the handling for the Daytona banking, just like on Indycars. When he asked for the same set-up he sent the whole crew into paroxysms of mirth. Of course, the Angry Ant took it in good humour.

After flag-fall, Chris Haldane and John ran across to the infield to watch the race and Chris remembered John being absolutely ecstatic when his two bikes went straight into the lead. But his high spirits were soon tempered by the early failure of one of his machines—Crevier was out, his clutch assembly having fallen off, the result of nothing more complicated than Broz's uncharacteristic failure to tighten properly the nut that held it on. Up to this point Lewis and Crevier had been sharing the lead and were doing so in such a convincing fashion that a first- and second-place finish looked like a shoo-in.[109]

All hopes now rested on the Angry Ant, and out on the track he was behaving like one, riding the Britten with aggressive confidence. Lap after lap he effortlessly retained command of the race and a win seemed a certainty at last. In the very closing stages, however, he slowed and was overhauled by Doug Polen, who went on to win for Ducati, the Britten coming home second. The second official explanation of the day from the Britten pits was that Lewis's strange fade was a deliberate strategy. Lewis, it was claimed, was under orders to ride conservatively if his team-mate dropped by the wayside—to ensure at least one high place for the Britten Team. Again, the press was happy to repeat the story, even applauding it as sensible, and again the seasoned racers at Daytona were left shaking their heads. Not one of them would have accepted an instruction to blow the win and they thought it unlikely that the Angry Ant would have done so either. They were right. The simple truth was that Paul Lewis was running out of petrol and he had slowed down to eke out what he had left in the tank to get to the line. As it was, he ran out at about the same time as he finished.

'It took John a while to learn that the fuel you use practising is always less than the fuel you use racing,' said Colin, 'and that it's better to be safe than sorry. He'd sent the bikes out with less than full tanks again.'

If he was kicking himself, John certainly wasn't going to tell the world about it. In an interview with the *Press* following his return, he said that 'second place was as good as a victory to me'.

'This was the first time in fifty years of racing at Daytona,' he was quoted as saying, 'that anyone has succeeded with a handmade engine of this size. I wanted to take on the global giants without a lot of money and show that there was still a place for the individual designer.'

He also gave a broad hint of what the future might hold for Britten Motorcycles, adding that he 'would not go back to Daytona unless he had a bike that was awesomely fast.'

'The present bikes,' he said, 'were designed three years ago and the factories are now slowly catching up. I would have to do an upgrade, which would not be difficult. There is room for development.'

Once again, it was clearly not enough for John simply to win, for that hardly seemed to require a new bike. Tightening the clutch-retaining nuts properly and putting enough fuel in the tanks would certainly have been sufficient to win easily this time around. In spite of the incontrovertible fact that it was only a combination of poor pitwork and poor strategy that had cost the Britten Team the race, it was almost as if he was looking for an excuse to dump his two bikes and start afresh.

In a letter to a friend about the race, he referred to a moment when Polen's Ducati was running between Crevier and Lewis as 'the Britten sandwich'. It was a phrase he would use whenever he could and he later referred to a similar episode as 'giving the Ducatis the good old Britten sandwich'. This attitude toward a company whose machines he had the utmost respect and affection for was curious. It seemed that for John the business of defeating Ducati had become peculiarly personal, as if the Italians had done him some deep and personal harm. It was not enough to win against them, it was not enough to win handsomely against them; he had to crush them utterly.

A party was held to celebrate the second place, which Allan Wylie attended along with a large gathering of John's friends.

> It was a great party and second place was worth celebrating. However, claiming that second was as good as first was pure horse-shit. It was typical, and I suppose understandable, that John would want to claim a moral victory or something, but that's not what motor racing is all about. Only one machine wins the race regardless of the

> circumstances of the machines that come in behind it. The Britten did not win and it would have made more sense to think about why that was so than to twist it around and call it a victory.
>
> John was always playing the underdog card although Team Britten had several advantages over its competitors. It was certainly one of the best-financed teams, although the money was spread thinly due to the wide scope of the operation. It also had one of only two modern engine designs in Twins or BEARS racing, the other being the 8-valve Ducati. Unlike that engine, which was basically a production item, the Britten was the only one designed as a pure race engine. This meant that no compromises had to be made in the design to reduce mass-production costs, to meet the noise or exhaust emission regulations that governed street bikes, or to accommodate a starter motor. The Britten bikes should have been winners from Daytona '90 onwards, and they would have been if the development and racing programmes had been managed properly.

Still, any excuse for a party was generally good enough for those present, and the gathering turned into a good old-fashioned piss-up. It culminated in the early hours of the morning with Broz firing up one of the machines on the dynamometer, filling the building with a solid, resonating noise that caused ripples to appear on the drinks, a physical yammering that filled the lungs, chasing thoughts from the head and feelings from the heart—a fitting pagan blast of celebration.

Shortly after the party, John sent a letter to all those he had invited acknowledging the contributions of the individuals who made up the Team. Allan felt that John had probably sensed rumblings of discontent from many who had given generously of their time and talent, and who had so far had little public recognition beyond the usual references to John's 'small but dedicated team'. Such rumblings had recently increased following the release of Harry Ruffell's video, which was titled somewhat pointedly *One Man's Dream*. Perhaps John had overheard less-than-impressed members of the Team refer to it as 'One Team's Nightmare'.

John also wrote in the letter that credit had been given to him in the video several times in a way that made him feel guilty. 'One of the main reasons I had the get-together was to acknowledge the huge contribution many people have made,' he wrote. 'Unfortunately I had too much to drink and forgot to do this so I'm writing instead.'[110] He then went on to list all those who had contributed and concluded with the words, 'Next year we are going to finish first and second!'

With his bikes now capable of running reliably, John might have been expected to expand his race programme, but when Paul Vink wrote to him to invite him to enter the BotT race at Assen in the Netherlands in 1991 his response was strangely noncommittal.

In his letter, Paul had warmly commended John on his machine's performance at the race the previous year, stating that the event's outstanding success had owed much to the presence of the Britten. He also drew John's attention to the substantial publicity the Britten had enjoyed subsequently throughout the Continent.

> I don't know if you are aware of the impact your one race appearance has had in Europe. In *SuperBike* Magazine you had three full colour pages and in Motorrad Magasin *MO* (Germany) you had even five. But the masterpiece of your presence was of course the fact that your bike featured on the front cover of our Ducati club magazine. The first time that a non-Ducati ever was on the front page. The 8th of September you are gladly invited to prove that Britten is best.

The reason for John's reluctance to commit to the race would soon become clear. He was, naturally, keen to accept the challenge but he was no longer sure that he wanted to do so with the race bikes he had. He now had a head full of plans for a new machine that made the old ones seem just that—old. And having reached that point he wanted nothing more than to consign them to history and move on.

In the meantime, both Fritz Egli and Pierluigi Marconi at Bimota had been waiting patiently for John to advise them of progress made civilising the engine with starter motors and so on. To keep the relationships alive, John sent them both a scenic book on New Zealand, along with a standing invitation to visit and stay as his guest. Although his invitation was not accepted in either case, the thought must have counted, for both companies remained enthusiastic in the face of little real progress. Then Gary Slot, of White Power Suspension, sent a fax to John alerting him to yet another potential customer.

'Hello Johnny boy!' he wrote. 'One of our customers is very much interested in your engine for a small production of street bikes. Erik Beull is now mounting engines from Harley-Davidson but is not able to get a good supply.'

Erik Beull was a former Harley-Davidson employee who had left to form his own company. The dynamic and talented designer and entrepreneur had set up a factory near Milwaukee (home of Harley-Davidson), where he installed Harley engines in geodesic frames of his own design. His machines were equipped with high-performance brakes and suspension and were clothed in streamlined fibreglass. He had learned early on the need for a proper dealer network, which he had now established, and was set to expand his business substantially. Unfortunately, he was also about to run out of the Harley-Davidson XR1000 motors that his machines were built around, having bought the last fifty made. It was difficult to imagine that he could ever have seriously considered the possibility of using an embryonic race engine to advance his plans.[111]

Predictably, the tentative contact with Britten Motorcycles soon withered away, but it must have seemed to John that such enquiries were like buses, with a new one along right after the last had departed. Soon after, Alan Cathcart woke John up with an early morning phone call to tell him that he had been talking to Federico Martini, the engineering director of the Italian motorcycle manufacturer Gilera. In a fax to Colin (who was still in Canada) to pass on the news, John said that Gilera were keen to build a V-twin-powered machine but needed a motor. Specifically, he wrote, they wanted a V-twin engine with four overhead, belt-driven cams and fuel injection that could be used as a stressed member. And, of course, a starter motor.

It is one thing to hand-build a small number of high-specification racing engines, but quite another to produce in volume a motor that can be maintained and serviced by everyday motorcycle mechanics in a commercial shop. The Britten V-1000 was obviously a highly strung beast and there is no way it could have been sold without considerable modification. The first obvious modification would be to drop the compression ratio from 13:1 to 11:1 so the engine could run on pump petrol. This would in turn reduce the horsepower to a manageable but still highly impressive 120 bhp, or thereabouts. John confirmed his thoughts on the compression ratio in the same fax to Colin in which he told him about Gilera's interest.

Other critical problems such as the tendency toward cold seizures would also have to be addressed, probably with a Nikasil bore to reduce clearances. The start point for any production attempt, however, would be a complete set of drawings, something that had yet to be even attempted. Once that point was reached, the engine would then need at least a year of intensive development to achieve an acceptable level of reliability for sale, even as a unit suitable only for race bikes.

The massive technical problems posed by the idea of turning the Britten V-twin into a production item were irrelevant, however, given the fact that, by John's own calculations, each engine cost at least NZ$40,000 to build. Even if volume production could somehow be achieved, this figure was unlikely to be reducible to a sum that would allow both Britten Motorcycles and any potential client to produce a commercially competitive machine—let alone make a profit.

In spite of this inescapable reality, John continued to give some thought as to how he could manage the actual production of engines, if somehow all the other problems could be solved, and he outlined them in a proposal he wrote to Pierluigi Marconi. He told Marconi that he would provide a complete set of drawings and would then oversee the appointment of Italian businesses to take care of such matters as the engine castings and engine-management systems. Britten technicians would work with Bimota engineers to iron out production bugs and to get the project up and running.

It was an ambitious suggestion but it immediately foundered on John's insistence that Bimota commit to a sum of money to buy the design of the engine. The problem, as they saw it, was that the engine was still, in spite of its obvious promise, an unknown quantity. As indeed was Britten Motorcycles. Nor was that the only, or even the main, problem. All over the world—with the exception of Harley-Davidson, which posted one record-profit year after another—the world's motorcycle manufacturers had been in the grip of a persistent, draining sales downturn since the 1980s. The timing for both Britten Motorcycles and the Europeans was wrong and all the correspondence between them, the preliminary agreements, the goodwill and the personal contacts so carefully nurtured would count for nothing.

It is possible that John's primary objective in writing to Marconi was to save face with a proposal he must have known the Italians would reject, as his thoughts were running in an entirely different direction. In the fax to Colin about the Gilera connection he also asked him to bolt a reversed front cylinder head onto the rear cylinder of one of the engines he had in Canada in order to see how badly the inlet trumpets interfered with one another. This was something that would need to be overcome if the trumpets were to share a common air-box. Clearly John was already thinking in terms of a new generation engine for an entirely new machine. Far from thinking about building a de-tuned prototype engine to explore the possibilities of supplying a powerplant for other people's street machines, he was planning a new Britten race engine with the sole objective of making more power.

Other individual enquiries that came in from riders and team owners wanting either to buy or hire a pure race replica were therefore of immediate interest, and there was now a steady trickle of them. Typical of such communications was one from a young German rider, Jens Hofmann. Jens actually worked for Dynotech but he was also a keen racer who, in the last European BotT Championship, had come third. Although both he and Hayri Winter had been promised factory bikes by a local Guzzi dealer they had failed to eventuate.

'Now,' wrote Jens, 'I talked to my other sponsor about the world's fastest, strongest and lightest twin all over the world and he is very interested.'

In his letter, Jens then went on to ask if he could hire a bike, along with a repair kit, for one season. He was also interested in purchasing a couple of engines.

In his reply declining the business, John told him that because he wanted to beat the factory Ducatis, he 'must do some work on my old horses. Maybe next season you can ride a Britten but you will have to hold on tight to the bars!'

Although John was now determined to concentrate on his plans for a sleek new thoroughbred, there would be one final gallop for one of the two 'old horses'.

Paul Vink had continued to press for at least one Britten to attend the BotT race at Assen in August 1992, telling John that a growing legion of fans demanded it. John was keen to oblige, but worried that participation in the race would interfere with work on the new bike. Fortunately, he had been contacted by another German prior to Jens Hoffman, who seemed to offer an answer to his dilemma.

Willy Abbrodatt was in the happy position of being able to draw sponsorship from his own company, Data Obsession, a manufacturer of computer hardware and software, to fund his own race team. The contact between him and John had also come about through Dynotech, which Willy used for all his static testing. Willy had written to John explaining that he had contracted German racer Hans Hoffman, to ride for him and wanted a Britten for the summer BotT series in Europe.

John had immediately called Colin (happily working back in Canada on his ski field) and asked if he would look after the spannering and the computer for the German team. Somewhat warily, Colin agreed on the condition that it did not cost him anything and for once, he said, it didn't. Within two weeks of receiving the call he was off to Frankfurt, where he met Willy, discovering him to be warm and personable.

They competed in the entire European BotT series, racing the bike for three months in Germany, Holland and the Czech Republic. According to Colin, the bike went reasonably well in the seven races they entered although it did not actually win anything. Hans crashed once, destroying a set of Marvic wheels, but Colin managed to patch everything up and with new wheels it had continued to go reliably and well.

> This was an amazing performance really. The bike we used was Number One, the same bike Chris Haldane had ridden, with a few bits from Number Two...Looking back, I have the feeling that we might have won a few with someone else in the saddle. Hans was good but I don't think he was that good. However, it was certainly an interesting cultural experience for me. Generally, I found the Germans to be thorough but hot-tempered. I've seen plenty of Kiwis go off at one another but that was nothing compared with the way these guys behaved. Hans particularly was an extremely high-strung character who would spin out completely whenever we had a problem. He would run around in circles kicking things and swearing in German while Willy tried to keep the peace. Willy kept saying, 'Hans we must try to understand!' I've seen riders lose it and I will put up with it a bit, but I've also worked with guys like Robert Holden who were always under control and easy to be with. I finally told Hans that I wasn't there to be abused and that I'd just as soon go home, after which he chilled out.
>
> On the other hand, although they were the hardest people I'd ever worked for, the Germans looked after me the best. Nothing was too much trouble and if I needed anything I only had to ask.

Because he was not winning, Hans complained often that the bike was not making enough power. This was to have a useful spin-off for the Britten Team because the bike was run up on the dynamometer quite frequently. Colin was impressed by the way the technicians at Dynotech would put a pen through the glitch spike that often tails off a reading, a spike he said John was always keen to read as extra horsepower. He was also impressed at the way they insisted that every test should be repeated three times before they would accept the data as valid. According to the Germans, the bike was consistently making a highly competitive 137 bhp. Colin assiduously picked their brains, gathering valuable information on testing procedures particularly, which he took back with him to New Zealand for his final brief stint as part of the Britten Team.

Not long after the race, John rang Hans Weekers and told him that he had thought over what Hans had told him about the impossibility of extracting further horsepower from the current motor. He had therefore decided, he told Hans, to build new heads. But that was not all. He also wanted to develop a 5-valve version of the new head in addition to the 4-valve. And he had also made up his mind to build a new bike with a completely new design.

Hans was staggered. 'I thought that he had achieved so much and that he would be content to refine what he had and win some more races. All I could say was "Geez John, why must you do so much?"'

Little did he know.

Not only had John decided to build a new bike, he had decided to build a bike where every single aspect of it was considered from an entirely fresh perspective. In many ways the design of the new machine would build on the first bikes, borrowing much from their engineering. However, nothing would be held over for the sake of mere convenience or economy, and no idea was off limits because of the difficulties of design or execution. It was a decision laden with risk and the prospect of failure and heartbreak, but now that John had made his decision there would be no turning back. He was going to build a legend.

CHAPTER TWELVE

Bullet on a Knife-edge

Some years later, standing in the stillness of his workshop on a peaceful Sunday afternoon, Allan Wylie looked back on his involvement in the Britten saga and mused that all he had wanted to build was a race winner and that, in his opinion, the bike that won races was last year's winner plus a one percent improvement.[112]

> So much of what John was doing was right, and my time as part of the Team had been an amazing opportunity for me to do things that I would never otherwise have done. But Team Britten seemed destined to repeat the same mistakes over and over again. Johnny always wanted to push forward into something completely new rather than getting what he already had working properly. During the time we worked together I had slowly come to realise that we had different goals. He wanted to win, make no mistake—he had a fiercely competitive nature and it showed in everything he did, large and small. But winning wasn't enough for John. He also wanted to dazzle.

As Allan surmised, John's decision to build something radically different probably did owe as much to his desire to dazzle as it did to anything else. This desire was probably more complicated, however, than a straightforward hunger for recognition, and was driven, at least in part, by a cool and calculating pragmatism. John was already well aware of the fact that he could hardly continue to justify the scale of the project as a hobby and, in the face of continuing difficulties snaring a big corporate partner, he now realised that building replicas of his new race machine for paying customers was perhaps the only way the project could continue.

We know that from the earliest days with Aero D One John had wanted to build a limited run of machines, and he reiterated this objective in an interview he gave to *Revs* magazine in April 1989 in which he said he hoped to produce bikes 'back in New Zealand and make them available as Pro Twins racers'. At some point not long after this he told another journalist that he would probably limit the number of bikes to just one dozen, a figure he quickly revised to ten. Without seemingly giving the matter any further thought, that then became the basis of the business plan for Britten Motorcycles.[113] Bearing this objective in mind, it made sense that his new machine should attract a great deal of attention, and to do that it would help if it was a very different motorcycle to his essentially conventional-looking fully faired machine. It was the end of the trail for his old horses.

Finally, only one of the two original Brittens would survive, although it was hard to say which, as it was an amalgam of both. In later years the excitement and drama of the creations that followed tended to eclipse the surviving machine as it sat in the Britten workshop gathering dust, and visitors tended to overlook it, even after it had been the subject of a painstaking restoration. In many ways, however, the first bikes were better balanced than their successors. Apart from the ground-clearance problem, they handled beautifully straight out of the box and if they were not beautiful they were certainly handsome. Chris Haldane remained convinced that with a few body and layout modifications the first two Brittens could have been relatively easily developed into enduring and dominant champions. But it was not to be. Already in John's mind a startling new creation had evolved, a machine he would later describe as a bullet on a knife-edge—the machine that would become the quintessential Britten V-1000.

When Hans Weekers realised that John was determined to go ahead with his plans for a new bike, he had only one stipulation before agreeing to work on the programme. This was that the approach would have to be a lot more scientific than it had been in the past, a demand John readily agreed to. After that it was a simple matter to strike up a deal, and Hans began work, initially on a new set of 4-valve heads. The plan, simply stated, was to build new heads to fit what they already had, with the objective of obtaining 145 bhp. And now Hans would be working with Rob Selby, who was still employed at the engineering shop.[114]

A freshly enthused Colin Dodge now returned to Christchurch from Germany to a scene of bustling activity.

> I could almost see the horsepower just waiting to be released when we were doing all the testing at Dynotech, and I came back all fired up. When I arrived in New Zealand the Team were about to run the ignition with Mark [Franklin]'s set-up for the first time while they waited for Hans to finish his work on the new heads.
>
> Mark had made a simulator to run the bike on and we started finding all these time lags in the programme. The problem was that the computer couldn't keep up with the ignition maps. The Germans had given me a computer so I would punch in new maps overnight to address the problem and then we would try them on the dyno.

> We started making some real progress. Mark had by now identified the deficiencies with the hardware and solved them and the project was humming along.

However, even though the new engine was on track and there was a fresh spirit of professionalism in the air, Colin's enthusiasm soon waned. He, too, had reached the end of the line.

> I was on the bones of my arse again and I got a call from Canada asking me back to the ski fields. Mike Brosnan was by now very involved and he was still being difficult. Within a fortnight I was off and I never really saw John again. I got a call asking if I could help at the next Daytona but I wasn't that enthusiastic. John said he'd talk to Mike Brosnan about it but I didn't hear anything further. A few years later I was back at home and there was a message on my phone from John saying it was Saturday morning and he was having a get-together that night for everyone who'd been in the Team and would I like to come. My phone had a timer on it and I knew the call had come in late on Saturday afternoon. He might have said, 'Sorry I forgot' but he didn't. I didn't bother going, I just got on with my life.

While awaiting the results of Hans's work John had been busy working out the layout for the rest of the bike. Much of this time was spent with Murray Aitken and Mike Sinclair, and everything seemed to fall into place with a kind of natural inevitability. John's acceptance of Murray into the inner design circle was probably a result of both Mike's enthusiastic endorsement of Murray's undoubted ability and a recognition of the fact that his own time was now limited by the inroads made by general project management. In fact, he struck it lucky with Murray, who was not only up to speed technically but was also able to manage his own time and push ahead under his own initiative. Actually, he was thrice blessed for Murray was also willing to work for some considerable time for nothing.

As regards the frameless construction of the previous Brittens, this seemed to require little refinement except for the steering head, the reason for this being that John had decided that there should not be one. He had built his own engine and he was satisfied that it was comfortably the most powerful V-twin in the world and that weight for weight his bike was damn near the equal of a Grand Prix 500 machine. There were reliability problems, sure, but these could and were being addressed. Essentially, his engine was strong enough to make the grade, the problems being only with the minor, if essential, adjuncts.

To a degree, John had achieved what he had by going to people like Jerry Branch and Hans Weekers—experts who understood the rules of combustion and aspiration very well—and in that sense the Britten motor was the last word in conventional wisdom. However, he had also acted in a way that many more conservative souls would have considered reckless and overambitious—and he had succeeded. If that bold approach had worked in the case of his engine design, why not look afresh at that Achilles heel of modern motorcycle design, that uncomfortable compromise of practicality and optimum engineering, the telescopic fork? Why not design a new front end all together?

Quite where the idea for a girder frontend came from is open to conjecture. John had always admired HRD Vincents and had spent some time examining a private collection belonging to Allan Bramwell, the well-known Christchurch motorcycle enthusiast. The big English V-twins represented the finest and most romantic expression of traditional motorcycle engineering, something that was bound to appeal to John. He had also admired the elegant simplicity of the girder frontend on a Norton ES2 that was often to be found at Phil Payne's shop.[115] In many ways John was always at heart a traditionalist, in spite of his fascination for avant-garde engineering.

A Christchurch photographer by the name of Colin Simpson, who had been the passenger on the Three Fools expedition, had yet another explanation for John's growing fascination with funny front ends. He remembered John visiting him at his home, where John showed a great deal of interest in an art-deco chair with a girder-type suspension system.[116] According to Colin, he could not leave it alone and he later came back to photograph it.

There were a number of adventurous individuals who were comparatively recent proponents of funny front ends and some of them had produced quite practical alternatives to telescopic forks.[117] Most of the patents that applied to the set-up John had in mind, however, were held by a Frenchman called Claude Fior, who had built a number of Grand Prix bikes that were subsequently raced with limited success. Some time earlier, Allan Wylie had collected material on work that had been done by Fior, and a number of others, and had sent it to John.

> In addition to Fior's work there was another gentleman who was very active with funny front ends called Andre de Cortanze. He designed a series of radical and spectacular racers that were built by the French Elf consortium. None of them were very successful but they were interesting and when I came across some descriptions and pictures of the machines I sent them to John along with some stuff about Fior. John and I had often talked about such things, as all motorcycle people do. But I only gave him the material as a curiosity. So many good ideas in motorcycling have been sacrificed for a funny front end. When I later slung off at his, he jokingly told me I was responsible because I'd sent him the stuff in the first place. I replied that I wasn't advocating a funny front end and I certainly hadn't meant for him to make one.

But make one he did.

There were both compelling reasons for making a girder-type front end and equally compelling reasons not to. On the negative side, there was the reality that a machine thus equipped would be far removed from known set-up technology. It would be trailblazing and, as someone once said, trailblazers get arrows in their back. The problems were manifold and were not restricted to the engineering challenges involved in designing and building something that worked.[118]

If the front end could not be made to work, however, then everything the Britten Team had achieved would be lost. And if a further problem were required then it was simply a matter of combining all the problems and adding the collective burden to a small, underfunded, overworked team struggling in a remote corner of the world to build an international race-winning motorcycle. It should also be remembered that this same team already knew they could win with the White Power suspension set-up they already had. For all they knew, the technology to render their efforts to date obsolete was already on the drawing board or, worse, circling the private test tracks of one of the world's established manufacturers. Indeed, it would have been unwise to ignore the inevitable emergence of just such a machine, and in particular of a V-twin-powered machine of comparable or superior performance. A window of opportunity was open but there was no way of knowing how long it would be before it slammed shut again.

The reasons in favour of a wishbone front end—for that was the set-up John had in mind—could perhaps best be understood in the context of Grand Prix racing, ironically an arena where such an arrangement was most unlikely to become popular in the foreseeable future in spite of some very obvious potential advantages.

According to Mike Sinclair, the biggest factor limiting Grand Prix racing is 'the front end on turn-in'.

> Riders want to throw bikes harder and harder into the corners and the tyres and forks can't cope. There are many reasons for this, but one of the main factors is that by braking heavily into the corner the rider compresses the suspension to the point where there is nothing left. Naturally, that severely compromises the road-holding. With the set-up John had in mind, dive under brakes can be totally controlled. It's even possible to set it up so the front end rises under braking if you want to completely flummox your rider. The point is that even if you dial in a bit of dive to give him the feedback he needs to control the thing, you can still avoid bottoming under braking. This means that as you tip into, and then power through, a corner the suspension can still absorb bumps that will chuck a bike with fully compressed forks off line.

If John had concerns about the risk attendant upon building and racing a machine equipped with wishbone front suspension, they were short-lived. In an interview he later gave to Alan Cathcart for *Australian Motorcycle News,* he explained his rationale for building a wishbone front suspension with the kind of confident enthusiasm that was almost his trademark. He identified the principal advantages inherent in the wishbone system, the first being his belief that such a set-up eliminated 'stiction' under braking loads. (By 'stiction' he meant the tendency for forks to bind somewhat under heavy braking when the braking forces were trying to bend the forks.) The second advantage, he said, was the elimination of the flex that was inherent in conventional forks design. Such flex, he claimed, resulted in the wheel accelerating and decelerating relative to the bike, which in turn set up chatter in the front brakes and/or tyre.

'A tyre,' he explained, 'is a spring with no damper. My front end maintains the wheel in a constant position relative to the bike, which promotes braking performance.'

When asked by Alan Cathcart why he had not simply adopted the front swing-arm layout that the Bimotor Tesi used so successfully, John's reported response was that the single wishbone geometry of the Tesi did not provide the same opportunity to shift the roll centre throughout the suspension travel.

> You can dial up any transition from pro-dive to anti-dive during overall suspension travel just by changing the angle or length of the wishbones to adjust the ratios. You only need to change the position of one end of one wishbone to have a uniquely tuneable front suspension. Finally the girder fork not only increases torsional stiffness at the front end but also reduces the weight, which, since you are dealing with one extreme end of the motorcycle, also decreases the polar moment and this improves handling.[119]

To obviate any long-term, and potentially costly, arguments, John contacted Claude Fior and asked permission to use what was virtually a Fior set-up. Alan Cathcart later reported that the front end was actually 100 percent Britten because Fior had never replied to John's fax asking for information. This was only half-true, however. John had spoken on the phone to Fior a number of times and Fior did at least give his blessing to the project. It is unlikely in any event that John would place himself in a position where he could be sued, or denounced, as a plagiarist.

In their conversations, Fior had explained to John that he was extremely busy and would not therefore be able to become actively involved in helping him to design his system. But John chose to ignore this and in a later fax to Fior he gently reminded the Frenchman that he still did not have a front end for his new bike.

He asked Fior to give the matter urgent consideration, appending a little drawing to the communication showing a motorcycle with a question mark where the front forks would normally be.

It may be that Fior did finally decline to supply details of the geometry of his set-ups, but drawings of his arrangements were available, if only through the International Patents Office. As it turned out, it was probably preferable that the Team worked out the details of the system for themselves, and Mike Sinclair and Murray finally did this. Murray produced huge simulated spread-sheets detailing both front and rear suspension in terms of lever ratios, rising rate, falling rate, and rake and trail characteristics through the range of travel and pro-dive and anti-dive. It was a remarkable achievement and it gave the team a first-rate start in mastering a complex and difficult proposition, one that, as has already been pointed out, held the potential for utter disaster.

During this period Murray also turned his attention to many of the details that had so often let the first two Brittens down, and a characteristic of his work was the spare elegance of the components he designed. Details such as the foot pegs and controls for brakes and gears, with levers acting on roller bearings, perfectly complemented the rest of the bike because they were so obviously right. Murray also had a lot to do with the selection of the characteristic big axle bearings, chosen because they offered a substantial surface for the carbon-fibre girders to bond to and also because they became an effective brace at the end of the girder.

The rear suspension was completely revised, a necessary step in view of the numerous failures the old set-up had suffered. A strong sub-frame attached to the front cylinder now cantilevered the top end of the spring further forward from the exhaust header into cool air. The spring-shock unit was also turned upside-down from the barn door set-up and was activated by a bell crank that was, in turn, activated by a push/pull rod attached, like its predecessor, to the swing-arm. This time, however, it all operated on the same plane. There would be no further trouble caused by the engineering of the rear suspension.

Before the subtleties of the body shape could be addressed, however, one fundamental problem had to be solved. At an earlier stage Allan had pointed out to John that the air entering the fairing on the first bikes really had no place to go, and that they really ought to do something about cleaning up their internal airflow. John had given the matter some thought and had come to the conclusion that there was no good reason to hide a narrow V-twin engine behind a bottom fairing that made the machine as wide as most transverse multi-cylinder bikes. He was already convinced that eliminating the lower fairing would make little difference to the bikes' aerodynamics, a conclusion he reached when testing the first bikes at South Eyre Road.

The Team had often run the old bikes without their lower fairings in place and seemingly had incurred no penalty in the top speeds achieved. John reasoned therefore that if the entire lower fairing was simply deleted he could probably reduce weight and increase accessibility without any significant drag penalty. He could also design the tank with lower sections that swelled out like vestigial stingray's wings. These wings would fair the rider's knees so that they would only be out in the wind when he was cranking into a corner—in other words, when any extra drag would be irrelevant, if not beneficial. The air whistling inside his lower legs could simply flow back, taking a bit of engine heat with it. In short, John could design a shape that cut through the air rather than push into it, the bottom half of the machine acting like a knife-edge while the top would resemble a bullet—a bullet on a knife-edge.

John was also more than happy with a layout that left his handsome, muscular engine in plain sight, and there was more than a little marketing savvy in his preference. Fully faired motorcycles tended to look much like one another while the one thing that most differentiated them, their engine, was hidden away. On the other hand, exposed power-plants looked purposeful and aggressive. These considerations had influenced motorcycle designers as far back as the 1950s, when, for example, the British company AJS had elected not to streamline its famous Porcupine racers, even though it meant losing races to opponents with full fairings. They had believed that to do so would offend their fans and cost them road-bike sales.

John had always preferred the more rounded forms of earlier bikes such as the English and Italian twins that preceded the slab-sided, squared-off era, and if he had not actually worked to achieve a somewhat retrospective look to his own engine he was certainly pleased that it had turned out that way. His preference for natural, rounded shapes extended to motorcycle body styles and he was keen that his new machine should incorporate a deliberately traditional aesthetic, an objective that was also served by leaving the engine exposed.

The only problem with these ideas, and it was a big one, was where to put the radiator. The old bikes had featured two radiators slung one on either side of the front cylinder, but clearly doing that again would ruin the knife-edge, as would mounting a single radiator in front of the engine. If a radiator could be relocated somewhere out of the slipstream, the aerodynamic advantages of the narrow engine could then be fully exploited. But how do you locate a radiator out of the very slipstream in which it needs to work?

John, Mike Sinclair and Murray thrashed out the possibilities. It is now difficult to say exactly who came up with the idea of sticking the thing under the seat. However, to paraphrase Sherlock Holmes, once all the possibilities have been eliminated you are left with the truth, and the truth was that there really was not anywhere else for it to go. The next step was to work out a way of making it function. Clearly, the way to achieve a flow of air through the radiator was to introduce air from a high-pressure point and exit it at a low-pressure point. The highest pressure point on the machine was undoubtedly the area immediately in front of the upper fairing's pointed nose and the lowest was probably the empty area beneath the tail and behind the engine. The only problem was that the fuel tank was smack in the middle, but there was nothing to prevent air being fed through it along an internal duct. Come to that, a second and third duct, running on either side of the radiator air-intake duct, could deliver air straight through the tank to the air-box.

The layout proved a simple and effective solution to what had seemed at first to be a complex problem, and in practice it was found that the radiator area could be significantly reduced because its cooling efficiency had increased markedly. This in turn resulted in a weight reduction of both radiator core and the water needed to fill it. Naturally, having the radiator mounted horizontally also achieved a huge reduction in drag, certainly over the more conventional mounting behind the front wheel, where it acted, in John's words, like the square sail of a windjammer.

The only major drawback of this layout, later revealed, was a tendency to overheat the engine if the bikes were kept waiting overly long for a starter's flag to drop, but that was hardly unique to the Britten Team. Portable, petrol-powered leaf-blowers later proved a complete solution to the problem, and were employed to push air through the systems when the bikes were kept waiting for lengthy periods while running prior to a start. In practice, however, this was hardly ever found necessary.[120]

Once it was decided that the radiator would live under the seat, it was a comparatively simple matter to design a carbon-fibre sub-chassis to support the seat and tail section and to mount the radiator. The new sub-chassis also included pick-up points for the front suspension's upper wishbone, while the lower wishbone was to be located onto a lug on top of the front cylinder head. Provision was also made to mount sundry items such as the battery, collector bottles for oil breathers and the header tank for the radiator on top of the sub-chassis, underneath the tailpiece. Of course, this meant the machines would boast a pretty big tailpiece, but that was no problem. John wanted a lovely big pointy tail to re-form the air behind the rider's backside, and to create a low-pressure zone to suck air through the radiator. A big flat section underneath it would also add a desirable venturi effect on the underside of the radiator, as well as smoothing the way for departing hot air from around the engine. Larger tailpieces were becoming the norm, and the elegant rear end on the Britten would soon look modest as Grand Prix bikes adopted bigger and bigger tails to knit the air back together in their wake.

With the basic design now settled, John proceeded to make the sub-chassis, the swing-arm and the girders for the front suspension. The sub-chassis would be created, like those on the earlier machines, with his tried and proven 'wet-lay' system, the structure being made up of carbon-fibre strands impregnated with uncured resin wound around aluminium rods. The rods would serve to locate the structure after it had been filled with foam, faced off with carbon-fibre and Kevlar sheet, and cured in John's home-made oven. This was essentially the way he had been making his boxed and triangulated swing-arms, and it was also the method he would use to construct the blades that comprised the girder forks for the new front end.[121]

The penultimate step in the manufacture of all three items involved hours and hours of finishing work, filling pinholes and other minor imperfections with resin, before painstakingly sanding with increasingly fine paper. Once all the surfaces had been smoothed to perfection John, gave the items to Bob who then buffed and painted them, leaving selected panels of clear-lacquered carbon-fibre.

By the time he was done, John had expended many hundreds of hours on the carbon-fibre and Kevlar structures, mostly in the dead of night, while working full time at Brittco during the day. Some idea of how long it must have taken him may be gleaned from the time it later took a properly organised body shop to do the same jobs—about 300 man-hours.

But for his troubles he was rewarded with relatively lightweight structures possessing considerable strength. For example, the sub-chassis supporting the radiator, the seat, the fuel tank, the fairing and the rider, in addition to providing the mounting point for the upper wishbone, weighed in at just 4.25 kg.

It was now time for John to turn his attention to the body that would partly clothe his new creation. With an old set of racing leathers stuffed with rags acting as a model, he set about building up the body shape in his workshop at The Stables by joining lengths of malleable aluminium welding wire with a hot glue gun. As he gradually built up the shapely filigree structure of wire, the dramatically organic nature of the new body emerged. This was John at his creative best, conjuring up complex forms, working in an ingenious and original manner that allowed him the freedom of a true artist. The result, even when it was still just a feathery skeleton of softly gleaming wire, was a confluence of harmonious curves that a glass-blower or a sculptor might have fashioned.

The smooth line of the low fairing turned under and ran back as a gentle curve that cut sharply into the substantial indent in the tank where the rider's knees would be. As he was determined that his machines would always have sufficient fuel, John sculpted a wide, generous fuel tank to offset the volume lost to the ducting that would run through it. This in turn meant that the indents had to be very deep in order for the rider to fit. John arranged the curved line of the indent to echo that of the nose, while the line formed by the top of the tank swept back and then descended gently to join the muscular curving bulge that ran aft on the graceful arc formed by the bottom of the tail. From dead astern, the tail resembled nothing so much as a python head, which would finally be completed with a round mouth for the breather outlet.

Once the lines were established, it was clear that fans and foes alike would have no difficulty recognising the new Britten at a glance, even from a distance. John had succeeded in referencing an older aesthetic, with echoes of BSA Gold Star and Ducati Super Sport, while creating something that was stunningly contemporary. The body shape was also glamorous, romantic and dramatic, from whichever angle it was viewed. That did not mean, unfortunately, that it was also ergonomically efficient, and many riders would later complain that the new Britten was an uncomfortable and awkward bike to ride. To most eyes appreciative of fine motorcycles, however, it was simply drop-dead gorgeous.

Like its predecessors, the new Britten motorcycle would be known by the same succinct and pared-down moniker, a name that perfectly suited its emerging character. The old Britten V-1000 had passed the torch to the new Britten V-1000.

If building the birdcage to form the body was challenging and time-consuming, it was at least clean. The next part of the process was quite the opposite. Two-pot expanding foam had to be spread all over the skeleton and then carefully filed and sanded back to the wire. The surface then had to be lathered with a layer of 5-mm-deep polyester filler, which would in turn be carefully filed and sanded back until a perfectly fair and mirror-smooth surface had been achieved. This buck would then be used to create a mould from which the final body could be formed out of carbon-fibre and Kevlar sheet.

As he contemplated this time-consuming and essentially unpleasant task, John received a phone call. It was from a young man who was doing year three of a four-year Diploma in Design at polytech in Wellington. Jason Monopoli was at a stage of his course when he was required to spend six weeks in the workforce in an area related to design and he wanted to know if John could use some help.

Jason had inherited an interest in motorbikes from his father and was, at the time, thrashing a NZ$200 Suzuki FA50 Scooter to and from polytech. He had read about John and tracked him down by calling various bike shops. John explained that he was working on a new project and then asked if Jason knew anything about fibreglass. When Jason replied that he didn't know a whole lot, 'John began to um and ah' but perked up immediately when Jason explained that his services were free.

'After that there was no more mucking about,' said Jason. 'He said that was great and I should come on down.' Jason recalled his first meeting with his new mentor as a somewhat rushed affair.

My father drove me down from Nelson and we arrived at this big, elegant complex. I thought it was far too flash after all this stuff I'd read about him struggling in a back shed and that the house must be on the other side of the railway line. When it turned out to be the right place my father whizzed me off to the nearest shopping centre where I picked up some new jeans and a t-shirt. We had just arrived back when John roared up in his white Benz with the top down. He waved and shouted that he'd be back in a minute and then he tore off again. I remember thinking at the time that it could only be his name that stopped him losing his licence when I saw the way he drove. Anyway, he soon returned and showed me the workshop. The wire frame for the body was nearly finished and he spent about fifteen minutes showing me how to put the two-pack foam on and shave it back. Then he raced off again and I began.

It was a bloody awful work. After the foam I had to put the bog on and I used masses of it. I'd think I was going well and then I'd hit a knot in the wire or something. I remember these 4-litre tins piling up—there were about sixteen by the time I finished. I worked for my six weeks and then stayed on for three weeks of my holiday. Then, at the end of the next term, I returned and worked through the Christmas holidays for another two-and-a-half months.

The school was almost ready to throw me out. John was just a nobody to them and they could not see what motorcycles had to do with design, but in the weeks I'd spent with him I'd learned more about design than all the time I'd spent at school.

I stayed in the spare wing [of The Stables] above the workshop where I was pretty self-contained. John would sometimes pop his head into the workshop for a quick word in the morning, and then he'd rush off to put in a full day at the office before returning to work through the night on the bike. I remember often hearing the birds before we knocked off. I also remember that John was always the last to leave. Usually there would be quite a crowd of us there. Harry the photographer, Bob the painter, Murray, John and occasionally Rob, who was doing all the engineering in another workshop. It felt very special to be a part of such a great team and I jumped head first into the project, really happy to do anything that needed doing.

By the time I arrived, John had started making the core boxes for moulding the new heads and so I also helped him with that job. We cut up and glued cross-sections of customwood to create the right pattern, and then Hans produced the porting and water jackets in resin from which we then made plaster moulds. I remember pouring the resin and sand mix into the core boxes at the foundry before melting these big chunky bits of aluminium. We had everything wired together to keep all the bits and pieces in place and we went through heaps of attempts to get it right. We would heat up the resin and sand mix, and sometimes it wouldn't stick and sometimes it burned. We eventually got it right and produced these beautiful, new heads.

With the head castings finished, Jason went back to forming the buck for the bodywork, laboriously sanding it with progressively finer paper until he had achieved a flawlessly polished finish. He also worked on the bucks for all the ancillaries, and when this job was also finally finished he smeared them with a releasing agent and painstakingly applied the fibreglass that would form the female moulds for the carbon-fibre bodywork.

The body was to be made up in six separate pieces and he started with the tank top and seat, which constituted one of the pieces and included the neck for the filler cap. He painstakingly laid four layers of carbon-fibre into the mould, with Kevlar layered into the lower edge of the tank where the bike would probably hit first if it fell over. The resin John had chosen for the job was again vinyl-ester. Next, Jason made the tank bottom, which was then laminated to the top with rovings around the jointing surfaces. The ducting for the air-box and radiator was then resined in place, along with the mount that sat on the sub-chassis. Happily, once the ducting was in place the tank was found to possess immense strength and rigidity.

Jason finished the job by adding a couple of laminates over the rovings and then rolled resin inside the tank to seal it.[122] The fairing and tank assembly incorporated deep flaps that extended down and slipped over rubber seals around the radiator and air-box. The seals reduced air leakage as far as possible, while the flaps located the tank and seat assembly onto the sub-chassis.

The fairing and tailpiece were then joined to this central body pod with Dzus clips, leaving only the blade for the fairing to be made to complete the upper body. This Jason created using a felt-lined female and male mould, which formed preheated Perspex into the desired shape, a shape actually more akin to a wind-deflector than a windscreen.

Having completed these tasks, Jason began finishing the body for painting, a job that took enormously longer than making it and one that was made infinitely more tedious by the necessity to make all the seams and joins even and neat. In spite of all the work that had gone into the moulds, they were far from perfect, so once Jason had achieved an acceptable fit for each part he faired the bodywork with automotive filler and sanding back began all over again.

While the body was being finished, all the other items needed, including the throttle bodies, were also being produced. John had decided that the throttle bodies should also be carbon-fibre—yet another first for Britten Motorcycles—and to make them he made up a metal mould.

The work ground on, day after day, as Jason gradually whittled away the list of carbon-fibre components yet to be completed and all slowly took their place on the shelf awaiting final assembly.[123] As always with John's projects, everything was made in a mad, blurred rush, with night and day folding seamlessly into one another as the workshop at The Stables slowly foundered in a sea of used tins and empty packets, off-cuts of materials, ruined, resin-coated tools, and other waste products of all descriptions.

Although the basic method by which the composite components were produced remained largely unchanged throughout the history of the Britten V-1000, one thing did finally change. Those who later worked on Britten V-1000s in a 'proper' bodyshop wore disposable gloves and safety masks and used convenient mix dispensers for the two-pack chemicals they dealt with. They also worked in an atmosphere with proper ventilation and in a space large enough for the proper organisation of materials.[124]

It was quite typical in most of the industries where these relatively new carbon-fibre and kevlar products were used, that the work was carried out in such a way that would later be seen as clearly dangerous. Many a New Zealand boat builder, for example, had their career cut short by a failure to protect lungs from resin dust and hands from a debilitating condition whereby the skin became chemically sensitive. Warnings of the dangers were there, both from manufacturers of the products in question and qualified medical personnel, but for some reason it took a long time for both individuals and industries to appreciate the inherent dangers of failing to ensure adequate protection. Like many beautiful boats built at the time, the Britten V-1000 may have been conceived as a thing of beauty, and even genius, but aspects of its execution were ugly and dangerous.

Next up were the wheels. John still had access to 'hardly ridden' Marvic magnesium alloy race wheels through Mike Sinclair, who had remained with the Kenny Roberts Team, but he decided against using them. That is to say he decided against magnesium alloy wheels altogether, not just Kenny Roberts' used Marvics. There is nothing more fundamentally common to all mechanical machines than the wheel, and it must have tickled him to contemplate building his own unique version, a carbon-fibre and Kevlar version of course.

John would later claim that the composite wheels he built were actually cheaper than the Marvic wheels he had used up to that point, but this seems highly unlikely. The value of the work that went into making the prototype wheels alone, had it been costed out on a commercial basis, was probably sufficient to buy enough low-mileage Marvics to keep Britten motorcycles rolling for some time. John's decision to build his own wheels also meant that the Britten Team would subsequently often suffer a chronic shortage. This in turn meant that many tyre changes had to be made under intense pressure because an insufficient number of rims could be set up with tyres in advance.

It seems a lot more likely that John built his own wheels because they were his own wheels. Once again, he was playing to the gallery. This was John the designer seeking to stun, not John the motorcycle builder seeking only to win. Composite wheels would be yet another thing for the motorcycle world to talk about and wonder at. They would occasion comment not just because they were structurally interesting but also because carbon-fibre was the very latest thing. Automotive and motorcycle designers and manufacturers were then discovering the extremely seductive aesthetic of carbon-fibre. The grey and black weft and weave of the material in the clear resin formed wonderful three-dimensional patterns and it was widely known to be strong, light and expensive space-age stuff.

John's wheels would not, actually, be the first carbon-fibre wheels, but they would be created using his own unique structural design.[125] He thought about the task as he beavered away through the night, and soon figured out a way to make skin and bones, three-spoke, front and rear wheels featuring his trademark oversized bearings. He was confident that the wheels he had in mind would be light and strong, because all the loads would be distributed reasonably evenly throughout the structure. Remarkably, he got it right first time and the method he devised would serve for all subsequent Britten wheels, although the design would change later to a five-spoke arrangement and many production refinements would subsequently evolve from the original.[126]

Once again he shut himself away in his workshop, neglecting to eat and to sleep, taking only the odd break to share time with his family, working his chemical alchemy with Kevlar and carbon-fibre. And then, some two weeks later, it was done. The first Britten composite wheel was a reality.

Days and days of finishing work followed, filling pinholes with resin and sanding with increasingly fine paper until at last, after expending several hundred hours in total to get to this point, the first wheel was ready for a final sealing coat of epoxy before painting.[127] And as always Bob Brookland did the job, buffing the wheel to a smooth sheen before applying coats of clear lacquer to give the it a lustrous, silky finish.[128]

With his first set of wheels under his arm John raced into Phil Payne's shop and demanded he put some tyres on them. Phil refused. He pointed out that it would be unreasonable for John to trust the safety of any rider to such untested components. John took the admonition seriously and roared off to find Mike Sinclair, who was in town at the time. Mike, as usual, agreed to help and together they went off to Mace Engineering—an old family firm in the city—where calibrated testing equipment was available to measure load and deflection. With simple jigs Mike and John were then able to quantify the rigidity and strength of a wheel against a production magnesium alloy item. To John's absolute delight, his wheel was found to have only 60 percent the deflection of the other, a finding that must have alleviated the distress of watching his painstakingly constructed wheel wrecked in the destruction tests that followed. Fortunately, the sacrifice confirmed that the wheel was outstandingly rugged. John then made a replacement for his ruined wheel and returned to Phil with his test results in hand, after which Phil happily clad them with rubber. From conception to execution, and then finally testing, just three weeks had elapsed.

As the suspension and bodywork for the new machine neared completion, attention was now given to items such as the brakes. From the outset of the new project John had decided to stick with the AP Racing brakes that had served him so well on the first bikes.[129] Something John had intended to change from the braking system used by his old bikes, however, were the cast-iron discs, which he wanted to replace, somewhat predictably, with carbon-fibre items. Unfortunately, and in spite of exhaustive enquiries made on his behalf by AP Racing, they proved difficult to secure, and finally their prohibitive cost and continuing performance problems persuaded John to stay with the cast-iron units. The only major modification in the braking department was one initiated by Chris Haldane, who insisted on different brake pads being used. He had good reason to do so. Normally, a wheel can be expected to act as a heat sink to draw heat away from the discs, but carbon-fibre is a poor thermal conductor. For that reason it was essential the pads be able to handle heat build-up, and the Performance Friction brake pads chosen by Chris were noted for their ability to do just that.

As regards the instrumentation for the new bike, not surprisingly John decided to do something different. Of course, something different meant something other than analogue instruments, a decision that many car manufacturers, enthralled by the design possibilities offered by *Star Wars*-electronic displays, had taken and lived to regret. The simple truth was that people found graduated dials with needles unambiguous and easy to read because they presented the whole picture, something that digital electronic displays generally did not do. John, however, was determined to find a new way to impart such vital information as how many revs the engine was doing, and so instead of a tachometer on the dashboard he fitted a red and a green light. This did not tell the rider how many revs the engine was doing but it did tell the rider when to change gear. While in the power band the green light would stay on, with the red lighting up when it was time to shift up. Having done so, the green would come back on.[130] Few riders ever liked it.

A second considerably bigger set of red and green lights on the dash gave warning, respectively, of falling oil pressure and overheating in the cooling system. Smack in the middle of the lot was the electrical socket the Team plugged into to download the data from the bike's computer onto a laptop in the pit.[131]

It was hoped this facility might prove useful in setting the bike up for different tracks and conditions, and initially John was confident he could market the telemetry to other race teams. Eventually, such information would be sent to the globetrotting Mike Sinclair down the phone line so that he could make his suggestions, and on the odd occasion that proved to be of limited use. Regrettably, the suspension recordings proved to be an interesting sideshow that was never of any real, practical value.

Meanwhile, Hans had finished his work flowing the 4-valve heads and the new engines were assembled. At the bottom of the assembly was a new crankshaft fresh from America. Some months earlier John had spotted an advertisement in an American performance car magazine for Crower crankshafts proclaiming that 'The World's Lightest Crankshaft Just Got Lighter'. Crower was a well-known American manufacturer of camshafts, valve trains, crankshafts, rods, injectors and clutches for high-performance engines. The company had developed an ultra-light crankshaft by carefully removing metal from non-stress areas, and had also perfected what it called a 'straight-shot' oiling system that worked with the centrifugal force generated by the spinning crank to reduce bearing wear and failure. John wrote to the company in California explaining that he was keen to reduce the inertia produced by the hefty 10-kg cranks that Rob machined out of 4340 billet.

'We currently run a balance factor of 55%,' John wrote, 'and this has proved most satisfactory. Our understanding of crankshaft stresses is that hollow crank pins can actually reduce the crank web stress levels by 50% if designed correctly. Can you help us at all with the correct proportioning of holes, web thickness and overlaps etc?'

After the usual exchange of letters John was satisfied that the Americans could help him, so he cabled Crower US$1500 and received a new crank for Christmas. It was an absolutely state-of-the-art beauty in flawless polished steel and it performed well.

Another company John was having negotiations with was the Swedish manufacturer Setrab, which made radiators for both oil and watercooling. He had been using their oil coolers as water coolers on the earlier Brittens but on the Swedes' advice he now considered ordering a special radiator for the ducted system. When he finally did so, however, he placed his order with a British radiator manufacturer called Docking.

Britten Motorcycles also ceased trading with White Power Suspension, in spite of all the personal goodwill that existed between them. There had been something of a corporate shake-up at the Dutch company, with key staff leaving, but the reason for switching to Ohlin suspension units from Sweden was that Mike Sinclair had clout with the company, through his association with the Kenny Roberts Team, and he was able to use this influence to order custom units especially fabricated to suit the new suspension of the Britten bike.[132] Amid the confusion of letters, faxes and phone calls, and out of the haggling and wheedling, specifying, ordering, confirming and chasing up, the bits that John would or could not make himself started to arrive.

As soon as the two new engines were assembled, Hans ran them up on the dynamometer, which the Team now had working. Hooking up the German software had not been easy and a fair volume of correspondence had been exchanged between John and Stefan Leiber at Dynotech. Not least of the problems was understanding the commands, and John sent one fax with a string of phrases such as '*Laufzitfehler—aufgetreten*' for translation. Stefan had patiently worked through the problems with John, and when Hans arrived from Auckland Broz had the machine functioning well. Of course, Hans understood the commands, which made life easier.[133] In their initial tests the motors performed well, and the usual process of mapping the EMS for optimum horsepower started, at which point Hans headed back home to Auckland.

'When we were building the engines John told me he wanted 145 bhp, and soon after I got home he rang me and said he had 160. I told him he was bullshitting me and then he told me he had made stroker kits. The engines were out to 1100cc. That explained the power gain but it was still very good progress.'[134]

Immediately after finishing work on the new 4-valve head Hans had turned his attention to the 5-valve John also wanted to build. Once again, it was typical of John that he should sally forth into a totally new area of engine development when the recent race at Daytona had shown clearly that his engines would be more than powerful enough to win, especially given the extra twenty-odd horsepower offered by the new 4-valve heads. For John, however, there was no such thing as adequate power. As always it was not enough for John simply to win; he had to win with crushing superiority. The fact that such technical forays cost valuable time and resources that could have been used to refine what was already working did worry him, and later he candidly admitted many such mistakes. His concern that he might be charging up a blind alley did not stop him, however, from trying everything that might give his machines an advantage. He was used to following his own convictions and ideas, even to the degree that this meant sometimes having the courage to make mistakes. And he was not alone; he had Jerry Branch in California to guide him.

In a letter to Jerry, he wrote that having gained second place at Daytona he could only think about how to get first in 1992. 'To beat the Ducatis my new heads are going to have to be outstanding. Your five-valve suggestion is the one I am dying to make. Not only for the reasons of added valve area but also because the reduced valve mass will promote faster rates of lift. I think there is room for three 1.1" to

1.2" inlet valves.'[135]

Jerry wasted little time in replying, and when he did he was most encouraging about the potential for a 5-valve version of the engine, something he had been keen to see developed since John showed him the heads of the very first Britten engine. He had run some tests on the new heads with a 5-valve set-up on his CAD (Computer Aided Design) and had come up with the necessary drawings and some very encouraging numbers.

In his response to Jerry's return fax, John wrote, 'Great to hear that things are coming right on the CAD. When I read the bit about "no problems with 173 hp" I just about went through the roof with excitement. I just can't wait to whip those factory Ducatis. I'll be eternally grateful to you, that's for sure.'

Once he had received Jerry's drawings of the 5-valve placement, Hans set about developing the ports and so on for the new head. He followed exactly the same procedure as he had with the 4-valve head and the work proceeded without a hitch. His initial opinion was that the 5-valve held considerable promise but he was disappointed with the final shape of the combustion chamber, which he claimed Rob 'for some reason or other' machined in such a way that it was not like the model.

> It worked OK but if you go back to the original flow figures it should have worked a lot better. John had purchased a water brake, which he couldn't get to work, so I helped him set it up. We ran the 5-valve on it and changed lots of things but it needed a lot more development than it ever got. It is hard to say just what was wrong because we had so little information, but I think the changes Rob made to the shape of the combustion chamber probably had a lot to do with it. With all those valves there was bound to be a problem achieving a good squish shape anyway. Certainly John always complained that he couldn't get the compression he wanted.

It must have been a keen disappointment for John, whose faith in Jerry to that point had never been shaken. By following Jerry's general prescriptions in the past, John had always realised precisely the performance outcomes from his engines that Jerry had predicted. He must have almost felt he had the 175 hp Jerry was reading off his CAD in his hand, but he didn't. The dynamometer print-out showed the 5-valve was making less power than the 4-valve through the mid-range by a small but infuriatingly persistent margin and a little more at the top end—and there it stuck.

What had worked, and worked in no uncertain fashion, was increasing the capacity of the 4-valve to 1100cc. The increase in power was instant and gratifyingly free of complications. The 1100 motors would soon deliver a staggering and reliable 175 bhp, enough simply to walk away from practically anything else it was liable to meet on a racetrack. John must have dreamed of 5-valve heads breathing like champions on the bigger bore and seen the magic number 200 light up—something that would have astounded the motorcycle world. Still, 175 bhp was nothing to be sneezed at. It was more than enough to win.

At that time there was no problem racing at the enlarged capacity in both the US and Europe, although the limit in New Zealand was set at 1000cc. However, it was a relatively simple matter to remove the stroker kit for races at home, where the reduced capacity set-up could be reliably produce a still outstanding 145 bhp.

Meanwhile, back at The Stables, Jason had been busy smoothing off the bodywork for bike Number Two and tweaking it to make it fit together, after which he turned his hand to making more wheels. While he was thus occupied, Bob painted the finished bodywork for Number One—with a colour scheme that was an example of John the 'dazzler' working at fever pitch. The combination of metallic electric blue and Barbie pink was so vibrant it bordered on being gaudy, yet the colours were also somehow so appropriate that it was immediately difficult to imagine a Britten in any other hues.

The inspiration for the pink guards and foot protectors may have come during one of the American trips. During Speed Week at Daytona the previous year John had shot a video tape while driving through the downtown traffic. Naturally, a great deal of the activity on the crowded streets revolved around the thousands of bikes that gathered every year for the most popular motorcycle race festival in America. In one part of the driving sequence John had frozen the frame on a collection of bikes, in the centre of which, in sharp focus, was a hot-pink road bike.

When he later explained the blue part of the colour scheme to the mayor of Christchurch at the time, Vicki Buck, John told her that he had wanted the bike to look like a New Zealand flag waving in the wind, hence the four red stars with white borders representing the Southern Cross constellation on the tank. However, the explanation he offered most often for the colour scheme was that he had purchased a glass starfish in the markets at Bali while on holiday there because he had been utterly entranced by its electric-blue colouring.

Using the starfish as a guide, Bob had painted the three-piece fairing, tank and tailpiece with a subtly metallic electric blue, while the front and rear guards and the streamlined 'foot-pod' were a striking pastel pink. The tank featured a stylised 'signature' reversed out in white, announcing the machine as a Britten. This was set between four red stars with white borders representing the Southern Cross.

Finally, there was the exhaust system to consider. From the twin exhaust ports on each cylinder four exhaust pipes writhed around the engine like mating snakes, or arteries about a heart, joining finally to form a massive and brutal-looking megaphone. Nobody knows what inspired the hue John chose for the sinuous piping, but once again it looked so right it was hard to imagine any other. John showed an artist friend, Gus Watson, the bike and enthusiastically asked Gus's young daughter Milly if she didn't think that 'Ming blue' was the only colour for an exhaust system. Like most subsequent fans of Britten motorcycles, she agreed. The colour, which could have been drawn from the heart of an oxyacetylene flame, looked both hot and cool.

Working furiously, the Team managed to complete 001 a few days before the Ruapuna round of the New Zealand Formula One Championship. The new generation Britten V-1000 had arrived with just weeks to spare before it was booked to appear at the Sound of Thunder meeting after which it would be crated up and sent off to Daytona. True to form, Team Britten was cutting things fine.

In town with a free week before the next round at Ruapuna and happy to accept the first ride was Chris Haldane, back in New Zealand after a season racing for Suzuki in America. He had purchased his own Yamaha OW01 Superbike to campaign back home and with it was leading the New Zealand Formula One Championship series.

> John had called me after my last race at Wanganui and he was obviously just itching to see how his new bike went. I looked at it and thought that it looked pretty cool. There was no doubting John's ability and I just wanted to ride it immediately. I told him it was definitely out there and he was pleased with the comment.

Mike Sinclair was also back in New Zealand doing his off-season windsurfing when he 'got the call' to come and join in the fun at Ruapuna. At that stage the suspension sensors that would later feed into the bike's EMS had not been fitted and John was keen to have Mike rig up a number of the independent data recorders used by the Roberts Team.

> I turned up in the morning before testing to make sure all was well and said hello to Chris, who was looking forward to the session. Then I went off windsurfing and returned later in the afternoon to find the bike in bits. Chris had been injured and there was a real question mark about his ability to complete the remaining two rounds of the championship. His position at the top of the points was looking very iffy.

To John's intense embarrassment, the front end had broken, spitting Chris onto the track and breaking his collarbone. The problem was the lower wishbone which in John's enthusiasm for carbon-fibre, he had fashioned with that material and had broken the cardinal rule by turning it through a right angle. The wishbones had predictably fractured at that point and even several years after John still winced when he spoke of the episode. Later, he told a journalist that, 'you get some talented guy who is about to win a championship and he generously agrees to test your new bike and you send him out and injure him. It was a terrible feeling.'

For Chris, the accident was literally the stuff of nightmares.

> I had done three laps when the bike just folded on me and fired me straight over the handlebars. It was like driving along in a car and having the steering wheel come off in your hands as you approach a corner. For ages after that I would wake up every night after being asleep for about three minutes and I'd be back there, flying over the bars. I'd almost jump out of bed the feeling was so horribly real. I left the track feeling really angry with John because it was the second time one of his bikes had collapsed underneath me and it looked like it was going to cost me a New Zealand Championship.

Chris's team carted him off to the hospital where his fears of a collarbone fracture were confirmed. The only thing that could be done was to put the arm in a sling after which Chris and his crew decided to seek solace in the bars of Christchurch. In addition to the two races at Ruapuna there were still two more rounds, at Teretonga in Timaru, to complete the season, and it really looked as if 1992 was effectively a lost cause. Chris and his team were still trying to revive their spirits with generous applications of lager when John finally caught up with them. He was short of breath as he had been running from one bar to another all over town. He was, according to Chris, desperately sorry about what had happened.

> He kept saying, 'What have I done?' I ended up feeling terrible for him he was so distraught. Obviously he hadn't meant to do it and the set-up looked sturdy enough. The break was a bad one but as the muscle trauma began to subside over the next day or so I began to feel a bit better. I had been racing for three solid months and I was very fit. John and I talked about building a foam structure onto the tank of the bike so that I could take my weight on my chest rather than on my wrists and I saw a sports physio who said I was mad but that I might get away with it. And so I decided to go for it. When John heard that I was going to go ahead he could not have been more helpful and we did the work around at his place.

On the day, and to everybody's surprise, the plan worked. Chris ran around the track for just long enough to make sure the bike was OK and then entered the preliminary race on the Saturday.

> I couldn't believe it when I immediately crashed. This guy on an RC30 got a great start and I followed him down the inside, but he braked about 20 metres early and I wound up squashed between him and a brick wall at the first corner. My leathers were all ripped around the damaged collarbone and I thought it was all over for good. However, it didn't hurt and the next day I won both of the next rounds of the series, the second of which was the New Zealand Grand Prix. I secured a first and a second at the following meeting at Teretonga and only had to manage better than a fifth at Timaru to take the Championship. I did that in the first race and then foolishly decided to do the second. Gassing the bike up coming out of the hairpin, I felt the bone break again and the pain was the worst I'd ever experienced. I don't know how I managed to stay on the bike but I made it back to the pits and just collapsed on the ground. Apparently, if you re-break bones when they are just beginning to mend, it makes the final recovery time a lot longer. The injury took about twelve weeks to heal but I had the Championship and that was the thing that mattered. I know it was also a tremendous relief for John.

Chris had been scheduled to ride the Britten at the following Sound of Thunder meeting but he was now highly uncertain if he would be fit for it. Doubtless feeling guilty, and therefore not wanting simply to replace Chris in spite of the odds against him competing, John offered to pay two air fares if Chris could bring a second, reserve rider from Auckland. John had already asked Chris and Robert Holden, who were both unavailable, to suggest an alternative rider for Daytona and they both came up with the name Andrew Stroud. And so when Chris flew back down to Christchurch he was accompanied by a lanky young man with a shy but engaging grin and a temperament off the track that suggested engineering rather than motorsport as a career. John was waiting outside the terminal in the Benz, and the two riders loaded their gear into the boot and eased themselves into the confined interior of the sports car, making themselves as comfortable as possible for John's usual 80 mph blast through the suburbs to The Stables.

For Chris it was the beginning of the end of a relationship in which he had invested a great deal of time and effort.

> By then it was obvious that I wouldn't be able to ride at the Sound of Thunder because of my collarbone and shortly after that I signed a deal to ride in the Malaysian Superbike series for Marlboro Yamaha on an OW01. The contract stipulated that I couldn't ride anything else during 1992 and 1993 and so that was that. I'd put a lot in for Johnny and I never made a cent out of it and I never got the big ride. It was disappointing but it was nobody's fault—it was just motor racing.

It was, as Chris said, just motor racing and it was inevitable that as the door closed for one rider it would open for another. In this case, however, the new man would prove more than a good match for the big, brutal V-twin. He would also prove to be, perhaps more than anyone else, John's brother in arms and his most profound travelling companion.

In a fax confirming Britten Motorcycles' race entry to the organisers of the Pro Twins race at Daytona in 1992, John appended one of his smiley faces alongside the enquiry, 'Do you know where I can find a rider who can beat Doug Polen?' The question was somewhat indulgent, as John's previous riders had shown they were more than capable of doing so. Indeed, Paul Lewis would have beaten him in 1991 had he not run short of fuel. However, even if John had not had any real misgivings about any of his other riders, Andrew Stroud would certainly become the one who inspired him with the most confidence. John went on to nickname him 'The Maestro' and would often say that when Andrew was on his bike it usually won.

Andrew Stroud, or Stroudy to his mates, had his first experience on a motor cycle when he was ten years old. A mate had a trail bike and he was allowed to ride it around on his friend's father's farm in the Auckland suburb of Howick, where they both lived. It was then a pleasant coastal village surrounded by countryside, a decade away from a housing explosion that would convert it to a sprawling suburb.

From the start, motorcycling was much to young Andrew's taste, but he had to wait until he was fifteen years old before he could buy his own bike and start riding in earnest. His first machine was a Suzuki TS90 trailbike, and he learned the art of motorcycle control on it, leaping, sliding and wheel-standing, wherever and whenever he could. By the time Andrew began his studies for an engineering qualification, he was ready to trade up to a road bike, which he was soon racing. He then worked his way through a prodigious number of motorcycles as he polished his new craft and quickly became bored and frustrated by the limitations of one machine after another.

> I had owned twenty motorbikes by the time I was nineteen as I traded my way up toward a decent race bike. The only problem was that I only made money out of one of them, a Suzi GT380 triple, which I bought for about NZ$250. I spent a hundred on it and after hand-painting it black I managed to get NZ$750 for it. In spite of my lack of success as an amateur dealer I had graduated to a Kawasaki KR250 by the time I was eighteen and came third in my first race, a club race at Pukekohe. I then raced the winter series and had some great battles with the likes of Mike Webb, Tony Rees and Brian Bernard at Bay Park, Taupo and Manfeild. I managed a few seconds and thirds after that in a number of club events, but there was no prize money and

while I was going to tech I had to survive on my NZ$33-a-week student allowance. It didn't leave much for racing.

By then he was convinced, however, that racing motorcycles was something he very much wanted to do. It was also obvious to his family. Andrew's mother, Barbara, had good cause to remember the day Andrew persuaded her to go for a ride on the back of his latest two-wheeled acquisition when, in spite of his father's admonition to 'take it easy', he wheel-stood the bike the length of the street as she hung on for grim death. His parents would prove, like so many motorcycle racers' parents, strong and consistent supporters of his efforts on the race track—immensely proud when he did well and equally understanding when he did not. Progress was steady though, as Andrew recalled.

In spite of the cash shortage I moved on to a TZR Yamaha 250 and did the National Series at the end of the year, coming eleventh.

Aaron Slight won every race that year and the quality of the riders generally was very high. For a while I struggled to find competitive pace but I felt my riding go up another level during the series, especially, for some reason, when we went to the meeting at Taupo. Everything suddenly clicked. My style changed completely and I became a lot more fluid, and a lot faster.

After the season this guy called Murray Carter called me up and offered to have his company, Shanton Apparel, sponsor me. He'd sponsored a few riders in the past and some had done pretty well. At the time I was working part-time at an engineering company called Stevens Chemical Industries for work experience, as part of my tech NZCE[136] engineering course. I was drawing up parts for packaging machinery and setting up machines for various production runs of things like toothpaste, shampoo and Valium. I was certainly ready for a diversion and so when I found myself on a race-ready Yamaha 250 for the summer series of 1986–87 I was pretty happy. I was even happier when I was able to beat Aaron and take the Championship.

I also raced a Yamaha 1000 in the second half of the National Open Production and the Formula One Series and won a few battles with Aaron and Bob Toomey. Bob was a Suzuki rider who went on to work for Kenny Roberts Junior. I just kept racing and a year later I managed a second place to Mick Doohan in a Formula One endurance race at Bathurst. And then in 1991 I won the New Zealand Formula One Championship. By then I knew it was what I had to do.

Andrew remembered his first meeting with John as a casual encounter that held no hint of the close friendship that would soon develop between them.

> I was at the do following a World Superbike race at Manfeild after finishing sixth on a Yamaha OW01, a bike I still have because the Japanese team I raced for gave it to me. John walked up and said who he was, but it didn't mean much because I really didn't know what he was doing. He told me he liked my race lines and that was it until Chris called and asked if I would like to ride a Britten. As I didn't have a ride organised for the Superbike series I said yes. I knew about Chris's tumble and he filled me in on the rest so I was aware of what I was letting myself in for, but I thought I'd check it out. John picked us up from the airport in his white Benz, which he later often gave me to use, and we went to his home. That's where I stayed while in Christchurch from then on. At first we were a bit guarded and awkward with one another. He told me he'd given up riding after he ground his foot down but he didn't seem to resent having other people ride his bikes.

It is hardly surprising that John was happy to hand his precious but ferocious machine over to a younger professional. He would often say that he started racing motorcycles late and it was true. Had he commenced racing, as Andrew had, in his teenage years there was no telling how far he might have gone. Moreover, when he did finally start racing, instead of honing his skills on 'proper' race machinery he had used up most of his racing years campaigning his Triumph Tiger. As we know, this was a brutal pig that demanded a peculiar style and rewarded courage and determination with dangerous unpredictability. In spite of that John had become a first-rate rider who deserved the respect he was given by those he raced against. In any event, he had done his stint on the track. He had won a few races, placed well in a few that mattered and he'd been injured. It was enough. He now knew sufficient about the game from the rider's point of view to build machines they could win races on and to appreciate their skill when they drew the best from his creations. In his forties, he was comfortable enough within himself not to resent his riders' abilities and confident enough of his role as a designer to celebrate their victories as his own.

Age would certainly not prove to be a barrier between Andrew and John, and they both came to realise that they had a great deal in common in spite of the fact that they came from different generations. Those who knew John well often describe him affectionately as 'a boy' and there was a quality of almost childlike wonder and enthusiasm in his nature. In Andrew he found a sympathetic and guileless friend whose easygoing attitude masked a keen mind and an aggressive will to win on the track.

In future, John and indeed the entire Britten Team, five or six at a time, would often stay with Andrew's family whenever they were in Auckland. Barbara Stroud remembered those visits as tremendously high-spirited romps that filled the house with the laughter and excited patter of the Team on a mission. In spite of the constant rush and pressure that seemed to travel with John, she also remembered that he was a perfect guest who cooked and cleaned and always left his room immaculately tidy.

> The Team were seldom home before five in the morning, except Andrew, who got plenty of sleep when he was racing. But John would always be up bright and early. He and I often used to talk about the things that could be done to the house. He redesigned it in his head the day he walked in and he had wonderful ideas. Gradually we started talking about all sorts of things. He was quite deep and he was looking for answers to the big questions in life. I had been through a lot of life's trials looking for my own answers and so we had a lot to talk about.

Andrew's sister, Melanie, was usually about during these invasions and she found that the developing friendship between John and her brother revealed a number of quite striking similarities between the two.

> They were both very good, evenly matched, chess players with a similar way of looking at things. Andrew also did the same engineering course as John, but it went deeper than that. They behaved like brothers in all sorts of ways that could at times be quite unnerving. They were both tall and gangly and they both scuffed their feet, even when they were sitting down. I remember once looking at them as they walked away from me and they both had this goofy stroll with their heads down and their right hands in their pockets. We all noticed the similarities and I remember my mother once asking John what on earth she must be if Andrew was his brother. John laughed and told her she would then be the youngest mother in the world. It was a typical remark for John to make. It wasn't cleverly witty or unctuous; it was just kind, warm and friendly.
>
> He was always interested in the things others were doing and so it was always lovely to have him around. I had a small shop selling kids' toys and I did a lot of my own design work. No matter how busy he was he always wanted to see my designs and to hear what I was up to. And he was so busy; his life never seemed to slow down. Once he was talking on his cellphone and a second call came in on another cellphone for him, so he had one on each ear. He looked at me and smiled and said, 'Now I'll get two tumours!'

With Andrew in the saddle and the whole Team in attendance, the debut of the new machine, with new metal wishbones, at Ruapuna in the 1992 Sound of Thunder, caused a sensation. Jim Sykes, who was then the president of the BEARS (and was to remain so for many years), said that John's previous bikes had had a powerful impact on the BEARS crowd but nothing had prepared them for the sight of the new V-1000.

> When we first saw the Denco thundering down the track in 1987 it was a tremendous morale booster and we all took pride in John's achievements with it. This was in spite of the fact that in many ways he was completely atypical of BEARS people, most of whom don't have a lot of money. For example, you'd often see some guy wandering around in his shorts and you'd know he hadn't scratched up the money to rebuild his bike after the last blow-up. But there was never a feeling that John was different, or considered himself any better than the rest of us. He was so quiet, you wouldn't know anything special was going on; he'd just be cruising around in his old black leathers. Although we loved the Denco we were totally overwhelmed by the first of the Brittens. The ground would shake and then the sound would drown out all the noise from every other bike on the track. Then as quick as you could turn your head it was gone. We were all even prouder of him for making it. But it was just a warm-up for the main event. When the first blue and pink bike appeared people were hysterically excited about it. They just could not believe their eyes and there was a huge crowd around it whenever it was in the pits. We have a kind of rule that if you always win you are too fast for your class and you ought to move on. Well those first Brittens had no class to move up to, but even though it soon became apparent that there was nothing in BEARS that could get anywhere near them nobody tried to get them handicapped out of contention. We were all so thrilled at what he had done nobody cared. We knew he used the Sound of Thunder to test his bikes, just like he was going to do this time, and that was fine by us.

Because of the rush to have the bike ready to race, Andrew only managed to squeeze in about half a dozen practice laps before the events commenced. He was entered in the last race of the day, the A-grade Flying Farewell, so the Team had little to do but talk to the crowd that was gathered about them. As always, Andrew was so relaxed that he actually spent quite a lot of the time dozing, a habit that amused the rest of the Team, who soon learned that it was wise to delegate someone with the job of waking him up before his race. John happily chatted to all his old mates, who marvelled along with everybody else at the radical new machine. Then finally, it was time to show them all what the new Britten V-1000 could do.

It would not be a cakewalk. A powerful field had gathered to do battle, among them Robert Holden astride his all-conquering Ducati 888, the same type of machine that had taken the world Superbike championship for the last three years. To make his job that much harder, Andrew was also riding with John's urgent shouted instructions to take it easy ringing in his ears.

He didn't.

I had so much power that I was able to go straight out in front, even though I found the bike awkward through the corners. It was hard to hang off the thing because of the slippery seat. The rubber bit in the middle was really narrow and when I slid to the side I was on this really smooth carbon-fibre. This became very uncomfortable very quickly, and I later had the boys put foam rubber strips on the side. My job was made harder because I wasn't getting the feedback from the front end I was used to. I couldn't really get it to do what I wanted it to do. The bike was incredibly light and manoeuvrable, but I couldn't go into the corners as fast as I wanted to because the front tyre would load up and start skipping. At that time all the teams were trying to make their bikes stiffer and stiffer but they were reaching the point where the riders lost the feeling of the bikes. The Britten was exceptionally stable but you couldn't get it to turn in because it was so rigid. The stiffness of the thing was later graphically illustrated when the Team put the front end in a jig and twisted it. It didn't flex, it just locked up the bearings. There was, of course, the advantage of having suspension travel left when under full braking and over bumps, but the reality was that the bike did not like having the front end loaded up. You couldn't brake deep into a corner and that was that. I had expected the front suspension to take some getting used to but I soon discovered that the rear was also doing strange things. Later, we established that the rear pivot point was about 10 mm too low, which caused the chain to pull the wheel up under acceleration, making the front end go light as the bike squatted at the rear. When the back end was loaded up like that the machine lost all its rear suspension travel, so I couldn't hammer it over bumps coming out of bends. It also greatly exaggerated the bike's tendency to wheel-stand. The problem could not easily be corrected because the swing-arm pivot went through the crankcase. The pivot was located just below the horizontal parting line in the crankcase, so it could not simply be moved further up.

The bike was also quite high, which made it more difficult to slide than something with a lower centre of gravity—something I particularly noticed later when I raced it in rain. However, the high stance did have some advantages as it allowed me to get hold of the bike easily and switch direction faster, as well as assisting in weight transfer fore and aft for maximum grip under braking and acceleration.

There was another aspect to the bike's handling, however, that was quite peculiar, although it was it was not all that obvious at Ruapuna. I was most aware of it when I came onto the main straight through the left-turning sweeper. It would not stand up and run to the outside edge of the track, which was where I wanted to be for the left-hander at the end of the straight. Instead, it stayed tipped over and wandered toward the infield.[137] On the plus side it had huge amounts of torque and

> a very smooth power delivery. I liked riding it but I could see that anyone who did not have fairly advanced skills in both road racing and motocross could struggle to ride it fast. From the start, however, I could tell that the potential was there to win and we proved it straight away.

English racer Mark Forsyth was at the meeting and he later recorded his impressions of the new Britten in an article for *Performance Bikes* magazine.

> For the first couple of laps me and my Ducati 888 were right up its chuff, holding second place. Then we came out of a long left sweeper onto the start finish line. The Britten played its ace card. The back end slewed sideways and it punted out of the third-gear corner leaving a long, black line, pelting me with shards of frazzled rubber and bits of track surface. The noise (like a nuclear holocaust) shook my chest cavity. Halfway down the straight the Britten was a dot.

After the meeting the bike was dynamometer tested and, in spite of its performance, and to everybody's horror, it was found to have somehow lost 30 bhp after just on three hours' running. The problem was traced to a drop in compression due to imperfect valve seating, and a full freshen-up of the motor was undertaken with different valve springs. To everybody's relief, a second quick session on the dynamometer revealed that the missing horsepower was back.

John had decided to take advantage of the larger capacity allowed in America, and so the stroker kit was fitted and the bike was once more a V-1100. As time had run out it was then hurriedly nailed into its crate and consigned to Daytona. Such was the rush to get the machine away to catch its flight that there was no time to re-map its computer following the final dynamometer run. Instead, the data from the run was printed out, to be downloaded into the motorcycle's EMS at the other end. As always, time was the one implacable enemy that no amount of will or dogged hard work could overcome. Once again, a Britten motorcycle would attempt to lick the Bowl with absolutely minimal running time to its credit.

Top: John and Roberto Crepaldi in front of "Black Beauty", Milano, Italy, April 1993, before leaving for Euro Races and the Isle of Man Tourist Trophy. (Photo: courtesy Roberto Crepaldi)

Left: John at the crash site, Isle of Man Tourist Trophy. (Photo: Harry Ruffell)

Top: Jason McEwen, Wigram, 17 January 1993. (Photo: Euan Cameron) *Bottom:* Jason McEwen leading Andrew Stroud, Sound of Thunder, 28 February 1993. (Photo: Euan Cameron)

Top: Andrew Stroud, Sound of Thunder, 28 February 1993. (Photo: Euan Cameron) *Bottom:* Andrew Stroud and Loren Poole, Manfeild 31 October 1993. (Photo: Euan Cameron)

Top: Loren Poole in the wet. Wigram, Christchurch, 23 January 1994. (Photo: Euan Cameron) *Bottom:* Jason McEwen, Russell Josiah, Loren Poole. Pukekohe, 13 November 1994. (Photo: Euan Cameron)

Top: Jason McEwen leads Andrew Stroud. New Zealand Grand Prix, Ruapuna 18 December 1994. (Photo: Euan Cameron) *Bottom:* Robert Holden and Andrew Stroud. New Zealand Grand Prix, Ruapuna 18 December 1994. (Photo: Euan Cameron)

Top: Andrew Stroud winning at Assen, 1995. (Photo: Alan Cathcart) *Bottom:* Andrew Stroud and Mike Edwards. Assen, 1995. (Photo: Alan Cathcart)

Top: Andrew Stroud winning at Daytona, 1993. (Photo: Alan Cathcart) *Bottom:* Assen, September 1995, just a few days before John's death. Britten Motorcycles wins the race (Andrew Stroud, first; Steven Briggs, second), and with it, takes the BEARS World Series (Andrew Stroud, first: on a works Britten; Steven Briggs, second: on a Café Racing & Superbikes Britten). *(Photo: courtesy Roberto Crepaldi)*

Top: John at Wigram Wings and Wheels, 19 February 1995. (Photo: Euan Cameron) *Bottom:* John's funeral, Christchurch, 8 September 1995. (Photo: Euan Cameron)

CHAPTER THIRTEEN

The Fifty-cent Connector

Andrew flew alone to Daytona, although in future he and John would invariably travel together.

> I soon after discovered that he was great to travel with because he was always wanting to have adventures and meet as many people as he could. Once, when we were in San Francisco, a beggar asked him for 'a penny from his heart'. John gave the guy money and spent quite a long time talking to him. The man said he'd been a schoolteacher who gave up because he liked begging. He told us he dressed in rags to look the part but made a reasonable living. John loved those kinds of people.
>
> That year Daytona was a full-on Duke [Ducati] effort with 888s galore. The favourite was a French-Canadian rider called Pascal Picotte. Picotte had an 8-valve 851 that was bored and stroked to 926cc. It was being campaigned by the Fast by Ferracci team who had won the World Superbike Championship with Polen on board in 1991 and 1992. The Ducati was a full works spec machine and enjoyed factory backing. It was as good as any Ducati then racing.
>
> I qualified twelfth on the grid because I couldn't get more than two laps in qualifying without the Britten overheating. I never even got a single good practice lap in before the race and, as it was my first time there, I had no opportunity to learn the track. I experienced enough, however, to know that it was very challenging. It was incredibly fast around the banking, where you were running right alongside the wall at well over 180 mph.[138]

The troubles had started for the Team from the moment they got Andrew out on the track. Once more, the intake-valve clearances were evaporating at the rate of about 0.005 in every forty laps. This was not in itself enough to prevent the bike finishing the race, but it was worrying. John eventually put it down to the new location of the injectors so close to the valves and the team simply continued to adjust the lash back in. The overheating problem, caused by a mysterious loss of coolant, proved more serious as there was no obvious leak. Fearing the worst, the Team stood anxiously by while Broz tore the engine down, only to discover a cracked cast-iron cylinder liner. This was something entirely new to the Team and it was a devastating development. There was just the afternoon and the night left before the race and the Team had no spare liner. Mark Franklin, who had come along to keep the EMS honest, immediately glued a phone to his ear and started a marathon phone-around which he eventually abandoned when he had exhausted every possibility for locating a spare within the remotest reach.

Jason Monopoli was also present, having been 'shouted a trip' by his parents, and he remembered the despondent atmosphere as the Team faced the prospect of a wasted journey.

> It was doom and gloom but we slowly cheered up because the place where we were working, which belonged to the AMA[139], had this dance on. It was totally bizarre. Broz was working on the bike in the corner and we were in the middle of all this food and wine. We were scoffing oysters and dancing with these really friendly strangers. When Broz drained the oil out of the bike someone accidentally knocked over the container he was catching it with and oil went all over the floor. Within moments there were people there with paper towels cleaning it all up, telling us not to worry about it
>
> Then John decided to braze up the crack in the cylinder liner. As far as we knew it had never been done before but we had nothing to lose. Broz heated it with the gas axe until John said nothing was going to change by pouring more heat into it. Broz agreed and just brazed it up. By four in the morning we were all playing hula-hoop. John was the best. As the sun came up Broz finished putting the engine back together and we reassembled the bike.

One further problem remained to be sorted out but it was at least something the crew was familiar with. The electronic fuel injection had acquired a lean spot that was stealing acceleration, so the fuel map program, loaded into the EMS only days before, was downloaded once again onto the laptop and the weak region was enriched. With that problem solved they finally heaved a collective sigh of relief. They had overcome the seemingly impossible. Now it was up to Andrew.

The problems had denied Andrew any opportunity to improve his twelfth place on the grid, and his best qualifying time of 2 minutes 2 seconds was well down on the lap record set by Doug Polen the previous year at 1 minute 53.8 seconds. However, when the flag fell Andrew found he was able to catch the race leaders and easily keep up with them. He also found a quick way around the banking.

> I ran about a foot away from the wall at the top at 189 mph, which turned out to be the top speed up until then around there, and then I'd carve it by dropping down through the turn, before drifting back up to the top through the exit. Running through the turn the suspension was squashed down and it was really hard to keep my head up. I was also getting wicked bruising on my chest and it would have been nice to have a bit of rubber on the seat too—there were just these wings of rubber on either side with hard carbon-fibre in the middle. On the other hand, the bike's incredible stability was very reassuring. While other riders were going around the banking weaving and wobbling and hanging on for grim death, I could actually lift my hand and wave to the crowd. I closed up on Picotte, who was leading, and decided to hang in there and follow him around, as I still did not know the track. Then some rain came along and they stopped the race.

Back on pit-lane the Team were in a state of intense nervous excitement. When Andrew came in during the rain break and told John that he was sometimes rolling off to three-quarter throttle in order to keep station behind Picotte, other nearby teams heard it and the word went down pit-lane like a brush fire. By the time the race restarted, the hype had built to an almost unbearable level. The tension erupted into all-out jubilation in the Britten camp as Andrew went straight after Picotte and latched onto him, running times that were only one-tenth of a second outside the lap record.

> It was an amazing motorcycle. It had really only done the twenty-odd laps at Ruapuna and a sprinkling at Daytona and there was still so much that was not right with it. The rear suspension was causing the thing to pull wheelies all over the place. It was great for the crowd, and it looked really cheeky, but it made it hard to accelerate. I felt like I needed wheelie bars. The underside curve of the fairing was also angled too high and that was causing high-speed lift, which made the wheelie tendency even more pronounced. I could lift the front wheel at 150 mph just by opening the throttle. It was simply incredible that in spite of all that, a brand-new, completely unsorted bike could still set the times that it did.
>
> Pascal Picotte got away a bit after re-start as he obviously realised there was some competition and I had to go after him at ten-tenths. When I caught him I was again happy to sit behind him and stay in his draft.

For lap after lap the Britten dogged Picotte, effortlessly closing on the Ducati with a great, fat burst of acceleration whenever the French-Canadian looked like clawing ahead. Andrew even pulled wheelies on the fast corner out of the infield, the only rider ever to have done so in the history of the track. As he gained confidence in the machine he began to draw right alongside the Ducati, and on one occasion that will for ever be part of Daytona folklore, he did so while on the back wheel. He seemed to toy with the hapless Picotte, and it became increasingly clear to the thousands of enraptured fans watching on the edges of their seats that the big blue and pink twin would eat up the Ducati either under braking approaching the chicane or powering out. In fact, Andrew had already made his choice.

'I'd decided to wait for the last lap,' Andrew recalled, 'and then close right up on him coming out of the chicane. Although the Britten was slow through that section of track, due to its reluctance to change direction, I knew I could be up his chuff, slip-streaming him as we approached the race to the line, where I'd be able to comfortably blast past him.'

Jason remembered the wild excitement that now reigned among the Britten team as the laps counted down.

> We were all shouting like lunatics. I was standing on the roof of our poor little hired van and I was jumping up and down so much I completely caved in the roof. John was doing his spastic disco war dance, whooping and yelling, punching his arms into the air. We all knew we were going to kick ass and it felt bloody marvellous. And then, just as we were certain we were going to romp home, the bike slowed down, spluttered around two more laps while everybody went past and then stopped. I walked back to the shed in a daze and by the time I got there the race was over. We hadn't even finished.

Sometime in the early hours of that last long night the rectifier had been wired up back to front. There were three bullet connections and two ended up with the wrong mates. Of course, it could not have happened if there had been a proper three-point plug and it would almost certainly not have happened if bleary eyes had not guided the hands that did it, along with a brain fogged by a lack of sleep. Perhaps it wouldn't have happened if Broz had finished the wiring rather than John.

It would not have mattered if the bike had not spent all the time that it did on the grid after surviving a rainstorm, waiting for the restart. It would not have mattered if the bike had not had to do all the extra laps after the race restart. But it did matter. The Britten had been slowly running out of electrical juice throughout the race. The battery was flat and the management system could not work. This time the use of a fifty-cent connector really had cost the Britten Team victory at Daytona. It is almost certain that the machine would have run the distance if the race had not been stopped and restarted due to the rain. But nothing is certain in motor racing and Picotte enjoyed an unopposed victory. He was followed home by no fewer than eight Ducati-powered machines.

There was scarcely time to mope and Jason remembered his absolute amazement at the scene awaiting him back at the Britten pit.

> There were suddenly all these people crowding about. John wheeled the bike in with his eight-year-old son Sam sitting on it and everyone went wild. They wouldn't stop clapping and cheering. I'm talking about a hell of a lot of people. They were giving us flowers and clamouring for t-shirts and so on. It was completely overwhelming. At one point I popped down to the Ferracci pit and there were about twenty people hanging around. Anyone who didn't know better would think they were the ones who lost.

An American tabloid television film crew turned up and the interviewer shoved a furry microphone in Broz's direction and asked why the motorcycle went so fast. If they had expected him to feel triumphant after losing a race, or placated by all the attention the Britten Team was receiving, they were about to be sharply disillusioned. Broz looked him square in the camera and said, 'I'm fucked if I know' and then went back to doing whatever it was he was doing. It has been said that the entire film crew was stone-cold flummoxed.

Andrew recalled that, 'John was deeply disappointed but he handled it very graciously.'

> He now knew we had the potential to win in any company and he took great comfort from that. All week we had this incredible amount of attention and interest from American race fans. They saw the bike as the radical cutting edge of motorcycle technology. And now it had proven itself. It was easily the fastest bike there and that was now plain for everyone to see. I watched the Superbike race on the Sunday and I remember thinking that the Britten could have been right up with the front-runners. Polen and Picotte were on their Fast by Ferracci Ducatis and they were doing lap times of about 1..53 to 1..54. Scott Russell was doing the same sort of times on his Muzzy Kawasaki ZXR750. The best I'd done was a 1..53.9, which was clearly competitive. Picotte was running in a strong second place at the halfway point of the race when he came in for fresh tyres. Unfortunately for him, he went too hard on them before they heated up and he fell off at the third corner. However, I knew I could beat him around that track and that convinced me the Britten was as fast as any Superbike in the world, even with its wayward handling. I knew that if we could sort that out it could be so dominant that the world would have to take notice, but I had strong doubts about the front end. It had promise but it needed a lot of development and there were no guarantees that we'd ever catch up with the very refined technology of telescopic forks. However, the girder had attracted a lot of attention.

Britten Motorcycles and its founder were now famous. *Cycle World*, the most prestigious and widely circulated motorcycle magazine in America, featured a gorgeous colour photograph of the bike soon after on its cover with the words 'STUNNER! Britten V-1100' above it. On the top right-hand side of the cover was the unequivocal message, 'THE WORLD'S MOST ADVANCED MOTORCYCLE. And it's not from Japan, Germany, Italy or America'. The cover story inside had been written by Kevin Cameron, the magazine's leading technical writer, a position he had occupied for many years at the magazine's illustrious predecessor, *Cycle Magazine*. His piece concluded with the words, 'Picotte rode well on a fine machine to win the race without further challenge. Britten, Stroud and crew were left with only the glory of all they had dared. And the bright prospect of all they seem destined to achieve. Soon. Very soon.'

The rest of the world's motorcycle press was quick to follow with a veritable flood of words on the Britten and its creator. If John had actually yet to dazzle the motorcycle world he had certainly strongly intrigued it.

And the starburst of attention in the American and European motorcycle media was noticed back home in New Zealand. Britten Motorcycles finally made the television news there, a medium with a long and inexplicable indifference toward the achievements of an equally long list of Kiwi motorcycle achievers. The story that was carried by New Zealand's two networks. Viewers were told that the Kiwi-built Britten motorcycle had been robbed of almost certain victory at Daytona because practically the only part of the bike that was not made by John Britten, a Ducati electrical unit, had failed.

Before the next big outing, in Italy at Monza, there was time for three additional Pro Twins races in America, the first of which was at the banked track at Charlotte in North Carolina, and Andrew and Broz made the long drive across the continent from San Francisco. It was the first time the two had ever spent any time together and Andrew remembered they got along very well.

> A lot of people don't understand him that well but I found him very genuine—you could always rely on Broz to tell the truth as he saw it.
>
> Anyway, we made it to Charlotte and I qualified up front but broke a cam belt and bent the valves. We then drove all the way back to Laguna Seca where, because I was a late entry in this race, I had to start from the back of the grid. We replaced the valves and I had a bit of a practice before the race. When we went out on the grid I found I was so far back I couldn't even see Picotte, who was up the front. However, I had a good start and more or less went straight through the field. I could see this guy in front I presumed was Picotte, and after blasting past him I thought I was winning. Unfortunately, I wasn't. The guy I passed was another Fast by Ferracci

> rider that I didn't know about and he was wearing identical leathers to Picotte. John had turned up and was in the pits, but he thought I knew Picotte was still out there so there were no signals. I started pulling wheelies and having a good time and it wasn't till I got to the winner's circle that I found out I'd come second.
>
> On the rostrum I said something really silly. I told everyone that the Britten handled better than the Suzuki 1100 I'd ridden the day before for another team, Dutchman Racing. The team's owner went berserk at me in front of John screaming, 'If you don't want to ride my bike just say so!'[140] John walked along with me after the trophy presentation and when I told him what a jerk I felt like he told me he could relate to someone putting their foot in it. He said he knew I didn't mean it the way it sounded and he made me feel a whole lot better. We were beginning to be pretty good friends. This guy from the local BMW dealership then lent us a little pick-up, so Broz and I crammed in and headed for Atlanta, where we broke the cam belts again in practice and withdrew from the race. Then it was time to get ready for Monza.

Once back in New Zealand, the bike was freshened up and was reassembled in time for Broz to have a crack at the 1992 BEARS Speed trials on it before it was shipped off for the Italian campaign. It was a ride Broz would probably have preferred to miss. In a letter to Mike Sinclair, who was in Sydney, Murray Aitken wrote that 'Broz ran 174 mph in the drizzle on slicks and only pulling 9200 rpm—he must be getting old as he thought it was dangerous—anyway it's 10 mph up on the old bike, suggesting 160 hp (crank).'

In fact, Broz had had the Britten wound out as far as it would go.

> It kept wheel-spinning on all the little bumps because it was so wet. I was looking down a narrow corridor with trees, barbed-wire fences and ditches on either side and I kept reassuring myself that there was no reason for it to want to go sideways—no reason at all! And I kept telling myself that as I kept it wide open, but the wheel spin meant that it would not go any faster. It was a relief to get to the end of the run.

Broz's efforts were at any rate sufficient to win the Cahill Cup easily, before the machine was crated up and delivered to the airport. Then Broz and Andrew flew ahead to Italy and cleared the machine through customs, before going to Monza to set the bike up at the famous old Italian racetrack. John soon caught up with them and when everything was in order he arranged a visit to the nearby Moto Guzzi factory. The Team was accompanied on the visit by Phil Payne who, like Team Britten, was back in Europe to race in the BotT races at Monza and at Assen.

For John, the visit to the Moto Guzzi factory was primarily an opportunity to renew his acquaintance with Dr John Wittner.[141] Since meeting the American

Guzzi-tuning guru at Daytona, John had kept in touch with him and they had formed quite a friendship. And Broz soon nosed out the dynamometer room, where he found a Guzzi V-twin singing away on full throttle, which it had apparently been doing for the past sixty hours. It was an impressive example of the lengths to which Dr John was prepared to go in order to ensure that the new 8-valve Moto Guzzi engines would perform reliably. Although there was little possibility that Moto Guzzi would ever have any interest in Britten technology, beyond perhaps the now fully functional EMS and some carbon-fibre work, the visit was not entirely social. Dr John Wittner was both an accomplished development engineer and an effective administrator and you never knew when you might require the services of just such a man.

For Andrew, the BotT race at Monza was to prove one of very mixed fortunes. The first hint of trouble came during qualifying when his front tyre began to deflate. Remarkably, in spite of having only 10 psi left in the tyre when he arrived back in the pits, Andrew had managed to qualify fifth.

> The Team had been plagued by a timing belt problem when testing the engine, which had been rebuilt following the trouble we had with the same thing in the States. However, they were sure they'd sorted it out and we were all very optimistic about our prospects. In the race I went straight to the front of the field, running easily with a factory Bimota, powered by an 8-valve Ducati engine, and a works Ducati 8-valve. Both bikes were built to contest the Italian Superbike Series and both were full-on factory machines. I was sure they'd be a real handful with professional riders on board but I actually found it relatively easy to stay with them. Unfortunately, I couldn't get past, as we seemed to have identical power, and so I just followed them both around. After a while I decided that I might as well have a play with the fuel-mixture dial on the dash and see if I couldn't find a bit more power. I leaned off the mixture by around 15 percent and the Britten instantly picked up about fifteen horsepower. I rocketed down the front straight, powering past both the Bimota and the Ducati right in front of the grandstands. At that point I was doing about 170 mph, accelerating strongly on my way up to about 186 mph before I started braking for the chicane.
>
> It was the first time the Italians had seen what the bike was capable of and their reaction was amazing. They went nuts! I could hear them above the noise of the bike and see them waving as I went past. Monza is a very fast track with very long straights, and as I now easily had the fastest bike there it should have been a picnic from then on. It had been raining a bit before the race but I'd decided to go with slicks, and as everyone else was on wets and it had dried out I thought I had the race in the bag. Unfortunately, the steering damper then sheared off at the bike end. There's a photo somewhere that shows it hanging down just before I crashed. I was aware of the

> problem because the bike began to tankslap violently. Somehow it flicked up and jammed between the engine and the header pipe and locked the steering on straight-ahead. I tipped the bike into the Parabolica and went straight down.

The Parabolica is a very high-speed sweeper[142] that just keeps on turning, and many had crashed there over the years. Andrew was going hard when he was abruptly dumped, and after a long slide both he and the machine stopped only a metre or so short of the Armco[143] bordering the infield. Phil Payne's race on the Alchemy had been over before it began with a fouled plug on the grid, and he was one of the first to reach Andrew, who was staggering about in a dazed and confused state. Fortunately, Andrew's worst injury was a broken big toe, and having been patched up he soon decided he was fit to race as planned for a ROC Yamaha GP team at the Hungarian Grand Prix before racing the Britten again at Assen.

By now John had been joined by CJ (Chris James) and Harry Ruffell, and the three decided that they would travel to Hungary to watch Andrew race. Before they departed, however, the crash damage to the V-1100 was repaired and the bike was taken to the Zolder circuit in Belgium, where it had been prearranged for Alan Cathcart to have a test ride. Having experienced the power of the first Britten two years earlier, the journalist was looking forward to sampling the new version with its extra horsepower. He had also recently ridden Doug Polen's world title-winning works Ducati 888 Superbike, in addition to his regular annual line-up of GP bikes, and was therefore in a good position to make a few meaningful comparisons.

After his test ride he did not hesitate to state his favourable impression of the new machine as reported in *Australian Motorcycle News* (Nov, 1992), offering the unequivocal opinion that 'the Britten's design and performance showed up the majority of current 500GP contenders as products of a pragmatic design philosophy rooted in the traditions of the past.'

'There is nothing,' he wrote, 'absolutely nothing on two wheels that can honestly compare with the experience, the thrill, of riding the V-1100.'[144] He went on to suggest that if the superior ability of the Britten to cut through rather than push the air, as the Ducati did, was added to its obvious power-to-weight advantage, 'there's only one conclusion: no contest'.

Nor was Alan's opinion of the Britten's superiority confined to the stark realities of relative grunt. The nimbleness of the Britten also impressed him mightily. 'This V-twin 4-stroke,' he wrote, 'is as powerful as the works 500s, and it's only 14kg heavier. What we have here is a motorcycle which not only has the performance and specification of a 500GP racer, it's also been honed to behave like one too—and that means ridden, wrenched, wheelied, nose-dived and chucked about in a way normal human beings can't comprehend till they try to do it themselves, and fail.'

Alan's overwhelmingly positive appraisal was, however, balanced by a number of reservations, among them his complete dislike of the new instrumentation. He rejected the green and red lights that substituted for a tachometer as totally impractical, complaining that, 'as an ex racer himself I am surprised Britten really convinced himself this was a good idea, because it's not. A track like Zolder gives you plenty to keep your mind busy when you're riding a device as potent and fast as the Britten without worrying about looking at lights.'[145]

Most concerning, however, was Alan's description of the bike's handling under braking. Stroud, he said, had the bike set up for an extreme riding position with the back jacked up for lots of suspension travel and a 53.5/46.5 front weight bias.[146] The result of this, Alan said, was that the bike had ultra-quick steering at the expense of stability under braking. 'Comparing it with the Tesi, which has a front swing arm,' he wrote, 'the Tesi was superbly stable when braking on the angle while the Britten wobbled about as if it was flexing the forks, which obviously couldn't be the case.'

However, if Alan had some misgivings about the bike's occasionally wayward behaviour there was no way he could finally resist the 'sheer rush of mega-power matched by the deeper thunder of the megaphone exhaust. Ain't nobody gonna catch me now, you think to yourself, as the front wheel paws the sky and you do your best to avoid chickening out and easing the gas. Okay—you think this sounds wimpish. Let me tell you, the Britten makes some 500GP bikes positively tame in comparison!'

After the test session, John, CJ and Harry resumed their journey, arriving in Budapest to find the ancient city's elegant stonework dripping from intermittent rain, with the prospect of heavy showers throughout the race. Ever the optimist, John thought the weather could prove helpful for Andrew, who had often done very well in the wet. He wasted no time in telling him so, Andrew recalled, urging his friend to seize the moment.

> He kept saying that I could win and I did feel confident that I could do well. I had been practising on intermediate tyres and the bike was going beautifully. The set-up felt perfect and I was really tempted to leave things as they were, but then the rain started falling a little harder and I decided to change to a full wet on the rear. At that time Dunlop had screwed up with their full wet front tyre, which had a strange profile, so I decided to leave the intermediate on the front. It had been working superbly in practice in the wet and when the race started I shot up to sixth place. I was trying pretty hard and on the second lap it nearly all came unstuck when the bike almost

> high-sided me. The back stepped out and we headed onto the grass. The television cameras caught the moment when the bike took flight after hitting a bump, causing me to do a near-vertical handstand on the handlebars before falling back down into the seat. On the video you can see the bike is sideways in the air. I got back on the pace and was in touch with the leaders again when the rain stopped and the track started to dry out. I was kicking myself for my tyre choice for the rest of the race. Eddie Lawson had opted for intermediate tyres on his Cagiva and he ran away from me and eventually won. I fought hard to stay in touch with the front-runners and Wayne Rainey later told my team manager that he'd found it really difficult to get past me. Unfortunately, as the track dried and shredded the rear tyre I slipped down to twelfth place.
>
> If I had managed a podium finish it would have probably meant a works ride, and looking back now I see it clearly as a turning point in my career, the moment I lost my best chance to make it as a GP rider. I was glad to have John around afterwards to cheer me up and help put it in perspective. And it was probably for the best. All the fame and money could have gone to my head and I might have ended up marrying an umbrella girl and living in Monaco.

After the race, John, CJ and Harry had a good look around Budapest. According to CJ, John particularly enjoyed looking at all the civic spaces, the bars and restaurants, the railway stations and other public buildings, and the three friends walked for hours and hours while he drank it all in tirelessly.

John's interest in public buildings, and especially in large traditional railway stations with arched ceilings of delicate ironwork and glass, went far beyond the curiosity of an enthusiast. He would often say that his interest in projects lasted only as long as it took to get to the point he could claim to have mastered the challenges involved. His motorcycle project had now clearly achieved everything he could have hoped for other than the sort of race-winning reliability that only comes with time and a constant regimen of detail development. It was also clear from the most recent losses that such race-winning reliability was close and that the Team was quite capable of achieving it. John Britten would never abandon his Team, nor the machines that brought him so much pleasure, but he needed a fresh challenge and to find it he had returned to another of his great passions—architecture.

Already in his mind's eye he was forming a building, drawing out the fine skeleton of a soaring glass roof, devising ways to turn stone pillars with twisting forms like giant drill-bits, assembling with his imagination a giant jigsaw that would be as daring in its own way as the motorcycle project—a building that would be every bit as monumental as the structures he so admired in Europe. He had already acquired the land for it, a parcel of buildings in the seedy part of Christchurch that lay on the eastern side of Cathedral Square, the magnificent open space that was the social, cultural and geographic centre of the city.

It would be a project demanding a huge personal input in time and, of course, a very substantial amount of money. Many people, and especially those friends of John's who were involved in property development, would see commercial folly in creating a huge structure that from the beginning was driven by consideration for those who would use it, along with uncompromising aesthetic values and a genuine passion to give something back to the city he loved so much. Many of those involved in the motorcycle project would also come to resent bitterly the attention the development demanded of him. None, however, would dissuade him. The building would be his development masterwork, his gift to the city. It would also be, in many ways, a repudiation of the values that had driven his earlier development of the Heatherlea high-rise, perhaps his most gracious apology to those who loved his city as much as he did.

In the meantime, however, there were other property developments to attend to and the family business to run. With mounting pressures on his available time, John could not afford to attend every race and even the time he could spend in the workshop was now limited mainly to the night hours, hours the rest of his increasingly professional team would rather spend in their own homes. In general, Britten Motorcycles would have to fend increasingly for itself in the day-to-day business of both racing and making motorcycles, a change that was marked by John's departure from Budapest, leaving Broz and Andrew to take care of business at the Dutch Ducati Club meeting in Assen without him.

In the week leading up to the race, Phil Payne had been staying with Kiwi friends Lyn and Peter Laurence in their comfortable old farmhouse in the south of France. The couple decided to accompany Phil to the Netherlands and had called John to volunteer their help selling Britten merchandise at the track. John accepted their offer gratefully, and then called back and asked if they could also video the race for him and perhaps provide a commentary over the phone from the tower, as Peter recalled.

> John organised the whole thing from New Zealand. He sent over a video camera, which Lyn took charge of, and I ended up doing the commentary. We both sold the gear, which was by then a pretty comprehensive collection of t-shirts, caps, posters and so on. Because our train fares back to France, and Broz's air fare home to New Zealand, were to be paid for out of the proceeds we needed to do well.
>
> We arrived on the Thursday night at about the same time as Broz and the bike. Then Andrew turned up, and after we started the thing on rollers he tore up the road on the wrong side and very nearly collected a bus. In the morning, Broz was being

driven mad trying to persuade the race number stickers to adhere to the curved bodywork, but Lyn saved the day by softening the stickers with her hair-dryer. With the numbers in place, Andrew then went out for a few qualifying laps and grabbed pole position with the fastest time, before taking off for an evening of revelry in Gronagan with Simon Crafar.

At 4.30pm we started the bike again for noise testing and were 10 decibels over the limit at 114 decibels. That was a big no-no. We shot off and picked up packets of polypads from a local supermarket, which we shoved up the exhaust. We tested again at 9.30 that night at 107 decibels and then again at 10.30, after shoving still more polypads into the boom-box, when we were 105 decibels. The officials finally said we were OK but added that they'd probably test us again on the grid. This would have spelt disaster as the bike could hardly run with all the crap up its pipe and it must have been clear to the officials that we intended for a great deal of it to fall out before the start. Throughout this Broz was becoming more and more stressed. All he had with him was a little toolbox and a briefcase with the laptop in it. At least the tools worked. The laptop didn't.

The engine was definitely off-song, but Broz couldn't reprogram the EMS without the laptop working properly. The bike would barely pull 10,000 revs and was clearly down on power. We were trying to help by liaising with John in Christchurch, but he wasn't able to tell us much and our calls were really pissing our landlady off because they had to be made at six in the morning to get hold of him. It was silly really. Only John would try to run a programme like that with one ill-equipped mechanic and an exhaust system that he must have known was far too loud.

It was soon evident to all those connected to the Team, however, that there was a snowballing level of interest in the bike, with huge crowds gathering around them while all the other machines in the paddock were virtually ignored, particularly after Andrew set the fastest lap time. By then, Lyn and Peter were almost completely overwhelmed by the growing clamour for Britten gear. The press of humanity only served to exasperate Broz even further, and when he yelled at them to 'get the bastards out of here' Peter and Lyn quickly arranged a cordon around the bike to keep people at arm's length. The enthusiastic attention, however, continued to grow.

'Everybody,' recalled Andrew, 'wanted the Britten to do well.'

If the crowd was overawed by the stunning blue and pink bike from the other side of the world, the tiny Britten Team was equally impressed by the sheer scale of the meeting and of the sophistication of many of the other teams, as Peter remembered.

Assen is a proper Grand Prix circuit set up especially for bikes, with all the pits in a row separated from one another by wire mesh running from the floor to the ceiling. We had the French Tuscon Vega team on one side and some Italians on the other, with Over Racing next to them. Over Racing and Tuscon Vega had huge semi-trailer motor homes and there were all these guys in monogrammed overalls running around on scooters. Being surrounded by such a lot of big-money outfits made us feel somewhat lilliputian. Phil was ensconced in our pits waiting for his race with the Alchemy, which he'd painted white with a big, silver fern on the tank. He'd been sorting the bike by burning up and down some Bavarian back road but had tuning problems that kept him out of the A race. However, he managed to sort it out in time to make the B event, in which he came second, which was bloody good going and won him a spot on the podium. So that worked out for the best and we were all pleased for him.

The big race started at 1 pm and when Andrew had still not returned from his excursion of the night before by 11.45am Broz began to get really edgy. However, Andrew strolled in at midday looking cool, calm and collected. We shook hands and his palm was slightly moist, but that was the only give-away that he might be just a little bit nervous, because the crowd by then was huge and the atmosphere had become absolutely electric.

When the race started Andrew blasted away from the rest of the field, and even though the bike was still choked up with the damned polypads and the wrongly tuned EMS he was still pulling fourth-gear wheelies down the back straight. If you had a Britten pass you could go anywhere and by race start I was up in the tower on the phone to John, who was back in the workshop with a crowd of people. I made myself at home and started relaying a blow-by-blow account. Meanwhile, Lyn was filming with Neil Mackley, a friend from Christchurch and a keen BEARS man, who was spotting for her. He'd tell her when the Britten was coming and she would shoot it as it whizzed by. We were pretty organised.

Out on the track the Britten was spluttering and misfiring at certain revs but Andrew found he could still comfortably outpace everything in the large field.

All the steel wool had messed up the tuning and knocked about 20 horsepower off but I still managed to get out front relatively quickly. This was despite the fact that the track really didn't suit the bike. There are a lot of banked corners at Assen and the Britten front end did not like the extra loads this put on it. I found it frustrating but I had to button off when I'd usually be pushing it. To make matters worse, the bike was not handling that well, even by its usual standards.[147] In spite of all that I still had so much more power than everyone else that we were going really well. By lap twelve of the fourteen-lap race I had opened up 200 metres on the next guy and I began to play with the tuning to see if we could go even faster. Maybe I dozed off

> a little, maybe I made things worse and lost some more power. Next thing this bike goes flying past me at about the same time that I saw the white flag. It was the last lap and I was suddenly in second place.[148] Apparently John, was at the factory with about twenty people listening to Peter through a conference speaker and they had all been very ecstatic, but now they suddenly all went deathly quiet and started chewing their nails. I'm glad I didn't know that at the time because I felt silly enough as it was. I quickly got the mixture where it seemed best and put my head down for that last lap. I knew it was going to be close.

From the tower Peter actually missed the overtaking manoeuvre, but he was shocked and dismayed to note that Andrew was suddenly running second. He was not alone.

> I glanced down to the pits where Broz was doing a sort of St Vitus's dance. Looking down from the tower he looked like a pressure valve going off. Thankfully, Andrew had woken up and he knocked two full seconds off his best lap time, setting fastest time of the race at an average of 158.47 kmh. However, he only just succeeded in closing the gap, and as the two bikes screamed neck and neck toward the finish there was a back marker right in the middle of the track. Oura—the other racer—went left and Andrew went right and then they flashed over the line. It was too close for me to call but Andrew had it by half a bike-length or so and two-tenths of a second. I made sure of it and then told John. I could hear the sounds of corks popping and yahooing down the line from 12,000 miles away. Britten Motorcycles had made their mark in Europe. That night there was a big party in the pits with a great blues/funk band and Broz and I pushed the bike up on the stage. Then he buggered off and left me to answer all these questions, which I did badly. I remember telling everyone it had a Yamaha gearbox while Broz sniggered at me from the back of the crowd. But it was a great night. We'd sold all the merchandise and could have sold a hell of a lot more. Lyn had actually given away her own t-shirt to some kid who looked like he couldn't handle the disappointment—she wasn't wearing it at the time I hasten to add. The bike already had this huge, passionate following before we even arrived but it had now blown out to a kind of cult. It was hard to take it all in.

When the bike was inspected after arriving back in Christchurch, one reason for some of the vagaries in the handling became immediately apparent. The wishbone inserts had been put in upside-down; a mistake that changed the pro- and anti-dive geometry along with, to a smaller degree, the rake and trail set-up. This would most definitely have contributed significantly to the adverse impressions Alan Cathcart had formed and to the difficulties Andrew had experienced. Of course, the person who could have prevented such a mix-up was the one person who really understood the suspension, and that was Murray. The fact that John had not considered taking him along on the European foray could only be seen as a false economy, particularly as Murray had a pretty sound understanding of the rest of the bike as well. Team Britten had succeeded anyway, but leaving Murray at home, and out of the loop, was a mistake John would persist in making, sometimes with serious consequences.

Andrew's prowess on the Britten had not gone unnoticed, however, and he had been poached to ride Ducatis in America, following which another ROC Yamaha GP team was eager to use his talents. While waiting for the word to head across the Pacific to the USA, he undertook an exhausting regime of testing with the Britten. The Team was frustrated to find that the front end continued to chatter even after the inserts had been set right, albeit not as severely. Worse, however, was the fact that little they did seemed to make any difference, as Andrew recalled.

> John was acutely frustrated about not being able to cure the front-end problem. The Team would go to Ruapuna and spend days and days testing, trying to nail down the problem. We had telemetry on the suspension so we could read out what was happening but we couldn't eliminate that patter completely. And of course any amount of patter, no matter how small, meant that we were that much further away from the machines with fully sorted forks. We tried every possible suspension setting and we even moved the engine back and forward as well as up and down. We could get it so that we could load up the front a bit more, but when it did break out it was more violent. We even put rubber in it to introduce a degree of flexibility, but that made it really hairy. I ended up doing about 1000 laps testing but we never nailed what caused it. Later, the Team began to suspect it might be binding up on the wishbones under twisting loads, and it may have been. Or it might not. It was never really bad but it stopped me going at ten-tenths because I just couldn't turn any harder. I do know that if we could have solved it the bike had the potential to blow everything away. I used to think there wasn't a Superbike that could come close if we'd refined it properly, especially on a tight track, because it was lighter than all the Superbikes and it had the horsepower. With a set of forks and a close-ratio 6-speed gearbox I believe the Britten could even have given most GP bikes a run for their money. In fact, with the right development, we could have had the fastest bike in the world, full stop. Whenever John and I talked about it I'd ask him to build me a bike with forks, but he always refused. He said it wouldn't be a Britten. And so we had to be content to have the 4-stroke with probably the highest power-to-weight ratio in the world and rely on its overwhelming grunt to win races.

In spite of the difficulties the Team continued to experience with the suspension,

John was confident that his bike was a winner, and with interest being expressed in sales enquiries from all over the world he decided to tool up for limited production. All the expressions of interest from other manufacturers had so far come to nothing, mainly because he had not answered their principal requirements for a road-bike engine, and in his heart he must have known that it was simply not an option at that time. With a huge infusion of cash, along with a couple of years of development time and a lot of new gear, it might have been otherwise. But it was not and there were no immediate prospects of change.

Building a limited number of bikes for wealthy race teams, however, seemed an obvious thing to do and it would allow his project to grow, thereby keeping the Team together. Of course, it was essential to keep the Team together in order to continue the motorcycle project, given John's increasing involvement in the new property development. He decided to build an initial batch of five bikes, with Britten Motorcycles providing a level of ongoing technical assistance to the race teams that purchased them, together with a guarantee of replacement parts as needed.

Where to build these machines was another matter. The current rented workshop would be inadequate for any kind of production run, no matter how limited, and it would be useful not to have to face the prospect of eviction. John began casting about for a suitable building to buy.

With Andrew committed to the American deal, John also needed another rider. Although he would not hesitate to put 'foreign' riders on his machines if he felt they promised a better chance for victory, he preferred to have New Zealanders riding for the Team. He was lucky to have a broad selection of exceptional local talent available to choose from, and his next choice proved just as auspicious as had those that preceded it.

Jason McEwen, who hailed from Palmerston North, was racing a 900 Supersport Ducati in the Australian Super Street series at the time and he was having a lot of fun doing it. A spray-painter by trade, Jason made an interesting contrast to Andrew. Off the track, Andrew sloped about with an easy grin for those he knew and the slightly distant air that is the preserve of the mildly preoccupied. Jason, on the other hand, had a manner in keeping with his wrap-around slitted shades and short spiky red hair. There was an intensity about him that existed alongside a wry and somewhat wicked sense of humour. His recreational roll-your-own enthusiasm had earned him the nickname 'The Hippie' and, on occasion, the ire of the powers that be. On the track, of course, like Andrew, Jason was fiercely aggressive, deadly fast and nerveless.

> I think Andrew had put a word in for me. We always got on pretty well and like most Kiwis who raced together overseas we helped each other out when we could. I

hadn't met John but I'd raced against the bike when Andrew rode it at Ruapuna. I was on the Ducati 888 belonging to the Anglo American Motorcycle Club and I fell off trying to keep up with it. The Britten had so much traction out of the turns with brilliant low-down grunt and a huge mid-range, so I was pretty keen to have a go on it and I jumped on a plane straight away after John called. He picked me up at the airport in his old white Benz and I stayed at his house. He showed me a video of Daytona and was obviously pleased with the way they'd gone there. I got the impression that the promise they'd shown at that race had a lot to do with him carrying on. He wanted to know what races I'd won and so I told him the story.

I got my road and race licence on my fifteenth birthday and I'd been racing ever since. I started on a liquid-cooled Yamaha RD250 and a 350 and did the North Island meetings, including the street circuits. After a really good debut season Dad bought me an Yamaha RZ350 and I acquired a rep for doing well in street races, although I couldn't say I'm keen on them. As far as I'm concerned, they're dodgy and I for one wouldn't mind if they just disappeared. Then came a GPZ600 Kwacka, and when I started beating guys I'd idolized I realised I might have a talent for it. I won the Junior Production Formula Two Winter Series on the 600 and the following year I moved up to a 750. I raced in the Senior Production events open to bikes of up to 1100cc, which forced me to ride harder. There were big fields and I ended up eighth overall. A Suzi dealer helped me into a 600 and an 1100 for the 1988–89 season. I didn't win a lot of races, except for a couple at the end, but I got lots of thirds and ended up second in the Championship. That surprised a few people. The next year Suzuki gave me the bikes and I won the Open Production and Formula One Championships against all the guns.

In the off season I did a bit of 600 Supersport racing in the States and managed a top-ten finish in that Championship, and then I rode Dukes for Bob Brown, Kevin Magee's old team boss in Aussie. That was followed by a stint in Don Bramich's team—again on Dukes. We were always underdogs against all the 750 Jap Superbikes, but it was good exposure and the fact that I had an 888 of my own made John feel easier.

John and I had a few beers together at The Stables that first night and then went testing the V-1100 at Ruapuna the next day. After a few laps I changed the steering-head angle and put a bit more weight on the front and altered the trail, which made it turn in faster than the way Andrew had it.[149] I was totally blown out to be on it. The 1100 was a handful but I've done faster times on it around Manfeild than I ever did later on the 1000, because they were pumping out about 10 extra horsepower.

The Britten had power from 4000 revs, which the Dukes don't, and I could pull the wheel up in fifth, which nothing else can do. I found I often had to feather in a bit of back brake on accelerating through second, third and fourth gear to keep the

> thing from looping the loop. I tried short-shifting, but nine times out of ten it would wheel-stand anyway. With a genuine 175 bhp available I suppose it was to be expected. All in all testing went really well and I was feeling confident by the time we got to Manfeild for the tail-end meeting of the 1991–92 World Superbike season.

The bike was entered at the meeting in a couple of BEARS races, with the main opposition expected from Robert Holden, who was racing Dallas Rankine's Ducati special 'Fast 'n Fragile'. However, after some close racing in the first lap of the first race, Jason was able to clear off to win by about 100 metres over Robert in a crushing demonstration of the Britten's superior power. The second race was an even more emphatic show, with the Britten simply disappearing from the rest of the field and coming within two seconds of the new lap record set earlier by Doug Polen on his Ducati Superbike. It was the last time the 1100 ever raced in New Zealand and it would be years before another Britten made the same power. But the bike was now reliable and, with the exception of the odd exotic import like Polen and his Superbike, the Britten Team was clearly miles in front of anything else on the New Zealand tracks. The front end was still a work in progress, but Jason had shown that its bad habits could at least be minimised if you nailed it down and put up with a hard and brutal ride—ironic, perhaps, given the reason for building it in the first place, but effective nonetheless.

At home, and in Assen, John had achieved at least one of his ambitions—his bike was indeed capable of utterly crushing the opposition. Barring bad luck or bad management there was no reason to suppose the Britten Team would not walk away with a Championship on its home tracks at least. Unfortunately, in motor racing it takes precious little of either to deny what might have seemed a predestined result, and in the case of the 1992–93 New Zealand National Superbike Championship there would be just sufficient of both to ensure that the Britten Team failed to win the prize.

Even if they did win practically everything else.

CHAPTER FOURTEEN

Battle on the Home Front

The decision to contest the 1992–93 National Superbike series heralded the permanent exit of the 1100cc configuration for the Britten Team. Under the governing Superbike rules, broadly similar to those in the International Superbike Championship, cubic capacity for multi-cylinder machines was set at 750cc while twin-cylinder machines were allowed 1000cc. While at first glance these limits may have seemed to disadvantage multi-cylinder machines, the reality was that anyone could make a twin if they wanted to. The fact that only Ducati chose to do so was indicative of the essential equity of the formula. Of course, the Britten was not based on a production machine, unlike all the other bikes it would race in the series, but there was provision in the rules for prototypes to race for a limited number of seasons. It was perhaps a bit of a stretch but it could be argued that the Britten might become a prototype for a production motorcycle. Who could say with absolute certainty? In any event, the national governing body, Motorcycling New Zealand, decided who raced and who didn't and they used their absolute discretionary powers to welcome the Britten to their Championship series. New Zealanders had always raced home-made specials, with both two and four wheels, against the best the world cared to land on their shores. It was a tradition.

At this stage things were looking good for the Britten Team. Losing the power the additional 100cc made was regrettable, it was true, but in other ways the smaller capacity 1000cc configuration made for a more balanced package and the Britten still possessed a comfortable excess of power over the Superbikes ranged against it. There was every reason for confidence, especially with Murray Aitken now being part of the race team.

The first races of the season were often held just before Christmas, the reason some series straddled two years as this one did, and this time they were held at Pukekohe. But after the usual mad rush the Britten Team turned up only to find that the bike suddenly would not run properly. They worked frantically to locate the trouble and for one of the very few times in his life John completely lost his composure. The bike was running, but only just, and he blamed the spluttering misfire on the computer. In turn, he blamed the supposed computer problem on Murray and Broz and roundly abused them in the pits, to the embarrassment of all present. Eventually, it was discovered that John had kinked a fuel line when fitting it so that fuel only came through in dribs and drabs. Unfortunately, by the time the problem was traced the day was over, and two rounds had slipped away without even being contested. It was a terrible start for the season.

The second round at Bay Park was no better, although the other riders in the series finally witnessed the potential for the V-1000 to eclipse them completely when Jason comfortably broke the lap record in practice.

One of the other riders was a young engineering graduate from the Bay of Plenty, temporarily on the dole and racing a Kawasaki that he'd built with his student loan. Loren Poole was a stocky farmer's son, fresh off the family's kiwifruit and commercial flower property. He could be aloof and reflective or heartily demonstrative by turns. His smooth, relaxed manner overlaid a quick eye for the main chance and a highly effective intellect sharpened by driving ambition and years of focused study. For the moment, however, the books had been tossed aside to indulge a season or two of motorcycle racing before life became serious once more.

Loren's mechanic, Tim Stewart, made an interesting contrast. Tall and whip-thin, with spiky, close-cropped, peroxide-white hair, he had a habit of looking straight through all but the chosen few he cared to acknowledge and he carried himself with a reserved air of quiet superiority. He was a gifted mechanic with an almost intuitive touch for discovering hidden horsepower. The two men had a mercurial relationship, but for the moment they were united as just another zero-budget race team out to steal as many places as they could from the professional outfits they were up against. Fortunately, Loren's ability as a rider, honed by years of buzzing about the family farm on a succession of trail bikes, and more recently racing in motocross events, was as impressive as was Tim's ability with an engine.

Loren remembered with sharp focus the impact the Britten had that day.

> It was the first time we'd really seen it run in the North Island, with their wash-out at Pukekohe. It was quite a revelation. Jason just blew everything away in practice, but of course with two DNFs at Pukekohe they had to start at the back of the grid. First race of the day I thundered off the line with an absolutely demon start and was going great guns when on the second lap this blue flash went past. It was Jason and he was hooting. I thought that would be the last I'd see of him but only a lap or so later he locked up and pulled off. Apparently they were trying these carbon-fibre sump baffles John had designed but they had been badly fitted and were rubbing on the

crank assembly. As a result, carbon and resin particles circulated in the oil system and totalled the bearings. So they were out for the second round. Naturally I was rapt. The failures at Pukekohe and Bay Park meant extra points for me. I had managed a sixth at Pukekohe first time out and was running third in the first race at Bay Park when I crashed on the last lap. The second race was better and I came home fourth.

I talked to Broz around the pits a bit and found out a little about their bike. The truth was I was already pretty interested in it. I had first seen the thing on the cover of a magazine, which I read lying on my bed in some cheap establishment in Kings Cross in Sydney. This was just after Andrew missed out at Daytona. I was over in Australia for a job interview the next day—selling pneumatic control valves. It was a good job but I read the article on the Britten and thought, that's where I should be.

I had run into John and Broz before the race at Bay Park because we were both using Robbie Dean's shop in Tauranga as a base and we all chatted. Andrew Stroud turned up at the after-match function and after about a million beers I wound up singing some Neil Young song with him and John on this karaoke machine. The best thing you could say about our singing was that we were well matched. By then I had the Sydney job and was due to start immediately after the race season. But the idea of selling valves suddenly didn't seem nearly as interesting as hitching up with John's outfit, and from that moment Britten Motorcycles were never far from the front of my mind.

Moving south, the Superbike circus paused at Wanganui for the annual, now non-championship, street race on the famous Cemetery Circuit. The Britten behaved and Jason showed that his reputation as a road-racer was fully justified when he took the Britten out front and kept it there to the chequered flag. The Team was finally in action.

Loren was also going well.

I managed to get third after Hepburn nailed me in the last couple of corners. It was pouring and I love the wet because I could really use the skills I learned riding motocross bikes. I did this ridiculous handstand on the bars going over the railway crossing but didn't fall off, and I could actually see Jason in front of me at the end, which was great. I was talking to the guys in the Britten Team and they were naturally happy after the race. Things seemed to have come right for them at last.

John Hepburn, the rider who had beaten Loren in the last few corners of the race, was a South Island truck mechanic and scrap-metal dealer who ran his own businesses in the provincial South Island town of Timaru. Hep, as he was generally addressed, was, like Loren, a former motocross rider who had taken up road racing after a bad crash in 1984 'buggered' his left leg. Since that time he had won a New Zealand 250 Production Motorcycle Championship and a string of other titles, including the New Zealand TT, the New Zealand Grand Prix and the Golden Handlebars, a competition that pitted motorcyclists against one another in motocross, scrambles, trials, enduro, drag and superbike racing.

Like all his fellow Superbike competitors through the summer of 1992/1993, Hepburn found the power of the Britten impossible to counter.

> Even if I could slip a wheel up inside the thing under braking, the twin-cylinder Britten put its power down so well it would just leap half a dozen bike lengths away coming out of the corner. If it was going well, and if it had a good rider on it, you had to be lucky to get near it—make a fortunate tyre selection in changing weather or some such thing. Of course, it was a peculiar beast and I know that Broz was always tearing his hair out trying to keep it running. For example, I heard that the valve angle to the cam lobe was wrong and it chewed out its cam followers, so Broz would pull the heads off after every race and slip in a new set.[150] But it set the standard and it made us all try harder. And it attracted a level of interest from the press and the public that the sport had never enjoyed here before.

The next two races in the series were back at Ruapuna, and the Superbike circus duly caught the ferry in Wellington and sailed for the South Island. Loren arrived in Christchurch and almost immediately met Phil Payne 'in some bar or other', and the two instantly hit it off.

'I ended up staying with the Doctor (as everybody called him due to his ability to fix sick Italian motorbikes) and used his workshop while I was there,' Loren recalled. 'Of course, Phil knew everybody, including John and the rest of the Britten Team, and we soon shot down to the Britten workshop where Murray showed us around. They had just moved in and were setting up separate workshops for machining, assembly and bodywork, as well as a dyno room. It was an impressive set-up.'

Indeed it was. Britten Motorcycles had now relocated to the stylish and spacious premises that would become its permanent home, the result of a deal John later said he could not afford to pass up. It was everything he could have hoped for, and even more to the point, it was cheap.

The New Zealand Railway shunting yard control centre in Carlyle Street dated back to the 1930s and was a solid concrete structure that presented its austere, largely window-free backside to the street. Access was through a single, heavy metal door located halfway along the building. The car park on the other side of the building, to all intents and purposes the 'front' of the structure, was accessed via a short lane on the eastern end of the property.

Out 'front', the generous car park was separated from the railway line by a chain-link fence. In marked contrast to the dark and usually chilly street frontage, the north-facing façade presented a pleasant industrial art-deco aspect of steel-framed windows topped by the shunting yard's master control room. This would once have enjoyed commanding views of what had been not long before the bustling epicentre of a thriving region's export trade.[151]

The Crown had recently earmarked the building as compensation to local Maori for colonial land confiscations, so John had negotiated an agreement with all the interested parties whereby he paid minimal rent for years, which was then deducted from an agreed equally minimal purchase price. It was an astute deal. A motorcycle wrecking company had used the property for several years and it was looking the worse for wear, while the surrounding area generally looked neglected and forlorn. However, it was only a minute or two from the central city and within a year of making the agreement, new, smart, light industrial buildings were springing up all around. A final, added attraction was the location of Auto Restorations not quite directly across the street.

Ratty old partitioning had been torn out to reveal two large workshops, a tea room, an office, a slightly smaller workshop (which became the dyno room), a huge changing room and ablution area (which became the body and paint shop), a 'dungeon' (containing the massive old diesel heating unit for the facility) and two offices upstairs, one of which had an en suite bathroom. There was also a small external storage area, ideal for hazardous chemicals, along with another smaller workshop.

John had the place spruced up with a coat of paint, installed remote-controlled electric gates, had Rob fabricate new door handles with the instruction, 'Make them exactly the same as the originals but twice as big', and screwed a discreet stainless-steel plate next to the steel door with the legend Britten Motorcycles Ltd on it.[152]

When the building had been purchased it had no street number, and it took some time, and the arrival of several neighbours, before it settled at 137. But by that stage the place was well and truly in business. A letter to Britten Motorcycles, Carlyle Street, found the right address from the beginning—as did a gentle stream of visitors.

Back at Ruapuna, the V-1000 again did everything it was supposed to do, with Jason winning both races handsomely. In doing so he also became the first rider to win a Formula One race on a New Zealand-built machine.

Russell Josiah, who came second, found that his bike was completely outclassed by the Britten and generously said so after the race.

'It was awesome watching Jason McEwen on the Britten,' he told reporters. 'He would come out of a corner, stand his bike up, open the throttle and disappear while I was still trying to get the power on.'

It was cause for celebration and the new workshops were given a thorough house-warming with John, as always, well to the fore. There was more than one wobbly head the next day, but everyone was required on deck as there was racing to be done before the Team went south for the next round of the championship.

The occasion was the annual, non-championship Lady Wigram Invitation, which as always was to take place around the temporarily converted runways of Wigram Airbase on the outskirts of Christchurch. Once again, it was no contest and Jason walked away with a win in both races and the first-ever 100-mph average lap.

As the circus headed south for the next two races at Teretonga, the fast, bumpy track just outside the city of Invercargill, the weather deteriorated to a good old-fashioned deep south gale and most present ended up partying hard again when horizontal rain set in on the practice Friday. Loren Poole had travelled south to race as well.

> Throughout the morning the wind had been knocking the bikes almost flat as we went past the gaps between buildings. It was getting silly. By midday the whole Formula One crowd was in the pub and by nightfall it was chaos. The next day people were as sick as chooks. Paul Gee ripped his helmet off on the dummy grid and spewed right there. Most of the others had already done so and a few hung on until afterwards. Jason won that day and the next while I nabbed a fourth and a third.
>
> That night I ran into Broz at about two in the morning at some bar and bought him a Sambucca test tube. We had a few more and ended up talking away most of the night. Of course, he was pretty happy. They were cleaning up.
>
> By the time we got to Timaru the whole Britten Team was there and they were feeling festive after Jason again went out and blew everything away in both races. I didn't fare so well, putting myself out with a crash, fortunately without damaging the bike or myself badly. Then we all came together again for the final championship race up at Manfeild.[153] Once more the Britten was way out front. Nobody could get near it.

Unfortunately for the Britten Team, Russell Josiah finished well in the points, as he had all season, and took the Championship.

Britten Motorcycles had come second.

The next race in the series was further north, around the streets of Paeroa, on the Coromandel Peninsula. Like the street race in Wanganui, it carried no championship points and John decided there was little to prove by going to the picturesque little town with its gold-rush history and bumpy street circuit. For the moment Jason was too depressed to care one way or the other.

'I had won every race in the season after the first two meetings were blown, with sixteen straight wins including the Lady Wigram Invitation. Unfortunately, it wasn't enough. Missing those first two races cost us the series and gave Russell the Championship. It was a bummer pure and simple.'

For Loren Poole, the Britten's non-appearance at the Paeroa street races was a stroke of luck, and against a very strong field, including entrants from Australia, he won all three races.

> I took home heaps of prize-money which was good after I'd emptied the coffers catching up on a time payment on the bike. I was on such a high I wrote to John, including a CV with the letter, and asked for a job as manager at Britten Motorcycles. I knew they needed it because I'd seen such shocking mismanagement around their pits. Murray was left shaking his head about everything. Broz was taking the piss out of John and John was running around like an idiot. He wrote back and said he'd like to hire me but he didn't have the dough. I was working for Waitakere Council on this biogas project by then, which flowed on from the engineering project I did for my degree. There were two of us involved and we had scored a government grant to do it, so I was busy for a while. In the meantime, I was still putting off the Australians. Letters went back and forward between John and me while I tried to sort something out and the months went by. Eventually, the Australians called and told me to forget it. So I wasn't destined to sell valves for big bucks to Aussies. Trouble was, I wasn't necessarily going to manage Britten Motorcycles either.

In an interview with the Palmerston North-based *Evening Standard*, John expressed satisfaction with the second place his team had scored in the Superbike series while avoiding any mention of the part his own errors with the crimped fuel line and the doomed carbon-fibre sump baffles had played in preventing the Team from winning the Championship. Instead, he blamed a shortage of spare parts, 'one of the hassles of being under-funded'.

He went on to say that he was 'dying to stop racing so we can begin testing', as 'there is so much more to squeeze out of the bike' and that a 'sister bike is only forty-eight hours away from completion'. The two machines, he said, would undergo rigorous testing before the next race, which he anticipated would be at Bathurst in Australia.

The 'sister' bike was in fact a 1000cc 5-valve, and its first competitive outing would not be at Bathurst's Mount Panorama but alongside 001 in March at the 1993 Sound of Thunder tenth anniversary meeting at Ruapuna. In a further refinement of what was by now a tradition for the team, the new bike was started for the first time only the night before, some seven weeks after John's announced forty-eight-hour deadline for completion. But on the morning of the race it was sitting outside the workshop in the sun—a brand-new, shiny blue and pink soul sister for the battle-tested V-1000 next to it. The Britten Motorcycle had again become Britten Motorcycles. The new bike was too much for John to resist, and for the first time in two years he took one of his own machines for a spin, helping to run the 5-valve in on the practice day. Afterwards, flushed with the pleasure of riding the beautiful new machine, he joked with the Team that his times were exactly the same as they had been when he last rode the Tiger 100.

But it was Andrew who John asked to ride the new bike, and he eagerly accepted the invitation. With Jason on the other machine for the first race of the meeting, and with the predictable support of the wildly cheering crowd, the two Brittens quickly put half a lap between themselves and their fellow competitors. Andrew diced with his team-mate for the crowd, until a problem with 'excessive' chatter at the front slowed him up and he contented himself with pulling wheelies the length of the pit-straight, comfortably retaining his second place behind Jason.

It had been a good opening for the show, but for some reason the wayward front end on Andrew's new machine proved unusually hard to pin down, even though the Team spent the weekend swapping suspension parts from one bike to the other. At one point long phone calls were made to Mike Sinclair in America, but by the end of the weekend the 5-valve was handling worse than ever.[154] In spite of the 5-valve bike's jitters, however, the team repeated the performance of their first race in the next Formula One event, with another one/two finish to the added delight of the still loudly enthusiastic crowd.

But as the meeting progressed, John was faced with a highly unpalatable reality. The meeting was proving a less-than-encouraging debut for the 5-valve, even ignoring the handling problems, and Andrew's experience on the track had confirmed the earlier findings on the dynamometer—the power the new engine made was flatter than the 4-valve in the first part of the rev range. This meant that the new bike did not jump out of corners as well as the old one. Hans had expected the 5-valve to go well straight out of the box, and both he and John now knew that it would not be easy to find more power. It might have been better if something had been obviously wrong, but the 5-valve was running like a dream. The worst outcome would be that the new motor was as good as it ever would be and as that was not significantly better than, or even as good as, the 4-valve there, was a disturbing possibility that the whole exercise had been an expensive waste of very precious time.

However, John had made the bike, and so when Lindsay Williamson, who was racing Black Adder, his Harley-Davidson XR1000 McIntosh special, challenged him to a race he decided he might as well enjoy a spin on it with a bit of opposition in tow. According to Lindsay, he and John arranged to have a few other fellows on modern Ducatis along for the ride for appearances' sake.

'We gave ourselves a bit of a handicap', he said, 'to make it look interesting, but not so much that we didn't think we'd win comfortably. We obviously got it all wrong because quite a few of them beat us.'

At the end of the race, however, John was in front of his challenger and John's fellow BEARS were in no doubt that he had given the new bike a good workout. They noted particularly the way the 5-valve twitched nervously when John wound the power on, which all agreed showed that at least he wasn't afraid to give the thing a good caning. After the race, John told a reporter that the 5-valve was actually a lot easier to ride than either the 4-valve or the 1100. Asked if he felt tired after his stint back in the saddle he laughed and said that he hadn't been going fast enough to get really weary.

'It's very nice to ride,' he said, 'I'm just not used to it.'

In April the two machines were packed up and sent to Australia to compete in a BEARS race at the Castrol Australian TT, the first TT to have been held since 1976.[155] The Australian press made much of the Brittens and of John, and he was kept busy doing interviews as public interest started to grow. Much was made particularly of the 15-bhp advantage the Brittens had over the best Superbikes, along with a supposed 25-kg weight advantage. The latter figure was somewhat suspect and it is hard now to know exactly where it came from. At the time, however, it was quoted widely and encouraged many race fans in the belief that the Brittens would be nigh on invincible. On the Britten Team's arrival in Australia, a television network organised to film John on a suburban street for an interview they had scheduled. They asked him to walk over the brow of a hill with the two bikes suddenly bursting into view from behind him and bellowing past on either side. It was great television and it ramped interest in the 'Kiwi wonderbikes' up to new levels.

The race weekend started with a disaster, however, when Jason was sidelined with a 'stuffed crank and set of main-bearings'. The bike had actually started to run the crankshaft bearings on the way up the famous mountain over which the track passes, but for some reason Jason elected to keep going. By the time he arrived back at the pits the motor had suffered major damage, an outcome that infuriated John, who made little effort to disguise his disgust with Jason. Half the Britten challenge was suddenly, summarily wiped out.

'We didn't have spares,' Jason recalled, 'which meant I was without a ride for the meeting. So Andrew went out on his own and won the BEARS races, but could only manage second in the Formula One event. We did OK but after all the build-up it was a bit of an anticlimax.'

The reason for the bearing failure on Jason's bike was, according to Broz, who was doing the spannering in Australia, a simple case of overheating.

> John had finally learned that running a huge, open megaphone was not acceptable at the race tracks where we competed and we had created boom-boxes. These were cast alloy units that looked like metal lungs attached to the back of the crankcase. The exhaust collected in the boom-box and then exited through two mufflers, one on each side, and it was designed to be big enough to cut the noise without spoiling the exhaust flow. On the whole it worked well, except for one problem. The metal boom-box naturally heated up with the exhaust gas and this in turn heated the crankcase. In Australia it was bloody hot anyway, so the bikes were operating at about 125 degrees Celsius—enough to melt the bearings. We had been aware of the potential for this to happen for quite a while, but John had not wanted to hear about it. After Bathurst he finally accepted the obvious, and the next generation of boom-box castings were separated from the engine casing, something that mostly solved the heat-transfer problem. Unfortunately, there was no time to do anything about it before we went to Europe and we also now had two pretty stuffed bikes on our hands. I argued that we should bail out of the European trip on that account, but John wouldn't hear of it and so we packed up both bikes and shipped them off.

In the meantime, Loren Poole had been waiting around trying not to consider the possibility that he might have made a serious mistake in letting the Australian job slip through his fingers. Finally, he decided that he had to force the issue.

> I called John to insist on an answer. However, he stole my thunder by telling me that he was off to the Isle of Man for the TT to race a bike. I was completely taken aback, as it was the last thing I was expecting to hear. It was hopeless trying to talk to him because he was really spinning out. He asked me some questions about milling machines and then promised he would sort something out when he returned. All I could do was continue to sit tight and wait.

With the BotT (now known as Pro Twins) race at Daytona in hiatus for the moment, while the rules were shuffled about, the number of venues at which the Brittens could race was suddenly somewhat limited. Nevertheless, the announcement, at the beginning of April, that Britten Motorcycles were sending not one but two bikes to the Isle of Man was something of a surprise. Few had anticipated that John would wish to contest the oldest TT still running and the toughest road race of them all. Certainly it was a bold decision.

All decisions made in motorsport carry an element of risk—risk of failure, risk of injury and ultimately risk of death. However, no single motorsport event had ever extracted such a price as the TT from those who dared to risk it. In many aspects the TT resembled nothing so much as the ancient Celtic contests that had once determined the fate of every man on the island, contests where dishonour was not an option and the only possible outcomes were victory or death.

The Team to go to the TT included a newcomer, a clothing retailer called Wayne Alexander. Wayne had first drawn the attention of John's wife, Kirsteen, who regularly bought clothing for John at Wayne's fashion emporium in Christchurch, and he and John had then become friends.

Wayne is a complicated individual who remains something of an enigma even to those who know him best. He had been an airforce mechanic and combined practical skills with a strong aesthetic instinct. He was also a committed Christian who nonetheless enjoyed a certain amount of good old-fashioned hell-raising and pushed himself hard keeping fit in physical activities such as boxing. In spite of holding strong and independent views on most things, with a tendency to promote them aggressively and competitively, he was also beset with a restless need to identify a mentor who could challenge him intellectually and creatively—one to whom he could attach himself with all the fervour of a disciple.

Wayne and John first met on holiday in Queen Charlotte Sound at Christmas in 1990, and Wayne immediately found in John the person he was looking for.

> John was there with his family and I was staying in the same beautiful bay. I made my way to the simple little bach they'd rented, where I was made welcome. Everything was down to earth and easygoing. I suppose the first thing that impressed me about John was that he had so much fun. He was extremely gregarious and he laughed often. That evening we played Pictionary, a game that was then becoming popular. Unfortunately, we didn't actually have the game, so we had to make it up as we went and wrote out our own words and so forth. The game suited John's lateral mind and because it's mostly a phonetic affair he did well in spite of his difficulties with spelling. Again the emphasis was on having a lot of laughs, but John was always competitive and he played like a demon.
>
> Some time later I went to the place in Lowe Street as the Team were finishing the first Britten Motorcycle for the 1991 race at Daytona, and when the bike raced in the New Zealand series, over the summer of 1991–92, I went to most of the races. By then I had opened a second shop in Christchurch and was beginning to outfit a third in Wellington, but I managed to fit it all in. I found the bike project utterly absorbing and I was really enjoying getting to know John. I have to admit that he intimidated me somewhat at first, and I spent most of the time listening. I was happy to do so.

> When the last round of the World Superbike series was held in Manfeild I took Rob Selby up from Christchurch in my Corvette. After the race meeting John was busy, but the rest of the Team, and practically everybody else who had been at the racing, ended up in this nightclub, before a few of the Team moved on to this eatery called the Cork and Fork. By then it was the wee hours and the barman was showing off by sticking blazing glasses of brandy to his hand, an old trick. I went one better by setting my brandy alight and sticking the balloon to my arse. I boogied about with it, waving around behind me. Then Murray and I got stuck into champagne and tequila slammers with a mate of his he'd brought with him. As dawn broke, Murray was outside spewing in the shrubbery while his friend chucked up inside the Cork and Fork. Somehow I got them both into the Corvette and we returned to the backpackers we were all staying in, only to find the rest of the Team had left. I rocketed down to Wellington with Murray and his mate passed out in the car and arrived just as the ferry was about to depart. When I opened the door, both of my passengers fell out onto the road at John's feet. He roared with laughter and told the story, to Murray's embarrassment, for years afterwards. But John was pleased we had made it and I think he decided then that I might be a person who could work under pressure. When he asked if I wanted to join the Team for the European trip I leapt at the chance. Of course, I had no idea at the time where it would all lead but I was happy to be on the journey. John was like that, he made you want to be around because that was where the action was.

The Isle of Man is a beautiful drop in the middle of the Irish Sea, populated by an ancient and independent people. The first Tourist Trophy (TT) motorcycle race was staged there in 1904. In more recent years the population of the island has actually doubled during the running of the TT, with some 70,000 spectators and 900 competing riders turning up on the ferries that unload in the ancient old port of Douglas. Invariably, when the invasion ebbs away some of them fail to return home. On average, at least a couple of racers and perhaps half a dozen fans are killed every year at the event, the latter mostly during Mad Sunday, the day when anyone who has a motorbike can have a bash at the course without risking the ire of the law.

In the hours leading up to the racing the previous year a young rider from Dublin had killed himself when he flattened his machine against a wall on the Handleys Corner section of the track. The next death occurred when a German motorcyclist hit a tipper truck off the course at Ballaleece Bridge. This was followed by a double fatality back on the course, when a local rider had a head-on at Greeba Bridge with a bike ridden by a German couple. Both riders were killed and the German pillion passenger was left fighting for life.

The reason the TT has extracted such a deadly toll from fans and racers alike is no mystery. It is, quite simply, the enigma of the course itself, a huge circuit that is unknowable in any absolute sense. For 37.73 miles it winds through villages, where riders brush past stone buildings that jut out to the edge of the street, rushes along flat-tack straights that undulate for miles across open farmland, and dives into dark copses of old timber with stone walls bordering one side of the road and stone cuttings the other.

To do well at the TT is to ride a hair's breadth on the sane side of flat-out, with the bike only partly under control, sliding through corners that rush up hill and down dale. It is to fly, tossed into the air by the many, many bumps. And it is to make a plan to get around the rider in front while tank-slapping along at 180 mph. To master the island is to know intimately the nature of Crosby, Ballacraine, Laurel Bank, Glen Helen, Cronk-y-Voddy, Kirk Micheal, Ballaugh Bridge, Sulby Bridge, Parliament Square, Gooseneck, Verandah, Bungalow, Sign Post Corner and Bray Hill—all points on the map and all places where riders have died. It is to know every section of road connecting those points, every corner, every dip and every minute variation in road surfaces—a lifetime of study. And you do not fail to negotiate a corner at the TT, not if you want to survive.

To do well at the island is to be part of a very select company, for nothing challenges man or machine as much as the TT. To win at the island in 1993 you would have to be able to turn in a 120-mph average lap consistently.

In the years leading up to 1993, winning usually involved riding a Honda. Beating the Japanese giant at the event it had quite reasonably come to look upon as its own benefit after winning it for years, was an ambition not seriously entertained even by the other Japanese giants. If a Britten motorcycle were to pull it off it would be like the New Zealand soccer team winning the World Cup—or any other ludicrous sporting improbability. But the Britten was there and it was undeniably quick and nimble. It was also extremely stable at high speeds and had a supple suspension that could soak up the bumps without the bike losing its poise. The front-end chatter was far less a problem on a circuit where most of the corners were high-speed sweepers and only maniacs on a death-or-glory mission tipped in at ten-tenths.[156] In fact, John had reason to believe that his bike's suspension could prove ideal for the island. Although the extreme stiffness of the girder and chassis seemed to unsettle the machine, both going into slower corners under heavy braking and then powering out, the set-up was most comfortable handling high-speed corners and bumps—of which the TT boasted plenty. Then there was the motor. If everything held together its massive torque was just the ticket for comfortably short-shifting around the track.

Going to the TT was not universally popular with the inner circle at Britten

Motorcycles. Gary Goodfellow, for instance, candidly admitted that he would not have chosen to race there for a stack of prize money, let alone the small purse then on offer. When asked his opinion of the place he simply responded with a question. Who went there? The answer, of course, was the English and the Irish, plus a sprinkling of representation from everywhere else—perhaps New Zealand more than most places. People like the Colemans, generations of them. Perhaps that was why there were heartbreakingly familiar native New Zealand cabbage trees growing on the island in profusion, a very deliberate Kiwi gift to the place. Exactly, responded Gary. The lunatic races, the English, the Irish and the mad dogs that travelled with them—they went there.

For many years the TT had paid start money when few other races had, and to a degree that had sustained private interest in the event. In 1973, however, the newly formed Grand Prix Riders' Safety Association—kicked off when New Zealander Kim Newcombe took a piece of paper declaring it to exist around the pits at Monza and had very nearly every GP rider sign it—blackballed the TT for its appalling safety record. Although the island continued to host a GP as part of the TT for years, it was largely ignored by the GP fraternity. (GP points continued to be awarded, however, to the largely non-GP riders who did contest it.) Start money paid out to the professionals to compete had gradually reduced to the point that it was financially marginal even for frequent race winners to go there. Steve Hislop, one of the top TT winners in the history of the event, with nine victories at the time, had been paid about £7000 by Honda the year before to compete for a first prize of just over £6000. The sum total compared dismally with the £200,000 first prize then being wrestled for on the English snooker circuit.

The men who had mastered the TT remained keenly aware of the dangers of the course. Hislop himself admitted that, 'the thought of a mechanical failure scares me shitless. I've been lucky to survive a high-speed crash when two top lads were killed on the same day and it's been on my mind ever since. When you've seen a good mate lying in the road in a body bag you wouldn't be human if it didn't do something to you.' [157]

Getting a dispensation to race a special at the Isle of Man was no easy thing. Britten Motorcycles clearly could not satisfy any homologation requirements for volume production and they were not a recognised manufacturer who might have expected some flexibility concerning the eligibility of prototype machinery. John was fortunate, however, in having a well-connected contact in the person of John Shand, or Shandy, a former Christchurch official in the Fédération International de Motocyclisme (FIM) who had forsaken his homeland for the manicured pleasures of Switzerland. Shand had some influence with the FIM race officials who ran the TT. It was also probably the case that Honda did not see the Britten as a serious challenge to their continued dominance of the event. If they had, it is probable that they would have had little difficulty in shutting Britten Motorcycles out.

After a month of negotiations, the Britten Team had been admitted and Shand had undertaken further negotiations on John's behalf to secure the services of well-known British rider Trevor Nation. Nation had won the TT on a rotary Norton two years earlier and engaging him would be a real coup for the Team. As neither Jason nor Andrew could race in the Senior TT, not having satisfied the rules of racing previously in a minor race, John asked New Zealander Shaun Harris to ride the second bike. Shaun had won the Best Newcomer Award two years previously when making his debut on the island. Known popularly as 'The Gremlin', Shaun had a nuggety stature more suggestive of a jockey than a motorcycle racer, but his hard and aggressive riding style was well respected by his fellow racers.

Shaun had first contacted John by phone after learning of the accident suffered by Chris Haldane while testing the first of the new machines.

> I'd never met John but I liked the sound of what he was doing. I told him that if he needed a fresh guinea pig I was his man. I didn't hear from him until he called out of the blue while I was in LA on a three-month contract developing a race bike for this Chinese-Canadian called Rodney Fee. He asked if I wanted to race the TT and maybe a couple of other races, and I agreed immediately. When the time came I flew from the US to Monza and joined the Team. I couldn't wait to get my hands on the thing.

In spite of the potentially significant advantages offered by the Britten suspension for the TT and the newfound reliability of the powerplants, John was under no illusions as to the size of the task in front of his machines.

'There are heaps of things that can go wrong,' he said in an interview with the *Press* in Christchurch on 2 April. 'I don't really have enough spares to keep two bikes going. They will probably cover about 800 miles and the factories have practice bikes, which I don't have.'

One thing he did have, however, was a lump of cash from Cardinal Network, in recognition of which the bikes had been officially entered as Cardinal Brittens. (The Cardinal Britten name was used exclusively for the V-1000s for some time.) Apart from the ever-present possibility of mechanical breakdown there were also critical considerations such as fuel consumption. Unless the bike could do two full laps, or nearly 80 miles, there was no way they could compete. John did his sums, made sharper by recent experiences, and concluded that it could be done, although it was a very long way to the finish, further than any Britten had ever gone.

The bottom line was that John believed going to the TT was worth the risk. If his bikes could do well he knew he would be generously rewarded by both the publicity that would inevitably follow and by the collective respect of the many thousands of fanatical race fans who attended the race every year and the millions who watched the brilliant television coverage.

A ground swell of media fascination threatened to overwhelm the tiny Britten entourage long before they even got to the race. The *Sunday Mirror*, which has a circulation of 2.6 million readers, ran a colour picture of the bike on the front page with a two-page spread inside under the banner 'Vision of the Future'.

The surprise announcement that Trevor Nation would not, after all, be racing a V-1000, which came a few days later, did little to dampen the rising enthusiasm among the growing legion of English fans for the auspiciously named Britten. John described the decision not to have Nation race, somewhat redundantly, as being correct because it would have given the bike too high a profile.

'You can't just bowl up to the Isle of Man and win,' he was quoted as saying.

As it happened he was right, but they would never come closer.

Soon after John and Broz met up with Shaun Harris in Monza, they made the acquaintance of Roberto Crepaldi, a congenial, wealthy Italian whose family had prospered after his father had founded one of the biggest Ferrari dealerships in Europe. Roberto was a wildly enthusiastic motorcycle aficionado who had taken up enduro riding at the age of fourteen and had eventually raced in such exotic locations as Egypt, Morocco and Tunisia. During the 1970s, Roberto, then in his twenties, discovered the joys of road bikes, and in particular the joys offered by English road bikes. While most of his mates were hankering after Ducatis and Moto Guzzis, and when he wasn't helping his father in the family firm, Roberto was hammering Norton Commandos and Triumph Bonnevilles around the beautiful northern Italian countryside. For most young men of his inclinations such a lifestyle probably seemed idyllic, but in 1981 he decided to step back from the family business to set up one of his own. In the home of sharp, high-performance, V-twin sports bikes, Roberto decided to hawk the world's oldest, and arguably the world's slowest, heavyweight V-twin. Roberto and his new business partner, Carlo, became the Harley-Davidson agency for Italy.

It was an almost prescient decision, for the venerable American marque was on the verge of a complete transformation, from a pig in a poke to a hog in hog heaven. Against all the odds and against all the trends in motorcycle design and sales, Harley-Davidson was about to become a global fashion icon. At first, though, Roberto recalled, taking on the agency had not been easy.

> It was a big decision. We had a small shop downtown where Carlo and I worked with just one other mechanic. To take on the business we had to raise US$200,000

> dollars to buy the inventory of parts and the bikes in stock. With so few sales it was a big risk, but we went to the banks and borrowed it anyway and it paid off. By 1992 we had sold 1800 bikes and in 1991 we also acquired a Triumph concession, which also did very well. By then I wanted to build my own very extreme performance bike—an out and out racer for a small niche market. I wanted it to be a V8 or V6 with the engine being the main structure of the machine. By then, however, there was trouble between my father's company and Ferrari, and the partnership between Carlo and me was also not so good. So, I took my share of the money and I was suddenly free to follow my own ideas. The next thing I did was to obtain a franchise for Jaguars and Aston Martins, and I have been selling them ever since at my company, Royal Cars.

By then Roberto had also set up his own race team, Café Racers and Superbikes (CR&S), in addition to acquiring a formidable collection of highly desirable racing motorcycles. He had initially been made aware of the Britten Motorcycle through various magazine articles, but his first look at the real thing was an epiphany. Later, he would say that his connection with the machine had been immediately and powerfully spiritual. In any event he had decided there and then that he had to have one.

His introduction to John was actually facilitated by New Zealander Hugh Anderson, the former World Champion motorcycle racer. At that stage Hugh was at Monza to race an ex-works Aermacchi and was having a somewhat difficult time.

> The Aermacchi, which was a 350 that had been bored out to 500, was suffering ignition troubles and I was having major difficulties explaining things to the bike's Italian owner and his crew. They produced this big, tall fellow called Roberto who spoke good English and he interpreted for us. You get to know a fellow under those circumstances, and Roberto and I had a cup of coffee and a chat afterwards and I introduced him to John. He knew about the Britten and he was already very interested in it, so the introduction was timely. I knew Roberto would also get on well with John. They were about the same age and they seemed to share the same restless energy, and they really hit it off.

And when they did meet, Roberto was certainly keen to talk business.

> I told John that I would like to explore the idea of doing something together. I think in the beginning he did not take me seriously and he told me that I should go to New Zealand to see what he was doing. I agreed to do so, even though he was being a little ironic maybe. In the meantime, I was able to help them out with somewhere

> to stay and work on the bikes. I introduced John to my best friend Sandro and he offered to look after the Team.
>
> Allesandro (Sandro) Saravelli was a fellow Milanese. He was fifteen years older than I was and I met him because he was a friend of my father's, and another Ferrari customer. Sandro made a lot of money with scrap metals and he was an old bachelor with no family. He was race crazy and back when he was a youngster he raced a Gilera. Then in the '70s he had a Formula Three team with a March Toyota. My father and I used to go to a bar near the workshop with him and I learned that he still loved to ride bikes. So before too long we had a small group of us who used to meet to go for fun rides. He became like an uncle to me and I learned from him what it was to enjoy life without limits, for he was filled with good humour and endless energy. His old metal yard was about 50 kilometres north of Milano at a place called Cusano Milanino. It was very big and Sandro had closed it down about three years before, so it was totally empty but still had a good workshop where he had serviced all his trucks and other machinery. It was perfect for Broz and Shaun Harris to hang out and they stayed there for the next five weeks as Sandro's guests.

The old warehouses and smelter covered some three or four acres and the pair rattled around in the vast and cavernous interiors without the distraction of a single soul other than Sandro. Broz stripped both bikes, which had been shipped from Australia, and found his worst fears realised.

> I found both motors had been cooked, although the one Jason had ridden was by far the worst. The primary gears had shattered and it was clear that I was only going to get one serviceable machine out of the two of them if I was lucky.

To add to his already considerable problems, Broz found that being on the opposite side of the world to the Britten workshop and the infrastructure of support offered by the Team's hometown, made everything doubly difficult.

> It was impossible to get work done properly. Roberto's father operated a customer workshop and we used the people he used to do the machining that needed doing. I sent this outfit the best set of rods we had, along with the best crank. They were to supply new bearings and resize the rods, which should have been straightforward. When the parts came back, however, the rods had deep marks on the webs where they'd been clamped up in a vice. They were obvious fracture points and I had to file them out before I could reassemble the engine. I'd never seen anything like it. After I'd put one bike together we went testing at Monza with Shaun. When that was done I had time on my hands again, so I worked in Roberto's father's workshop for a week.

I saw more of the same shit with brand-new Ferraris. I couldn't speak the lingo and we had to communicate with sign language, but we got on all right.

When I wasn't sorting out sick Ferraris I spent my spare time with Sandro, who was absolutely brilliant company. We did all the usual things, but he had three friends who were dying of cancer and I also used to go with him in the evenings to visit them. Although he loved to fool around and make jokes Sandro took the responsibilities of friendship very seriously. He was a top bloke.

The test sessions at Monza had been used primarily to try out a number of suspension refinements. Monza was only about half an hour away and two sessions were undertaken, unfortunately without positive results, as Shaun recalled.

John had found these fancy rubberised rose joints that he hoped would introduce a certain amount of flex into the front end. The idea was that this would help eliminate the front-end patter. The idea worked to a degree, but the moment the bike started to bump-steer or otherwise lose its poise the situation would get worse and worse. The bike would start weaving viciously and I quickly came to the conclusion that the new rose joints were not going to work. We also tried different length pull rods for the back-end suspension, with no appreciable improvement in the handling. The only good thing about the sessions was that I got to know the bike a bit. At one point I saw Broz waving frantically at the pits, so I came in immediately thinking something dire had happened. He told me the clutch was slipping and I was about to completely wreck it. I told him it wasn't, but he insisted he could hear it as I was coming out of the Parabolica. I told him it was wheel-spin. He found that hard to believe as the Parabolica is a high-speed corner, but he checked it out and sure enough—that's what it was. He'd never heard that happen before so he knew I was going for it.

Wayne arrived shortly after the test sessions, having been 'lost' for a few days en route in Bangkok, and he and Shaun whiled away the time racing scooters around the complex to stave off boredom. Finally, John showed up and the Team enjoyed a welcome change with a visit to the Ducati factory, where they were received with some enthusiasm.

The famous Italian company had just started building their new Supermonos, and John and Wayne met Pierre Terblanche, an expatriate South African who was in charge of styling at Ducati. Wayne recalled that he was delighted to talk to them.

He told us that the Britten had exerted some considerable influence on his thinking and that this had happened without his conscious knowledge. He said that he had

> simply found himself drawing shapes that echoed those of the Britten. For a while this really concerned him as he was, after all, a highly original designer, but he finally decided to stop fighting his instincts. He told us that he realised the reason he kept returning to those forms was because that was where motorcycle design had gone and that was where he had to go too.

In spite of such diversions, Broz and Wayne were impatient to get moving and it was with a sense of relief that they finally took leave of the old foundry. They loaded the good bike onto a huge bus that Roberto had outfitted for his race expeditions and set off for Belgium, where they were entered in a road race.

'The bus formerly belonged to a motocross team,' said Roberto, 'who had used it for touring. After I bought it I completely stripped it out and refitted it to suit my street-racing friends. It was an old Fiat, but it had a strong motor and it looked very smart. I made it black inside and out, and the moment John saw it he christened it Black Beauty. We still call it that.'

Recalling their time in Milan, Wayne echoed Broz's sentiments.

> Roberto and Sandro were joyful company and as John was flying in to meet us at the events it was mostly just the five of us. Sandro was a natural clown. He had a strange finger that had been cut off in an accident and stitched back on. It had ended up at a funny angle and he couldn't bend it. We all used to laugh when he drank coffee because it stuck up in the air like some English dowager taking tea, and he found it just as hilarious as we did. I remember him complaining that when he cleaned his teeth it used to poke him in the eye. Roberto was a big, bouncy fellow with the capacity to see beyond the immediate need to look after business day to day. He really could see the big picture all the time. They were both deeply philosophical in spite of their totally unselfconscious habit of enjoying every moment. There was something quite childlike about them mixed in with something very old and wise. [158]

The race at Mettet in Belgium came to a grinding halt when, like its stable mate, the bike shattered its primary gears. The team loaded it into the bus and drove back to Italy, where Broz rebuilt both engines, two new sets of primary gears having by then arrived. He then checked everything again meticulously, tidying up a few things here and there. The plug leads and caps were beginning to look a bit tatty, so John had him replace them with a very smart set he had found locally. Broz had comfortably completed his ministrations when it was time to load up Black Beauty once more. They headed for Mallory Park, a racetrack located in the Midlands about halfway between London and Liverpool, where they would catch the ferry for the Isle of Man and where John would join them once again.

Shaun was convinced that the engine on the bike he had tested at Assen, the bike the Team intended running in the TT, was running hot, and he had persuaded Broz to fit a temperature gauge to the sump. A few laps at Mallory Park confirmed that the engine was indeed cooking in its oil, and it was decided that a sandwich block should be made up to move the oil filter away from the engine heat and further into the cool air stream. Rob was contacted back at the workshop and told to make the piece with some urgency and have it airfreighted out.

The rest of the trip was uneventful, and the Team arrived at the Isle of Man in good time and met up with John. After the Team had set up in the pits John and Wayne decided to have a good look around the island. They found themselves at the industrial museum at Laxey, where an early Victorian lead and zinc mine had been preserved. The centrepiece of the museum was a huge wheel built in 1854, part of a pumping system capable of removing 1100 litres of water per minute from tunnels 457 metres below the surface. With a diameter of over 23 metres, the cast-iron and timber structure, known as the 'Lady Isobella', was the largest water-wheel in Europe, and possibly in the world. The Lady Isobella—as famous a symbol of the island as the cats with no tails and the succulent kippers from the surrounding seas—had been more or less functioning continuously since it was originally commissioned. While they closely examined the structure, consisting mostly of timber with half-inch iron-rod bracing, Wayne casually mentioned that it would be possible to step onto the inside rim of the wheel from the brick structure surrounding it and to go round a full circuit by hanging onto the bracing rods. He immediately regretted coming out with the thought.

> John jumped on the idea and wouldn't let it go. We did the usual tourist thing, looking at everything, and I kept hoping he'd forget about it, but he didn't. He kept telling me that I had to do it now because I might never be back there again. I gave in and did it. He took photographs of me upside-down, way the hell up in the air hanging on for grim death and wishing I'd said no.
>
> The wheel was quite slow and the steel rods were biting into my hands, and for a few moments I genuinely feared that I would not be able to hang on. Later, John stuck a couple of prints of the photos he'd taken on the smoko-room wall at the workshop. About two years later we had the big chief of the Isle of Man tourist board visit and the prints caught his eye. He was absolutely horrified. It was apparently not the approved way to kill yourself on the island.

John had already told reporters that he was going to the TT on a learning mission, saying that he hoped 'people don't get the idea we're here to show them how to do it'. Even with such modest ambitions, however, his first view of the course where the teams were already practising was both sobering and intimidating.

'Shit!' he said. 'It's fast, isn't it.'

Practice at the racetrack started in the rain and the team immediately had a problem on their hands.

'I had only just got going on my first practice lap,' said Shaun, 'when I over-revved the motor and buggered a valve. It was my fault entirely, but there was nothing to be done except fix it as fast as possible so I could get back out and practise.'

He fired up the bike again after hurried repairs, just as the weather cleared, but once more the bike failed before he had even completed a lap this time, when the computer packed up. Electronic interference was suspected, and John thought that a local microwave navigation link was the culprit. So they tried wrapping the plugs in lead and tinfoil, but there was little, if any, improvement. Frantic phone calls were made back to Mark Franklin in New Zealand and under his instructions some circuits were modified. This involved the installation of a watchdog circuit, after which the computer fired up again, but it was not a perfect solution and the EMS continued to give trouble. And the infuriating problem continued to frustrate them as practice time slipped away. Finally, it was discovered that the entire problem was the fault of the fancy new Italian plug leads and caps. The caps had no suppressers and the electrical field they were generating was messing up the computer. It was of course, a relief to have the engine working properly again but the fiasco had been costly—Shaun had lost critical testing time.

> The practice sessions were over and I had managed to complete just one full lap. It was bad enough when you could use all your allotted time. Even with a week to test and set up the bike you'd only get about five sessions and a dozen laps, all going well. We needed all of that given the range of chassis adjustment we had to contend with. Compared with most race teams, who were concerned mostly with spring and damping options, we had to set the rake, trail, wheel-base, steering offset, front pro- and anti-dive, rear pro- and anti-squat and, of course, the normal spring and damping options. With no time left I just had to more or less go with what we had but even with the little riding I had managed to get in between problem-solving sessions I knew that the bike's set-up was way out of the ball park.

Shaun confessed his misgivings to a reporter, telling him that, 'the suspension is way too hard and the front end is slapping while the rear is skittering all over the place. And we're not even going fast yet.'

Frantically, the Team switched the spring/shock unit for the front suspension for a softer one, and then by further softening the damping, increasing the trail and dropping the rear end 15 mm they got to the point where Shaun was ready to give it a go. It was far from satisfactory, however, and other less tenacious riders might have been forgiven for hanging up their helmets and heading for the pub.

The trouble the Team was having with the suspension set-up went beyond the lack of practice and loss of time. Between John, Shaun, Broz and Wayne, all of whom were putting their individual oars in, there wasn't enough real knowledge of the suspension to do anything other than splash about. The only person who could have really done something useful was Murray, and he was again staring gloomily at the walls in the workshop on the other side of the planet.

Then the race was on and it was too late for Shaun to do anything other than grit his teeth and press on. Unfortunately, he found that the bike wasn't so much pressing on as pogo-ing off the bumps, which had the effect of throwing him dangerously off line.

> Generally, bikes are set up for the island with about half the usual amount of compression damping as they would have anywhere else. Otherwise the handling on the very high-speed but uneven surface is a little like throwing a brick down the road. As I clung on, it occurred to me that I might as well play with the compression damping on the front-suspension Ohlin damper, which I could do as the canister was mounted on the dash. It could hardly make matters worse. I adjusted it twice, putting less compression into it each time.

To his surprise and delight, Shaun found that his ad hoc refinement actually made the bike handle 'heaps better' and remarkably he was able to get into a groove. At the end of the first lap—in reality only his second for the meeting so far—he was sitting in eighteenth position. Three laps later he had worked his way through to eighth place, slicing his way through the traffic in no uncertain fashion. He was now in top company, with Joey Dunlop immediately behind him. Of course, the TT is a time trial and as machines start at different times his real position was probably further down the field. All the same, it looked like a top-four finish was definitely on the cards, with the possibility of doing even better as Shaun began to get the measure of the Britten. He reached speeds of close to 187 mph and on the short start–finish straight he was officially timed at 165 mph, the fastest reading of the race and more than 3 mph faster than the 4-cylinder Honda that eventually won. The commentary eagerly reported that the Britten was the fastest motorcycle in the race, and the crowds began cheering Shaun on with rising enthusiasm as he thundered along, hustling the waywardly handling Britten down the long and winding road.

Back at the pits, John heard strange reports that groups of spectators had been observed crouched on the ground with their bums in the air. Later he learned that it was indeed true. At various points on the circuit groups of new Britten fans were listening for its arrival with their ears to the ground. The legend was growing. The last time a twin-cylinder bike had won at the TT was Mike Hailwood's historic victory against all expectations on a Ducati back in 1978.

Then, with a lap to go, the newly fitted threaded adapter holding the oil filter cracked and the oil leaked away. Shaun stopped at a pub, and after borrowing more oil from a spectator, he managed to limp along a bit further.[159]

'I couldn't believe it when I saw that Rob had used aluminium tooling plate for that part,' Broz later complained bitterly. 'With all the wind buffeting on the filter it was bound to fail. In spite of all our problems we were set for a high finish and then that happened. It was sickening!'

There was nothing for it but to try to be philosophical about what had happened and to learn the hard lessons the island had to teach.

'Next year,' John ruefully told reporters at the press conference after the race, 'that piece will be made of steel.'

Obviously, the failure of the bike was disappointing, but it had not disgraced itself and it had enjoyed enormous and positive media attention. Also it had won for John his first sale. In the same press conference he announced his intention to build a further eight replicas of the race bike.

'These,' he said, 'will sell for US$75,000 dollars each and Italy's biggest Ferrari dealer, Roberto Crepaldi, has just placed an order for one. Mr Crepaldi intends racing it at the TT next year.'

He went on to make a second announcement. Britten Motorcycles had started work on a 550cc single-cylinder 4-stroke. The new engine was being built to power an 'affordable road/race bike and the keynote for the new design was simplicity'. As usual, John was being somewhat premature, driven perhaps by his glimpse of the new Ducati single at the Ducati factory and the knowledge that he might never have a better time to talk to the world's motorcycle press. When he made the announcement the engine was still forming in his head and far from proving simple, his plans, once hatched, would be for an engine of enormous complexity. However, he had decided to make the first machine and his decision would prove, as always, to be final. Roberto and those closest to John were in no doubt that the prospect of building a Britten to contest the Sound of Singles races in Europe excited his imagination as much as building the big twin had.

Back home, however, the announcement of a pending single was received with some scepticism by most members of the Team, who could see many cogent arguments against the idea, not the least of which was the fact that they now apparently had another eight V-1000s to build and were still learning how to campaign the V-1000s they already had. If the TT had shown anything it was the danger of being under-resourced. The biggest disincentive to undertaking such a project, however, was that it was difficult to imagine exactly who would buy a single from them.

While it was true that the Sound of Singles race series had won widespread international success, it was pursued mostly by cash-strapped amateurs who found the challenges of doing it themselves part of the fun. Big single-cylinder trail-bike engines were being slotted into road-bike frames and so on with absolutely minimal expenditure. The parts suppliers were more often the local wrecking yard rather than the specialists who made things like titanium rods. Even if John could significantly reduce the cost of the bike, it was unlikely to find widespread acceptance among that fraternity, regardless of the odd well-heeled customer cleaning up with a sharp Britten weapon. However, it was unlikely that Britten Motorcycles would be able to reduce the costs sufficiently to suit even the exceptionally wealthy unless at least semi-volume production could be achieved. Simply eliminating one cylinder from the V-twin did not significantly reduce the material costs or the amount of skilled labour needed to produce the finished article.

Of course, John didn't see it that way. He saw a challenge to build the most eloquent and potent version of the simplest form of the motorcycle yet. And it was true that the racing 4-stroke single-cylinder engine was one of the last engineering frontiers in the motorcycle world. The established manufacturers had in recent decades generally concentrated on singles as a power source for off-road machines or cheap commuter bikes. Road-race engines, on the other hand, had been somewhat neglected. It was an area where a significantly different approach might win widespread acclaim, if not acceptance. No doubt the minimalist nature of the single-cylinder motorcycle was also something that held enormous appeal for John, and there was the attraction of further usage for the technology. If he could build a successful high-performance single—and his proposed 550 would need to develop about 90 bhp to be really dominant—then he could build simpler versions of the engine for light aircraft.[160]

There were also John's ambitions to build a Third World car, which could share a simplified version of the single-cylinder. This project, like the ornithopter, had been in the back of his mind since he was in his early twenties and at some stage he actually made a model of it.[161] Finally, as mentioned, there was the fact that Ducati had built a single-cylinder engine, an ingenious device that had a counterweight whizzing up and down instead of a second piston, thereby maintaining the perfect primary balance enjoyed by the 90-degree twin. The Supermono was a winner and no doubt John enjoyed the thought of taking a stick to his self-appointed rivals in a completely new arena. Of course, the simplest way to achieve his objective would have been to lop off one cylinder of his V-1100, but that would not achieve the objective of doing something brand new and different. Nor was it likely to achieve the horsepower he had in mind.

Meanwhile, the Team drove the big black bus to Newbury near Reading, where a mate of Shaun's had a motorcycle shop. Here Broz tidied up the bike for their last race in Europe before going home. The race was on the famous old circuit at Donington, where Shaun, who was off the pace for some reason, finished well down in the field.

Two months after arriving in Europe the Team began packing up the spares to ship home from the workshop in Newbury. They had spent the entire time living in Roberto's bus, and with Assen coming up John had decided to leave the bike with the bus for Roberto to store. According to Shaun, the stress of the previous two months was really beginning to tell.

> Wayne and I almost came to blows on a number of occasions. One time he wanted to extract some start money from various race organisers and I suggested that my race record should be included with his application. For some reason he disagreed. It was a stupid thing to argue about but he didn't know the race scene and I did. I now accept I could have been more accommodating. He and Broz were also having trouble, and because Broz was my spannerman I always stood up for him. Under pressure Broz became more than usually grumpy and the aggravation began to grow between the two of them.

For Wayne, the stresses of managing the Team had come mostly from Shaun.

> Shaun fancied himself a manager and he was always correcting me, so it was usually Broz who kept the peace. Broz constantly reminded me that you had to keep the rider happy at all costs and I did my best to do that. At the same time I was doing all the washing for the team and cooking them three meals a day. It was hard work and we were all getting up each other's noses after living all this time cheek by jowl in Roberto's bus.

The night before the Team was due to leave, matters finally came to a head. Wayne laid the blame for what happened next squarely on the doorstep of the Indian restaurant next to the workshop they were using.

> They only had this low-alcohol beer and you need a good amount of the real stuff if you're going to devour a few big curries. I told them they couldn't serve that stuff to Kiwis but it was all they had. John was with us that night and he produced this bottle of really high-octane Navy rum, which we put in the beer to give it some oomph. So it was John's fault as well.

Shaun watched as the evening unravelled and all the accumulated tensions burst forth, although it was the peacemaker who ended up on the floor.

> Broz got plastered and he was waving his finger under Wayne's nose. Wayne told him to back off or he would sort him out. Broz kept going and Wayne stepped back and decked him. Apparently he was quite a keen amateur boxer and I remember thinking at the time that I was glad it was not me on the other end. Broz got up a few times and the same thing happened, and then he finally gave it up. There was no real damage, no broken nose or missing teeth. It seemed to clear the air and there has been no lasting animosity. Blokes are funny that way; it sort of made us friends. All in all it was just a bloody tough trip.

The campaign had obviously been one of mixed fortunes for the Team but there was much to draw solace from, not least the growing reputation of the bike. And so, once again consoled with 'the glory of all he had dared' and with one firm order in his pocket, John headed for Japan.

CHAPTER FIFTEEN

The Junction

The failure at the Isle of Man was, in many respects, similar to the successive failures at Daytona that preceded it. In each case the obvious potential of the Britten to win against all the odds had mightily impressed fans and pundits alike. After the last near miss at Daytona, for example, David Edwards, the influential editor of *Cycle World* magazine, had actually declared the Britten to be the winner.

> The biggest winner in the exotic bike sweepstakes has to be the Britten V-twin race bike which packs more innovation between its two wheels than most NASA space shots. Straight out of its Air New Zealand shipping crate, John Britten's avant-garde beauty came within a wrongly wired battery of winning the Daytona SuperTwins race. If I were a head honcho at a motorcycle company in Japan, Germany, Italy or America I'd march right down the hallway with a copy of the *Cycle World* story on the Britten and ask how it is that one man working in a shed in Christchurch could have out-teched my entire engineering department.

Whether any head honchos stormed around the corridors of their establishments brandishing the magazine article is not known, but many would not have to wait long for John to pay them a visit to tell them himself. He had already visited Moto Guzzi and Ducati and, encouraged by the performance of his machine at the Isle of Man and by all the publicity the campaign had generated, he decided that before returning to New Zealand he would stop in on the manufacturers in Japan. He intended to sound them out about either buying elements of the new bike's technology from him or having the Britten Team work for them on a consultancy basis. Harry Ruffell and CJ, who had both been at the Isle of Man, were also keen to look through the factories in Japan, so the three friends travelled together.

CJ remembered they were delighted on arrival to find themselves guests of *Riders' Club*, a major Japanese motorcycle magazine, which generously looked after them.

They had run big spreads on the bike in their magazine, with long articles about it, and they sold hundreds of thousands of copies. They had also started quite a fan club among their readers. They wanted to pay John to bring a bike over to Japan to race and generally they couldn't have been more helpful. We booked into a hotel room in Tokyo that was about the size of a bathroom, which made us claustrophobic, but it was a buzz just to be there. We were driven everywhere in this beautiful white Benz with white leather upholstery, courtesy of the magazine. The weather was hot and sticky and we seemed to be in one perpetual traffic snarl-up all the time we were in the city, so the car was a real oasis.

Our first port of call was Honda, and after driving for hours we finally arrived at this huge industrial complex where I was amused to see this guy in the car-park giving the parked cars a flick over with a feather duster. One of the perks I suppose. Inside, we were shown to this boardroom and then a guy came in with an interpreter and asked John who he wanted to talk to. John said he wanted to talk to the guy who did the same things he did in the Britten factory. The fellow then asked exactly what part John played in building the bikes and so he gave him a quick run-down on his role. Then we waited again and presently about fourteen guys in white coats trooped in and sat down. John told them about the bike in detail and they sat there and listened.

He stopped for a break and asked if they wanted to ask questions, and there was a bit of a confab and then the interpreter asked John if he would tell the truth now about his big factory. At that point we decided to roll some of Harry's video, which showed John heat-treating a casting and working with carbon-fibre in the workshop at Matai Street. They were aghast, looking at him as if he was from another planet, and then asked a flood of very precise technical questions. John was giving these comprehensive answers and they were scribbling it all down as the interpreter interpreted, and I became more and more concerned until finally I couldn't hold back and kicked him under the table. He winced but it didn't stop him. Later he said he'd held stuff back, but I wasn't convinced. I think he gave them everything they wanted.

When the meeting came to a close John asked to see the factory as they had previously agreed to let us do, and there was another confab and then the interpreter said 'No'. He said John could steal all their secrets and set up his own factory. John was stunned. He said, 'What secrets could I possibly want to steal from you!' It was a bummer really and then the same thing happened at Yamaha. The only difference here was that John talked to the racing team and they were great. They were interested in having John build carbon-fibre tanks and stuff for them and we got the feeling we were talking to real enthusiasts. However, we were too depressed by the way both companies had shut us out from their operations to even go to Suzuki or Kawasaki. The magazine people threw us a party and we ended up drinking sake in this little place off a busy street. We enticed these lovely Japanese girls who happened to be passing to join us, which freaked everyone in the restaurant out. It wasn't done. By then, however, we were pretty tanked up.

There was this guy at the table who was leading all these drinking games and we were matching him glass for glass, determined to uphold the honour of the nation and all that. But he didn't seem to get pissed. I got suspicious and followed him to the toilet, where I caught him sticking his fingers down his throat and throwing up. He was a professional drinker hired for the occasion! The effects of all the booze had me flying but for John it was different. I'd never seen him look as sick as he did the next day. We went somewhere in the beautiful white Benz and he suddenly threw up all over the immaculate white leather. He was horrified and embarrassed after the wonderful hospitality we had enjoyed from these people, but he was in a bad way. It took him days to get better and I started to wonder if something more than a really bad hangover was going on. Finally, we decided to get some fresh air, so we got on a Bullet train and zapped out into the countryside. There was a schoolgirl reading an English textbook, so we asked her where we should get off. We were just pulling into a station and she said we should go to this resort that was nearby. Of course we'd gone miles out into the country in a very short time because the things go so fast, and the place was way out in the middle of nowhere, right under Mount Fujiyama.

The Seven Pools Hotel gave us robes to put on after we'd haggled the price down from about NZ$700 a night to NZ$300, and then we just wandered from one aromatherapy hot pool to another, lying on these big slabs of warm marble. It was brilliant and slowly John started to look a bit better, although he still seemed to be out of sorts. After we got home he was uncharacteristically bitter about the way we had been treated by the Japanese factories and he started to make noises about preventing the Japanese buying up land in New Zealand and so on. It was probably the only time I ever heard him venture any kind of political opinion and it seemed out of proportion to what actually happened to us in Japan. I mean some of those people treated us very well indeed. I was worried because something still seemed very wrong.

Once back in New Zealand, John began to cast around for a rider to race the second Britten at Assen. He had intended that only the machine left in Europe would contest the meeting, but with fresh sponsorship cash from Roberto Crepaldi and his Café Racers and Superbikes team John decided to mount his preferred two-pronged attack. English rider Jim Moodie was quickly contracted to ride the second bike, which was flown out from New Zealand along with Shaun Harris and Broz. All seemed well when John arrived shortly before the race to see Moodie set pole with Shaun behind him, and the crowd was eagerly anticipating a battle royal. When it started to rain shortly before the race the Team was not too concerned—

they had both wet and intermediate tyres and both Britten riders were adept in the wet.

For the first couple of laps Moodie led the race, with Shaun not far behind, but as the rain began to bucket down he found, to his dismay, that his brakes completely disappeared.

'I was pulling the lever right back to the bars,' he said later, 'and still nothing happened. It was frustrating.'

By the end of the second lap German rider Hans Fischer had taken the front spot, but Moodie held on gamely to second place in spite of his lack of stoppers, until lap eleven when a second Ducati, ridden by Mike Edwards, slipped through. Britten riders were by now equipped with brilliant blue and pink leathers, and it was ironically the bright colours beckoning through the rain in front of him that had encouraged Edwards to greater efforts. At flag-fall Jim was a distant third, with Shaun, who had experienced similar difficulties, finishing way down in tenth place, though Broz saw it philosophically.

> We knew bugger all about racing in the wet at that stage. If we had we'd have slotted the brake pads and there wouldn't have been a problem. However, we didn't and when it started absolutely pissing down the bikes had no stoppers at all. Moodie had a few sharp words with John about the way things had gone. It takes a special temperament to race a big experiment like the Brittens because anything can go wrong. Moodie was maybe a little too hot-headed to really understand what he was dealing with. But he did well to get where he did. Real well.

In spite of the disappointing finishes, the Brittens had done enough to draw considerable attention, particularly when Moodie had posted the fastest time around the track. The two bikes had enthralled the crowd throughout the meeting with their striking looks, blistering acceleration and deep-booming exhaust notes (albeit now sufficiently muffled to pass the noise tests). One way or another a legend was building.

Once back home, John started to tool up to produce the next run of Britten V-1000s (various rule changes having relegated the 1100 to history) and decided that he would build an initial batch of five. He also turned his attention to the single-cylinder race bike he had announced at the Isle of Man. From the beginning of the project John intended that it would compete at the TT, and John Shand was given the task of ensuring that there would be no rules to get in the way if something totally, mind-blowingly original suddenly turned up. Accordingly, he lobbied the FIM against the imposition of minimum weight limits on the Sound of Singles class, an important consideration for John as he was determined that his single-cylinder racer would be more powerful and lighter than anything else in the world. Finally, in November, Shand was able to inform John in a fax that he had 'put forward your proposals against considerable opposition from the Italians who wanted a 120 kg limit'. He was pleased to report that the new class, to be known as 'Supermono',[162] would be for normally aspirated, 4-stroke machines up to 800cc without minimum weight limits.

'You owe me a beer!' he concluded.[163]

Soon after, John Shand was in touch again, this time to report that Steve Hislop might be available to ride a Britten at the next TT. Hislop, Shand wrote, was unlikely to accept a ride with Honda the next year as a new, major Honda sponsor had insisted that Phillip McCallen, the winner of that year's Senior, be made number one rider.

'Hislop,' he claimed, 'would never settle for the number two spot. With Hislop and Holden on two bikes ex NZ and Roberto running his bike with Shaun on it we should be able to knock Honda off their perch.'

It is hard to imagine that John did not grimace slightly at Shand's extravagant predictions as he read the fax. Having three bikes ready by the time the next TT rolled around would be a tall order, let alone 'knocking Honda off'. But he had already decided to give it his best shot. If two bikes were better than one then why not take three?

While work on the new V-twins geared up around him, John got busy roughing out plans for the new single-cylinder engine. It was his intention to get the ball rolling before he was taken away from the workshop by his other commitments. The Team would then be able to carry it on whenever there was an opportunity through some delay in the programme with the new V-1000s.

Hans Weekers was quickly roped into the project and remembered that John more or less had the whole thing planned in his head before anything was put on paper. The significant technological variation he wished to pursue lay in the valve area. He wanted six.[164]

If the keynote for the new motor was to be simplicity, it certainly did not extend to the valve arrangements, as Hans recalled.

> The set-up John had in mind would require asymmetric cams and nobody made them. I had an idea whereby we could run the four inlet valves off two cams without rockers, using two bath-shaped buckets actuating two valve stems apiece. The exhaust valves, of course, would each have a conventional round bucket.
>
> John was very sceptical, so we made up a test rig and set it up in the lathe. We spun it up and it worked. He loved it, so I set about doing a complete set of drawings for the new motor, the first for any Britten engine. I included three plugs because I

> knew getting good squish was going to be a real bastard. Then the factory set about building it, using the bottom end of a V-1000 to get it running well enough for the dyno. It was not a priority, so it was done in fits and spurts, but John was very serious about it and he would never let it rest completely.

For whatever reason, John's life was now building to a crescendo of activity. As we know, he had in the past told a select few people that he did not see himself on earth for a long time and he now began to work as if he wanted to realise all his dreams at once. Building a handful of V-1000s and developing a new engine for an as yet unspecified number of Britten Supermonos, as well as running a demanding business, ought to have been enough to tax the grit of the most stalwart of men. For John Britten, however, motorcycles and motorcycle engines were but one area in which he wanted to explore his creative vision and leave his mark. His passion for Christchurch, the only city he could imagine living in, transcended proud parochialism and he regularly spoke of his desire to contribute in some way to its material well-being. And, for John, that meant a building, one fusing traditional aesthetics and applied technology. He had already identified a place within the city where he might build such an edifice, in the run-down area referred to earlier, immediately to the east of Cathedral Square.

He began purchasing properties across an entire block, driving a succession of hard deals and, there is no doubt, picking up a great deal of prime real estate at bargain basement prices. This was only partly because of the general seediness of the area and the fact that all the 'smart' money was building bars and cafés on the other side of town along the river. John got even better deals than many would have expected because he used all his considerable skills and cunning as a negotiator and trader. He called in favours and promised future ones. He charmed, cajoled, begged and bluffed, and then it was there—a massive site just around the corner from Cathedral Square.

From the outset, John was confident that his development would be so dominant that existing seedy businesses such as the massage parlours would shy away like bats from the light and wing off elsewhere. In the same way, he was confident that the attractions offered by the new watering-holes across town would not detract from his plans. He was not yet entirely sure exactly what form his edifice would take, but it was beginning to gel and one of its characteristics would be that it blended in with the finest traditional architecture Christchurch had to offer. In keeping with this objective he decided to retain as much of the existing period buildings on the site as possible. His determination to retain the older façades along one street in particular would greatly add to the expense and complication of his project, but he was still haunted by his demolition of the original Heatherlea.

More and more he rallied to the defence of threatened old buildings he had grown up with, sometimes pleading their cases to those who wished to demolish them. When he heard, for example, that the United Services Hotel, an inner-city building he admired, might be in danger of demolition, he begged the owners to allow him to clean the façade at his own expense so that a decision could be made with the building looking its best. His offer was refused and the building duly bit the dust. The wreckers in this instance were established family friends with long associations through Bruce, and John was particularly disappointed by their stubborn insistence that only their own immediate interests mattered. He was beginning to view the city as an entity, a living organism with a life-force that could only thrive in an atmosphere of harmony and beauty. His visits to the ancient cities of Europe had left their mark on him.

John hired architects Warren and Mahoney to draw up plans for the site, and they came up with a design, which they christened Press Crescent. This incorporated apartments down one side of the site and retail shops on the other. Stylistically, the plans represented an extension of the attractive late 19th-century two-level terrace-style shops that lined either side of New Regent Street, the street that led directly to the site. However, the concept failed to enthuse John and he asked Wayne Alexander to draw up a list of activities for the site that would reflect a strong New Zealand theme. There had to be generous space devoted to providing the public with a harmonious and relaxing environment to simply enjoy. Wayne was in sympathy with John's ideas.

> We were picture painting in each other's heads and I felt I could see clearly the structures he could see. I have enjoyed that kind of creative empathy and communication before and since with certain individuals but nothing was ever as powerful as that time I spent with John. Before our next meeting I drew a perspective of one section of the building I believed we had been talking about and then extended it by sellotaping another piece of paper to it. I ended up with a huge drawing that covered my entire dining-room table, and when it was done I folded it up and sent it to John. He was ecstatic and he took it straight along to Warren and Mahoney. They were actually bloody good about it considering it was nothing like their idea and it hadn't come from fellow architects. They told him they liked it, and so the idea for Cathedral Place, as we now called it, was born. In many ways the new proposal was modelled on the atrium at The Stables and John intended building it in much the same way. It was to be a building crafted and gilded by artisans and artists.

In place of an open road between terraces, the plan was to cover the entire site—the better part of a large city block—with a massive glass ceiling, reminiscent of the big-city railway stations John had so admired in Europe. This would allow him to build mezzanine floors within the structure, leaving a central atrium soaring above the access and running throughout its length. The immense arched ceiling was to be supported by delicately proportioned steel girders, in Meccano-set fashion. These were in turn to be supported on the south side of the development by twisting stone columns, which were to be turned and drilled on the site. On the north side the ceiling was to rest on huge fabricated-metal 'cabbage trees'. John often told his friends how much he loved these trees, describing them as a New Zealand icon. He attributed a curiously spiritual quality to them, possibly because they were often the only living link to the ancient forests, the only natives to have survived the early settlers' clearing of the forest for farming.

Functionally, the building was to be a retail complex incorporating restaurants, bars, a nightclub and an area for artists. (The original Artists' Quarter still existed but it would soon be demolished.) The apartments idea was completely discarded.

Russell Boddington, Bruce's protégé, had now left Brittco to explore his own ideas and initiate his own projects. It was a friendly and positive parting of the ways, but John now needed his own right-hand man and he asked Wayne Alexander if he would be interested.

> I think John was quite surprised when I agreed immediately to join him. He knew I had just opened a second shop in Wellington and that I was pretty committed to my business, but from the moment I got involved in the project I didn't want to do anything else. Of course, I learned later that you can't leave a business like I did and expect it to carry on, and it caused me all sorts of problems, but I never regretted my decision.

Wayne's new role in John's life was far from popular with a number of John's old friends. Some, like Robin Judkins, viewed Wayne as a kind of Svengali, a man far too uncritically supportive of John's every whim for John's own good. This attitude was undoubtedly exacerbated by the strong reservations many harboured about the entire Cathedral Place development. It was certainly true that the proposed structure was relatively expensive, given the area of useable space it would yield, and that it would require rental returns from retailers in excess of current rates in order to be profitable. John's answer to those who advanced such misgivings was that retailers would surely see value in paying a little more to be located in a place that was simply the most elegant, exciting and welcoming place in the centre of the city. They could not help but see value, he argued, in a location that would naturally attract large numbers of people to go there. And if they really were too stupid to see it, then he would let the space to talented and committed individuals who would manage different businesses on his behalf. It was this final idea that caused some of John's oldest friends the gravest concerns.

One such friend was Kevin Brookfield, the man who had run the sandwich shop in the old days at the Artists' Quarter. He had remained in retail, finally owning a number of record stores, and he now watched with some growing concern as the massive project quickly enveloped John, not only in its construction but also as its future commercial operator.

> John's talents were not in the dog-eat-dog world of retail. John was a practical artist with a unique fusion of design and engineering skills. I learned that the first time I met him, the day he turned up in my sandwich bar looking like David Bowie with the biggest pair of flares I've ever seen on the end of a bloke's legs. I only had to talk to him for a few minutes to realise he was different. He became a great friend to my wife Judith and me even though his life then was miles away from our settled domesticity. Jude and I had married when I was eighteen and she was sixteen. John, on the other hand, had serial relationships with one woman after another until he eventually married Kirsteen. When I met him I was working hard selling sandwiches while he was just sort of swanning around. At heart, however, he was very family-oriented and he respected our lives. When Jude and I finally built a home he gave us this amazing spiral staircase for it made out of a tree trunk, which had steel pipes running horizontally through it into the railway sleeper treads. It was a clever, overwhelming gift.
>
> I know he saw the development as something for the future of his family, but I was convinced that being the owner-operator of such a vast business would suck him dry financially, emotionally and creatively. I know that as time went by the development worried him increasingly, but he wasn't happy to hear anything against it. Nevertheless I made a point of talking to him about it and the more I did the more concerned I became. It was eating him up but he couldn't back off. His reputation and his pride were at stake. At the same time I couldn't help feeling that if anyone could pull it off he could. And I think looking back that this kind of faith probably added to the pressure on him.

With his time increasingly dominated by Cathedral Place, John had little left for the management required within Britten Motorcycles to build five bikes and to continue the race programme. Nor did he have time to carry on with research and development and to pursue new engineering projects, both of which he was eager to do. He was seriously overstretched. For months he maintained a crippling regime of hours, working at Brittco during the day and then toiling the night away at Britten Motorcycles.

Of course, with friends like Chris James around life could never be entirely serious, and in spite of all the various pressures in his life John still found himself dragged into the hoaxes his friend still enjoyed springing on the world. Over the years CJ had taken root in New Zealand, not least because of his friendship with John, and had graduated from itinerant hippy to highly successful property owner with a diverse portfolio of rental accommodation in Queenstown and Dunedin.

But CJ's success had failed utterly to dampen his enthusiasm for the absurd, and in the grip of one of his recurrent bouts of good-natured mania he decided to mount a challenge for the 1994 America's Cup.[165] Unfortunately, CJ's challenge, on behalf of the Doctor's Point Boat Club—Doctor's Point being located on Lake Wakatipu in Queenstown—was received just ten minutes after the deadline for challenges had passed. He was told, however, that if he turned up with a late entry fee of US$10,000 the San Diego Yacht Club would be pleased to consider his case. Wasting no time, CJ jetted off to San Diego and arrived at the club with US$10,000 in cash. He was surprised to find a good representation of the international press were gathered outside the club to report the dramatic late entry by a Russian syndicate. The Russians eventually turned up after everyone had gone home but in their absence the reporters had turned their attention to CJ. A British television news crew filmed the exchange and a number of people who knew John Britten then witnessed the subsequent news item on British television. They saw CJ standing in front of the San Diego Yacht Club waving his bundle of cash at the forest of masts that surrounded him in this, one of the most exclusive marinas in the world. And he was shouting gleefully that he was not in the least intimidated by it all and that the Doctor's Point Yacht Club from Queenstown, New Zealand, was 'going to clean everyone up!'

'What kind of boats do you have at the Doctor's Point Yacht Club?' a British reporter asked politely.

There was a pause while CJ seemed to take a mental inventory of all the various craft represented by the club.

'The Doctor's Point Yacht Club currently sails two windsurfers and a couple of dinghies,' he announced, 'but we will of course be commissioning a new boat and John Britten, the brilliant Christchurch designer, has agreed to design her.'

The first knowledge John had of this new venture came when the world's yachting press, having established that the John Britten referred to by CJ was indeed the Kiwi motorcycle guy, inundated him with phone calls at his home. By then the local and national press had also latched onto the story. Privately cringing, John was pressured into allowing press photographers to take shots of him sitting at his drawing board while pretending that the uppermost blank sheet of paper was covering an America's Cup racing yacht design rather than further sheets of virgin paper.

He soon got into the spirit of the thing and announced with a straight face that he was looking at a double-ended, symmetrical racing yacht that could sail both ways. This, he said, would give an invaluable advantage in manoeuvrability. As a final afterthought, he told them that the boat would also feature a carbon-fibre mast.

He then fobbed off the press from all further interviews until CJ returned from San Diego, with his US$10,000 still safely in hand and a firm refusal by the club to consider his late entry. By then the press had more or less forgotten the matter. However, John had not. He greeted CJ with an enthusiastic endorsement of the challenge and urged him to put more pressure on the San Diego Yacht Club to reconsider their rejection. The idea of a reversible yacht, John told CJ, actually had merit. Of course, the cup defenders saw no point in changing their minds about the Doctor's Point Yacht Club challenge, but John's suggestion that carbon-fibre was the best mast material was to occasion some considerable interest from the New Zealand syndicate that did contest and eventually win the cup. Various meetings were set up to discuss the matter and, of course, carbon-fibre masts, and many other parts, became common on top racing yachts. This would inevitably have happened anyway, but as always John was in the vanguard of such developments.

Such respites, however, if respite is the right word for CJ's artfully choreographed mayhem, were rare as John's life became increasingly cluttered with the competing demands of his various projects. On the motorcycle front alone, John was drowning in a morass of paper. There were quotes from suppliers to request and bills from suppliers to query when they varied from those quotes. There were paper wars to wage with those whose products failed. There were duties and taxes and an endless parade of shipping documents to deal with, as parts came in and bikes travelled to and fro internationally. There was also a veritable seam of public gold in the form of government development grants, marketing grants, employee subsidies and tax breaks to be assayed, a rich mother-lode hidden behind an avalanche of paper. There were customers and potential customers to deal with. The profuse correspondence between John and Roberto Crepaldi, for example, was a clear indication of just how involved one sale could be even when it was being transacted with a man who could not have been more accommodating or understanding. It must have been excruciating for John, who positively hated writing, to have had do so much of it.

He desperately needed someone to write his letters and someone to set up a basic accounting procedure for Britten Motorcycles. He needed a manager. Bean-counting had never been of the slightest interest to John, and probably the kindest thing that could be said of his accounting skills was that they were loose.[166]

With Wayne's assistance John had greatly increased the inventory of Britten Motorcycle merchandise, and the business was becoming increasingly successful and, of course, correspondingly complex. The merchandising range had begun simply enough with t-shirts, designed and screen-printed by Bob Brooklands, but it now included caps, coats, pants, badges, pens, cups, computer mouse pads and a host of other branded items. At its height, the company would sell nearly NZ$3 million's worth of product in a single year.

For a time, John personally dropped off boxes of Britten merchandise at various shops, but he later had little idea of who had what. He urgently needed help and it wasn't just with the books.

Of the entire original motorcycle crowd, apart from independents such as Mike Sinclair and Bob Brookland, only Rob Selby was left. (He had left his last employer to work full time with Britten Motorcycles when John secured the place at Lowe Street.) Of course, Broz had also come on board full time by now but more hands were urgently needed. Rob could hardly be expected to handle all the machining on his own and Broz could not reasonably be expected to construct eight new bikes and service both the Team's race bikes as well as those of Britten Motorcycles' customers. Clearly the business needed at least another couple of mechanics and a machinist. John also knew that he needed to retain the services of Jason Monopoli, his designer, and Murray Aitken, his development engineer, neither of whom had yet been paid a wage.

Then there was the matter of machinery. Ideally, the company needed a decent milling machine, but John balked at shelling out the NZ$100,000 required for a small CADCAM mill. Computer Aided Design and Computer Aided Manufacturing machines were a relatively recent technology that allowed the operator to machine practically any shape from computer-generated drawings. Having set the mill up to do the job once, it could effortlessly repeat the process every time the operator called up the design. Clearly such a machine would have revolutionised Britten Motorcycles production, but it was not to be.

Instead, John began to cast about for a cheaper alternative, and shortly before leaving for the Isle of Man he had spoken to Loren Poole about it. Loren had prepared a report on the different equipment available with a summation of each machine's cost and capabilities. It was a succinct document that impressed John even though he finally elected not to follow any of Loren's recommendations. He eventually purchased a relatively old mill while in America, and in doing so encumbered all that used it, and relied on its output, with endless delays and frustrations. However, Loren's report did persuade John that he should give him a two-week trial at the workshop as a de facto manager and the invitation was duly made and accepted.

> When I arrived I found Rob sort of running things, but he didn't seem to know what to do with me and there was no sign of John. I helped Jason sand down a fairing for

a few days and then Rob put me on a lathe making shims, the first time I'd operated one since school. Two weeks and a lot of shims later John and I finally got together and talked about the company and the way he wanted to see it develop. We agreed that I would start full time in July before he went to the TT.

Slowly but surely Britten Motorcycles evolved from a hobby to a business, a transformation that would eventually see the company employ sixteen highly skilled people. Predictably, the transition was often haphazard, and Loren was somewhat surprised when John called him weeks before the date agreed as a start time to tell him he was needed immediately.

I told John I needed at least two weeks to get myself organised, but he called again sounding quite distraught. He asked if I wanted the job or not, and I assured him I did and more or less abandoned everything and hit the road. I had only just arrived at the factory when John walked in, dumped everything to do with the company in front of me and told me to look after it. We talked later that night and confirmed everything, but from that moment on I managed the place, although I was never officially given the title. This subsequently caused a lot of anguish. The front office was John's and Broz was living upstairs in the office with a bathroom, so the only place for me to go was the smoko room, where everyone could see and hear me. It was an uncomfortable arrangement to say the least.

I did all John's letters and got more and more involved in the deals to sell bikes and nail sponsorships. He would tell me what he wanted to say and I would write the letter. Then we'd get together and he'd make any changes that needed making, although we got to know each other so well it was seldom necessary. The hunt for sponsorship cash began well when Bob gave me a name in ICI and I followed it up. We eventually secured about NZ$20,000 from them. It was a good deal and I was later able to go further in the UK with the parent company for even more loot.

The decision to start the new bike programme by building the batch of five race bikes had just been taken, and we desperately needed to get organised. I assembled a parts list and gave everything a parts number, and we made up build sheets with full specifications for everything. I also put together a list of suppliers with all the contact details. There were boxes everywhere with bits of paper in them and often no one knew what parts they were actually using. I started to record the vast amount of information that had accumulated over the years. Then there was all the merchandise. By then it was getting to be a reasonably big business that urgently needed to be taken in hand, with proper stock control and so on.

In addition to getting the paperwork under control I was able to help the team to address some of the persistent problems with the bikes.[167] In some areas refining what we had was not simple, and one of the biggest problems I faced was John. He had this idea about development that was utterly unrealistic. He told me, for example, that Andrew knew what he wanted and Broz could fix it for him, something that just didn't stack up when you looked at the complexities of setting up racing bikes. The engineers were just left out of the loop, something that proved to be enormously counterproductive.

I think a lot of John's attitude stemmed from a desire not to involve other engineers more than he had to. I still don't completely understand, for example, his attitude toward Murray but now wonder if he wasn't just a bit threatened by him. Murray was a bashful, modest fellow but he was also a doctor of mechanical engineering. When he and Hans redesigned the engine they obviously worked well together because they both operated at a fairly high level.[168]

Murray ended up doing a hell of a lot on his own initiative that John really did not appreciate. If anyone wanted to know how big or how strong something needed to be they would ask Murray. Often these questions needed a lot of engineering work to come up with the right answer, and only those who actually did it could understand the work involved. Because Murray was so good at what he did it was easy to underestimate the effort and take the results he achieved for granted. In many ways John and Murray were almost bound to misunderstand one another. Murray is a straight up and down character and he has no time for bullshit. If John had one big blind spot it was that he often didn't want to hear the harsher realities, whereas Murray had no qualms about stating them.

Prior to the 1993 Daytona race, Murray worked for six months around the clock and got the odd NZ$10 for petrol, but that was about it. He and John had done a lot of work on the carbon-fibre wheel project, working on the design of a winding machine to make them on a volume-production basis. Later on, Murray would get pissed off when John patented all that for himself but that's the way it turned out. By the time I got there, however, Murray had drifted away and was working for a company called Industrial Research Limited. When I managed to hook into a Business Development Grant to pursue the wheel project and other stuff, Murray was hired out to John as a consultant by them for about NZ$120 an hour. This was crazy. I suggested to John that we should deal with Murray directly because it would obviously cost us a lot less, and he finally became a paid member of the team. Both Murray and I then worked under contract as consultants to Britten Motorcycles and charged our time to the grant. Officially we could work on the V-1000, the wheel project, the single and general design work. Within six months of arriving I'd secured about NZ$200,000 in grants of one kind or another so we were in good shape.

I started keeping set-up sheets and records of everything that happened at the track, both racing and in practice. Murray upgraded all the computer files and we consulted with people like Paul Treacy, Mike Sinclair and Mike Watt to sort out the handling.[169] The bikes were a real mess after they got back from Europe. Nobody knew what the rake or the spring rate and pre-load should be because nothing was written down. The set-up was miles away from where it needed to be, which really pissed Murray off because he'd worked so hard to get it right, and it was kind of embarrassing to have the other guys there because we had no idea where to start with the testing. There was no baseline.

Once we got organised things improved almost immediately. We spent a day with our three 'consultants', which actually proved quite useful.[170] We developed into the most high-tech race team in New Zealand to the point where we could confidently take on the likes of Robert Holden on a Ducati Corsa. Eventually we had two mechanics and at least one engineer as part of the race team. We were smartly turned out in the Team kit, we had all the merchandise properly displayed, and of course we had a tent. If we hadn't got organised Andrew would not have been able to take on Robert or many of the others in the next New Zealand Superbike Championship.

Things also improved for me at the workshop, mainly because Broz bought a house and I was able to move out of the smoko room. He took his lathe, his welding gear and his tools with him, which annoyed John, who then had to buy all that gear new, but at least we now had a reasonable lathe. I think that there was a period there when money got really tight for John and he began to spin out a bit. I also moved out of John's house where I had been staying and lived upstairs at the workshop for a while. (I discovered the folly of that soon enough and moved into digs with the Doctor, which was a vast improvement.)

The big task tool-wise was to sort out this antiquated old CNC [Computer Numerical Control] mill that John had picked up cheap in the States. It had these horrible old international standard controls that required 1S0-G codes to be typed in to determine the cutting position and the feed rate. I approached Desktop Engineering, a Christchurch company who sold Gibbs products—Gibbs specialises in software for Computer Aided Machining—and managed to secure a sponsorship deal. We ended up with a NZ$30,000 program for NZ$5000. The only hardware we had to buy were the Mac computers, while we were able to use the Vellum 3D package for our CAD. We could then export the data into the Gibbs, which in turn generated the 1S0-G codes. Unfortunately, Gibbs didn't make a post-processing program for such old machines and so we had to find someone to do it. It was tricky work and we knew that finding the right person could be a nightmare.

Luckily, however, the right person found them. Quentin Rowe had seen a Britten motorcycle on a local Canterbury television show and had immediately sent his CV to John. He was working for a local electrical fittings manufacturer at the time as a toolmaker and felt that his work, which was mostly in packaging, was taking him too far away from the engineering disciplines that were his passion. When John did call out of the blue some six months later Quentin mentioned that he had had a go on a CNC mill at PDL[171]. John jumped at that and Quentin was offered a job, which he accepted with alacrity.

> I was expecting to work in this tin shed at the end of his garden, and when I saw this substantial building I couldn't believe it. It was a very pleasant surprise although the full-on racing environment was a real wake-up after cruising along at PDL. I read through the machine's manuals to see if there was anything I could do, and realised that I could write some software and get the thing working for them so they could use it to create cases and so on. My job was to get it to the point you could feed in a program and have it spit stuff out, but that proved impossible. So much was against us. There weren't enough numbers, there were no drawings, there wasn't enough to practise on, we were running out of time and it was constantly crashing.
>
> Broz was singularly unimpressed with the thing but it would more or less do the job. He and Rob got used to it because they had no choice, but it caused so much trouble and frustration that it was hardly economic. Halfway through milling something the circuits would pop and you'd have to set it up all over again. Worse still, it wasn't that accurate. If John had spent another NZ$30,000 we would have had something that could really have cut the work out. But we made do. I found myself drawn into all sorts of work at the factory, some of it of a nature I would not normally consider doing. My speciality is obviously working metal, but I also found myself milling carbon-fibre and we would sometimes finish it with a belt sander. I soon realised that it is great stuff if you can get other people to work with it. It blunted the tools and I probably ended up with a lung full of it, but it was the kind of place where you just got on and did what had to be done. These days, however, I stay away from the organic bits on bikes.

When Loren had first applied for the job with Britten Motorcycles he had noted his race experience but had refrained from mentioning it further to John. He had been hired for his engineering and management ability and he felt that it would be inappropriate to push for a ride. However, he was keen to keep his hand in and when Broz organised for him to race his mate Jeff Ballinger's Ducati at the Sound of Thunder meeting he was quick to accept. Jeff, who was the son of Ned Knewstubb, the well-known New Zealand motorcyclist, had a unique Fast by Ferracci-developed, air-cooled 851 Ducati that had been imported and previously raced by Jeff Nash. Loren, who was delighted to find himself in charge of such a hot machine, wound up winning a race on it although it then stripped a timing belt, which put him out of the last feature race.

> The meeting was observed by people like Lindsay Williamson, who must have reminded John that I had some ability, and it wasn't long after that that John asked Broz to take me to Ruapuna and give me a shot on a bike. From then on I was able to assume more and more test duties, and Murray and I often went to the track to try out different things we were working on. In the meantime, however, we were getting further and further behind our schedule. John now wanted three of the new bikes at the Isle of Man and we had sold them all on the basis that the owners would have their bikes raced at the island with a rider of their choice. A mechanic and everything else required, including parts, was to be supplied by us. Roberto's bike was to be finished first and delivered in time for him to race in the Italian Championship, but it soon became clear that we were so far behind schedule that his bike would not be ready in time. It took ages for Rob to get through all the machining of the heads and it was increasingly obvious we needed more hands.

The first person to sign up for another bike after Roberto was an American called Jim Hunter. Jim was from a wealthy Massachusetts family that had made a great deal of money in the rag trade.[172] For thirty years the big, cheerful American had owned at least one bike and in recent times had acquired nine more machines, mostly older Ducatis and Triumphs. He had raced his Ducati 450 in classic events for several years, but had switched to a Supermono and had occupied the pits next to the Britten Team at Daytona in 1993.

When he phoned the workshop, Loren took the call and spoke to him about the plan to sell bikes for the new owners to race at the TT. Jim was immediately interested. After some correspondence the deal was struck. Not long after this a friend of Jim's, an American called Dr Mark Stewart, signed up for the third bike, also agreeing to the plan to race it at the TT. It was an encouraging start for Loren and a fillip for the Team generally. With three firm orders to fill, however, it was clear that still more hands were needed.

So it was that in late November Jason Monopoli received a message via his parents that John had called and that he was most distressed that Jason was not at the workshop. This was somewhat surprising to Jason, who was at that point unaware that he was even being considered for a position. He had recently finished his diploma and had taken his Suzuki 400 away for a holiday to the far north. When his parents managed to pass on John's message to him he was at Cape Reinga, which is as far north as you can get in the North Island of New Zealand without getting your feet wet. Although it was ten o'clock at night, the urgency of John's message was such that Jason immediately packed up and started south. He rode through the night, caught the early morning ferry across Cook Straight and then rode straight through to Christchurch, arriving at the workshop just after midday. He then went directly to work.

> I took over the chassis and bodywork, actually all the composite work. John didn't want to spend any money, so we used the moulds I'd already made, although they were makeshift in the first place. As a matter of fact, they were used right up until the end. The pace was crazy. John would finish at the office and come in for an hour, and then he'd race home to be with his kids for an hour, and then he'd come back for the night.
>
> Because Andrew had complained about the fairing lifting at 180 mph we made it a different shape and angled it down further, as well as making the tank bigger. We lowered the seat base and redesigned both guards. Andrew had somehow caught the rear guard on the tyre at Daytona and I actually saw it go with a big pink puff at the back of the bike. We put ribs in the new ones for strength and redesigned the front guard to give more downforce, although it was further changed later. I was not having an easy time because I was beginning to react to the resin we were using. The skin on my hands was thickening and swelling and my eyes were always streaming. My face was all bloated and puffy, and I was generally beginning to resemble the Michelin Man. It never occurred to me to stop doing what I was doing in order to recover though. I was caught up in the urgency of the task as we all were. We gave our best and then a bit more. We were driven by this sense that we were different—we were special and we were on a very special mission.

Although the production of the five bikes was obviously a priority it did not mean that all racing was suspended. The test programme also continued unabated throughout this period as John searched particularly for the elusive key that would rid the Britten of its tendency to chatter the front wheel. To a certain degree they were beginning to enjoy some success at this and, according to Loren, the history of the bike's handling from about that point on was one of pushing the patter further and further away.

> The first task had been to get the front end working as it had been designed to work by getting the set-up within the design ballpark. When it was set up reasonably well it would still load up the front, but it did it much later. You could tip it in harder and the handling was suddenly reasonably competitive. We no longer had to rely on vastly superior power to win races, which was just as well as the competition wasn't standing still either. Much later I came to the conclusion that the ball joints that attached the girders to the suspension arms were too light for the job. We started giving them

> a gentle squeeze in a vice before fitting, and the handling would be superb until they loosened up. It was a real shame we didn't try heavier units, because we were getting so tantalisingly close to a totally competitive race set-up.

Of course, the only way to test the improvements was to take to the track and race, and at the end of October the team travelled to Manfeild to do just that in round one of the 1993–94 New Zealand Formula One Series. They took two bikes, one for Andrew and one for Loren. With both the 5-valve and the first 1100 versions of the engine now permanently retired, battle was recommenced with the new shorter stroke engine. Boasting 985cc and with a bore of 99 mm and a stroke of 64 mm, the hugely under-square engine was now pumping out 160 bhp on the dynamometer. But, as Loren recalled, things were still not quite right.

> In practice both bikes were again chattering badly and we couldn't seem to get to the bottom of the problem. The engines were also behaving in a strange way, with one delivering more top end and the other delivering more power in the mid-range. Looking back, I should have taken more notice then of the fact that Britten motorcycles, and especially Britten engines, were seldom the same. However, we looked the part with matching leathers (I borrowed Jason's) and for a while we went pretty well on wet tyres in the fairly wet conditions. By the third corner Andrew was leading-with me right behind him. I matched him lap for lap, just hanging in 20 metres back, power sliding through every corner, feeling fantastically at home on the machine and wondering if it would be all right to pass him. I decided that would be both pointless and bad-mannered and I elected to stay where I was. I was comfortable, Andrew was cruising and we had a huge lead on the rest of the field.
>
> Then it stopped raining. As the track dried John Hepburn, who was on slicks, started to catch up. My tyres began to melt as I pushed the bike on the rapidly drying track. Then the front end started sliding stupidly. I almost crashed on one corner and then damn nearly crashed on the next. Hep got past me on the second-to-last bend but I knew I could blast past him down the straight. Unfortunately, the bike was so out of shape getting around those last corners I couldn't quite do it. Andrew was still only 60 metres in front when he blew up with this huge cloud of white smoke, the result of yet another dropped valve. Hep and I flashed past him just before he clutched over the line for third. When I got back to the pits I found I had a hole in the front tyre and there was only four pounds pressure in it. It was a bitch because I knew I should have won that one. John gave the bike to Andrew for the second race, but I'm not complaining about that. I just couldn't help being pissed off about the first one. It felt like burglary.

In spite of the fact that Andrew won the second race, the meeting was a less than heartening performance for Britten Motorcycles and for a few days John toyed with the idea of entering all the rounds of the Championship in order to battle-harden his machines before the TT. It was a matter of acute frustration that the improvements the Team had so assiduously wrested from the front suspension had failed to materialise on the track at Manfeild, and he was keen to see a real contest with his machines at their best. He eventually decided against further racing, although there would be one more outing before the TT. Ironically, it would not require the rider to negotiate any corners whatsoever. The next time a Britten raced it would be purely against time with a wild blast down a country road in hot pursuit of world speed records.

CHAPTER SIXTEEN

Streamliners and Speed Records

It was none other than the mercurial Jon White, first encountered during South Island race trips in the 1980s, who was now responsible for one of the most extraordinary episodes in the history of Britten Motorcycles. Over the years Jon had won a deserved reputation for clever and meticulously engineered specials, including a very beautiful and successful Triumph Trident BEARS racer. Jon and Greg Atkinson were responsible for building Lindsay Williamson's[173] first Harley-Davidson special Black Adder using a frame and bodywork fabricated by Ken McIntosh. Jon's engineering and fabrication skills were not restricted to motorcycles, and among a number of automotive projects he had completed, was the immaculate restoration of a basket-case De Tomaso Pantera.[174] His father had been a motorcyclist in his early years, riding with the Pirates Motorcycle Club, whose emblem had been a skull and crossbones (the club later became the Corsairs Motorcycle Club with whom the BEARS had affiliated). He had later become a powerboat racer of note, as had Jon's older brothers Dennis and Gary. Dennis was a founding member of BEARS, but it was Jon who really lived to ride. While still in his early teens he was recognised as a hard and effective race rider. Tall and wiry, he had a brooding intensity that matched his reputation for having a violent and often uncontrolled temper. He was also, it must be noted, a founder member of BEARS, and his fellow racers recognised that he was, in his own way, a talented and driven visionary. When he told them of his dream to build a land-speed record streamliner powered by a Britten V-1000 engine they knew that he would shift heaven and hell to make his dream a reality.[175]

Jon's interest in breaking records went back to the days of his earliest memories. He had worshipped the land-speed record heroes of his youth, and indeed of earlier times, and longed to be counted among their number. On one occasion at Hawkesbury he defeated Dr Rodger Freeth, the celebrated racing astrophysicist, who was riding a factory-framed Yamaha TZ750 equipped with a stove-hot engine and his own aerodynamic winglets and tailpiece. The two subsequently became friends and Freeth stayed with Jon when he was in Christchurch. Freeth was also an enthusiast of speed records, and in 1993 he set the outright New Zealand land-speed record in an Indycar open-wheeler with a speed of 191 mph.[176] Tragically, he was killed in an accident in the rainforests of Queensland in 1993 while navigating for Kiwi rally champion Possum Bourne,[177] but his example was to be a lasting inspiration to his friend Jon White. In time, Freeth's all-out New Zealand speed record would be one of the barriers that Jon would seek to smash on his way to a motorcycle world record. It was natural, if ambitious beyond all normal, reasonable expectations, that Jon would use his proven talents and undoubted courage to pursue international motorcycle speed records. It was his destiny.

From the beginning Jon had little interest in breaking only national records, although they would have to fall along the way. His goal was to set international records; specifically, he wanted to be the fastest man on two wheels in the world. Having conceived the idea, he threw himself into the project with such ferocious and single-minded determination that he succeeded in attracting a significant level of support.

> You have to sacrifice everything if you want to go for world records. Everything! The project cost a total of about NZ$250,000 and I raised the lot. My brother Dennis cut through all the red tape to organise the officialdom, which was just as well as they couldn't have made it any harder. We were selling electric-blue models of the streamliner with '200 MPH' written on the sides behind the Britten logo to raise funds. I gave some models away while one guy gave me NZ$20,000 for his. We got sponsorship from people like Mobil and Highway 61 chipped in. (I got a lot of flak for having their name on the streamliner, but they earned it.) An old mate from Auckland called Bill Wallace put about NZ$50,000 in the kitty. Old Bill had been in charge of electroplating at Air New Zealand and when he later set up his own business he did really well. He became like a father to me, full of wisdom and kindness, and he couldn't do enough to help.

Jon was able to commission Ken McIntosh to build a frame for his cigar-bodied special, which he christened 'White Lightning', and enlisted the help of well-known yacht designer Digby Taylor to design the shape. Streamliners present a number of unique and complicated design challenges. They must be as slippery as possible and that means they cannot generate downforce to keep them on track, as this only constitutes speed-sapping drag. On the other hand, for obvious reasons, they cannot generate lift. They must be perfectly neutral and must be stable at high speed.

The shape that Taylor evolved was a thing of rare and dynamic purpose, a beautifully proportioned torpedo that was extensively refined following comprehensive wind-tunnel testing. As Jon recalled,

> We made a model out of welding rods that ended up being the exact structural model for the real thing. Then it was a matter of making triangles with the rod until we had the complete structure. Next we put a skin on it and tested the model in the wind tunnel at Canterbury University. I was there for about two years off and on making sure we were on track. The professor used to treat me like one of the students, telling me off when I played up or did something wrong. Along the way we had to make various modifications to our initial design, like deleting the hump over the front wheel because it was causing turbulence. We also shortened the body up when we found that left cleaner air behind. We ended up with a really slippery and stable shape.

Streamliners also present a huge challenge when it comes to the construction of the body. Basically, the smallest asymmetricity will cause pressure on one side or the other, which will in turn slowly cause the machine to get sucked off course or worse, as speeds rise. The body must therefore be perfectly regular and flawless.[178]

The end product, after two years of dedicated graft, was a stunning carbon-fibre and Kevlar sandwich skin that slipped around the McIntosh skeleton, the whole unit fitting Jon White's narrow frame like a glove.

For months Jon had fed NZ$1600 a week to Ken to work on the streamliner, casting himself in the role of assistant. 'I was just part of the team and just another one of the boys during smoko, even though I was paying the wages. The only thing I could do to claw a bit back was to trash Ken's phone with toll calls, but he knew. He is every inch the wily Scotsman and you couldn't ever put anything past him. But boy they made a beautiful job of it.'

Ken McIntosh recalled his role as being the journeyman to Jon's design team. 'The front end, the frame, the rear suspension and so on were all designed by Jon's team,' he said, 'but ours was still not an easy task. For example, I had never had to stand on a box on a table for days on end to weld something up before. That was one week I didn't have to go to the gym.'

The biggest problem with Jon White's dream to hurl a Britten-powered streamliner into the land-speed record books, however, was that he never really discussed the matter of an engine with John Britten. When he finally did, John was far from enthusiastic, but he eventually agreed on the proviso that Jon pay NZ$5000 for the use of the engine, a minimal sum that would help cover the cost of the rebuild that would inevitably be necessary after the attempt. He also demanded that Jon agree to pay for the engine if he broke it. Loren then drew up an agreement, which Jon signed, and the deal went ahead. However, it was far from an easy matter to slot the engine into the streamliner's frame and the effort largely forced a halt to the work being done on the new motorcycles.[179]

Jon's immediate target was the outright New Zealand land-speed record set by Rodger Freeth in the Indycar, during which attempt, all going well, he would also snare the flying-mile and flying-kilometre records for motorcycles up to 1000cc (then standing at 190.44 mph and 185.74 mph). His final objective in New Zealand was to crack the 200-mph barrier, and then it was off to the salt flats of Utah to go for the big one, the world motorcycle land-speed record. Jon was not alone in seeking to set new speed records in New Zealand. His partner, Alice Walby, was a speed queen in her own right and she intended to set speed records for production motorcycles on her 1200cc Triumph Daytona.[180]

Hans-Gunther Von Der Marwitz, a German FIM official, was contracted to supervise the event and arrangements were made to close South Eyre Road, site of the BEARS speed trials, which was duly surveyed to ensure that it met gradient requirements and so on. In obtaining FIM cooperation, Jon was greatly assisted by the ever-helpful John Shand, but the costs of bringing Hans-Gunther out were still prodigious.[181]

A week prior to the record attempt Jon had a trial run with the 5.3-metre-long streamliner at Wigram airfield. Because no one really knew how to pilot a streamliner he elected to do the trial without the bodywork. He squeezed into the cockpit with a helping downward push from a team-mate and waited for the engine to reach its operating temperature of 80 degrees Celsius. He stalled the engine on his first two attempts to take off but the third attempt went smoothly, with the little jockey wheels retracting into the belly of the sleek beast as he accelerated down the runway. He cruised to the other end of the runway, where his jockey wheels kissed the tarmac gently while he braked to a halt. The return run did not begin so well as he lifted the jockey wheels too early. The accelerating streamliner wobbled off course and headed straight for a television cameraman who was filming in front of his parked van. With nowhere to go, Jon buttoned off and flopped the streamliner on its side, skidding to a halt at the cameraman's feet.

The damage was remarkably minimal, and during one trial on the runway the next day Jon engaged third gear at 160 mph, wheel-spinning the rear tyre as he accelerated up to about 170 mph. He was extremely satisfied with the run, afterwards pronouncing the Britten engine to have 'an awesome amount of grunt'. Only a few modifications were found necessary as a result of the trials. When the body was finally fitted, for example, Jon found the cockpit visor restricted his vision, so it was removed. It was also found necessary to run the streamliner without the engine covers owing to overheating problems. There was much discussion about the effects this might have on the aerodynamics of the streamliner, the final consensus being that there was at least a possibility it would make no difference. A final run up and down the runway convinced him that he still had a sweet-handling machine that became more stable the faster it went. He was ready.

At first light on the morning of Saturday 27 November 1993, the stunning-looking projectile sat growling on idle at the white start line painted across South Eyre Road. A shimmer of heat haze wavered around the open engine compartment as a thin stream of exhaust smoke mingled with the still, dense morning air. Conditions were judged ideal for the attempt, even if the location left many feeling distinctly apprehensive as they peered into the distance down the narrow, steeply cambered road between the trees and telephone poles that studded its verges. One observer was later quoted in the Australian magazine *Performance Cycle* saying that, 'the road looked dangerous, the complete opposite of Wigram. Someone muttered it was like looking down the barrel of a gun, from the wrong end.'

When all was ready, Jon dumped the clutch and accelerated strongly. He quickly lifted the 'trainer' wheels and the 260-kg streamliner almost immediately started to weave, and then it drifted off the steep road camber to the left, flopping over on its side on the grass verge and sliding to a halt.

'The rough chip surface of the road created this horrible noise inside the shell with the gear down,' Jon recalled, 'and with the bodywork acting like a drum-skin the deafening din made it almost impossible to function. I lifted the wheels too soon again just to be rid of it and then couldn't steer the machine.'

As before, the damage was not substantial, being largely confined to the tail, and Jon elected to have a second run without it.

> I got it up to about 150 mph in the second mile and settled down before starting to feed it some more throttle. It accelerated so smoothly it felt effortless. I don't know exactly how fast we finally went but I remember that with the power of the Britten engine and with so little air resistance it felt as if it would just keep going faster and faster and faster. But it was bloody hard to see where I was going. I wanted to lift my head to see over the nose at the centreline but couldn't. Instead I had to look down the side and gauge my position from the edge of the road. However, I finished the run all right and we turned it round and lined it up for the drive back.

The return run proved a different story. Jon got into third gear and was accelerating hard at about 120 mph when the machine went suddenly out of control. It fell on its side and slithered along the verge, finally coming to rest after bouncing off a wire fence. Thankfully, Jon emerged again unscathed save a damaged finger on his right hand that would remain 'buggered' for the rest of his life. However, he had been extremely lucky and he would also always carry the memory of a huge old macrocarpa tree tearing toward him as he viewed the world sideways, before it whisked past only inches from his head.

This time the damage included the front and rear sub-frames and further harm to the bodywork. Ken McIntosh and Nick Williams examined the machine and decided that although largely superficial, the damage was sufficient to warrant a trip back to Auckland for repairs.

'It was over and I just had to accept it,' recalled Jon. 'I remember thinking that there was some glory in it, running down a narrow little country road with the throttle wide open, squinting into the sun, fighting the camber of the road and trying to stay in the middle. But it was over and we hadn't achieved anything.'

Many members of the Britten Team were present, and Loren remembered some discussions among them about the set-up Jon had on the front end.

> It was Jon's set-up, not Ken McIntosh's, and he had the rake and trail set so it was very steep and we felt that might have contributed to the machine's instability. Later at Bonneville [Salt Lake] other teams advised him to rake the thing right out. After the crash we all went to the pub feeling gloomy, and then someone suggested we put a 'dustbin' on one of our bikes. There was one around apparently and someone knew someone who knew where it was.

The dustbin, a great blob of a fairing that encased the entire front wheel, was of quite recent provenance, although it looked as if it should have belonged to an earlier era. The man who suggested it was Neil Mackley, proprietor of the Wasp Factory, Christchurch purveyors and restorers of classic Italian scooters. He knew that a couple of keen BEARS men had a dustbin for the 982 Moto Guzzi they were campaigning. This was a copy of 1950s Moto Guzzi Grand Prix bodywork that was brilliant for speed trials but was not allowed on the track. As the dustbin had largely languished since the six-month project to build it had been completed, Neil was sure its owners would be more than pleased to have it finally prove useful. John had watched the proceedings from something of a distance up to this point, but now decided to get the Team involved. Loren recalled:

> John felt strongly that White deserved a fair crack at the record and he decided we should go for it. When the dustbin arrived we set to and made a mould, from which we made our own dustbin, cutting four nostrils in it to feed the radiator and the air-box. We used plenty of duct tape to hold it all together but it worked out pretty well.
>
> We had to get up at five each morning to be at the course before the wind came up, and on the Sunday I did a run on a stock bike and went through the flying mile

> at 183.86 mph. Jon had a run on Alice's Triumph and posted 160 mph and then Alice went a couple of miles an hour faster. An Australian named Lionel Simpson had come over with his old push-rod Rob North Triumph Trident and his rider Des Mathews was only a second or so slower, which was phenomenal. On Monday it was raining so we spent the time in the workshop.[182]

The first test run of Blue Thunder, as Jon White's machine was now known, was made in light rain on Thursday.

'John had me perched on the bike like a jockey,' said White. 'I had to remember to test the computer button and when I forgot he really got stuck into me. Other than that everything seemed set and so off I went.'

The crowd watched as he roared off into the mist, the drone of the unrestricted exhaust finally fading in the distance. On his return run he got the machine up to 180 mph, in spite of the conditions. The computer revealed that he had been using only 10,000 revs, which allowed a further 1700 revs before the limiter cut in. This gave a theoretical top speed of about 200 mph, a figure the team were convinced could be achieved as the engine would be making peak horsepower at those revs.

On Friday morning a light wind cut speeds back and activities were abandoned when the engine started overheating inside the fairing. The longest time a Britten engine had ever run at full noise prior to this was for sixteen seconds at Daytona. Now it was being asked to keep it up for up to 6 km with less than the normal flow of air through the radiator. Back at the workshop, further holes were cut in the fairing for additional cooling ducts and the engine was run up on the dynamometer. Saturday morning was the last opportunity to run on the closed road, and the day dawned calm and clear, with a light frosting of fresh snow on the mountains. It was now or never.

A small but enthusiastic crowd had gathered for the day and the air was charged with quiet excitement. If the dustbin's heritage was too recent to be considered vintage, the same could not be said of Bob Burn, one of those gathered to witness the record attempts. Bob had occupied the chair when he and Russel Wright set the world record for a bike and sidecar on a similar Canterbury road with a 1000cc Vincent Black Lightning back in 1954. Remarkably, their record speed of 167 mph still stood, although Russel was long gone and his solo record, set the same day, had been eclipsed soon after. Bob smiled happily while talking about the old times, at least when he was not watching with the concentrated anxiety of one who knows first hand the dangers of speed-record breaking.

Out at the course there was trouble with the timing system, however, and tension mounted as Mark Franklin worked with quiet determination to trace the fault. The tension built even further when someone gave permission for a truck with a wide load to proceed. The truck crawled down the closed road at a snail's pace, while exasperation and impatience boiled over into anger. But at last the road was clear, the timing equipment was functioning perfectly and the attempts could be made. Loren was the first to trial the further refined bike.

> I did a couple of runs and the machine seemed kosher, and then Jon White had the first serious blast, which was right because he was thinner across the shoulders and could get in behind the fairing. He took the flying mile at 188.092, mph an outright motorcycle land-speed record for New Zealand. Unfortunately, it wasn't quite enough to take the flying kilometre. Then I had a go. I had imagined it would be boring but it was pretty tricky, more like flying than riding. I couldn't really steer and found I had to totally relax. The road had a gently undulating surface but at that speed it was more like a motocross track. All I could hear was the back tyre breaking traction and then biting again, and my vision narrowed to a tight, blurred tunnel. The air still wasn't getting through to the radiator in sufficient volume and the temperature warning light came on halfway through the run, so I backed off slightly. When we tore the engine down later the bores were quite badly scored. The boom-box got really hot inside the fairing and both Jon and I burned the inside of our legs. My run ended up half a second slower than Jon's, which was disappointing, particularly as we didn't have the flying kilometre record. I know that with a week's extra prep we could have done things like build a longer swing-arm and easily have gone 10 mph faster, and that 200 mph was a definite possibility.
>
> By then it was 9.30am, and as conditions were still good we decided we might as well have a go at the international acceleration records for the standing quarter-mile, kilometre and mile. We changed the gearing, lost the dustbin and put the front suspension back to the usual height. We had to change the timing over and then I went to the far end for the first run. There was only time for one go at it. Someone dropped their hand and I did the best clutch start I'd ever done. The front end came up 2 in and stayed there for the duration. The boys then raced to move the timing gear to the other end and I did the return run, which went just as well. We had set three records, including a time of 10.759 seconds for the quarter- mile. The guy from Germany was absolutely blown away and John was over the moon.

However, most of the acceleration records were for categories that had been established by the FIM but for which there were no existing records to beat. Jon White had his national record, but the day was obviously a crushing disappointment for a man whose dream had been fixed so unerringly on breaking world records.

The day was more successful for Alice Walby, who broke the World Women's Motorcycle Record with a speed of 169.141 mph on the Triumph. This really was a remarkable achievement considering that the machine was practically stock. John had thought to bring flowers for her, and he produced them from the back of the van along with a bottle of champagne to toast their success. He pronounced the proceedings 'not bad for a morning's work!' And it wasn't. The records were real even if a Britten had gone faster on the banking at Daytona.

After Hans-Gunther departed, Jon was left to contemplate the events of the past week with a mangled finger, a permanent scar on his leg and a bent streamliner. Suddenly, his brother Dennis, who had been going through the recorded times, let out a shout of surprise. And Jon was surprised.

> My brother was flicking through these papers when he said, 'Hang on, I think you have set a world record!' And I had. I'd set a new international record for a 1000cc motorcycle. Luckily, the timing gear was still set up and we could do all the technical things that needed to be done at the end. The big problem was that there was a time limit on having the FIM official sign it off, and he'd shot through. We finally caught up with him as he was catching the ferry to Wellington and got him to do his bit. He seemed to realise that I had taken the record and so I asked him why he had not told me. He said it was up to me to inform him and that his duty did not include letting me know. But we were in and the record was ours.
>
> The press had made a real big deal of Loren's records but I was completely overlooked after that. I'd risked everything but they weren't about to make a hero of me. I saw Loren's New Zealand record certificates on the wall at Britten Motorcycles a while later and asked if they had mine. Apparently, there was a NZ$250 fee payable to the ACU for each certificate to get the paperwork done and they hadn't bothered with the records I'd taken. Some money was sent to them and I waited, but nothing happened. Finally, I called them and they said they had sent the certificates to Dennis. He hadn't seen them and so I asked for new ones to be sent. Six years later I finally got these pieces of shit with the word REPLACEMENT stamped on them. I never bothered to put them on the wall. Thankfully, I did receive my world record from the FIM without any of the hassles I experienced with our own national body.

The streamliner was repaired and had one more opportunity to prove itself—at the salt flats at Bonneville, Utah, in the famous Speed Week. Tim Stewart, who was now an employee of Britten Motorcycles, travelled with the entourage to look after the engine, which Jon had shipped out ahead. And it did perform faultlessly throughout the week. At Bonneville the Team joined forces with Rick Vesco, brother of Don, the famous world-speed record-holder on both two and four wheels. Both he and the other teams present were tremendously impressed with the streamliner, then the most compact machine of its type ever seen on the salt, and a photograph of it ended up illustrating its class in the following year's rule book. Unfortunately, it pencil-rolled in an early run while doing about 180 mph, damaging the oil cooler and again bending the tail. The oil cooler was fixed, and in spite of considerable pain from injuries sustained in the spectacular crash, which included a very sore neck, Jon made several attempts to post the two-way 210-mph average passes over the 5-mile course he needed to take out the 1000cc Utah Salt Flats Racing Association record he sought. Each attempt went perfectly up to the 4-mile marker, where he was doing well over 200 mph and still accelerating hard. At that point, however, the bent tail started to drag the machine off course and he had to ease off the throttle to avoid crashing again. Sadly, and in spite of coming so tantalisingly close, the record eluded him. There was nothing for it but to pack up and go home. Even that, though, was far from straightforward.

> I had absolutely nothing left in the kitty by then. I already had a ticket, but my luggage had taken up all my weight allowance and I had no choice but to carry the engine. It weighed 61 kg and I had to stand around pretending it weighed hardly anything at all. Unfortunately, the ticketing people insisted on putting it on the scales and charged me an extra 200 bucks to take it aboard. I called a Yank I knew and he came and bailed me out. When I arrived in Auckland I called Bill Wallace and he came out and gave me NZ$500 to get back to Christchurch. We talked about the way things had gone and he suggested that I should buy a Britten engine so we could really go for it next time. When I got back to Christchurch I negotiated a price of NZ$50,000 for a motor and Bill gave me ten grand as a deposit. I made an appointment to meet Loren with Bill, but he didn't show and Bill, who wasn't impressed by Loren's no-show, decided to flag it for the moment.

Although the Bonneville expedition had failed to snag any records, Jon was far from despondent. The fastest average run he had been able to make on the salt may have been only 187 mph, but the potential of the machine had been comprehensively demonstrated. Jon was convinced that the streamliner could be geared to achieve 300 mph and that became his ultimate target. He now decided that the next all-out assault on the record would take place the following year on the salt surface of Lake Gairdner in Australia. He made plans to manufacture the special wheels and tyres he would need to survive at three times the ton and prepared to sort out the streamliner's wayward handling, primarily a matter of straightening out the frame.

For whatever reason, John Britten decided against loaning another engine to the project, a decision that seemed to kill all possibilities of running the streamliner again. Broz recalled that White continued to press John for another chance until finally Broz told him to give it up. It must have been a bitter disappointment.

However, the story was not quite over. Showing yet again the tenacity that had got him to the salt flats in his streamliner, Jon painted the machine in the yellow and black colours of Roberto Crepaldi's CR&S race team. After trying for some years to persuade the Italian to buy it, he finally succeeded and the graceful ship was packed off to Italy.

'I always found the thing too tight to operate comfortably,' Jon said finally, 'and I wouldn't want to have another go as the pilot. I keep telling Roberto we need a skinny Italian kid with no mother. Then we'll really have a crack at it!'

For the Britten crew, the record-breaking effort had been good fun, a time of focused, spontaneous, unified and exuberant purpose. John had led the Team with all his old enthusiasm and drive, infusing the atmosphere with good humour and a sense of almost boundless possibility. In many ways it was the last time things would be that way, as the countdown to the TT continued in a mood of increasing tension, anger and frustration. In spite of the fresh hands, progress on the new bikes was still agonisingly slow and the pressure was beginning to tell. As the Team struggled against time and exhaustion, the aroma of the Isle of Man seemed to drift across the oceans, a distant scent of mist, cold woods, wet stone, Castrol R and blood.

CHAPTER SEVENTEEN

Licking the Bowl

On 19 December 1993, under a slate-grey sky, Andrew Stroud swung his leg over a Britten to contest round six of the 1993–94 New Zealand Superbike Championship at Ruapuna. In the first of the two races, the second of which was also the New Zealand Grand Prix, he started from the second row on the grid, having contested only one race in the season (previous finishing positions, as always, determining grid places). The opposition was expected to be formidable, with a number of new machines set to do battle. Among them was a very tricky Muzzy Kawasaki ZXR750 with Russell Josiah on board. Andrew's machine was built largely to the same specification as the Superbike that Australian Robbie Phillis was then campaigning very effectively in the International Superbike Series. The Kawasaki was beautifully turned out, with the same good engine bits, state-of-the-art swing-arm and big brakes as its Superbike brethren, as well as being considerably lightened by the careful paring away of every ounce of superfluous metal.

The expected rain held off, and in dry conditions the Team was disturbed to witness Russell Josiah beat Andrew fair and square. Even worse was the fact that Andrew had a real struggle defending his second place against John Hepburn's Suzuki.

But when the rain did start, and in earnest, the second race took place on a track that was all but under water. The main opposition in the wet conditions was expected to come from John Hepburn, an acknowledged rainmaster, and sure enough he took his Suzuki GSX-R750 into the lead from the start, keeping Andrew at bay for four laps before a huge new sheet of water at the end of the main straight caused him to run off the track. Hepburn recovered without dumping the bike and lit out after Andrew, who was now in front. On the last lap Hepburn succeeded in overtaking Andrew, only to encounter a red flag. Another crash had caused the race to be cut short and places were allocated according to positions on the previous lap. John therefore came second behind Andrew, who had struggled to keep the

Britten on course in the atrocious conditions, later admitting to about thirty hairy front-wheel slides and a dozen at the rear.

After the race, John Britten looked at Hepburn and shook his hand, telling him that the race had, by rights, belonged to the Suzuki rider. Hepburn recalled that:

> He was really good about it and the truth was we always got on pretty well. I really admired everything he had done and regretted that he never asked me to ride his bike. I guess I was the only Southerner who was an obvious choice to do so, but the rides always went to Northerners. I always believed that if the Britten had had a set of forks up front it would have been damn near invincible. I remember following Andrew around and I was absolutely amazed at the way his front wheel chattered about under braking. I asked him later if it was always like that. He said it got a lot better when it had worn in a bit, but I always thought the girder front end really held the bike back.

The two races were a somewhat inconclusive way for the Team to close the year, but there was some satisfaction to be drawn from the performance. One way or another they had won the New Zealand Grand Prix, and the machines were beginning to show the benefits of the new regime of testing and refinement. More importantly perhaps, the new bikes under construction were finally, if belatedly, coming together.

To placate his waiting customers, John had written to them reporting on the progress of their machines and promising them a scale model of the real thing by way of an apology for the delay in delivery.[183] Unfortunately, the model ended up taking longer to make than the full-size articles.

Allan Wylie's brother, Jim, a former professional model maker, was responsible for creating the masters from which the 1/12-scale models were manufactured. He had first considered the idea of building the model when it was suggested to him by John during the 1992 BEARS Speed Trials. An enthusiastic sporting motorcyclist, Jim had built many kit models of motorbikes and he therefore had a good idea of the magnitude of the task, but even he had little idea that fully 3000 hours of work and two years would elapse before the scale model was ready to be put into limited production.[184]

Model production found a home in the small room off the assembly workshop at the Britten factory, and after two years of painstaking work at Jim's home, limited production of the pewter models, which were to be sold both fully assembled and as kit-sets, began.[185]

The new workshop was proving a perfect location for the expanded Team and everyone involved was working well together, in spite of the frenetic schedule. A mood of cautious optimism for the future pervaded the place, buoyed by the fact that the fame of Britten motorcycles continued to grow with the constant stream of features about the new machines in the international motorcycle press. The parade of admiring visitors who came to Christchurch from all over the world also suggested that the Britten star was shining brightly and was bound to attract a heavy-hitting corporate partner before long.

One of the visitors was none other than the celebrated engineer Keith Duckworth, the 'worth' of the famous English race-engine constructors Cosworth.[186] He was left in the care of Rob Selby, who showed him the around the factory and inside the engine he was assembling. The Englishman expressed his approval of everything he was shown with a few brief nods of his head, and the visit ended with Rob driving him to Christchurch Airport to catch his flight out.

'I gave him my card,' said Rob, 'which he accepted with a smile. Then he told me he didn't bother to carry them himself because everybody seemed to know who he was.'

The growing international recognition for the company was somewhat offset, however, by the final rejections from the Japanese manufacturers John had visited for Britten Motorcycles' services.

After the trip John, had written to Mr Hiroyuki Omata, head of Honda's research and development facility, offering to sell the designs of the ducted cooling system, the carbon-fibre swing-arm and the girder front end, but his efforts had failed to arouse any interest. His correspondence with Mr Sakurada at Yamaha's Motor Sports Division had at first seemed far more promising, and the company had actually gone so far as to request a quotation for a prototype race bike featuring many of the Britten's unique features with a Yamaha race engine. Unfortunately, the quoted price of US$200,000 was higher than Yamaha had expected and the project was put on the back burner.

'As you know,' wrote Mr Sakurada, 'the motorcycle industry is now in depression. I regret to say nothing can be decided nor promised. If there are any other persons interested in your idea and with whom you can do business don't hesitate.'

Clearly, the business of Britten Motorcycles would remain the construction of Brittens for some time to come. In the meantime, however, exciting things were afoot on the property development front. Specifically, Cathedral Place was about to become Cathedral Junction.

With the building site cleared of all unwanted structures, John had set up a stone-turning machine under a big green tarp among the rubbish and the rubble. Because of the atmosphere of destruction, and the somewhat makeshift nature of his plant, the site had then became popularly known as 'Little Bosnia', a reference to the nightly television news images of that unhappy country's ruination at the hands of Serbian and Croatian artillery. However, work was proceeding apace on the restructuring that was needed to beef up the old façades John wished to retain, and it was only when this was well advanced that he learned about a development that fired his imagination and forced him to rethink his plans completely. The news that so excited him was that there were moves afoot to bring trams back to Christchurch and they were to pass within a block of his site.

The idea to reintroduce trams to Christchurch had been put forward by individuals within the city's Ferrymead Transport Museum, who wanted to run their vintage units through the city using rails that had become surplus with the closing of a nearby railway branchline. Their suggestion had met with a warm reception in the council, which saw the idea as a great tourist attraction for the city, and had quickly become an established plan. As soon as he heard of it John began to lobby the council to have the lines run through his development, and in doing so he made a powerful friend in the person of the mayor of the city, Vicki Buck. The enormously popular mayor had made quite a reputation as a go-getter and an innovator who warmed to like-minded individuals. This was just as well. John was by any usual council criteria so late with his request that the body, which had already decided upon a route, would normally have refused to even give him a hearing. To complicate matters, the only way John could get the tramline into his site was by running it up a street that was not even part of the approved route.

However, according to Vicki Buck, the shop owners whose businesses lay along the accepted route had even been disappointingly lukewarm about the idea and some had been downright negative. On the other hand, when John put his proposition to the shopkeepers along his preferred route, and furthermore suggested to them that their street become a mall, they were keenly supportive. Once he had demonstrated to the council that no additional rails would be needed, he was home and dry. His plan won the day and he decided to rechristen Cathedral Place with the name Cathedral Junction.

John's victory was far from complete, however, because it suddenly occurred to him some time later that without a serious rethink of the track layout his development would not be a junction at all but the end of the line. This, he decided, would never do—trams, like people, must flow. By now some time had elapsed since his appearance at the council and he knew they would be reluctant to reconsider their plans yet again. He also knew that they had ordered the rails, including all the curves, nine months before and that he would never persuade them to order more. With the council due to put the final big tick to the project the next day, time was fast running out. After working all night he came up with a plan that, with considerable shuffling, would effectively give him the branch line on the site he needed without requiring a single inch of additional railway.

'He arrived with his plans half an hour before we were due to vote our final approval for the second route,' recalled Vicki Buck, 'and told us all why he wanted to change it yet again, explaining the benefits. He then offered to show us how it all worked without extra line. We said, "Never mind. We'll take your word for it!" And, of course, he was right. It was one hundred times better his new way.'

John raced ahead, acquiring many parts needed to complete his huge jigsaw, with an eye open for a bargain. An escalator, for example, was snatched up for a song when it was made available by the redevelopment of Christchurch Airport. He also continued to build the jigsaw of human resources he needed to pursue his increasingly demanding and complicated professional life. One leading priority had been to find a person who would act as a foil to his creative fervour. He was after a cautious type with financial experience who would keep a careful track of all money matters and act as an advocate for the kinds of conservative values he respected but seldom acted on. An old friend, Merrin Corcoran, with whom John had set up a fashion emporium in London to sell New Zealand products, suggested that her husband, Tim, might be ideal, and after some negotiations he was hired. It was a portentous appointment.

Corcoran's training was in law, but his professional preference lay in accounting and he had combined the two by becoming a tax specialist. For a number of years New Zealand-born Tim had resided in the UK, where he indulged a passion for breeding horses. He was often quoted as saying that he preferred horses to people, a statement that seemed to some to betray a somewhat curious attitude to humanity. In the future, his often abrupt and punctilious manner would cause some friction and even bitter anger among those who worked for and with John. In many ways, however, it was inevitable that his overriding desire for neat and predictable outcomes would clash with the overwhelmingly creative bias of those around him.

His first task was to initiate proper accounting procedures, a job that included, as he put it, 'working with Inland Revenue to change Britten Motorcycles from a hobby-based culture to a business structure'.

To a particular degree Tim was on a collision course with many members of the Britten Team from the beginning. It was not so much that they disapproved of any moves to make the company more professional, but they were most definitely against any moves to impose a regime that failed to recognise that most had contributed well above and beyond their effective remuneration to date. There was also a common suspicion that Corcoran's previous work in the tax-minimalisation area had already attracted the critical attention of the Inland Revenue. When Broz subsequently became a target of the taxmen it was suspected that he had been thrown to them as an offering to draw attention away from other more corporate areas. Whether there is any truth in the suspicion or not, the zeal with which Corcoran attacked the job of turning Britten Motorcycles into a properly conducted business soon created bitter resentment.

In the final wash there would be a significant number who felt betrayed and unfairly treated by the business-first attitude that now held sway, particularly when they were expected to deliver a selfless 110-percent effort for minimal or non-existent reward. However, regardless of everything that later transpired it is undeniable that Corcoran enjoyed John's confidence, in spite of the many occasions when the latter angrily overruled decisions made by the former and rejected his advice. Because everything was done, at least ostensibly, in John's name, any perceived injustices that followed could not be laid solely at the lawyer's doorstep. Brittco and Britten Motorcycles had grown beyond the stage where John's somewhat chaotic administrative skills could reasonably be expected to cope. He needed a manager for his growing business, and he did his best to get the best he could.

John also hired designer Barry Read, a man he had known since the 1970s, as architectural designer for Cathedral Junction. Barry had quite recently returned from a long sojourn in London, where the BBC had employed him as an art director, working for ten years with such luminaries as English film director Dennis Potter. On his return to New Zealand, Barry had been a part of the design team for the new Museum of New Zealand,[187] and having completed his work there he was glad to accept John's offer of work.

> The museum project was a real 'design by committee experience' and I knew working with John would offer far more creative freedom. The first thing he asked me was what I wanted in my office. It seems such an obvious thing to ask but it was a first in my experience. We discussed using CAD, but he didn't like computer images and wanted drawings. I wound up doing about ninety of them.
>
> In his initial briefing he told me that Cathedral Junction was to be the Christchurch equivalent of [New York's] Grand Central Station. It was to be a civic space open twenty-four hours a day. Much of the space, he said, was to be devoted to people who were pausing while travelling. This was part of a bigger picture he saw, which was to expand the tram system to run from the Junction down all these alleyways to hook up with the railway services that went to the suburbs and Lyttelton. A stack of beautiful 1950s railcars was lying around at the Ferrymead Museum, and he saw them being upgraded and restored to operate alongside the existing rail commuters. At the time he was putting time aside to talk to other inner-city property owners about the benefits of such a network to Christchurch in general and Christchurch's retailers in particular, and he was winning them over. It was a visionary plan, particularly compared with the council's intention of ripping up Cathedral Square to install a bus terminal. With John pushing it was no pipe dream. He was very persuasive when he

wanted to be and he was determined that those in power would understand his vision.

And at the hub of this marvellous integrated system would be Cathedral Junction. His vision of the place itself was one of comfort, elegance, space and beauty. Both the architecture and structural engineering were to owe much to the Edwardian age, while the interior employed an art-nouveau theme featuring New Zealand icons. It was to be built to last for hundreds of years out of timber, steel, stone, concrete and glass.

Because the tram-track curved through the length of the building, Cathedral Junction was to be a completely asymmetric structure, and this created many unique challenges in addition to various technical and engineering problems. Among the latter was the design of the giant doors that allowed the trams in and out of the project. John intended that the opening and closing of these doors would be a kind of regular theatrical event. They were to be 6 m high, made of glass in steel frames with timber mouldings. It was great having the Team down the road because I could go to them for help, and I did so on this occasion when Rob Selby and I got together to solve the door challenge.

I was constantly amazed at the hours John worked and at the way he took on so many of the detail problems himself. For example, there were to be soaring stone columns supporting the glass roof and some of these stone columns were to be a spiral design. Cutting the spirals represented a complex engineering challenge, but John just set his mind to it and worked out exactly how to move the cutter to create them.

He also sifted through huge amounts of information to glean ideas. Someone told him about the work Hitler's architect Albert Speer had done and he went out of his way to find out more. John became especially fascinated by something Speer did in the early days of Nazi power when he turned a stadium in which Hitler was going to address a mass rally into what he called a 'Cathedral of Light'. He achieved this by dragging all the anti-aircraft searchlights in Germany to the site and then arranging them around the perimeter, shining their beams straight up so that the columns of light fused thousands of feet overhead into a big luminescent pool. John loved the idea and intended to have searchlights shining vertically along the ramparts of one face of the development so that the building would produce its own distinct loom, visible from the Kaikoura coast to the top of the Alps.

The key to my relationship with John lay in something he said to me shortly after I started working for him. We were getting ready to do the lift face, which was to be made of carved stone, and he decided that the two of us would do it together. He said he never got to know people closely by going to the pub with them. He got to know people by working with them.

One of the major design difficulties presented by a building that was, essentially, a giant greenhouse, was to ventilate, cool and heat the massive interior space. As always John sought out the individual with the knowledge he needed and the attitude to think outside the conventional 'power-hungry' square. He found him in the person of Murray Thurston, a consulting engineer in Auckland. Thurston Consulting had previously been based in Christchurch and had worked with Warren and Mahoney, the well-respected architectural firm John had retained for Cathedral Junction, on a number of large and prestigious local projects, including the Parkroyal Hotel. The company specialised in 'building services', namely the control of the things that move around a building that are not usually seen, such as air, water and refrigeration. Both firms were known for their ability to handle large commercial commissions and unusual briefs, among the latter being the provision of 'push-button' snow for the Antarctic Visitors Centre in Christchurch.

Murray had met John on a number of occasions in Christchurch, most notably when he and his wife purchased some leadlight lamps from him for their Sumner home in Christchurch, and the two already 'knew one another to say hello'.

> John came up for a meeting in Auckland and outlined his plans for Cathedral Junction, and we were all immediately enthused by his vision and were keen to be a part of it. He wanted the interior of the building to be a very New Zealand environment and he was keen to carry the theme through with ecologically sensitive technologies within it.
>
> The first thing we recommended was that the glass ceiling should be double-glazed. Obviously, this would add significantly to his initial materials costs, but once done it would make it possible to achieve efficient heating and cooling in what was, after all, a vast space. He immediately saw the sense in that and agreed.
>
> I then came up with a plan to air-condition the interior by building a vertical wall of dripping greenery through which we could gently push air. I envisaged a structure 10 m high and 10 m wide, consisting of a frame covered in mesh to which a carpet of sphagnum moss was attached. Sphagnum moss was an ideal material to use because it was available in quantity from the West Coast and it could hold a lot of water. Other water-loving native ferns could also be hung on the wall to create the look of a lushly clad bank dripping water into a forest pool. The water would collect in the pool below the bank, to be continuously pumped back up to the top of the wall. Large fans set into the ceiling would suck fresh air from the outside and pressurise the void behind the wall, causing a large volume of slow-moving, moist air to flood into the interior of the building. Because Christchurch has such low humidity, the moisture in the air would then evaporate, causing the air to cool. In addition to cooling the space with comparatively little energy consumption, the system added the

advantage of humidifying the air. To assist the process we further proposed that large fans be set into the ceiling to suck out the rising heat. The job of these fans would be greatly assisted by the fact that the intake fans would gently pressurise the entire building. Of course, the pressure would be lost when the giant doors opened, but as the wind generally blew from one end of the building or the other these events would actually assist with ventilation.

The overall effect of the slow movement of large volumes of air would have been very similar to the cool atmosphere that suffuses a damp forest. The sound of falling water would be a bonus.

To achieve warmth in winter we decided to bury big water tanks in the basement, which would be heated during the night using cheap, off-peak electric power. When heating was needed during the day, blowers would push air through heat exchangers to supply warm currents to the interior above. Because it was impractical to heat the entire space, we planned to create overlapping 'warm zones' with the flow of heated air. This was to be assisted by the strategic use of radiant gas heaters and gas flares, which would have been visually exciting as well as providing immediate, tangible comfort to those within the structure. It was a tremendous opportunity for us because John loved people and companies that thought creatively and independently. He did not accept 'no' for an answer when he encountered obstacles in the way of a desired objective, but always worked to find a way around such barriers, invariably by returning to first principles.

I remember that the whole office used to become very excited when he was coming up and our brain-storming sessions were always positive, stimulating and invigorating. We could see that Cathedral Junction would be a magnificent showcase for the 'green' technologies that are the way of the future.

Although Cathedral Junction was becoming all-consuming, it was not the only building project that John was working on during this period. When he had needed a wall to enclose Heatherlea, he called for tenders and was predictably uncomfortable with the quotes he received. Once he had rejected the idea of hiring someone to do the job, he naturally looked for a better way to do the work himself. Typically, he did not just examine the conventional technologies on offer but looked for an entirely new way to go about it—a way that would not only be cheaper but would produce a superior product.

Many Christchurch buildings had been, and continued to be, constructed from limestone, removed with surgical precision from the southern landscape at Oamaru. John looked closely at the way the massive steam-powered chainsaw at Parkside Quarry in Oamaru carved out huge cubes of the earth-toned material to be further cut to produce building blocks. Perhaps, he thought, the limestone could also be finely sliced to make building-block-size fascias. Instead of solid blocks, each fascia could be used as internal and external facing, with high-density, closed-cell urethane foam in between. He soon worked out a way to achieve his objective and tried out the new system on the wall around Heatherlea. It was an instant success.[188] In many respects the structure resembled the traditional limestone walls common in France, but the final result was the first modern, structural masonry system in the world. The wall combined high strength, thermal efficiency, cost effectiveness, lightness and, of course, the appearance of solid stone.

He had then built a number of similar walls around Christchurch, including one in front of Harry Ruffell's photographic studio. A garage for a cousin had followed, before John moved on to other things. His experience with the system had convinced him that it was suitable for the big challenge—building a house.

Now, finally, he had his chance to do it, for it so happened that two old friends, Derek and Rebekah McCullough, were in the market for a new house. They had just purchased an elevated site on Cannon Hill, a coastal Christchurch suburb offering magnificent sea views to the north and a pleasant vista back toward the city over Ferrymead Museum. When John explained the system to them and showed them the walls and the garage, they became enthusiastic and gave him the go-ahead. John had worked closely with long-time friend Roland Logan[189] on the system and so they both became involved in the construction, which in addition to establishing the viability of a new type of housing offered the further challenge of being located on quite a steep slope. However, the terrain was just the first obstacle to be overcome, as Derek explained:

> John worked with our architect to produce the plans we needed to submit to council for approval. It was then that we ran into the kind of officious little prick that will not, under any circumstances, co-operate. Unfortunately, he had the power to grant or refuse our permit. We did not mind having to show that the design met all the building codes, but the lengths we had to go to were ludicrous. We did tests at the University of Canterbury, when we made up a panel and subjected it to all the usual load tests. Unfortunately, the instruments could not measure any significant flex even after we had put every available weight on it. So we got a whole lot of students to stand on it. I think one even had his motor scooter up there. Still no flex. The horrible little man actually tried to tell us that because there had been no measurable flex we had therefore not measured anything and he could not certify our plans. He kept bleating that he had to think of future owners. In the meantime, the present owners would have been climbing the walls if we'd had any. By then we literally had nowhere to live.
>
> Finally, we got the go-ahead and John and Roland turned up to make a start.

> However, it was soon apparent that the system John had devised was too slow. It was impossible to brace up to the stud height we wanted so that the foam could be poured in one go. John and Roland downed tools just two days into the project and retired to the Ferrymead pub to redesign the bracing system. A month later they were ready to have another go. Of course, they hadn't spent that month in the pub but making the new system took time. By then we were living in John's holiday home in Church Bay, which meant hours of commuting, but at last there was progress.
>
> Midway through construction John was so overwhelmed with the bikes and Cathedral Junction that he had to hand over the project to Roland, something that made him very apologetic because he felt a responsibility to see it through to the end. However, everything was going really well by then and when it was done we were absolutely enraptured with our new house. It has the most outstanding thermal qualities. We get sea mists here and temperatures can plummet, but the house is never cold. The walls radiate warmth in the winter and keep us beautifully cool in the heat of summer. It's simply magic. The house was well and truly broken in with a series of great shindigs and I am glad to say that John enjoyed some of the best of them. He knew how to have a good time and we continue to follow his example in our 'Britten' house. It gives us great pleasure to think that John was responsible for it—the only one he ever did. The only way we will ever leave is when they carry us out to bury us.

At the time, the successful development of the world's first modular, composite-masonry building system went largely unnoticed and it remains to be seen if it will ever win wide acceptance. However, the project did illustrate the depth of both John's ingenuity and his capacity to operate effectively on a number of fronts simultaneously. To conceive and refine such a radically different building system to the point where it could be marketed successfully would have been a commendable achievement for a talented innovator who was able to dedicate every waking moment to the project. To do it while juggling the demands of two other hugely demanding projects showed more than clever and determined management. It showed character.[190] Barry Read was finding the pace of work at Cathedral Junction exhausting but exhilarating.

> John used to arrive at the office every night to look at the drawings I had made that day. He would pour us both a glass of wine and we would settle down to discuss any alterations or corrections he might want, before discussing the next drawing he wanted. By then it might be midnight, but we would often go down to the site and crawl under the security fence to talk about the next part of the project *in situ*.

With Cathedral Junction taking an increasing toll on his time John, had few opportunities to relax and he made the most of those that came his way. He continued to drive his jet-boat at every opportunity with the kind of reckless abandon that he could no longer indulge by racing motorcycles. It was in some ways a strange exchange, as the challenge offered by the jet-boat was largely technical while the challenge posed by racing motorcycles was quite the opposite. Bikes demanded a Zen-like state of absolute physical and mental engagement. Jet-boats, on the other hand, required little more than a commitment to try. Could it get to the top of the flow; would it fall back? In the end it was usually less a test of skill than a pure gamble. But if it was only a gamble how better to dignify it than by making it a win or lose all gamble? And so John sank his boat. He sank it in Lyttelton Harbour. He sank it in the rivers of Canterbury.

John's jet-boat was different from most and it was different in a way his motorcycles never were because it was so compromised. Powered by a modest Chevrolet V6, the heavy 16-foot boat featured a solid aluminium deep-vee hull, very much deeper and heavier than the light, shallow riverboats favoured by the jet-boating fraternity. He had it built that way in order to use it in both the ocean and in the back blocks, and while most jet-boats could operate in as little as 10 cm of water John's required a reasonable channel to float. The craft was garaged in a boat-shed at Church Bay, a few miles further along the road from his old haunt at Teddington, where John had bought a retreat for himself and his family. 'Birdsong', as it was christened, was a comfortable old bungalow set at the bottom of a steep, shingle track and had a front yard that ran down to a shelly beach. (In the months following his purchase of the property the boat came in handy carting furniture across the harbour from Lyttelton.)

John Harris, a close family friend, shared many jet-boating adventures with John, starting in the summer of 1993 when he and John took their boats south to Alexandra in Central Otago to explore a tributary of the Clutha River. Locals advised them that no one would be swimming or fishing because the water was 'dirty' from recent heavy rain and the river was dangerously high. To compound matters, the local weather forecast predicted further heavy rain. Everyone familiar with the mountain-fed streams and rivers of South Island New Zealand knows that such conditions are not to be taken lightly. The most innocent and picturesque tributary, meandering gently between far-flung shingle banks, can turn in a matter of hours into a churning maelstrom of the most malevolent power, able to wash out bridges, undercut roads and railway lines and bring down hillsides. Southern rivers are not to be trifled with, especially when the omens portend trouble. Lucky escapes in these unpredictable waters featured in several of John's jet-boat adventures, including the Clutha River trip, as John Harris recalled.

We got up as high as this old railway bridge, where the river began to climb up a narrow gorge. Because of the flooding, the rapids were actually more like waterfalls and I decided to call it quits. I just looked at the ferocity of the flow and thought 'Wow!' John wasn't finished though, and he persuaded us to transfer to his boat before he started powering up these things, managing quite a few before the jet unit hit a rock and the bow swung around and jammed on another. We got the boat free using the oars and turned around in the pool below the next fall, but the steering had been totalled. It was a big boat and the bottom was slamming on the rocks as we gathered speed on our way back down the waterfalls. It was a wild ride and I really didn't think we'd make it to the bottom without being battered to bits and sunk. However, we made it somehow and then careered up a steep shingle bank that was piled up against the sheer cliff face. The water poured over the transom, and the thing was dragged back into the current and sank until only the front third of the boat remained high and dry.

After securing the thing as best we could on the shingle bank, John and Kirsteen floated off down the rapids in their lifejackets to get help while I went overland with this young guy who was with us from America. He was actually CJ's surprise son and the two had met for the first time only a week before, so he had really been thrown in the deep end. I wasn't feeling the best because the day before I'd just about scalped myself on a heavy cable that was stretched across another river we'd been exploring and I had all these stitches and yards of bandage keeping the top of my head on.

We found an old fisherman camped out who drove us in his Landrover back to my boat, where we caught up with John and Kirsteen. CJ was there as well, waiting to pick up his son. The fisherman then towed my boat on its trailer back up to a place about a kilometre below where John's boat was where we launched it. We motored up the river and got a line on John's boat and then towed it flat out upriver, with CJ and his son bailing furiously while the water sloshed out the back. We nearly succeeded in emptying it, but then we ran into the first of the waterfalls and had to stop. John's boat sank again and because the nose was buoyant it slowly turned over on its back in the strong current. It then disappeared completely for a while but eventually surfaced again, and we turned it over once more and jammed it up another steep shingle bed. Using a winch we borrowed from the Landrover guy, we finally dragged it up high enough to empty it and then drifted back down in both boats. By then it was 9.30 at night and the promised rain had started.

That night there were spectacular thunderstorms and a drenching, persistent downpour. By the next day the whole of the South Island was in flood and the river we had been on had become a roaring torrent that would certainly have completely obliterated John's boat—and anyone unlucky enough to be caught in it.

The next time John lost his boat was at this place called the Hurunui Shoots, a piece of violent water that runs out of Lake Sumner. The shoots are a series of powerful falls that have to be taken all at once, and John had made it to the last of them when moments from the top his engine cut out. Later, we wondered if water had flicked up from the universals and soaked the electrical system, but someone might have knocked a plug lead off. He nearly flipped backwards when the transom was driven under at the base of the shoot, and then with the boat mostly sunk he was swept all the way back down. How he didn't lose it altogether was absolutely beyond me. All I could do was power back down beside him, but somehow he and the boat survived and came to rest still just afloat in the calm at the bottom. He bailed it out and after drying out the system he had it running again.

There was a third occasion in the sea that I was not along to witness. Apparently, he was out fishing near the Heads at Lyttelton when he had another engine failure and the boat was swamped by the steep swell that was running. He got a tow in and once more survived by the narrowest of margins. His attitude to jet-boating was steeped in the early pioneer ethos because he'd been a part of it. Those guys never seemed to worry about wrecking their boats and were always pushing the odds. He used to say, 'Where there's falling water there is pooling water,' and then he'd do something crazy. But when he did get in a jam he refused to give his boat up when most people would have called it quits. He just didn't know how to give up.

John also continued to make time for the friends he had met through motorcycling. Although it might have been more comfortable to encourage Roberto to remain on his own side of the world, given the fact that his bike was way behind schedule, John encouraged the Italian to visit. And despite the fact that it was now obvious that the promised Christmas delivery date would not be possible, Roberto decided to accept John's offer and travel to New Zealand. By then, however, he was determined to purchase another New Zealand-built motorcycle. In the end he would buy three.

Roberto landed at Auckland International Airport and then went by taxi to see Ken McIntosh, the man Hugh Anderson (Roberto's New Zealand friend and 50cc and 125cc World Grand Prix Champion) had recommended in connection with Manx Nortons. Roberto had not thought to phone first, so the visit was something of a surprise for Ken.

This big Italian just wandered in off the street and asked to see Mister McIntosh. I told him he was talking to him but he looked puzzled and asked if my father was around. I guess he expected some ancient geezer from the old days. Once we had sorted out who was who he immediately ordered a Manx from me. He looked at the streamliner we were building for Jon White, which interested him immensely, and

> then he noticed my Vincent special, which I'd based on an Egli Vincent. He became very excited and told me that he wanted to buy that as well. I told him it wasn't for sale but I'd make him one if he found an engine, and he said that that would be fine. He then shot off down to Christchurch to see how his Britten was getting on and telephoned me from the factory. He said, 'You build Harley-Davidsons!' I told him I didn't but he insisted I did. He told me he'd seen a picture of one on the wall in the Britten smoko room. I said, 'Oh, you mean Lindsay Williamson's Black Adder!'[191] I explained that the bike was a one-off and that to build another I'd need an XR1000 motor. I added that as they were as rare as rocking-horse shit I couldn't see it happening. He answered that he had just such an engine and immediately ordered a replica of Black Adder as well. Not long after he arrived back in Italy he sent me the Harley motor and a Vincent engine. He was a fantastic fellow to deal with.

Once he was comfortably ensconced at The Stables, Roberto believed he would finally have an opportunity to discuss the possibilities of doing further business with John. He soon discovered, however, that John had other ideas.

> I expected to find a small business in Christchurch and to talk deals, but instead I found a free individual who was more like a hippy. He was very funny, and as we began to know one another he and I spent more time laughing than anything else. He kept telling me to forget the idea of making money for a while and to enjoy the immediate prospect of building, developing and racing the motorcycles. In the end I agreed—it was stupid to always be looking for a deal. I began to relax and think more about the challenge of racing Brittens. We became *simpatico* and from that time on we were always on the same wavelength. He became a very good friend.

To make up for the lack of progress on Roberto's bike, John decided to give the Italian a real experience of the mountain country to the south, a landscape that had always been close to his heart. Accordingly, he contracted a trail-bike tour operator to take most of the Britten Team and Roberto deep into the mountains. To get there, the Britten van was pressed into action and the crew piled aboard for the trip.

'It was like a big family,' said Roberto, 'and that was the way John liked things to be. We put an old armchair in the back and I was sitting in it smoking joints with everyone. It felt so free, the way life should be all the time.'

Loren also recalled the free and festive atmosphere as the Team crammed into the old van John had recently purchased as their official support vehicle and headed south.

John, Roberto, Broz, Jason Monopoli, Wayne, Perry Rees, Shandy (who was also over for the festive season), Al Wylie, John's son Sam and I all travelled in the van to Queenstown. We had an absolute hoot all the way. In Queenstown we met up with Perry Rees, who had ridden his BMW K75S down from Christchurch, and then hooked up with this mad guy called Dennis, who we immediately christened Mad Dennis. Mad Dennis ran tours into the hills and he had a collection of off-roaders. He had a bike ready for each of us. Roberto had a new GR350 and I had an old smoky one. There were also 250s in various conditions and Mad Dennis himself rode a XT600 with his twelve-year-old son on the back.

We headed into the hills and pushed up into the snowline in the mountains over some really gnarly territory. Roberto was a big boy but he was really good. Shandy and I were both experienced, so the three of us rode with Mad Dennis, who took off like a scalded cat. Jason had never ridden offroad before, but he quickly got the hang of it while the others got further and further behind. We were riding ridges thousands of feet up in the clouds, getting bogged from time to time in these strange alpine swamps.

Eventually, Mad Dennis called a halt way the hell up in the mountains, but the rest of the Team was lost and it took ages to find them. Once we were all together again we headed back down to join a road that led to an old hotel at one of the mountain passes. By the time we made it to the road it was half-dark. Mad Dennis had Sam on the back of his bike by now, while his son, who was an absolute demon rider, was on Sam's bike.

They hurtled off on the cam and we chased them along gravel roads in a huge cloud of dust. Wayne ran off the road and busted a rib, and both John and Perry had taken plenty of spills through the day. We were all buggered and some were really hurting, but when the stragglers finally made it to the hotel we found the energy for a great session. The next morning we were off at first light, tearing across this rolling pumice country, hurtling over massive paddocks where we only encountered a gate every hour or so, and splashing through clear mountain creeks and rivers. Broz fell off and broke his collarbone and I had to click my shoulder back in after a tumble. Broz ended up sitting behind Mad Dennis, and again there was a mad dash in the dark back into Queenstown at the end of the day, where we all got thoroughly pissed in a restaurant.

Roberto was absolutely rapt, and in some ways I think those two days were the high point of my time with the company. It was the way it should have been all the time but I could sense it slipping away. In the end the TT finished us. We never got that happy, carefree mood back again.

Although he may have consistently beaten the odds in his jet-boat on the southern rivers, and was obviously fit enough to attack the Southern Alps on a trail bike, it was clear by the end of that summer that John was fighting another, harder battle. John Harris's wife, Liz, who was Marguerite Martinis' sister, worked as a travel agent and handled all the arrangements for Britten Motorcycles. She remembered witnessing a strange new kind of behaviour by John that concerned her deeply.

> He would come into the agency to discuss some arrangement or other, and then he'd sit at a desk in the office and just stare blankly into space. I thought he was there because it offered some peace and respite, so I'd leave him alone and eventually he'd come to and join the world again. He was suffering one flu after another and he always looked bone-weary. When we visited we would often find him taking a nap and again that was totally out of character. We knew something was wrong but his doctors apparently could find nothing.

Another old friend who noticed that all was not well was Charlotte Thodey, who was visiting for the summer from her home in Australia, where she was now an established artist.

> I had known John since we were both about thirteen and I knew something was wrong as soon as I saw him. My parents had an old bach at Kakanui on the east coast, and the family was gathered there for the Christmas holidays. John turned up for a visit and I was very concerned at how unhappy he seemed. He took me for a drive and he was belting along these narrow country roads so fast that I had to ask him to slow down. I told him that I didn't want to die because I had a painting to finish. We talked a lot and he told me that the more he had the less he was able to sleep. At the bach he opened the refrigerator, which had hardly a thing in it, and said, 'How wonderful, an empty fridge and loose tea!' He seemed to think he'd lost something precious and simple from his life.

Because nothing obviously wrong could be identified, John simply squared his shoulders and forced himself to attend to all the many things that demanded his attention. Although he was still operating with his customary eye for clever, simple solutions to often complex problems, his fatigue was beginning to affect his behaviour and his outlook. He became uncustomarily sharp when things failed to run smoothly and some of his closest relationships, like that with his sister Dorenda, became strained by an equally uncharacteristic intolerance of any dissension from his views. Increasingly, those who questioned the wisdom of Cathedral Junction encountered a curt, and even angry response that made it clear such opinions were unwelcome.

As 1994 got under way, the Cathedral Junction crew acquired an addition to the team, designer Shaun Craill. Shaun had recently arrived back in New Zealand from the UK, where he had worked as an ergonomic designer in a specialist studio closely associated with British Rail that designed cabs for high-speed trains. The job had offered a few interesting perks including the right to travel anywhere he wanted to go in the cab with the train driver. Relaxing back at home in Auckland, he had picked up a magazine and read a piece on John Britten that mentioned John's enthusiasm for designing his own domestic taps. Shaun wanted to talk to him about the possibilities of employment, so he cast a few of his own. At the same time, to show he was comfortable working in the world beyond plumbing, he drew up a hot-rod that resembled a cross between a jet fighter and an old three-wheeler Morgan. It featured long aerofoil section arms splayed forward, with wheels steered by differential braking. A Britten V-1000 engine behind the double inline cockpit drove two fat tyres sitting cheek by jowl with the chain running between them. It looked like a dangerous, petrolhead's fantasy, just the sort of thing John would appreciate. In spite of all the work Shaun put into the bait with which he intended to catch a job, however, John saw neither the graphic of the tricycle, nor the taps. In the end they were not needed.

Shaun had attended a Kiwi wedding in London, and two years later the now repatriated couple had decided to have a belated reception for their New Zealand friends to attend in Christchurch. Shaun took advantage of his time in the city to call John and make an appointment to see him. At the appointed hour he arrived at the workshop, only to find that John had forgotten the arrangement and could not be contacted. He settled in to wait as long as it took, and when the night was well advanced John finally turned up. By the time he had quickly shown his portfolio it was one o'clock in the morning, and so he was somewhat surprised when John then offered to show him the proposed route for the tram tracks and the Cathedral Junction site.

> We went around in his Benz. It was late January and still quite warm but an earlier drizzle had left the streets slippery. I was struck by the fact that John did not wear a seat belt or give any indication that he ever did. Later I found out that the only times he bothered with them were when he was strapped in for racing. He was sliding on every corner and I remember thinking that it was a different way to get a design brief. Although the car looked quite tired it went very well and he drove it fast, all the time. After our little skid around town he gave me the job of building a model of Cathedral Junction.

The finished model was about 2 m long and included a painstaking amount of detail.

According to Jason Monopoli, and all that saw it subsequently for that matter, Shaun made a beautiful job of it.

'That model,' said Jason, 'finally showed people exactly what John had in mind.'

One of the first people outside the project to see it was the mayor, Vicki Buck, and she was impressed.

> I thought it was one of the best things I'd ever seen. It was going to be the most beautiful, magnificent building, an edifice the city could have been proud of for ever. He had done a lot of really fascinating research into what people wanted and had proceeded from that point. His focus was on how it would feel to be in that space. He told me that he wanted to achieve an environment that children would love and a space that worked for the local community. He said he wanted a building that would look as if it had always been there so that it would never date. In my opinion his design would have achieved that and more.

After the model's completion, Murray and Jason both suggested to John to keep Shaun on to help in the acutely short-handed body shop. John immediately agreed. Shaun started just before the sortie to the 1994 Daytona Pro Twins race and was instantly caught up in the usual desperate slog to get things finished in time.

> I was living in the guest wing at The Stables, going to work at nine in the morning and returning the next morning at three. On Sundays we had a break and didn't go to work until midday. It was four months before I could get back home to get clean clothes, so I just wore stuff straight out of the merchandise collection. The Britten workshop was a bit of a brutal awakening. I was working with Jason on the carbon-fibre bits and the first thing I noticed was how shocking he looked. His face was all puffy and his eyes were constantly streaming. We were working on the carbon-fibre with these Black & Decker power files that came with a twelve-month guarantee. We'd cut them out in a matter of weeks because the carbon-fibre dust would short them out while the Kevlar dust wrecked the bearings. We kept taking the broken machines back to the store, but after half a dozen had been returned they drew the line and refused to replace them. After that we tried putting dust masks over the air intakes and they lasted a little longer.

Progress on the five new engines was such that it was obvious they would not be available for Daytona in 1994, and the only option was therefore to run one or both of the first two machines. Work on the five new bikes thus slowed in order to freshen up the old ones, and then ground to a halt altogether when John decided the older bikes needed 1100cc engines to be competitive at the horsepower-hungry bowl. His decision seems to have been a response to rumours of fabulous new bikes waiting in the wings for the resumption of the Twins race, although, in fact, the only probability was that the long-awaited Harley-Davidson racer would finally show up.

The original 1100 motor had been based on an engine from one of the earlier machines and that motor was now retired. Changing two of the next generation engines to the bigger capacity therefore involved Rob making up new crankshafts and spacers for the heads. Of course, given the usual flow-on effects, the work did not stop there. The spacers made the engines taller, which in turn altered the relative height of the suspension pick-up points on the sub-chassis, which was bolted to the heads. As a result, Murray had to recalculate and reconfigure the geometry of the front end, a huge, time-consuming task. Once again, a last-minute decision by John had taken focus away from the immediate task in hand—building the five V-1000s in time to test and refine them to the point where they were finely honed and reliable weapons with which to do battle at the TT. And once again, there would be a price to pay somewhere down the line.

The first competitive appearance of a Britten motorcycle in 1994 was at the annual Lady Wigram Trophy Meeting at Wigram Airbase in Christchurch, held on 16 and 17 January. Robert Holden had been doing some testing for the Team and John had decided that he should ride in the event. Loren duly organised his air fare from Auckland and went to the airport to pick him up, but found that Robert was not on the flight. Due to a booking mix-up, his ticket had been organised the wrong way around.

> I went back without him and John decided I would have to ride in his place. Everybody thought I'd done it deliberately but I hadn't. In fact, I'd missed practice and because I'd also had a big night the night before I wasn't feeling the best. I led the first race for a while until John Hepburn got me, but I was beginning to learn the track and kept second place. Hep had this absolute weapon, a GSXR Suzuki 750 Superbike with a fully worked 1100 in it. He'd decided it was going to be his weekend and he arrived determined to kick Robert's butt. Of course, he had to settle for kicking my butt instead.
>
> John was a bit glum after the first race. He really didn't want to be beaten that day in front of a home crowd just before we left for Daytona. Before the next race it pissed down and we all went out on wets. Hepburn got away from me from the start and pulled out about 300 m. It was like that for all but the last three laps, when I got in a groove and pulled 100 m a lap off him. I loved the Britten in the wet. There was such a good throttle connection, you just dialled up the revs and it went there instantly. I passed him just before the last corner. There's television footage showing us both with our feet on the ground, as we got around it with these huge slides. I didn't

> know he was doing exactly the same thing behind me and expected him to come through underneath me. I jumped on the gas and the wheel popped up just before we went over the line for the win. John was ecstatic.

There were two further appearances before the bike left for America. The next one was back at the airfield, where both the 5-valve and the new 1100 gave demonstrations at the Wings and Wheels meeting. Because their part in the event was strictly non-competitive, John felt comfortable riding the 5-valve again while Broz put the 1100 through its paces. (John may have been further encouraged to take to the saddle by the presence of a film crew, which came along to record some final footage for a film they were making about him.) The demonstration went well, with both machines running strongly until suddenly the 5-valve went badly off-song. Instead of stopping, however, John forced the spluttering machine from the furthest point of the course all the way around the track to the pits. By the time he got it there, it was sounding, according to Broz, like a concrete-mixer.

> I think it probably broke a valve spring and then lunched a valve. It was hard to tell because John had completely destroyed the head in question by carrying on as he had. It was a shame, because although the 5-valve clearly needed more development so much work had gone into it and it had tremendous potential. The heads were pulled off and stuck on a shelf in the workshop, where they remained from then on. That was the end of the 5-valve.

The surviving 1100 was then rushed across town to win at the Sound of Thunder, where it won both its races with Andrew riding. Following that there was just time to crate it up and then it was off to the airport to be buried in the belly of a jetliner for the trip to America. It was that time again.

Now reinstated after being missing from the calendar the previous year, the Pro Twins race at Daytona was sadly, no longer a part of the famous Speed Week. But if the number of spectators was down there was renewed enthusiasm for the event among the competitors.

Race-bike master-builder Ken McIntosh was at Daytona to take part in the classic racing that now accompanied the Pro Twins event, and he was on hand to welcome John, who had experienced some difficulties at the airport.

> John was late getting to the track because he'd run into a spot of bother with US customs at the airport. He had all the Britten t-shirts and stuff in the crate with the bike and it was all travelling under the same carnet. Of course, that meant that everything had to go back out of the country again when he left. US customs were natu-

rally sceptical that the merchandise would leave and he had to work pretty hard to sort it out.

Rod Coleman had taken seven bikes he'd restored, intending to sell them at Daytona to the wealthy enthusiasts who go along every year. He'd also taken along a team of riders, one of whom was me, to race them. When John arrived with the Britten Team they set up with us and we ended up calling the place 'Kiwi Corner'.

The Barber Dairies Team was one of the biggest race teams at the meeting and they had a beautiful marquee in the pits. I knew a few of them, and I took John along and introduced him to all the guys. It was really sumptuous, with great catering, and we were treated most hospitably. John Surtees [the only man to ever win World GP Championships for both bikes and cars], who I know quite well, was there and he was his usual straightforward, on-the-ball self. John enjoyed meeting him and the two had a great chat. The Barber Team had a Ducati 8-valve Superbike that they had bought from Fast by Ferracci. It was only a season old and it was beautifully prepared. They had a good rider called Steven Mathews to race it and we certainly examined it with some respect. I remember telling John that it would be one to watch. Back at 'Kiwi Corner', John's bike attracted huge attention but I particularly remember one guy just staring at it for hours. He turned out to be Kevin Cameron, the leading technical writer for *Cycle Magazine*—later *Cycle World*. He was the guy who'd labelled the Britten 'The Most Advanced Motorcycle in the World' on the cover of the magazine the previous year. Obviously he was still fascinated by it.

John met Andrew Stroud at the airport the day before the race, and the next morning Andrew went out and took pole position, setting the fastest time in practice.

Ken McIntosh watched with John as the Britten snarled around the banking. 'Boy that bike was fast,' he recalled. 'It was just miles quicker than anything else there.'

Armed with what was clearly the fastest bike in the race, Andrew could afford to be quietly confident and he took advantage of every opportunity to catch up on some badly needed sleep after the long flight from New Zealand.

I was suffering badly from jet lag and I was having trouble staying awake. We were kept on the dummy grid for some time and I fell soundly asleep on the bike. Someone had to tap me on the back when the bikes moved out. I snapped straight out of it and went into the lead from the beginning. Then I started to feel a vibration up the front and I began to think that the tyre might be coming apart, which they are prone to do at Daytona because of the extreme loading they are subjected to running along the banking. They can get big blisters and then just pop.

When you are doing speeds up around 180 mph that's something you obviously

> want to avoid, so I buttoned off a little to cool the tyres. The bike started to move around anyway, especially coming out of the turn on the banking. It was leaving black lines all the way to the wall as it moved sideways, but it wasn't enough to really slow me down and I stayed pretty much wide open through that section. The rubber used at Daytona is a lot harder than most race tyres in order to take the punishment and they tend to slide around a little anyway. This year for the first time Harley-Davidson had their Superbike running and it was pretty quick. Because I'd slowed a little Ron McGill, who was riding for them, managed to catch me up. I didn't mind and it was better for the crowd. I let him past and then retook him a few times, and then a couple of laps from the end I put my head down and left him behind. I always had it under control.

Chris Haldane had stopped off to see the race on his way to the UK, where a works ride in the British Superbike Championship on a Honda RC45 awaited him. Once again, he watched the race with John from the infield.

'As Andrew got closer and closer to winning the thing,' he recalled, 'John got more and more excited, until he was doing everything but turning back flips. When it was won he was absolutely ecstatic. He was laughing and crying and in general he was just utterly overwhelmed. It was great to see.'

It was the end of a long road. On 7 March, after four years of trying and with just one machine, Britten Motorcycles had finally won the Pro Twins race at Daytona.

The celebrations that night went on into the early hours. 'Kiwi Corner' had done well, including Ken McIntosh.

> I was ready to party because I'd also had a fantastic time, coming ninth out of a field of seventy-five on Rod's Manx in the classic racing. I had told myself before the race that if I came home in the top third I could pat myself on the back, so the result was really satisfying. Rod had also done pretty well overall with his sales effort, and with Andrew's victory in the bag we had a rip-snorter at the prize-giving banquet where Rod got up and spoke. He said it was a proud day for Kiwis because John's bike hadn't just beaten the opposition, it had blitzed them. In fact, he said, it had completely annihilated them! He thought it was glorious and he didn't care who knew it.[192]

Back at the workshop in Christchurch, however, the mood was very different. The Team gathered around the big table in the smoko room and listened to the race over the speakerphone. Shaun Craill recalled that news of the win was received with tired relief rather than enthusiastic celebration.

> Loren had organised the media to come around and we popped some champagne for the cameras, but the truth was our hearts weren't in it. We were all too buggered. Jason didn't want to talk to the television people, so he was wearing the old overalls he kept for such occasions with 'Fuck off!' painted all over them. A reporter asked if he was gong to take them off and he just replied, 'What do you think?' and carried on fiddling away on something at his bench. Someone said that we wouldn't have to work so hard for a while and that was really all we could think about.

A few drawn faces at Britten Motorcycles, however, were not going to deter the media from trumpeting the victory as a triumph over the best the world's motorcycle industry could produce, although the media made little, if any, effort to quantify the real strength of the opposition. And it was true that Britten Motorcycles had beaten Harley-Davidson, who had expended a considerable amount of effort in making and developing their new road racer over quite a few years. Later, Ken McIntosh would write in the programme for the next annual classic race meeting at Pukekohe that, 'To compare the design of the Britten with the Harley-Davidson Superbike shows the difference between a team of competent factory engineers employed by a big company and the dreams of one man. And look who won the races!'

It was a fair point. The Britten had also thrashed a well-prepared and well-ridden 8-valve Ducati Superbike. However, without the presence of factory-supported outfits such as Fast by Ferracci, the Pro Twins race at Daytona was no longer the place to prove the point that John wanted to prove—that his motorbike really could beat the very best the world had to offer.

Two hundred miles of a road notorious for the pounding it delivered bikes and riders alike was a very different challenge to 200 miles on a smooth racetrack, but John's determination to mount a full on assault on the TT at the Isle of Man with three machines was unwavering. He was returning to a place that had already scared and defeated him, the most dangerous mongrel of a road race in the world, a place so alienated from mainstream motorcycle racing that it had produced, mainly by a process of elimination, a special breed of iron-arsed riders who were absolute specialists. He was going back to contest a race that only survived because it had become a tradition so burned into the psyche of the riders and fans who went there that no amount of death and carnage could stop it. He was also going to the only race he had an outside chance of earning an absolute place in the big book of motorcycle history. Mostly, though, he was going for the same reason that Edmund Hilary went to Everest. He was going because it was there.

CHAPTER EIGHTEEN

Fame

At home in New Zealand there was suddenly no need to wonder if John Britten and the motorcycle that bore his name belonged in the big book of local heroes. Days after the victory at Daytona, the documentary 'Backyard Visionary' was shown on television and the smattering of media coverage that the project had attracted suddenly became a deluge. Such is the power of television that overnight John and the bike were famous.

Harry Ruffell had recorded key events in the Britten story from the very beginning on videotape and had entertained some hopes of making a documentary film himself for television. After failing to attract interest and, more importantly investment for the project, he eventually called Ian Taylor, a filmmaker who owned a Dunedin-based company called TaylorMade Productions. Although Ian did not know of John or the bike he sent a writer to Christchurch to view Harry's footage. On his return, the writer told Ian that the footage was 'all over the place like a dog's breakfast' and would require an enormous amount of work, but that the story was magnificent. It was not a bike yarn, he said, it was an account of an epic struggle against the odds by one brilliant and charismatic individual. Ian was soon convinced and he took a summary of the proposed film to TVNZ, the publicly owned national network. He was disappointed to find that they considered the story be of no significant interest.

> I tried them three times and the first two times they didn't even respond. The third time they said it might be appropriate for a sports programme segment. I was so discouraged by their negative attitude that I almost didn't bother taking it to the only other network in the market, TV3. However, I knew someone there who loved cars and I managed to sell him on the idea, so he took it further up the line. After the usual suggestions that we do a two-minute filler for a sports programme, they finally got the picture and saw the dramatic potential. They then decided to give it the

> go-ahead and we were in business. I shot the additional material we needed to complete the documentary and the rest is history.

It was history of a sort at any rate, and of a sort that enjoyed widespread popularity. It was television history, and like a lot of television history it needed only a star and few extras to tell its simplified story, in this case the slightly hokey saga of a shy genius who had almost single-handedly created the best motorcycle in the world in a backyard shed.

And so John became a popular folk hero, a man defying the odds alone.

'When 'Back Yard Visionary' went to air,' said Ian, 'the network was inundated with calls congratulating them and asking for it to be shown again, which they soon did. It really was quite unprecedented. We were swamped with orders for copies of the film from motivational courses, rehabilitation clinics, prisons, hospitals, retirement homes and God knows how many individuals.'

Although Andrew's victory at Daytona was added as a trailer, the near miss the previous year was the dramatic heart of the documentary. For many reasons the story of noble failure against overwhelming odds resonated deeply through the nation, touching a well-spring of admiration. The next day, radio talk-back programmes around the country ran hot with calls about John Britten, the amazing, solitary genius. Such an impression was almost guaranteed to upset the Team.

Murray, for one, refused to watch the programme, while others that did so found some of its contents positively infuriating. It was bad enough that the film focused on John largely to the exclusion of nearly everyone else who had been involved, beyond the inevitable fleeting references to John's 'small but dedicated Team'. What was worse, however, was that some of the few references that did exist were insulting. One sequence showed a highly stressed John complaining as he struggled to finish the first new generation V-1000s in time for the 1991 race at Daytona that the toolmaker he had hired was at home with his new baby being all 'maternal'. The toolmaker was, of course, Rob Selby. It was understandable that injudicious outbursts such as the one directed at Rob were natural, if regrettable, under the twin pressures of threatening deadlines and chronic fatigue, and John did not exercise any editorial veto over the finished product. However, he had allowed Harry to offer that particular slice of footage, and when Harry marketed his own video, *One Man's Dream,* John elected to leave the sequence in that production as well. Clearly he felt the somewhat capricious slap on the wrist was deserved, a less than worthy sentiment given Rob's years of patient hard work. Although Rob shrugged the insult off, his wife was so upset that John would begrudge Rob a little time with their first-born that from that point on she had as little to do with John as she could.

There were, however, moments in the documentary that were destined to become part of New Zealand folklore, primarily because they were so patently real. In the scene that had been recorded late at night by Harry, when John attempted to quench a hot casting in the washing-machine tub containing an insufficient quantity of water, he was shown ruefully berating himself for the near disaster. The episode endeared John to the people of New Zealand more than almost anything else in the documentary, certainly more than a revelation that other talented New Zealanders were also part of the story could have hurt him. It also struck a chord with the Britten Team, whose members were always aware of the ever-present potential for John to be distracted.

The effect of the film on the New Zealand public at large, and on the corporate sector, was nothing less than a transformation—from total indifference to passionate support. Prior to the televising of the film Zak Pullen, a former TV3 employee, who had a couple of months free after leaving the network before joining his girlfriend in the UK, had approached Loren with a deal. He had a gut feeling that the documentary, which he had seen prior to broadcast, was going to be big and he wanted to publicise the film and to manage Britten merchandise for a percentage of the take. A deal was struck and he swung into action. Working like a demon, he stuck up posters of the bike all over town with a message urging everyone to watch the film, a local marketing exercise that complemented the daily advertisements he placed in the national papers. His strategies paid off handsomely, and in the week following the documentary screening the company sold NZ$30,000's worth of t-shirts.

In the meantime, Ian Taylor finally met John when he was invited to join a think tank for a day to contribute ideas to the MONZ, the monolithic Museum of New Zealand, then under construction in Wellington.

> It was strange because I found myself sitting between Sir Tim Wallis, the famous southern aviator responsible for the hugely successful Warbirds over Wanaka airshow, and John Britten, both of whom I'd made films about. The two of them made me feel like a mental slug. During a lunch break John and I walked around the museum, which was copping some serious flak at the time for being ugly. I still think some aspects of it resemble a public urinal, but John had this wonderfully keen insight into the way the building would work and his positive enthusiasm forced me to re-evaluate my own judgements. Whenever I go back there now I walk around it with him in my mind. He also remains a part of my life as a kind of touchstone. There are two things I often think of when I seem to be in deep shit. The first is a scene in the film *Apollo 13* when this guy who is contemplating the seemingly impossible task of retrieving the astronauts stranded in space says, 'Gentlemen, failure is not an option.'

> The second is John and his overwhelming determination. I'm not surprised he inspired the whole country; he certainly inspired me.

John was by now no stranger to media attention but hitherto it had been expressed mostly in the international motorcycle press. For a number of years he had been widely known within New Zealand by the community of sporting motorcyclists, but the widespread national celebrity that now engulfed him was something quite new. Many who knew him intimately found his attitude to fame something of a puzzle and most doubted that he ever sought it for its own sake. However, when it came he handled it easily with a self-deprecating shyness that easily could have seemed self-serving in others. But other friends saw in him a driving need, which Allan Wylie described as 'a craving for something very like fame, perhaps recognition or attention'. He had first noted it when they were away at Daytona in 1989.

> After Britten No 001 died at the first corner there was a steady trickle of visitors to our garage to look at the funny bike. I felt like slinking away with my tail between my legs. We'd shown up with this radical-looking bike, which promised much, but we ended up failing miserably. John, though, was basking in the attention and it suddenly occurred to me that John and I had different goals in the project. I wanted to win races, and if any recognition should come my way as a result that would be nice. John wanted to win, too, but if he could get the recognition without first winning a race then he'd settle for that. It seemed that, for him, recognition was the main goal and winning races just a means to an end.

However, if he did find satisfaction at the level of recognition he suddenly enjoyed, John also found it often bizarrely peculiar. Not long after the film was shown, a pedestrian wearing a Britten Motorcycles cap roundly abused him while he was stuck in traffic. The man was angry with John for some real or imagined lack of consideration, and John repeated the story often because to him the episode encapsulated the absurdity of celebrity. After the documentary was shown, he also received a number of letters from people who told him that his example had actually prevented them from committing suicide, admissions that both astounded and humbled him. On the other hand, John found the uncritical attention of people who were clearly attracted only by his celebrity status irritating and ridiculous. On several occasions he referred to himself as Chauncey Gardener, the ingenuous character portrayed by Peter Sellers in the movie *Being There*, whose inane utterances are mistaken for profound statements by gullible and easily impressed sycophants.

Robin Judkins and John spoke about fame on a number of occasions. Robin said that to a degree fame was simply another manifestation of a quality that John had always possessed.

> It was clear from the time I first met John that he had an unusual and powerful ability to win over those he met without effort, something he seemed quite unconscious of. I believe he remained unaware of it for most of his life. When I first met him as a young man he had this eclectic collection of fascinating friends whose natures ranged from the catatonically depressed to the outrageously hysterical. It never occurred to him that he was the only common denominator in their lives and the sole reason they were a group. It was only in the last few years that he understood that he had the capacity to charm and beguile and, furthermore, discovered that he could use it to his advantage. It was not something he felt comfortable with, however, and the knowledge that he had probably used this gift to cajole and manipulate all his life caused him to become quite reflective. By the time real fame came along he was ready to deal with it. In any case, it was not really in his nature to play the star. Although I recognised early on that he was unusually engaging, he was so thoroughly humble and unprepossessing it took years for me to realise that he was also a genius.

Sometimes celebrity manifested itself in immediate ways that could bemuse John. On one occasion he was strolling through an alleyway downtown with a group of his friends in the middle of the night (not an altogether unusual occurrence) when a motorcycle suddenly howled up and skidded to a stop. The youth astride the bike tore off his helmet and demanded to know if he was addressing John Britten. John reluctantly admitted that he was, whereupon the rider produced a marker pen and asked John to sign his fuel tank. John's first reaction was to refuse, but when his friends urged him to do it he reconsidered and signed his name with a flourish.

In fact, John found many of the expressions of recognition he encountered delightful and amusing. He may have been essentially humble, but he was never a victim of false modesty and the sight of a woman with pink and blue hair at a racetrack, or a man with a wheel-standing V-1000 tattooed across his shoulder, really tickled him. So did the many letters and drawings he received from children who seemed to love the colourful bike and its creator. Partly as a result of the documentary, the school reader on dyslexia that John had contributed to became a huge success in more ways than one.

'My kids have no interest in motorcycles,' Ken McIntosh later remarked, 'and they and their friends only really know of two. One is the Harley-Davidson and the other is the Britten. I'm sure he didn't mean it as such, but that reader was one of the best marketing tools he could have devised.'

Gifts from fans occupied pride of place in the workshop, usually in the smoko room. On the window ledge, for example, lived an exquisitely executed bent-wire model of the V-1000 sent to John by a local barman. Letters and cards were thumb-tacked to the walls. A huge canvas painting of a Britten at speed was hung carefully in the workshop. John seemed truly to appreciate the effort.

Nor did fame blind him to the achievements of others, and when a couple of designers from Burt Rutan's aircraft company in America dropped in to see him at the workshop he regarded the visit as a thrilling and signal honour.[193] Even more significantly, perhaps, he never lost the capacity to derive sincere, unaffected pleasure from his own achievements.

'I never tire of looking at the bikes,' he told a reporter after the documentary was shown. 'I can just wander around them looking at them from different angles and find something fresh in them each time. But when I see one of the best riders in the world on one going past another on the back wheel it just blows me away!'

It should also be recorded that he did not suddenly expect the world to recognise him. Wally Sledge, an elderly South Island gentleman who, as it happens, was a keen racer of venerable Jowett motorcars, related a story that illustrated the point. John had been attending a garden party in honour of some worthy cause or other, where he befriended an elderly lady who seemed in need of company. He spent the afternoon talking to her and generally attending to her needs, and she left with a lasting impression of a gentle and courteous man. The lady later saw a repeat of the documentary on television and wasted no time contacting her friend Wally.

'That man on the television,' she told him excitedly, 'is the same one I was telling you about. And you know he never mentioned a word about himself or any of the amazing things he has done all afternoon.'

In fact, John's genuine and open curiosity about others was something that characterised him all his life. As a teenager he had hero-worshipped a daring and accomplished skier named Gus Watson, who had hardly noticed John at the time because he in turn worshipped John's older sister Dorenda. Gus later became wheelchair bound after a skiing accident in which he tumbled onto a rock just below the snow's surface, and the two saw little of each other for years before meeting up once again. When they did, Gus, who was now a successful artist, was heartened and encouraged by John's uncomplicated reaction to his disability.

> It struck me that he was the kind of person who would take the time to find out what you had to offer no matter how busy he was, and he was the only person who ever came out and asked me how I was. He wanted to know all the grubby things that people in wheelchairs can't wait to discuss that nobody wants to hear. How did I go to the toilet? Could I still get it up? The second thing that struck me was how much he loved to share what he was doing. Once I went round and he was blowing a hairdryer over bits of cotton that were stuck on a motorcycle body. He was very

> excited. 'See,' he shouted, 'it drags air out from under the seat!' He was such an affable fellow—it was really only the intensity of his eyes that betrayed the fire that burned within. No matter how famous he became he never seemed to lose that open friendliness.

In the end, however, John was famous and that was that. There was little point in denying it, or in being coy about it, or, in fact, in doing anything other than accepting it gracefully. And, by and large, that is exactly what he did. Of course, his growing celebrity was, as he had anticipated, extremely useful for Britten Motorcycles. Prior to the documentary Loren had been struggling to secure sponsorships for the race programme, with most companies slamming their doors before he'd even secured a hearing. Suddenly, however, the phones at the workshop were ringing hot with offers of money and product.

'It was fantastic,' said Loren. 'I was transformed from a pushy sales type to Mister Wonderful overnight and I didn't have to lift a finger!'

There was time now for one final motorcycle outing in New Zealand before two Brittens were due to compete in an Irish road race called the North West 200, which John had decided to contest prior to the 1994 Isle of Man TT.

Britten Motorcycles had accepted a challenge to race against a Pitts Special stunt plane and a Hughes 500 helicopter, at the airshow that was held every two years over the Easter weekend on the shores of Lake Wanaka. Overshadowed by the spectacular mountains of the Southern Alps, Warbirds over Wanaka, as the show was known, featured military aircraft and, in particular, World War II fighters. These included two Spitfires and a number of other classic fighter aircraft belonging to Sir Tim Wallis, a man of almost legendary status among aficionados of classic aircraft and the select band of hell-raising helicopter pilots with whom, in the late 1970s, he had established the deer industry in the South Island.

Although Sir Tim belonged to an older generation than John, the two men were friends and the challenge to race one of his machines against two aircraft was far too bold for John to turn down. John was most eager to have photographs of one his motorcycles taken with the Spitfires, which had always held a powerful attraction for him. The similarity between the deep and resonating engine notes of the Britten V-twin and the Merlin V12 had already been noted by a number of writers and it was a comparison that John found pleasing.

He had therefore taken Loren south to race the bike, where they hoped his recent experience setting the acceleration records along South Eyre Road would prove to have been useful practice for the task. Both knew Loren would have his work cut out for him, as the bike would only just turn within the width of the runway and the race was from one end to the other and back again. However, on the first outing Loren managed to nail both the plane and the helicopter in spite of the fact that both aircraft pulled full Immelmann turns—outside loops that culminated in a roll to right the aircraft as they headed back down the strip and a manoeuvre not usually associated with helicopters.

The following day the two pilots insisted that they should all race up and down the runway three times. Loren was not so keen, but it was a challenge.

> I knew it would be difficult because I had to come almost to a complete halt to turn around. The guy in the helicopter was really confident that he would trash me because I would only have the jump on them through my superior initial acceleration. This had been enough to hold them off for two runs, but they were counting on a third being of decisive advantage to them. This made me even more determined to do well. Apparently, lots of flash machinery like full race Ferraris had tried it before and the aircraft had always cleaned up. Anyway, I gave it death and we won by miles. John was amping throughout the show with all these people wishing him well. On the Saturday night we had this huge session by the lake and he looked happier and more relaxed than I'd seen him for ages. It was a wonderful weekend. He was so funny about getting the photographs of the bike with the Spitfires. I had to go and change back into my leathers and he went to a lot of trouble to find a professional shooter.

In fact, John had approached Sir Tim, who as usual was watching events through a pair of binoculars, to ask him to recommend a photographer. John first apologised for interrupting him and then asked his question, and when Sir Tim made no sign of responding John concluded that he had not been heard above the noise of a looping Chipmunk. He repeated himself more loudly. Sir Tim then reluctantly dragged his attention away from the now upside-down Chipmunk, which he had been paying close attention to, and turned to John. As John repeated himself yet again he saw the Chipmunk bellyflop onto the ground over Sir Tim's shoulder. Sir Tim turned back immediately but he had missed the crash that had killed the pilot instantly. For a moment both men were at a loss to comprehend what had happened and then Sir Tim rushed away, leaving John in a mute state of shock. It was a sudden and brutal reminder that death was only ever a heartbeat away. And in some strange and uncomfortable way it made John feel gauche. Typically he repeated the story later with himself cast in the role of the insistent pest.[194]

Back at the workshop, the race to complete the new machines reached a new pitch of feverish activity. After his test sessions Robert Holden had added his voice to those who had previously recommended a sprag clutch. Although, as we know, this was nothing new, Loren was around to take up the advice and he began to push for action. The Isle of Man circuit has a relatively good surface for a main road, but the dips and bumps that are nothing worse than gentle undulations for motorists become launch pads for racing motorcyclists. On any given lap a bike would take to the air dozens of times. Each time it did so, the engine would hit the rev limiter and cut, before being spun back up again by the back wheel as the bike landed. Naturally, such behaviour was hard on everything and the sprag clutch was designed to provide a highly desirable cushioning effect for the drivetrain as well as making the machines easier to ride. Sadly, however, there was now insufficient time to act on it before the TT. Indeed, it was beginning to look as if the bikes would not be finished in time at all.

Roberto had waited patiently for his bike, even though the promised Christmas 1993 delivery date had long passed. John had written a number of letters explaining that the delays resulted from Britten Motorcycles' determination to ensure that Roberto's machine had all the latest technology under development, an excuse that was beginning to wear a little thin. Roberto had his heart set on contesting an Italian 'ride what you brung' championship, and had by now organised a race team consisting of a manager, a mechanic and a rider. He was raring to go.

To honour his promise that Roberto would be able to run a Britten in the Italian series, John decided to send him the 1100 that had won Daytona after equipping it with Roberto's bodywork, which was finished and painted, and converting the machine to 1000cc. Of course, making the new body fit the older machine presented the usual headaches, but eventually the bike stood resplendent in the black and white chequerboard pattern with yellow highlights that Roberto's designer had come up with. Painting the complicated CR&S livery had certainly presented challenges but the result was a credit to Bob's artful skills with the spray gun.

Sending the bike to Europe actually served two purposes for John, as it also gave him an opportunity to have two of the riders he wanted to race at the TT try it out.

John's erstwhile FIM contact, John Shand, had recommended that Steve Hislop be approached, but this had come to nothing. However, it looked as if Robert Holden would be a starter.[195] And to make up his trio of riders John had been talking to impressive TT performers Englishman Nick Jefferies and Irishman Mark Farmer.[196]

Although the two riders seemed quite different on the face of it, one being a middle-aged Yorkshireman and the other being a young Irishman, John had selected by good luck or good management two highly rated individuals who for some reason favoured the challenge of racing on a rank outsider. Both men would turn down works rides to go with the Britten Team—from Honda in Nick's case and Ducati in Mark's. In doing so they ran considerable risks, one being of failing to live up to the high, and highly improbable, levels of expectations that John Shand had whipped up in the media. Already the press was talking of the 'first serious challenge to Honda's supremacy in years' and in doing so they were beginning to focus on the riders who would front it.

When finally confirmed, the three riders constituted a formidable line-up of talent, which served to hype the hype even further.

Although Robert Holden had yet to crack the magic 120-mph average lap—to join Jefferies and Farmer—he was the fastest Kiwi ever to have lapped the circuit, with an average of 119 mph, then one of the top ten times ever recorded. In addition to being entered on the Britten, he was also set to ride a FZR600 and a Ducati Supermono. His ambition to take a podium finish was as well known as his ability and determination, and he was rated a real contender in all three classes. If he succeeded in doing so he would be the first 'foreigner' to have stood on the rostrum since 1984.

The bike was shipped to London and then transported to Bradford, where Nick Jefferies uncrated it, having arranged to test the bike the next day at Mallory Park racetrack. The fax he fired off to confirm its arrival betrayed his unbridled enthusiasm at his first look at the new bike. 'What a bike! Mind blowing. I want to ride it NOW! Everyone here is spaced out. It's definitely the business.'

The next day the Britten was taken to Mallory Park, where Nick was sufficiently impressed with it to tell the press the bike was fast enough to win the TT.

'It's surprisingly light and very powerful,' he enthused. 'And boy is it fast!'

His appraisal was not without some reservations, however, and he added that 'the engine braking is phenomenal and takes some getting used to, especially around the slow corners. The front suspension also gives a strange feeling as the bike hardly dips under braking.'

The next day the bike was shipped to France, where Peter Laurence, who had once more been pressed into action, picked it up in a hired van. He took the machine to the Paul Ricard circuit, where Mark Farmer tested it. Like Nick, Mark was tremendously impressed and told Peter that he couldn't wait to race it. The New Zealander then took the bike on to a French bike show, where he sold some merchandise to a disappointingly small crowd. He hit the road again for Milan, where Roberto was champing at the bit to have a go at the opposition with the beautiful new weapon his friend had crafted for him on the other side of the world.

Broz had already arrived in Italy to spanner for Roberto, part of his job being to teach Roberto's Italian mechanic the intricacies of Britten tuning, repair and maintenance. But without a manual and with set-up sheets written only in English, the task was completely unrealistic. The bike's subsequent inglorious flop on the racetracks wasn't all down to poor preparation, however. More often than not, the team fielded a bike that was running well enough, only to watch it putter about at the back of the field. Nangi Dones, the rider chosen by Roberto, had been a test rider for Ducati, but Broz became convinced that the Britten intimidated the Italian. Broz complained when he called the workshop that the EMS readout showed that the engine was almost never revved above about 8000 rpm.

Back at the workshop, new hands had been pressed into service. Jeff Ballinger, the man who had given Loren the ride in the Sound of Thunder, was no stranger to Britten Motorcycles. He had finished third behind Andrew and Jason in the 1992 Sound of Thunder and second behind Andrew in 1993. He recalled complaining to John after the latter race that John was standing in his light. John, he said, just gave him a wry smile.[197] Jeff had also visited the Addington workshop when Rob, Broz and Murray were there on a number of occasions.

> Murray was just a skinny little fellow then and Broz was continually grumbling about students who thought they knew everything. Of course, Murray mostly did. It was a good crew. Broz built the dyno under my house at Lyttelton and my bike was the first or second to run the big wheel up. I was around at Broz's a couple of months before the bikes were due to leave and he told me they weren't going to make it. I offered to lend a hand and the offer was accepted. I found myself doing things like the finishing work on the swing-arms. We'd get black snot from the carbon-fibre, which was horrible, and everything was done in a huge rush.

Somehow the Team stayed on track, buoyed up by John's arrival each night after his evening stint on the domestic front. But the brutal hours were grinding them down and each of them was beginning to wonder when they might come up against the limits of their own endurance.

Since his departure from the electrical fittings manufacturer to join Britten Motorcycles, Quentin Rowe had found that his new job had completely taken over his life. Like the rest of the Team he found his main challenge was maintaining his concentration in the face of an almost overwhelming desire simply to fall asleep.

> We had the odd distraction, like the parade of visitors coming through the place during the day, and quite a few of them were absolute babes. One time this gorgeous French photographer came in and we were all so knocked out we were afraid to use the mill in case, in our completely buggered state, we crashed it. Loren went absent without leave with her for a day and we were all utterly consumed with jealousy. The big challenge, though, was trying to solve problems in a state where our minds just went blank.

As none of the new machines would be ready in time for the North West 200, the challenging Irish road race John and Roberto wanted to compete in before the TT, Broz was summonsed home with the machine that had been campaigned in Italy. John had decided to refurbish the machine so that it could run in the Irish race with its older sister. It had been a disappointing series in Italy, but that had not dampened Roberto's enthusiasm for Britten Motorcycles or his eagerness to receive his own bike. Nor had it dampened the affection in which he held the Britten Team. Nestled in Broz's luggage was a very low-mileage Ducati Monster engine, a present from the Italian in gratitude for Broz's efforts through the Italian series. However, the foray represented more than a failure on the racetrack; it had also added enormously to the burdens already weighing down the frazzled team in the Britten workshop. It was a trying time, as Loren recalled, but not unrelieved for him.

> The business of running the bike in the Italian series had again cost us a huge amount of time and effort when we desperately needed to concentrate on the main business at hand. Broz was taken away when we most needed him and I was tied up with paperwork, organising shipping as well as transportation once the thing had been delivered. We were trying to do too much and it showed in the lack of results in Italy. By then it was absolutely imperative that we secured the services of at least two mechanics to take up the slack caused by Broz's departure and to boost the new bikes along. I pressed hard for Tim Stewart to be taken on board and John took my advice. Tim had completed an apprenticeship as an automotive engineer with a company in Whangarei. One of the older guys there was a brilliant race mechanic with a lot of experience with Cosworth BDA engines and he taught Tim a lot about setting those motors up. It was a fantastic way to learn about the ins and outs of dealing with high-performance engines and it gave Tim a great edge when he joined Britten Motor cycles. The other mechanic hired was Guy Kingsbury, a highly experienced automotive mechanic with a meticulous and conscientious approach to his work.

Guy and Broz had been friends for a few years and the latter had introduced Guy to John. The mechanic had subsequently spent some time 'hanging out' with John and Broz prior to his appointment and was, to a degree, acclimatised to the somewhat impatient and autocratic nature of John's management.

Tim Stewart, on the other hand, had served his apprenticeship mastering the exacting art of automotive machining before becoming a race-engine mechanic. He had been taught to shun most shortcuts and that optimum results could only be achieved through a regime of order and focused deliberation. He soon realised that the only way he could maintain his exacting standards, while at the same time managing to satisfy the frenetic demands of his new employer, was by working a punishing number of hours.

> To keep up with John's schedule I usually worked from eight in the morning until three the next morning. From the beginning I loved the project and, although I'd occasionally become overwhelmed with exhaustion, it was such a buzz being there it never occurred to me to stop. Sometimes, when there was a push on to get a bike ready and crated to ship out to a race, John would be there too. We were quite alike in terms of the hours we worked, and played. When such a job was finally done John and I would often head out to a favourite bar, like the Dux Delux on the river, and see who could last the longest getting utterly trolleyed. It was always dawn before we gave up. As I got to know Britten Motorcycles I realised that many of the problems the Team had experienced over the years were the result of John's optimism and a certain amount of stubbornness on the part of others at the workshop. There was an understandable reluctance to revisit problems that were considered more or less solved. For me, however, more or less was not good enough. I wanted to cure the problems full stop. The other thing I discovered early in the piece was that rejecting John's designs outright didn't work. He'd just dismiss your opinion and leave things as they were. The only way to progress was to take John's basic design and engineer it so that it worked. When John saw something he'd come up with re-engineered so that it functioned better he would be delighted. I quickly discovered an ally in Murray, who was also driven to refine and develop the technology. We began to talk and soon these talks evolved into a plan of action that would see us work our way through the bike, from one end to the other. That programme went on, mostly at night and for a long time in secret. Along the way we would solve most of the problems until we had a bike that was in a completely new class, a Britten with a reliable and ever more powerful engine that handled the way it was supposed to. I also realised that there was a desperate need for a manual for the bikes, so I started writing one from the moment I got there. Off and on I kept working on it for the rest of the time I was there.

For the time being, however, any talk of development was curtailed. In addition to maintaining the new bike programme, an urgent, if cursory, freshen-up of both the original new generation V-1000s had to be completed so they could be shipped to the UK in time to meet up with Roberto and Sandro. Café Racing and Superbikes were taking the bikes to Ireland to do a spot of racing. They were also going to take Loren, who was more than happy to be leaving.

> John and Shand had by then put our NW200 and TT effort together in terms of riders. Nick Jefferies and Mark Farmer were confirmed, while Robert was to join the team to ride the third bike at the TT. I was not asked to manage the Team and had not intended leaving the workshop, but when Shand told me he could organise a Honda 600 for me to ride I told him that would be cool if John agreed. In fact, John

was pleased for me to go because I could handle all the paperwork getting the bikes through customs and so on. And so I paid for my own ticket and went.

The guys in the shop were going mental with just a month to go before the TT because the bikes were way behind schedule, and it was a relief to escape. In fact, it felt like a huge weight had been taken off my shoulders and I was really looking forward to seeing Roberto and to taking a real break with Chris James [CJ] after the NW200. We planned to have a good look around Europe and generally take it easy for a few weeks before the TT. As I exited customs into the Heathrow Airport terminal, the first thing I saw through the glass wall overlooking the parking area outside was the word Britten written in huge letters along the side of an enormous black bus. Roberto and his best friend Sandro were waiting with open arms and killer espressos and glasses of grappa. The bus was insane. It was totally deluxe with accommodation for about eight people, a kitchen, shower, lounge; everything you could ask for. We drove north through the UK and got the ferry across the Irish Sea. John had not sent any mechanics at all and we were totally reliant on this poor Italian Broz had tried to teach. Of course, there were no manuals and he and Broz had not really understood each other's languages, and we immediately ran into even more problems because the engines really were not up to doing that race. They had simply done too many race miles without a comprehensive rebuild. And this was a hard race.

The course is enormous, running between three towns—Colrane, Port Steward and Portstown—a distance of about 9 miles. There are huge long straights, including one that's 4 miles long. It's possible to go from the front to the back of the gaggle you're in four times by the time you get to the end of it, with slip-streaming loops favouring everyone except the guy in front. We had terrible bore-scuffing problems and Nick's bike was puffing oil.

The poor Italian mechanic pulled Nick's engine down to see if he could fix the problem. I was running around trying to organise parts for it, and then the end of one of the plugs on Mark's bike fell off and the valves got damaged. So that had to be fixed as well. The banjo bolts that secure the oil lines feeding the camshaft bearings contain jets that meter the flow. As the oil is under pressure, these jets are absolutely critical. Without them too much oil is delivered to the camshaft bearings. The Italians didn't know that, of course, and they replaced them with ordinary banjo bolts when they put Mark's engine back together. Consequently, when the race started Mark rocketed away and then the top end filled up with oil, causing hydraulic lock under the buckets, and the thing shat itself halfway round the first lap. Nick finished seventh, which was absolutely remarkable under the circumstances, but it was a shambles, with Team Honda complaining about the oil coming out the back of the bikes. It was really tough on Mark, who was determined to do well and who basically loved the bikes. He deserved better. So did Nick, although he was more philosophical about it than Mark, who was gutted.

I was riding for the Ron Grant team and he gave me the worst bike in his stable, saving the best for this American who was supposed to be a real hotshot. I think Ron picked my engine up from a wrecker, and of course everyone else was on really trick machinery. I still had a great time in a qualifying race in the wet, coming in about fifth. In the race itself I came in around twelfth out of about eighty riders and got a prize as 'Fastest Newcomer', which was some compensation. Ron was pissed off that he'd given the good bike to the American, who didn't come anywhere, and he promised me the good one for the TT.[198]

Although Loren was not officially part of the Britten Team, he was beginning to feel distinctly uncomfortable with the way John Shand had presumed to take the position of Team manager upon himself and speak boldly to the media on behalf of Britten Motorcycles.

After the race he was interviewed on radio and television, and he told the world that he was the Britten Team manager and that we were going to do 200 mph at the TT. It was true that we had done 180 mph in the speed trials and there was a big long straight that ran downhill at the TT, but he was really pushing it. He said we had 15 bhp more than the Hondas and that we were going to do them like a dinner. He was also telling Roberto how to set the bikes up, and to make it worse Roberto was listening to him. I was supposed to start my holiday with CJ, but John called up and said he needed the heads from the two bikes back in New Zealand to freshen up as spares for the new bikes, which were due to leave for the TT in a couple of weeks. Shand had organised this dodgy little workshop in Chester with this old motorcycle character, and instead of looking at the wonders of Europe I found myself knee-deep in crap. I was glad to get the job done and join up with Sandro on the bus. We drove to Mark Farmer's house and parked outside, and that's where we stayed for the next few days. Mark was really great and he and his girlfriend Terry looked after us and generally made us welcome.

A few days later we took the bus on an outing to the racetrack at Snetterton, where Mark did well on a Yamaha, and we met up with Andrew Stroud, who won his race. Then it was time to motor in Black Beauty to the ferry that would take us to the Isle of Man. Sandro was driving and I hooked into the vino and laughed all the way, glad to be moving again. When we arrived, however, I was brought down with a sharp thump. The boys had turned up from New Zealand by then, but instead of a happy reunion the atmosphere was pure poison. Broz looked like he wanted to kill me and the others were hardly talking to me at all. John, who arrived a few days later, knew there was a problem, but he just shrugged it off and told me to concentrate on my own ride. I was flummoxed. When I'd left everything had been sweet, now it was horrible.

It was hardly surprising that the mood back at the workshop had deteriorated in the weeks that Loren had been away. Quentin remembered the atmosphere during the final days before the bikes were due to leave as a kind of collective high, brought on by sleep deprivation and exhaustion.

> Just before we left John asked how I felt and I said, "This is real life!" That's how it felt. It was as if I had never given everything I had to give in order to achieve something before. Meeting that challenge was very, very satisfying and I felt I was on the same trip as John. I know it's absolutely unhealthy but I'm really glad I did it. Somehow I lasted all the way to the UK on the flight, and then I just crashed big time. Everyone was in the same condition.

Jeff recalled:

> It was already apparent that it wasn't going to be a good trip. None of the bikes were tested because there simply wasn't time. Two were fired up on the dyno the night before they left and one was blowing oil. The third was only started briefly the morning it departed.
>
> Loren was helping to get the bikes together and there was plenty to do. We had set-up sheets and everything, so we were covered there, but John really was way over-confident about the reliability of these brand-new machines. Broz and Tim were ignoring me but when Murray arrived he was still the same, thank God. He was just cruising along being himself. With him there I could walk away.

The root of the tension lay in the somewhat curious relationship that existed between Tim Stewart and Loren, a relationship that seemed to deteriorate from affectionate companionship to open hostility on a cyclical basis. The tension in the relationship was brought into sharp focus by the ragged exhaustion the whole Team was suffering. It was all too easy to resent Loren's earlier departure from the stresses of the workshop and to accuse him of ducking out when the pressure came on.

'They had gotten really wound up about me having an easy time,' Loren complained, 'and because it dovetailed with all the negative stuff they were going through they spat it back out at me when we met up again.'

Whatever the reason for the aggravation, it was a dangerous development. With the Team emotionally and physically 'tapped out', such negativity could easily develop into a major, destructive schism. That danger would be greatly increased by John's predictable refusal to take charge with an application of incisive leadership, a failure that led to precisely such an outcome.

In the meantime, Quentin had perked up a little after more or less falling unconscious following his arrival in the UK. However, his first impressions of the Isle of Man were far from reassuring.

> It was my first time out of New Zealand and the place spooked me. I was aware of this ancient energy all around, which I found quite intimidating. I couldn't help feeling that the bikes were like broadswords being wielded in a medieval battle. Everybody knew that people would certainly die, but that didn't stop it. It was humbling and it was scary. Jeff and I met up with Chris Haldane, who had hired a car, and we went around the course on Bloody Sunday. All these boy racers were hanging their knees out on their bikes and Chris was carving them up in this Vauxhall because he knew the line so well. I was sure we were going to die there and then, but he kept telling us that we were safe because we had four wheels. There were 200 corners on that circuit and it just boggled my mind how anyone could learn it.

The Team was beset with problems as the practice sessions wore on. One particularly persistent and frustrating development was that the bikes kept breaking timing belts. Later, it was discovered that in the hurry to finish the engines Rob had not machined the drain holes beneath the buckets in the same way as the pre ceding engines, and it was suspected that the old hydraulics problem might have resurfaced. A succession of different belts was tried, and finally the problem seemed to be under control, but no one could confidently predict how long they would last during racing.

Wayne Alexander accompanied John on the long journey from New Zealand and he remembered that at some point over the Atlantic, in spite of everything he had to think about, John suddenly became very excited because he believed he'd finally figured out the answer to a two-stroke conundrum that had been bothering him for years.

> He really felt that he'd solved some fundamental shortcoming inherent in two-stroke technology, although he didn't really explain exactly what it was. When we arrived in London we went straight into the city to the Patents Office. It was late and the only person who could show us where anything was, was the charlady, but she knew her way about and took us where we needed to be. John pored through all these files and finally found something. This was bad because obviously he didn't want to find it. However, it seemed that some Pom had figured out the same thing some years before. Apparently, he sold the technology to an Australian just six weeks before we

arrived at the Patents Office. John was disappointed about it, but we were on a mission so he soon forgot about it. Whatever it was.

Shaun Craill had also made his way to mainland UK and thence from there across to the Isle of Man. He was determined to remain with the Team until the end of the mission.

> I didn't have an official job so I ended up being in charge of presentation, which meant cleaning the bikes mostly. John and I had made a deal whereby he paid my fare, enabling him to claim the GST [Goods and Services Tax]. He then recovered all the money by not paying me for a few weeks. We arrived without John and set up the workshop, saw to the bikes and worked out the road routes and so on. You had to be onto the road routes or you could easily get stranded somewhere when they closed roads for practice and racing. When John arrived with Harry Ruffel, who was doing some filming, the quiet efficiency we had established as a Team was instantly reduced to shambles and stress levels quadrupled. It was the last thing we needed. I don't know why, or even quite how, John did it but somehow he created a sense of crisis. It was as if he needed things to be on the edge, barely happening in the nick of time. He made decisions as Team manager that floored me. For example, the course was so bumpy that the front guards were sometimes belting the underside of the fairings, and this caused the dashboard, which locates the fairing, on one machine to crack. It wasn't critical damage, but the crack could easily have spread and then it might have become a problem. I worked out that I could grind out the damaged area and put in fresh material, and have it cooked off with a hairdryer overnight. However, John decided I should take off all the ICI sponsor's stickers instead and replace them with fresh ones. The stickers, which were stretchy vinyl jobs, dissolved in oil and they took hours and hours to scrape off. And then one of the bikes raced with a bodywork crack that could have become quite dangerous.

To add to the general tension, the Team was kept busy for an entire night when Robert Holden's bike scuffed the bores in its engine. The all-night session saw the bike back together by early morning, when Shaun and Tim took it to Jurby airfield. Tim ran up and down the airstrip, bedding the engine in, and they managed to get back to the pits just before the roads were closed for the day. In the meantime, one of the two spare bikes had been uncrated and assembled, regrettably with the wrong bodywork, which had been more or less jammed into place. (As no two machines were the same, each had to be married to its individual bodywork in a process that required hundreds of hours of painstaking adjustment and modification.) Shaun had secured the body as best he could and then fitted the tailpiece.

Unfortunately, no one had thought to connect the oil-breather pipe through to the tail outlet, and when Robert took the bike out it leaked oil onto the rear wheel, almost causing him a high-speed crash.

'It was the kind of thing that happens when you are working in such a high-stress environment,' said Shaun. 'Robert did one lap and then walked away. He was doing well with his 600 and he decided to put all his effort into that.'

It was not an acrimonious departure. Tim Stewart recalled Robert as being disappointed but resigned.

> It was obvious to everybody that we were overstretched and the general consensus was that it would be better to park up his bike as a spare. He had enough to do with his other rides. As usual we were working around the clock. On a good night we got to bed at about three and then grabbed about three hours' sleep. Those who had managed to get to bed at a more sensible hour would get up really early to drive the van to the pits before the track shut. Then the rest of us would stumble out of bed and stroll a couple of kilometres over the paddocks and join them. We were always a bit knackered but the atmosphere was great. There were lots of guys we knew around, and in between sessions of frantic activity it could be quite social.

In 1994 there were actually more New Zealanders racing at the TT than had ever done so before. Among the sixteen Kiwi riders were nine who made up a team, led by Robert Holden, that intended competing for the Maudes Trophy, an award given for team success.[199] This team was entered in the Supersport 600 event and qualifying had gone exceptionally well. Jason McEwen was one of the team's nine riders, and when Robert Holden decided not to ride the Britten after all John asked Jason if he would. Why he suddenly wanted the complication of running three bikes again is hard to know, but Jason readily agreed. Unfortunately, Jason only managed one-and-a-quarter practice laps before coming to a halt with water in a plug lead. His next outing, as he recalled, lasted only a further quarter of a mile.

> A belt broke after a lap and a half while I was going flat knacker. The bike handled it pretty well considering that I declutched immediately I felt the power loss. It stayed on track even though it had no drive, and we only had to replace a couple of bent valves. I had gone fast enough on the 600 to qualify for the Senior, but because I was new they wanted two full laps from me. I didn't know if I was going to be allowed to ride or not.

By the Thursday afternoon Mark Farmer and Nick Jefferies had qualified and all seemed reasonably under control, although the decision on Jason was yet to be announced.

Also well under control were the preparations of the formidable Castrol Honda RC45 team of Steve Hislop, Joey Dunlop and Phillip McCallen. The evening before, Hislop had clocked a sizzling average 121.30 mph on his very first practice lap, a feat that must have seriously disturbed him. Back in the pits he complained to reporters that the 750s were now too fast to be safe on the circuit. He must have known that his comments would not be greeted sympathetically by either the fans or his fellow competitors. With a certain amount of faint jeering sounding from the hills, he assured everyone that he was just making a comment and he had no intention of withdrawing. Far from it, Team Honda was strong and confident.

Back at the Britten camp pits, Mark Farmer was now happy with the set-up of his bike and had decided to call it a day. Mark was riding Roberto's machine, which was, according to Shaun, probably the best prepared of the three. However, at the last moment the Irish rider changed his mind and decided to do one final practice lap. He had turned up late that morning and had missed the first practice session, so his decision was prompted by no more than a desire to grab a bit more time in the saddle before the event. His bike was hurriedly made ready and he took off just before Steve Hislop came flying past on his Honda RC45.

> Approaching Hawthorn, I saw a bike in the distance going well, and I recognised it as Mark Farmer on the Britten. I closed in on him at Ballacraine, and eventually got past him going into Laurel Bank One. I never saw him again. When I got back my mechanics told me I had done over 123 mph on the flyer. I changed the gearing and did another lap, but I was slowed at the Black Dub by yellow flags. Going past I recognised Mark's Britten and realised he must have crashed right behind me on the previous lap.[200]

Mark had crashed at perhaps the slowest section on the course, but with a number of off-camber sweepers and blind 140-mph bends it was also one of the most difficult. Mark Farmer was dead, the third racer to die at the spot since 1978.

By some kind of fateful irony the first riders at the accident site were Andrew Stroud and Chris Haldane. Andrew recalled the tragic scene.

> We were getting in a final practice session, and as we came into Black Dub I saw a trail of yellow and black wreckage on the road. I knew immediately it was from Mark's bike. Then I saw a body on the footpath and Chris and I pulled over. A doctor and a marshal were already there and they told us not to look but we did anyway. He was pretty banged up because the bike had squashed him against the stone bank. I'd known Mark quite a while through racing in Asia, at Macau and so on. The night before, he

> and Chris and I had been at a nightclub getting loose on the dance floor. My last memory of him was of him doubled over with laughter surrounded by happy people. Chris and I got back on our bikes and got on with it. There was nothing else to do.

Nick Jefferies and John heard the news together with Perry Rees in the pits. Harry Ruffel joined the group as they left for the crash sight and asked John if he wanted film taken. Grimly, John agreed and the group left immediately. 'As we arrived, Hislop went past going like the clappers,' Perry remembered.

> The eruption of noise and the flash of colour seemed unreal in the silence after he was gone. Black Dub is this absolutely beautiful spot with a stone wall down one side of the road and a stone cutting on the other. The trees form a tunnel overhead, so the road is nearly always in shade and it was quite dark. There's a little stream just a few metres off the road that adds to the dampness and the place is notorious for traction problems. The body and the bike had been taken away by the time we got there, but there were small bits and pieces of the bike's bodywork here and there. I've never seen a human being look as devastated as John did. Nick's best friend, Rob Vine, had been killed at exactly the same spot two years before. We looked around and John picked up a bit of wreckage and just stood there staring at it, before he pulled himself together and we started to try to figure out what might have happened. We noted these black lines on the road, evidence of a huge slide. It seemed obvious that the back had come around on Mark under power, and the computer read-out later confirmed that he was near peak horsepower at about 8000 revs in fourth gear. Of course, they impounded the bike and John went through hell before they finally announced it was rider error and not some mechanical failure. He wanted to pull the pin and go home, but Nick Jefferies was adamant that Britten Motorcycles should still race. He held it all together and we stayed.

Interviewed soon after by Hamish Cooper, John acknowledged that it was Nick's positive attitude that had kept the challenge on track.

> Nick had been fantastic to us. It's hard to explain how you make a choice to keep racing here. The riders and the families accept the risks but it doesn't make it any easier to continue after something like this happens. Mark Farmer was a really nice guy and a great rider with a reputation as a hard charger. His bike was the best in the Team and he was happiest with it. He loved the high-speed stability of it. The bike was set up the way he liked it and each time he came in he was beaming from ear to ear. It's just tragic.

John's agony over Mark's death was compounded by the horrible possibility that a mechanical failure had caused the accident. Although no one had witnessed the crash, a marshal located a few corners away reported that he had heard the bike seize. Quite how anyone could detect a seizure in that way is hard to imagine, but his comments were taken seriously. When John and Murray were allowed to examine the wreck, they spent two-and-a-half hours going over it. It must have been a bitter relief to find that the suspension still seemed to be in excellent condition, although they were not allowed to touch the bike to see if the engine was turning freely. It was some considerable time before the Team was finally able to recover thc bike and strip it in front of track officials when it was clearly demonstrated that the engine had not seized.

In spite of the official finding that rider error was to blame, debate over the cause of the crash would further divide the Team. Some of the crew blamed a particularly hard compound tyre that had been fitted to the rear wheel immediately before the bike went for that last fatal run. John later complained that Michelin should never have included it in the tyre selection, but again it is unlikely that Mark would not have known exactly how his bike was handling by the time he got to Black Dub. Although the tyrc would have been slow to warm up, it was characteristic of the circuit that tyres would cool down on the long straight sections anyway. In other words, even though tyre warmers had been on the bike for some time before it went out, Mark would have known that the tyres would have been relatively cold at that point.

Shaun Craill suspected something simpler and he later wrote a report on the subject for the company.

> In the report I noted that the Britten was an awkward fit for most riders. I wrote that the ideal rider would have been an orang-utan, a fellow with very long arms and legs and a very short torso. Of course, we never found anyone who matched that description. Poor old Andrew was too tall and suffered constant buffeting, even after we made the screen higher for Daytona. He had to take the padding off the back of the seat to fit the thing, which made an uncomfortable ride even worse. Jason, who is also quite tall, used to get bruising on the insides of his arms. It was even more uncomfortable, however, for riders like Mark, who had long arms, a long torso and short legs. He had the most radical ergonomic set-up I had ever seen, with especially fabricated foot-pegs which shifted his feet forward about 25 mm and an extra 60 mm of padding in the seat. The Britten required a very forward riding position anyway, but these modifications and his build meant that he had his weight even further forward than most. His head was also taller than the screen, so a special higher one was fitted and the clip-ons were raked right back. He had a tendency to brake late and

> throw his bodyweight forward, which would have greatly reduced the load on the rear tyre. This allowed him to go for lighter and lighter rear shocks, which would have improved traction to a point, but once it unhooked it would be in a very sudden manner that would have made recovery difficult.
>
> I heard him complain after a test session at Jurby that it was like riding a brick, and Jefferies said his teeth hurt because the suspension was so hard. Mark had the rear end squirming under braking and he asked for a softer spring. They gave him what he wanted but after further testing he complained again. I heard Murray say incredulously, 'You want to go lighter again?' After that he declared that he was really chuffed with the set-up. That really was the way he liked to ride.
>
> When we looked at the accident site we noticed a seam where fresh seal met up with older seal right where the skid marks started. There was a shallow indentation between the new and old material with a thin ribbon of water in it. It looked to me like he simply lost traction and swapped ends. The way he rode, and the set-up he preferred, made that a very likely scenario. When we looked at the tyres the back was scarcely scuffed up but the front showed signs of having been worked very hard.

Wayne Alexander, who examined the crash scene not long afterwards, offered yet another explanation for the fatality.

> The local council, or who ever it is that looks after the road, had trimmed the bush growing along road edges with weed-eaters and had turned what had been a soft landing zone at head height into a lethal palisade of vicious spikes. One of them had gone through Mark's helmet. That spike alone would certainly have killed him. I pleaded with John to speak up about it but he wouldn't do it. They are probably still trimming the roads the same way just before each TT to make it look pretty for the visitors.

It is likely that quite a few factors combined to create the fatal circumstances that led to the crash, but there is a common belief that Mark had been unable to resist the temptation to take off after Hislop. One of the most successful men in the history of the TT, Hislop was at that critical moment engaged in one of the fastest flying laps ever recorded.

This is a view shared by Shaun Harris. After the previous TT Shaun had been promised a ride in 1994 by John and he had been bitterly disappointed when he learned that he was not to be a member of the Team. His anger at what he perceived to be a blatant betrayal was further compounded by the immense sadness he felt when he learned of Mark's death.

> When I learned that the computer print-out showed Mark had been at full throttle when he crashed I could almost see the accident happening. The year before, I found I had to short-shift through that particular part of the track as, for some reason, the bike always tried to spit me off at that spot.

Whatever the cause, Mark's death had brought the total toll of racers killed at the Isle of Man to 166.

Although in the end it was impossible to know exactly what had happened, one thing was clear to those who knew John well. Despite the fact that he handled the tragedy with a quiet and tightly controlled dignity, they felt that he took full responsibility for the accident onto his own shoulders and that from that moment on he was never quite the same, as Quentin recalled.

> While the bike was still impounded there was a female reporter asking questions that made it clear she wanted to put the blame squarely on this experimental, home-made bike. John handled her as best he could, but that tin-arse, back-shed bullshit was suddenly blown out of the picture. Farmer was dead. We were a professional race Team and we had to deal with it that way. It was time to dig real deep to see what was down there.

The next day, Nick and Jason took the two surviving bikes out to the starting grid for the Formula One race. It was only then that Jason learned that he would not after all be allowed to ride, and so the Britten challenge came down to one rider and one bike, a situation many of the team would like to have seen from the very beginning. However, the race was postponed owing to rain, but in the rerun Nick started well with a standing-start lap average of 117 mph. He was going strongly, well in touch with the leading gaggle, when his rain-soaked plug leads shorted out and killed the ignition. It was a simple problem that had plagued the Team throughout the TT, but it had proven difficult to eliminate. The race had given a tantalising display of the Britten's potential and many professional observers noted that while the Hondas were weaving badly at speed in spite of their uprated suspensions and gusseted frames, the Britten was rock steady.

The next clash was the Senior TT and it proved to be a repeat of the earlier event for the Britten, with the bike again posting a blistering standing-start lap-average speed of 118 mph before the gearbox gave way at Ballacraine on lap two. The Britten challenge was over.

By then the Team was simply living for the time they could go home, and Jeff Ballinger waited with the same dull, stunned resignation as the rest of them.

> I ran into Quentin and told him I was glad we were nearly out of there. He just stared at me and then shook his head and told me Loren was missing. We waited around feeling sick and then Broz came along and told us he'd heard Loren was dead. Thankfully he wasn't, but it must have been a close thing. The people who first got to the accident had ignored Loren while they attended to the other rider involved, because they were quite certain that Loren could not have survived the smash. When they did have a moment to look at him they were surprised to find that although he looked munched up he was still very much alive, and both riders had been taken to the hospital by helicopter. We all visited him later but he was totally zonked out on painkillers. It was a weird place, with a mortuary full of bodies, including Mark's, in the next room.

Up until his accident Loren had been doing well. He had enjoyed a good twelfth-place finish in the 600 race on the Honda and had been awarded a Silver Replica after posting an impressive 113.6-mph lap, second only by a fraction of a second to Robert Holden. Although Jason McEwen had beaten him in the race, Loren's faster lap time had also won him an invitation to race in the Senior TT. Naturally, he had accepted.

> I had a reasonable start in the Senior and I was humming along behind this German rider called Helmut Dahne. He had years of experience at the TT and he was well liked and respected by the racing community. He had actually won the TT in 1976 on a BMW R90S, but they had an absurd handicapping system in place for a couple of years that saw him robbed of his victory. He was an elegant, fast rider but even he couldn't cope when his engine suddenly started blowing oil out the breather and over his back tyre. He went down immediately in front of me, and although I managed to avoid his bike I collected poor old Helmut. I smashed into his leg at about 230 kph [143 mph] and flew off the bike, tumbling through the air for a couple of hundred metres. There was enough time for me to think I was as good as dead, before I hit the road and bounced back into orbit. I cleared a brick wall but bowled off three unlucky spectators who were sitting on it, and then slammed through all this scrub, luckily without hitting any big trees. I was knocked completely senseless so it took me quite a while to realise I was still alive. It came as a shock to the people who found me as well. They'd attended to Helmut first because they thought I was ready for a body bag. I'd broken the top of my pelvis and ripped up my right shoulder. My head was heavily bruised and I'd torn the ligaments in my right knee. For a while I was expecting a lot worse. Helmut's leg was badly smashed up and he never rode again at the island, although he remained interested in the racing.
>
> When I turned up at the TT a couple of years later these German guys found

> me and gave me a good luck postcard from him. I was in the hospital for a week and then I was able to go to Assen with Tim and Murray. It was good to be alive.

Murray and Tim were also keen to visit their piston supplier, Omega, Birmingham and they did so after leaving Assen. It was an instructive visit, as Tim recalled:

> We took a few pistons along to show them the kinds of problems we had been having and they were really helpful. This guy Fred took us through the place and showed us the forging process and so on, and then sat down with the pistons. He seemed really confident that he knew what the problem was and sure enough after that we largely stopped having piston failures. It clearly demonstrated that although there might have been some advantages in being on the other side of the world, being so far away from the guys whose products we used could be costly. But it was good progress and Murray and I were very encouraged.

With the Team all packed up and ready to leave the island, John still had one sad duty to perform. The Team had farewelled Mark with a simple but heartfelt gesture when, in the silent wood beside the low stone wall, they gathered to plant a tree. It was frowned upon by officialdom to leave any memorials to those who died at the TT, but the tree was planted next to a small bronze plaque that had been placed there in memory of Rob Vine. For John, however, the moment was not enough. In Ireland road racers are national heroes, and when one falls the Irish like to give them a huge send-off. And so John made his way to the little Irish village where Mark Farmer had lived and he walked for 2 kilometres in the funeral procession down the main street. His attendance was made more painful by the fact that Mark's partner, Terry, was beginning to believe that John was personally responsible for the accident. Although nothing much was said, the threat of an ugly lawsuit hung in the air. It would remain there for many months until finally Andrew Stroud's mother, who met Terry when Andrew later started taking her out, persuaded her that she should let it go.

In late June Nick Jefferies wrote to John and summed up the Britten effort 'warts and all'. He discussed the 'character clash' between Broz and Loren, describing it as most unfortunate. He had nothing but praise for Loren, however, calling him an excellent ambassador for the Team who could succeed at anything he tried.

'What a pity he wanted to ride as well,' he wrote, 'because his input would have been invaluable. I felt that without his management the day to day problems we encountered were exaggerated.'

He then listed ten items that he considered 'would be pertinent to a full-blown attack on winning the TT next year'. They were to improve the reliability and handling of the bikes, to appoint a capable team manager, to arrive earlier for testing, to prevent Michelin from controlling tyre selection, to equip the bikes with quick-release rear wheels, to choose only two riders and give them 1000 miles of testing each, to take three bikes plus two engines, to house the team together and to clean up the look of team members with corporate-style clothing. And in conclusion he wrote:

> I know that some of these items represent an oversimplification but if every one of them had been attended to we would almost certainly have finished at least runner up in either the F1 or the Senior. It was a great privilege for me to ride your wonderful bikes and to be involved with all the great guys that came over with you. No one could have foreseen what was going to happen and we should take nothing away from your great achievement in actually being there and competing at the highest level. I do hope you continue. I am sure that success will come your way and when it does it will be one of the happiest days of your life.

Quentin recalled John's efforts to rally the Team and boost morale:

> John wanted desperately to pull everything together after we got back, but everyone was shattered and all for different reasons. He set up a suggestion box and asked us to write down each other's strengths and shortcomings. He tried to start the ball rolling by reading us his version of everyone's pluses and minuses and did his best to make light of it. He meant well, but the idea went down like a lead balloon and he very pointedly neglected to include himself. We all hated the idea and nobody joined in.

Thankfully, the best medicine for the Team was waiting in the workshop. The three bikes, including the wreckage of Roberto's bike, needed to be rebuilt and delivered to their owners. While they were at it John decided that the Cardinal Network bike should also enjoy a thorough restoration, and this was duly accomplished before the bike was delivered to Gil Simpson at his company's headquarters in Christchurch. The debt owed by Britten Motorcyles to Gil had been settled in part when he acquired a half-interest in old Number One, the original 1100. Long ineligible to race, the bike had been taking up workshop space and John felt it was high time his friend and benefactor should enjoy the machine himself.

The delivery of the newly glittering Britten was a surprise for Gil, who was delighted when Guy, who had been responsible for the bulk of the beautiful restoration, woke up the 175 hp within and rode it into the atrium foyer. Gil was then photographed by the press, whom John had alerted, sitting on his new machine wearing an old leather flying helmet and goggles, with a huge grin on his face.[201]

John's funeral, Christchurch 8 September 1995 (Photo: Euan Cameron)

Top: Andrew Stroud, Pukekohe, 26 November 1995. (Photo: Euan Cameron) *Bottom:* Andrew Stroud, Pukekohe, 26 November 1995. (Photo: Euan Cameron)

Top: Andrew Stroud, John Hepburn, Steven Briggs, Murdoch. New Zealand Grand Prix Ruapuna 23 March 1997. (Photo: Euan Cameron) *Bottom:* Steven Briggs NZGP Ruapuna 23 March 1997. (Photo: Euan Cameron)

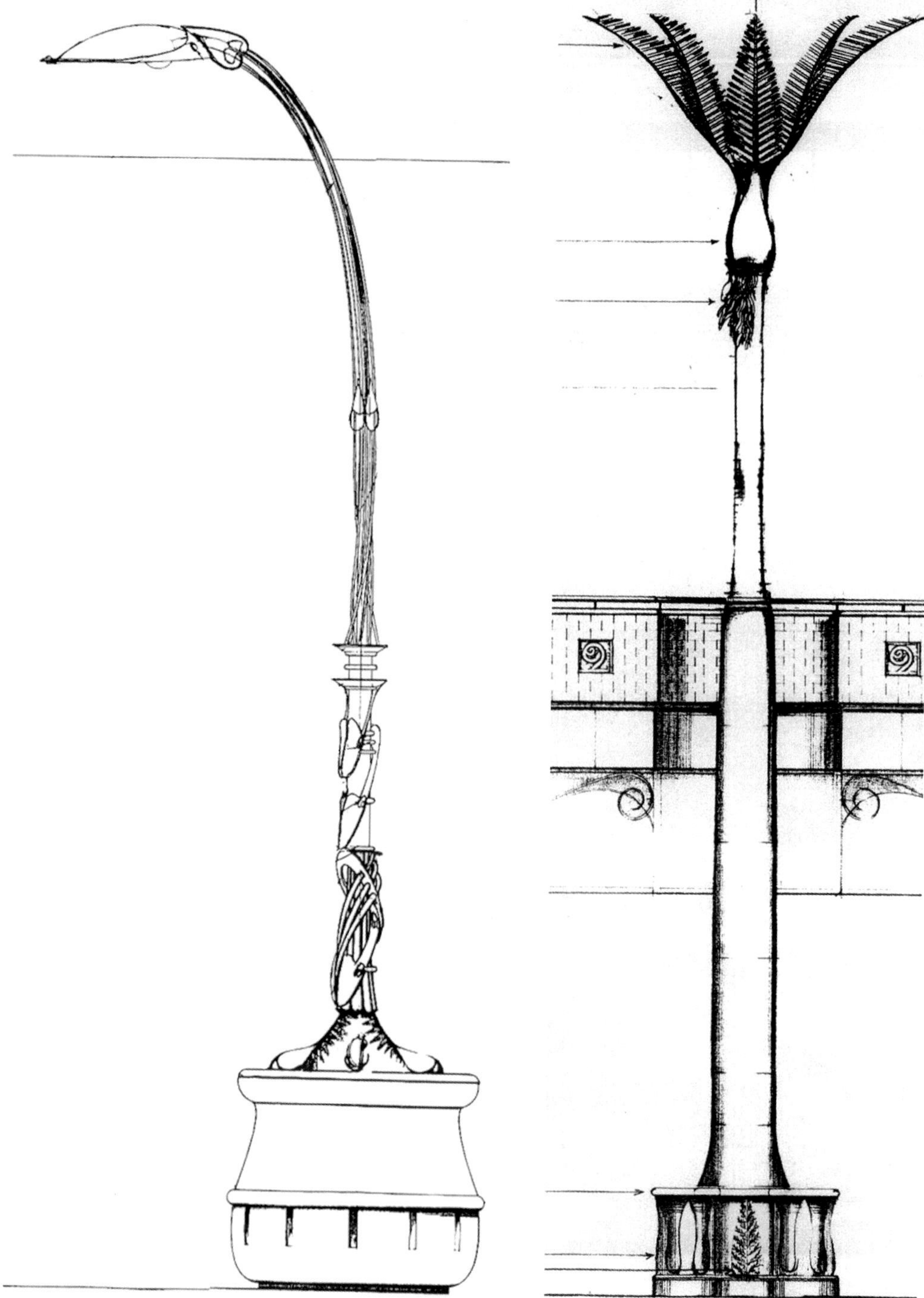

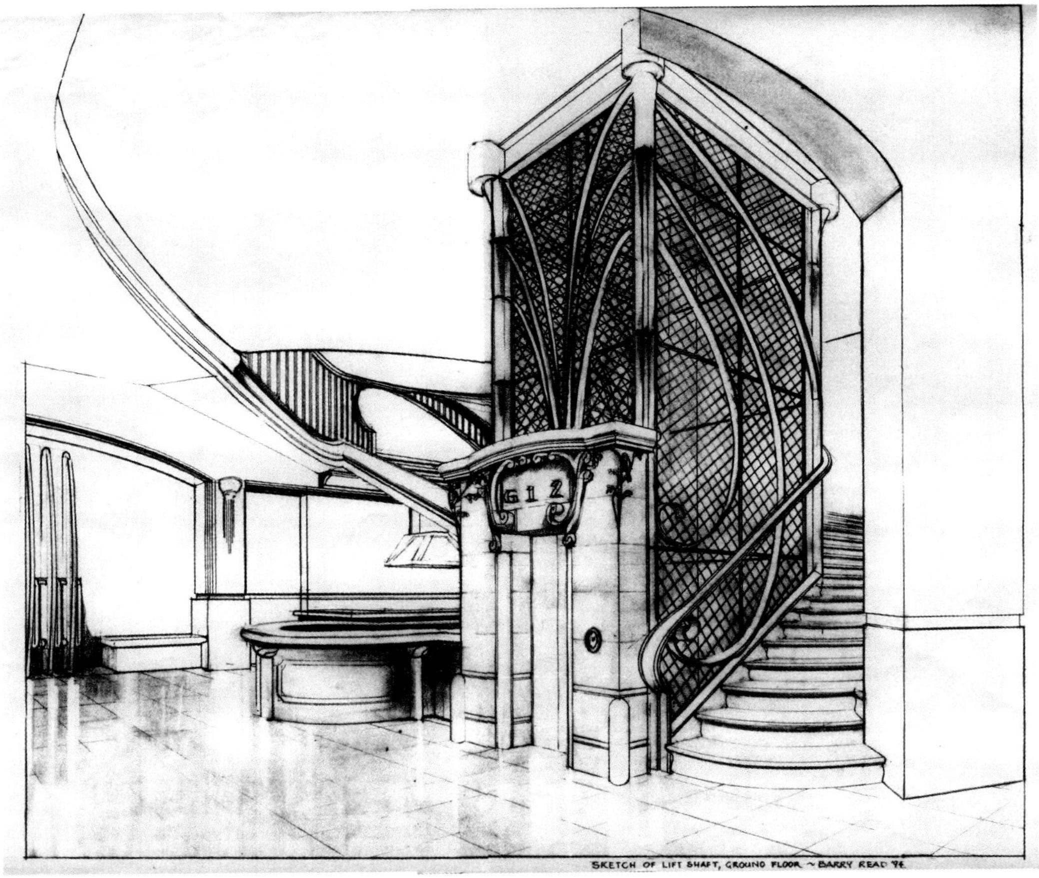

SKETCH OF LIFT SHAFT, GROUND FLOOR ~ BARRY READ '94

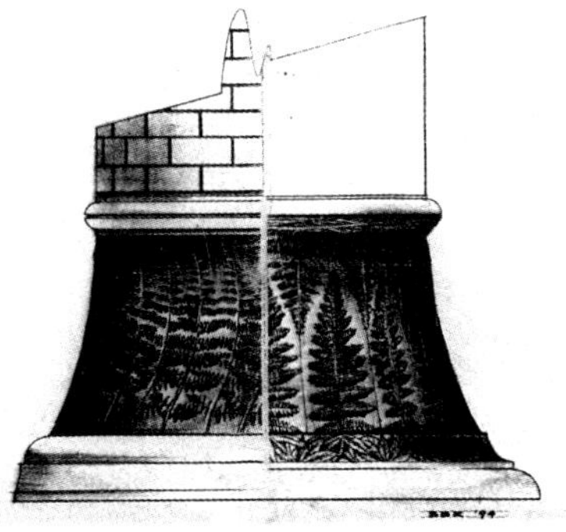

COLUMN BASES AND CAPITALS ~ SCALE 1:10

Cathedral Junction

This building would have been John Britten's other great life's work. Even as he was dying he worked with artist Barry Read to produce a comprehensive prescription for a magnificent edifice combining New Zealand icons with flowing art nouveau architecture. Over 100 of these drawings were made but many were apparently lost after John's death. Barry retained copies of most drawings and along with the usual plans, elevations and a full scale model of the structure they collectively detail a building of mostly public space that could have been the pride of the city. (Illustrations: Barry Read)

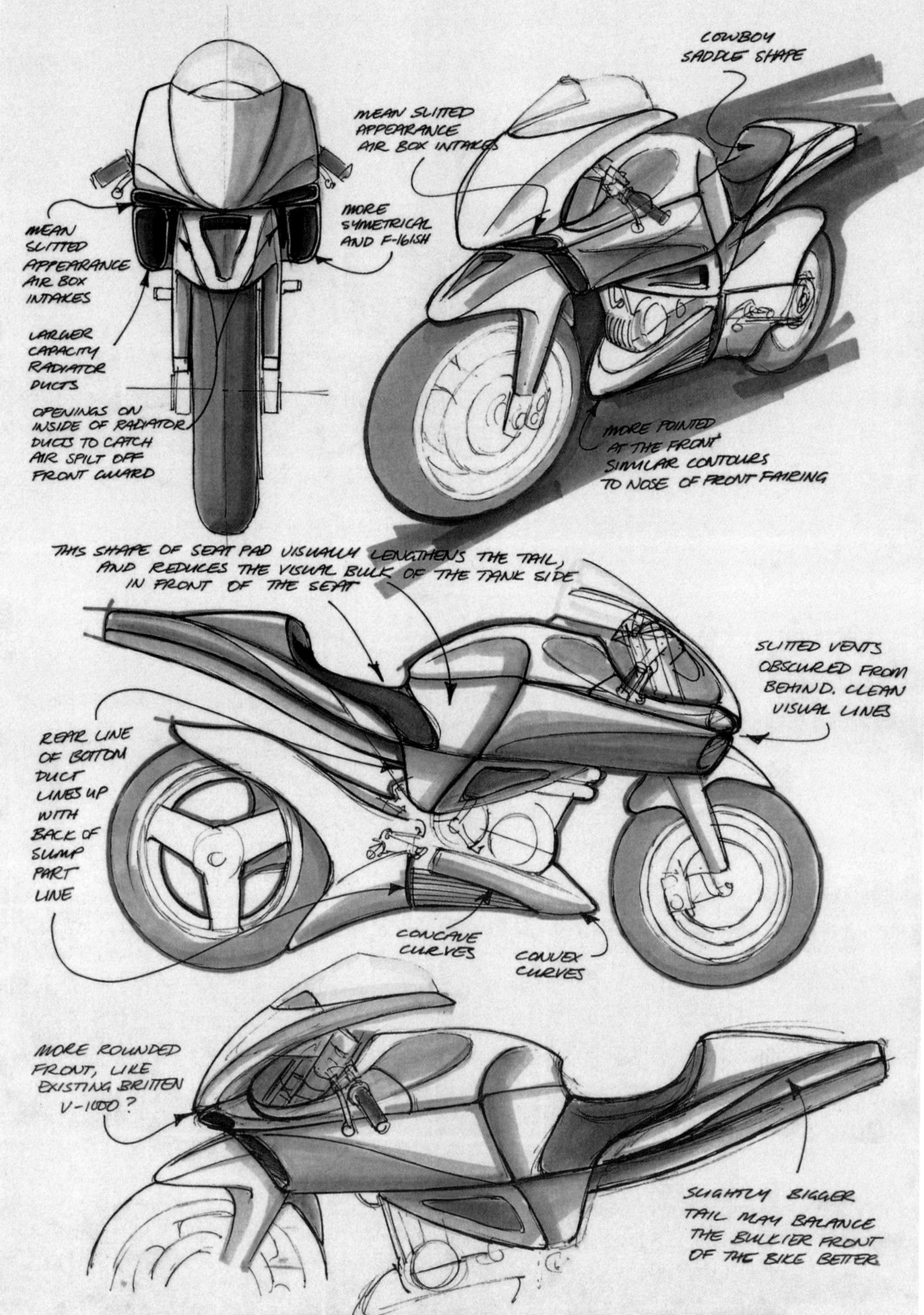
COWBOY SADDLE SHAPE
MEAN SLITTED APPEARANCE AIR BOX INTAKES
MEAN SLITTED APPEARANCE AIR BOX INTAKES
MORE SYMETRICAL AND F-16ISH
LARGER CAPACITY RADIATOR DUCTS
OPENINGS ON INSIDE OF RADIATOR DUCTS TO CATCH AIR SPILT OFF FRONT GUARD
MORE POINTED AT THE FRONT
SIMILAR CONTOURS TO NOSE OF FRONT FAIRING
THIS SHAPE OF SEAT PAD VISUALLY LENGTHENS THE TAIL, AND REDUCES THE VISUAL BULK OF THE TANK SIDE IN FRONT OF THE SEAT
SLITTED VENTS OBSCURED FROM BEHIND. CLEAN VISUAL LINES
REAR LINE OF BOTTOM DUCT LINES UP WITH BACK OF SUMP PART LINE
CONCAVE CURVES
CONVEX CURVES
MORE ROUNDED FRONT, LIKE EXISTING BRITTEN V-1000?
SLIGHTLY BIGGER TAIL MAY BALANCE THE BULKIER FRONT OF THE BIKE BETTER

Left and above: Drawings by Shaun Craill of the proposed Indian race bike, a machine that could also have become the basis of a production street-legal sports bike. Based on a sketch by John, that he made by drawing over a picture of a Britten V1000, the drawings eventually led to a full-size clay mockup. *Top:* One of a number of similar proposals for an Indian cruiser. (Illustrations: Shaun Craill)

Building a Britten V1000—the assembly of P006.

Top left: Assembly starts with the bottom end. Crankshaft modeled on Crower item. Note short skirts on pistons, titanium rods that cost John 'as much as a decent bike'. *Bottom left:* The crankcase bottom end assembly. Also shown is the primary drive and the Suzuki sourced gearbox.

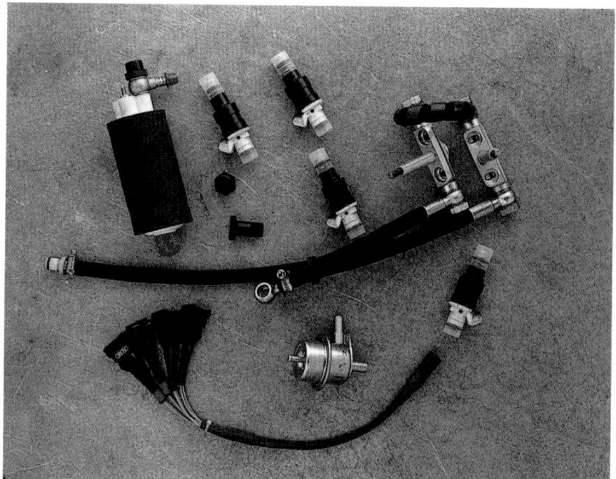

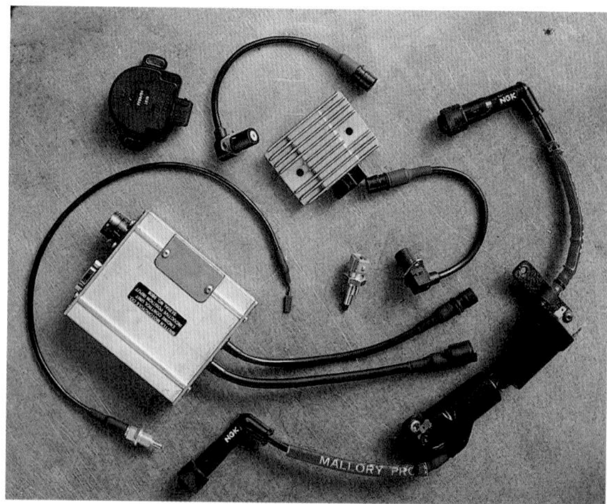

Top right: Fuel injection parts. *Bottom right:* Engine management system and ignition parts. The bigger box is the computer that manages the engine—the source of so much trouble and vitriol. The computer was eventually manufactured by Britten Motorcycles under license. The smaller box is the voltage regulator. (All photos: Graham Thompson)

Top left: The cylinder head assembly showing valves, valve springs, valve followers, buckets, camboxes and heads. *Bottom left:* Heads with cams installed, bolted onto the block. Note the absence of part-line at the base of the cylinder. Sump baffles are installed. (All photos: Graham Thompson)

Top right: Cylinder heads showing clearly the twin exhaust ports. *Bottom right:* Lower crankcase with gearbox and oil pump installed.

Top left: Top engine case, view from the timing side. Crank sensor, alternator and cam drive assembly now installed.
Bottom left: View from the primary side.

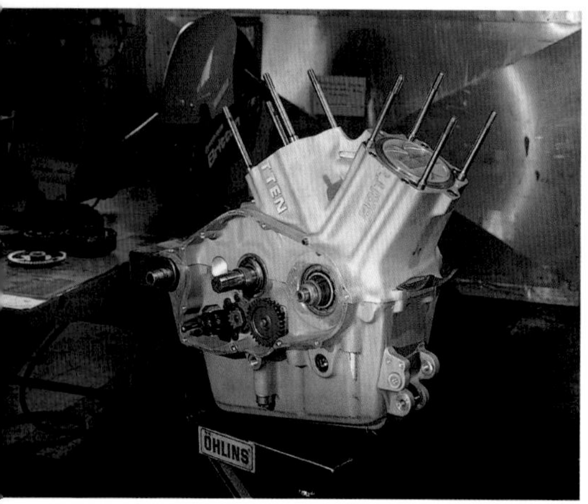

Top right: Cam caps installed, primary cover in place, and clutch assembly mounted. *Bottom right:* Cam belt backing covers, cam belt, cam belt pulleys, carbon fibre cam belt cover, alternator, and alternator cover in place. Water pump, injectors, and water plumbing installed. (All photos: Graham Thompson)

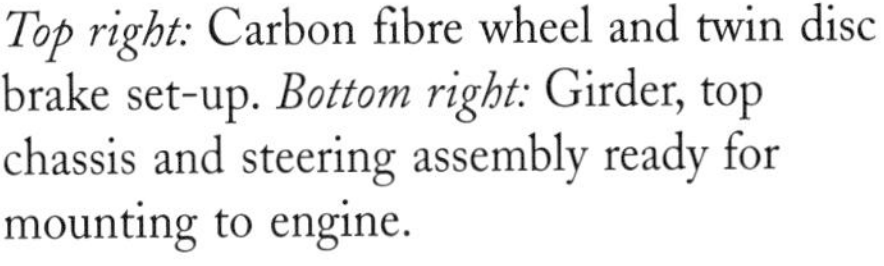

Top right: Carbon fibre wheel and twin disc brake set-up. *Bottom right:* Girder, top chassis and steering assembly ready for mounting to engine.

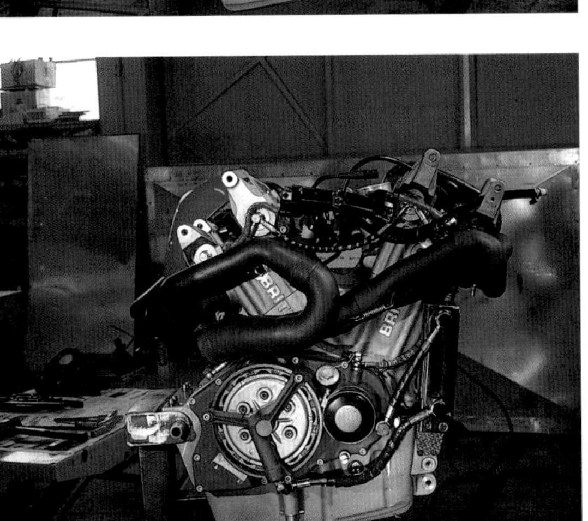

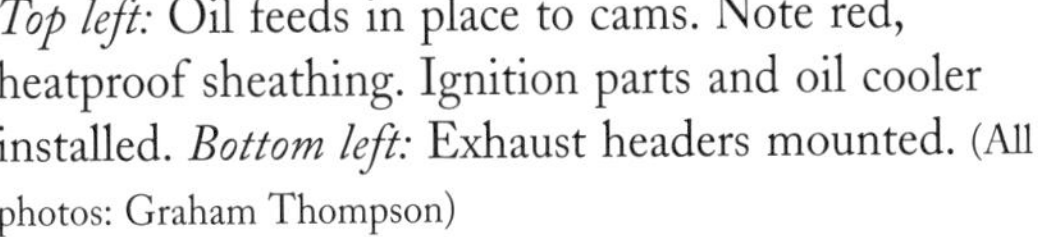

Top left: Oil feeds in place to cams. Note red, heatproof sheathing. Ignition parts and oil cooler installed. *Bottom left:* Exhaust headers mounted. (All photos: Graham Thompson)

Top: Swingarm installed on engine. Rear suspension in place. Tyre hugger mounted on swingarm. Foot peg assemblies mounted. *Bottom*: Primary side view of engine and rear suspension. (All photos: Graham Thompson)

Top: Bodywork waiting to be mounted. Note the three pieces: nose, tank and tail. Boombox and silencers, front end, and radiator/seat, with sub chassis ready to be mounted. (The boombox was made by welding flat panel steel together and then inflating it with compressed air.) *Bottom:* Rob Selby assembling front end to engine. (All photos: Graham Thompson)

From top: Primary side. *One down:* Timing side. *Two down:* Timing side with exhaust in place. Note that on this, the second to last V1000, the boombox is separate from the crankcase to obviate heat transfer from the exhaust to the bottom of the engine. Carbon fibre covers in place on boombox. Bodywork and radiator sub chassis mounted to the top of the engine. *Three down:* Primary side. (All photos: Graham Thompson)

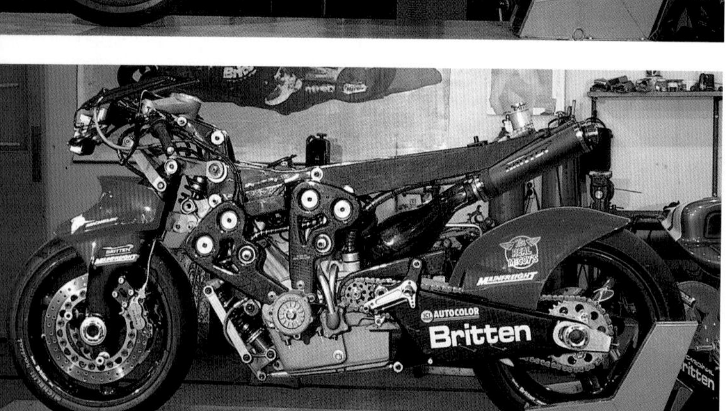

The completed machine: Top picture shows the primary side; bottom, the timing side. Soon after these shots were taken the bike was wheeled down to the dyno room, just as its predecessors had been, and fired up on the big wheel. The EMS was then programmed and with 165 hp on tap it was ready to roll. After the factory had raced it in Japan and Germany, it was freshened up and painted gold for delivery to Gary Turner in Holland. (All photos: Graham Thompson)

P006 behind F003—'the Waterbike'. Note that the Waterbike's exhaust system is the now superseded alloy arrangement—bolted directly to the crankcase. (Photo: Graham Thompson)

The pace of work was calmer, the hours sustainable, and slowly the Team knitted back together. It was time to regroup and refocus, and, as if heaven sent, a brilliant opportunity to achieve everything that John could possibly have imagined for Britten Motorcycles landed right in his lap. The company was suddenly poised to become the prototype design house he had always wanted, with a project that would allow full rein to his own talents and those of the individuals around him. Best of all, it would be in creating and developing a new range of motorcycles.

It did not matter that they would not be Brittens. For John it would almost be like returning to the point where it had all started, both for him personally and for motorcycling generally. The new project would involve nothing less than breathing fresh life into one of the greatest names in motorcycle history.

CHAPTER NINETEEN

Politics

Amid the confusion and sadness of the Isle of Man John had received what would otherwise have been very exciting news indeed. Now, with a little time and distance to clear the air, he was able to take stock of what seemed on the face of it a remarkable offer. He had been asked to play a vital role in nothing less than the building of two prototype machines to relaunch one of the oldest and most revered names in American motorcycle history. Ambitious plans were afoot to ensure that the mighty Indian would ride again.

There had once been a plethora of manufacturers of motorcycles in America, but once revered names such as Ace, Henderson, Big X and Rex Acme had largely disappeared with the Great Depression, and as America geared up for war, only Harley-Davidson and Indian remained as serious manufacturers.[202]

Although the Indian company had finally faded into oblivion in the 1950s, various attempts had subsequently been made to cash in on the illustrious history of the marque. In the 1970s a range of Italian mini-bikes sold quite well with the Indian name on their tanks, and over the years a number of other machines with engines ranging from Harley-Davidson to Chevrolet V8 were sold by various groups owning bits of the trademark.

One of these part-owners, an entrepreneur and ex-motorcycle traffic-cop named Wayne Baughman, amassed a lot of money from about 1990 selling franchises and taking orders for what he claimed would be a new production Indian. However, in the four years Indian Motorcycle Manufacturing Inc (IMMI), based in Albuquerque, New Mexico, collected money, he succeeded only in producing a pair of prototype machines. Of the two, only one had a real engine and it barely ran. Hundreds of dealership franchises were sold and deposits on hundreds of motorcycles taken.

Dave Tharp, a writer and Indian enthusiast, attended an Indian rally in Albuquerque, where Baughman had promised to unveil his running Indian and give test rides to journalists.

'I knew the project was in trouble,' he later wrote, 'when I met engine designer Cyril Batten. He was wearing a badge with the title "Mr Titanic". Like the ship, my hopes sank when the promised test ride never happened. Wayne said that one of the bikes—which were hidden inside a curtained-off tech area much of the time—had "wheelied away from a test rider". A malfunctioning fuel injection system was blamed, and all rides were off.'

Not long after that, IMMI's business accounts were seized by the Massachusetts bankruptcy court and all those who had invested in it learned that their money had evaporated. They were not alone. The court was, in fact, already handling the assets of the previous Indian company, run by one Phillip Zanghi. Zanghi's attempts to breathe new life into the Indian name had also collapsed into bankruptcy after he, too, had spent millions of other people's money. On that occasion there had been no motorcycles whatsoever to show for it. With Baughman's failure coming hard on the heels of Zanghi's, it appeared that Indian Motorcycles was destined to remain a distant memory, or at best a disparate collection of other people's bits and pieces.

Harley-Davidson, on the other hand, had emerged from a period of hard times with a remarkable resurgence that began in the middle of the 1980s and yielded record profits every year. Although the company stuck pretty much to its knitting by producing the kinds of big-capacity V-twin heavyweight cruisers that the market apparently wanted, it also successfully managed to diversify, by selling accessories in a big way. Soon this side of the turnover accounted for fully 30 percent of their business.

The prospect of grabbing a slice of such an obviously lucrative market was too attractive for the old Indian name to be allowed to pass away quietly, and a Western Australian businessman, Maurits Hayim-Langridge, in association with a New Jersey lawyer, Michael Mandelman, acquired Indian trademarks from the bankrupt business. The route by which this occurred was typically mired in litigation.[203] Nevertheless, the two men were confident enough of their cause to approach John Britten to design and build them a number of prototypes.

The agreement was actually a three-way split between Britten Motorcycle Company, Liberty Holding Company Incorporated of Wisconsin and Indian Motorcycle Manufacturing Company Incorporated of Nevada. Because of the complexities arising out of the fact that, what was once America's most popular and successful motorcycle company had by now been sliced into numerous portions, progress was inevitably painful and laborious. There were, it seemed, many Indians but none could produce a chief worthy of the name. In spite of the difficulties, however, Mandelman and Hayim-Langridge slowly settled their plans for the public float they hoped would supply the boatloads of cash they would eventually need to avoid sinking. At the same time, with John's assistance, they also evolved a comparatively modest plan to put Indians on the road, Indians on the track and Indian merchandise in the shops.

Initially, it was thought that a Britten race bike with special Indian bodywork could re-establish the name by competing around the world, much as the Brittens had been doing. The plan also called for at least a couple of heavy, traditional cruisers of differing capacities and with civilised engines to be developed concurrently. In fits and starts, the possibility of the Indian making a comeback slowly gathered credibility. But it would be a long haul and for the moment the battle was mostly fought on paper.

A great deal of detailed project planning was already in place by the time John received confirmation that the Indian project was to proceed, and when Michael Mandelman flew over to meet with John an agreement was quickly negotiated. By April (1995) the first of a number of contracts had been signed and the project was ready to roll. The money the partners agreed to advance was supplemented by further funds from a New Zealand Government Business Development Investigation Fund, given to help develop a street version of the race bike. What would eventually emerge was an agreement whereby Britten Motorcycles sold access to key aspects of its technology—namely the ducted radiator design, the stressed engine concept, cylinder head design, wet sump design, belt-driven cam system, tank design incorporating ducting, engine-breather system, girder and carbon composite technologies, and the technology whereby the swing-arm was mounted directly to the engine.

It was, certainly, a recipe for an exciting new American motorcycle. In an outline of the project prepared by Britten Motorcycles for Dr John Wittner, who John was keen to have manage the project, it was written that the 'Indian will succeed because their range will be high-tech performance motorcycles. This is unlike Harley where they are only relying on an image, their product is second rate.'

Specifically, the agreement called for Britten Motorcycles to produce concepts for a race bike based on the Britten V-1000 with different 'Indian' bodywork, from which the street-legal Indian Superbike would be developed. Various subsequent agreements also called for a 1400cc heavyweight cruiser, to be called the Chief, and a 1200cc middleweight the Scout. The engines for the latter were to be modular units developed from the race engines, suitably modified for volume production and for use as everyday transportation. The agreement further specified that Britten Motorcycles would build and race two of the Superbike prototypes at Daytona and other yet to be determined events, and that the bikes were to be ready within an eighteen-month timeframe. The company was then to be given the option to produce the finished articles, which were to be reverse-engineered by Britten

Motorcycles for volume production, with cruiser prototypes being developed later. A business plan, developed at the same time, anticipated 300 units being built in 1996—the first year of production—growing to 10,000 units by the year 2000.

Meanwhile, Baughman had somehow burst back on the scene and was making threatening noises. Because of the possibility that Baughman, or indeed a number of others, could make life complicated (at least three manufacturers were making motorcycles with the Indian brand using various powerplants), the project was shrouded in secrecy. Confidentiality agreements were signed and the team selected to work on the project was sworn to secrecy.

While waiting for the money to come through, John gathered the Indian team together, promising key members permanent positions in the company with market-rate salaries. Generally, the contract was promoted within the group as a way to sort out all the conflicting needs of the fragmented organisation and as a way to formalise the roles of all involved.

For Shaun Craill, however, who had been asked to be part of new team, the situation turned out to be less than ideal.

> John already had the nucleus of a first-rate design team. John, Murray, Rob, Jason and I had all the skills that were needed, and we could draw on Mike Sinclair and Hans Weekers when we needed them. In terms of pure design, Jason and I perfectly complemented each other. He was better than I was at seeing things in three dimensions but I was able to do the drawings. The way the Indian contract was drawn up, John was actually sub-contracted to the partners as an individual and then contracted Britten Motorcycles to do the work.
>
> My understanding was that he would take out a million of the 3 million they had agreed to pay for the whole project, which he wanted to put into Cathedral Junction. It all sounded wonderful, but from the very beginning things started to sour. Because I'd been promised a 'proper job' I drew up a contract and gave it to John for his consideration. I don't think he even read it and Tim Corcoran came back with another, which he presented as a 'sign it or fuck off' deal. The job description said that I would do anything the company wanted me to do. It was a crazy document because it meant that while there was any work to do I could not be fired. So I signed it. The promised salary never eventuated and I'd have to say that in the end none of the promises were honoured, but we tried to gradually change things while getting stuck into the project.

Part of the problem in forcing Britten Motorcycles to treat its employees with all the dignity usually afforded talented and skilled professionals was the number of talented and skilled professionals who were prepared to work for nothing. Quentin

Rowe recalled seeing faxes and letters every week that arrived at the factory from individuals within New Zealand and all around the world who wanted nothing more than an opportunity to work with John.

> Some of the CVs were mind-blowing. Obviously, the efforts of those who were there to force the company to pay for the hours we worked were undercut by this constant stream of offers of free services. On the other hand, we now fitted together and that's no small thing. We had become a highly professional unit.

In spite of all the uncertainties, however, Jason Monopoli was beginning to thrive with a fellow designer to encourage and inspire him, and he, too, found the confidence to tackle John on the sticky matter of the future.

> Shaun had been working overseas and it was a real thrill to be working with a designer from the real world. We got together and discussed the things that bothered us, and one of them was the fact that John treated us as if he was doing us a favour letting us work there. We told him we were professional designers and we wanted to be paid overtime. He got really snaky about that and said that he didn't want to work with uncommitted people, but we continued to press for a certain degree of recognition and respect. John was losing the company as a hobby as we drove toward an increasingly professional approach and he fought that for a while. However, we knew we had to make the place realistic and we just kept going down that track.

Shaun recalled asking John

> ...what sort of process we should follow design wise and got the distinct message that we were to be like the old Italian school where he as maestro would approve and sign off our work. It's not a particularly pleasant way to proceed but that was the way it was and we accepted it. However, the question of the general direction the company should take was a more complicated matter.
>
> In many ways John was adept at telling people what they wanted to hear, so everyone had a different idea of what we were trying to be. However, I do remember a barbecue at Church Bay in 1993 when we were all invited over and he clearly wanted to listen. I often wondered later if he had an inkling that he was ill at that point. It was a bit of a thank-you for all the effort but he clearly wanted us to discuss the future. He asked for contributions but no one put their hand up, even though he made it very clear that he was there to hear us out. They all just sat back with their snags and beers and said nothing. I hadn't been there long so I was reluctant to put myself

> forward, but in the end I did say I'd like to see us develop into a design studio. But that was about it, so some went home thinking we were a race team, some thinking we were a prototype studio and some thinking we were motorcycle manufacturers. And, of course, every one of those things had different needs and often conflicting priorities. The confusion did not promote harmony.

With the Indian project finally beginning to fire, however, all concerns for the future were put on hold and the design team, consisting of John, Shaun and Jason, went to work with a will. The start point for the Indian race bikes was an image John produced by drawing with felt pens and crayons on top of a photocopy of a photograph of a Britten V-1000. Describing the look he was after, he later said that the Indian Superbike was to be 'more flamboyant, more aggressive, more sinister looking than a Britten—like a Corvette compared with an E Type Jaguar'. It was also to have telescopic forks in place of the front girder suspension.

Shaun produced a front view of the machine from John's drawing and then worked his way around the bike with a three-quarter front view, a three-quarter rear view and a view from dead astern. He began with the fixed points of the V-1000, and a reasonably detailed picture of the new machine quickly emerged. At the same time he took advantage of the opportunity to make the bike a great deal more ergonomically friendly than the Britten V-1000. Other new features, such as the varying box-section titanium exhaust John wanted, were drawn in, even though the engineering required to locate it, without transferring heat to the rider's seat, was uncertain to say the least. And there was much more to deal with, as Shaun recalled.

> The exhaust also presented interesting challenges in arriving at the best compromise between flow and noise suppression. John wanted a sound-absorbing 'sock' to run up its guts, and I suggested a number of counter-rotating turbine blades driven by exhaust pressure, which would 'break up' the sound waves instead. He thought that idea worth pursuing.
>
> We were also looking forward to addressing some of the build and design problems inherent in the V-1000. For example, the air ducts on the V-1000 went through tortuous curves and the intake air and cooling air were not separated. Murray always wanted to keep them apart because it was possible for the intake to scavenge air from the wrong side of the radiator under certain conditions. The finish on the insides of the V-1000 ducting was also as rough as hell, which must have induced turbulence in the airflow and slowed it down. We wanted it perfectly smooth in the Indian.
>
> The production plans for the prototype called for the factory to invest in a CADCAM mill, which meant that we could build a full-size clay model and then

scan it to take the lines off. The program could then correct any dints or wavers and do a flip side so the design was perfectly symmetrical. With the digital information thus acquired, the mill could then carve a perfect shape out of foam, from which we could make equally perfect moulds. After struggling for years with asymmetrical bodywork, the body shop could have multiplied its productive capacity in one fell swoop.

Jason did one side of the clay and I did the other. I have to say his side was better, but in the end it was a pretty mean-looking machine and John loved it. We had a big poster of an F16 on the wall and we both drew inspiration from it. When Mandelman came over to have a look I met him for the first time. Murray liked him and was looking forward to working with him, and he was a nice guy although he didn't do much other than taking a lot of notes. He was obviously committed to the project but he had difficulty understanding technically what we were on about. At one point we suggested that perhaps the steering head should be adjustable so you could dial up a set-up for racing and another for cruising. He thought we meant something like a big hinge to extend the forks like a chopper and had difficulty grasping that we were talking about tiny adjustments.

I drew up some concepts of the cruiser for his consideration, taking as a start point a drawing of an original Chief. I was surprised and concerned when he immediately pointed to the drawing of the original old machine and said emphatically that that was what he wanted. He was a vegan and he brought over all his own juice. That meant we couldn't go out and have a drink with him, so it was hard to really know what he was thinking. We didn't seem to reach any decisions, which I found worrying, and after the clay was finished progress seemed to grind to a halt for the time being. We still hadn't been paid properly because there was some money snafu, and at one point John was going to sue them for breach of contract. I believe they settled that, but while it seems John's outstanding accounts were paid our wages shortfall was never addressed. And so we waited to see what might happen next and went back to general duties on the five V-1000s we were building.

Tim also found himself doing all sorts of odd jobs, sometimes spitting parts out on the lathe for weeks at a time.

I did everything. It was the same for Broz. When we were not doing our specialist jobs we mucked in and did whatever needed doing. That was the way the place worked and nobody complained. John came in one day and gave me a sketch for some girder spacer he had come up with. It was a tricky thing with flats and threads, and one part had to be bored to a very precise depth to fit into the other. I looked at it and said it wouldn't fit together, but he got more and more insistent that I make it. In the

> end he just told me to make same swarth. So I did. He came back later and beamed at the big mound of swarth on the floor. I said, "Here you are Johnny, just as you ordered. Now try them." Well, they didn't fit and just as he always did when something went wrong he threw his hands up and said, "I just don't believe it!" After that he tended to listen a little more to me and in the end he largely left me to my own devices.
>
> Sometimes things got a little tense when John had someone trying to make something from a pie-bag sketch he'd given them that had a bit of mince in the wrong place. He had a sixth sense about someone wanting to have a bit of a go at him and he knew just how to diffuse it. I don't think he did it consciously but he'd nearly always hurt himself. He'd bounce in and stub his toe or bash his head on a shelf. I remember him telling Rob, who was fuming about something and hadn't yet had a chance to say anything about it, that they should get out of the place and go out dancing. I don't think Rob's ever danced in his life, but John broke into a little jig as he sat next to Rob and then he got carried away and leapt to his feet and brained himself on Rob's mill. Of course, Rob couldn't be mad at him when John was all dazed and hurt. Somehow he kept the Team together; it was part of his genius.

It was at about this point that John began to be aware that fame was a two-edged sword and that the consequences of having a certain amount of the world's attention were not always welcome. He had long recognised that 'information evaporation' was an inevitable consequence of living in the small world of motorsport, even if his headquarters was hidden away on the 'dark side' of the earth. This had not prevented him from being furious when Roberto laid bare the inner workings of his Britten engine for Italian journalists to photograph. Worse, however, was to follow. For some time now Alan Cathcart had enjoyed a somewhat privileged position with Britten Motorcycles, and John did not hesitate to tell him about the Indian project, having first impressed upon him the need for extreme discretion. John was therefore utterly dismayed when a story written by Alan revealing the Indian plans was syndicated around the world.

In the article, Alan revealed details of the proposed prototypes and the identity of Maurits Hayim-Langridge. John was quoted as saying that Maurits and his people had invested US$2 million of their own money getting the project to the point it was at, and that he had a full-scale mock-up of the Superbike in his workshop. Less critically, Alan also revealed details of the new Britten Supermono, writing that John had "divulged" that the 600cc engine would be an ultra short-stroke that could rev to 12,000 rpm and more. John was also quoted as saying:

> There will be plenty of valves—more than four—and plenty of ports and, of course,

> it will be water-cooled and fuel injected. I've designed a novel system of camshaft drive: the cylinder head, cylinder and sleeve will be cast in a single piece, like an air-cooled aircraft engine, but with the flange much lower than usual and no cylinder head bolts. That makes the crankcase much smaller than normal and it will be made from carbon-fibre using my patented space-frame construction.

Working with Hamish Cooper, John immediately sent out a press release saying that, 'Everything published so far has been pure speculation dressed as facts. I'm angered and the Britten factory is concerned that some journalists, desperate for a scoop, are resorting to these tactics.' It would seem, however, that he had jumped the gun by blaming Alan for the leak, as the source of the journalist's information was none other than Maurits Hayim-Langridge himself as Alan later confirmed.

> John, whom I continued to meet, correspond with and have dinner with whenever we could, never made any complaints about what I wrote and I never betrayed any secrets because I was 'desperate for a scoop'—since anybody who knows me and my journalistic work knows that's not the way I operate. In fact, the person who revealed to me the existence of his collaboration with Britten was none other than Maurits Hayim-Langridge himself. My wife's family live in Perth, Western Australia, which is where he is/was based. On a family trip out there, I went to interview him on the record, after being directed to him by my friend Dr John Wittner, who made an introduction for me, for an article that was published around the world in the summer of 1994. In it, he referred to the Britten connection, and I suppose he did this because he was trying to attract outside investors for the Indian project, and the idea of a Britten-designed Indian was obviously an attractive one. If Maurits got upset about this being published as a result of our interview, he had only himself to blame. I feel no remorse for what I did—I acted professionally and correctly at all times. As far as the Britten Supermono is concerned, I specifically discussed revealing the existence of this project with John, who only asked me not to reveal how many valves it had—hence my specific wording of 'more than four valves' (Yamaha already had five!). The reason I wanted to write about the bike was that the Supermono class, in which I was a leading protagonist both off the track and on it, needed every boost it could get to get the FIM to adopt it as a category, as indeed later happened as a support class for World Superbike. John knew this, which is why he discussed the outline existence of the bike on the record.

John now had little choice but to admit that the project was indeed happening, while drawing attention to the confidentiality clauses in his agreement that prevented him from commenting further. It was a vexatious development. For years he had touted the Britten workshop as a place where other manufacturers could quietly develop new technologies away from prying ears and eyes, and now, in one fell stroke, any such reputation was in tatters. It was a harsh lesson. Fortunately, his somewhat intemperate and unjustified outburst against Alan caused no ill-feeling and the two men remained close friends.

While all this was going on, work continued on the remaining two of the batch of five bikes, and the testing and development programme was resumed using the original two new generation V-1000s. As a result of this work, three important refinements occurred that brought about vastly increased reliability and a significant improvement in handling.

The first refinement was the development by Hans Weekers and Murray of a twin-belt, cam-drive system.[204] However, the extended dyno testing that Broz had to do to test the new belt arrangement was causing him some concern.

> I began to experience some very unpleasant health problems. Avgas [aviation petrol] has a very high lead content and basically I was poisoned. Of course, we had an extractor system to suck the exhaust gases from the pipe and I kept putting in more fans, but some invariably leaked out. I started to experience numbness in my legs and I had these terrible headaches. I used to quite like the smell of petrol but now it just makes me puke. Years later I'm only just beginning to come right.

The second significant improvement—that of better handling—came with the belated procurement of a sprag clutch, which rider Jason McEwen was soon able to appreciate in action.[205] With Andrew busy elsewhere, Jason and Loren were given the task of riding for the Team in the forthcoming New Zealand Championship. During testing with the new clutch at Ruapuna, Jason was immediately able to knock one full second off his lap times.

> Before we had the sprag I had been slipping the clutch going into corners. Now I could ride the bike in harder and tip it in with confidence. It didn't get out of shape so much and I reckon it killed about 90 percent of the front-end patter. I was also able to use the much smoother engine braking and the ride was generally a hell of a lot more comfortable.

Partly to counter any negative impressions left by the tragedy at the TT, Hamish Cooper, who increasingly acted as a de facto press secretary for the company, organised for English racer and journalist Mark Forsyth to ride one of the new bikes. (This was the same Mark Forsyth who had been so impressed by the Britten he had raced against at Ruapuna some four years earlier.) In his story, which appeared in *Performance Bikes* magazine, Mark reported that he was still uncomfortably aware that the front end tended to chatter when pushing through turns in spite of all the improvements. However, he found the handling generally superlative, which would indicate that John's funny front end was finally beginning to realise its potential.

'The Britten,' Mark wrote, 'continues to rewrite the rules on what a 1000cc twin can do. A big Ducati (916 or 888) is an unruly, barely manageable pig. The way the Britten flicks left, right, through the chicane belies its true capacity. The way you can brake deep into corners and maintain a brain-frazzlingly high corner speed should be the territory of small two-strokes, not a hairy chested V-twin four-stroke.'

Mark also revelled in the power on tap. 'A charge through the first three gears towards a right hand kink gets the Britten wheelying after the change into fourth, through the kink. Yes, a throttle only wheelie. What a feeling. Coming out of slow turns requires a great deal of fine throttle control and bodyweight over the front end to stop yourself looping it over backwards. It's mental. Completely mental.'

Meanwhile, the pair of bikes ordered by the two American friends had been refurbished and Jim Hunter's machine was shipped off to take part in a race at Road Atlanta. Dr Mark Stewart's bike remained behind, however, and was actually raced over the following season in New Zealand.

'We didn't hear from Dr Stewart for ages,' recalled Loren. 'He just seemed to be a very cruisey guy who wasn't in any kind of hurry to get his bike back. So we kept it and used it.'

Loren and Broz accompanied Jim Hunter's bike to the race at Road Atlanta, where American rider Nick Ienatsch, editor of the American magazine *Sport Rider*, was set to race it. The two New Zealanders had recovered their earlier friendship and it was a pleasant trip. However, it was far from a cakewalk. The bike was spitting gobs of oil out the back and they suspected for some time that the rings may not have bedded in. To compound their troubles, the new oil coolers on the bike leaked and Loren had to run around looking for someone who could crimp new lines up.

> Jim Hunter made me pay for all that out of my own wallet. I think he was telling us it was time to get our shit together. Then when that problem was solved we had an electrical fault. The wiring had been routed incorrectly and the alternator wires were rubbing somewhere, so the bike would run for a lap or three and then cut out. Nick [Ienatsch] missed a practice session while Broz sorted it out, and we were all tremendously relieved the next day when the bike finally ran perfectly.
>
> Nick was impressed with the way Broz and I worked to solve the problems and

he enjoyed the way we could set the bike up with his input once it was running right. He was good at giving quality feedback and we made rapid progress. However, he was especially intrigued when I downloaded the bike's computer into my laptop and then downloaded the laptop into the hotel's fax machine via the phone line. This allowed us to procure a continuous print-out of the bike's behaviour because the fax machine printed out on a roll of paper. He was fizzing about that.

He was only able to qualify the bike in fourteenth place, but improvements made between the last qualifying session and the race itself were such that he was able to take the bike into sixth place early in the race.

Even though we were sidelined soon after with a broken belt and bent valves, the collaboration between the mechanic, the engineer and the rider had clearly confirmed that this was the way to race the motorcycle. Effectively, I looked after the suspension, allowing Broz to concentrate on keeping the bike going. Hunter was pissed off with the failure to win a result, but Broz was rapt. We knew we'd done well. It was just a shame that the lesson had still to be fully learned back in New Zealand.

It was ironic that while Jim Hunter was somewhat annoyed and disappointed with his machine's showing, it had confirmed a previous positive impression with another potential buyer. During the meeting, a man who introduced himself only as Geoff approached Loren and explained that he worked for a Mr Barber, the man who owned Barber Dairies, the same Mr Barber whose racing team had played host to the inhabitants of Kiwi Corner the previous year at Daytona. Apparently, Mr Barber also had a huge collection of bikes in a big industrial complex out of Atlanta, which Loren was invited to have a look at, along with Broz.

When we accepted Geoff drove us there in his Chevy Impala. Boy, that place was an eye-opener! There were literally hundreds of classic road and race bikes, each in its own glass case, on this vast racking system. There was a huge workshop within the complex, with six immaculate workstations, and they had their own dyno room. The place wasn't open to the public, so we had the place to ourselves. Broz and I were just bowled over. We were invited to spend the night at the home of this young guy who rode for him and the next day we flew out. We never met Mr Barber, who apparently only ever dealt through Geoff, but we eventually sold him a bike.

Nick Ienatsch faxed Loren soon after his return and confirmed his favourable impression of the bike, writing, 'I know that riding that thing was the highlight of my ten years as a journo.' He went on to express his hope that he would see the team at Daytona in eight weeks and invited them to hit the town with him if they could tear themselves away from the racetrack.

'It's hard to believe the women, bikes and women,' he joked. 'Of course I know you guys like to spend the extra hours working on your bike over at the Mechanics School! Don't worry, if you do make it we'll sneak off and see life away from the track. Did I mention the women?'

Back on the home front, the team was making final preparations for a two-machine attack on the 1994–95 New Zealand Superbike Championship. Bob Brookland's offer to manage the race team, gratis as always, had been accepted by John, while Tim Stewart had been given the job of spannering for Jason. Guy Kingsbury was to look after Loren's bike.

Before the race season had even begun, however, there was a challenge to the Team that almost hobbled them. The drama began when Motorcycling New Zealand (MNZ), the body that represented those involved in the sport, was asked to impose a minimum weight requirement of 160 kg (about the weight of a Ducati) for the Superbike class. With the Britten weighing in at 144 kg this would have meant carrying ballast, a particularly odious notion to John, who had worked so diligently to reduce weight to an absolute minimum.

For some time he had been aware of the scheme, which was being promoted by road-race riders within the motorcycle clubs of South Canterbury, Otago, Taumarunui and Auckland, but refused to take it seriously. John's only comment was to dismiss the idea by pointing out that any minimum weight requirements should be matched by maximum power limits, the two having an equal bearing on how fast a motorcycle would go. Believing that the road racers' suggestion would be seen by MNZ and the majority of the other race teams as a blatant attempt to punish the superior design of his machines, he thought little more about it.

John's decision to ignore the suggested minimum weight requirement and his failure to lobby his side of the issue more vigorously backfired badly when the idea suddenly gained considerable traction. It happened at the Annual MNZ Conference, when a raft of remits, including the minimum weight requirement for Superbikes, was fielded out to a road-racing workshop. At the workshop all the clubs involved threw their support behind the Otago Club remit that recommended that 'rule 14-15-3 be instituted to read that Superbikes should have a minimum weight requirement to promote better parity within the class and closer racing'.

It was quite normal to refer remits to various workshops because of the large volume such conferences had to deal with. The recommendations of the various workshops on the remits, few of which were in any sense contentious, were then passed in blocks by the conference. The road-race workshop in question took place on Saturday night and was, somewhat predictably, lightly attended. In spite of the obviously contentious nature of the minimum weight remit, the small number of people who did turn up nevertheless advised it be automatically passed by the conference the following morning as part of a package of recommended remits.

At that point, however, alarm bells began to sound among those at the conference who regarded John Britten's motorcycles, and the high public profile they enjoyed, as the best things that had happened to New Zealand motorcyling in living memory, if not in its entire history.

With the conference in recess for morning tea, Kevin McCleary, the immediate past president of MNZ and a lifetime member, frantically rallied opposition to the remit and Errol McCabe, another MNZ life member soon joined him. Together they spread the word of the impending rule change among conference members.

'I had been attending a trials workshop while the road-racers were hatching their plot,' Errol said, 'and I was most concerned when Kevin told me what was up. He said, "If this thing goes through they will have eliminated the Britten!" I thought the road-race guys were very pushy and self-centred, and I wasn't going to sit by and watch them get away with it.'

Ken McIntosh, who was at the conference as a member of the Classic Register, was also intensely angered by the remit and he approached Tim Gibbes, the MNZ executive in charge of public relations, to see if there was anything that could be done to defeat it.

'I asked Tim what he thought, and he put his head in his hands and asked me how on earth he was supposed to put a positive spin on such an action. The most popular bike in New Zealand was about to be nobbled and he felt gutted about it. By then, however, there was a good bunch of us and we decided to challenge it after the break and see how we went.'

'Kevin McCleary led the charge,' recalled Errol.

> He stood up and said he wanted to exercise his privilege as a lifetime member to address the conference. Errol Conaghan, the president, gave him the OK and Kevin promptly asked him if it was true that the conference had the previous year voted to present John Britten with a special medal for his contribution to motorcycle competition in New Zealand. The conference fell dead silent as Conaghan answered that it had.
>
> McCleary then asked him if the medal had been presented and, when he was told that it had not, suggested that it be made out of at least 20 kg of lead. That way, he said, it could be screwed straight onto the bike to satisfy the minimum weight requirement for Superbikes that was about to become law!
>
> Well, there was a bit of an uproar about that, and I hopped quickly to my feet and moved a motion that the remit be opened to the full conference for discussion. Tim Gibbes quickly seconded it. I stayed on my feet and told the conference that I wasn't going to sit down because the matter would just be swept under the carpet.

> Conaghan finally ruled that he would take it as a 're-occurring' remit, which meant that it would require a two-thirds majority show of hands to pass. We all spoke against it and then the vote was taken. I was still on my feet and I looked around and reckoned about 95 percent of the sixty delegates had their hands up to support the nays. And so the attempt to force the Britten to carry extra weight failed. One of the road-race guys screamed out some crap about his sponsors, and Tony Rees, Grant Ramage, Russell Josiah and John Hepburn walked out. I thought that would be it, but of course it wasn't.

'The media tried to blow it up into a major confrontation between John and I,' claimed John Hepburn, 'but it was never personal and we continued to get on well. The stink over the weight limit remained a hot issue, however, and in the end there was a special hearing in Auckland, which MNZ flew us all up to. I was talking to John beforehand and I explained that we just wanted the rules clarified as we wanted one rule for everyone.'

And so the lines were drawn. On one side was the clique of Superbike riders, who believed they had little hope of beating the Britten twins as things stood, and on the other were the mostly older enthusiasts, who wanted to watch them try, including Errol McCabe.

> Kevin McCleary rang me up and told me he hoped I'd be there as he couldn't make it. The road-racer guys had appealed against the decision on the grounds that the conference had behaved unconstitutionally. They just couldn't accept that they'd lost. Instead of being decisive and telling them where to go, the executive decided to discuss it with a special meeting of the conference delegates. I know it's a hard job with people sniping at you, but they should have just said, 'Nah!' Anyway I assured Kevin that there was no way I was going to miss it.
>
> When the special meeting convened at the Waipuna Lodge in Auckland, John was sat down on one side of a table with six or seven road-race people on the other. He had prepared this comprehensive submission, but Conaghan chopped him down and said there wouldn't be any new material introduced and it went directly to another vote. I was sitting beside Len Payne, who was another past President of MNZ and another lifetime member. He passed on not long after this but he was there that day to vote for John Britten. Him and quite a few others.

One of the others was Ken McIntosh, who recalled that,

> There were about twenty delegates in all and I estimate they voted two to one for the Britten. It was strange, though, to witness the intensity of the group in favour of

> the weight penalty. Robert Holden was very vocal about it and so were Don O'Connor and Dallas Rankine. These were guys who would go out of their way to help you but they also seemed to go out of their way to debunk the claims made for the Britten. They had built a Duke especially for Daytona a few years before and it hadn't worked out, and I later wondered if they resented John's later success there. I couldn't imagine what else might lie at the bottom of their really negative attitude toward the Brittens.

Immediately after the meeting, John Hepburn and John Britten were interviewed by TV3 standing next to the lodge's landscaped pool.

'With the cameras rolling, John gave me a little push toward the water,' recalled John Hepburn, 'and told me he'd hate to have to chuck me in. We both laughed about it. He'd made his point and he'd won. There was talk of a Britten Hate Club but that was crap. We didn't hate each other.'

For Ken McIntosh, however, the affair had shown both a good and a less than appealing side to competitive motorcycling in New Zealand and he wondered if John Hepburn might have been lucky not to end up in the pool.

> When I spoke at the conference against the remit I described it as a blatant attempt by a bunch of sore losers to misuse the rules to achieve something they couldn't achieve on the track. I guess that was the down side. However, the way the conference, and particularly a number of the life members of MNZ, stood up against it was magnificent. In some ways I suppose getting a life membership could be regarded as being a bit like being invited to join a private club and a good excuse for the odd piss-up. But those guys earned the honour through their contributions to the sport and were given it, in part, because the sport did not want to lose their input. In other words, they were expected to bring a certain wisdom to the table and that is exactly what they did.

With all the politicking behind them, the Team turned up at Pukekohe for the first meeting looking sharp and feeling confident. For the first time they were immaculately attired in Britten gear, and with Murray along all seemed set for a brilliant season. The first meeting brought mixed fortunes, however, and a disturbing view of the future for Loren when he crashed in practice.

> I'd asked the boys to put a 5 ¾ in rim on the back instead of the 6 in to get more side grip, but when I gassed the bike up coming out of Railway onto the back straight it high-sided me. I slid along on top of the bike and hurt my shoulder and leg, still trying to figure out what on earth had happened. Back at the pits I found out that I

> still had the 6 in rim on the back. Bob was livid about his paintwork, but I tried to stay focused and dusted myself down before we duct-taped the bike up and I went out for the first race.

The race went brilliantly for Jason, who cleared out to win by several hundred metres, but Loren found himself battling hard with Robert Holden for the second spot. To Loren's consternation, Robert seemed to have little difficulty blowing past on his Ducati down the straights.

> He was on his latest Corsa-spec machine and he had more top end than I did. That meant that I had to take him under brakes. With Robert that was never easy to do and it certainly wasn't the way to race a Britten. We swapped places for the last three laps. On the final lap he took me on the back straight again and I got him at the hairpin. He then drove out underneath me, so I came through on the ripple strip on the left-hander before the bridge. We rubbed elbows and I pushed him out wide. I knew he'd come at me again, so I went narrow on the next corner to 'shut the door' but then had to really tip the bike in going over the hill corner onto the finish straight. The bike got a big nasty slide toward the concrete wall and he came through to beat me by half a bike length.
>
> I couldn't figure out why I wasn't way out in front with Jason and decided I still couldn't have been pushing hard enough. That set the tone for the season. I didn't know then that I was down on power and the atmosphere within the Team toward me just got steadily more negative. John never got personal and always treated me like a professional, and he could see what was happening within the Team. However, he maintained a hands-off attitude and just let the situation continue. If he'd taken the lead we probably could have sorted out the problem straight away, but instead it grew steadily worse.

In the second race, Loren missed the warm-up lap and was late joining the grid because of difficulties starting his bike after a last-moment tyre change. Because he was idling up to his grid position with the clutch out when the flag dropped, he was able to roll on the power and wheel-stand right through the pack to lead at the first corner, before he was forced to button off to let his tyres warm up.

> I got comfortable with Robert about 150 m in front and with Jason in front of him. I put my head down and got within 50 m of Robert when the front began to slide. It got worse and worse, and after two laps of it I pitted to find that John had left the cap off the tyre valve and it was nearly flat.[206] We pumped it up and I headed back out and got back in the groove a lap down. Unfortunately, because I'd missed that

first sighting lap I had also missed seeing the marshals pointing out some oil on the track. Next thing I knew I was sliding along on the grass toward the barrier. Boy was I popular then. It was almost a relief when Jason also lost the front end and fell off. So we ended up with a win and a third.

By the next round at Bay Park I was really fired up. Russell Josiah got the jump on his Kawasaki ZXR, with Jason behind him. Robert was third and I was behind him. Suddenly Robert's bike seemed to blow up in front of me in a big white cloud. He was still going at full noise and I was dodging around behind him to avoid what I thought was oil, but it was water. He pulled off a few corners later and I went after the other two, but could only finish third with Jason taking the win.

In the second race my bike stopped halfway around the first lap. Someone crashed and the race was red-flagged, so I set about pushing the bike back to the pits. It was a stinking-hot day and I arrived feeling totally knackered. Unfortunately, the disc on the end of the crank that slices through the Hall Effect pick-up had cracked, so there was no ignition and that was that. Jason won the restarted race and went on to win every single race for the rest of the series.

At Manfeild we had trouble with noise, so we fitted these droopy pipe ends, which seemed to work. Guy was running surface-discharge plugs in my engine on the day that robbed three or four horsepower for some reason, so the bike was even slower.[207] My main job was to beat Russell, who was leading in the points at that stage, but my bike was almost unrideable. There was no power down low and then it would suddenly cut in on full noise. Jason and Robert took off and I diced with Russell, passing him on the last corner for second place. I beat Russell in the second race as well, but it was a struggle. Tony Rees on Andrew's old OW01 passed me under power down the front straight early in the race and I had trouble shaking him after I got him again. Robert had two DNFs that day, which helped our cause, and John was really happy, but the atmosphere in the pits was pure poison.

The atmosphere outside the pits was hardly any better, and when an opportunity to accuse the Team of cheating arose, other teams were quick to take it. The episode was driven by a series of unrelated events that seemed, to a number of Team Britten's hard-pressed competitors, to add up to a conspiracy.

The storm started to brew when they noticed an unusual fuel drum that the Team had been given at Daytona. The drum had contained a very high-octane fuel, which the Fast by Feracci Team had generously donated for the Britten Team to try. Rob Selby had actually run a machine on the dyno with the mix and found that it made no difference, and it was not used again. The drum it came in, however, made a handy container for the Number One aviation fuel the race bikes did use. Unfortunately, the 'Elf' labelling attracted suspicious attention and rumours of dark goings-on at the Britten pits began to circulate. Such suspicions were enhanced when Tim Stewart decided to add a product called Red Line Water Wetter to the coolant. The non-glycol-based additive contained a corrosion inhibitor and lowered the boiling point of the coolant, a desirable property given the heat of the day and the fact that Jason's bike had been running hot. (In fact, the problem with the bike was a leak caused by corrosion at the point where the front water spigot went into the head, a leak Tim later cured by gluing in a small piece of green metal snipped from a piece of Steinlager beer can with fast-acting Araldite. The green metal is there to this day.)

> We were pretty sure the stuff was OK as it was non-glycol, but I still had the door shut just to be sure. Suddenly, Jason tried to come in but Guy was leaning against the door. When Jason called out, Guy told him we hadn't quite finished making a few fine adjustments and he should come back in a while. The guys in the pit next door heard this and assumed we were up to no good.

Before long, the rumour that the Britten Team was pepping up their fuel illegally had swept through the pits and yet another formal complaint had been made to the steward. The fuel in the offending drum was consequently tested and found to match the aviation fuel sold at the outlet approved for the meeting, and the complaint was dismissed. Unfortunately, one of the courier companies entrusted with delivering the fuel sample to one of the two labs commissioned with the task of testing it lost the sample. Although they later found it, and the second test confirmed the first, the circus had long left town and the findings were never widely circulated. This gave rise to fresh rumours that the results had been suppressed. The episode struck yet another note of discord in a season that was rapidly being characterised by such antagonisms, and the 'them and us' attitude continued to grow in both camps.

The next round of the Championship was at the Team's home track, and John was determined that the Ruapuna meeting would be nothing less than a tour de force for Britten Motorcycles. He therefore entered three machines, the third to be ridden by Andrew Stroud, who was available on the day. Unfortunately, the conflicts between the Britten Team and leading elements among the rest of the Superbike circus continued to fester, fed now by the certainty that the V-1000 was almost impossible to beat on the track and in the Championship. It erupted again on the morning of the meeting with a protest that seriously threatened Andrew's right to race in the event, as John Hepburn explained.

> Before every race there is a riders' briefing, which is compulsory. Stroudy and I go

> back a way and I know he's always late for everything, but he didn't turn up at all. If anyone else had done it they would have been banned from competing. The unrest this caused was part of this continuing perception that the Britten Team was getting a special deal. Anyway, a hat was passed around and money was collected to put in a protest. I ended up being the muggins that took it to the steward, who told me he'd hear it after the meeting. That wasn't good enough and I insisted that it be heard straight away. In the end we had a meeting with Andrew and John on one side and Robert Holden and I on the other. Andrew was sitting there laughing at us but John was furious. The steward gave Andrew a private briefing to solve the problem, but it just reinforced this feeling that we were not all playing by the same book.
>
> Throughout the season there seemed to be two sets of rules. Shand was powerful within MNZ and I'm sure that had a lot to do with it. Also Britten Motorcycles was paid to turn up while we had to shell out for our sport out of our own pockets.[208] Effectively that meant that MNZ always wanted them to race and so they gave them special treatment, which rubbed the other teams up the wrong way. For example, we knew they had a big-bore kit but could never get their bikes measured. I'm not saying it was out to 1100, which would have been illegal, but we didn't know for sure. Every time I've won a Championship my bike has been stripped down and checked, and I prefer it that way. But the Brittens were never checked.[209]

With the drama of the missed riders' briefing played out, all was in order for a Britten field day. John was confident Andrew would win both races, and when Tim Stewart backed Jason he was quick to accept a bet on the outcome.

> I had a lot of faith in Jason, and I was also confident that we had a good set-up and a great engine. I told John I'd put up a hundred bucks that Jason would beat Andrew and he was quick to shake on it. The boys all told me I'd never see it even if Jason came through, but I expected him to make good. I knew I'd have to pay him if it went the wrong way.

Loren's dismal season remained true to form and he complained that his bike was now even further down on power.

> I was placed fourth place on the grid behind Russell, Jason and Robert. Andrew hadn't raced that season, so he was right at the back. When we hit the main straight two bikes went straight past. Again I thought I couldn't be going hard enough out of the corners. I really cracked it on and got back behind Russell. The second right-hander is a big, looping corner and I almost took him, but he was tight so I hung back. Then Andrew turned up and took me, so I followed him into the dipper. When I gassed it

> up on the exit, the bike high-sided me and down I went with the bike coming to rest on its side minus the rear brake lever and a foot-peg. I picked it up and was so pissed off I did a wheel-stand the length of the front straight with my foot on the swing-arm. Then I passed a couple of stragglers and thought I might as well keep going. In the end, I climbed back up to seventh and it was just as well that I did. The two points I collected ultimately secured me third place in the Championship behind Jason and Russell.

While all this was going on Jason was locked into an epic battle with Robert Holden for the lead.

'Robert had to win here to have a chance of taking the Championship,' recalled Jason. 'I'd nearly caught up with him in the points and if I won both races I'd take it. He didn't often fall off, but he was prepared to push to the very limit if he had to. I was trying really hard, and in the end he crashed heavily and Andrew came in second behind me.'

Back in the pits, Robert limped over to consult with Russell Josiah. It was time to enlist some support and talk tactics.

'Robert told me that we had to stop the Brittens scoring a trifecta in the next race,' recalled Russell, 'and I agreed that it was all or nothing. We were going to have to go all out.'

Loren also became involved in a post-mortem back in the pits before setting off once more.

> Bob was giving me berries about his paintwork again. He told me if I crashed again I was finished. I had serious bruising from the crash and I went out for the next race with a hurt body and hurt pride. I got in behind Jason, Robert and Andrew, and then Robert crashed again. I was only really going through the motions because by then I was convinced something was wrong with the bike and I wasn't going to push to make up for it. Then Russell steamed past me on the back straight and crashed a couple of corners later in front of me. So after all the carnage we ended up finishing first, second and third.

Back on the side of the track, Russell was left ruefully examining his torn-up leathers and smacked-about Kawasaki.

> When I took Loren I thought he'd stay right up my chuff, so I pushed on hard. Then I overcooked it and the bike let go. I bounced off the track and while I was flying through the air I saw that Loren had actually fallen well back. I just had time to think what a bastard it all was before I landed again with a big thump that knocked the

> wind out of me and bruised me all over the place. I picked myself up and Robert came over, limping worse than ever. His leathers were also all torn up and he was bleeding. He was really pissed off. 'Why did you have to go and fall off you silly bugger?' he said. 'You had the bastard!'

The second win secured the Championship for Jason and for Britten Motorcycles. Afterwards, he had nothing but praise for the support he had enjoyed from the Team and from John. For him, the dissension pulling the Team apart was nothing but background static. Such is the power of winning.

'I'd had an excellent season,' he said. 'Tim was a brilliant spannerman and we communicated easily. If I wanted something done he'd understand what it was and do it. Bob was really good to me, too, and I enjoyed it when John was around. He had a tendency to spin a bit in the pits but he kept it under control and I found him really positive.'

After the race the bikes were all put on the dyno back at the workshop and it was immediately apparent to Loren why he had experienced such a disappointing season.

> John didn't like doing dyno testing during the season as it was hard on the bikes, so I'd had to wait until it was over to confirm my suspicions. But it was even worse than I'd imagined. Jason's bike was making 150 bhp and Andrew's 152 bhp. Mine was down at 142 bhp. On the second run my engine dropped a valve and lunched the engine. All in all, it was one of the most miserable periods in my life and it should have been one of the best.

With the Championship safely tucked away, the Team looked forward to a big celebration at the prize-giving. For most of the evening it was just that, and Tim was pleased when in addition to settling the NZ$100 bet John had lost to him he also presented him with a bottle of champagne. However, the evening was blighted by a nasty and destructive conclusion.

The situation had its origins in a tax audit that had been visited on Brittco some weeks previously, and the unpleasant episode that unfurled was the forerunner of a number of future situations that closely resembled it in several particulars—all involving expectations, agreements and money.

If Broz had ever regarded his part at Britten Motorcycles as being a career move, or even a proper job, he had long since been disillusioned. On the contrary, the only way to accommodate his experience within the company and to remain motivated was to view the project as belonging to a collective of individuals who contributed every bit as much as John. Within such a dynamic Broz did not follow

John's dreams so much as share them—he was not a servant; he was a partner in a splendid adventure. If John was sufficiently well-heeled to slip Broz a bit of survival money, then he was entitled, Broz conceded, to put his name on the project.

After the first year of hanging about on call when he had received nothing, Broz had been paid a modest hourly rate in cash during the years he had worked for Britten Motorcycles, although there were thousands of hours of unpaid overtime for which he never received a cent. Basically, Broz regarded the money as having been slipped to him under the table, a modest stipend to pay his out-of-pocket expenses and keep him afloat. He also believed that his annual 'wage' was actually below the minimum tax threshold; certainly he did not believe that John expected him to survive on what he earned minus income tax.

Unknown to Broz, however, John had kept a careful note of all the payments, and when Tim Corcoran came across the box containing all the slips of paper recording them he did not hesitate to claim the tax write-off for wages paid. At the time, the Inland Revenue Department was auditing Brittco and there were, as stated earlier, some suspicions that Broz had been flung to the wolves as a sacrifice. Whatever the circumstances may have been, Broz suddenly found himself summonsed to the IRD's offices in Christchurch, where he was 'put through the third degree by officers who clearly knew all there was to know.' The first interview was but a precursor to what was to follow, and by the time they were done with him Broz had acquired a file of paper over an inch thick along with a tax bill of some NZ$27,000. Facing the loss of everything he owned Broz asked John to help him, but John backed Tim Corcoran, who maintained it was entirely Broz's problem. It did not help matters that John picked up his brand-new TVR sports car the same day that Broz was finally told he was on his own.

A Team photograph, snapped on the afternoon after the three Brittens had taken the podium places at Ruapuna along with the Championship, shows Broz standing proudly in the line-up in his Britten t-shirt. Within a couple of hours of it having been taken, however, he had been fired.

It was an uncomfortable situation for everyone, as Quentin recalled.

> Broz had a skinful and wanted to take John on about the tax thing. Then Kirsteen put her oar in and when Broz told her to butt out she threw a huge wobbly, so that John felt he had no choice but to fire Broz on the spot. Broz had been a big part of it for a very long time, but he hadn't really had much credit and I think that was chewing away at him. Loren was the opposite. He knew how to claim his dues and he was pretty cunning at making sure they came his way, while Broz just got frustrated. But the tax money was at the bottom of it and I think John felt guilty about it. Even though he had fired Broz he didn't seem to want to accept it had happened

> and Broz continued to go to work. I think both he and John wanted to make everything right again, the way it had been, but Kirsteen remained insistent that Broz had to go. John discussed it with all of us, which we didn't like. We felt it was his call.

At least one idea came out of the consultations, however, when John took up a suggestion that he make Broz's renewed employment conditional on him seeking psychiatric treatment. If the idea had been calculated to offend Broz it could not have succeeded better, and when the idea was put it to him in a letter he finally stopped showing up for work.

In a letter he had once written to the Netherlands Ducati Club, John had described Broz as 'the Britten mechanic and engineer, a man who can make anything and everything and do a superb job of it'. It was scarcely surprising therefore that he was still reluctant to accept that Broz had really left, and he made his way round to Broz's flat with CJ to talk the matter through. But once in the presence of his old friend, John seemed to fall into his old state of awkward silence and the opportunity to resolve the situation was lost.

'John just sat and said nothing while CJ did all the talking,' said Broz. 'I told them I wasn't interested and they left.'

In the end, Broz was given two months' severance pay and an extra month's wages after refusing to do outwork for either Britten Motorcycles or Cathedral Junction.

It was a sad sundering for such a long and profound association, doubly so because in the end there would scarcely be time to mend the tear, even with the best will in the world, which there was not.

John decided to wind up the season further north by contesting the road races at Wanganui and Paeroa with just a single bike. Jason easily won the street races at the Cemetery Circuit in Wanganui but then decided against racing at Paeroa. For the moment he had had enough of dangerous street circuits and he regarded Paeroa, which boasted longer straights and faster corners than Wanganui, as being more hazardous than most. Andrew was then offered and accepted the ride, but when he had to rush off to the UK to test for a Grand Prix team John turned to Loren.

> John warned me against crashing and I got the distinct impression that Bob would go ballistic if I wrecked his paint again. I got Jason's bike for the event and the extra power was a revelation. So was the way the bike handled—it was so hard. Jason's front-end set-up almost bounced me out of the seat, so I had Tim dial in more trail until it felt good to me. Paeroa was the biggest meeting of the season, with 15,000 spectators, and I was so nervous before the race I got diarrhoea. I knew it would be the only chance I'd get to make up for the terrible season I'd just been through—the only

> opportunity I'd get to show that I could handle a Britten.
>
> In the first race I was fourth into the first corner and then I just picked off the guys in front one by one. I didn't need to indulge in any heroics around the corners and I took most of them comfortably on the straights. I'll never forget the way I just opened the taps to blow past Russell and I kept wishing I'd had the power during the New Zealand series. I got out in front and then cruised off into the distance. Although Robert wasn't there I still felt I'd made my point when I won by miles. In the second race I also torched everyone. It felt like a total vindication.

And so the season ended with two convincing victories to add to the 1994 New Zealand Superbike Championship and Jason's dominance in Wanganui, underscoring what was now patently obvious to all that followed motorcycle racing in New Zealand. Barring accidents or bad management there was no combination of rider or machinery that could get near a well-ridden, well-sorted Britten.

CHAPTER TWENTY

The Fraternity

Although John had promised Kirsteen that he would no longer race, he had specifically excluded classic motorcycle racing and racing anything with four wheels. He had ordered a 5-litre TVR Griffith through his friend Paul Pannel, who was by then the New Zealand agent for the English car-maker, but had not been content simply to await its arrival. Instead, he had flown off to England to spend time with the builders, many of whom became firm friends. For some reason John assured Paul that the car was more or less standard, but when Paul received vague but substantial invoices for additional work he suspected John was being economical with the truth. When, as was his right as the company's agent, Paul eventually picked the car up from the wharf, his suspicions were soon confirmed.

'I fired it up and it went weeeeeeoowh!' he said. 'It was unbelievably rapid.'

On the day that John took delivery he ended his first drive in a ditch. The Team was amused to note his somewhat sheepish expression as they arrived to find him completing repairs to the car's fibreglass body, which was still wearing dealer's plates, after an all-night session in the workshop. As they arrived they were all roped in to help, and it was soon understood by all concerned that John had no wish for his escapade to become known domestically.

Kit Ebbett was taken for a 'quick flick' in the TVR and had good reason to remember the experience.

> We roared around the streets of Riccarton and Fendalton at speeds well in excess of 100 mph. When we got back to the house a couple of guys from the Team were waiting for him. They'd been waiting for half an hour but decided to hang on because they could hear the car circling in the distance and knew we would soon return.

It would not be long before John had the car out on the track but in the meantime he had an opportunity to indulge his enthusiasm for classic racing motorcycles.

His promise to race only historic motorcycles was somewhat hollow, because classic racing is not some slow version of the real thing. Former World Champion Hugh Anderson, for example, was still recovering from the effects of crashing a Ducati 900 SS into the concrete wall skirting the high-speed right-hander that led onto the front straight at Pukekohe.

Historic race meetings were social get-togethers like most race meetings, but they were, like all race meetings, about racing more than anything else. John must have suspected that his much-used Triumph would undoubtedly inflict sorrow and pain sooner or later—probably the reason he had left it in several parts in the dark. However, you can only keep a sporting motorcyclist down for so long.

The opportunity for John to go racing again came with a personal invitation from Ken McIntosh to attend the annual Classic Motorcycle Festival at Pukekohe, just outside Auckland.

'John and I both attended the Rodger Freeth Memorial Dinner some months before the Classic Register meeting,' Ken recalled, 'and when he told me that he missed racing his old Triumph I suggested he bring one of his machines to our next meeting.'

Although John was aware that the invitation carried with it the promise of a ride on practically anything that caught his fancy, and he was happy to have Andrew Stroud ride a Britten at the meeting, he was initially lukewarm about the idea of attending himself. However, Bob Brookland, who was taking his 1917 Indian flat-tracker north for the event, finally persuaded him to attend and they met up with Andrew at the track. In the end, it was a brilliant meeting for everyone and Bob was delighted to see John enjoying a weekend that he later described as one of the best times of his life.

When John had started racing motorcycles one of the things that had most attracted him to the sport was the easy camaraderie that usually existed between competitors. (This was not to say that the occasional clash while racing was not carried on at the side of the track or back in the pits. Typical of such episodes was one when two riders had crashed because one had been trying too hard, and the wronged party complained that he would have thumped the other party except the other party was already in so much pain he couldn't bring himself to do it.) However, as is always the case when enthusiasts gather, there were different levels of acceptance.

In the beginning, John had fought hard and lived dangerously to win acceptance within club racing as 'Sack of Shit' Britten, the eccentric on the Tiger. He had then fought equally hard, and with just as much risk to life and limb, to win a place among the fraternity of hard and serious motorcycle racers. Now he was an internationally recognised constructor and he was back with the people who had first attracted him to motorcycles—the passionate enthusiasts who had always been at the heart of it.

With the sun warming his back and the aroma of Castrol R and freshly mown grass in the air, and with the smiles of all around him to warm his heart, everything for once was well with John's world. All the gnawing doubts about the amount of time and effort he had invested in what can so easily turn into the cruellest of sports were for once allayed. It was time simply to relax, have fun and enjoy the love and respect of his fraternity.

And it was a fun time, as Bob Brookland recalled, albeit marked by some disappointment.

> John was absolutely blown away by the goodwill of people. All weekend they were giving him different bikes to ride in every race and he became his old self. I was absolutely flat out on the Indian, doing about 95 mph through the dog-leg on the back straight, when I felt a tap on my shoulder. It was Johnny with a huge grin on his face. He rode about five different bikes and he was giving away rides on the Britten. Unfortunately, when it was Ken McIntosh's turn it blew up underneath him.[210] That was a real bastard because it was my turn next and I still haven't ridden one. John got on the cell phone straight away, and the factory just managed to catch the last overnight truck coming up and they squeezed another bike across the very back of the load. John said that people had paid money to see a Britten demo and they were going to get it.

As it had been Ken McIntosh who first suggested that John attend the classic meeting, it was somewhat ironic that the V-1000 had decided to blow up while he was astride it. However, the machine stayed together long enough for Ken to get a real taste of what riding a Britten V-1000 was all about.

> When John let me have a crack on the Britten it was a real high point in my riding career. I expected a quick ride, but unless you have experienced a Britten first hand it is impossible to understand just how fast they are. It was blindingly, staggeringly quick. I had four laps before it blew and the thing that really impressed me, apart from its sheer speed, was the steering. If I had somehow not known about the front end I would not have twigged that it wasn't equipped with forks. It was that good. The other thing I loved was the handling. I let it find its own way over the hump onto pit straight and then wound it on, and it felt utterly stable. I had it flat knacker in fourth, so I was up to between 140 and 150 mph and it felt absolutely relaxed.
>
> Among other things, John rode a Vincent during the meeting that belonged to a customer of ours. As it had hardly been ridden, following a complete restoration,

> the girder front end was not set up at all well. After John's ride the owner, Ian Neilson, asked how he'd liked it and John told him the front end had a lot of promise. I had a laugh with Ian about that later. I told him that anyone other than John Britten would have told him it was a load of crap!

After the weekend, Ken contacted John and asked him to write a review of the meeting for the *Register*, the official organ of the Classic Motorcycle Association. 'I hounded him to do it,' said Ken, 'and John finally agreed. He wrote it out longhand on a flight to the States and the piece wound up being the editorial in the March/April issue.'

Entitled 'Britten's Pukekohe', the piece was probably the only occasion John ever recorded a general account of an event of any kind, and his words offered an interesting insight into both his mood at the time and his attitude toward his chosen sport.

> Great weekend away from it all, a chance to relax. That's a very rare opportunity. Polished from head to tyre a Vincent awaits its first ever lap. The owner asked me to run it in. He doesn't even know me. I don't even know his name but his face is full of kindness and trust—all those old fashioned virtues that seem to be as scarce as hen's teeth, especially, I'm afraid to say, at the modern motor racing championship that my Britten has just completed.
>
> In 1976 I bought a 1946 Tiger 100 for three hundred dollars and raced it in Classics for ten years. 'Any Old Iron' I called it. The poor man's motorcycle. So my perspective of the weekend is from a lover of classics but one who never made the quality machinery division.
>
> Ken McIntosh has certainly got the same golden heart as Ian [Neilson]. He works like me—around the clock. As if it's not hard enough to build classic bikes for a living and bring a gaggle of them out to a race meeting for friends and customers to ride he's got to organise the biggest classic meeting ever held in New Zealand. I'm standing like a one-legged tap dancer practicing tapping my foot up and down. No trouble—just the reverse change pattern to the Britten V-1000, with the right foot, not the left. I'm the type who always pulls the 'push' door and pushes the 'pull' door—so I'm a bit apprehensive. All that foot tapping and the thought of doing it wrong to any of Ken's precious bikes sends my bladder into panic mode and I'm back to the urinal again.
>
> I'm now having so much fun on Ken's bike (one of his Manx Norton replicas) that I offer him a ride on the Britten V-1000 that has been sent up from Christchurch to frighten fearless motorcyclers later in the programme. Ken's away, quickly settling in. After you get over the fear of 160 odd hp, you quickly realise the bike's as friendly

as a little 250, doing exactly what you want with no effort. The white flag comes out. I know Ken will enjoy it, it's closely related to his passion—big bore, high torque engineering. It's a sort of classic of the future.

Someone had to be the first to experience it. The totally fail proof bottom end just lasts forever. We run the titanium forged rods I bought in '87. They've got an unlimited life…so the story used to go. Luckily we use a sprag clutch so on this lock up the rear wheel still turns. This made things less frightening for Ken at speed at the kink on the back straight when that big end ended.

During the day I raced the following bikes. 1—a Vincent Comet 500, 2—a 1937 Manx 500, 3—an AJS 7R3, 4—a Norton 250 Manx, 5—a Norton 1962 Manx 500 and 6—a BSA 1971 works replica Rocket 3.

Yes, a once in a lifetime experience—if you're lucky. To savour the history, the character and the performance of these bikes that influenced motorcycle history. I will be forever grateful to the owners for this opportunity.

The Comet was smooth and hard in the chassis. It could be ridden very hard without handling limitations, that is after the carb is set up to get the mono making power. Even with the carb right I think it will lack torque. Perhaps a bit of hotting up is required. But it is very rideable and smooth at speed. The sex appeal of the all silver machine is unbeaten in my opinion.

Then the 1937 Norton Manx 500—very special—Ken warned me – 'You'll have more fun on this than anything.' At my level of riding it's easier to reach the limit of a bike's performance when there are handling inadequacies inherent in the bike's frame and suspension, before tyre adhesion becomes a problem. The '37 had instant power and much more than you would expect but the factor governing speed was chassis flex. Not in an uncomfortable way at all, more just a friendly low frequency wallow. The wallow seems about ten percent under the adhesion limit and works like a safety warning system. That made it fun. It's always good to outperform many bikes in the field on the oldest one.

Bike 3. It's the supreme honour to ride the AJS 7R of Rod Coleman's. This time I even had Ken McIntosh gritting his teeth with envy. It was a very exciting experience. I would travel a long way to gaze at this bike. I expected to see a little, hand painted sign saying 'Do not touch—Please keep behind the ropes.' To sit on it, to race was such a privilege. I decided to ride it as hard as if it was my own bike (well almost) as I really yearned to know just how good it could be. Taking off from the grid as the flag dropped I was the meanest I've ever been on a clutch in my life, including when I got my wife's car stuck in a riverbed.

Having tried unsuccessfully to get it rolling in the pits and having Rod's instructions not to let it drop under 8000 on the line, I did what was necessary. I just stared at the rev counter and kept the throttle at MAX and accurately feathered the clutch to keep it between 8000 and 8500. I soon caught the field up, the people with normal engines. Once rolling the 7R3 handled beautifully—smooth, small and very well behaved. With extensive carb work and a look at the ports or timing to find where the low down and mid racing torque is hiding, Rod would have not only one of the most beautiful bikes in the world, but one of the nicest to ride as well.

Number 4 was the rarest bike—there's only one. It's owned by a gentleman named Brian Thomas. If I could make a wish I'd wish that Brian could come and work at the Britten workshop. There is no engineer in New Zealand that could hold a candle to him in the 'do it yourself' stakes, from the foundry pattern to the track. It's a long distance with a lot of stumbling blocks.

I've got his 250 'scaled' (500-style) Manx Desmo singing through the field. The tiny engine feels to be working at maximum torque. Not loaded up and not ranging out. It feels strong. I glance at the rev counter whilst whistling past a couple of bikes—10,500 rpm—expletive deleted! I wonder how Brian can make that Manx nightmare of a Desmo do this reliably. If only the factory had known then the history books could well read differently. I'm six foot one but I didn't feel uncomfortable at all on these scaled motorcycles. Many thanks Brian.

Number 5. The classic of classics. I've often thought that if I could trade my Triumph in on a proper classic it would be a late Norton 500 Manx. That's fourty [*sic*] thousand dollars less three hundred dollars equals thirty nine thousand and seven hundred dollars. I'll think about it. Thanks to owner Billy Apple I get my first ride. Yes, the motorcycle world opinion isn't wrong. It's a beautiful bike that does everything as perfectly as you would ever want in a classic. But my smile was bigger on the '37 Manx.

Lucky last. The people at this meeting are so happy and kind. I've even got Warren Barry offering me a ride on his bike. This one's got disc brakes, well sort of. It's also called a Rocket. And a rocket it is. Another name for it would be 'missile'. It's made for someone who rides fast and in a more modern style. It's so modern it even patters at the front end. It handled like a mid '80s 600 Pantah Ducati. The sound I love. Once I read a journalist's description of the sound of a Lamborghini V12 at high revs sounding like 'tearing a sheet'. This is the motorcycle equivalent.

After Andrew completed his demonstration on the Britten V-1000 there was a standing ovation from the wonderful audience. Classic lovers with open minds, happy to enjoy the sight of modern machinery and rider. Andrew is a maestro. One of the greatest riders in the world. I believe. I stood beside him and said, as the clapping continued, 'Even if you become world champion one day I bet you won't ever be appreciated as warmly as these people appreciate you today.' If you weren't there you missed one of the best displays of balance and skill ever demonstrated on a motor cycle. It filled my stomach and heart with pride. Pride in Andrew, pride in my

> machine, pride in the people who helped me to put it together. Lastly pride in my fellow motorcyclists with whom I felt so comfortable having my weekend off.
> P.S. There's a rumour going around that I was beaten by an 83-year-old. It's true. Only a bike length separated Robert Holden—first, Len Perry—second and me—third in a handicap race. Len should be an inspiration to others who think they are old. He is still riding fast. Long may we all.

Brian Thomas, the man who had constructed from scratch the 250cc scaled-down desmo-headed Manx that John had so enjoyed racing, was a spry and gentlemanly senior citizen who went on to construct a number of other such machines.[211] He recalled that his first bike had only really completed a limited test programme at Manfeild before he gave it to John to ride at the Classic Festival.

> We had run it around the track at Manfeild at a couple of thousand revs, and when it didn't go pop we did another lap at 2500 rpm. Gradually, we worked our way up to just over 8000 rpm and decided to pencil in the red line at that. When I gave the bike to John up at Pukekohe he asked how high he could rev it and I told him to use his judgement. After his race I asked how he'd found it and he told me it was still pulling really well at 10,500. So we kind of rubbed out the old red line and drew in a new one. I saw him quite often after that. On more than one occasion I received a phone call from him while I was at home in Feilding—usually at about six in the morning—to warn me that he was coming to visit. I'd ask where he was and he'd tell me he was on his way up my driveway. I didn't mind. He really was a splendid fellow and I was always glad to see him.

The Pukekohe weekend ended with a free-for-all dash around the track by all who wanted to join in, with the crowd being told that 'as long as you have a bike, a helmet and a pair of boots you can have a go'. It proved a somewhat reckless invitation. Bob Brookland and John were reduced to hysterical, knee-buckling laughter at the sight of a large man flying along on his old 'Pom bomb', cellulite flapping in the breeze, clad only in the requisite helmet and boots.

CHAPTER TWENTY-ONE

Final Lap

Back at the Britten workshop, the effort to develop the machines continued. The third breakthrough in improving the handling occurred after Loren closely examined a photograph of Robert crashing at Ruapuna with Jason and Andrew immediately behind him.

> I could see that the back wheel on Jason's bike was at a strange angle. I had been puzzled ever since my bike had spat me off under power, as I was used to being able to power-slide sideways out of corners on the Kawasaki. In fact, everyone who'd ridden a Britten had complained about how hard to slide the bikes were. Now it seemed we might have an answer. We knew the later swing-arms had less material in them than the early ones John made, part of the never-ending quest to reduce weight, and wondered if they were flexing.

In fact, Murray was already looking at the problem with Tim, part of the secret development programme the two were working on. Tim recalled that the collaboration actually began when Murray mentioned how handy it would be to have jigs to measure the torsional rigidity of various parts of the bike as well as the whole machine..

> I told him to make me some sketches and that I would then build whatever he wanted. The first thing he wanted to check was the swingarm, so I built a jig and we measured the degree of flex under load. Murray then sent the results to Mike Sinclair, who was so surprised at the figures he advised us to check the jig. He said that if the results were accurate we had 'one floppy swing-arm'. We knew that the rubbery swing-arms probably helped to get the power down when driving out of a corner, but we also knew it would cause problems down the track. They had to be fixed and Murray came up with a redesign to solve the problem. We then carried on and tested the

> girders. Rider feedback from the Isle of Man had suggested that the girders were in fact too rigid, so Murray decided to change the design to introduce a little side flex. He proposed to do this by altering the proportions of carbon-fibre and Kevlar and by changing the arrangement of the skeleton somewhat. He also wanted the girders to be a little thinner.

John seldom visited the workshop any more and in many ways the Team began to thrive, as they became confident in their own abilities to take initiatives and make improvements. This new confidence was soon expressed when Jason Monopoli and Murray set up a meeting with John to talk about building new swing-arms and girders. Jason recalled:

> Murray and I told him we had a plan to build better ones but he vetoed the idea. We decided to do it anyway. In two days we were able to produce a swing-arm that was lighter and stronger than the old ones and it didn't crack up. I think the total cash outlay developing it was about NZ$100. We then made the new girders and we were able to put both the new girders and the new swing-arms on the bikes being refurbished and finished.

Shaun and Jason also looked carefully at the way the company identified itself, as Shaun recalled.

> We considered that the Britten Motorcycle Company was swamped in logos and that none of them were really as good as they should be. First of all there is John's signature, which appeared on the bike's tank. It's actually his sister Dorenda's signature, which John appropriated. He could never remember how it went, and when he was asked to autograph something he'd have to stop and think, but writing was never his strong suit. Then there's the big 'V' symbol, the Britten 'Swish' and the Kiwi 'B'. Different typefaces saying Britten appear all over the bike. Most manufacturers would be content to proclaim their name once, but he said it on the tank, the engine, the wheels, the girder suspension, the muffler and the swing-arm. We wanted to clean the whole lot up and he agreed. For some reason, however, he hired someone outside the company and then changed their design to italics. Italics are not good on a vehicle because from one direction they always end up looking as if they are leaning backwards. We couldn't figure out why he wouldn't let us loose on the thing but he may have wanted to remind us that there were other designers out there. There was plenty to do so we just shrugged it off.
>
> John still occasionally came to us with an idea he wanted us to develop. Some were really clever and some were frankly loony. One of the latter arose out of a prob-

lem we were having with conrods splitting. The drop-forged titanium Jet rods we had used went out of production because the Indy engine they were used in became obsolete. We could have bought some but only by placing a minimum order for about 200. John felt that was prohibitively expensive, so we bought over-length rods and Jet modified them for us.[212]

John had an idea that we should make some rods out of carbon-fibre and he made up a jig to do it. We couldn't for the life of us work out how the big ends could be bolted together or how we could torque them up even if we could work out some arrangement. However, the idea was tried.

Tim Stewart was roped in to make up the jig and he remembered the episode with some amusement.

The good thing about the carbon-fibre conrod was that we were pretty sure it wouldn't work. We weren't 100 percent sure because you never could be, even with Johnny's most out-of-it ideas. But we were reasonably sure and that meant we wouldn't waste a lot of time on it. What would hurt would be to spend eight days making up a set of headers for a bike, only to have Johnny wander in and hacksaw it in half because he wanted to try something. He did that to me once because he was dying to try a splitter in the exhaust that some drunken Irishman had told him about in a pub at the TT. Gobs of free extra horsepower just shouting to be released and so on. For some reason we couldn't put it in a vice and we couldn't find any vicegrips, but he told me to go ahead and weld it while he held it. I told him I'd burn him but he was so impatient he insisted, so I welded while his hands blistered. It didn't make any difference when we tried it out on the dyno but he had to try. Anyway, when he made the conrod with his skin and bones method he bent the rovings over in the same way he had with the lower wishbone that collapsed on Chris Haldane. Murray had told him then that it was not the way to go with carbon-fibre and he told him again this time, but Johnny had to do it that way to avoid ending up with a shape like a pyramid. We all gathered around as it was spun up in the jig, and the thing was creaking and groaning and zinging like a banshee. A rod at full noise might grow by a thousandth of an inch but this baby stretched about a quarter-inch. It was pretty funny and even Johnny had a little smile on his face. We shut it down before it failed completely. It was crazy but he had to try it. It was great working with him on things like that but if we saw him pick up a spanner we'd do our best to get it off him. If he was undoing a nut his mind would be on why whatever it was we were fixing had failed and what needed to be done rather than the nut. Suddenly, the head on the nut would be rounded and a two-hour job had just escalated to an all-night session.

Meanwhile, dynamometer testing of the new engines had revealed a new problem, as they would, in Loren's words, 'hoick up great gobs of oil and spit them out the oil breather. It was a strange problem in so far as it only affected the new engines, and we had lots of trouble solving it.'[213]

By now Tim and Murray had embarked on their mission to chase the gremlins out of the Britten engine, and they suspected that the oil was being expelled primarily by compression blow-by. They believed this was a consequence of the sloppy clearances that had been adopted to prevent the partial seizures that had plagued the Team in the past. As the pair proceeded, Tim began to appreciate further the difficulties the Team had always laboured under, one of the main ones being the lack of a second test motor, against which they could do comparative testing.

> The fact that we could not test something new against a benchmark was always a problem and so was the general lack of parts. When we ordered something it was always just enough for our immediate needs. We ordered pistons by the pair, for example; something that was bound to make us a low priority for Omega and gave us no leeway for mishaps. However, when the next set did arrive it was clear Fred had made some changes and I couldn't wait to try them. I also remember that as John held them I could almost hear him thinking that he could have bought a decent car or something for the same money. However, they worked well and we more or less halved the piston clearances without any problems, although I always allowed a bit more for faster tracks like Daytona. This was because the more open throttle tracks always resulted in the pistons growing a little more as the heat was retained.

The pair spent more and more of their sleep time in the dyno room, running up engines as they tried different set-ups. They were careful to ensure that no one knew what they were up to and would beaver away on other things until everybody else had left the building. It was a curious way to work, and later the pair would win John's confidence to the point where such subterfuge became completely unnecessary. For the time being, however, they had to behave like a couple of spies, a reality Tim was prepared to live with.

> Johnny didn't like testing that much because he felt it wore stuff out and he was the one who had to pay for it. He was right, of course, but the reason he had people like Murray and me was because we were driven by a curiosity to go further. Otherwise neither of us would have been there working for NZ$9 an hour. And there were others besides Johnny who might have been a problem had they known what we were up to. For example, Rob had his own theories and ideas that he wanted to try. With more time I would like to have looked at them, but Murray and I had to stay on a

really tight track so we kept it from him. And there were others who would have, quite naturally, wanted to know exactly what it was we were looking to achieve with each step we took. The reality was that often we were just looking for a direction. So much in race-engine development is trial and error, and that was well demonstrated when we tried a couple of old pistons. We were doing cam-timing comparisons and we cracked a piston. We didn't have any more spares other than a couple of old flat, top jobs out of the original 1100. We weren't worried about the compression for the work we were doing, so I turned them down and machined in the valve pockets. The following night I stuck them in the engine and suddenly we had another 3 hp showing on the dyno at peak revs. This was exciting so we immediately welded up the sides of the combustion chambers to get the compression back, and after machining the heads up found the engine had more power in the mid-range as well. It was a big improvement, and riders who tried the new set-up soon after said their bikes had been transformed into jets.

I was also curious about the appetite V-1000's had for exhaust valves. Murray and I suspected it was a resonance problem so I was measuring the thickness of the casting and so on to see if we could perhaps put in a little extra metal and cure it. To be honest we were not getting too far when I realised that one particular bike hadn't munched a valve for quite a while so I stripped it to see if I could find out why that was so. I discovered that someone, and it might have been me, had inserted an inlet-valve guide instead of the exhaust guide by mistake. The inlet guide is longer than the exhaust guide and it had obviously suppressed the problem resonance. All this was great news and when we told John he was really chuffed. We started getting customer's engines back and mowing off the tops of pistons, welding up combustion chambers and putting inlet guides with the exhaust valves. We found we could do test sessions of hundreds of laps at Ruapuna without problems.

The greatly improved engine reliability gave John confidence to invite Ken Nemoto, the president of the prestigious Japanese publication *Riders Club*, to travel to New Zealand to try his hand on a Britten. Ken's magazine, which published a great deal of Alan Cathcart's work, had long been a supporter of Britten Motorcycles, and the former All Japan 250 Champion accepted the invitation with alacrity, promising an extensive coverage of the test in the July 1995 issue of his magazine.

Murray and Tim accompanied Ken to Ruapuna, and Ken duly donned his leathers and took the bike out for a few quiet laps. Tim remembered that he and Murray were somewhat surprised that a man who was clearly in his mid-sixties would want to take on something as powerful as a Britten, but they were confident he could manage at the somewhat pedestrian pace he was running.

> He puttered around for a few laps and then came in to make some changes. I think he wanted the throttle position altered slightly and a few other minor things. Once that was done he went out again, and boy did he show us a thing or two. He was one of the smoothest riders I have ever seen on a Britten and he was right on the pace. Very soon he was getting around in times that were only just below Andrew's lap record and he made it look so effortless. They had a small team to do the assignment, including a photographer, and when the July issue came out they had dedicated pages and pages to the story with the most stunning photographs. It was great.

The refinements to the engine were achieved without a major mishap on the dyno, but this was about to change. Fortunately, Tim was testing an engine with Hans Weekers when it all went wrong, and there was little anyone could say.

> Hans had come down from Auckland to try a pair of heads he had been flowing and we'd set them up on a bike in the dyno. When testing you always ran the engine up to thirteen grand after warming it up and pulled in the clutch the precise moment it got there. There was a green light wired into the system that let you know the moment the engine was doing it and the dyno would then measure the friction in the system while the big wheel rolled on. Once that was established subsequent readings could be corrected. I was poised to pull in the clutch when I saw a shaft of metal rise up out of the front injection trumpet. Although everything happened in a fraction of a second, Hans and I made eye contact and in that moment we exchanged a whole heap of information, most of which could be summed up by the words "What the…". I hauled in the clutch a microsecond before the green light came on and we watched in stupefied amazement as the metal sliver sank back down into the trumpet, and then it all came to grief with a god-awful bang. Everything was dead quiet again before we had really registered what had happened. The next day Johnny had a look at the wreck and wailed, "I just don't believe it." And it was wrecked. The front rod had split up the oil gallery like a banana and pounded the piston into the head, while the rear rod had snapped off under its piston, bent over backwards and jammed itself into the gearbox, smashing everything up as it went. It happened because the Jet rods had done about 1000 hours, which was probably about 960 more than they were supposed to do. But they were all we had.

Generally, things at Britten Motorcycles were on the up and up. When the Museum of New Zealand Te Papa Tongarewa enquired about the possibilities of purchasing a Britten for public display, Loren was able to secure the best price yet—NZ$175,000.

The museum wanted a machine with history, and so it was agreed that they would get the bike that had won the New Zealand Grand Prix Championship. Unfortunately, at the time that particular machine had the only reliable engine in the Britten stable, so the bike they actually received was an amalgam of parts, although it was the correct bodywork. Of course, a lot of parts switching and swapping always went on and soon after the delivery it would have been impossible to reassemble the bike the museum thought they had.

In the meantime, the secret nocturnal development continued and Murray and Tim turned their attention to such matters as the cooling systems.

> We found the cooling system was cavitating, but soon sorted it and any tendency to overheat was cured. As time went by we looked at everything. We came up with a better boombox for the exhaust and then we turned our attention to the air-box. We knew the air-box was pretty useless and we wanted to build a much bigger one that could seal properly. The bikes had way too much fuel capacity for sprint races, so we wanted to build an alternative set-up that sacrificed fuel space for air-space. Murray was also looking carefully at the whole front-end set-up and soon we were testing all sorts of refinements. Whenever Mike Sinclair was in town he and Murray would disappear upstairs and go through all sorts of stuff together, looking at results from our testing in the various jigs we eventually made up, coming up with solutions to all sorts of problems. They were both really interested in the front end and both were really keen to eliminate the collywobbles. Eventually, Murray would redesign the thing altogether, but that was a little further down the track.

With the bikes delivering better handling and increased reliability, and, with an evolving maintenance and race-management programme, the dark days of the TT were finally left behind. There was cause for optimism. The company had won world renown for its engineering and design achievements, and there was an understandable and palpable pride within the workshop. There was a huge depth of talent, both within the company and waiting eagerly in the wings. Britten Motorcycles had grown far beyond the point where it was one man's anything. It had become a complex and capable organisation, a perfect vehicle for a busy creative mind to pursue a plethora of bright enthusiasms with the balance offered by other fine minds.

There can be no doubt that John Britten had big plans for his now grown-up creation, even if many of his musings on the subject seemed a little ad hoc. His baby had hopped out of the bassinet and torn off into the distance, and that took a little getting used to. So did the knack of leading without relying on personal friendship and loyalty—and the ability to delegate. However, there can be little doubt that John had the tenacity and the energy to achieve his goal of creating a sustainable creative entity. In fact, in many ways, given just a little consistent direction from the top, Britten Motorcycles was already there.

It was also true that John's immediate plans for Cathedral Junction had suffered some reverses, but most seemed of a fundamentally superficial kind. For example, saving the façades of some of the old buildings for the project had cost more money than most developers would contemplate and perhaps more than John intended. It was also undeniable that the returns per square foot, by the standards of most developers, were not enormously attractive. But, according to Tim Corcoran, John had the money to finish the project comfortably and still have sufficient funds left over to be considered wealthy. Nor was he under any great pressure to finish the development quickly. He could easily have slowed things down, so that it emerged over a period of years—like the Gaudí cathedral in Barcelona if necessary—with a handful of artisans toiling publicly for an indefinite period at a popular and rewarding project. After all, Cathedral Junction had been designed from the outset as an important and enduring structure that could be realised in elegant stages.

Many of John's friends later suspected that he had a growing premonition that time was rapidly running out, and this would seem a credible explanation for his increasingly obdurate attitudes and his apparent growing concern over Cathedral Junction. Looking back on the events that were about to unfold, Quentin Rowe offered the opinion that 'if ever there was a time in a man's life to fuck up, this was the time for John to do it. And if ever there was a time for a man to be forgiven for doing so, this was also it.'

John had started complaining of fatigue soon after returning from the Isle of Man, although a number of visits to various doctors failed to reveal anything serious. Following his accident on Aero D One, his ankle had healed with the ligaments attached incorrectly, and when the ankle began to give him trouble it was decided he needed an operation. However, he put off the operation in order to race the TVR that summer and the surgery was scheduled for the following February.

In the meantime, the licence to operate the trams had been let by the council to The Helicopter Line, a company well versed in tourist ventures and with a highly successful helicopter service headquartered in Queenstown. They operated other successful businesses, including the famous jet-boat tours that swept tourists up the wild waters and narrow gorges of local rivers. Wayne recalled that John had conducted a number of meetings with the company's CEO and that he had generally engaged in some 'fairly serious sucking up'. Even the urgent needs of business were not enough, however, to curb John's exuberant enjoyment of speed and his irrepressible desire to win. The CEO concerned had an immaculate Porsche 911 and was a keen amateur-club car racer. But he found himself up against John in his

TVR, and in his usual mood to take no prisoners, in a Country Gents race meeting at Wigram. Wayne was there to witness the event.

> John went howling past the guy in the Porsche and lost it going into the next corner. He sort of ran off the track a bit, and got all crossed up and just shut the door on the guy behind. The Porsche driver slammed on the anchors and a beautifully prepared BMW 2002 behind him went straight up his chuff. There was a big crunch. In the meantime, John had sorted himself out and just drove away in this great cloud of dust. Afterwards we had a look at the Porsche and there was a crease in the roof. John took one look at that and said the whole car must be rooted for it to bend like that. He was mortified. When the race season ended John went into hospital and had the operation on his foot, but for some reason the general anaesthetic knocked him around terribly and from that time on he seemed to gradually lose energy.

Kit Ebbett and others were also aware of a change.

> We were all very concerned, but from time to time to time he seemed to recover his old spirits and we'd heave a sigh of relief and hope everything would be all right. He had always found time for Mum, and when she died in March 1995 he spent several days with us and spoke at her service. It was the first few days he'd had off in a long time and he was recovering from the operation on his foot. Everyone was commenting on how well he looked and he was a great comfort to have around. He was positive, caring and supportive, all the things that made John the warm individual he was. But he wasn't getting better and it was not long after that that he took a turn for the worse and his health started to really break down. He was suffering a severe flu that never seemed to go away, and he began to look even more drawn and weary than he had after Mark Farmer's death.

Derek McCullough knew that John had a problem when he saw him refuse a joint. 'I'd never seen him do that before,' said Derek. 'Not in all the years I had known him.'

When John's symptoms persisted through autumn and into winter he was given yet another thorough check-up. This time the results were devastating. He had cancer and the doctors could only promise him a matter of months of life at best. Tragically, the cancer had reached his liver and the condition was now too advanced to treat surgically.

John kept the news within his family for a weekend before calling his close friends to tell them of his condition, asking each to keep it private 'for business reasons'. Lindsay received his call, as did most, with shocked disbelief. 'I told him that he'd win out against it but he knew it was no good. He said, "I'm buggered mate." I still couldn't accept it. I kept thinking he'd be all right—that other people had beaten it and he would too.'

'The news was kept secret from the Team at Britten Motorcycles for a while,' said Allan Wylie, 'but I believe he may have kept it secret from everybody for some time prior to June. One of the doctors whom John consulted said he had diagnosed John's cancer at about Easter time, which suggests that he may have known about it for two months before he told anyone at all.'

Finally, however, it was time to tell the Team. The man given the job was Tim Corcoran, and he wasted no time mincing his words. He assembled the Team and told them that John was dying and that there would have to be some urgent changes made, a pronouncement that left little doubt that he meant job losses. It was all over in a matter of minutes. Tim Stewart was actually overlooked in the muster and had continued to work at his bench, but he was soon put in the picture.

> It was totally devastating. Corcoran came into a place where every single person there was dedicated to making something wonderful. Handled properly, the Team would have continued to a man working on the dream. Everyone would have fought to find a way to keep it alive. Instead, after Corcoran left we could scarcely talk to each other. In those few minutes he tore the heart out of the place.

Quentin remembered the next day he went into the workshop and found John saying goodbye to everybody. He told them that he would shortly leave for Australia to investigate a new cure that was being touted in alternative health circles.

> He seemed to be glowing with vitality, and in spite of what I was hearing I had this strong feeling that everything was going to be all right. But we had not even had a chance to talk about it among ourselves after he left before Tim Corcoran came in again and told us that it was time for some rationalisation. We all knew what that meant.

Jason Monopoli was also there that day.

> John walked in and gave me a hug and he was crying. I felt really close to him; we'd been through so much. After he left, Corcoran came in and fired me. I had been overpaid a bonus the Christmas before and it came to light shortly after this. Corcoran called me and demanded it back immediately. I'd just taken a new flat and couldn't do it, but he wasn't willing to give me a couple of weeks. He wasn't interested in the 2000 hours of unpaid overtime I'd racked up either. Corcoran rang me the next day

> and when I told him I still needed time he hung up on me. John somehow formed the impression that I'd refused to give the money back and was apparently ranting about it. I never saw him again, so it was a sad way to end our relationship.

Shaun Craill's departure was equally acrimonious.

> Because of the ridiculous job description Corcoran presented me with I couldn't legally be made redundant while there was work to be done. My job in the body shop was taken by a guy on a work experience scheme, even though it was a breach of contract to use them to do 'real' jobs. The firings were illegal anyway because we were supposed to be given the right to respond, but Corcoran rode roughshod over all those niceties. He was damn lucky that out of consideration for John none of us took issue with his treatment of us. Corcoran then promised me two things and subsequently reneged on both. The first was that he'd do everything to help if I continued to freelance to the company, including paying fair market rates for my work. The second was that I'd be given a great testimonial. The first freelance work I did for them was the renderings for the cruiser that the Indian people suddenly wanted. After I produced them Corcoran cut my invoice by two-thirds and told me I could take it or leave it. Then, after blocking me from having any influence on the content, Loren presented me with a testimonial that was both useless and insulting. It said that I was good at drawing other people's ideas. I tried to point out to Corcoran that the document was unfair and that I couldn't use it, but he refused to do anything about it. In the end I reflected that as John had cancer in the liver and the other guys were struggling on I'd go quietly, but it soured my experience of the company and there was really no need for it to be that way.

Although Loren Poole assembled with the rest of the group he had actually learned of John's illness a few days before the announcement. He remembered his reaction to the news as a deep-sinking sensation that left him feeling listless and curiously detached. However, a meeting with John following the release of the news quickly snapped him back into sharp focus, for there was racing to be done and John was determined to do it.

Alan Cathcart had worked tirelessly to promote the idea of an international BEARS series and his efforts had finally paid off. The movement that had been started by a collection of twenty motorcyclists in a bar in the Ocean View Hotel at Governors Bay on Banks Peninsula in 1983 had spawned a full international series a dozen years later, with a simple set of rules that banned Japanese bikes and 8-valve Ducatis.[214]

The first round was to be contested alongside the impending Pro Twins race at

Daytona, with the balance of the series being held in Europe. There was no way that Britten Motorcycles would not contest them, for in spite of the sudden, brutal reality he faced, John wanted his machines there and he wanted them to win. Loren was asked to set the ball rolling.

> John was positively bubbling with enthusiasm about the series and he was absolutely determined to take the Championship. He gave me the job of organising everything and I prepared to go to Europe. Roberto's bike had been fully rebuilt and it was shipped out to Daytona. Roberto, Sandro and a couple of friends jumped in a plane and flew over from Italy for four days, while John flew over from New Zealand. Jim Hunter, who had been trying to win the race for years, watched Roberto's bike win with Andrew on board while his broke down. He later complained with a huge grin on his face about the general injustice of life. 'That Roberto,' he said, 'he just flies in, eats all my food, wins the race and then flies home!' However, before he left, Roberto watched with John as Andrew also won the very first round of a new International BEARS Championship. It was a brilliant start to the season and John was tickled pink about it.

Roberto and John also took time out to go to Disneyworld in Orlando, where they rode all the rides, taking several shots at the huge roller-coaster, which was a firm favourite of John's. For Roberto those hours with John gave him pause for reflection.

> I think the V-1000 project was over in John's mind by then. He had already moved on to the single and he had a good idea of what it would be like. John believed that everything should be as simple as possible, as close as he could get to the essence of whatever it was he was building. To him that meant, in motorcycle design, a single cylinder. We talked it through and I ended up with a very clear picture in my mind of the machine he wished to build next. It would have a small, light frame to introduce a little flexibility, because he was convinced the V-1000 was a little too stiff for the best handling. Because the single was to be so much lighter he was going to only use one side of the girder suspension and only one side of the swing-arm.
>
> There was to be one intake on one side for the air-box and the radiator was to be under the seat. He believed he could achieve 100 kg as an all-up weight, with perhaps 90 hp. This one-to-one ratio would endow the single with similar performance to the V-1000, but with its lighter weight it would be able to brake harder and be driven faster into bends with less tyre stress.
>
> He had lots of other ideas that I found very interesting. For example, he wanted a straight exhaust pipe that could fold like a telescope. A servomotor would adjust it

to different lengths according to the throttle and revs. As always, it was a pleasure to hear him thinking out loud. His way of looking at things was often upside-down, just like New Zealand, and often it was extreme. But there was always a philosophy behind the ideas, something that was deeper than just building a brilliant thing. In the case of the single it was part of his search for simplicity, and I totally agreed with him. Today I am building a special single with a Rotax engine, but it will just be a nicely built conventional machine. It will not be my version of the bike he wanted to make. That would not be right.

That day, playing at Disneyworld, was the last time I ever saw John and I am glad it was such a fun time. Of course, we talked about everything and I knew exactly what he faced and we were both so sad about that. But I learned something from him that changed my life. I learned that you can achieve anything if your mind is free. And his mind was completely free. Death was nothing to fear.

John returned to New Zealand and threw himself into the Cathedral Junction project with more vigour and determination than ever as Barry Read recalled.

After John became sick we really started moving fast. Not only were we working through broad-stroke concepts but we were also dashing out detail drawings when the foreman ran up the stairs demanding them. The crane was just a few feet behind me, through the office wall, and I felt like I was really in the thick of the project. John's commitment and energy in the face of his illness was just amazing, and I kept on spitting out drawings, which were then sent over to the architects Warren and Mahoney, who put them onto CAD. He wanted that building finished and he was determined that his own impending death would not stand in the way.

Back on the bike front, events were also moving fast.

Roberto's bike had returned to New Zealand from Daytona for a complete health check and had then arrived back in Italy on the last day of practice for the second round of the International BEARS Championship at Monza. Tim Stewart, who had rebuilt the bike, had accompanied the machine most of the way and he recalled that it was lucky to make it to the track at all.

The bike was apparently bumped off the flight in Singapore to make way for some perishable freight. I arrived at this airport just out of Milan and was picked up by Sandro and driven to Monza. We met up with Roberto and Shandy. Everyone expected the bike to be there but it wasn't, so we sat around and waited for hours while practice time ticked away, but it didn't turn up. Eventually, Roberto traced the bike to Milan Airport and he and Sandro and I drove back to find it. It was a Satur-

> day and the place was half-asleep. The airfreight agents didn't seem too concerned until Roberto pulled this huge roll of cash out of his pocket and started laying notes, one after another, on the counter. Various people came and went to pick up their share, and finally we got the paperwork to take to customs. By then Roberto's roll was quite thin but he started laying down notes on the customs counter again until he ran out. At that point Sandro pulled out his giant roll and started oiling the wheels. Eventually we ended up in a warehouse, where Sandro gave the last of his wad to the forklift driver and we had the bike.

Dario Marchetti, a rider for the Kawasaki Italia Team in the World Superbike Championship, had agreed to ride the machine. In spite of a rear shock absorber breaking he managed a very creditable second place the following day behind Alan Cathcart's Saxon Triumph.

After the race Roberto and Sandro loaded the bike into the back of Black Beauty and drove through France to catch a ferry to the UK. In the meantime, Tim flew back to New Zealand, where he prepared Jason's ex-bike (the machine Andrew was to ride), in time to meet up with Roberto and Sandro at Gatwick Airport. They cleared the bike through customs, this time without any need of paper lubrication, and proceeded to Thruxton, an 'airfield' racetrack located about an hour and a half south-east of London, for the third round.

Roberto had given the remaining rides for the season on his machine to a young up-and-coming New Zealander called Steven Briggs, and he was out practising when Tim arrived.

> I was busy changing the oil in the blue bike, but I was aware of the fact that Steven's lap times were a bit ordinary. When he brought the bike in I changed the oil in that as well, and was dismayed to see bits of sump baffle and locking wire streaming out of the sump. I called Roberto and Sandro over and showed them. They were devastated. By then it was early evening, but I told them I needed a welding set and they took off and found one while I started stripping the bike. When they got back I suggested they go to bed and leave me to it. They wandered over to Black Beauty with their shoulders down looking like the unhappiest Italians in the world. I had just got off a plane from New Zealand and I was feeling pretty buggered, but I just couldn't let those two guys down. I got on with it, dismantled the engine, welded up the baffles, replaced a bolt in the system after drilling a hole though it that it needed, and put everything back together again. It was sunrise when Sandro came out of the bus and saw me slipping the fairing back on. He couldn't believe it and he started yelling for Roberto to come out. They were instantly the two happiest Italians in the whole world.

> After that Sandro could never do enough for me. If I wanted a drink I could have anything, including French champagne. If I wanted smokes he'd whizz off and get me three packets. He always called me Mister Tim and his hospitality was boundless.[215]

Steven Briggs had previously raced 250cc machines in his home country, and in light of this Roberto's choice for him to ride his machine seemed somewhat curious. However, Steven had also recently met John Shand and he had promoted Steven to Roberto with some enthusiasm.

In spite of his inexperience with large-capacity motorcycles, Steven soon showed what a capable rider he was, rapidly coming to grips with the big V-twin. Looking back on the season he spent with Roberto, he does not hesitate to describe it as one of the most enjoyable episodes of his life.

> I had taken the 1993–94 Formula Two Championship in New Zealand on a TZ250 Yamaha against pretty stiff opposition because the rules allowed 750cc twins in my class. Robert Holden was aboard a Ducati 750 supplied by Dallas Rankine, and although my two-stroke Yamaha TZ250 had to run on pump gas they were allowed methanol. That Ducati was very fast. All the rounds were in the North Island that year, and in spite of Robert's presence I took the Championship and broke every lap record for the class along the way. Afterwards I decided to go overseas, and because my girlfriend is Dutch we based ourselves in Holland. The Hank De Vikes Race Team, who were the biggest Yamaha race team in Europe, needed a rider because their rider, Geoffrey De Vikes (who oddly enough was no relation of Hank's), had broken his leg. I filled in and immediately managed a fourth place on a YZF600 at Assen in a European 600 Championship race. The team was pleased and so was I, as I'd never raced a big bike before. When a fax arrived from Roberto asking me if I'd like to race his machine I said yes immediately. I had been an admirer of the Britten project for some time and had followed their fortunes with keen interest. I had met John at the Isle of Man and we had talked for about half an hour, but it was not long after Farmer had been killed and things were obviously stressful for him, so we hadn't discussed anything much to do with the future. Roberto invited me to Milan and told me he'd arranged for someone to pick me up from the airport. That's how I met Sandro, one of the most engaging nutcases you could ever imagine. Sandro was driving some old heap of a Fiat and he took me to this abandoned factory he owned, which became my home for about four months. Later that day I met Roberto, who turned out to be an exceptionally nice fellow who was totally crazy about motorcycles and we all drove to Thruxton together.

The two Italians always apparently enjoyed themselves but the BEARS Championship was a time of especial joy for both of them. Looking back, Roberto was particularly happy about the relationship that developed between Sandro and Tim.

> Sandro was always the resident lunatic on our team. We would be in the middle of a meeting with officials and he would suddenly start singing opera. Many people found him very difficult to understand. He formed a very close relationship with Tim after that night. Sandro spoke very little English and Tim spoke no Italian but they evolved their own language. I remember one time when they were chatting away to each other and Steven, who was always in the background with his girlfriend, said to me, 'What are they saying?' I told him that I was sorry but I had no idea, only they knew. Tim was totally dedicated to the machine, and I found him some mornings asleep by the bike with his hand on the engine after working until he dropped off from exhaustion. My job was to drive Black Beauty and to act as the team manager, but I didn't have to do much managing. Everyone got on very well together; we were a good team.

Sandro wasn't always difficult to understand, however, as Steven remembered, especially when it mattered.

> Sandro managed to get his message across when he wanted to, usually with Roberto or Tim's help. He told me not to worry about winning pole once Tim had sorted out the bike at Thruxton but to get comfortable on it first. However, he then told me about all the riders who had gone out and won straight off the bat. In fact, he kept telling me all about them from then on and I was under no illusions about what was expected. I went out and found I had to completely change my style, because corner speed is everything on a 250 and the wrong way to race a Britten. Generally I found it excellent on the really fast European tracks but awkward on anything slower. Unfortunately, the handling was somewhat inconsistent. I was to discover that it would be good on one track and then terrible on the next, even if the two tracks were similar and we had anticipated that the same set-up would be ideal.
>
> I knew that I'd gone reasonably well after my qualifying session and came in to find Sandro stretched out on his plastic deckchair with a cigarette in his hand. He was wearing his usual shades, so I couldn't see his eyes, but he pointed his finger at the sky and said, 'Bravo! Meesta Briggs, number one!' I knew then that I had pole.

He also had a team-mate.

After Daytona, Andrew had flown off to Europe to join an Italian 500 Grand Prix team that was supposedly in the throes of signing off sponsorship to contest the season with a Yamaha. Unfortunately, the sponsorship deals largely fell through and he found himself struggling with little money through the first and second rounds, after which the team ran out of funding altogether. Andrew elected to take the bike to Japan without team support and managed a remarkable twelfth place, the first 'privateer' home.

'I raced in another three rounds,' he said, 'with just the mechanics who were not being paid. We were doing it for ourselves. However, the bike kept breaking down and there was no money for parts. In the end I didn't even feel like putting on my leathers.'

Walking away from the Grand Prix circuit did offer Andrew one major compensation, because he was now able to contest the remaining rounds of the BEARS Championship. With four rounds remaining there was still a good chance to take the Championship, and his offer to race was accepted with alacrity by Loren on behalf of Britten Motorcycles, and he immediately organised for a machine to be flown out to London. As he packed to go to the UK, Andrew received a further fax from Loren that concluded, 'Thanks for all your support Andrew. We must win this series for all of us, especially John!'

Although the second bike had only arrived from New Zealand with Loren the previous day, Andrew was able to qualify second, behind Steven and in front of Alan Cathcart's Saxon-Triumph, the Harley-Davidson Superbike of Ron McGill and the Raceco Moto Guzzi of Paul Lewis.

Before leaving for Europe, Loren had caught up with John in Christchurch after the latter's arrival home from Noosa, where any hope for a miracle cure had been dashed.

> John had briefed me as he always did and I took about three pages of notes. In spite of his situation he had cheeky comments for everyone for me to pass on, and he was generally very excited about our prospects in the BEARS Championship. I was to be Andrew's spannerman while Tim continued to spanner for Steven on Roberto's bike, so John also ran through his mental checklist of all the things that had to be ticked off before each race. He told me not to forget to make sure the bikes had enough water and so on.
>
> I had business with ICI in the UK after meeting their marketing manager the previous year at the TT. We nutted out a great sponsorship deal for Britten Motorcycles and ICI. I called John and told him all about it and he was really pleased. He always loved sponsorship money.

The race at Thruxton was held in torrential rain and Andrew emerged out of the grey vapour a clear winner. For Steven, however, the race was a damp squib.

'I was going through a slow second-gear corner when the throttle jammed open,'

Steven recalled. 'The cable had been routed so that it jammed between the shock and the chassis top member. Basically, the back just drove around and I fell over, bent a foot-peg and took off a tiny bit of paint. The damage to the bike and me was minimal but I was out of the race.'

Immediately after the race Andrew tore off to catch a plane to Japan, where he practised for the up-and-coming Suzuka eight-hour race before flying back to Austria for the next BEARS round at Zeltweg. His schedule was so tight, he had time for only four practice laps there before qualifying. Steven was also on the track.

> Andrew was slightly faster than I was and we were easily the fastest there. Unfortunately, there was a problem with the timing equipment and we ended up about fourth and fifth on the grid with a number of back markers in front of us. We weren't too concerned, although there were a number of ex-GP and Superbike riders there. The Saxon-Triumph with Alan Cathcart was quite fast and Paul Lewis was really quick on this Raceco Moto Guzzi. Mike Edwards was also a contender on the Tigcraft Harley Superbike. As expected, however, Andrew and I blasted through to the front and we would have finished that way except that my rear shock shaft sheared clean in half. I'd done a few practice sessions by then, and it was actually the fourth time it had happened, but it was always a potentially dangerous situation when it went.
>
> When Tim balanced an engine he always did it a certain way that promoted smooth running, but this was not done automatically at the factory. Roberto's bike was not balanced Tim's way and the resulting vibration actually snapped the shock. I remember thinking that I really should give up as I was riding on the rear spring alone. The bike was pogoing under throttle so much I couldn't see because my vision was so blurred. It was a shame because the bike really suited the track, but I kept going anyway and somehow finished fourth. I was actually just pipped on the line by an Austrian called Andy Hoffman on a Guzzi for third.

Once again Andrew had taken a comfortable win, after which he screamed off down the autobahn to the airport to make his flight back to Japan. There he managed a highly creditable eighth place with team-mate Tamaki Serizawa on a Yoshimura Suzuki in the eight-hour race, before flying back to the UK once more to await the fifth BEARS round at Brands Hatch. During his absence, Steven and Tim had returned to Sandro's old factory in Milan where, just as the Britten Team had done in 1992 and 1993, the two dragged some old scooters out of hiding and got them running so they could race each other around the massive buildings. Roberto's Britten had now done a high number of hard racing hours and it was beginning to tell, but Tim gave it the benefit of his superior attention and had it running well. All seemed set for Brands Hatch, where a victory for Andrew would give the Britten

Team the Championship. It was only then, Steven recalled, that he and Tim learned of the hopelessness of John's illness.

> Roberto called us in for a meeting at his office and we made our way to his Jaguar dealership, which was right in the middle of Milan. It was an extremely elegant place with what was virtually a private motorcycle museum underneath the complex. Roberto loved race bikes and he had about forty of them lined up. He regarded them as treasures rather than assets and he liked to keep them in exactly the state they were in after finishing their last race—they weren't even cleaned. He liked British stuff and he had a number of Nortons, including the JPS Rotary Norton ridden by Ron Haslam and Robert Dunlop in 1992, a sister machine to the one on which Steven Hislop won the 1992 TT.
>
> However, this time we were shown into his private office, which was accessed through an electronic door. I got the feeling that not a lot of people ever went in there. The room was quite dark, with heavy wood panelling and lots of leather furniture, including a huge leather-covered desk. There were lots of sharp little lights in the ceiling illuminating cabinets full of race trophies. I also remember these two carved, highly polished wooden horses that stood perhaps a metre and a half high. They were statues of Ferrari's prancing horse. Roberto greeted us and then he told us that John was not going to live much longer. He stated it quite simply, and then Tim and I went back to the factory and prepared to go to the UK.

The fifth round of the International BEARS Championship at Brands Hatch was run in front of a huge crowd, nearly 80,000 strong, as a support race for a round of the world Superbike series. Although Andrew posted pole comfortably, Steven was again plagued with reliability problems.

> We had the same electrical glitch bugging us all season. It had really affected us at Zeltweg and it was another consequence of the balance problem. Basically, we kept cracking the pick-up for the Hall Effect on the end of the camshaft. When it happened the engine would make only about 8000 revs, and it would invariably happen after about eighteen laps. When it happened early on at Brands Hatch we only had one spare, so I had to qualify the bike as it was. I still managed to get second place on the grid, and then Tim put the new pick-up in and we found the extra revs. However, when our race was due to start we were held up on the line for ages and the temperature began to creep up. By the time we did the sighting lap it was off the dial and people were pointing at the bike as I went past. I looked down and saw water pouring out at such a rate I was sure the engine must have blown. I resigned myself to an early retirement, but by the end of the lap the temperature gauge seemed to

> have stuck at 98 degrees Celsius. I decided to cruise slowly in about sixth place until it came down to about 80 degrees, when I felt confident to pick up the pace. I could see Andrew ahead having a real fight with Paul Lewis, so I caught up and sat behind Paul, waiting for him to crash. On about the fourteenth lap I suddenly had an opportunity to take both of them, which I did, and the next time I looked back Paul was gone. I then let Andrew pass and we cruised through to take the championship.

In fact, as Andrew recalled, the race between Paul Lewis and Andrew had been a bit of a jack-up.

> Alan Cathcart knew we were going to run away with the race and he wanted a good show in front of this enormous crowd to make it exciting. He was trying hard to promote the class and he asked me if I would make a bit of a race of it. I thought about it and decided I might as well. After the race started I got out in front, and then when I got to the back of the circuit where there were a lot of trees and not many people I eased off. Paul Lewis would come thundering around to find me cruising along and he'd close right up. Later, he was laughing about it and he told me that every time he saw me idling along he'd shout, 'You beauty!' The crowd really loved it too. I could see them on their feet cheering away. Then Steven got in on the act and went past both of us. By then there was only a couple of laps to go, so I put my head down. I easily knocked about three seconds off my lap times and took the win. But I was lucky to make it. Back at the pits I found out the bike only had about half its oil left. The rest had jetted out the breather, due to a shot ring or something pressurising the crankcase. Luckily, it had gone all over the hugger and the bottom of the seat rather than on my back tyre or the track.

As always after a race, Loren called John but, ominously, he found him in hospital.

'John's voice was very weak,' said Loren, 'but he made no mention of his illness. He was over the moon about the Championship and we had a wonderful, joyful conversation about it. He was just ecstatic.'

Andrew and the Britten had earned a niche in motorcycle race history. They had won the first International BEARS Championship. More significantly, however, it was also the first time a New Zealand-built bike had ever won a World Championship and it had been achieved with a New Zealand rider. Andrew remembered it well.

> I was determined to win for John, and I definitely put in a bit extra. I was prepared to risk a lot for that Championship. I was on the phone to him all the time and his heart was really in it. He often expressed his disappointment that he couldn't be there

> to see the races. The next and final round of the Championship was at Assen, and when I won that as well he was very emotional. He felt he did not have long to go and he really wanted me to go back and see him.

In fact, the victory at Assen was twofold. A new crankshaft had been sent over for the CR&S Britten and Tim had rebuilt the engine after having it balanced to his specification. Steven's girlfriend had an aunt in Holland who had a small garage with a well-equipped automotive workshop near Assen, and she very generously invited Steven, Tim and Sandro to stay while the work was done. With the balance problems solved, the electrical problem could also be properly addressed and Steven was able to take third place comfortably, behind Mike Edwards and in front of the other Harley Superbike. It was a conservative performance but it was sufficient to take second place in the Championship. And so the first International BEARS Championship ended with a Britten one/two victory.

After Andrew had spoken to John on the phone, John asked to speak to Steven.

> We were in the phone booth at Assen and his voice was very weak, so it was hard to hear with 30,000 people around, but he was really thrilled about the results. He told me that he had not dared to hope for the top two places and he congratulated me warmly for securing the second spot. I was only twenty years old and largely inexperienced in the bigger stuff, and I guess he must have thought I had little chance of doing well. After that all the pressure was off and I felt free to go for it in this Super V-twin race we had entered at the same meeting. It was packed out with top 8-valve Dukes and Bimotas, and Andrew and I knew we'd really have to push it. [216]

Out on the track Andrew and Steven found the going every bit as tough as they had anticipated it would be. As Steven recalled:

> We were doing one minute and twenty-seven-second laps, which was only about one second slower than the top Superbikes. It was very, very fast. Andrew and I had great starts and went straight out front. I was content to follow Andrew and learn a bit more about riding Brittens, and we just let rip. I remember thinking just how much fun it was as we took first and second place in front of this huge, cheering crowd.

Back at home, John told the people of New Zealand of his absolute delight with the win and second place in the inaugural International BEARS Championship through a recorded message that was played on television over pictures of Andrew taking the final chequered flag. His voice was laboured and weak, but his message was strong. He said proudly that it was a great win for the Team and for all those who had put so much into Britten Motorcycles. Allan Wylie visited him not long afterwards and found him sitting up in bed with the BEARS trophy, a huge glass cup, nearby.

> I told him that I considered the second race that Andrew won at Assen was even better than the Championship because it was a twins race and it was open to 8-valve Ducatis. They were there in numbers and there were some very professional outfits. He agreed that it was pretty significant. There were not that many occasions when a Britten was put up against really top-drawer opposition like that and it was great that on that occasion it was able to take the win.

With his bikes finally making the podium consistently, fulfilling all their promise and drawing huge crowds and critical acclaim around the world, John marshalled his own inner forces to battle the death sentence he had been handed. He had scanned the Internet for information on his illness and called specialists all over the world to educate himself as best he could about his condition. One thing had rapidly become very clear. The only people who had survived cancer of the kind he had at the stage his had reached were a tiny minority who had somehow experienced a miracle. Miracles, he learned, were invariably the preserve of the faithful. Without a rock-solid belief in God they simply did not happen.

Such religious intensity was not new to John. His extended family had always been strongly religious, and whenever she saw him his grandmother Isabel never failed to ask John when he was going to be saved through Jesus. He started to reflect on her simple message and then one day he opened the Bible she had given him with the inscription inside the cover that read, 'What shall it profit a man if he shall gain the world but lose his own soul.' He got out of his bed with the Bible clutched to his heart, knelt on the floor and asked for forgiveness. John, ever the dealmaker, ever the lateral thinker, then asked God for the miracle he needed. In return he would commit the remainder of his life to Him, using his celebrity to draw others into the fold.

In spite of all his troubles John was still capable of having a good time with his friends. His forty-fifth birthday rolled around and his sister Dorenda invited them all to attend a party at Heatherlea (John stayed here for a period after falling ill, before returning home), asking that each of them do a performance of some kind. Some sang, some danced, some recited verse and some repeated old party tricks. David Turner, for example, ate a whole packet of marshmallows, no mean feat, as all that have ever attempted it will know. Finally, it was time for John to receive his surprise of the evening. The guests escorted the frail figure to the garage, where the old Indian, still resplendent in the red paint Bruce Garrick and John had painted it with all those years before, stood on its stand. Bruce clambered onto it and kicked it into life. After a thorough tune-up in the Britten workshop, and for the first time since it was pushed into the ditch in Gore and perhaps for years before that, the bike ran sweetly. Bruce slowly looped around the garage on the machine while John, his face glowing with excitement, ran after it laughing. It was a wonderful and welcome respite from the relentless onslaught of the cancer that was now voraciously devouring him.

Having made the decision to find faith, John strove with all his strength of character to become a true believer, struggling with the conflicts that inevitably arose, as he grew weaker and weaker. He knew the deal, however, and he stuck by it. He had to believe that he would be saved or he would die.

When Marguerite Martini, a former girlfriend with whom John had lived for a while, flew over from Mexico, where she now lived, she found it difficult to get over the shock of John's gaunt appearance. However, he was so overjoyed to see her that she eventually found herself talking enthusiastically about old times, old pranks, and old and beautiful memories.

> He loved life too much to stay down. Too much even for me to stay down! I slept on a makeshift bed next to his in the guest wing at The Stables and he woke me up in the middle of the night when there was a full moon and the room was flooded in light. He wanted to dance and we so we did. He was so light it was like holding a child. However, soon the time came round for me to leave him with his family and to go home to mine. I knew I'd never see him again. Of course it was terrible saying goodbye to him. Just terrible.

Although John now insisted that he would not die, he nevertheless meticulously planned his own funeral, justifying his actions by pointing out that a bus could hit him. It was to be a grand affair that he jokingly referred to as his megalomaniac service and it was planned to the smallest detail. Included in his instructions, for example, was his wish that after the service the choirboys be given lamingtons—a Kiwi party favourite of sponge-cake cubes dipped in chocolate and rolled in coconut.

He had friends with him at all times now, usually right beside him in a camp stretcher so he could talk to them whenever he wanted to. One night, when the house was in darkness and all were asleep, Wayne, who was sleeping in the stretcher that night, was awoken by the sound of someone creeping about down below. He quietly crept down the stairs into the atrium and almost bumped into a surprised intruder, who took flight. Wayne took off in hot pursuit and a game of hide and seek around the neighbouring streets ensued.

> At one point I could hear someone whispering in the darkness quite close and so I decided there must be two of them. Then, a little later, I heard a cell phone ring. I think that was the way they were keeping in touch. I lost them in the end and made my way back to the house. John was wide awake and demanding to know what was going on. I told him we'd had burglars and he demanded to know why I hadn't woken him up. 'We could have had them,' he said.

Back in Europe, Andrew had been enjoying a little time off, but a telephone conversation with Karen, a young Christian who had been reading the Bible to John, convinced him that he should return immediately.

> When John first called me in England and told me about his illness he was desperate and had no idea who he could turn to. We talked about God, and a few days later he called me again and told me that he had had a visit from a favourite aunt and they had prayed together. I had only recently come back to the faith myself, and I was probably too awkward and self-conscious to be that useful to him, but from that point on we spoke about faith all the time. He was excited and positive, and that was tremendous. I guess I thought that John would be all right, but I suddenly understood the urgency of the situation after I spoke to Karen. I didn't know then that Karen was going to be my wife, but as soon as she spoke to me I knew I had to take her words very seriously.
>
> I had intended spending time in Auckland, but everything was booked except for one seat going straight through to Christchurch. I grabbed that and went from London to Christchurch Airport and then straight to his home. I found him physically very changed—a shadow of his former self. There were about twenty people in the room but he cried with joy when he saw me. I had already sent the BEARS Championship Cup back to him and I kicked myself later for not having it in my hand when I walked in. The mayor, Vicki Buck, was waiting to present this civic award and we had to ask her to wait a little while longer so we could compose ourselves.

In fact, the award was something that Kit Ebbett had suggested to the mayor when he discovered that there was no time to recommend John for a 'proper' gong on the annual Queen's Birthday Honours list.[217] But when the award was presented, Vicki Buck found the occasion was more than just the formality she had initially expected.

> The award was granted by the city for excellence and it was just a little greenstone thing. I knew he was close to death and I thought it might be best if I sent it around

> to him in a taxi, as I didn't think it would mean that much to him. Also, my own father had died of cancer just twelve months before and I wasn't looking forward to seeing John suffering in the same way. However, he insisted that I bring it to him and so I went. I was only going to stay for a moment, but once I had seen him and talked to him it felt really lovely and I stayed for the afternoon. And he was utterly thrilled with the award, it really meant a great deal to him. I know he loved his city and he was really pleased to think that the city admired him.

After the presentation, when all the guests had finally left, Andrew found himself alone again with John. This time there were no tears and John calmly asked Andrew if he would stay.

> John didn't say for how long he wanted me to stay and I didn't ask. I just told him that I would and he said I could have the guest bedroom and it was settled. And so I stayed until the end, two weeks later. He was in good form, cracking jokes and laughing, and he never complained. The morphine obviously helped but there must have been times of huge discomfort and pain. In spite of everything we still had a lot of laughs. A karaoke machine was brought in for a party for one of the kids and it was sitting forgotten downstairs when I went out for an afternoon. I picked up the microphone and said, 'I'll see you soon John.' It was switched on and my voice reverberated around the rooms and the atrium, and up to the wing where he lay. When I returned later he told me that God had spoken to him. He laughed and laughed when he learned the truth. We spoke a lot about God and at some point he obviously realised that although he would be saved it would not be in this world.
>
> One day he lay drifting in and out of consciousness while Karen and I sat at the foot of the bed, holding his feet, silently praying. John suddenly sat up, his face suffused with joy. He was laughing with pure happiness. He kept saying, 'I never knew it could be like this! I never knew I could feel like this!'

In spite of all the pain of his illness, John continued to receive a string of other visitors, treating all with warmth and good humour, asking questions of them and listening carefully and respectfully to their answers. He also continued to share his dreams, urging those who came to see him onwards and upwards.

His twin sister Marguerite arrived from Australia, where she now lived, and spent time with him. He also continued to work, especially when the Indian project, which had lain dormant for some months, suddenly fired back up again. Murray acted as a conduit to the others involved in the project, primarily Shaun Craill, who then translated John's ideas into a series of superb graphics. Working this way they refined the designs for the big cruiser, the only machine the now beleaguered Indian Motorcycle Company was interested in pursuing. Clearly John was still concerned that Britten Motorcycles should have a future, even if he would not be around to see it.

He urged those left at the workshop to get the prototype single-cylinder engine running, and it was Murray who finally fired it up on the dynamometer, where it ran sweetly enough but delivered only about 50 hp. Determined to get the most he could out of it, he persisted, persuading more and more fuel and air into it as he worked away at the EMS. By the time Murray was ready to call it a day, he had coaxed a credible 75 hp out of it. Hans, who had been aiming at 90 hp, was naturally disappointed with the result but it had run and made reasonable power. Clearly there was much potential for development and John was delighted.

In the meantime, a number of John's friends had been working to arrange a last outing for him, and some final contact with his sister Dorenda. On the day, John was duly carried down the stairs and placed carefully into a car. The driver, an American who had long admired John and had often turned up at the workshop 'to supply the dope and do my gee-whizz thing around the resident genius', drove John, Dorenda and Wayne carefully to architect John Trengrove's new home in the country. The extensive garden was relatively new but it was already magnificent and John was slowly driven through it. He stayed out for the better part of the morning, until he announced that he was tired and the party headed for home.

The next day he had an appointment at the hospital, and afterwards, back at home, Wayne, Andrew and Ruth McCracken carried him upstairs. Suddenly his colour changed and they knew the end was approaching. CJ arrived up from Dunedin in the late afternoon. At about 7.30pm on 5 September 1995, at the age of forty-five, John Kenton Britten finally stopped the clock. He was survived by his wife Kirsteen and their three children, Sam, Isabelle and Jessica.

In London, Merrin Corcoran put down the phone in her fashion emporium and slowly wandered outside. She had made the voyage back to New Zealand to be with John only weeks before and had been expecting the news since business commitments had forced her return to London. Now that it had come, however, she found herself in a curious emotional vacuum that added to the final shock of the loss. With her husband in New Zealand, she realised that there was absolutely no one who could possibly understand the impact the news was having on her. Walking aimlessly, she suddenly encountered Robin Judkins doing exactly the same thing. They stared numbly at each other. Neither had ever really known the other well but they knew John had been a good friend to each of them. They sat down at a café and had a coffee together, enormously relieved to be with the only other human being in London who understood how they felt.

'Before we went our separate ways,' said Merrin, 'I told Robin that only John could have organised our meeting. He was capable of great caring. I felt he was looking after us.'

Tim Stewart had flown in from Europe the night before and had slept through most of the following day.

'I woke up thinking that it was time to go and see John,' he said. 'I had been pretty tired after the flight home and I was feeling refreshed and ready to face whatever the day might bring. Then I found out he was dead. It was too late.'

The funeral was the nearest thing New Zealand had seen to a state funeral since 1974 after the sudden death of the then Labour Prime Minister, Norman Kirk. Christchurch came to a complete halt as the funeral procession, led by Andrew Stroud on a bellowing V-1000, slowly made its way to the cathedral. Also in the funeral procession was the International gypsy caravan, which had been shipped up from the Queenstown Motor Museum to carry the flowers.

Kit Ebbett recalled the scene.

> It was daffodil season, a flower that John had always loved. The cathedral was packed with great yellow mountains of them. It was also absolutely packed out with people, as was Cathedral Square itself. It also seemed that the entire city centre was crammed full of motorcycles. The press of people outside the cathedral was such that some of the official pallbearers could not make their way to the hearse to uplift the coffin. I was on the spot, however, and I just looked around for familiar faces. It was marvellous really. I felt that John was guiding me to gather together the people he wanted to carry him in. Roland Logan was there, and David Purdue, Wayne Alexander and Willy Trengrove.

A profound silence fell over the huge crowd both inside and outside the cathedral as the service was read, and for an afternoon the entire city paid homage to a man it would sadly miss having around. Inside the cathedral, the beautiful, traditional, stone edifice that was the very heart of the city, a single shaft of light suddenly pierced the gentle gloom through a massive stained-glass window and fell upon Andrew Stroud as he read the lesson.

When the casket was finally carried out it was preceded by a solitary Scottish piper. His melancholy notes skirled through the hushed cathedral, but as soon as the procession emerged into the bright light outside his mournful dirge was abruptly drowned out by thousands and thousands of motorbikes exploding into life, creating a wild, thunderous roar that filled the air and rattled the windows downtown. John Britten did not go quietly.

CHAPTER TWENTY-TWO

Legacy

The Britten Motorcycle story did not end with John's death. For a start, there were sufficient parts to build two more motorcycles either already at the factory or on the way from suppliers, and there was a race team still with bikes to race.

Before his death John had often floated the idea of having his sister Dorenda take over Britten Motorcycles, a prospect that had much to recommend it to those who still wanted to press ahead with the company. She was a talented and conscientious administrator, an established designer in her own right (at the architectural end of interior and furniture design) and a great supporter of the motorcycle programme. She had accompanied the Team on various missions and had proven a popular travelling companion who always found a way to be useful. However, John's estate[218] opposed the plan and the opportunity was lost.

In his will, John left up to 49 percent of Britten Motorcycles to a selection of the people who had worked with him over the years—recognition at least for a few of those whose often unpaid efforts had contributed so fundamentally to the successes of the motorcycle project. Furthermore, the list represented a canny melding of the talents and characters that the company would need if it were to go on to greater things.

Quite where it was to go to was, of course, another matter.

The first order of business was the pair of V-1000s that remained to be completed, in addition to which John had been vehement that the single-cylinder motorcycle should be built. On the face of it, this was a sound idea. It would buy the Team some time to settle down to a future without John, and it was probable that a ready market existed for a small number of the new machines, enough at least to cover the building of the prototypes and to keep everything turning over. Roberto, for example, still insisted that he wanted one.

Then there was the idea of operating as a prototype design house. With Murray still on board, there was really very little that the company could not have undertaken in that area, particularly if Shaun Craill and Jason Monopoli could have been persuaded to overlook the indignity of their departures and accept work on a contract basis.

From the beginning, however, the new regime, which was effectively Tim Corcoran operating on Kirsteen's behalf, seemed determined to discourage those who had the company's best interests at heart. The tone was set when they elected to give only 30 percent of the company to the new shareholders, a decision that left the minor shareholders with such small percentages that Broz, who was given 2.55 percent along with Loren and Murray, described the bequest as 'nothing more than a piece of paper with some very small numbers on it'. Rob Selby did best, with 10.14 percent of the shares, and Bob ran second with 7.62 percent. At the other end of the list, Tim Stewart, Guy Kingsbury and Roberto Crepaldi were each given 1.53 percent of the company.

Of course, it was entirely legal to reduce these shares from a maximum of 49 percent of the new company to any figure at all, and Corcoran justified the move in a letter to the new shareholders by claiming that the percentage withheld from those shareholders elected by John might be needed to attract a new manager or partner.

However, when Perry Rees was given the job of general manager, his name selected from a short list left by John, no mention was ever made to him of the possibility of receiving a shareholding. From the beginning, his tenure was blighted by the way the newly reformed company was set adrift without the benefit of any of the assets and patents developed or acquired during the lifetime of the old company, these having been retained by or transferred to the estate. The new company was also saddled with a high level of debt after being made to settle the full book value of all stock held with an immediate payment.

If these circumstances were not challenging enough, Perry was additionally hampered by the estate's insistence that his primary function was to find an equity partner—a white knight to sink money into the company. To fulfil this brief he had to overcome several fundamental problems, the first being that there was no clear picture of just what it was the company would do even if it had access to funds—a situation made worse by the loss of key personnel under circumstances that made it extremely unlikely that they would ever again contribute to the company's future. Another problem was that he could not find partners to invest in specific aspects of the technology developed by the company, as the estate owned all the rights to them. For example, the production method for carbon-fibre wheels that Murray had designed, largely without payment, John had patented under his own name (to Murray's enduring disgust). The technology might have had some commercial future as a stand-alone operation under the Britten umbrella, and such an enterprise could have exploited the huge branding potential offered by the Britten name. Without control of the patent, however, such a plan was largely unworkable.

Perhaps Perry's greatest obstacle to success, however, was the fact that the estate would not relinquish any degree of control of the company by reducing its shareholding below 51 percent. Obviously, no potential partner was going to accept junior standing in a company that clearly did not believe it could survive without their capital.

In spite of the impossibility of his mission, Perry dashed around looking for an equity partner. But one never emerged despite the fury of meetings, letters, phone calls and faxes he initiated.

Shortly before he died, John had spoken to Bob Brookland about his hopes for the future of Britten Motorcycles and said that he had left the Team the oyster and that it was up to them—his successors—to find the pearl. It was unfortunate that he did not also elect to leave them the shell. Instead, he left instructions that the new company was to enjoy a rent- and licence-free holiday for long enough to establish itself, a period the estate set initially at twelve months, after which time the situation would be reviewed. Clearly, the now valuable real estate under the Britten Motorcycles workshop was vulnerable to sale at any time beyond that date.

For a few months prior to Perry's appointment, Loren had continued to manage the company and discovered a formidable ally in the person of Howard Paterson, one of John's trustees. Howard was an astute and successful businessman in Dunedin and Queenstown, and for a while he worked with Loren, and later with Perry, to try to restructure the company to get it up and running. 'We should do it,' he told Loren, 'for John.'

And Loren agreed.

> Before John died we had been talking about publicly floating a company to make the single-cylinder race motorcycle. We knew a lot about going public because we had so much information from the Indian deal and we'd done so much critical path-planning and costing. The only thing I disagreed with was building the single that way instead of a twin, and Howard agreed. The more we looked at it the better it seemed and we began to get together some pretty heavy-duty corporate support to carry the company forward. The dream, of course, was to build a production bike for the street and the track. At the time we believed that there was enough support in New Zealand to make that a reality.

The idea of a second-generation V-1000 was not new of course. The Indian sports bike was just that, and with a conventional front end and a 6-speed gearbox an out-and-out race version would have been a nice place to start. If all failed it could be sold, like its predecessor, in very limited numbers as a factory-supported race bike to independent race teams.

Andrew Stroud was keen to see just that happen and he volunteered to assist in any way he could.

> I went to the factory a few times and I was really keen that we have a go at building a third-generation V-1000. I believed that with minimal development the V-1000 could still race competitively against the best Superbikes in the world. So much of it was right. All it really needed was a little more flexibility in the structure, which a bit more frame and forks would have provided so that it could be pushed harder into corners, along with another gear to keep it cooking. We could simply buy a front end, so that was no problem. It would have been a really worthwhile thing to do and I'd love to have had the wherewithal to do it.

Sadly, the 'wherewithal' would become a retreating and diminishing illusion, and its final disappearance with a scarcely audible pop, would leave some of those who had contributed most to the project in an atmosphere of the deepest gloom.

One of those who suffered most from the growing realisation that everything that had been learned was destined finally to turn to dust was Murray Aitken, but for some time he remained 'on call', ready to help in any way he could. When Kirsteen was told that a 6-speed gearbox would allow the two new machines to set a whole new run of track records, she had agreed that they should be made and the newly appointed board of directors had duly voted to spend the money needed to do so. (The new board was made up of Kirsteen, Tim Corcoran, Rob Selby, Bob Brookland and John Shand, and had its first meeting on 7 November 1995.) Although Murray had actually drawn up the new arrangement and given the drawings to Rob to follow through, Rob did nothing about it and the new gearbox became, like so much else, just one more cardboard cut-out in the phantom 'What if?' jigsaw.

By then Murray had also finalised his design for a new girder front end that he believed would finally vindicate John's faith in the system. He and Tim had by now gone through the entire suspension system and had come up with a number of modifications to the front end that significantly improved it. As Tim recalled:

> We put needle rollers everywhere we could and paid particular attention to the ball-joints in the girder set-up. I machined up special carriers for ball bearings that attached to the ball-joints and these looked after all the vertical movement in the suspension. This left the ball-joints only in charge of steering movements, which greatly

> reduced wear and meant we could hold a good set-up for longer. The real answer was a system without ball-joints that was a lot like earlier pushbike systems, and Murray designed just such a set-up. Unfortunately, when we told Kirsteen and Corcoran that it would cost between NZ$10,000 and NZ$12,000 to build and develop it they flatly refused to consider the idea, so that was that.

Naturally, it was a great disappointment to learn that the quite incredible progress that Tim and Murray had made developing the V-1000 would go largely to waste. Years later, Tim would look back on the time he and Murray spent in the dyno room and describe his affair with the Britten engine as 'unfinished business'.

> We knew the engine flowed 210 hp. All we had to do was come up with a head that could burn it. Murray was well on the way to developing it, and with his new front end he'd designed, the V-1000 could have had a whole new life in front of it.

For Murray the refusal to continue was an even greater disappointment.

> We could have had 300 people making motorcycles and a whole range of industrial design, but the big picture was completely lost. I used to get angry that so much effort went down the drain. Finally, I just wanted to forget all about it.

Also going down the same drain was John Britten's other great masterwork—Cathedral Junction. Barry Read, the designer John had hired, had remained in Christchurch after also being summarily fired by Tim Corcoran, working on a local television production. He often walked past the deep-frozen project at Cathedral Junction on his way to the studio, and the sight of the deserted lot always left him feeling sad and disappointed.

> Cathedral Junction was designed in stages so that it could grow organically. Although the money was apparently there to finish the job completely, it did not need to be done all at once if money was an issue. At the point that the project was shut down we had finished all the expensive work on stage one—all the structural work to convert the old façades to our new use. If we could have just finished that stage it would have eventually generated the money to move to stage two and then stage three and so on. The team to do the job was in place and we could have managed without John. He had already left an explicit and detailed plan for the project. In a way his part was done. It was a sad folly that it did not go ahead, even at a much reduced pace.

Vicki Buck echoed this sentiment.

> I had a strong impression that the people left in charge didn't understand that project. We even had a request that the tram tracks be ripped up. Without John there was no one left in control with any passion for his vision, and that was tragic for the city. As a council we would have bent over backwards to see it happen, but the interest simply was not there from the other side.

So instead of any further work being done, the site was cleared of debris and coated with fresh gravel for car parking. Concrete tubs were dragged in and planted with a handful of wispy trees, while the massively strengthened and restructured façades stood as hollow sentinels guarding nothing more than a forgotten dream. The cheerful ding-ding of the trams' bells announced their regular arrivals and departures, but there was no reason to get off and there was seldom anybody waiting to get on. In fact the site remained empty until developers finally purchased it, in the year 2002.

Barry Read was invited to join the resurgent project, but one look at the new plans that had been drawn up was enough to persuade him he wanted nothing to do with it.

> When I saw what was proposed I was utterly disgusted. The new development was to be a basic tilt-slab construction with wiggly lines cast into the concrete as a sop to the ideas John had been pursuing. John had been after clarity of form and function, and while he had loved curves he would have hated the way the developer was plagiarising details without any understanding of the basic idea behind John's vision. In all respects this new plan had nothing to do with John.
>
> I found out that the architects Warren and Mahoney had actually lost or destroyed the final hundred drawings done for John in his life, drawings that were bringing to form his last dreams. It made me deeply unhappy to consider that this was the way Christchurch treated a man who was, after all, considered one of New Zealand's greatest designers.
>
> My sadness turned to anger when I later saw a television news item concerning a boutique hotel that had opened in one of the original, retained buildings. Claims were made about 'realising John Britten's dream', claims that couldn't be further from the truth. One of the hotel's exterior windows featured a two-dimensional man 'creeping in', a joke apparently that it was claimed John would have enjoyed. He wouldn't have. The thing was a travesty and an insult to his memory.

By that stage, however, a more fitting memorial had already been established on the windswept ridges of the Port Hills, where the city council had purchased a block of land to 'preserve its unique scenic, environmental and ecological qualities'. At the request of the previous owner, Winston Robinson, the council named it after John Britten.

Kit Ebbett recalled that he and John had often climbed up to the isolated spot, in the shadows of a set of massive radio aerials dominating the skyline, to stand against a strong east wind and have a rave. It was a beautiful spot, and it was for ever inviolate—a fitting and wholly adequate place to remember an exceptional life.

CHAPTER TWENTY-THREE

Swansong

For those who had been let go it was a time to find new directions. Broz had already returned to work as a forklift mechanic, and after paying off his tax bill with a bank loan he set about rebuilding his life. Along the way he created yet another Ducati-powered special to replace the now retired Aero D Zero, a machine as meticulously engineered as its predecessor. However, after two crashes broke and fractured more bones than even the most hardened sporting motorcyclist can stoically sustain, he gave up racing, bought a house on a bit of land in the country, got married and became considerably less grumpy.

Quentin Rowe and Jeff Ballinger teamed up to form an engineering and design business, while Guy Kingsbury bought a service station.

Shaun Craill landed a job designing kitchen and bathroom hardware and returned to Auckland. He subsequently had one final episode with the Britten Motorcycle Company following his nomination of the Britten V-1000 for a New Zealand Design (or BEST) Award. Shaun had discussed the idea of entering the awards with John but apparently he had not wanted a bar of it. In spite of John's attitude, Shaun proceeded anyway and entered the bike under the names of the entire Britten Team. After John's death the governing committee of the BEST Awards then decided a special award, to be called the John Britten Memorial Award, should be created instead. The new award was to be given for outstanding achievements and would not be granted automatically every year. [219]

For some, however, putting Britten Motorcycles behind them was far more difficult. Jason Monopoli, for example, eventually ended up where he wanted to be, working for top international designers, but he did so only by the narrowest of margins. Just over a month after John's death he had started to feel ill as he worked at his design board. He began vomiting blood and then passed out. A doctor was called and Jason seemed to recover somewhat, but then he had a second episode. He was put to bed and the next day felt well enough to have a bath. However, when he was unable to summon the strength to get out of it he was admitted to hospital. He went in on a Friday night and by the following Sunday he had lost a further eleven units of blood. His veins were collapsing and he was by then losing blood faster than the medical staff could get it into him. With life slipping away an emergency operation was scheduled, and a blown artery was discovered and repaired. Finally, his weakened body could retain the life-sustaining blood it was given and he began to recover. A month later he accepted an invitation to attend a job interview at the Triumph Motorcycle Company in the UK. Triumph and Jason were not destined for each other, but he did land a job with the famous British design company Seymour Powell. His health remained good and his career as a designer flourished.

Back at the workshop, what was left of the Team was determined to run at least one last campaign together before it was all finally over—the 1995–96 New Zealand Superbike Championship. It would be run with just one machine and one rider against formidable opposition. And there was only one bike for the race, said Loren.

> We had now completely repaired Roberto's bike after its return from the TT and we asked him if we could race it. He was happy to agree and announced that he and Sandro would come down for the season. It was really good that we could use his bike as it gave us a chance to test the new package in an environment that was more sympathetic than the Isle of Man, and we had access to our own workshop. However, we were under no illusions about the size of the challenge—we knew it would be tough.

Obviously, those who had been denied the winner's podium in the past by John Britten's V-twins now had a raft of new machines with which to take on the ageing Britten design. However, the V-1000 chosen for the job was handling better than ever, with a new swing-arm and sprag clutch, and the heart of the beast, the magnificent V-twin engine, remained potent and competitive. Loren and Andrew worked together on a comprehensive test programme at Ruapuna to fine-tune the bike for the coming season, and Andrew quickly whittled his test lap times down with a best of 1..33.6, close to the lap record.

Tim was chosen to wield the spanners, with Murray on call should he be needed, and by the time the first race of the season at Manfeild came along Loren felt they were ready.

'We had to be,' he said, 'because Robert Holden was back with a vengeance. Don O'Connor of Eurobike Imports, the New Zealand agent for Ducati, had teamed up with Dallas Rankine and they had imported a stove-hot 955 Corsa from England. They were determined to beat us fair and square on the track and they had the set-up to do it. We were equally determined to win one last series for John. If we had not continued to develop the bike, however, we would have been dog tucker.'

The 955 Corsa in question might not have been the quickest factory twin in the world, as the works obviously had further significant set-up tweaks for the machines they supplied their own riders. At the time, however, it was a top Superbike in the UK and in every sense a full factory, state-of-the-art, purpose-built race bike that had been methodically developed and set up over a full season of racing. Dallas Rankine, the driving force behind so many of the Ducatis Robert Holden raced, was a talented and determined team owner/manager, and with additional backing from the Ducati dealers in New Zealand he had the resources to back his plans. With Dick Huurdeman along to keep the machine at the pinnacle of peak performance, the team represented a formidable combination.

'Robert took his racing very seriously,' said Andrew. 'He never raced for the money—it was always the challenge. There was a lot to him. He knew what was going on in the whole scene and I often thought he would have made a brilliant crew chief. Most riders just think about how they are going in a race, but Robert remained very aware of the characters around him. He could always relate to the way other riders felt and he would use that to get past them.'

In fact, Robert knew his opposition all too well. He had been one of the riders responsible for the refinement and development of the V-1000, and he knew intimately both its strengths and weaknesses. Given his outstanding abilities as a development rider he probably knew them better than anybody else.[220]

Robert was not the only one who believed that Andrew and the Britten might be vulnerable to the pressure the Ducati Dealers Team could apply. Many people still questioned just how good the Britten really was—partly the price of its celebrity. John had always believed that his countrymen would eventually turn on him and often talked of the 'Tall Poppy Syndrome'. The TPS was a view, espoused here and there over the years by a number of social observers, which held that New Zealanders tended to bring down their heroes, the negative flip side of an egalitarian society. In John's case the syndrome had spectacularly failed, and his early death had put him beyond its hooked fingers, but it was possible that his machines might begin to suffer the TPS in his stead.

Whether or not this might prove to be the case was a matter of only academic interest to the main protagonists, however. Both the Britten Team and the Ducati Dealers Team knew that the 1995–96 New Zealand Superbike Championship was going to be a hard and bruising encounter between two of the most gifted motorcycle racers in the world on two of the fastest motorcycles in the world. And so it proved to be.

The first round of the season was held at Manfeild, and the Britten Team ran into immediate problems as the bike blew huge backfires on the rollers and refused to run. However, this proved to be only a momentary set-back, as recalled Loren.

> Tim pulled everything apart but could find nothing wrong. We got Murray on the blower, and after listening to Tim describe the symptoms he told him it had to be the ignition. Working through Saturday night with Murray on the line, Tim finally found that the top camshaft Hall Effect pickup was not correctly tuned with the one on the end of the crankshaft. He sorted it and we were ready for the race the next day. The race itself was a perfect start for the season. Andrew followed Robert for most of it and then pulled the pin at the end and won. The second race was much the same. Score round one for us.

If the Team thought for a moment that the rest of the season was going to be easy, however, the next rounds of the Championship at Pukekohe soon disabused them of the notion. Andrew was the first to be disappointed.

> Robert hole-shotted me and took off like a missile. We were circulating nearly a full second below the lap record, way faster than I wanted to be going. I was losing the front end twice a lap on the fast sweepers where there are no run-offs. The wheel kept tucking under and I was occasionally scraping the side pods on the track because it was quite bumpy at the speeds we were going. We were very close and often we rubbed fairings. I could brake later than he could and we were often side by side going into the hairpin. On one lap I went around the outside and he ran me onto the grass coming out. After the race he told me that he could not have gone any faster and that every time he looked around I was there. But I never got him.

As it had been at Manfeild, the first and second races played out the same way, only this time the Britten was cast in the losing role.

Score round two for the Corsa.

The meeting at Pukekohe had thrown up old conflicts and Loren had one more power play to win in order to conduct the rest of the season the way he wanted to.

> At Pukekohe Andrew had wanted the springs too soft. The preloads were wrong and the bike was bottoming out, so it just could not go any faster. I could calculate all that and fix it by lifting the bike and making the necessary suspension adjustments, but Tim prevented me from doing my job by dealing directly with Andrew and cutting me out of the loop.
>
> After the meeting I asked Perry to tell Tim that it had to come through me and

> he did so in no uncertain matter. I then had the authority I needed to get on with my job, but we had already blown the race meeting.

The next stop was Ruapuna, where Robert anticipated the Britten would out perform him on the stop-start track, predicting that the final result of the four-round series would be decided at Teretonga. A victory at Ruapuna would also present the winner with the New Zealand Grand Prix. On the way south Robert had absolutely blitzed all his opposition at the Wanganui Street Race (which Britten did not contest as it carried no points in the Championship) and he was really fired up. Robert may have predicted a victory for the Britten at Ruapuna, but he would move heaven and hell to prove himself wrong. The meeting began badly for him, however, when he dropped the Ducati 916SP he was racing in the Sports Production class during a tyre-scrubbing session in the morning. His troubles then continued in the first Superbike race of the meeting when the Corsa developed an injection problem. This allowed Andrew to romp away to an easy win, with Robert the runner-up in spite of a persistent misfire. By the second Superbike race, however, the Corsa crew had sorted the injection glitch and the battle was rejoined. And Andrew was ready for it.

> With all the thousands of laps I'd done at Ruapuna, the fastest time I ever did was 1..33.2, about the lap record. In the last race that day Robert was pushing me so hard I did a 1..33.0. I saw the time on the pit board and thought that ought to do it, but when I looked around there was Robert, right behind me. I put my head down and really let rip! The pit board said 1..32.6 next time I went past, but when I snatched a glance back Robert was even closer. That's when I totally went for it, pushing the bike so hard it was sliding at both ends. The next time I went past the pit board it said 1..32.0. This time when I looked back Robert had gone. I found out later he had fallen going through the esses when his front wheel had tucked under and the bike had low-sided him, dumping him hard and hurting his leg. He tried to restart the Ducati but it was no go. It was typical of Robert to try until he fell, he was such a competitor—not that he often fell, he was too good for that. But he was prepared to push that hard if he had to in order to win.

Score round three for the Britten.

Roberto and Sandro had arrived to watch the racing at Ruapuna, and they had cheered themselves hoarse urging Andrew on to victory. With the prospects of a Championship victory looking positive, and with the New Zealand Grand Prix safely in the trophy cabinet, the two Italians were satisfied with the performance of the Café Racers and Superbikes Britten. However, neither felt like celebrating.

'Both Sandro and I found it not so easy staying as guests of Kirsteen in the home where we had such good times with John on our two previous visits,' Roberto said later. 'It was very sad, but he was gone. We both missed him terribly and things were just not the same without him.'

However, once the circus had moved south to Teretonga, just outside Invercargill, the two perked up. There was the Championship at stake and, just as Robert had predicted, it all came down to these last two races.

The weekend began badly for the Britten Team, when late on Friday during practice a stone flicked up into a drive belt and a part had to be flown south from Christchurch. The next day, however, Andrew threw down the gauntlet by unofficially breaking the lap record set by Robert on a Suzuki GSXR1100 in 1988, by almost a full second. But the first race on Sunday visited further mechanical woes on the Britten when a brake line burst, showering Andrew with brake fluid.

'I was never sure if I was going to stop or not,' he recalled, 'and although it turned out that the anchors were always there it did take the edge off my performance.'

Robert screamed away on the Corsa to lead the twelve-lap race from start to finish, officially breaking his old Superbike lap record by 0.21 of a second on one blistering lap, with Andrew hanging on for second place. For Robert it was a remarkable feat of grit and determination. His injured left leg was now a mass of black bruising from the knee down. (The Teretonga track is nearly all left-hand corners, where riders use their left legs constantly.) While waiting for the start of the second race, his leg cramped badly, but he was still confident that his bike had more top end than the Britten and that he could still take it and the Championship. He gritted his teeth and prepared to go out and do it again.

Roberto and Sandro were now very nearly mute with tension, and they waited in an agony of suspense to see if Andrew could fight back and save the day and the Championship. Everything depended on the last race.

They had nothing to worry about. With his front brakes fixed, Andrew simply rode away from the Ducati, breaking Robert's brand-new lap record by 0.078 of a second. On the last lap he pulled a huge triumphant wheelie all the way down the home straight to the roar of the crowd. None roared louder than Roberto and Sandro, in spite of their ragged, raw throats, as Andrew took the chequered flag and the Championship. Andrew would meet up with Robert just one more time.

> I saw Robert in Wellington about a week later. I had arranged to go on a mountain-bike ride with him but he had this massive haematoma on his leg, and as his doctors had advised him it could send a clot up through his system to his heart and kill him he thought it wise to bow out. He was then thirty-seven years old and he told me he was going to retire. He said he wasn't going to do another round of road circuits in

> Europe, but the lure of the TT was obviously too much. He definitely wanted to do a 120 mph lap. He was very, very good at the Isle of Man, a real contender. And he finally did it.

In fact, the 1996 TT looked like being a real Robert Holden benefit. He set the fastest time in qualifying for both the Senior and the F1 race on a Ducati Corsa and the fastest qualifying time for the Sound of Singles race on a Ducati Supermono. He also set the third-fastest time on his Ducati 916SP road bike, and when he joined John Hepburn for dinner he was in a buoyant mood.

'We were talking about the track, as you do,' said John, 'going over various aspects of it. At one point we discussed a particular corner that we had both always found a bit of a challenge. Robert told me that he was sure he could take it flat out, something neither of us had yet been able to do. The next day we found out that he couldn't.'

The Isle of Man had claimed another champion.

On 17–18 February 1996 the thirteenth Sound of Thunder was held, and it was dedicated to the memory of John Britten. Andrew rode the only Britten entered and cleaned up the meeting, winning both his races. Writing in the New Zealand motorcycle magazine *Kiwi Rider*, Rex Knight reported that the most spectacular sight was Andrew Stroud on the Britten after the last race. He spun it round and round in a perfect doughnut on the start/finish line, until bike and rider disappeared in a huge cloud of rubber smoke, then, with precise control, he launched the machine down the front straight in a near-vertical wheel-stand, like an Apollo rocket blasting out of earth's orbit on a moon mission.

As bikes Number Nine and Number Ten slowly took shape back at the factory at something approaching a snail's pace, Loren joined the ranks of the dispossessed, although in his case he drifted away before he was formally cast off.

> I was very satisfied with the way the bike had gone in the New Zealand series and I was keen to work with Perry and Howard to find a way forward. I would have accepted almost any deal to be a part of it, even if it meant just keeping in touch. There was still a lot of goodwill and the recent victories hadn't done us any harm. We resumed our conversations with the corporate types we'd been negotiating with and then, as things were looking exciting, Tim Corcoran made it clear there was no point in continuing and that was that.

The future would continue to involve Loren in motorcycle racing, and his next stop was as a designer in a 500cc Grand Prix motorcycle programme. His new patron, Bill Buckley, was a keen speedway competitor and an Auckland industrialist who had made something of a killing producing particle accelerators for nuclear scientists who wished to study the nature of the universe and manufacturers who wished to zap circuits onto computer chips. (In the field of advanced electronics this is the modern equivalent of writing the Old Testament on the head of a pin.) It was apparently doubtful that any modern computer gear did not have some input from Mr Buckley's company and he had been well rewarded for his efforts. To celebrate his success, he began to spend a considerable part of his good fortune building a 500 Grand Prix machine.

Loren designed the BSL 500s, as they were called, after introducing CAD tools such as solid modelling to the project. Later, Jason Monopoli left the Kenny Roberts Team—which he had joined following his time working for Seymour Powell—to return home and design the bodywork, while Tim Stewart, with Loren's help, scored the task of sticking the two bikes together. Somewhat irrelevantly, Buckley claimed that his project owed nothing to John Britten, but it was hard to imagine that many of the key people driving it felt the same way. Soon after, Loren left the project and joined Team New Zealand with responsibility for all the 'appendages' on their America's Cup boat.

But that, and the Buckley project, are part of another story.

Perry was determined to fly the Britten flag at every opportunity, and in spite of the vagaries and conflicts of his job he managed to stitch together an impressive race programme.

At the end of February 1996 he and Andrew travelled to Daytona to contest both the Pro Twins and the BEARS race using Jim Hunter's bike. Tim Stewart had arrived earlier to fit Hunter's bike with new cylinder heads, pistons and swingarm, as well as generally breaking the machine out of hibernation.[221] The new heads featured the refinements made by Murray to the shape of the combustion chambers. His work had been particularly effective, and with an extra 7 hp the team was quietly confident of victory.

Before the start of the BEARS race, with the field assembled on the dummy grid and the air thick with fuel vapour and nervous anticipation, there was a quite remarkable moment when the entire track came to a complete standstill as a tribute to John Britten. For a full minute the crowd stood quietly, while in the pits the rustle of tools was stilled. Even the gentle beat of the air compressors ceased as all machinery at the track was turned off. Then, with the passing of that single silent minute, it was back to business as usual and the harsh cacophony of motorcycle racing broke out as if wired to a single electric switch.

The start of the race saw Andrew storm into the lead and charge away from the pack. His machine continued to run faultlessly throughout the meeting and he was finally able to smoke the field in both races. The tribute paid to John Britten by both the crowd and the competitors at Daytona was gracious and generous. At the end of the day, however, the tribute paid by Andrew on a Britten motorcycle was even better.

It was also a successful meeting for the business of selling motorcycles, as Perry was able to finalise the sale of Britten number six (number one being the first of the girder bikes) to Barber Dairies. While negotiating the deal Perry was introduced to Mike Canepa, a man who seemed to have unlimited amounts of cash and his own race team—10K Racing. Before long he, too, was negotiating the purchase of a Britten, to add to his considerable motorcycle collection of classics at San Jose.

Although due to a lack of funds, the Team was unable to defend its previous world BEARS title, Steven Briggs rode Roberto's bike at Assen for the fifth round of the Championship and managed a predictably popular win.

And at the 1996 TT, the spectre of the Isle of Man was exorcised to a degree when Shaun Harris rode Roberto's bike right through to the finish, bringing it home in thirty-second place, the second twin home in a field of eighty-four, with forty-eight retirements. A slow pit-stop had dropped him fifteen places and it was hardly a performance to cause consternation in the Honda camp, but Shaun was under orders to keep below 10,000 rpm and he did manage the mileage.[222]

On the way back to New Zealand Perry and Andrew stopped off in America, where they were guests of Jim Hunter. They took Hunter's bike to Loudon in Maine, where Andrew put on a demonstration at the local track in front of a substantial crowd. Mike Canepa was also there with his 10K outfit, and he and Perry were able to get together and clinch a deal for Britten number seven.

Back in New Zealand, Perry organised for Jason McEwen to climb onto a Britten just once more, eighteen months after he last rode for the Team, at the first annual Robert Holden Memorial Race at the Cemetery circuit in Wanganui. Jason set up Roberto's bike with his favoured rock-hard suspension and won easily after a slow start. He also took Roberto's bike to Australia, where a round of the national BEARS championship was to be run as a support race for the Australian round of the World Superbike Championship at Philip Island. The Britten made up for the Team's somewhat lacklustre performance on their previous visit to Australia when Andrew easily won the race in front of a very supportive crowd.

Roberto then generously gave his bike to what was left of the Team to campaign in the 1996–97 New Zealand National Superbike Championship, with Steven Briggs on board. The Team was therefore able to mount a two-pronged attack, with Andrew riding Number Two, which was still owned by the estate, although Andrew could not join them until the circus arrived at Ruapuna. However, while Andrew's mount had undergone a complete refit, Roberto's machine was beginning to suffer the effects of a prolonged period of hard racing, as Steven recalled.

> Although I'd raced the same bike at Assen and won the BEARS event on it, it was no longer performing up to par. It was very worn and really it should have been rebuilt or retired. Tim found he could not even keep oil in it. It wasn't so much leaking at the seams as just weeping through the castings. The cases had had it really and I suspect the gearbox-bearing housings were so worn that they allowed the shafts to get out of line. We had a lot of mechanical failures and I had to put up with jamming and jumping gears.

At Ruapuna Andrew took his place in the Team to contest the New Zealand Grand Prix. With all the new modifications his machine proved to be the best-handling Britten he had ever experienced. Ironically, however, these very improvements would cause him to crash quite spectacularly and heavily.

> In addition to the sprag clutch and the new swing-arm and girder blades, the back end had finally been modified with an eccentric axle for the swing-arm, which lifted it another 5 mm to the point it should always have been. I won the first race easily, but Chris Haldane got out in front on his Ducati 996 Corsa in the second. It was the last race of the day and I was running behind Steven. I remember four of five times in a row he shut the door on me as I was trying to get past—I suppose he wanted to beat me. I also remember thinking that the bike was gripping so much harder than it ever had before, particularly under acceleration. I was able to get the bike underneath Steven and out-brake him going into a right-hander. Usually the bike would slide a bit under power, but this time it just gripped when I wound it on. We went over a bump and it slid sideways just a little, but the rear suspension spring was not compressed, as it would have been before the swing-arm pivot-point modification. It suddenly gripped again and kicked back from left to right, tipping me off. It only just got me, but it was a hard fall and I chipped a bone in the back of my knee. I still have problems with it.

John Hepburn was behind Andrew when it happened and he saw Andrew fly clear over Steven. He watched aghast as Andrew and the bike, which was trailing a comet tail of pink and blue bits, then slammed into the bank on the side of the track. Hepburn completed a further lap, convinced that Andrew must have been seriously hurt—or worse—by the crash, and he was both relieved and surprised to see him on his feet by the wreckage when he next passed the spot.

It would not be the last time a Britten would throw Andrew.

'Later, doing two demos on successive weekends, I had the suspension jam on some of the cabling,' he said, 'and I had two hard falls that really hurt. If you are going to take a Britten motorcycle to a track it really has to be a fully supported effort with mechanics that know the bike and so on. They don't like being trifled with.'

In spite of the somewhat shaky start, the Championship finally fell to Andrew, with Steven taking third place.

'I didn't manage to win a single race in the series,' said Steven, 'and a lot of people felt that indicated I was not up to the job, even though I came in third. That's motor racing I guess. For a while I felt pretty bad about it for Roberto's sake.'

As 1997 wore on Perry continued to seek equity investors to revitalise Britten Motorcycles, but really there was little to sell other than the company name. At the same time, the Indian Motorcycle Company imploded in a black hole of allegations, denials and litigation, finally bringing to a halt any possibility of a revival of Britten fortunes from that direction. The outcome was a great shame for all those who were genuine fans of the redoubtable old name—although there were any number of keen players waiting to kick the corpse—and, who knows, maybe one of them will actually administer the kiss of life to the famous marque some way down the line.

As the number of salaried staff was quickly whittled down by the man who had now earned the nickname the 'Mean Beanie', or 'Rambo@london.com' for the apparent equanimity with which he 'bulleted' people from the other side of the world, the survivors fell out with one another. The workshop staggered on in an atmosphere of surly resentment that often boiled over into acrimony. Murray described one such day in an email to Shaun Craill, when he wrote, 'all the toys ended up outside the sandpit'. And then there was an extraordinary episode when psychiatrists were brought in at great expense to sort everyone out in the head department. It was a peculiar and predictably unsuccessful thing to do when the heart of the problem was quite simply that those who were left were just waiting to be summarily dismissed.

Perry continued to go racing whenever he could, funding the campaigns with sponsorship money and the sales of merchandise. For the first time ever, Britten Motorcycles was actually showing a profit, but it was a hard slog with no obvious end in sight. Perry had arranged to deliver Canepa's bike to him at Daytona in March, when the annual BotT race was to be run alongside the first round of what was now known as the Sound of Thunder World Series, and he managed to wangle funding to take Andrew along with him. Before leaving, they won the BEARS National Finals Race at Ruapuna. At Daytona, 10K Racing, Mike Canepa's race team, had organised American rider Tim Barnes to ride their bike, so Andrew rode Jim Hunter's machine and won both races, with Barnes managing second place in the Sound of Thunder event.

By this stage Perry's one-year contract with Britten Motorcycles had run its course, and although he continued to direct operations for several more months there was no talk of renewing it and his final period with the company was unpaid. Saddened and somewhat disappointed, he eventually gave up and Britten Motorcycles was once again left adrift without a hand on the helm.

In spite of the absence of a manager at the factory, Pukekohe businessman Kevin Grant was able to negotiate a deal with the estate to purchase V-1000 number two, which would thence forward be known as the Waterbike, after Kevin's irrigation company Water Dynamics. Although it was retired from active racing, the bike would in future often appear with riders such as Chris Haldane and Andrew Stroud[223] on board to thrill crowds at Pukekohe with electrifying displays of power and dexterity.

Back at the workshop, Tim Stewart, who had left the BSL project for the time being, finished building Britten Number Nine and, as he had a relatively free hand, it was very much his machine. Meticulously assembled and incorporating all his ideas on tuning and balancing, Number Nine would prove to be an absolute demon, possibly the fastest Britten ever. Tim also finally finished writing his manual.

Sean Chamberlain, an ex-boat builder, now looked after the bodywork department. He had lost a leg in a motorcycle accident and his wages were paid under a local rehabilitation scheme. It was a stroke of luck for Britten Motorcycles as his commitment to quality was absolute. Everyone who saw the machine agreed that the bodywork on Number Nine was the best yet. And, as always, Bob Brookland was there, still 'hanging onto the dream like you wouldn't believe', to lay on his beautiful paintwork, this time a stunning gold and black livery.

Once it was ready, Number Nine was dispatched to Japan along with Chris Haldane as rider and Tim as spannerman. It was a first visit to the country for any Britten motorcycle, and huge crowds at Tsukuba racetrack received it with rapture when, in the sixteenth round of the International Battle of the Twins Series, it turned out to work its magic. Wayne and Bob were also there, and for a while it was just like old times; the Team was back. Chris was astonished at the wild reception the bike enjoyed, with tens of thousands of fans trying to climb into the pits to get a glimpse of the V-1000. The considerable quantity of merchandise the Team had brought with them was soon gone. Chris recalled the event:

> It was a big event anyway, with lots of All Japan Superbike riders present. We were told it was the biggest crowd they'd ever had at an All Japan Championship event and that the record attendance was apparently down to the presence of the Britten. God knows what the numbers were, but it was certainly the biggest crowd I'd ever seen.

It was an incredibly competitive race, with a host of really fast 8-valve Ducatis being ridden hard out by absolutely fearless and talented Japanese riders, in addition to a number of Miriwaki Honda twins, factory-supported machines that really jumped out of the corners and handled extremely well. I was quite envious of the way they could be tipped into the big, high-speed sweeper that led onto pit straight as I was struggling with it. The front end on the Britten was not happy when cranked over on the gas, and the patter was so bad going through that section that my vision was blurring and it felt like the front wheel was going to leap off the ground. However, the motor was pure dynamite. It felt like my Corsa with an additional 1500 revs and it made power all the way up—very much how I imagine the latest factory Ducati Superbike would be. I knew that Tim had created a monster that would absolutely do the business, but I also knew it was not a long-term proposition. Nothing that hot can hang in for long.

We arrived at the track with minimal practice time left, but I was pleased to qualify on the front row and decided that a lightning-quick start to grab the clear track offered the best strategy. Unfortunately, just as the light went green, something let go in the clutch with a bang and the bike promptly assumed a vertical attitude, with every prospect of looping over on its back. In fact, I'm convinced that it would have if I'd had just 100 extra revs. I hung on like a clam and closed the throttle and waited for it to come back down again. When it did I nearly stalled the bike because, of course, I couldn't clutch it, so we slowly chugged off in dead last place. I felt like a complete dork, and as I didn't really know the track that well and it was only a short race, our immediate future looked pretty sad. However, I still had all that power and I started to blast my way back up through the field, going quicker all the time. It was tricky running without the clutch, but I managed not to miss any gears and ended up in fourth place, just missing third as the flag dropped. The crowd was going wild and under the circumstances I was pleased to claw back a bit of dignity.

After the race the media were tripping over each other to get photos of the bike and so on, and the crowds in the pits around the bike were bigger than ever. It was mayhem.

Because there was a very good chance to sell Britten Number Ten to a German who had been expressing interest in the machine for some time, Britten Motorcycles had also decided to contest the next round of the series, which was at the Festival of Ducati at Oschersleben in Germany. We turned up and settled in, and then the most peculiar thing happened. Tim had altered something in the suspension but the set-up was pretty much as always, and once again I figured I'd have to use all the power I had to get out in front to overcome the handling peculiarities. We arrived at the track on Sunday morning and I went out to warm the bike up and scrub the front tyre in. I mentally braced myself for the usual struggle at the places I would have

> expected the bike to patter, but there was nothing. I pushed it harder and harder and still it behaved absolutely perfectly. In fact, I was going far faster than I'd ever have thought possible and still there was no sign of the dreaded patter. I had all this brilliant power and a bike that suddenly handled like a champion. The Britten was suddenly everything John could ever have dreamed it could be, and as I waited for the race to start I kept thinking, 'This is going to be out of this world'.

Chris's partner, Vanessa, was watching from the pits as Chris took an 'awesome start', jumping cleanly away from the rest of the field.

'We lost sight of the bikes as they went around the back of the circuit,' she recalled, 'but Chris was well in the lead. By the time they came back into view he was miles out in front. He had blown away the rest of the field so badly I was almost embarrassed.'

Out on the track Chris was still going faster and faster.

> The first lap was out of the box, and as I got to the end of the main straight on the second lap I had a quick look behind to see where everybody else was. To my amazement the track behind was completely empty. I sat up and had a longer look back, thinking that the race must have been red-flagged, but then this Honda VTR with a German Superbike Champion on it came around the corner and I knew it was still on. So I got on with it again and started stretching out my lead. For the next three laps I was thinking that this Britten had to be the most amazing bike in the world, when suddenly the patter began to return. I could see Tim making ease-up signals every time I went past the pits. He knew that engine was close to the edge and he was beginning to get nervous.
>
> I won the race reasonably easily but by the time I'd finished the bike was handling just the same as ever, pattering away whenever it was tipped over under power. I only experienced it working faultlessly that one time and it made me think there had to be something simple about the set-up that we hadn't quite understood. I know John always felt that way and that it had frustrated him badly that he couldn't quite nail it, but it was a case of so close and yet so far. The bike was sent back to Japan for one of their motorcycle magazines to have a test rider put it through a session back at Tsukuba before it returned to New Zealand, and I think he managed about five laps before the engine Chernobyled itself.
>
> For me the German race was a great way to bow out of the Britten story, and for a while there I am quite sure I was riding the fastest bike in the world.

Brittens continued to race here and there as their owners felt the inclination. Michael Canepa kept the flag flying in the US, with American rider Michael Barnes on his bike taking yet another Daytona victory in 1998 after Tim had fettled the machine for fresh action.[224] It was perhaps ironic that now that John had gone his bikes had at last achieved the crushing superiority he had sought in the races they had been designed to win. This latest success at Daytona showed clearly that there was absolutely nothing that could challenge a well-prepared Britten. The Team repeated the victory in 1999.

In Italy Roberto's enthusiasm for competition was battered by the sadly precipitate death of his friend Sandro, yet another victim of cancer. However, Roberto remains a staunch enthusiast for the Britten motorcycle and no doubt the day will come when the proud chequers of the Café Racers and Superbikes V-1000 again grace the racetracks of Europe.

Number Nine's engine was rebuilt for its new owner, Gary Turner, and his bike is now set for a hard racing career at all the old haunts—Assen, Daytona and, perhaps, who knows, the Isle of Man. Gary also purchased a generous inventory of spares to keep it cooking.

Number Nine and Number Ten, the last two bikes built, were eventually sold for US$100,000 each, which were the highest prices yet paid. Britten Number Ten was the lightest ever, with a magnesium kit replacing many of the aluminium parts. With Tim Stewart now working back on the BSL project it was largely assembled by Rob Selby and it was destined to occupy pride of place in its new owner's living room in Nevada. For the first time, Rob took charge of mapping the ignition as the shining new machine sat on the dynamometer. He called in a mate who had some experience of such things and together they hunched over the computer screen in the small office in the dynamometer room and puzzled over the meaning of the words, *Laufzitfehler—aufgetreten*, the same words that had stumped the Team years before. In spite of the difficulties, the machine eventually produced all the right numbers on the screen and it was crated up and sent to Las Vegas. Years later, it was still in its crate, its proud owner apparently happy to leave it that way indefinitely.

Wayne Alexander came back into the picture, this time with the title Race and Prototype Manager, of a new company called Britten Prototypes Limited, which he set up with the estate. For a while motorcycles were back on the agenda, specifically a motocross machine with yet another funny front end featuring hydraulic steering and a radical new two-stroke engine. When a second private investor became involved, a further company, Dashfoot Limited, was established. The new company's objective was to produce prosthetics for athletes, and one of the first such projects was a new artificial lower leg with an ankle joint of hard but flexible nylon and a lever to change the angle of the foot for cyclists. The new company enjoyed some success with its prosthetics, but after Britten Prototypes experienced financial difficulties the estate sold its shareholdings in both companies to Wayne for a nominal consideration. He then continued to pursue his projects only as a tenant in the factory.

And so the dream flickered on into the following century, while individuals such as Perry Rees continued to seek a role for a restructured company to carry the Britten name. Slowly but surely, however, the light was fading.[225] Ironically, Broz would be the very last employee of Britten Motorcycles recalled to rebuild first the Waterbike for Kevin Grant and then Gary Turner's machine. By then there was no one else to turn to. Another machine may eventually assume the mantle of the big, bold, Britten V-1000 when twin-cylinder machines gather to race. Such is the nature of progress. It is hard to imagine, however, that it will capture the hearts of admirers in quite the same way that the Brittens did. Inherent in the history of Britten Motorcycles is an element of pure fantasy that turns out, on close inspection, to be wonderfully grounded in truth. And the achievements of the man who dreamed up the fantasy and of the small team of individuals who designed, crafted, developed and raced Britten motorcycles are hard to over-estimate. Over a decade after the first steps were taken to create them, the Britten V-1000s remained outrageously different to every other machine they raced against. They also remained savagely powerful contrivances that could foot it in almost any company, contrivances that furthermore, require individuals of rare talent and courage to extract the best they had to offer. Fortunately such individuals were always available to do just that.

It has been remarked that when all is said and done a lot more is usually said than done. In the case of John Britten and the Britten Team, however, it may be fairly said that they made their mark and that they did it at the place that really mattered—out there on the track. It is also possible that the most remarkable quality of the Britten V-1000 may yet prove to be the longevity of its racing career. And there is something more. Where the Britten motorcycle is concerned, the shared dream is so powerful that many passionately want to see it go on. They come from all over the world, and they come from every background imaginable. Some love motorcycles, some simply love dreams and dreamers. They have not, and they will not, easily forget the man and the machines that made such a powerful statement about both the power of the individual and the power of teamwork.

John's good friend and former team-mate Allan Wylie once remarked that John wanted to win races but, even more than that, he wanted to win international acclaim as a designer. John undoubtedly knew that it was only by doing so that he would also win the freedom to spend his life exploring his remarkable imagination. That John Britten's motorcycles won many races, and continued to win races for years, is a matter of record. However, it is indisputable that John Britten also achieved his primary objective—international recognition as an outstanding engineer and designer.

In 1998 the curators of the Solomon R Guggenheim Museum in New York mounted a major exhibition called 'The Art of the Motorcycle', and the unique Frank Lloyd Wright-designed building was ideally suited for such a show because the single gallery had been constructed as a continuous spiral from bottom to top. The museum had gone to considerable trouble to stage the exhibition, mounting special polished stainless-steel panels on the walls that perfectly set off the parade of machines, and it proved to be the most successful exhibition in the museum's history. Later, the exhibition would move to the Field Museum in Chicago and then to Germany via the new Guggenheim in Bilbao, Spain, attracting huge attendance numbers in each place. Finally, it would prove to be the most popular exhibition of this kind ever staged anywhere in the world.

At the very bottom of the Guggenheim's spiral was the steam-powered Micheaux-Perreaux, built in 1868 and the first of 100 motorcycles arranged on the spiralling gallery floor. Over 300,000 visitors to the exhibition in New York wound their way up the gentle incline, passing a cavalcade of significant motorcycles, all carefully chosen to illustrate the evolution of the machine and to celebrate each step of the journey. At the very top, at the end of the line, they encountered two machines arranged in such a way that it was impossible to know which was the penultimate and which represented the pinnacle of the art of the motorcycle. One was a blood-red racing Ducati. The other was a blue and pink Britten V-1000.

Endnotes

CHAPTER 1

1 The distance between New Zealand and the rest of the world's major populations was eloquently demonstrated in 1917 and 1918 when the German raider *Wolf* captured and sank a number of ships off the North Cape of New Zealand before meandering home. On its completion the voyage represented the longest distance in recorded history that anyone ever travelled to attack someone else.

2 The ballast rock was quarried from the headland at Church Bay, the very place where John Britten would later buy his holiday home.

3 Corporal punishment was abolished in New Zealand schools in 1988.

4 The downturn was the beginning of a vicious seesaw that wiped out many businesses while the economy wobbled between recession and depression, a situation that persisted for many years.

5 It is likely that Bruce would have stayed in the airforce longer had his father's failing health not forced him to give it up to run the family business.

6 It is not recorded if Bruce personally knew Bill Hamilton, the high-country farmer credited with being the father of the jet-boat, but he certainly knew many who were closely connected with that illustrious gentleman.

7 John persisted with letter writing and reached the point where he could pick someone's brains on the other side of the Pacific about often complex technical matters. Many of these communications took the form of faxes, which over the years revealed both a lingering frustration and a final acceptance of his limitations. One hand-written fax, for example, had one word misspelled and crossed out a half-dozen times. Then, before continuing with the business of the fax, John wrote, 'I wish I could spell.' Many letters written by John showed evidence of having been written with a ruler under each line to keep everything on the level and a proficiency of spelling that clearly indicated painstaking and doubtless frustrating use of the dictionary.

8 Various domestic and international motorcycle magazines published Fred's motorcycling adventures, which generally featured Fred—a dog of highly flexible morality—coming unstuck as a result of one of his many flaws of character.

9 When John Bain grew up he and his brother Gavin opened a business specialising in classic machinery and all manner of items automotive, marine and aeronautical. The business, called Fazazz, was located in a large, old, industrial brick warehouse in downtown Christchurch that was rather similar to buildings once occupied by Butler Cycles (now demolished) and the printworks owned by David Turner's father. Fazazz became justifiably well known for its displays of classic cars and motorbikes (mostly of a performance nature), and for the wonderful arrays of books and automotive memorabilia that crammed the antique display cases.

10 Some time later, John also ruined a cork floor in the house when messing about with fibreglass in the course of making his own pair of ski boots.

11 Little did anyone know, of course, that one day the boy tinkering with the long-interred Indian would own a company with a contract to design a complete model line-up to resurrect that ancient and worthy marque.

12 This attitude was probably made more singular by the very large number of old jalopies that remained in reliable service in Canterbury long after most had gone to scrap, a result, it is said, of the undemanding flat landscape.

13 When Allan Wylie, who later became a key player in the development of the Britten motorcycle, heard this tale he was sceptical about the offered Mustang swap. 'John actually advertised the truck for sale in *Road and Track* magazine in the USA and I happened across the ad in an old issue many years later. I can't remember the exact wording but the ad asked, somewhat naively, I thought, for a new American car in exchange for the truck. I'm not sure if the car was specified but Cadillac comes to mind. As for turning down a Mustang, I don't believe it.' A logical explanation for the Mustang story might be that John was already learning the advantages of talking up the market.

14 John Hughson died at the age of ninety-two in 1971.

CHAPTER 2

15 It was Charlotte who gave John the book about the flying pioneer Richard Pearse.

16 While attending the polytechnic John started work on an exquisite caravan to carry on his second International truck, which was now largely completed.

17 The Triumph featured a free wheel device and David Turner remembered John being 'very chuffed' about it. In marked contrast to the single-minded all-out approach he took with most his projects, however, the Triumph was restored only two decades later. Kit remembered him saying toward the end that the car had seemed so very old when he bought it but he'd ended up owning it longer than all the previous owners put together.

18 The beautifully executed wooden caravan boasted leadlight windows, a bunk and a compact galley.

19 The M1 had been built by the highly successful New Zealand racing-car driver and constructor to explore the prospects of manufacturing a supercar. Apparently, he had greatly enjoyed driving the low, gullwing-doored, mid-engined prototype and had continued to do so after the project was finally shelved right up until he was killed testing one of his race cars. He had willed it to his friend and number-one driver fellow Kiwi Denny Hulme. Denny may have been a Grand Prix world champion, but off the track he liked to drive nice and steady, and he apparently detested the M1 as much as Bruce had liked it. In any event it was now for sale.

20 Pounamu is the Maori word for jade, in New Zealand often also referred to as greenstone.

21 Toward the end of the nineteenth century, a theory that symbiosis could act as an evolutionary mechanism had been briefly popular but it was soon discredited and had fallen into ridicule. Peter reasoned, however, that it was entirely rational to suppose that some organisms would parasitise others to the point where the two might entwine to create a new organism. Human hair and animal fur, he argued, could have once been blood-sucking worms. They may have passed,

through a process of symbiosis, from being a life form completely separate to their host, to become an integral part of the host organism. Birds, he believed, were probably small surviving dinosaurs that took to the sea in order to survive whatever it was that wiped out the rest of their larger brethren, where they were parasitised by a feather-like organism called a sea plume. The sea plume is a master of hydrodynamics, able to maintain its equilibrium in sea currents by constantly varying its aqua-foil shape. Why should it not therefore have facilitated flight when the birds emerged from the water? Although this thinking enjoyed something of a resurgence in bona fide scientific circles, mainly following the publication of work by biologist Lynn Margulis in the mid-1960s, Peter was then quite alone in his views on birdology on the remote West Coast of the South Island of New Zealand.

22 Thirty years later Peter continues to wander out along the narrow track that leads to the edge of his eroding headland, where even the sea seems determined to get him. He still talks to the gulls as they hover so improbably in the turbulent wind and they seem to listen. He remains a solitary man in a strangely intense and half-forgotten corner of the world where everything can change with an overnight flood or a slip, and yet where so much seems to stay the same.

CHAPTER 3

23 The old mansion and its magnificent gardens had been bequeathed to the city and both had survived handsomely—along with the original and very splendid gatehouse.

24 By the time the old buildings that made up the Artists' Quarter were demolished, John had long since moved out, but his time there had left a significant impression on him. Years later he planned to build a new Artists' Quarter, part of the complex he intended to be his crowning achievement as a developer.

25 The company name, J K Britten Glass Works, was to appear on John's cheques for many years and even, during an Inland Revenue Department audit, on the tank of his Triumph race bike.

26 The range of lights steadily increased to include items such as tulip shades and magnificent parrot lights. The lead-light parrot featured compound glass curves and was perched on a stand. Kit recalled that John spent some time learning to curve glass for his lights, heating it up and slumping it into metal moulds. Although the process was clearly similar to that he had employed making the watch-face for his former girlfriend, Kit remembered that the 'workshop was ankle deep in broken glass before he got it right.'

27 One friend recalled ordering a light that was finally delivered three years later. By then she was not even sure if she had ordered it, or if it had been offered as a gift, and she was uncertain if an offer of payment was appropriate. John soon disabused her of that notion, however, and she duly coughed up. Typically, the light became a treasured possession.

28 In time, Allan's talents would take him to Auto Restorations Ltd, a company with an outstanding international reputation for the exemplary work it carried out on some of the world's rarest and most valuable classic cars. A visit to Auto Restorations might have found Allan assembling a bronze Weber carburettor, manu-

factured from scratch by the firm for a gleaming red mid-1930s Grand Prix Alfa Romeo prior to a day of classic racing at Ruapuna. Or he might be found sorting out a bug in a blue Bugatti. This is not to say that the company confined itself to maintenance and repairs. A second Grand Prix Alfa Romeo, a sister to the first, was a powerful testament to the company's skills. Re-created from a surprisingly small collection of original parts, the fabulous racer sported a host of 'new' parts, including wheels, brakes, suspension, steering, body, fuel tank, cockpit interior, engine parts (including the engine block, superchargers and carburettors) and exhaust—all built meticulously to the original specification.

29 Through the most crucial years, Colin was to be a loyal and tenacious supporter of the Britten motorcycle project, working without reward and ultimately with little in the way of recognition. It was a testament to his strength of character that he looked back on the past with an affectionate and somewhat detached view.

30 The episode did not dampen John's desire to fly like a bird, and a few years later he and another couple of mates purchased what was at the time a very high-performance hang-glider. They trooped out to the Port Hills, the steep volcanic range that separates Christchurch from Lyttelton, to take a few elementary lessons before soaring off into the wild blue yonder. An instructor who was present at the time recalled his misgivings when he realised that the three were not listening to a word that was being told to them. The inevitable accidents happened—John cracked his pelvis, one friend broke a collarbone and the third novice acquired a buttock full of thistles.

31 John never really grew out of his sugar addiction. It was said that while climbing Mount Aspiring he kept himself going with pockets full of jellybeans.

32 It will come as no surprise that John's favourite musician at the time was David Bowie.

33 Paul later bought the car after 'stuffing my own TR2 into a ditch' and then, some years later, sold John the pagoda-top Mercedes Benz 280SL he would own and sometimes race for the rest of his life. On one such occasion Paul captured him on film indulging in what Paul laughingly described as 'an appalling display of driving', with the Mercedes completely sideways while he pressed on with his arm out the window to keep the door shut.

CHAPTER 4

34 This was but a variation on a theme for Marguerite, who also survived lots of 'spin-outs' in the Healey and many more moments of absolute terror. On one occasion she and John were being flown in 'some ancient biplane' that clipped a fence when landing in a field. Fortunately, the only damage was a little torn fabric on a wing.

35 The 'Hub', as it was popularly called, was a transitional model between the rigid rear-end model that John had and the swing-arm machines that followed. The Hub achieved a certain amount of rear springing with springs located between a special hub and the axle, obviating for a time the need to change the frame design.

36 The engine specification now included a 750 Bonneville inlet cam and an E3134 exhaust cam in a carefully flowed head featuring considerably enlarged inlet ports.

Triumph Trident intake valves were utilised and fuel was delivered by the bored-out Amal concentric carburettors, which were mounted on handmade manifolds. At the bottom end of the engine a one-piece 650/750 Triumph-type crankshaft was used, which increased the capacity to 512cc, a capacity that surprised many familiar with the Triumph when they learned of it. It was commonly presumed that Allan must have bored and stroked the engine to extract the power that he gained from it.

37 A few years later John had another crack at whitewater rafting with CJ. According to CJ, it was midwinter and the water was icy. He fell out of the raft and struggled to the surface, only to find John waiting to push him back under again. 'I didn't know if I was going to drown or die of hypothermia. I couldn't wait to get back to a hot tub, but when I finally got out of my wetsuit and jumped in I damn nearly scalded myself to death. Something had gone wrong with the thermostat and it was nearly boiling. John was never a cruel person but he couldn't resist the absurd and he thought it was hilarious.'

38 John's welcome stood in contrast to the Country Gentlemen's refusal to allow Allan to race his Ford Coupe—either because they did not consider Henry Ford's V-8 pukka sahib or they didn't want another John on the track. Finally, however, they realised that Allan was a talented driver, a gifted engineer and a fine fellow to be with. 'I was eventually invited to race the coupe in '92,' he recalled. 'By then I had got to know some of the Gents and I earned my ticket to the Wheels and Wings meetings by doing scrutineering. I'd also raced a Moto Guzzi, a trio of Straight 8 Alfa Romeos, an Aston Martin DB3S and a few other things, which certainly improved my standing with them.'

39 BEARS racer Mark Franklin, who was a highly skilled electronics technician with Air New Zealand at Christchurch Airport, installed the timing equipment. Mark specialised in the repair and maintenance of instruments and his skills would later prove invaluable to John.

40 When English motorcycle journalist Alan Cathcart came across the burgeoning BEARS scene in the Antipodes, it was obvious to him that the proven popularity of the mix augured well for an international affiliation. He went on to achieve just that, with considerable help and encouragement from one of the original founders. By then, John Britten needed an international arena for his own machines to compete in, and BEARS would eventually help to provide it.

41 Having Mike Sinclair onside was like having a direct line to the coal-face of Grand Prix technology. When Mike later accepted a top job with the Kenny Roberts Marlboro Yamaha Team he became a key insider in the largest and most powerful motorcycle race team in the world at that time. 'King Kenny's' team was so well resourced and funded that competitors nicknamed it 'The Evil Empire', and with Wayne Rainey riding they would eventually clinch three 500cc World Grand Prix Championships.

42 Somehow it later became widely accepted that they actually finished sixth and Allan suspected that John might have been guilty of some small exaggeration. They did finish sixth in class but were beaten by a couple of smaller machines in addition to the five in their own class.

CHAPTER 5

43 Dennis was Jon White's older brother and was also a founder member of the BEARS.

CHAPTER 6

44 Pearse's aircraft in nearly all respects anticipated future development far more than did that of his American counterparts. How a solitary farmer managed to do this in a place so removed from anywhere remotely connected with the fledgling technology of powered flight, using such common materials as cut-down sheep-dip tins for his propeller blades and old irrigation pipe for his cylinders, is a story to inspire the most jaded imagination. But he did so and on 29 March 1903 a small crowd saw him splutter into the air and fly straight and level across a field into a hedge. This singular achievement was discounted mainly because Pearse himself did not consider his first flight to have been sufficiently controlled to qualify as 'flight'. His modest denial of the significance of his own achievements encouraged a certain amount of ridicule and earned him the unfortunate nickname 'Bamboo Dick'. The fact that he ended his days as a solitary, angry figure in a psychiatric hospital simply added a sad piquancy to a truly heroic story.

45 Hamilton, a high-country man who loved adventure every bit as much as John did, slipped away from the family farm in his youth to go to England, where he raced Bentleys at Brooklands, the famous English oval track. After returning home to resume farming he dammed a river running through his land and built his own hydro-electricity generator. He then used the power to manufacture his own unique heavy-digging and earth-moving machinery, training up his farm-hands to be skilled metal workers and engineers. He won a reputation as a brilliant engineer and innovator for his pioneering work with hydraulics, and was credited with inventing an excavator that could swing its bucket right over the driver to load a truck waiting behind it. Obviously, this saved a huge amount of time because the machine no longer had to turn away from the face it was working on.

46 Newcombe had done well in New Zealand and Australia racing speedway and motocross, and had eventually caught the eye of the agents for the German motorcycle manufacturer Maico. The company, known primarily for its excellent motocross machines, offered him a place in its factory as a mechanic and a works rider in Europe the following season. At the time, Kim worked in Melbourne for the agents of Konig Outboards, and he had been tremendously impressed with both the elegant simplicity of the German machine's design and the quality of its engineering. He had proven these qualities for himself racing a Konig-powered hydroplane in Australia, and when he arrived in Germany he contacted Dieter Konig, the founding owner of the outboard motor company. The two immediately hit it off and instead of taking up the Maico contract Kim accepted a job in Berlin with Dieter. In between racing hydroplanes with his daredevil boss and preparing racing engines, Kim found time to build a Grand Prix motorcycle using one of the company's demon 500cc race engines. When he couldn't find an experienced rider willing to take on the job of developing and racing the new bike, he did it himself, winning five races in Germany to gain his international race licence. At the same time he began to develop a Konig-powered sidecar and con-

structed a number of motorcycles for other riders.

In 1972 Kim entered the West German Grand Prix and came home third. The sudden, electrifying presence of the complete unknown on a water-cooled, 4-cylinder, 2-stroke machine, a machine utterly and bewilderingly different to anything else then racing, was a shock to the motorcycle hierarchy. However, it was nothing compared with what happened the next season. Incredibly, with three Grands Prix run, Kim Newcombe was out in front, leading Phil Read and Giacomo Agostini, both of whom were racing works MV Agustas, in the championship. Phil Read finally overhauled Kim in the points chase and at the end of the season he was second. Tragically, Kim was not around to accept his trophy having been fatally injured in an accident during a non-championship event at Silverstone prior to the final Grand Prix in Spain. It was not quite the end of the story, however, as a Konig sidecar won the world Grand Prix Championship in 1975 and 1976.

47 At Daytona in 1972, now being a member of the factory team, Geoff was given a works 500 to ride only to find his Kiwi-prepared engine was stronger. And so he rode the Lawton machine and was cruising home for an easy win when his chain broke on the last lap. Shortly after that his career came to a premature end in July 1973 when his Pan Am flight crashed into the Pacific, killing all on board.

48 Roberts built the machine in two bites after Geoff wrote off first the front end and then the back end.

49 The 500 Suzuki frame Roberts built for Keith Turner to contest the 1971 500 World Championship was the fourth such item he had created—basically it was a refined version of the TR Suzuki tubular frame equipped with a square-section swing-arm featuring Timken roller bearings. This arrangement offered outstanding strength and superior handling. The package of a Steve Roberts frame and cycle parts and Dick Lawton's engine was good enough for Turner to take second place in the championship behind Agostini.

The following year, the Steve and Dick combo produced a more powerful tubular-frame machine for Turner along with a radical monocoque version. The latter featured a welded and riveted sheet-alloy frame and proved blindingly fast in testing. Unfortunately, a long wait on the start line for the first race in Singapore, in searing heat, cooked the monocoque's motor, and so the idea of an airbox fed by cool air from an inlet remote from the engine was born. This was incorporated in all Steve's subsequent designs and eventually in practically all race bikes.

Steve continued to build frames for 250 and 500 machines, and when Dave Hiscock, a New Zealander who had competed brilliantly in Australia and Europe on a McIntosh-framed Suzuki, approached him to build something different for the 1982 season, he again opted for an aluminium monocoque. Quite apart from the fact that this offered superior strength for a weight that was at least comparable with the conventional machines it would race against, it was also different enough to attract the kind of attention that might secure Dave a factory ride the following season.

With new V4 Hondas and new lightweight works Suzukis ready to race in the 1983 season, Dave needed to come up with something radical or face the prospect of withdrawing from international racing altogether. For a while the latter seemed inevitable, but he was finally persuaded by Steve that they should have a go with the new composite materials, then regarded by those who knew something of their immense strength and light weight with almost mystical awe.

The idea of building a monocoque motorcycle with non-metallic materials had occurred to Steve when he originally saw a Lotus Elite, the world's first production sports car with a monocoque structure of fibreglass and polyester resin that hit the market in 1958. It was not until 1967, however, that Steve began to play with such materials after taking up motocross racing. His home-built race bike featured a tank, airbox, seat, number plate and back mudguard in one fibreglass unit, which he found tremendously difficult to remove from the mould because of its rigidity and strength.

Steve also largely restored Rod Coleman's fabulous collection of classic racing motorcycles and classic cars. Not least of these was a very early Stutz Indianapolis race car, which he completely refurbished from a basket of bits for Len Southward's museum. In time, Steve would restore a number of machines for Len, whose collection of outstanding classic cars is justly renowned throughout the world.

50 The fact that the front end and bodywork could be then parked in a gallon drum, leaving the factory 16-valve Yoshimura GS engine, with rear suspension attached, completely at the mercy of mechanics, was to prove extremely useful later in the pits.

51 Farrow eventually became manager for New Zealand International Superbike rider Aaron Slight.

52 When John Britten and Steve eventually met it was, according to Steve, a real pleasure. 'I guess I ran into John three or four times altogether, but I remember one occasion at Manfeild very clearly. John had by then built this fantastic machine and he was selling raffle tickets to help take it to Daytona. I bought a couple and then had a good look at the bike. He had the tank off it so all was visible and I congratulated him on his achievement, telling him that I considered he'd really cracked the Buddha. He was so open and friendly he just lit up and answered all my questions. There was no hint of professional jealousy about John because he was a genuine enthusiast.'

53 These parts eventually included Bert's overhead valve heads, cylinder liners (machined from old gas pipes), wheels, pistons and rods, carburettors, magneto innards, cams, valves and flywheels.

With good-humoured equanimity Bert endured endless blow-ups and a number of high-speed accidents. He was fond of saying that if an engine blew up before crossing the line it was too highly tuned, if it blew up over the line it wasn't tuned enough and if it blew up on the line it was just right. In 1967 he and the Indian (equipped with his own cobbled-up streamliner body) managed a mean two-way average speed over the Bonneville at Salt Lake in Utah of over 190.07 mph, breaking several international speed records in the process. (Bert was clocked on several occasions at over 200 mph!) When Bert died peacefully aged seventy-eight in 1978, he was carving two new con-rods from a DC6 aircraft propeller and was planning yet another foray to the salt. It is sad to think that John might never have met Bert, but it is also entirely possible that he did. One thing John did speak of, however, was his admiration for Bert's remarkable achievements and he acknowledged the old speedster as an inspiration on a number of occasions.

54 Unimpressed with the slow steering of his Ducati 900GTS, Broz opted for a steep steering-head angle of 24 degrees, while the forks were Ceriani units taken from a 750GT that were fitted with especially made heavy-duty springs and heavier fork oil.

55 This swing-arm was essentially the same shape as the carbon-fibre swing-arms John developed later.

56 The under-slung rear spring was a Formula Ford automotive Koni, which supplied excellent damping, although locating the correct strength spring proved difficult and Broz had a succession of them made by local company Gerrard Springs. The bike rolled along on a Morris magnesium-alloy wheel at the rear and a similar-looking Campagnolo wheel on the front, both wearing Michelin slicks.

57 Broz eventually won the coveted Cahill Cup at the annual BEARS speed trials several times, and was the first competitor to break the 150-mph mark in 1988. When in 1990 he set his highest recorded speed to date over the flying quarter-mile with a run timed at 153.98 mph, he also won the 'Guess your speed' sweepstake by failing to meet his estimate by just 0.25 mph. Given the motor's only moderate power, the very respectable top speed clearly indicated that John's aerodynamics had something to recommend them.

Broz's efforts on the bike were far from restricted to straight-line drags, and he was a consistent podium finisher in local BEARS races and other club events. In 1989 he took a hard-won second place in the inaugural BEARS TT Championship, beating the likes of Paul Pavletich, Robert Holden, Owen Coles and Jason McEwen, all of whom were on state-of-the-art machines that made Broz's Aero D Zero look positively vintage, at least in terms of its technical specifications. He also took second place in the New Zealand BEARS Formula One Championship behind Glenn Williams on a Ducati 851.

Broz finally retired the bike in 1990 after winning a fifth place in front of a big crowd in a BEARS race at the World Championship Superbike meeting at Manfeild. The race marked the end of an effective racing partnership between a talented and doggedly determined rider and a beautifully balanced machine. Because the bike still had an alternator, a kick-starter and provision for the required lighting, Broz considered converting it to a street bike, but he finally decided to allow the machine to rest in peace among his other 'toys', and there the story of Aero D Zero ends—for the moment at least.

58 These included Jack Shuttleworth and his sons, who were famous for their exploits in *Tru Jen*, an Allison aero-engine powered hydroplane. At the time it was profitable to purchase war-surplus Allison and Rolls-Royce Merlin aero-engines, brand new in their maker's cases, from the Royal New Zealand Airforce purely to recover the expensive metal used in the poured bearings.

59 Colin Lyster died in Nelson in 2003.

60 Colin Lyster also became quite heavily involved in the areas of streamlining and braking. In 1999, he recalled his career in Europe:

'About then the all-enveloping "dustbin" fairings were outlawed and there was a lot of activity in the area of streamlining. The dustbins were banned because they were so dangerous. However, the new open-wheel fairings were not very stable and they were the subject of much experimentation. I used to go to Vickers Armstrong and pick the brains of the old boys who could still remember low-speed aerodynamics. I'd run something past them and they might say that it would work up to 300 mph and I'd say fine, that's more than we need. Sometimes they might even give me a foil, a shape that worked.

'During 1965 and 1966 I tried putting a wing behind the rider's head. The wing was adjustable and would revolve around to a vertical position under braking to act as an airbrake. The FIM banned it and so I tried canard wings and all sorts of other things. By then I'd stopped racing and had constructed a special Manx for David Croxford to race. The only thing that wasn't mine was the motor and even that was more mine than Norton's. The bike featured a space frame like an aircraft and it was very fast. I worked with Rob Quaife on a new gearbox and he built his first six-speeder for me. We also made the bike stop properly, and if you read the old books they accredit me with being the father of the twin-hydraulic disc brake on motorcycles after I developed a set-up for the Norton. That led to a stint working for Ferrari on their disc set-up and later with Jaguar who were also experiencing some problems. Next was a job with Chrysler building a race version of the Hillman Imp to deal to the Mini Coopers. The Imp went on to beat Roger Clark in his works Escort. He couldn't believe it.

'My work with aerodynamics also took me to Ford and the GT40 programme after they had taken control of the project from Lola. After that I was persuaded to go to America to work with Honda on both braking and aerodynamics for two years.'

61 A 2-litre, 4-valve-per-cylinder, twin-cam, 4-cylinder engine almost attracted sufficient local investment in New Zealand to make limited production as a marine engine.

62 This was the same accident referred to in Chapter 5, caused by the Truimph's cracked oil tank.

63 Typical of such experiences was that of Bruce Kennedy, an Auckland driver who raced at Western Springs Speedway.

'Bob built an air-cooled, 4-valve-per-cylinder, quad-cam, horizontally opposed flat-four. It was like a big VW and it seemed to have heaps of potential. It was so low, and light and compact. At the time half the opposition drove American VW-based engines like the SCAT and Autokraft, all them being between two and two-and-a-half litres. The other half were in Ford Cosworth BDPs. There was always a lot of innovation and experimentation in speedway, with blokes doing all sorts of things to engines. In the early days, some blokes were using 4-cylinder Rugby engines supercharged with aircraft-cabin blowers and Jeep motors ported and bored to the max. One bloke was making cylinder heads by doing them in two pieces, a top and a bottom, so he could machine all the waterways and so on. Later on we sawed a Chevy V8 in half and made a big V4. Others sawed them the other way and made straight slant-fours. But we hadn't seen anything that was entirely built here until the Denco came along.

'The engine was just under two litres and although it's hard to say exactly how much horsepower it made it felt like about 140, which was pretty good. We built a car for it and it was a very neat little set-up. Unfortunately, it was hard to keep it going. The basic engine was OK but the motor needed another year in the workshop to sort out the bolt-on bits. Bob built quite a bit of the fuel-injection system, including the throttle bodies and the injectors, and it was really hard to make it work. We ended up making a lot of bits and although my father Doug was pretty good at that stuff it was very challenging. Perhaps Bob should have just bolted on Hilborn injection in the first place. The camshafts didn't have any keyways to locate the cam-belt drive pulley and we had to send it back to him after four or five meetings because we just couldn't time it. He then sent us Allan Palmer's upright 4-cylinder to keep us going and, as we never got the flat-four back, we used that until 1990.

'Allan had raced it quite a bit and had won a few championships in Christchurch but the opposition was a lot lighter down there. Since 1938, for example, the annual National Championship has only been won two times by South Islanders. Allan did bring the car to Western Springs Speedway a few times, but although he was quite competitive he never made the podium.

'When we got the motor Bob had put it back together as a 2.1-litre 4-valve and we had some hopes for it. And in truth it went pretty well. However, things were changing. I started racing for someone else and the big American production engine-based fours arrived. The 166-cu-in Chev-based Brayton, for example, developing about 360 horsepower, along with the Gaerte and Esslinger and so on. I lent the car to a friend who campaigned it for a season or two and it made a good B car.

'I always felt Bob was bored by the stuff he'd already made and simply did not put in sufficient time to make things work properly. And that was a pity because they had a chance there to really achieve something.'

64 The idea of using fibreglass to build the 12-metre boats to compete for the oldest sporting trophy in the world had been considered before, but such thinking was always stymied by the fact that the rating required that the boats be built to Lloyds of London (English maritime insurers) specifications. However, the New Zealand team had come up with the idea of having two Lloyds surveyors present during the entire time the hull was being constructed, to supervise the preparation and application of all materials in order to verify that they were being used precisely to the manufacturer's specification, thereby achieving certification.

Although *KZ7*, one of the three 'Plastic Fantastics' prepared for the team, would narrowly lose the right to challenge Australia at Fremantle to American Denis Conner, the impressive performance of the boat sounded the death knell for metal construction of America's Cup boats.

65 As always, John did not hesitate to pump Jerry for further advice on a number of other matters, including the optimum size of the carburettor jetting. 'The front head will still use our down draft converted carb,' he wrote, 'but we will adjust it so it sits at about 45 degrees. We feel we might be able to bore the 38 mm smooth bore Amal Mk 2's out to a maximum of 40 mm. Is this enough?' He also asked if, in Jerry's opinion, he should make a two-into-one exhaust system to save space (a move bound to incur the disapproval of Bob, who believed that with such systems 'you always got a dud shot on the twin and that killed them stone dead').

66 According to Allan, all estimates of where the red line was were largely specula-

tive because the rev counters, which had been sourced from Mike Sinclair, could never be persuaded to work. The real limit may well have been 1000 rpm below the lower figure.

67 In 1986, the year prior to Aero D One's appearance, Phil Payne, a former New Zealand National 250 Champion who had also won the Castrol Six-Hour race in what was then a record time, had taken the cup on a 1000cc Moto Guzzi with a speed of 142.8 mph. John often dropped by Phil's motorcycle-tyre shop, which was a favourite hang-out for sporting motorcyclists, for the odd social session. The two had met when John and Broz first attempted the Six-Hour and had become close friends. Because of his prowess as a mechanic Phil was known universally as 'The Doctor', and in 1982 he had worked with Mike Sinclair for the Suzuki Factory team in the UK.

By 1987 Phil was back in New Zealand doing what he enjoyed most—racing motorcycles. Although Phil would never become part of the Britten Team, he would become one of those highly select outsiders to whom John sometimes turned when he needed a fresh approach to talk something through. Or when he simply felt like having a bit of fun.

The following year Broz took the cup back with a top speed of 150.82 mph. His fastest winning top speed ever on Aero D Zero was 153.98 mph, posted in 1990.

68 Gary then contracted fellow Kiwi rider Robert Holden to race his bike for the rest of the season and Robert wound up winning western Canadian and Canadian/American Championship titles.

69 The race itself was as dramatic an affair as ever, when in the fourth session race leader Dominique Sarron crashed his Honda into the foam blocks on the side of the track and became entangled in the ropes holding them together. Sarron was co-riding with Wayne Gardner, then leader of the 500cc World Championship and the winner of the two previous Suzuka eight-hour races. Although Sarron eventually fought his way free, the team had dropped to about tenth place on a machine that was clearly no longer running right. The crash meant that Gary and his team-mate Katsuro Takayoshi, who had been running strongly in second place after qualifying ninth, looked certain of pulling off a huge upset win. Australian champion Kevin Magee was chasing hard, but with 7:55:00 showing on the clock and with just 6 km remaining he was still 12 seconds behind and was no longer making up ground. Then, as it so often does in motor racing, disaster struck. Takayoshi clashed with a back marker, damaging the fairing. Although he was able to continue, Magee had slipped through for the win on his Yamaha. A keenly disappointed Pop Yoshimura in the Suzuki pit had to be content with second place.

70 Ken McIntosh was an Aucklander who had built a number of extremely successful race bikes for riders like Dr Rodger Freeth. In particular, he was known for the quality of the frames he designed and fabricated. In more recent times he had become justly respected for the quality of the replica Manx Nortons he built.

71 Hugh Anderson, the former 50cc and 125cc Motorcycle World Grand Prix Champion, was a close friend of Alan's and he ventured the opinion that both the accident and the harsh words that followed were a result of what he described as

Alan's overwhelming enthusiasm.

'He had only just started his writing career and he was blazing with this desire to ride and report on all that was new and exciting and different. Obviously John's bike fitted the bill and I think Alan, who is quite an emotional person, was hurt on more than one level when it rejected him. Later, after he'd ridden and reported on heaven only knows how many different machines, he matured both as a writer and a rider and I know he regretted bursting into print like that. But he never lost his absolute enthusiasm for doing what he did, and when he later crashed badly on one of Ken McIntosh's Manx's I was sure it was simply a result of being so stimulated to find himself on such a superb machine at Pukekohe in New Zealand. I can't say too much about it because I crashed straight into a concrete wall at full bore the next day, but I can say that Alan always really loved his work.'

72 Years later it still rested in peace, and in pieces, beside the Triumph in the dark dungeon beneath the building that was, by then, the Britten workshop. (The dungeon was accessed by a big trap door in the foyer floor and was the home of a huge New Zealand Railways regulation diesel-powered central-heating unit.)

CHAPTER 7

73 When Mike later saw the amount of work that was being done on the V-twin, he revised his opinion and told John that he might as well have done a 500 after all. By then, however, the Britten V-1000 was well on the way.

74 Allan Wylie later nicknamed the somewhat pregnant body shape 'The Barn Door'.

75 This arrangement was designed and developed first by Swiss engineer Ernest Henry for the Grand Prix Peugeots raced before World War I. The American race-engineering genius Harry Miller, among others, had developed the set-up to a fine degree by the early 1920s and had gone on to enjoy great success with it. However, after World War II the 4-valve layout had largely fallen by the wayside and attempts to revive it, by the likes of Walter Hassan of Coventry Climax fame, had largely failed to deliver any performance advantages over the then current 2-valve technology. It was left to Honda to reinvent the 4-valve engine in 1967, which they did with a vengeance. Their radical 50cc twin, 125cc 5-cylinder and 250cc 6-cylinder racing motorcycles were suddenly unassailably dominant, and the 4-valve technology they sported became immediately the new state of the art for both bikes and cars.

76 This was essentially the same arrangement as the HRD Vincent V-twin, except that in the case of the earlier machine the metal sub-frame doubled as an oil tank. John had examined a number of HRDs closely, including a quartet of the machines belonging to Alan Bramwell, the man who had established the Country Gents. Later, John would rent space from Alan when the motorcycle project moved out of The Stables.

77 When Keith Duckworth, one of the partners behind Cosworth, the famous race-engine builders, later visited the factory, he looked down a port and remarked that he would have put the injectors further up. He did not seem to regard the location as being particularly critical, however—a view supported by later dyno-testing of the engine with the injectors in different locations.

78 Eventually, this decision had to be reversed after some difficulties were experienced with the engine advancing and retarding as the belt stretched and recovered. More seriously, the single belt would also sometimes flick over the sprocket teeth, resulting in bent valves and worse.

79 The cam bearings were, like all the bearings in the engine, larger than was conventional. John believed that bigger bearings were not only stronger but that they reduced the tendency for heat build-up, thereby increasing reliability and reducing horsepower-sapping friction. At either end of the camshafts two ball races were paired together and mounted into their respective bearing holders. Oil to lubricate the cams was fed into the bearing holder on the right side of the engine and thence into the hollow camshaft exiting through 2-mm holes on the leading side of each lobe. This was a common practice that ensured delivery of lubrication to the exact point it was needed, and it worked well. During a later test the effectiveness of this system was graphically illustrated. The cam assembly was set up with the buckets on a lathe and spun up to 5000 revs—effectively an engine speed of 10,000 revs as the cams spin at half the engine speed. At this speed it was impossible even to see the assembly owing to the mist of oil. Pressure lubrication was also delivered to the big ends, the gudgeon pins and the gearbox shafts.

80 In later engines Omega pistons of a similar specification were used.

81 Nikasil is an extremely hard compound made up of nickel and silicon, and is applied to an alloy cylinder to obviate the need for an iron liner.

82 Initially, the bore-piston clearance was set at 0.005 in, but this was later reduced to first 0.0045 in and finally 0.0035 in. At these tolerances the performance of the piston was satisfactorily reliable for a racing engine, although there was always a need for extreme care to avoid cold-start seizures.

83 Owing to the narrowness of the angle of the two cylinders, this in turn meant that the cylinder barrels had to be cut away at their bases because they now overlapped inside the crankcase. The two rods featured conventional split-bottom ends and ran side by side on plain bearings on the one-piece crankshaft. The Team had to make one final modification to the rods as they were too broad at the top to fit the pistons, but after a slight shave they were made to fit.

84 Rob continued to do most of the machining at night. He enjoyed the luxury of a new lathe but it lacked a digital readout. As the machine's controls clicked around in multiples of five, it was decided that the Britten engine should also be machined in multiples of five. This certainly helped to simplify matters but inevitably some anomalies crept in. The first block, for example, was intended to be 195 mm high, but after setting up the casting in the lathe Rob accidentally fired it up with the cutter in reverse. By the time he had machined off all the mangled metal, the height of the block had become 193.25 mm, which it then remained for all subsequent engines.

85 This was not counting a set of carbon-fibre baffles John later tried that fell apart and quite literally stuffed up a motor, costing him a New Zealand Championship.

86 On later bikes the swing-arm was painted black, with a clear-finish carbon-fibre feature on the sides of the highly visible component.

87 The Daytona 200 is, as the name implies, a 200-mile race for production motor-

cycles. The rules are basically the same as those for European Superbike racing. It was, and remains, the main event during Cycle Week.

88 All the Suzuki parts were sourced from the Wanganui importers South Pacific Suzuki Distributors, formerly Percy Coleman Motorcycles, which was now run by Percy's son Rod. The company received a regular stream of orders from Britten Motorcycles for replacement parts for the gearboxes, which from the beginning struggled to handle the power of the Britten engine.

89 For a while John toyed with the idea of making some, and he could well have sold a run of such items to other interested parties. Certainly Allan was capable of undertaking such an exercise and he did later build bronze Webers from scratch for a Grand Prix Alfa Romeo. Neither Allan nor Rob, however, could see the point.

90 Information in the blue book included the following:
Bore 94 mm
Stroke 72 mm
Comp ratio 13:1
Balance factor 55%
Injectors Bosch 0 280 150 036
Oil pump Holbourn-Eaton-type full-flow filter
Fuel pump Walbro model 5530
Plugs Champ g58
Conrods titanium as well as valves
Primary drive by straight-cut gears ratio 1.717:1 46/79; later changed to 1.7027:1 37/63
Gearbox gears straight-cut constant-mesh all indirect drive
Ratios first 2.5:1
Second 1.777:1
Third 1.380:1
Fourth 1.125:1
Top 0.961:1

91 Eventually Don Knit came through with a generous amount of sponsorship money and the bike later raced in their colours. At Daytona, however, the bike simply sported one of the company's stickers.

92 The Colemans had enjoyed as much sporting success as they had commercial success. Percy Coleman was one of the earliest stars on the grass tracks that were popular in New Zealand from 1908 until the 1920s. He raced a variety of machines but Indians and Harley-Davidsons were his favourites. His success in New Zealand earned him a crack at the high-speed, banked asphalt surfaces in America immediately after World War I. In 1930 Percy raced a Douglas at the Isle of Man and became the first name on a long and ever-growing list of Kiwi participants. Later, his sons Bob and Rod carried on this family tradition with highly successful New Zealand and international careers. Both raced at the Isle of Man, Rod as an official rider for AJS. Riding one of their machines, Rod won the 1954 350 Junior TT.

CHAPTER 8

93 In 1989, for example, Dr John Wittner had just received prototypes of the new

4-valve 'cam-in-heads' heads from Moto Guzzi and his machine was running Weber/Marelli fuel injection for the first time. He could count on perhaps 100 bhp at about 6900 revs.

94 The second such machine was purchased and raced for many years by Phil 'The Doctor' Payne. Vee Two Engineering would go on to become a highly successful company specialising in the manufacture of Ducati speed equipment, ranging from engines carefully modified to produce substantial and reliable power to replica Alchemies.

CHAPTER 9

95 Ignition maps were entered into the computer that ran the engine management system during the programming of each engine on the dynamometer. Basically, the throttle control offered seven lines between zero revs and 13,000 revs, with an advance degree for every one hundred revs on each line. Once all the entries had been made, the engine would theoretically run at peak power for all throttle openings. In practice, it was often necessary to fine-tune the map for different racetracks to make allowances for such factors as altitude, which would vary the density of the air and alter the fuel-air ratio. Spiking was a sudden surge of electrical energy in the management system that zapped the ignition map into disarray.

96 South Eyre Road had been popular with BEARS riders for some time as a place to test their machines. It was dead straight, reasonably flat and, being a rural road, relatively free of traffic.

97 Among the canny New Yorker's many acquisitions were nearly all the factory 3-cylinder race bikes from BSA and Triumph, plus the entire stable of ex-racers from the extensive Harley-Davidson collection, purchased at a time when such items were not regarded as being particularly valuable and when Harley-Davidson was in dire financial straights. Ianucci had very nearly driven himself broke preparing and racing his fabulous assortment with a variety of invited riders under his banner Team Obsolete. The New Yorker's ultimate coup was to come some years later when he negotiated the purchase of all the exotic, multi-cylinder works MV Agustas from the moribund Italian company.

98 Manfeild hosted the final rounds for the Agip World Superbike Series in 1989 and 1990. In 1989 American Freddy Merkel was crowned champion at the track and the following year Frenchman Raymond Roche took the honours. Unfortunately, a lack of sponsorship prize money, an unwillingness to invest in improvements at the circuit and local opposition to the noise generated by the racing resulted in New Zealand losing the event.

99 The aluminium casting that bolted to the top of the engine to hold the bell-crank later fractured when the bike was raced in Canada by Gary Goodfellow. As a result, the rear tyre collapsed onto the bodywork, producing billowing clouds of smoke as Gary fought the weaving machine to a halt. Colin felt obliged to tell Gary it had happened before and recalled feeling deeply embarrassed by the second failure, which, he said, made them look like amateurs. A Canadian engineer then examined the arrangement and pronounced it unsound, after which it was pinned with an additional strut. Various successively stronger arrangements were then tried

in an effort to produce something so solid it could not fail. Colin disliked all of them just as much as the original, but the problem was only really solved with the next generation Britten, which finally had everything working on the same plane.

100 For Robert, the problems with the EMS were a most unwelcome complication on top of an injury that occurred earlier in the week, when he had taken a nasty tumble off his Honda Superbike. The accident had left him with a badly gashed arm requiring fifty stitches, and so the persistent misfire of his Britten added frustration to pain as he continued to be thwarted in his attempts to learn the difficult circuit, where he had never raced before.

CHAPTER 10

101 'Gary had secured this position on only his third lap,' Paul Vink said, 'on a partially damp track that he didn't know, something that clearly demonstrated the phenomenal potential of the Gary Goodfellow/Britten combination.'

102 Paul Vink also thought the Britten would win: 'Of course we were all very disappointed that the wonderful Britten was out but the crowd now switched their attention back to the tremendous dice that was still going on between Robert Holden and the race leader Oliver Schmidt. This only ended when Holden retired with a mechanical problem on the tenth lap. The same lap saw Mike Edwards steal the lead before Hans Fischer, a very likeable Dutchman, was cheered on to take second place from Schmidt, who ended up third. Kees Doorakkers, who had at last come to grips with the Dr John Guzzi was the first non-Ducati home in fourth place.'

103 Decompression levers were common on large single-cylinder engines equipped only with kick-starts and were used to get the engine past compression. This gave the kicker a fair chance of actually turning over the motor, the momentum already achieved helping to push through compression when it came around again. John reasoned that a hydraulically activated version could allow a much lighter starter motor and battery to be used. It was a promising idea but one that sadly would never be tested by Britten Motorcycles.

104 Egli had made his name equipping his trademark spine frame with engines ranging from Vincent V-twins (which he eventually remanufactured) to Kawasaki Z1000s.

CHAPTER 11

105 Colin's appraisal of John's ability to manage a racing team was endorsed by Allan Wylie, who observed on many occasions the same blind spot to the very immediate dangers involved in the sport—in spite of John's own close calls and painful accidents.

'He never got to grips with it,' recalled Allan, 'because he lacked the temperament for it. He liked to take risks, but one of the key steps to success in racing is to reduce risks to the absolute minimum. In spite of its glamorous public image racing is a game where sound methodology, discipline and attention to detail are essential to success. John never had time for that sort of thing; it was far too dull. He preferred the chaotic approach.'

106 After racing the Britten through the summer, Chris had gone on to win the New Zealand Sports Production Championship for the 1990/91 season on a Yamaha FZR1000, a strong performance that had won him the invitation.

107 It is also probable that John was unaware that Chris would be at Daytona and, given the outstanding run of success the young rider had been enjoying, he may just have rued the additional monies he had paid out to get Lewis—especially as the AMA had declined his request for financial assistance for air fares.

108 In 1989 Crevier became the first Canadian rider to win three championships in one year and in 1991 he would win for Kawasaki both the Canadian Pro 750 Superbike Championships and the Pro 750 Productions Championships, setting outright lap records at every circuit on the Canadian National Tour along the way.

109 The official explanation given by John to the press for Crevier's retirement was a somewhat lame claim that the clutch cable had broken, a statement that the press was happy to repeat but one that left fellow racers shaking their heads. They knew perfectly well that an operating clutch was no requisite for success and all of them could race perfectly well without one once underway. Of course, a detached clutch assembly was a different matter.

110 In the letter John wrote that he wanted to 'thank Rob for his enormous contribution alongside Allan Wylie and Colin Dodge, Ron and Steve Hall in the foundry, Alan Roberts for the crankshafts and so on, the team at Auto Restorations, Gary Goodfellow, Mike Brosnan, Murray Aitken, Mark Franklin and Mark Cawston for all the exhaust system designs. And Bob Brookland for his magnificent paintwork.'

111 Beull overcame his engine supply problem by designing a brand-new chassis to take the RS1200 Evolution engine, a move that finally resulted in Harley-Davidson taking a controlling stake in the company.

CHAPTER 12

112 Allan's views on winning races were echoed by Mike Sinclair. 'In professional racing you don't do anything radical, you do last year's winner plus a small margin of refinement. John would have hated my job, it's so conservative.'

113 In a similar fashion he also later added the further objective of building 100 500cc single-cylinder motorcycles.

114 Hans worked with Rob (who was still, at this stage, working at the engineering shop) on the new heads and got the ball rolling by having Rob build a jig that defined the space available for the new ports.

To determine the best shape for them, Hans bolted the buck to his flow-bench and measured the flow over the bare seats with the valves opened. He led the flow to the seats through short bell mouths that he fabricated from a malleable material. (A secret substance, the nature of which he steadfastly refused to divulge to anyone.) Having thus established a base line, he then began to build up the port lengths, using the same material and adjusting the shape as he went so that the flow was maintained as the ports grew longer.

He first established the shape of the exhaust ports and then turned his attention to the inlet ports, leading them away from the valve stems at the required degree angle and building them up carefully until he reached the intake flange

When setting out the pattern of rovings for each structure, John took great care to avoid right angles, or even tight turns, as they weakened the finished item. In many ways, in fact, the characteristics of carbon-fibre resemble wood and the technology therefore favours gentle curves and organic shapes. On the one occasion he later compromised this principle, he ended up with good cause to regret it.

Once John had finished winding the rovings, he clamped up the mould and baked the assembly overnight in his oven at 50 degrees C. The mould assembly included internal plastic bags, which John inflated to provide constant pressure to force the material against the mould, and outlets for any excess resin.

The following day he popped the structure out of the mould and cleaned it up prior to filling it with expanding foam. (This practice was later discontinued on the girders when John grew concerned that the foam might be putting pressure on the rovings. Structurally, it was found to make no appreciable difference.)

122 The tank was designed to hold a generous 20 litres of fuel, easily enough to complete the races John intended to contest and with a margin for error. There was no metal unit inside the carbon-fibre skin.

123 The components were the dashboard, the bottom pod, the boot protectors, the foot-peg holders, the chain-guard, the shock-reservoir bracket, the coil brackets, the oil-cooler bracket, the battery box, the timing-belt cover and the air-box bottom. Eventually, a highly organised Britten Motorcycle Company body shop would produce the entire list of carbon-fibre components needed for one machine in about 600 man-hours. When 001 (or the first of the 'Slimlines', as some members of the team soon christened the new design) was built, however, there was simply no way to know just how long the job had taken.

124 This was a change in John's attitude from back in the days when he made leadlights and was warned by a nurse that the fumes produced by the furnace in which he melted lead were highly toxic. He and Roland were actually tested for lead levels, and although the results showed some cause for concern John apparently still did little about ventilation.

125 Freddie Spencer, World Grand Prix Champion, had had a carbon-fibre wheel on his works Honda 500 collapse under him in about 1984, the result perhaps of not employing Kevlar in the mix.

126 John started by making moulds for the rims, spokes and hubs, the last two being made in one piece. The spokes and hubs were made by cutting four oversize layers of both carbon-fibre and Kevlar matting and folding them into the mould, wetting them out as he went, the carbon-fibre being laid first to form the final exterior covers.

He then secured rovings to three hooks attached to the outside edge of the central aluminium spool, which would become the axle-bearing housing, and wound them around and around to form the outside edge of the housing. Next, he led the rovings back and forth from the hub to pairs of pins in the termination point of each of the three spokes. The pins were so spaced that the rovings, which crossed over one another, followed the eventual shape of the spokes where they flared to meet the rim. The spokes were made over-length so that when they were trimmed to fit they would not contain any turning rovings. Care was also

5 Such a front end was so different to that being used by every other race team meant that it might take years to develop the technology, and the materials technology in particular, to give reliable and safe race performance. If any proof of this was required one had to look no further than Elf.
6 For all the above reasons, it might be unreasonably dangerous for a rider to take the machine to the very edge where competitive motorcyclists raced.
7 In order to make a girder front end strong enough to handle the loads imposed by racing it was also probable that no weight reduction could be achieved.
8 For all their faults, conventional forks had become so good that it was only at the very sharpest edge of motorcycle racing that their current limits were apparent.

119 Disappointingly, as we shall see, chatter under braking would actually prove a real problem for Britten riders and it would take years to refine the system to a point where it was almost tuned out of the set-up. Similarly, John's predictions on weight savings would prove optimistic.

120 The ducted, horizontally mounted radiator was so successful that it is difficult to understand why it was not very quickly adopted by the world's manufacturers of V-twins and single-cylinder motorcycles, who years later continued to locate their radiators out front. Of all the contributions the Britten V-1000 made to motorcycle design, this was possibly the most immediately and obviously useful. Of course, when powerplants were wide 3- and 4-cylinder affairs it scarcely made any difference.

121 John proceeded by first creating moulds for the various pieces, from which he then produced the 'skins' that would eventually cover the rovings, or bones, of each structure. To make the structure's skins, he cut oversized patterns of carbon-fibre and Kevlar matting, and then placed them into the moulds in layers after wetting them out with resin. The carbon-fibre, which provided structural strength, was the first material placed into the mould as it would create the final exterior finish. The layers of Kevlar that followed provided high-impact resistance. (Bulletproof vests are made out of it.) The excess material was left lying out to the sides of the moulds while he laid in the four alternating layers of carbon-fibre and Kevlar that would eventually encase the bones. Having reached this point, he then folded the excess layers back into the mould, one over the other, finishing up with a skin that was about ten layers thick.

In the same way that he had previously created the bones of his structures, he next wound carbon-fibre in continuous strands, or rovings, four strands at a time, around spools located on a jig. He did this in sequence, back and forth, taking care not to kink or break a roving. (Had he done so he would have had to start all over again because the structural integrity of the finished product would have been compromised.) As always, he kept an even tension on the rovings by feel, dragging them between the four rollers in the resin bath. Surprisingly, at least to people familiar with such materials, he filled the bath with a two-part vinyl-ester (with a retarding agent added to it) rather than an epoxy. He did so because he had discovered that vinyl-ester offered better wet-out properties than most two-packs (compounds that 'set' when one part was added to the other) and could therefore be more thinly applied.

When setting out the pattern of rovings for each structure, John took great care to avoid right angles, or even tight turns, as they weakened the finished item. In many ways, in fact, the characteristics of carbon-fibre resemble wood and the technology therefore favours gentle curves and organic shapes. On the one occasion he later compromised this principle, he ended up with good cause to regret it.

Once John had finished winding the rovings, he clamped up the mould and baked the assembly overnight in his oven at 50 degrees C. The mould assembly included internal plastic bags, which John inflated to provide constant pressure to force the material against the mould, and outlets for any excess resin.

The following day he popped the structure out of the mould and cleaned it up prior to filling it with expanding foam. (This practice was later discontinued on the girders when John grew concerned that the foam might be putting pressure on the rovings. Structurally, it was found to make no appreciable difference.)

122 The tank was designed to hold a generous 20 litres of fuel, easily enough to complete the races John intended to contest and with a margin for error. There was no metal unit inside the carbon-fibre skin.

123 The components were the dashboard, the bottom pod, the boot protectors, the foot-peg holders, the chain-guard, the shock-reservoir bracket, the coil brackets, the oil-cooler bracket, the battery box, the timing-belt cover and the air-box bottom. Eventually, a highly organised Britten Motorcycle Company body shop would produce the entire list of carbon-fibre components needed for one machine in about 600 man-hours. When 001 (or the first of the 'Slimlines', as some members of the team soon christened the new design) was built, however, there was simply no way to know just how long the job had taken.

124 This attitude had been apparent back in the days when John made leadlights and he was warned by a nurse that the fumes produced by the furnace in which he melted lead were highly toxic. He and Roland were actually tested for lead levels, and although the results showed some cause for concern John apparently still did little about ventilation.

125 Freddie Spencer, World Grand Prix Champion, had had a carbon-fibre wheel on his works Honda 500 collapse under him in about 1984, the result perhaps of not employing Kevlar in the mix.

126 John started by making moulds for the rims, spokes and hubs, the last two being made in one piece. The spokes and hubs were made by cutting four oversize layers of both carbon-fibre and Kevlar matting and folding them into the mould, wetting them out as he went, the carbon-fibre being laid first to form the final exterior covers.

He then secured rovings to three hooks attached to the outside edge of the central aluminium spool, which would become the axle-bearing housing, and wound them around and around to form the outside edge of the housing. Next, he led the rovings back and forth from the hub to pairs of pins in the termination point of each of the three spokes. The pins were so spaced that the rovings, which crossed over one another, followed the eventual shape of the spokes where they flared to meet the rim. The spokes were made over-length so that when they were trimmed to fit they would not contain any turning rovings. Care was also taken to arrange the rovings so that the spokes would end up hollow, with the rovings lying against the laminated shells. John completed the spokes by folding the outside flaps of the laminates over onto themselves, then closed up the moulds over the rovings, bolted them together to apply compression, and baked the unit in the heat-box overnight.

After extracting the completed hub and spokes assembly out of the mould, he docked the ends of the spokes so they could be mated to the rim. He then cut and shaped Dyvinicell foam to fit inside the hollow spokes, pushing it home after soaking it in resin. Next, he pushed wetted-out carbon-fibre wrapping into the end to form a plug before grinding the ends off each spoke flat. Finally he laminated two carbon-fibre caps over the ends of the spokes to form a bonding surface for the rim.

He now made the rim, again cutting carbon-fibre and Kevlar cloth over-width before winding the materials into the mould, wetting out as he went. About forty turns completed the windings, after which he stretched an inner-tyre tube around it. The hub and spokes were then located against the rim through holes in the mould and the tube was inflated to about 80 or 90 psi, forcing all the laminates together and against the mould and the spoke ends. Next, John placed the assembly in a clamp and put it in the heat-box for twelve hours. After the assembly had baked to perfection, he sent it off to a machine shop with a form tool that was able to turn the outside of the rim to accept a tyre. When it was returned, the outside of the wheel had the right profile and was perfectly smooth.

127 This was eventually cut back to about sixty hours per unit when the Team became proficient in their manufacture.

128 The weight of that first front wheel after painting was 2.9 kg, while the rear wheel, which John made next, was another kilogram on top of that. Although this was by most standards extremely light, the wheels were not significantly lighter than the best racing magnesium alloy wheels. Later magnesium alloy wheels would weigh in at a featherweight less than the Britten composites, but nonetheless there was one significant weight advantage—the rims on the Britten wheels were lighter than those on magnesium alloy wheels, leading to a useful reduction in rotating mass and inertia.

129 Automotive Products, an English subsidiary of the Lockheed Company, manufactured competition brakes and componentry. Later, when testing the first of the new bikes, Alan Cathcart would be less than impressed with the brakes, comparing them unfavourably with the Brembo units on the Tesi he raced, but he would also be careful to acknowledge the pedigree of AP's product. It may have been that the machine he tested was suffering the effects of some hard racing, because there would be few other complaints about the way the bikes stopped. However, the relationship with AP was not destined to last and later Brittens switched to Italian Brembo braking systems when the costs of AP Racing products no longer seemed justified on performance criteria.

130 The green and red lights were to be accompanied on the dashboard by two knobs. These would permit adjustment of the management system while on the go. The right knob would handle ignition and the left would look after the fuel mixture. A complete turn on the right knob would produce up to a 30 percent increment

in either advance or retard, while the other produced leaner or richer running, and the graduation of the knobs was also easily adjustable. The ignition knob was found to be a mixed blessing when riders actually started to play with it and was soon deleted.

131 Information thus recorded would soon include suspension movements, from data supplied to the computer by a number of linear sensors. If the rider wished to record the behaviour of the bike's suspension through a particular section of track, he could punch a button and leave a marker on that particular cycle for later downloading on the trackside laptop. Graphs of the engine's revs and the power being made during the same period, all of which were also marked when the rider hit the button (along with such information as the engine and air temperature, throttle positions, fuel and air flows and voltage) could then be overlaid if desired to show also the revs and power the bike was making.

132 The first two bikes would prove something of a headache for Ohlins who had no data on shock-absorber piston behaviour for the particular lever rate selected for the new bike. It was finally changed to a lever rate they were familiar with for all bikes built after Britten 002.

133 Hans was able to tell them that *'Laufzitfehler—aufgetreten'* meant 'operating mistake—system shut down'.

134 The new 'big-bore' engine featured an even shorter stroke than the first ones and the new crankshaft had therefore been ordered to provide a stroke of 72 mm for a bore of 99 mm, giving a total volume of 1108cc. The included valve angle had been steepened by half a degree and was now 29.5 degrees.

135 John also wrote that 'the capscrews that hold the heads on are in the way of the outside buckets for a three-valve head. I can lower the capscrews to below the buckets and let the bucket break into the capscrew hole. This will probably work. How long will it take you to prepare some information for me?'

136 The New Zealand Certificate of Engineering was the same course that John Britten had done.

137 Eventually, the machine's unnerving desire to lie down was attributed to the gyroscopic effect of the much reduced, but still substantial, 12 kg-crankshaft, an effect that was probably exacerbated by the machine's relatively high centre of gravity. (The trait was not eliminated until the next generation of Britten engines abandoned Jerry's thinking on the desirability of a heavy crankshaft with a further reduction in crankshaft weight to about 5 kg.)

CHAPTER 13

138 'I eventually set the fastest speed for the meeting around the banking at 189 mph,' Andrew recalled, 'but it took a while to get used to it.'

139 American Motorcycle Association.

140 'I should have said just that,' said Andrew later, 'but I did ride it and we finished second in the AMA Endurance series. In spite of that he refused to pay me, along with all the other guys who rode for him. Of course, I didn't know then that he was going to turn out like that so I felt terrible.'

141 At the time of the visit, local industrial strife and the general world recession had

choked the shipping of the delectable Italian V-twins and the factory was awash in a sea of red motorcycles, a sight that awed and fascinated the Kiwis.

142 Sweeper is a common term for a sweeping corner.

143 Armco is the metal railing often used as a barrier around racetracks.

144 To underscore his point he compared the power-to-weight ratios of the Britten and Polen's Ducati. The Ducati, he reported, weighed 141 kg without fuel and was insignificantly lighter than the empty-tank Britten, which weighed in at 144 kg. However, he pointed out, the Britten had 171 hp at the back wheel compared with the Ducati's 135 hp.

145 Alan also complained that the 320-mm AP front brakes had a lot less bite than the Brembos on the Bimota Tesi he was used to riding 'in spite of their GP lineage'. The throttle action also came in for some stick, being described as somewhat abrupt compared with the delicate delivery of the injected Ducati, a circumstance that he claimed made it ridiculously easy to unhook the rear wheel.

146 'The steering head angle,' he wrote, 'was a very steep 23 degrees in combination with 29mm offsets giving 97mm trail and lots of pro-dive'. He reported that the set-up caused 'the front end to dip significantly under braking, further steepening the front end and reducing trail'.

147 'Later,' Andrew said, 'I realised that the Britten taught me to ride slowly round corners, which wasn't very good for my chosen career. I'd get on a bike with forks and have to consciously speed up. The Superbikes were doing about 1.23 that year at Assen and the best I managed on the Britten was about 1.27 flat. Of course, the Superbikes got about four-and-a-half hours of practice to chip away at it whereas we had only a couple of twenty-minute sessions. Even so, I would hardly have been competitive in their company and I am convinced that a set of forks would have made the difference. If my Britten had been equipped with them I could have carved at least a couple of seconds off each lap, and with the bike running right I'm sure we could have run up front with the Superbikes.'

148 The rider who had surprised Andrew was none other than Sin-Ichro Oura, the grand old hand of Japanese motorcycle sport. His beautifully constructed and prepared Yamaha TRX850-powered, Over-framed special was no slouch and he was determined to add a win in the prestigious BotT race to his earlier victory in the Sound of Singles (SoS) event.

149 On the Britten this was achieved by adjusting the offset on the front wheel at the girder, either with an eccentric adjuster that could be turned one way or the other, or by changing the adjuster for another one altogether. The effect was the same as dialling in more offset on the triple clamps of a conventional set-up. Jason also 'changed the swing arm-geometry. John had the rear end up in the air for a steeper front-girder angle but it didn't work and the bike felt better balanced once the arse had lost a bit of altitude.'

CHAPTER 14

150 The rumour about the cam followers was but one of a number that seemed to circulate around the pits as fast as the Britten circled the track, and there was often an element of truth in them—in this case, the fact that Broz often had the

heads off the engine. However, the reason he so often delved into the top end was not to slip in a new set of cam followers, but to replace the valve springs.

'We did have problems getting the correct valve-guide lengths and the valve-seat materials right but by then we had them sussed,' Broz remembered. 'The persistent problem we still had was with valves failing because the valve springs would crap out. This was especially true of the exhaust valves. Whenever a spring went ping it destroyed the valve and that caused an awful mess. You could anticipate it happening because the bike made a different noise when it was coming at you. Sometimes we were actually able to call the rider in before it blew and save ourselves a whole lot of heartache. It was a design problem with the springs themselves and it had been troublesome from the beginning of the project. Initially, a number of different Japanese production valve springs had been used, but when they failed German Schmethelm springs were tried. Schmethelm were regarded as one of the best sources of racing valve springs, but unfortunately these quite often failed as well.

151 The railways had declined, however, as a result of policies generated by a government-sponsored think tank in the 1970s, which had been led by prominent trucking interests. This somewhat biased group had been entrusted with the task of planning New Zealand's future transportation needs. Not surprisingly, it had recommended that the country largely abandon publicly owned rail in favour of privately owned trucks, and the decimation of the rail network commenced with almost religious zeal. As a consequence, buildings such as this were surplus to requirements and going for a song.

152 John also had a 20-foot-long sign consisting of cut-out steel letters prepared that was to be mounted on the roof, and it would doubtless have looked very stylish. However, he decided against it and the letters were tossed into a jumble in a dark corner within the factory, where they remained.

153 'I'd missed a payment on the bike and it got repossessed on practice day at Manfeild,' said Loren, 'but the sidecar boys gathered around the repo-agents and asked if I wanted them beaten up. The sidecar riders and swingers are a great bunch, every bit as crazy as everyone thinks they must be. I can't imagine a better stoush than one between repo-agents and outfit operators, but I said thanks but no thanks. However, the repo-agents were impressed with the fact that the sidecar operators were prepared to stand up for me and they gave me my bike back for the day. Unfortunately, I was distracted by all the drama and couldn't manage a decent place in either race.'

154 It later took an extensive back-to-basics sort out-by Murray in the workshop before the handling finally improved to the level of the older bike.

155 The meeting would also be the first time bikes had been seen racing at Mount Panorama since the 1980s, when a series of confrontations between race fans and huge contingents of police had erupted into episodes of mass violence, apparently pursued with relentless enthusiasm by both sides. The riots were fuelled by a combination of larrikin high spirits, drought-breaking quantities of alcohol and a determination, finally frustrated, on the part of the police to keep strict control.

156 Such maniacs included Yorkshireman Carl Fogarty, though he hardly made a habit of it. In 1992 'Foggy', as he was universally known, had set what was then an

unbelievably fast lap with an average speed of 123.61 mph on a Yamaha 750—unbelievable to the point that many informed parties believed the engine had to have been bored and stroked.

157 Hislop aroused the ire of race fans by suggesting that competing machinery might sensibly be restricted to 600cc, a position he was quickly pressured into abandoning. He was not, however, the first high-profile rider to question the sporting ethic of killing a constant number of contenders. Giacomo Agostini, arguably the most successful motorcycle racer of all time, with 122 Grand Prix victories and fifteen World Championships, mostly on MV Agusta 3-, 4- and 6-cylinder race bikes, included ten TT Seniors in his portfolio of victories. His disenchantment with the event was well publicised, but he would only say that his decision not to continue racing on the island was personal. It was one that dovetailed with more acrimonious departures. Barry Sheene, for example, roundly condemned the TT as a treacherous and pointless anachronism, and most Grand Prix riders followed his lead in declining further participation. As the 1970s rolled on the TT largely become the domain of specialist road racers.

158 Another person who had some extended contact with the two Italians was New Zealand wool-seller Perry Rees. Perry had become friendly with John not long before through his wife's friendship with Kirsteen, and he enjoyed joining up with the Team whenever his international travel arrangements allowed. Later, he would leave his job to take over the management of Britten Motorcycles, but for the moment he was just a fan, albeit well connected. He met the two Italians on a number of occasions and they made a lasting impression on him.

'They had this real European flair and an absolute lust for life. They enjoyed everything they did. At the time John was telling the press that he had orders for five or six bikes, but the truth was Roberto was the first and only punter to ante up with the loot at the time. That's not to say John didn't have interest from all over the world, because he did. Unfortunately, a lot of the enquiries were for the 'road-going version', and although he told people they were welcome to put lights and such on the bike to conform with local requirements it was obviously never a realistic proposition.

'Roberto badly wanted to race a Britten. He was utterly passionate about the things he loved and bikes were high on his list. He had an incredible collection of Harleys and Nortons, including a number of Norton F1s, but he wasn't at all spoilt by his wealth. I was constantly amazed at the profound things that would roll off his tongue. Sandro, his best mate, was another beautiful human being. He was totally eccentric and although he was also incredibly wealthy you'd think he slept on the streets, because he loved looking like a slightly ridiculous bum. He was a gourmet and I remember him using his very odd finger as a probe to sample bottles of home-made jam at a stall on the Isle of Man, shouting, "Good taste! Good taste!" The stall-holder was horrified, but then he bought just about every bottle she had and suddenly she loved him. His joyful mood was irresistible to most people after only a few moments. When the two Italians arrived at a race meeting in this huge, black bus with everything in it you could possibly want, as well as the Britten and the Team, they were a sensation. But they hardly seemed to notice. They were very cool in this totally unaffected way and they always seemed to be having an enormous amount of fun.'

159 Andrew Stroud later did something similar when he started to run out of petrol and left the track long enough to go to a service station for a fill-up.

160 The horsepower yardstick for a racing single had been established by the radical rotary-valve, fuel-injected Fuchs/Suzuki—with 90 bhp at the crank.

161 Quite where the model got to seems to be a bit of a mystery. When he spoke of the car to Kirsteen's brother Brent Price, John told him to 'put out of your mind everything you think a car should be'. This one, John said, would be shaped like a turtle shell and constructed with organic material (like flax) moulded with resin into a top and a bottom section. To fit inside the shell, the rear passengers would face to the rear. It was to be a three-wheeler (like a side-car outfit) and it was to be powered by a big single-cylinder petrol engine with enough torque to obviate the need for a gearbox. Some versions were to be amphibious and the car was to be designed so that most of its manufacture could be achieved in the Third World.

CHAPTER 15

162 John confidently told Alan Cathcart in an interview for syndicated publication that the Britten Supermono would have an all-up weight of just 90 kg and that he had revised the capacity for the engine from his initial figure of 800cc to 600cc. He had done so, he explained, once he had decided the engine would have more than four valves and an extremely short stroke. Although Alan reported that he was not told the exact bore/stroke ratio he made 'an educated guess' that it would be about 110 x 63 mm. He was able to report that unlike the oval pistons being used by some high-performance single-cylinder engines the piston would 'definitely be round'.

163 In the same fax John Shand also reported taking the tourist board out for dinner. He had been happy to learn that the board had decided to 'continue the precedent set by Britten Motorcycles the previous year whereby they would deal with teams for sponsorship deals as opposed to only dealing with individual riders'. This meant that John could continue to pay his riders out of a lump sum given to him by the board, if indeed he was forced to pay them at all. The arrangement had certain obvious attractions, the main one being that if the riders were paid only a minimal amount the balance of the sponsorship money could be used to defray expenses.

164 Six valves would represent the greatest valve area for cylinder area yet achieved, which promised excellent breathing characteristics if a decent squish chamber could be devised with all those valve pockets. Hans thought the idea worth pursuing, but was horrified by John's plans for multiple, complicated rockers, which he saw as a huge stumbling block.

165 The upcoming contest was eventually destined to result in a New Zealand victory.

166 Russell Boddington later said that John had composted his accounts on the floor of his car.

167 'One of the first things we looked at was the cooling system,' Loren said. 'John drew up a better, deeper radiator, which helped but we still had problems. I think the water pump may have been cavitating but there was not, in any case, a lot of

water around the bores. This had come about because the bore size had been increased, making the jackets thinner. To solve that, Rob got the bog out and we increased the capacity of water in that area by adding extra volume to the moulds before casting the cases for the next five engines. We also moved the studs out to accommodate the increase in the jacket size.'

168 'Murray had known that a bigger bore and shorter stroke with increased valve area was the way to go with the second-generation Britten engine,' Loren said, 'an opinion that John had not at first shared. It was Murray who worked out a computer program to establish optimum cam profiles and valve sizes, duration and lift overlap, and then generally organised and orchestrated the whole project. And in the end it was Murray who had been proven right.'

169 Mike Watt came from Loren's home town of Tauranga and was a hands-on shock specialist at a GP level. Paul Treacy was another Kiwi with the Kenny Roberts team and he and Mike Sinclair set their own data-acquisition system on the Britten suspension, which they also hooked up to the throttle pot and rev counter.

170 Loren elaborated on this point: 'Eventually we set up our own data-acquisition system by utilising some spare channels on the EMS to record suspension movements and so on. We made new buttons for the front end and new spacers to make it behave more like a fork, with pro-dive to steepen the angle under compression so you could tip into corners better. Jason [McEwen] had been winning through sheer hard mental riding with a rock-hard set-up. He could make it work but it was really close-to-the-edge stuff. Generally, you need some suppleness in the front end so that when you throw your weight on it going into a corner the rake changes and the thing turns. Otherwise it feels like a board. Andrew was telling us what it was doing and we were telling him what he needed. Basically mechanics were left to spanner and engineers engineered. After just a few trips to Ruapuna we had the lap times down from 1.38 to 1.33.'

171 PDL is a well-known Christchurch manufacturer of electronic hardware.

172 Over the years Jim had developed a diverse portfolio of investments, including a significant shareholding in a company that specialised in collecting rainforest plants with medicinal potential, which were then propagated in an enormous greenhouse facility.

CHAPTER 16

173 Williamson was a motorcycle racing enthusiast and co-owner of the then Christchurch Motorcycles, at the time a highly successful dealership located near the Artists' Quarter.

174 The De Tomaso Pantera is an exotic Italian supercar powered by a mid-engined Ford V8.

175 Motorcycle streamliners are cigar-shaped devices with totally enclosed cockpits and small side wheels that are retracted as the motorcycle gathers speed and lowered when it is about to stop. They are powered by all manner of engines and usually feature a driven rear wheel rather than a jet or rocket engine.

176 The successful attempt was made on a closed public road in the North Island, a reasonably straight but unreasonably narrow and bumpy road running across the Hauraki Plains, an experience Freeth described as the scariest thing he'd ever done.

177 Possum Bourne died on 30 April 2003 of injuries sustained in a collision with a fellow competitor while inspecting the course of the famous Queenstown hill-climb 'Race to the Sky'. He had won seven consecutive Australian Rally Championships and three Asia Pacific Rally Championships. Subaru had given him factory backing to compete in the 2003 Production World Rally Championship.

178 Nick Williams of Tsunami International, the successful manufacturer of surf skis and snowboards who had first helped John unlock the secrets of composite construction, was drawn into the project to achieve this perfect form. He had Digby Taylor generate wafer-thin sections of the body shape around a central longitudinal axis so they could build the mould up slice by slice.

179 'Many, many hours were put in by the guys in the workshop,' Loren recalled. 'The exhaust system had to be set up, along with the chain sprocket, the throttle linkages, the radiator and a whole host of other details. We also remapped the computer to give more power at higher revs.'

180 Alice was no stranger to Triumph motorcycles, having won the 1992–93 BEARS Clubman series on Jon's red-hot T160. She would attempt to take the national women's outright speed record, previously the property of Heather Spurle, who had managed a two-way average of 168.8 mph (271.6 kph) in a hydroplane in 1990.

181 'It cost ten grand to fly the German out,' complained Jon, 'because he insisted on going first class all the way with his wife. We also organised a Mercedes sports car for him to drive and first-class accommodation. He really racked up some big bills for us while he was here and that was a real burden when we had all these other ongoing costs we had to pay, like three-and-a-half grand for the ambulance for a week. I was going through money like water but that was just the way it was.'

182 According to Loren, 'The race bike we had used had some damage to the front piston and rings, which was thought to have occurred as a result of an airlock in the coolant. After consultations with the streamliner crew it was decided to remove the engine from the streamliner and install it in one of the new, incomplete race bikes. While Broz worked to complete the task, John was busy working out the mounting points for the dustbin, which Bob had now sprayed blue before adding the team's sponsors' logos. Broz lowered the front end of the new bike and put in the highest final gearing they had, with work continuing through till Wednesday, when the dustbin was mounted.'

CHAPTER 17

183 The idea had been tried successfully once before, when in the early 1930s the American tycoon Everett Cord sent models of the stunning supercharged car bearing his name to customers who had placed orders following its unveiling at a New York automobile show. Deliveries had been delayed due to teething problems with the front-wheel drive system, but one look at the model was sufficient to persuade most of Cord's customers to hang in and wait for the real thing.

184 The first job, of course, was to work out how to make it. Injection moulding was rejected as being too complex and expensive, and the decision was made to spin-cast the models in pewter. Every part of the real machine was then photographed

and the photographs were turned into scale drawings. Once this process was completed, it was possible to hew all the parts for the model from solid brass. Often the time taken to make the part on the model matched the time taken to build the full-scale item. The exhaust, for example, took Jim about eighty hours, the same time as the real thing. Copper wire of the correct gauge was heated and bent to make up the correct curves, before each pipe was silver-soldered to the collector. The detailing was exacting and precise, even down to the Britten script on the engine casting, which was engraved onto thin strips of brass that were then fixed to the engine master. Soldering very fine mesh onto the rear sub-frame created the under-seat radiator. When all was done on the masters, Jim turned his attention to the instruction booklet by photographing the parts as they would appear relative to one another during assembly and then holding enlarged photocopies over a light box so he could trace out the line drawings for the exploded diagrams.

185 At this point Jim, left the project to take up a position at the Canterbury Museum and another Wylie brother, Andrew, took over and started to make up the kits. By then the real bike had won at Daytona and so the machine chosen to represent the marque was the machine that Andrew had ridden. The seventy exquisitely detailed parts for the model included moulded rubber tyres, a vacuum-formed PVC windshield and exhaust heat shields, coolant and breather hoses, plus all the appropriate decals. Priced at just under NZ$300 the baby Brittens sold well, with 1400 kits finding a home by the time the last full-size V-1000 rolled out of the workshop.

186 The 'Cos' part of the name Cosworth came from Duckworth's partner, Frank Costin.

187 The Museum of New Zealand has since become formally known as Te Papa Tongarewa, meaning 'Our Place' in Maori.

188 Basically, the facing blocks were machined with slots to accept long horizontal plastic mouldings produced by extrusion dies. Snap-in plastic clips placed into these mouldings held the outside and inside fascia in place. Once the complete hollow wall had thus been assembled, expanding foam was added to make up a fully structural composite wall.

Pre-cast foundation beams, made with special moulds and linked with a poured beam on the top of the structure via steel tie rods, held it all together. There was no grout or mortar in the wall, or indeed any other finishing required.

189 Roland Logan was one of the early friends at The Stables. He and John had remained close.

190 Later, John willed his invention (which he had fully patented) to Roland who continued to build homes, and the system seems inevitably destined for success. This is especially evident when the cost of building one of these stone-faced structures is compared with cost of building in other materials. According to Roland's estimates, the structural masonry is at least 40 percent more cost efficient than any other type of fully insulated and lined walls.

191 This was Black Adder number two, the first having been written off in a race at Ruapuna when Lindsay crashed at speed and the bike ended stuck up a tree. One of the few parts to survive was the exhaust heat shield with the legend 'XR1000'

cut into it.

192 Ken McIntosh recalled events following the win: 'A couple of Barber's riders accepted an invitation to attend the next of our classic festivals back at Pukekohe and when they turned up we organised them a ride on a Britten. They bought one not long after that. We also put John Surtees on one. He does not usually ride other people's bikes because he is still very serious about being on the track. He reverts to Grand Prix mode, totally focused and very fast. However, he made an exception for John's bike and gave it a good caning. He still raced with his open-face helmet and he later told me that he was fine up to 140 mph. Above that, he said, his helmet was trying to strangle him. Being Surtees he pressed on anyway, and he was very complimentary about the bike afterwards.'

CHAPTER 18

193 Burt Rutan was famous mostly for a series of high-performance ultra-light aircraft that he designed and manufactured. He was also responsible for a twin-engined aircraft that flew non-stop around the world and a pedal-powered craft that crossed the English Channel.

194 It was not the first time John had witnessed a plane crashing onto a runway. Years before, in France, he had attended the Orly Air Show and through the lens of his camera had followed a damaged Soviet fighter as it plummeted onto the runway after colliding with its twin. Remarkably, the pilots of both aircraft ejected successfully. John had captured the distant puff of tar, dirt and aluminium when the Soviet aircraft crashed, a small but sharp explosion right in the middle of the frame.

195 Shand had also let it drop to the press that the hugely successful Kiwi rider Graeme Crosby might be enticed out of retirement to ride the Britten, but in fact the latter had only been considering turning up to make a film for television about the event. Although the press referred to 'further talks' being planned, he was never actually approached with the idea, one that the decidedly retired racer would have turned down flat in any event.

196 Nick Jefferies had won the Formula One race the previous year on an RC30 Honda. The forty-something-year-old Yorkshireman had previously made a habit of placing second in a considerable number of TTs over a long racing career, and his maiden victory came exactly twenty years to the day after his older brother Tony collected his final TT win. He had underscored his achievement with yet another second place in the Senior TT and many had then expected him to retire. However, retirement was far from his mind and he was determined to do well in 1994 after being dropped by the Honda Britain squad. His knowledge of the course and of its history was legendary, and he was a popular and tenacious competitor who had first joined the exclusive 120-mph average lap club in 1992.

Mark Farmer was also a member of the 120-mph club, having set fastest lap in the Formula One event from a standing start the previous year before retiring with mechanical problems. The Crawley-based Irishman's best TT result to date had been a fourth place in the 1991 Supersport 600 race, but his electric form on the mainland during the 1993 season had persuaded many observers that a TT podium finish could not be far away. In accepting the Britten offer he wrote, 'As modesty is not one of my strong points I can assure you that I will achieve a good result for you and will give 100%. For your records my best average time around the TT course is 120.68 mph which I achieved in 1992 riding for Team Loctite Yamaha, my team mate being Mr C Fogarty.'

197 In 1994 the Britten Team stayed away for most of the meeting and Loren was able to win the main event on Jeff's Ducati.

198 The fact that Loren had a ride at all was a source of some irritation to John Hepburn, who had been awarded a scholarship to ride at the TT, courtesy of the NZMA.

'Shandy was supposed to organise a bike for me but he gave it to Loren. I complained bitterly because the whole deal was beginning to look like an expensive waste of time, but I finally managed to stitch together a ride and it worked out far better than it I expected. I went home with the Best Newcomer's Award and two Bronze medals, with a nineteenth place in the Junior TT. That was enough to earn me a start in the Senior, where I managed twenty-sixth place overall. Shandy's deals often seemed to turn to custard like that and I decided not to get involved with him again if I could avoid it.'

199 The team was racing new, identical Yamaha YZX600 Thundercats that had been procured from Yamaha for the event by the ever resourceful John Shand. He had also extracted substantial money from the TT organisers to assist the Kiwi contingent in getting to the event, money that in some cases fully covered both air fares and accommodation.

200 Hislop had a camera on board and the video taken actually showed him overtaking the Britten, which appeared stable on the road.

201 Within a couple of weeks the bike had left the smart atrium foyer, with its polished granite floors, soaring glass ceiling and fern-shrouded waterfall, for its first bike show. From that point on it would spend about half of its life resting in its smart corporate home and the balance touring the country.

CHAPTER 19

202 The history of Indian Motorcycles had actually began in 1901, when the then American High Wheeler Bicycle Champion George Hendee and an engineering wizard from New York called Carl Hedstrom put a small petrol engine in a bicycle to help train pedalling athletes. It was America's first 'motocycle' (they left the 'r' out to form a trademark). The little machine, given the name Indian, attracted attention and the partners quickly started making and selling them. In 1902 they won the first motorcycle race in America and in 1903 built their first V-twin. Two- and 3-speed gearboxes, swing-arm suspension, electric starter motors (the very first on a motorcycle), fully electric systems and increasingly powerful engines had all been incorporated into the bike's design by 1913. By then, Indian Motorcycles were the largest manufacturers of two-wheelers in America, producing 20,000 units a year.

The Indians proved popular all over the world following race victories not only in America but also at the Isle of Man, where they came home first, second and third in 1912. Classic machines like the Scout, the Chief and the Sport Scout won over converts as far away as Japan (Soichiro Honda, the founder of the company that bears his name, rode a 101 Scout for twenty years). When in 1927 Indian took over the Ace Motorcycle Company, it added a brilliant range of 4-cylinder in-line motorcycles to an already distinguished model line-up.

Unfortunately, the company had by now been acquired by a group of financiers, who introduced lousy management and not much else. World War II temporarily disguised their incompetence, and both Indian and Harley-Davidson supplied hundreds of thousands of machines to the military. However, whereas the Harley contracts were negotiated with skill, the Indian contracts were such that the company was almost broke soon after the cessation of hostilities. New single-cylinder and vertical twin motorcycles were marketed in place of the promising shaft-drive in-line V-twin (similar to a Moto Guzzi) that had been developed during the war, and the company's doors finally shut in 1953. Under the new ownership of Associated Motorcycles Ltd—the British parent company of AJS, Matchless, Royal Enfield, Velocette and Norton—a few parallel twins dribbled onto the market through the late 1950s and then they, too, ceased production.

203 Hayim-Langridge was a successful Harley-Davidson dealer in Western Australia and he had paid Baughman US$30,000 for the Australian franchise for the new Indian that the latter was supposedly about to produce. He then discovered that Baughman did not actually own the rights to the Indian trademark in Australia, and when Baughman refused to return the money he and Mandelman successfully sued and bankrupted Baughman, acquiring in the process the trademarks that Baughman did legitimately own.

Hayim-Langridge then apparently paid an additional US$2 million to the Massachusetts court, and a further US$1.2 million to a northern Californian Indian parts manufacturer, in order to acquire further rights to the Indian name. Of course, he and his partner Mandelman then assumed the mantle of prime target for a queue of future litigants, some of whom wanted the Indian motorcycle they'd been promised and some of whom wanted to wrest away the right to build them.

204 Hans recalled, 'Murray reading…this article by Keith Duckworth where he complained about the trouble he had experienced with the mechanical cam drive of the DFV engine. He wrote that he wished he'd known how reliable belts were. It made us laugh! However, we knew that many of our problems stemmed from having a single belt to drive both camshafts. We were not convinced by the hydraulicing theory and believed the belt simply became overloaded under certain conditions, although we never really understood what those conditions were. We worked out as much as we could on the computer and then drew up a system we called the "Y-Front".

'This system had a single belt driving a very wide idler cog, which then drove separate belts to the cams. Rob made it up and it worked well enough, but we eventually eliminated the idler and had two full-length belts, which proved very reliable.'

Looking back, Broz felt that the primary reason the belts had overloading was the fact that the bottom sprocket on the crankshaft had too few teeth. It had not always been so. When Hans narrowed the valve angle as part of the quest for more power the camshaft sprockets had then interfered with one another, resulting in new sprockets with two fewer teeth each being fitted. This in turn necessitated a new bottom sprocket with one less tooth, one less in total than the manufacturer's recommended minimum.

According to Broz, the problem at the Isle of Man had not been so much a problem of breakages as of stripped teeth.

'With such a light crankshaft, the belts were unable to cope with the way the engine spun up when it landed after some high-speed jumps. The Y-Front was a sound answer to the problem and I spent about three months testing it on the dyno, where it worked really well. However, it made the engine a couple of inches wider and it didn't look that flash, so John decided not to use it. The two-belt system we ended up going with was a better system than the single belt but it still gave some troubles.'

205 Loren had tracked down the company in Australia that originally made the clutches for Ducati and ordered one to test. The resulting improved handling was achieved as the final drive was able to slip to a degree on the overrun. Essentially the back wheel was no longer hopping about as it tried to turn over the V-twin against the compression under trailing throttle.

206 Tyre valves required caps at racing speeds because the centrifugal force generated by the turning wheel could overcome the spring holding the valve shut, thereby allowing air to leak out slowly .

207 Guy ran discharge plugs because of earlier experiences when the ends had fallen off conventional plugs. Tim elected to stay with the conventional plugs but had to remember to change them frequently to avoid the same thing happening again.

208 John had indeed persuaded race organisers to pay an undisclosed sum of appearance money to Britten Motorcycles.

209 According to Tim Stewart, there would have been little point. 'The original 1100 was long retired and if we had been using the stroker kits everyone would have noticed the fat spacers under the heads. The whole idea of the bikes being 1100cc was plain silly'.

CHAPTER 20

210 Ken McIntosh was, in fact, the only person ever to experience a complete bottom-end failure on a Britten motorcycle, fortunately on the 'slow-down' lap and fortunately after it had been fitted with a sprag clutch, which prevented the rear wheel from locking up. Like John Britten, Ken was a constructor of racing motorcycles. His part in the Britten streamliner and in the construction of specials like Lindsay Williamson's Black Adder has been noted, but the record for his race bikes was far more formidable.

Ken had started 'messing around with old Nortons' as a schoolboy and began making frames for a long line of specials while still in his teens. Although he only ever rode at a club level, his machines completely dominated New Zealand motorcycle racing in the early 1980s. Most McIntosh victories came with the redoubtable Dr Rodger Freeth in the saddle, but David Hiscock, Bob Toomey, Mike Pero and Norris Farrow also enjoyed significant success on Ken's products, with many Championship victories in 250, 350, Superbike, Formula One, TT and Grand Prix racing.

Nor was Ken's success confined to New Zealand. In 1982 Freeth took a McIntosh Suzuki to a surprise win at Bathurst in the Arai 500, the prestigious endurance race that ran alongside the Australian Grand Prix. Over 100 McIntosh Suzukis, in both twin- and mono-shock guise, were finally constructed and sold, along with the superb series of one-off specials that included his own beautiful Vincent-powered race bike. Later, Ken had won acclaim among Norton cognoscenti at home, and around the world, for his superb restorations of Manx Nortons, and for a number of brand-new replicas constructed mainly from his own spare-parts catalogue. (In fact, he was able to build everything from his own parts, with the exception of the top end of the engine.) He had also been a member of the Classic Register since its inception in 1980, and as a committee member had played a leading role in organising and promoting their increasingly spectacular annual race meetings at Pukekohe.

211 Brian Thomas went on to produce a number of different engines, including a 500cc twin-cam desmo, a racing engine planned but never produced by Norton. He did this in association with the original British designer, communicating with a constant stream of email.

CHAPTER 21

212 They did this by cutting the little ends off and shortening the rods. Then the little ends were rewelded back on and the finished rod was heat-treated. The work was carried out by an individual who worked for Jet who took raw castings home and finished them off to Britten specifications. The arrangement had worked well enough, according to Tim Stewart, although he always found it frustrating that no one thought to ask the man to procure extra castings, so that he could make them up when required without long lead times.

213 It was suspected that the oil baffle plates in the sump were now too close to the cases and had turned into little oil pumps owing to capillary action, which caused pressure to build up in the narrower gap. When little grooves were put in the plates to let the oil drain away, it helped but did not entirely solve the problem.

214 Later the Japanese would be allowed in, but the rule remained that eligible machines could not have desmodromic valve actuation, fuel injection and four valves per cylinder. (Entrants were allowed any two of these features but not all three.) Basically, this eliminated 8-valve Ducatis, and left the Brittens as the only serious rivals.

215 Tim remembered further: 'From then on whenever we stayed at his old scrap-metal yard he would take me to dinner quite regularly at this restaurant that belonged to a friend of his. Although it looked like any other Italian restaurant the food was absolutely exquisite and the wines were superb. Looking at the other customers it was obvious that the place was a preferred eatery among the very, very rich. I was never allowed to see a bill but I know they were big. We usually went with a friend of his called Rocco. Rocco was part of the bike scene with Roberto and Sandro, and although he spoke no English we all got along very well. Strangely, Sandro would always disappear at the end of the main course leaving Rocco and I to get absolutely wasted on liqueurs over dessert. Later on, I found out there was a special little room out the back where the gamblers gathered. Sandro would be out there playing double or nothing with the restaurateur for the bill.'

216 Among the more competitive machines they were up against was an 8-valve Ducati Corsa being campaigned by a team owned by an expatriate South African with the name of Gary Turner. Back in the infield, Loren had organised two people to help sell merchandise to the Britten-crazy crowd, who were buying it as fast as they could put it out. One of his helpers was a New Zealander who had a bike shop in Holland, and he introduced Loren to Gary Turner. The two immediately started talking deals, which resulted in Turner eventually buying Britten Number 9. 'It was a great way to sell bikes,' said Loren.

217 Later, Kit would discover that no Queen's awards could be made posthumously, and so the simple civic award, presented without pomp or ceremony, would be the only such recognition John ever received.

CHAPTER 22

218 The trustees of the estate of John Britten were Kirsteen, Tim Corcoran, Chris Weir (John's lawyer), the late Howard Patterson (a highly successful South Island businessman who had become a close friend to John) and Chris James.

CHAPTER 23

219 'I was surprised and disappointed that yet again the Team was going to be denied any recognition, but I thought the Award itself was a terrific idea,' said Shaun. 'The first one was given at the annual dinner to James Coe, who was an ex-president of the Ergonomic Society and the founder of the New Zealand Design School. He was highly deserving of it, so it was a good way to start the thing off. There was one bum note on the night, when Kirsteen got up and addressed the dinner. I had written an obituary for John for a professional publication called *Pro Design*. For some reason they forwarded it to Tim Corcoran at Brittco for approval without telling me and Kirsteen now read large tracts from it to the gathering as if it was her own work. I was quite embarrassed when my obituary was subsequently published. I looked like a plagiarist.'

220 John Hepburn recalled a conversation with Robert about the Britten test programme that offered some insight into Robert's opinion of their mutual adversary.

'Robert told me that Stroudy was useless as a test rider because he was too good. Earlier in the year Robert had been at Ruapuna to do a couple of weeks of testing for the Britten team. He did his first test lap and came straight back in because he reckoned the rear suspension unit was shagged. The Team said it couldn't be, because Andrew had been riding it and he hadn't complained and he'd been doing good times. But when they checked it out it was completely gone. Andrew was able to ride around a problem like that, and he naturally—automatically—did. Robert could ride fast in spite of all sorts of problems as well, but he was a brilliant development rider. He really knew what a bike was doing and why. John Britten knew Robert possessed that talent and he used him whenever he could. From the beginning, though, Robert never really liked the Britten's front end. Apparently, he always said the same thing to John after every session—"Mate, put a set of forks on it!"'

221 Tim recalled the moment: 'When we started the thing up it fired all these dog-

food pellets out of the exhaust. Some furry little creature had been living in the boom-box and had filled it with stolen grub. I don't think it was home when the bike fired up.

222 Shaun Harris continued to go to the TT, year after year, driven by an unflagging determination to win. Finally, in 2003 he won both the 1000cc Production Race, on a Suzuki GSX-R1000, and the 600cc Production Race, on a Suzuki GSX-R600.

223 Andrew would continue to race while he and his wife Karen raised their family of three children. In 2000, after a brief spell in retirement, he won the popular four-hour endurance race at Manfeild on a Suzuki GSX-R750. The following year he won the New Zealand Sports Production Championship on a Suzuki GSX-R1000. In 2002 and 2003 he won the New Zealand Superbike Championship, again on a Suzuki GSX-R1000. At the time of writing he was working to put a New Zealand Superbike Team together to contest the World Championship.

224 Tim Stewart spent a number of years working for a top Superbike team in France, before returning to New Zealand to work for Chris Haldane at his Ducati dealership. He would finally focus on the good times he enjoyed with Britten Motorcycles, although he would always regret that there was not more time to explore the outer limits of John's dream. He would also express a readiness to do it all again.

'I had a huge amount of fun with those guys and learned so much, not just about building and racing motorbikes but about life itself. I wouldn't do it for money because there never was enough to justify the effort. But I would work with all those guys one more time to build another bike that we could all own. I reckon an 1100 with the 5-valve head, a 6-speed gearbox, Murray's new girder front end and all the other improvements could break a whole lot of lap records before we stuck it in a box for our retirement fund.'

225 Although the prospect of a new Britten motorcycle might have been fading, the memory of John Britten was not. In 1996 the Discovery Channel sent a film crew over from New York to make a programme about John and his motorcycles. Andrew Stroud was interviewed sitting on a Britten and other footage was used from the documentary *Backyard Visionary*. Years later, Andrew reported that he was still recognised from the documentary at odd moments all over the world.

'The documentary was apparently viewed initially in 30 million homes, but it was so popular it kept being shown again and again. It was still being rescreened in 2003. As the years went by I started receiving more and more invitations to speak, particularly to young people, about John and the bikes. New Zealand has one of the highest youth suicide rates in the Western world, and the message about pursuing your dreams and having faith that obstacles could be overcome was a really powerful message for them. I continued to race but my speaking engagements became more and more important to me. By 2003 I was in a position to dedicate a substantial part of my life to talking to young people. There is a proverb that says that without a vision the people perish. I believe that John's example still helps others to appreciate the simple truth of that reality.'

Index